Frommer's®

Virginia
9th Edition

by Bill Goodwin

Here's what the critics say about Frommer's:

"Amazingly easy to use. Very portable, very complete."

—*Booklist*

"Detailed, accurate, and easy-to-read information for all price ranges."
—*Glamour Magazine*

"Hotel information is close to encyclopedic."

—*Des Moines Sunday Register*

"Frommer's Guides have a way of giving you a real feel for a place."
—*Knight Ridder Newspapers*

WILEY

Wiley Publishing, Inc.

About the Author

Born and raised in North Carolina near Hampton Roads, **Bill Goodwin** has lived in northern Virginia since 1979. He was an award-winning newspaper reporter for the *Atlanta Journal* before becoming a legal counsel and speechwriter for two U.S. senators, Sam Nunn of Georgia and the late Sam J. Ervin, Jr., of North Carolina. Now a full-time travel writer, Goodwin also is the author of *Frommer's South Pacific, Frommer's Tahiti & French Polynesia,* and *Frommer's Fiji.*

Published by:

Wiley Publishing, Inc.

111 River St.
Hoboken, NJ 07030-5774

ISBN 978-0-470-17591-0
Editor: Jennifer Moore, with Kathleen Warnock
Production Editor: Suzanna R. Thompson
Cartographer: Andrew Dolan
Photo Editor: Richard Fox
Production by Wiley Indianapolis Composition Services

Front cover photo: Chincoteague Island: A wild pony on the beach
Back cover photo: Westover Plantation House

For information on our other products and services or to obtain technical support, please contact our Customer Care Department within the U.S. at 800/762-2974, outside the U.S. at 317/572-3993 or fax 317/572-4002.

Wiley also publishes its books in a variety of electronic formats. Some content that appears in print may not be available in electronic formats.

Manufactured in the United States of America

5 4 3 2 1

Contents

List of Maps

An Invitation to the Reader

In researching this book, we discovered many wonderful places—hotels, restaurants, shops, and more. We're sure you'll find others. Please tell us about them, so we can share the information with your fellow travelers in upcoming editions. If you were disappointed with a recommendation, we'd love to know that, too. Please write to:

Frommer's Virginia, 9th Edition
Wiley Publishing, Inc. • 111 River St. • Hoboken, NJ 07030-5774

An Additional Note

Please be advised that travel information is subject to change at any time—and this is especially true of prices. We therefore suggest that you write or call ahead for confirmation when making your travel plans. The authors, editors, and publisher cannot be held responsible for the experiences of readers while traveling. Your safety is important to us, however, so we encourage you to stay alert and be aware of your surroundings. Keep a close eye on cameras, purses, and wallets, all favorite targets of thieves and pickpockets.

Other Great Guides for Your Trip:

Frommer's Maryland & Delaware
Frommer's Washington, D.C.
Frommer's The Carolinas & Georgia
Frommer's Exploring America by RV
Frommer's USA

Frommer's Star Ratings, Icons & Abbreviations

Every hotel, restaurant, and attraction listing in this guide has been ranked for quality, value, service, amenities, and special features using a **star-rating system.** In country, state, and regional guides, we also rate towns and regions to help you narrow down your choices and budget your time accordingly. Hotels and restaurants are rated on a scale of zero (recommended) to three stars (exceptional). Attractions, shopping, nightlife, towns, and regions are rated according to the following scale: zero stars (recommended), one star (highly recommended), two stars (very highly recommended), and three stars (must-see).

In addition to the star-rating system, we also use **seven feature icons** that point you to the great deals, in-the-know advice, and unique experiences that separate travelers from tourists. Throughout the book, look for:

Finds	Special finds—those places only insiders know about
Fun Fact	Fun facts—details that make travelers more informed and their trips more fun
Kids	Best bets for kids and advice for the whole family
Moments	Special moments—those experiences that memories are made of
Overrated	Places or experiences not worth your time or money
Tips	Insider tips—great ways to save time and money
Value	Great values—where to get the best deals

The following **abbreviations** are used for credit cards:

AE	American Express	DISC	Discover	V	Visa
DC	Diners Club	MC	MasterCard		

Frommers.com

Now that you have this guidebook to help you plan a great trip, visit our website at **www. frommers.com** for additional travel information on more than 3,600 destinations. We update features regularly to give you instant access to the most current trip-planning information available. At Frommers.com, you'll find scoops on the best airfares, lodging rates, and car rental bargains. You can even book your travel online through our reliable travel booking partners. Other popular features include:

- Online updates of our most popular guidebooks
- Vacation sweepstakes and contest giveaways
- Newsletters highlighting the hottest travel trends
- Online travel message boards with featured travel discussions

What's New in Virginia

Here's a recap of developments in Virginia since we prepared the previous edition of this book in 2005. You can also check for more recent developments at www.frommers.com and at my personal website, www.billgoodwin.com.

NORTHERN VIRGINIA WTOP Radio, which gives traffic reports every 10 minutes, has switched frequencies from 1500 AM to 103.5 FM. It's the most popular station in traffic-plagued northern Virginia.

In Alexandria, **Atlantic Kayak** has closed its Old Town store and now operates exclusively in Maryland.

The ideally situated **Holiday Inn Select** on King Street is being turned into the more luxurious **Hotel Monaco** by Kimpton Hotels (www.monaco-alexandria.com). The massive renovations completed in early 2008, and the Monaco is now open. Meanwhile, the Radisson Old Town Alexandria has already morphed into the **Crowne Plaza Old Town Alexandria** (© 800/972-3159 or 703/683-6000).

Arlington National Cemetery has a new neighbor: **The United States Air Force Memorial,** on Air Force Memorial Drive at Columbia Pike (Va. 244) (© 703/247-5859; www.airforcememorial.org). Its stainless-steel spires, which soar out of the ground like a "bomb burst" precision flight maneuver, can be seen for miles around.

Mount Vernon now sports a state-of-the-art orientation center and an educational museum at its entry, and employees are once again making whiskey at **George Washington's Distillery.**

Out in the Hunt Country, Leesburg's **Dodona Manor, Home of George C. Marshall,** 212 E. Market St. (© 703/777-1880; www.georgecmarshall.org), has reopened after being restored to its appearance when the great World War II army chief of staff and postwar Nobel Peace Prize winner lived here in the 1940s and 1950s. You'll see his leather easy chair and early black-and-white television.

The Smithsonian Institution no longer provides a shuttle between the National Air and Space Museum on the D.C. Mall and the **Steven F. Udvar-Hazy Center** near Washington Dulles International Airport.

For complete information on this region, see chapter 4.

FREDERICKSBURG & THE NORTHERN NECK You can explore Fredericksburg's historic architecture with **Hallowed Ground Tours** (© 540/809-3918; www.hallowedgroundtours.com) on Thursdays and Fridays during summer, and commune with local spirits with **Ghosts of Fredericksburg Tours** (© 540/654-5414; www.ghostsoffredericksburg.com).

On I-95 about halfway between Alexandria and Fredericksburg stands the modernistic **National Museum of the Marine Corps,** 18900 Jefferson Davis Hwy. (U.S. 1) in Triangle (© 877/635-1775 or 703/784-6115; www.usmcmuseum.org), whose exhibits impressively chronicle the Leathernecks' exploits from

1775 to the wars in Iraq and Afghanistan. It's a treasure-trove of high-tech exhibits.

Among Fredericksburg's restaurants, **Austine's, The Smythe's Cottage and Tavern,** and **Feast-O-Rama** are history in this historic town. In their absence, you can get a refined Southern-style meal at **Bistro Bethem,** 309 William St. (℃ 540/371-9999), and a fine light lunch at **Caroline Street Cafe & Catering,** 1002 Caroline St. (℃ 540/373-1645).

Kilmarnock on the Northern Neck is now blessed with **Swank's on Main,** 36 Main St. (℃ 804/435-1010), a sophisticated bistro that would make any large city proud.

For complete information on this region, see chapter 5.

CHARLOTTESVILLE   The **Hardware Store** and **Northern Exposure** restaurants have closed. Taking their places are **Himalayan Fusion,** 520 E. Main St. (℃ 434/293-3120), offering Nepalese and Tibetan twists to Indian fare, and **Mono Loco,** 200 W. Water St. (℃ 434/979-0688), where south-of-the-border food is a mere pretext for the chef's creativity.

Tickets to Thomas Jefferson's **Monticello** now have specific mansion tour times printed on them, which has greatly reduced the long lines in summer and on spring and fall weekends. And you can buy them in advance at www.monticello.org.

James Madison's **Montpelier** has a new welcome center housing a "Treasurers of Montpelier" exhibit of the Madisons' furnishings and personal belongings, including a lock of the fourth president's hair.

For complete information on Charlottesville, see chapter 6.

THE SHENANDOAH VALLEY   The Shenandoah National Park has added air conditioners and televisions to some units at **Big Meadows Lodge** and **Skyland Lodge,** the park's only hotels.

Front Royal now sports the lively **Soul Mountain Café,** 300 E. Main St. (℃ 540/636-0070), where the fare ranges from

Southern-style catfish to Jamaican jerk chicken.

The fabulous **Inn at Little Washington** has added two cottages and a Victorian home to its inventory of awesome accommodations, but has done away with its Presidential Retreat.

Near Luray, the Jordan Hollow Farm Inn has changed its name to **Jordan Hollow Inn** to reflect its many recent improvements, including six new deluxe cabins sitting atop a hill with great views of the Blue Ridge. In Luray itself, the **Mimslyn Inn** is closed while being transformed into a modern hotel.

Built in 1924 but used for other purposes since the 1960s, Staunton's **Stonewall Jackson Hotel & Conference Center,** 24 S. Market St. (℃ 866/880-0024 or 540/885-4848; www.stonewall jacksonhotel.com), has reopened after a $21-million restoration.

Staunton also has two new restaurants offering excellent fare: **Staunton Grocery** (℃ 540/886-6880) and **Zynodoa Restaurant** (℃ 540/885-7775), both bistro-style establishments on Beverley Street in the heart of downtown. The former is more formal and creative, while the latter is more relaxed and affordable. Both are very good.

Out in the countryside between Staunton and Lexington, the lodgelike **Fox Hill Bed & Breakfast,** 4383 Borden Grant Trail, Fairfield, VA 24435 (℃ 800/869-8005 or 540/377-9922; www.foxhillbb. com), is a perfect place to stay over and relax while touring the scenic area around Raphine. It has a fine view of the Blue Ridge Mountains.

In Warm Springs, I no longer recommend the inexpensive **Roseloe Motel,** which serves weeknights as lodging for workers at a huge real estate project.

In Lexington, **James River Basin Canoe Livery** is now **Twin River Outfitters,** 917 Rockbridge Rd. (P.O. Box 99), Glasgow, VA 24455 (℃ 540/258-1999; www.canoevirginia.com).

Downtown Lexington has seen a change in the restaurant guard. Gone are the excellent **Willson-Walker House Restaurant** and the vegetarian **Blue Heron Cafe.** The reserves have been sent in, however, with the eclectic **Bistro on Main,** 8 N. Main St. (℗ **540/464-4888** admirably filling the gap.

For complete information on this region, see chapter 7.

ROANOKE & THE SOUTHWEST HIGHLANDS The **Art Museum of Western Virginia** is building itself a new modern home on Salem Avenue at Williamson Road. It will not open until the fall of 2008, but you already will see its dramatic steel-and-zinc roof mimicking Roanoke's Blue Ridge Mountain backdrop.

Ruby, the Siberian tiger who starred at Roanoke's **Mill Mountain Zoo,** has gone to big-cat heaven.

The **Wyndham Roanoke Hotel** was in need of renovation during my recent visit and reportedly was about to go under the knife and reappear as a Sheraton hotel. Until that happens, I would stay elsewhere.

In Abingdon, **The Martha Washington Inn** now has a full-service spa and indoor pool. The **Starving Artist Cafe** has closed after many years catering to the town's artistes. Occupying a Victorian house is the new **Zazzy'z Coffee House,** 380 E Main St. (℗ **276/698-3333**), where you can get a caffeine fix, buy a book, check your e-mail, and have a deli-style lunch.

For complete information on this region, see chapter 8.

RICHMOND Carytown's excellent **Acacia** restaurant is moving to an undisclosed location. In its absence, you can wander over to the lively **Can Can Brasserie,** 3120 W. Cary St. (℗ **804/358-7274**), for French fare. The Jefferson Hotel's **Lemaire** dining room was in the process of switching from French. In the meantime, you can sample very good American comfort food at **Comfort,** 200 W. Broad St. (℗ **804/780-0004**).

Next door to the Richmond National Battlefield visitor center at Tredegar Irons Works, **The American Civil War Center Museum,** 500 Tredegar St. (℗ **804/780-1865;** www.tredegar.org), does an excellent job of explaining the war's causes from three perspectives: North, South, and African-American.

The **Virginia State Capitol** has reopened after a massive, multiyear restoration. The new underground welcome center is at 1000 Bank St., at 10th Street, on the capitol's south side. Guided tours depart on the hour daily until 4pm.

The Federal Reserve Bank's **Money Museum** is closed until 2009 during renovations.

Richmond Raft Company no longer has white-water rafting in Richmond.

For complete information on Richmond, see chapter 9.

WILLIAMSBURG, JAMESTOWN & YORKTOWN The **Boomerang** bus between Williamsburg and Virginia Beach is no more.

A substantial renovation has added the **Abby Aldrich Rockefeller Folk Art Museum** to the **DeWitt Wallace Decorative Arts Museum.** They share underground quarters behind the Public Hospital and are collectively known as **The Colonial Williamsburg Museums.**

Busch Gardens Williamsburg is now known as **Busch Gardens Europe,** which accurately reflects the character of its European villages.

The **Williamsburg Lodge** has returned to its 1930s appearance after a massive renovation. **The Fife & Drum Inn** now has a Colonial-style cottage around the corner, so guests don't necessarily have to climb the 17 steps up to the main inn.

Artifacts uncovered by extensive digs at Historic Jamestowne, site of the original Jamestown colony in 1607, are now displayed in the **Archaearium,** a first-rate archaeological museum.

The **Mariners' Museum** in Newport News has opened the marvelous **USS** *Monitor* **Center,** where you can see the remains of the famous Union ironclad, recovered from the floor of the Atlantic Ocean off Cape Hatteras, where it had rested since sinking during the Civil War.

For complete information on this region, see chapter 10.

NORFOLK Hampton Roads officially became a cruise-ship port with the opening of Norfolk's new **Half Moone Cruise and Celebration Center,** downtown next door to NAUTICUS, The National Maritime Center.

Admission to the **Moses Myers House** and the adjacent **Norfolk History Museum** is now free, with donations recommended. NAUTICUS and the *Victory Rover* are selling tickets combining NAUTICUS admission and a cruise. The **Tugboat Museum** has sailed away to Florida.

On the Granby Street restaurant scene, **Voodoo Rouge, Jack Quinn's Irish Pub,** and **The Blue Hippo** have all closed, as has **Cora** in Ghent. On the other hand, the pace has never been faster on Colley Avenue between Maury and Spotswood avenues in the heart of Ghent, where the legions have been joined by **The Green Onion,** 1603 Colley Ave. (© 757/963-6100).

For complete information about Norfolk, see chapter 11.

VIRGINIA BEACH Originally designed by Pete Dye and Curtis Strange for the Professional Golfers Association, the **Tournament Players Club of Virginia Beach** is now the **Virginia Beach National Golf Club.** It has the same phone numbers but its website is now www.vbnational.com.

Spiffed-up and renamed **Ocean Cove Motel/Angie's Guest Cottage** no longer is a bed-and-breakfast, but it still is one of Virginia's few official international youth hostels.

Dining choices now include the spectacular **Catch 31,** in the Hilton Virginia Beach Oceanfront (© 757/213-3472), where you can consume fresh seafood while taking in the summertime entertainment in Neptune Park next door. My favorite breakfast joint is now **Doc Taylor's,** 207 23rd St. (© 757/425-1960), the daytime version of the adjacent Tautog's Restaurant. Right by the beach, **Waterman's Surfside Grille,** 415 Atlantic Ave. (© 757/428-3644), has been totally renovated but still serves my favorite crab cakes.

For complete information on this region, see chapter 11.

CHINCOTEAGUE & ASSATEAGUE ISLANDS The **Driftwood Inn** has reemerged from extensive renovations as the **Best Western Chincoteague Island** (www.bestwestern.com/chincoteagueisland).

New to Chincoteague is the inexpensive **Mr. Baldy's Family Restaurant,** in middle of the island at 3447 Ridge Rd. (© 757/336-1198), where the quite bald Robert Zoller serves a variety of traditional fare, all of it very good value.

For complete information on this region, see chapter 11.

1

The Best of Virginia

In 2007 Virginia celebrated the 400th anniversary of the landing of the first permanent English-speaking colonists in North America. That small band of gentlemen and tradesmen had a rough start at Jamestown, but within a few years this beautiful and bountiful land had greatly rewarded them for their courageous efforts. They first set foot on a sandy Atlantic Ocean beach at Cape Charles, at the mouth of one of the world's great estuaries, the Chesapeake Bay. Beyond them lay a varied, rich, and scenic land. They settled beside one of the great tidal rivers whose tributaries led their descendants through the rolling hills of the Piedmont, over the Blue Ridge Mountains, and into the great valleys beyond.

Today, the history-loving Commonwealth of Virginia abounds with historic homes and plantations, buildings that rang with revolutionary oratory, museums that recall the bloody Civil War fought on its soil, and small towns that seem little changed since Colonial times. Conservation efforts have kept a great deal of Virginia's wilderness looking much as it did in 1607, making the state a prime destination for lovers of the great outdoors. Virginia has an abundance of places to indulge your passion.

Given so much to cover in relatively few pages, this entire book could be called *Frommer's Best of Virginia*. In this chapter, I choose what I consider to be the best of the best. You'll surely come up with your own list as you travel through the state. Be sure to see the destination chapters later in this book for full details on the places mentioned below.

1 The Best of Colonial Virginia

- **Old Town Alexandria:** Although Alexandria is very much part of metro Washington, D.C., the historic district known as Old Town evokes the time when the nation's early leaders strolled its streets and partook of grog at Gadsby's Tavern. See "Alexandria" in chapter 4.

- **Mount Vernon:** When he wasn't off surveying, fighting in the French and Indian Wars, leading the American Revolution, or serving as our first president, George Washington made his home at a plantation 8 miles south of Alexandria. Restored to look as it was in Washington's day, Mount Vernon is America's second-most-visited historic home. See "Mount Vernon & the Potomac Plantations" in chapter 4.

- **Fredericksburg:** Not only did the Fredericksburg area play a role in the birth of a nation, it was the boyhood home of George Washington. James Monroe, who as president kept European powers out of the Americas by promulgating the Monroe Doctrine, lived here before he moved to Charlottesville. The great Confederate leader Robert E. Lee was born near here a generation later. Fredericksburg still retains much of the charm it

Virginia

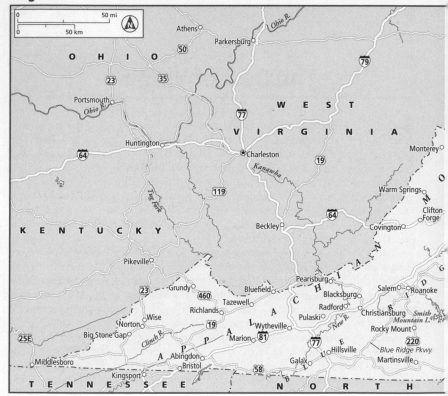

possessed in those early days. See chapter 5.

- **Charlottesville:** If Washington was the father of the United States, then Thomas Jefferson was its intellectual genius. This scholar, lawyer, writer, and architect built two monuments—his lovely hilltop home, Monticello, and the University of Virginia—that still evoke memories of this great thinker and patriot. See chapter 6.

- **Williamsburg, Jamestown & Yorktown:** Known as the Historic Triangle, these three towns are the finest examples of Colonial America to be found. Colonial Williamsburg looks as it appeared when it was the capital of Virginia in the 18th century. The original Jamestown settlement is now a national historical park, as is Yorktown, where Washington defeated Lord Cornwallis to end the American Revolution. See chapter 10.

2 The Best of Civil War Virginia

When the Civil War broke out in 1861 and the Confederacy moved its capital to Richmond, the state became the prime target of the Union armies. Virginia saw more battles than any other state, as Robert E. Lee's Army of Northern Virginia

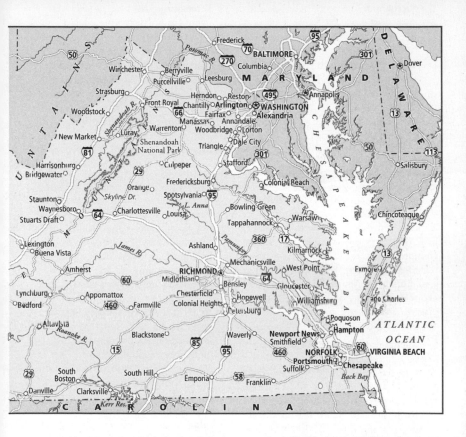

turned back one assault after another. Today you can visit the sites of many key battles, all of them national historical parks.

- **Manassas:** The first battle of the war occurred along Bull Run near Manassas in northern Virginia, and it was a shock to the Union (and thousands of spectators who came from Washington to watch) when the rebels engineered a victory over a disorganized Union force. They won again at the Second Battle of Manassas. See "The Hunt Country" in chapter 4.
- **Fredericksburg:** No other town in Virginia has as many significant battlefields as Fredericksburg. Lee used the Rappahannock River as a natural line of defense, and he fought several battles against Union armies trying to advance on Richmond. You can visit the battlefields in town, and at Chancellorsville and the Wilderness, in a day. See chapter 5.
- **Appomattox Court House:** After the fall of Petersburg in 1865, Lee fled for little more than a week until realizing that continuing the war was fruitless. On April 9, he met Grant at Wilbur McLean's farmhouse and surrendered his sword. America's bloodiest conflict was over. The farmhouse is preserved as part of Appomattox Court House National Historical Park. See "What to See & Do" in "Charlottesville," chapter 6.

• **Richmond:** The capital of the Confederacy, Richmond has many reminders of the war, including the magnificent Museum of the Confederacy and the White House of the Confederacy, home of President Jefferson Davis. Monument Avenue is lined with statues of the rebel leaders. The city's eastern outskirts are ringed with battle sites, part of the Richmond National Battlefield Park. See chapter 9.

• **Petersburg:** After nearly 4 years of trying to capture Richmond, Union Gen. Ulysses S. Grant bypassed the Southern capital in 1864 and headed for the railroad junction of Petersburg, the lifeline of the Confederate capital. Even there, he was forced into a siege situation, but finally, in April 1865, Grant broke through and forced Lee into a westward retreat. See "An Easy Excursion to Petersburg" in chapter 9.

3 The Best of the Great Outdoors

Virginia has hundreds of thousands of acres of natural beauty preserved in national and state parks, national forests, and recreation areas. Especially in the mountains, you can find more than 1,000 miles of trails for hiking, biking, and horseback riding. The Chesapeake Bay offers boating and fishing, and the Atlantic beaches are among the best on the East Coast.

• **Shenandoah National Park:** Nearly two million visitors a year venture into the Shenandoah National Park, which straddles the Blue Ridge Mountains from Front Royal to Rockfish Gap. Many visitors merely drive along the 105-mile Skyline Drive, one of America's most scenic routes, but the park has more than 500 miles of hiking trails, including 101 miles of the Appalachian Trail. Many trails start at the Skyline Drive and drop down into hollows and canyons, some of them with waterfalls. Even on the Skyline Drive, you are likely to encounter deer, and you might even see bear, bobcat, and wild turkey. See "Shenandoah National Park & the Skyline Drive" in chapter 7.

• **Running the Rivers** (Front Royal, Luray, Lexington, Richmond): The South Fork of the Shenandoah River twists and turns its way between the valley towns of Front Royal and Luray, making it a perfect venue for rafting, canoeing, and kayaking—or just floating along in an inner tube. The James River can be swift and turbulent as it crosses the Shenandoah Valley, cuts through the Blue Ridge Mountains, and courses its way across the Piedmont to Hampton Roads. Depending on the amount of rain, you may be able to raft down the James through metropolitan Richmond. See chapters 7 and 9.

• **Mount Rogers National Recreation Area:** While you won't be alone in Shenandoah National Park, you could have a hiking, biking, horseback-riding, or cross-country skiing trail all to yourself in Mount Rogers National Recreation Area. This wild land in the Southwest Highlands occupies some 117,000 acres of forest and includes its namesake, Virginia's highest peak. Two of Virginia's finest rails-to-trails hiking, biking, and riding paths serve as bookends to the 60-mile-long recreation area: the New River Trail, near Wytheville, and the Virginia Creeper Trail, from Abingdon to White Top Mountain. See "The Great Outdoors in the Southwest Highlands" in chapter 8.

• **Back Bay National Wildlife Refuge/ False Cape State Park** (Virginia Beach): You can't sunbathe or swim on the beach of Back Bay National Wildlife Refuge, but you can hike through the dunes or take a canoe into the marshes, which are on the Atlantic Flyway for migrating birds. You can sunbathe and swim at the adjoining False Cape State Park, but it's so out-of-the-way that you'll have to bring your own drinking water. See "Parks & Wildlife Refuges" in the Virginia Beach section of chapter 11.

- **Assateague Island:** Of all the natural areas in Virginia, none surpasses Assateague, which keeps the Atlantic Ocean from the back bays of Chincoteague. Here you will find the famous wild ponies in Chincoteague National Wildlife Refuge and relatively tame humans strolling along some 37 miles of pristine beach. Assateague Island is also situated directly on the Atlantic Flyway, making it one of the best bird-watching sites in the country. See "Chincoteague & Assateague Islands" in chapter 11.

4 The Best Scenic Drives

The Old Dominion has some of America's most beautiful scenic drives.

- **George Washington Memorial Parkway** (northern Virginia): Stay away during rush hour, when it becomes a major artery into and out of Washington, D.C. But any other time, the "G.W. Parkway" is a great drive along the Potomac River from I-495 at the Maryland line to Mount Vernon. The views of Washington's monuments are unparalleled. See "A Scenic Drive along the Potomac River" in chapter 4.
- **The Presidents Route (Va. 20;** Charlottesville to Montpelier): Thomas Jefferson and James Monroe would travel the 25 miles north to visit their friends James and Dolley Madison by a winding wagon trail. Today that road is known as Va. 20, and it's still a scenic wonder through the modern vineyards and expensive horse farms of the Blue Ridge foothills. See "James Madison's Montpelier" in chapter 6.
- **Skyline Drive** (Shenandoah National Park): Few roads anywhere can top the Skyline Drive, which twists and turns 105 miles along the Blue Ridge crest in Shenandoah National Park. The views over the rolling Piedmont to the east and Shenandoah Valley to the west are spectacular, especially during spring, when the wildflowers are in bloom, and in fall, when the leaves change from green to brilliant hues of rust, orange, and yellow. See "Shenandoah National Park & the Skyline Drive" in chapter 7.
- **Lexington to Hot Springs:** Va. 39 runs from Lexington to Hot Springs via the Goshen Pass, a picturesque gorge cut by the Maury River. You can make a loop by continuing north from Hot Springs via U.S. 220 to the beautiful village of Monterey in "Virginia's Switzerland." From Monterey, you can cross the mountains via U.S. 250 to Staunton and I-81. See chapter 7.
- **Blue Ridge Parkway:** A continuation of the Skyline Drive, this road continues along the Blue Ridge crest south to the Great Smoky Mountains National Park in North Carolina. Of the 218 miles in Virginia, the most scenic are north of Roanoke. See "The Blue Ridge Parkway" in chapter 8.
- **Colonial Parkway:** It's not long, but the Colonial Parkway between Jamestown, Williamsburg, and Yorktown has its scenic merits, especially the views of the James River near

Jamestown and of the York River near Yorktown. See chapter 10.

- **Chesapeake Bay Bridge-Tunnel:** A man-made wonder, the Chesapeake Bay Bridge-Tunnel runs for 17 miles over—and under—the mouth of the Chesapeake Bay between Norfolk and the Eastern Shore. You can barely see land when you're in the middle. See chapter 11.

5 The Most Charming Small Towns

Virginia's many lovely small towns capture and nurture the state's history and culture. This is especially true in the Shenandoah Valley, where I-81 and U.S. 11 follow the route of the Colonial-era Valley Pike, thus continuing to string together Winchester, Strasburg, Staunton, and Lexington, all possessed of 18th- and 19th-century brick and stone buildings.

- **Middleburg:** The self-proclaimed capital of Virginia's Hunt Country, Middleburg takes up barely 6 blocks along U.S. 50, small enough to be digested in an afternoon. Some of the world's wealthiest individuals keep their horses near Middleburg, and the town has a host of upscale shops in buildings dating from the 1700s. See "The Hunt Country" in chapter 4.
- **Monterey:** Over Shenandoah and Bull Pasture mountains from Staunton, the village of Monterey appears more like New England than Virginia, with its white churches and clapboard homes in a picturesque valley. Thousands of visitors make the trek over the mountains to the annual Highland Maple Festival in March. See "Staunton–to–Warm Springs via Monterey" in chapter 7.
- **Staunton:** There's Shakespeare to be seen at the Blackfriars Playhouse in Staunton, an old railroad town that was formerly most famous as President Woodrow Wilson's birthplace. The replica of The Bard's 17th-century indoor theater has spurred a downtown renaissance, with new restaurants and shops opening all the time. A don't-miss for kids, the Frontier Culture Museum, is here, too. See "Staunton: A Presidential Birthplace & the Bard's Playhouse" in chapter 7.
- **Lexington:** One of America's best small towns, Lexington has a lively college atmosphere in addition to a host of sights. It's home to the Virginia Military Institute (VMI), where Gen. Thomas J. "Stonewall" Jackson taught; its students went off to the Civil War at New Market. Afterward, Robert E. Lee came here as president of Washington College, now Washington and Lee University. VMI was the alma mater of Gen. George C. Marshall, who won the Nobel Peace Prize for his plan to rebuild Europe after World War II. Jackson, Lee, and Marshall are buried here, and there are museums dedicated to them. See "Lexington: A College Town with a Slice of American History" in chapter 7.
- **Abingdon:** Daniel Boone opened Virginia's Southwest Highlands to settlement in the 1770s, and a thriving town grew up at Abingdon. Homes and buildings dating to 1779 line Main Street, making it a wonderful place to stroll. The town is home to the Barter Theatre, Virginia's state stage, where you can still barter for a ticket. See "Abingdon: A Show-Stopping Town" in chapter 8.

6 The Best Family Vacations

The majority of Virginia's visitors arrive by car, and most of them are families. Accordingly, the state's major attractions and resorts are well equipped to entertain and care for children. It's a great place for kids to learn about American history while enjoying a good time at the beach or one of three major amusement parks.

- **Shenandoah National Park:** Two lodges in the most popular part of Shenandoah National Park make this a great place for family vacations. The kids can participate in ranger programs, hike to waterfalls, or go for a pony ride in the forest. See "Shenandoah National Park & the Skyline Drive" in chapter 7.
- **Colonial Williamsburg:** The Historic Area of Colonial Williamsburg is the best place for children to get a quick lesson in American history. On the streets, they might run into Thomas Jefferson (actually, an actor) and have a conversation about the Declaration of Independence, or drill and march with the 18th-century militia. As soon as they get bored, head for Busch Gardens Europe or

Water Country USA, two nearby theme parks. See chapter 10.
- **Virginia Beach:** First there's the beach, 4 miles or so, with lifeguards during summer—but that's not all. Rainy days can be spent at the local Virginia Aquarium & Marine Science Center, the state's most popular museum. Norfolk's NAUTICUS, Hampton's Virginia Air and Space Center, and Colonial Williamsburg are all just short drives away. See chapter 11.
- **Chincoteague & Assateague Islands:** The fishing village was the setting for Marguerite Henry's classic children's book *Misty of Chincoteague*, and there are plenty of wild horses (called "ponies") in Chincoteague National Wildlife Refuge on Assateague Island, which also has a guarded beach for swimming during the summer. The best time to see the horses is during the annual pony swim the last week in July, but the kids can ride one in a small equestrian center. See "Chincoteague & Assateague Islands" in chapter 11.

7 The Most Unusual Virginia Travel Experiences

A museum devoted to hounds, a stalactite organ, an 18th-century version of today's Jacuzzi, a stuffed horse, and a cruise to Elizabethan times all make for unusual travel in Virginia.

- **Chimes Down Under** (Luray): One of the most fascinating caverns in the Shenandoah Valley is at Luray. Through huge subterranean rooms comes beautiful music—in the form of hammers striking million-year-old stalactites. See "Luray: An Underground Organ" in chapter 7.

- **Ancient Hot Tubs** (Warm Springs): Eighteenth-century travelers couldn't climb into the Jacuzzi after a rough day on the road—unless, that is, they pulled into Warm Springs. Since 1761, travelers have slipped their weary bodies into these natural rock pools whose waters range from 94°F to 104°F (34°C–40°C). You can, too. See "Warm Springs & Hot Springs: Taking the Waters" in chapter 7.
- **Mounting Little Sorrel** (Lexington): After he died of wounds accidentally

inflicted by his own men at the Battle of Chancellorsville, Gen. Stonewall Jackson was buried in Lexington, where he had taught at Virginia Military Institute. Thanks to taxidermy, Jackson's war-horse, Little Sorrel, stands in VMI's museum. Robert E. Lee's horse, Traveller, is buried just outside Lee Chapel, his master's resting place. See p. 184.

- **Splashing with Harbor Seals** (Virginia Beach): Children and adults will love the Virginia Aquarium & Marine Science Center's **Harbor Seal Splash.** Accompanied by an animal care specialist, you get into a pool and splash around with the resident harbor seals and participate in a training session. See p. 306.

- **"Hoi Toide Tonoit"** (Tangier Island): Out in the Chesapeake Bay sits remote Tangier Island, whose residents have been so isolated that they still speak with the Elizabethan brogue of their forebears. Out here, "high tide tonight" is pronounced *hoi toide tonoit*—as in "hoity-toity"— and narrow 17th-century lanes barely can accommodate modern automobiles. Cruises leave from the Northern Neck and the Eastern Shore. See chapters 5 and 11.

8 The Best Country Inns

With all its old homes and gorgeous countryside, Virginia is a hotbed of country inns and B&Bs. Some have been in business since Colonial times; a few are among the best around. Our picks barely touch the surface.

- **Red Fox Inn** (Middleburg): In the center of tiny Middleburg, this rambling inn maintains the romantic charm of early Virginia in its original 1728 stone structure. There's a cozy dining room downstairs. See p. 99.

- **The Hope and Glory Inn** (Irvington): The state's most fascinating country inn occupies a converted 1890s schoolhouse, and it has cottages in the garden, but what really sets it apart is an outdoor bathroom complete with claw-foot tub. That's right: It's outdoors, albeit surrounded by a stockade fence. See p. 121.

- **Clifton** (Charlottesville): Thomas Mann Randolph, husband of Thomas Jefferson's daughter, Martha, built this clapboard house as a trading post in 1799. Today it's a luxury-laden but relaxed country inn. The restaurant itself is worth writing home about. See p. 129.

- **The Inn at Little Washington** (Washington): For the best, you need look no further than the Blue Ridge foothill village of Washington, which everyone in Virginia calls "Little Washington." An English decorator designed the rooms here, but it's the romantic restaurant that draws the most raves. See p. 164.

- **Fort Lewis Plantation & Lodge** (Millboro): One of Virginia's most unusual inns, the Fort Lewis Lodge occupies an old mill and rebuilt barn on a farm beside the Cowpasture River, just over the mountain from Warm Springs. A spiral staircase ascends to three rooms inside the old silo, and there are two log cabins with their own fireplaces. It's a great place to show urban kids a bit of farm life in beautiful surroundings. See p. 180.

- **The Martha Washington Inn** (Abingdon): Gracing Abingdon's historic district, the center portion of this Greek Revival inn was built as a private home in 1832—and as if to prove it, the plank floors creak loudly as you enter the gracious lobby. You can sit in white-wicker rocking chairs on the front porch and watch the traffic on Main Street—or imagine Daniel Boone's dogs being attacked by wolves nearby. See p. 212.

9 The Best Luxury Accommodations

With deep-enough pockets, you can enjoy some of the Mid-Atlantic's best luxury accommodations in Virginia.

- **Morrison House** (Alexandria): More like a country inn in the middle of Old Town Alexandria, this small, luxurious hotel isn't that old, but it looks exactly like the Federal-period homes surrounding it. The dining is marvelous. See p. 75.

- **The Tides Inn** (Irvington): A venerable boating and golfing retreat, The Tides Inn stands among Virginia's elite resorts. The style is more British Raj than Old Virginny, but the facilities are first rate, including a spa with treatment rooms overlooking Carter's Creek. The golf course is one of Virginia's best. See p. 121.

- **Boar's Head Inn** (Charlottesville): A 19th-century gristmill serves as the centerpiece of this lakeside resort, on the outskirts of Charlottesville, and lends ancient charm to the Old Mill dining room, one of the best places to sample Virginia wines without trekking to the vineyards. Modern amenities include a full-service spa and access to Charlottesville's best-equipped sports club. See p. 127.

- **The Homestead** (Hot Springs): Outstanding service, fine cuisine, and a myriad of activities characterize this grand old establishment, in business since Thomas Jefferson's day. In fact, Jefferson was the first of seven presidents to stay here. The Homestead offers accommodations ranging from standard rooms to plush suites. PGA pro Lanny Wadkins presides over its golf course, one of Virginia's finest. See p. 178.

- **The Jefferson Hotel** (Richmond): A Beaux Arts landmark with Renaissance-style balconies and an Italian clock tower, the Jefferson was opened in 1895 by a wealthy Richmonder who wanted his city to have one of America's finest hotels. See p. 221.

- **Williamsburg Inn** (Williamsburg): An establishment with three fine golf courses, the Williamsburg Inn was built as part of the Colonial Williamsburg restoration but looks like it might have been here in 1750. If staying in the main inn with its superb service and cuisine won't do, you can opt for one of the restored houses and taverns that have been converted into accommodations. See p. 262.

10 The Best Moderately Priced Accommodations

Virginia has too many fine, affordable lodgings to mention them all here. The following are some we like best.

- **Richard Johnston Inn** (Fredericksburg): Elegantly appointed rooms await in these two 18th-century homes across from historic Fredericksburg's visitor center. See p. 110.

- **Frederick House** (Staunton): A cross between a boutique hotel and a B&B, this collection of Victorian houses is in the heart of Staunton, a quick walk to both Woodrow Wilson's birthplace and the Blackfriars Playhouse. See p. 172.

- **Inn at Gristmill Square** (Warm Springs): A naturally warm spring used to turn the water wheel of the gristmill that makes up part of this comfortable inn. Some rooms are in an old barn and silo. See p. 179.

- **Hampton Inn Col Alto** (Lexington): No ordinary Hampton Inn, Col Alto is an 1827 manor house converted into a comfortable B&B-type hotel. Even if you stay in the modern motel buildings next door, you'll eat your continental breakfast in the period dining room. See p. 186.
- **Hotel Roanoke & Conference Center** (Roanoke): The grand, Tudor-style Hotel Roanoke stood in a wheat field when the Norfolk & Western Railroad built it in 1882. It was closed in 1989, but a $45-million renovation completely restored its grand public areas to their original appearance and rebuilt all its rooms to modern standards. See p. 200.
- **Summerfield Inn** (Abingdon): Ideally situated a block behind the Barter Theatre, this bed-and-breakfast offers spacious rooms in a converted carriage house, one with a two-person hot tub and walk-in shower. See p. 212.
- **Linden Row Inn** (Richmond): This row of Victorian-era town houses has been renovated but not restored, which has left the rooms with 12-foot ceilings, a mix of late Empire and Victorian pieces, and marble-top dressers. See p. 222.
- **The Fife & Drum Inn** (Williamsburg): Upstairs over the stores of Merchants Square, this charming bed-and-breakfast has Williamsburg's Historic Area right out its front door. For those who can't handle climbing up the stairs, owners Billy and Sharon Scruggs, themselves Williamsburg natives, have a Colonial-style cottage to rent around the corner. See p. 265.

11 The Best Inexpensive Accommodations

Virginia has many clean, comfortable motels of the budget-chain variety. But for something a little more special, check out the following choices.

- **Fredericksburg Colonial Inn** (Fredericksburg): Don't be surprised to see Blues and Grays toting Civil War rifles in the lobby; this place is very popular with reenactors. An avid collector, the owner has laden the rooms with antiques. See p. 110.
- **Best Western Cavalier Inn at the University** (Charlottesville): The University of Virginia owns and spotlessly maintains this older motel, a half-mile west of the Rotunda, the center of campus. See p. 128.
- **Big Meadows & Skyland lodges** (Shenandoah National Park): With stunning views from atop the Blue Ridge Mountains, these two rustic but charming inns are surprisingly affordable. Just be sure to reserve as early as possible. See p. 151 and p. 152.
- **Llewellyn Lodge** (Lexington): This B&B within an easy walk of Lexington's many attractions is made special by owners John and Ellen Roberts, who willingly share their knowledge not only of the town but the surrounding wilderness. See p. 188.
- **Luray Caverns Motel West** (Luray): This old-fashioned motel sits across the highway from the famous caverns, which owns it and keeps it spotless. See p. 166.
- **Anderson Cottage** (Warm Springs): A real warm spring courses behind this charming B&B in one of Bath County's oldest buildings. It's stocked with so many of owner Jean Randolph Bruns' family heirlooms that it seems as much museum as place to stay. See p. 179.
- **Colony House Motor Lodge** (Roanoke): This older but clean and very well-maintained motel is convenient to both downtown Roanoke

> (Fun Fact **Virginia's Gourmet Contributions**
>
> A native of Newport News, the late author William Styron once said that the French consider salt-cured Virginia hams to be America's only gourmet contribution to the world's cuisine. Virginians love their ham (especially stuffed into hot biscuits), and they are crazy about rockfish (sea bass) and crabs from the Chesapeake Bay and shad and trout from the rivers. Virginia's farms produce a plethora of vegetables, and its orchards are famous for apples. And let's not forget the peanut, one of Virginia's major crops, which has been used in soup since Colonial times!

and the Blue Ridge Parkway. Doors to the rooms have louvers to let in fresh air but not light—an unusual touch for any inexpensive hotel. See p. 200.

- **Quarterpath Inn** (Williamsburg): You can walk to Williamsburg's Historic Area from this clean, family-owned motel east of town. See p. 264.

- **Belvedere Resort Motel** (Virginia Beach): With the Atlantic Ocean out its back door, this comfortable, clean establishment is the last family-owned motel on the Virginia Beach oceanfront. See p. 308.

12 The Best of Virginia Cooking

You can dine on all types of cuisine in Virginia, but the highlights are produced from recipes handed down since Colonial times—dishes such as peanut soup and Sally Lunn bread—or that put a modern spin on local ingredients. Here are some of the best places to sample Virginia's unique and very historic cuisine.

- **Gadsby's Tavern** (Alexandria): George Washington said goodbye to his troops from the door of Gadsby's Tavern in Alexandria's Old Town. This former rooming house and the tavern next door look much as they did then, and a waitstaff in Colonial garb still serve chicken roasted on an open fire, buttermilk pie, and other dishes from that period. See p. 76.

- **The Inn at Little Washington** (Washington): Chef Patrick O'Connell constantly changes his menu to take advantage of trout, Chesapeake Bay seafood, Virginia hams, and other local delicacies in his romantic dining room. The service at Virginia's finest restaurant is wonderfully attentive and unobtrusive. See p. 164.

- **Mrs. Rowe's Restaurant and Bakery** (Staunton): Every town has its favorite "local" restaurant, where you can clog your arteries with plain old Southern favorites like pan-fried chicken, sausage gravy over biscuits, and fresh vegetables seasoned with smoked pork and cooked to smithereens. In business since 1947, Mrs. Rowe's somehow manages to cook great veggies without all that lard. See p. 174.

- **Roanoker Restaurant** (Roanoke): Another local, favorite the Roanoker regularly changes its menu to take advantage of the freshest vegetables available. And every day it serves the best biscuits in Virginia, hot from the oven. See p. 203.

- **King's Barbecue** (Petersburg): Like all Southerners, Virginians love their barbecue, and it doesn't get any better than at the two branches of King's.

Pork, beef, ribs, and chicken roast constantly over an open pit right in the dining rooms, and the sauce is served on the side, not soaking the succulent meat and overpowering its smoked flavor. See p. 243.

- **A Chef's Kitchen** (Williamsburg): You don't just go to dinner at veteran Chef John Gonzales's table, for he puts on an entertaining and highly informative cooking show for nearly 3 hours. See p. 268.

- **Old Chickahominy House** (Williamsburg): Named for a nearby river, this reconstructed, antiques-filled, 18th-century house is one of the best places to sample traditional Virginia fare, such as Brunswick stew and Virginia ham on hot biscuits. See p. 269.

2

Planning Your Trip to Virginia

Whether you plan to spend a day, a week, 2 weeks, or longer in Virginia, you'll need to make many "where," "when," and "how" choices *before* you leave home. In this chapter I explain how best to go about planning your trip.

1 Virginia's Regions in Brief

First of all, you must decide where to go. I can't make that decision for you, but I briefly tell you what the state has to offer.

Virginia has three distinct geographic regions. Along the eastern coast, the **Tidewater** is a flat coastal plain dominated by four rivers—the Potomac, Rappahannock, York, and James—that empty into the Chesapeake Bay, one of the world's largest estuaries. The Chesapeake meets the Atlantic Ocean at Hampton Roads, one of the world's most immense natural harbors. The rivers divide the Tidewater into three *necks,* as we call them: the Peninsula between the James and the York; the Middle Peninsula between the York and the Rappahannock; and the Northern Neck between the Rappahannock and the Potomac.

Heading west, the flat plain gives way to the rolling hills of the **Piedmont** in central Virginia, from Richmond and Charlottesville to the Hunt Country and suburban sprawl of northern Virginia. This farm country rises to meet the foothills of the **Blue Ridge,** a skinny mountain chain running the entire length of Virginia. Between the Blue Ridge and the Allegheny Mountains to the west, gorgeous valleys—including the Shenandoah—extend from the Potomac in the north to the Southwest Highlands near the borders of Tennessee and Kentucky.

NORTHERN VIRGINIA My home area in northern Virginia is the fastest-growing, wealthiest, and most densely populated part of the state—with horrendous traffic to prove it. Our northern counties once were a suburban bedroom for workers in Washington, D.C., but not anymore. Areas such as Tysons Corner have become de facto cities in their own right, with employment in high-tech service industries outstripping that of the federal government. Just across the Potomac from the nation's capital, **Arlington** is best known for its national cemetery. The historic Old Town district of **Alexandria** offers fascinating daytime walks as well as good restaurants. To the south lie the Potomac plantations, including George Washington's **Mount Vernon.** To the west, I enjoy driving out to Virginia's hilly **Hunt Country,** where the first major battle of the Civil War was fought at **Manassas.**

FREDERICKSBURG & THE NORTHERN NECK I always look forward to visiting **Fredericksburg,** whose quaint cobblestone streets and historic houses recall America's first heroes—George Washington, James Monroe, John Paul Jones—as does the quiet Northern Neck farmland, where Washington and Robert E. Lee were born. Military buffs love to explore Fredericksburg's Civil War battlefields.

CHARLOTTESVILLE   Located in the rolling Piedmont hills known as "Mr. Jefferson's country," **Charlottesville** boasts President Thomas Jefferson's magnificent estate, Monticello, as well as the University of Virginia, which he designed. Drives south bring you to Poplar Forest, his beloved retreat; Patrick Henry's final home at Red Hill; and Appomattox Court House, where the Civil War ended when Robert E. Lee surrendered to Ulysses S. Grant.

THE SHENANDOAH VALLEY   Some of Virginia's most striking scenic views are from the **Skyline Drive,** which follows the crest of the Blue Ridge Mountains through magnificent **Shenandoah National Park,** where you can explore a host of hiking paths, including part of the Maine-to-Georgia Appalachian Trail. Down below, charming towns like **Winchester, Front Royal, Luray, Staunton,** and **Lexington** evoke the Civil War, which flowed over the rolling countryside of the Shenandoah Valley, the South's breadbasket. In another valley high in the Allegheny Mountains to the west lie the famous mineral waters of **Warm Springs** and **Hot Springs.**

THE SOUTHWEST HIGHLANDS Beyond the vibrant railroad city of **Roanoke** rise the highlands of Virginia's southwestern extremity, a land of forests, waterfalls, and streams seemingly untouched since Daniel Boone led settlers along the Great Wilderness Road into Kentucky. The **Blue Ridge Parkway** wanders along its eastern border. Here the state's highest point, **Mount Rogers,** sits surrounded by a national recreation area teeming with trails for hiking, mountain biking, and horseback riding. Down in the Great Valley of Virginia, the quaint town of **Abingdon** features the famous Barter Theatre, begun during the Great Depression when its company traded tickets for hams.

RICHMOND   The state capital has few rivals among U.S. cities for its historic associations, among them St. John's Church, where Patrick Henry said, "Give me liberty, or give me death." But it was Richmond's role as the rebel capital during the Civil War that brings visitors to the Museum of the Confederacy and the Richmond and Petersburg battlefields. Fine arts and science museums, cafes, lively concerts, and theater add to Richmond's cosmopolitan ambience, and children can get their kicks at nearby Paramount's Kings Dominion amusement park.

WILLIAMSBURG, YORKTOWN & JAMESTOWN   Coastal Virginia's "Historic Triangle" is one of the country's most visited areas, and with good reason. **Jamestown** is where America's first permanent English settlers arrived in 1607 (and some of my own ancestors in 1613). **Williamsburg** immaculately re-creates Virginia's Colonial capital, and **Yorktown** commemorates the last battle of the American Revolution. Adding to the triangle's allure are theme parks and world-class discount shopping. From here it's an easy excursion to see the recovered gun turret of the USS *Monitor* at one of the nation's premier maritime museums in the shipbuilding city of **Newport News.** Historic **Hampton** may be the country's oldest continuous English-speaking settlement, but it boasts a modern, high-tech air and space museum.

NORFOLK, VIRGINIA BEACH & THE EASTERN SHORE   The great harbor of Hampton Roads is home to the resurgent cities of **Norfolk** and **Portsmouth.** You can play in the surf at **Virginia Beach,** whose boardwalk and 20 miles of sandy beach are lined with hotels, and commune with nature in **Back Bay National Wildlife Refuge** and remote **False Cape State Park.** Drive across the 17-mile Chesapeake Bay Bridge-Tunnel to the Eastern Shore, an unspoiled sanctuary noted for the fishing village of **Chincoteague** and nearby **Assateague Island,** whose wildlife refuge and national seashore have protected the famous wild ponies and prevented any development on almost 40 miles of pristine beach.

2 Visitor Information & Maps

Each city and town has a visitor information office. I list contact information for these offices in the following chapters.

The best source for statewide information is the **Virginia Tourism Corporation,** 901 E. Byrd St. (P.O. Box 798), Richmond, VA 23219 (© **800/847-4882** or 804/786-2051; fax 804/786-1919; www.virginia.org). It publishes or distributes a host of information, including a statewide travel planner; official state highway maps (including the state's "Civil War Trails" and a very useful "scenic byways" map highlighting the state's many beautiful routes); lists of hotels, motels, country inns, and bed-and-breakfasts; an outdoor guide to the state; a golf directory; a biking guide; a state park directory; a list of Virginia wineries and wine festivals; and a guide for travelers with disabilities. Most are available on, or can be ordered from, its website.

When driving into Virginia you can stop at roadside **Welcome Centers** in Bracey, on I-85 near the North Carolina border; Bristol, on I-81 near the Tennessee border; Clear Brook, on I-81 near the West Virginia border; Covington, on I-64 near the West Virginia border; New Church, on U.S. 13 south of the Maryland border; Fredericksburg, on I-95 southbound between U.S. 17 and Va. 3; Lambsburg, on I-77; Manassas, on I-66; Rocky Gap, on I-77 near the North Carolina state line;

Destination Virginia—Pre-Departure Checklist

- Did you make sure your favorite attraction is open? Many Virginia attractions are closed on Monday, for example, so call ahead for opening and closing hours.
- Do you need to book any theater, restaurant, or travel reservations in advance?
- Do you have a safe, accessible place to store money?
- If you purchased traveler's checks, have you recorded the check numbers and stored the documentation separately from the checks?
- Do you have your credit and debit card PINs? Is there a daily withdrawal limit on credit card cash advances or from an ATM?
- To check in at an airport kiosk with an e-ticket, do you have the credit card you bought your ticket with or a frequent-flier card?
- Did you bring your ID cards that could entitle you to discounts such as AAA and AARP cards, or student IDs?
- If you're flying, are you carrying a current, government-issued ID, such as a driver's license or passport? You also will need them to visit attractions on military installations such as the Norfolk Naval Station.
- Did you bring emergency drug prescriptions and extra glasses and/or contact lenses?

> **Tips Dial 511 for Info**
>
> You can dial ℂ **511** from anywhere in Virginia and receive up-to-date travel, traffic, and weather information.

---

and Skippers, on I-95 north of the North Carolina border. The centers are open daily from 8:30am to 5pm.

A good regional source is **www.visit hamptonroads.com**, operated by the Hampton Roads Partnership and covering Norfolk, Portsmouth, Virginia Beach, Hampton, Newport News, the Williamsburg area, and other localities in southeastern Virginia.

Another is the **Shenandoah Valley Travel Association,** 277 W. Old Cross Rd. (P.O. Box 1040), New Market, VA 22844 (ℂ **877/847-4878** or 540/740-3131; www.visitshenandoah.org), which covers the valley from Winchester to Lexington.

The **National Geographic Society** (www.nationalgeographic.com/maps) publishes excellent maps of Shenandoah National Park (map no. 228) and of Mount Rogers National Recreation Area (no. 786).

I post updates to the information in this book on my personal website, **www.billgoodwin.com**.

3 Entry Requirements

PASSPORTS

All visitors to the United States are required to have a valid passport. For information on how to get a passport, go to "Passports" in "Fast Facts: Virginia," later in this chapter. The websites listed provide downloadable passport applications as well as the current fees for processing passport applications.

For information on entry requirements for a specific country, go to the Entry/Exit Requirements section in the Consular Information Sheet for the country you are interested in at http://travel.state.gov/travel/cis_pa_tw/cis/cis_1765.html. *Note:* Children are required to present a passport when entering the United States at airports. More information on obtaining a passport for a minor can be found at http://travel.state.gov.

VISAS

For specifics on how to get a visa, see "Visas" in the "Fast Facts: Virginia" section at the end this chapter.

The U.S. State Department has a **Visa Waiver Program (VWP)** allowing citizens of the following countries (at press time) to enter the United States without a visa for stays of up to 90 days: Andorra, Australia, Austria, Belgium, Brunei, Denmark, Finland, France, Germany, Iceland, Ireland, Italy, Japan, Liechtenstein, Luxembourg, Monaco, the Netherlands, New Zealand, Norway, Portugal, San Marino, Singapore, Slovenia, Spain, Sweden, Switzerland, and the United Kingdom. Canadian citizens may enter the United States without visas; they will need to show passports and proof of residence, however. *Note:* Any passport issued on or after October 26, 2006, by a VWP country must be an **e-Passport** for VWP travelers to be eligible to enter the U.S. without a visa. Citizens of these nations also need to present a round-trip air or cruise ticket upon arrival. E-Passports contain computer chips capable of storing biometric information, such as the required digital photograph of the holder. (You can identify an e-Passport by the symbol on the bottom center cover of your passport.) If your passport doesn't have this feature, you

U.S. Entry: Passport Required

All persons, including U.S. citizens, traveling by air between the United States and Canada, Mexico, Central and South America, the Caribbean, and Bermuda are now required to present a valid passport. Similar regulations for those traveling by land or sea (including ferries) were expected as early as January 1, 2008.

can still travel without a visa if it is a valid passport issued before October 26, 2005, and includes a machine-readable zone, or between October 26, 2005, and October 25, 2006, and includes a digital photograph. For more information, go to **www.travel.state.gov/visa**.

Citizens of all other countries must have (1) a valid passport that expires at least 6 months later than the scheduled end of their visit to the United States, and (2) a tourist visa, which may be obtained without charge from any U.S. consulate.

Many international visitors traveling on visas to the United States will be photographed and fingerprinted on arrival at Customs in airports and on cruise ships in a program created by the Department of Homeland Security called **US-VISIT.** Exempt from the extra scrutiny are visitors entering by land or those (mostly in Europe; see above) that don't require a visa for short-term visits. For more information, go to the Homeland Security website at **www.dhs.gov/dhspublic**.

MEDICAL REQUIREMENTS

Unless you're arriving from an area known to be suffering from an epidemic (particularly cholera or yellow fever), inoculations or vaccinations are not required for entry into the United States. If you have a medical condition that requires **syringe-administered medications,** carry a valid signed prescription from your physician; syringes in carry-on baggage will be inspected. Insulin in any form should have the proper pharmaceutical documentation. If you have a disease that requires treatment with **narcotics,** you should also carry documented proof with you—smuggling narcotics aboard a plane carries severe penalties in the U.S.

For **HIV-positive visitors,** requirements for entering the United States are somewhat vague and change frequently. For up-to-the-minute information, contact **AIDSinfo** (© **800/448-0440,** or 301/519-6616 outside the U.S.; www.aidsinfo.nih.gov) or the **Gay Men's Health Crisis** (© **212/367-1000;** www.gmhc.org).

CUSTOMS

For information on what you can bring into and take out of the U.S., see "Customs" in the "Fast Facts: Virginia" section at the end of this chapter.

4 When to Go

Virginia is a gorgeous place in October, during Indian summer when the turning leaves blaze orange, red, and yellow across the state. October also is the most crowded time in the western part of the state, when throngs of visitors mob the mountains during this "leaf season." (You can find out the approximate dates for peak color in the Shenandoah Valley by calling © **800/434-5323.**)

Otherwise, Virginia is busiest during summer, when the historic sites, theme parks, and beaches draw millions of visitors—and hotel rates are at their highest. The least crowded—and least expensive—time to visit is in spring. That's when the dogwoods, azaleas, and wildflowers are in a riot of bloom from one end of Virginia to the other.

Virginia's Average Temperatures

	Jan	Feb	Mar	Apr	May	June	July	Aug	Sept	Oct	Nov	Dec
High (°F)	44	46	56	68	75	84	90	88	81	69	57	47
High (°C)	7	8	13	20	24	29	32	31	27	21	14	8
Low (°F)	26	27	38	45	54	62	66	65	59	48	39	28
High (°C)	−3	−3	3	7	12	17	19	18	15	9	4	−2

THE CLIMATE

Virginia enjoys four distinct seasons, with some variations from the warmer, more humid coastal areas to the cooler climate in the mountains. Wintertime snows are usually confined to northern Virginia and the mountains. In summer, extremely hot and humid spells can last several weeks but are normally short-lived. Spring and autumn are long seasons, and in terms of natural beauty and heavenly climate, they're optimum times to visit. Annual rainfall averages 46 inches; annual snowfall, 18 inches.

VIRGINIA CALENDAR OF EVENTS

For an exhaustive list of events beyond those listed here, check http://events.frommers.com, where you'll find a searchable, up-to-the-minute roster of what's happening in cities all over the world.

January

Whale-Watching Boat Trips, Virginia Beach. The Virginia Aquarium & Marine Science Center sends cruise boats out looking for whales. Sightings are not guaranteed. Call ℂ 757/437-2628, or go to www.vmsm.com. January 2 to mid-March.

Lee Birthday Celebrations, Alexandria. Period music, plus house tours at Lee-Fendall House. Call ℂ 703/548-1789, or go to www.leefendallhouse.org. Fourth Sunday in January.

Open house at Stratford Hall on the Northern Neck, Lee's birthplace. Call ℂ 804/493-8038, or go to www.stratfordhall.org. January 15.

February

George Washington Birthday Events, Alexandria, Mount Vernon, Fredericksburg. Old Town Alexandria puts on the dog to celebrate GW's birthday: walking tours; symposia; black tie or Colonial costume Saturday-evening dinner followed by a birthnight ball at Gadsby's Tavern; a parade on Monday (ℂ 800/388-9119 or 703/838-4200; www.funside.com). George's home at Mount Vernon also gets in on the act. Call ℂ 703/780-2000, or go to www.mountvernon.org. Down in Fredericksburg, special activities are held at Mary Washington House and George Washington's Ferry Farm. Call ℂ 800/678-4748 or 540/373-1776 (www.visitfred.com). Presidents' Day weekend.

Maymont Flower and Garden Show, Richmond. A breath of spring, with landscape exhibits, vendors, and speakers at the Greater Richmond Coliseum. Call ℂ 804/358-7166, or go to www.maymont.org. Late February.

March

James Madison's Birthday, Montpelier. Ceremony at cemetery and reception at house. Call ℂ 540/672-2728, or go to www.montpelier.org. March 16.

Patrick Henry Speech Reenactment, St. John's Episcopal Church, Richmond. "Give me liberty or give me death" resounds once again. Call ℂ 804/648-5015, or got to www.historicstjohnschurch.org. Closest Sunday to March 23.

Highland Maple Festival, Monterey. See maple syrup produced, pour it over pancakes, and visit one of the state's largest crafts shows. Call ✆ 540/468-2550, or go to www.highlandcounty.org. Second and third weekends in March.

April

Thomas Jefferson's Birthday Commemoration, Monticello, Charlottesville. Wreath-laying ceremony at gravesite, fife-and-drum corps, and a speaker. Call ✆ 434/984-9822, or go to www.monticello.org. April 13.

Norfolk's International Azalea Festival, Norfolk. The brilliant beauty of azaleas in bloom is the backdrop for ceremonies in the Norfolk Botanical Garden saluting NATO countries, including the crowning of a queen who reigns at a parade and other festivities. Also features a military display that includes an air show, visiting of ships, and aircraft ground exhibits. Call ✆ 757/441-1852, or go to www.azaleafestival.org. Second to third week in April.

Virginia Arts Festival, Williamsburg, Hampton, Newport News, Norfolk, Virginia Beach. Famous performers appear at venues from Williamsburg to Virginia Beach during this month-long festival. Call ✆ 757/282-2800, or go to www.vaartsfest.com. Mid-April to mid-May.

Virginia Fly-Fishing Festival, Waynesboro. Anglers gather beside the South River for demonstrations, lectures, casting instruction, live music, and wine tasting. Call ✆ 703/403-8338, or go to www.vaflyfishingfestival.org. Third weekend in April.

Historic Garden Week in Virginia, statewide. The event of the year for garden lovers—a celebration with tours of the grounds and gardens at more than 250 Virginia landmarks, including plantations and other sites open only during this week. For information, contact the **Garden Club of Virginia,** 12 E. Franklin St., Richmond, VA 23219 (✆ 804/644-7776 or 804/643-7141; www.vagardenweek.org). Last full week in April.

May

Shenandoah Apple Blossom Festival, Winchester. Acres of orchards in blossom throughout the valley, plus 5 days of music, band competitions, parades, the coronation of the queen, footraces, arts and crafts sales, midway amusements, and a carnival, with a celebrity grand marshal. Call ✆ 540/662-3863, or go to www.thebloom.com. Usually first weekend in May.

Virginia Gold Cup Race Meet, Great Meadow Course, The Plains. Everyone dresses to the nines for the state's premier steeplechase event. Call ✆ 800/697-2237 or 540/347-1215 (www.vagoldcup.com). First Saturday in May.

Seafood Festival, Chincoteague. All you can eat—a seafood lover's dream. Get tickets in advance from **Eastern Shore Chamber of Commerce,** P.O. Box 460, Melfa, VA 23410 (✆ 757/787-2460; www.esvatourism.org). First weekend in May.

Jamestown Landing Day, Jamestown. Militia presentations and sailing demonstrations celebrate arrival of the first English settlers in 1607. Call ✆ 888/593-4682 or 757/253-4838 (www.historyisfun.org). Early May.

Michelob Ultra LPGA Open, Kingsmill Resort & Spa, Williamsburg. The nation's best women golfers tee off in the state's top tournament. Call ✆ 757/253-3985, or go to www.michelobultraopen.com. First week in May.

Reenactment of Battle of New Market, New Market Battlefield State Historical Park, New Market. Call

© **866/515-1864** or 540/740-3101 (www4.vmi.edu/museum/nm). Weekend closest to May 15.

New Market Day, Virginia Military Institute Campus, Lexington. Annual roll call for cadets who died in the Battle of New Market. Call © **540/464-7000,** or go to www.vmi.edu. May 15.

Oatlands Sheepdog Trials, Leesburg. Dogs compete in sheepherding contests. In addition, there are crafts, food, and house and garden tours. Call © **703/777-3174,** or go to www. oatlands.org. Late May.

Virginia Hunt Country Stable Tour, Loudon County. A unique opportunity to view prestigious Leesburg, Middleburg, and Upperville horse farms and private estates. Sponsored by Trinity Episcopal Church, Upperville. Call © **540/592-3711,** or go to www.middleburgonline.com/stable tour. Memorial Day weekend.

Shenandoah Valley Music Festival, Orkney Springs. Music from classical to country fills the mountain air. Call **Orkney Springs Hotel** at © **800/ 459-3396** (tickets only) or 540/459-3396 (www.musicfest.org). Concerts start Memorial Day weekend and run on weekends through August.

June

Vintage Virginia Wine Festival, Great Meadows Steeplechase Course, The Plains. Taste the premium vintages from 35 wineries at this Hunt Country festival. Arts and crafts displays; food; and jazz, reggae, and pop music. Call © **800/277-2675,** or go to www.vintagevirginia.com (for information about this and many other wine festivals statewide). First weekend in June.

Harborfest, Norfolk. Tall ships, sailboat races, air shows, military demonstrations, and fireworks. Call © **757/441-1852,** or go to www. festeventsva.org. Mid-June.

Boardwalk Art Show, Virginia Beach. Works in all mediums, between 14th and 28th streets on the Boardwalk. Call © **800/822-3224,** or go to www. vbfun.com. Mid-June.

Ash Lawn Opera Festival, Charlottesville. James Monroe's home is the setting for opera, musicals, and concerts. Call © **434/293-4500,** or go to www.ashlawnopera.org. End of June to August.

July

Independence Day Celebrations, statewide. Every town parties and shoots fireworks in honor of the nation's birthday. Contact local tourist information offices. July 4th.

Pony Swim and Auction, Chincoteague. Famous wild horses swim the Assateague Channel and are later herded to carnival grounds and auctioned off. Return swim to Assateague on Friday. Call © **757/336-6161** (fax 757/336-1241; www.chincoteague chamber.com). The carnival-like festival is last 2 weeks in July; swim on last Wednesday in July.

August

Virginia Highlands Festival, Abingdon. Appalachian Mountain culture showcase for musicians, artists, artisans, and writers. Area's largest crafts show has an antiques market and hot-air balloons. Call © **800/435-3440** or 276/676-2282 (www.vahighlands festival.org). First 2 weeks in August.

Old Time Fiddlers' Convention, Galax. Dating to 1935, one of the largest and oldest such conventions in the world. It also coincides with the Fiddlefest street festival. Call © **276/ 236-8541,** or go to www.oldfiddlers convention.com. Early August.

September

American Music Festival, Virginia Beach. Top entertainers perform on the sand. Tickets are first-come, first-served. Call © **800/822-3224,** or go to www.vbfun.com. Labor Day weekend.

The Irvington Stomp, Irvington. Guests actually stomp grapes in the European fashion during this fun-filled event at White Fences Vineyard & Winery. Call © **804/438-5559,** or go to www.irvingtonstomp.com. Saturday of Labor Day weekend.

State Fair of Virginia, Richmond Raceway Complex, Richmond. Rides, entertainment, agricultural exhibits, pioneer farmstead, and flower shows. Call © **800/588-3247** or 804/228-3200 (www.statefairva.org). Ten days in late September.

October

Chincoteague Oyster Festival, Chincoteague. A feast of oysters—but for advance ticket holders only. Call © **804/336-6161,** or go to www.chincoteaguechamber.com. Early October.

Waterford Homes Tour and Crafts Exhibit, Waterford Village. This tiny Quaker town grows to some 40,000 on this one weekend. Call © **540/882-3018,** or go to www.waterfordva.org. First weekend in October.

Virginia Film Festival, Charlottesville. Tribute to all things celluloid. Call © **800/882-3378,** or go to www.vafilm.com. Mid-October.

Yorktown Day, Colonial National Historic Park, Yorktown. British surrender in 1781 celebrated with a parade, historic house tours, Colonial music and dress, and military drills. Call © **757/898-2410** or 757/898-3400 (www.nps.gov/colo). October 19.

International Gold Cup, Great Meadows Course, The Plains. Fall colors provide a backdrop to one of the most prestigious steeplechase races. Call © **800/697-2237** or 540/347-1215 (www.vagoldcup.com). Third Saturday in October.

Marine Corps Marathon, Arlington. More than 18,000 men and women run a 26.2-mile course from Arlington through Washington, D.C., and back. The U.S. Marine Corps' "People's Marathon" is open to all (there's even a wheelchair division). Call © **800/786-8762** or 703/784-2265 (www.marinemarathon.com). Third or fourth Sunday in October.

November

The First Thanksgiving, Charles City. Reenactment at Berkeley Plantation. Call © **888/466-6018** or 804/829-6018 (www.berkeleyplantation.com). Early November.

Assateague Island Waterfowl Week, Chincoteague. The only time of the year when visitors can drive to the northern end of Chincoteague National Wildlife Refuge on Assateague Island. Guided walks for pedestrians. Call © **757/336-6122,** or go to http://chinco.fws.gov. Thanksgiving weekend.

December

Mount Vernon by Candlelight, Mount Vernon. See Washington's mansion as he would have, by the light of candles. Tickets required. Call © **703/780-2000,** or go to www.mountvernon.org. First week in December.

Grand Illumination, Williamsburg. Gala opening of holiday season with fife-and-drum corps, illumination of buildings, caroling, dancing, and fireworks. Call © **800/447-8679** or 757/220-7645 (www.colonialwilliamsburg.com). First Saturday in December.

Christmas Candlelight Tour, Fredericksburg. Historic homes welcome visitors. Call © **800/678-4748** or 540/373-1776 (www.visitfred.com). First weekend in December.

Monticello Candlelight Tour, Charlottesville. Experience authentic Colonial decorations. Call © **804/984-9822,** or go to www.monticello.org. Early December.

Historic Michie Tavern Feast and Open House, Charlottesville. The old tavern puts on two Christmastime feasts. Reservations required. Call © **804/977-1234,** or go to www. michietavern.com. Second weekend in December.

Jamestown Christmas, Jamestown. Jamestown Settlement is all decked out 17th-century-style. Call © **888/593-4682** or 757/253-4838 (www.history isfun.org). Second to fourth week in December.

5 Getting There

BY PLANE

The major international gateway to Virginia is **Washington Dulles International Airport** (IAD; © **703/661-2700;** www.mwaa.com), about 25 miles west of Washington, D.C. Dulles is also a regional hub for domestic flights, and fares can be less to fly in and out of here than other airports in Virginia.

Domestic carriers serving Washington Dulles include **AirTran Airlines** (© 800/247-8726; www.airtran.com), **American** (© 800/433-7300; www.aa.com), **Continental** (© 800/525-0280; www.continental.com), **Delta Airlines** (© 800/221-1212; www.delta.com), **JetBlue Airways** (© 800/538-2583; www.jetblue.com), **MaxJet** (© 888/435-9626; www.maxjet.com), **Midwest Airlines** (© 800/452-2022; www.midwestairlines.com), **Northwest Airlines** (© 800/225-2525; www.nwa.com), **Sun Country Airlines** (© 800/800-6557; www.suncountry.com), **Southwest Airlines** (© 800/435-9792; www.southwest.com), **Ted** (© 800/225-5833; www.flyted.com), **United Airlines** (© 800/241-6522; www.united.com), **US Airways** (© 800/428-4322; www.usairways.com), and **Virgin America** (© 877/359-8474; www.virginamerica.com).

Among the major international airlines are **Aeroflot** (© 888/686-4949; www.aeroflot.ru), **Air Canada** (© 888/247-2262; www.aircanada.ca), **Air France** (© 800/321-4538; www.airfrance.com), **Aer Lingus** (© 800/474-7424; www.aerlingus.com), **Alitalia** (© 800/223-5730; www.alitaliausa.com), **ANA/All Nippon Airways** (© 800/235-9262; www.fly-ana.com), **Austrian Airlines** (© 800/843-0002; www.aua.com), **British Airways** (© 800/247-9297; www.ba.com), **Korean Airlines** (© 800/438-5000; www.koreanair.com), **Lufthansa Airlines** (© 800/645-3880; www.lufthansa.com), **Northwest/KLM Royal Dutch Airlines** (© 800/225-2525; www.nwa.com), **SAS Scandinavian Airlines** (© 800/221-2350; www.scandinavian.net), **Swiss** (© 877/359-7947; www.swiss.com), **South African Airways** (© 800/722-9675; www.flysaa.com), and **Virgin Atlantic Airways** (© 800/862-8621; www.virgin-atlantic.com).

Also serving northern Virginia is **Ronald Reagan Washington National Airport** (DCA; © **703/685-8000;** www.mwaa.com), on the Potomac River 2 miles north of Alexandria. With the major exception of **Air Canada** (© 888/247-2262; www.aircanada.ca), it mostly hosts domestic carriers such as **Alaska Airlines** (© 800/252-7522; www.alaskaair.com), **American** (© 800/433-7300; www.aa.com), **ATA** (© 800/435-9282; www.ata.com), **Continental** (© 800/525-0280; www.continental.com), **Delta Airlines** (© 800/221-1212; www.delta.com), **Frontier Airlines** (© 800/432-1359; www.flyfrontier.com), **Northwest/**

Tips **Getting Through the Airport**

- Arrive at the airport at least 1 hour before a domestic flight and 2 hours before an international flight. You can check the average wait times at your airport by going to the TSA **Security Checkpoint Wait Times** site (**http://waittime.tsa.dhs.gov**).
- Know what you can carry on and what you can't. For the latest updates on items you are prohibited to bring in carry-on luggage, go to **www.tsa. gov/travelers/airtravel**.
- Beat the ticket-counter lines by using the self-service electronic ticket kiosks at the airport or even printing out your boarding pass at home from the airline website. Using curbside check-in is also a smart way to avoid lines.
- Bring a current, government-issued photo ID such as a driver's license or passport. Children under 18 do not need government-issued photo IDs for flights within the U.S., but they do need passports for international flights to most countries.
- Help speed up security before you're screened. Remove jackets, shoes, belt buckles, heavy jewelry, and watches and place them either in your carry-on luggage or the security bins provided. Place keys, coins, cellphones, and pagers in a security bin. If you have metallic body parts, carry a note from your doctor. When possible, pack liquids in checked baggage.
- Use a TSA-approved lock for your checked luggage. Look for Travel Sentry certified locks at luggage or travel shops and Brookstone stores (or online at **www.brookstone.com**).

KLM Royal Dutch Airlines (✆ 800/225-2525; www.nwa.com), **Spirit Airlines** (✆ 800/772-7177; www.spiritair.com), **United Airlines** (✆ 800/241-6522; www.united.com), and **US Airways** (✆ 800/428-4322; www.usairways.com).

See the destination chapters for details about Virginia's other gateways: **Richmond International Airport** (RIC; ✆ 804/226-3000; www.flyrichmond.com), **Norfolk International Airport** (ORF; ✆ 757/857-3351; www.norfolkairport.com), **Newport News/Williamsburg Airport** (PHF; ✆ 757/877-0221; www.nnwairport.com), **Charlottesville/Albemarle Airport** (CHO; ✆ 804/973-8341; www.gocho.com), **Shenandoah Valley Regional Airport** (SHD; ✆ 540/234-8304; www.flyshd.com), and

Roanoke Regional Airport (ROA; ✆ 540/362-1999; www.roanokeregional airport.com).

Many flights to these regional airports are of the "commuter" variety, and you likely will pay higher fares to fly into them than into Washington Dulles.

ARRIVING AT THE AIRPORT IMMIGRATION & CUSTOMS CLEARANCE Foreign visitors arriving by air, no matter what their port of entry, should cultivate patience and resignation before setting foot on U.S. soil. U.S. airports have considerably beefed up security clearances in the years since the terrorist attacks of September 11, 2001, and clearing Customs and Immigration can take as long as 2 hours.

People traveling by air from Canada, Bermuda, and certain Caribbean countries can sometimes clear Customs and Immigration at the point of departure, which is much faster.

FLYING FOR LESS: TIPS FOR GETTING THE BEST AIRFARE

- Passengers who can book their ticket **long in advance,** who can **stay over Saturday night,** or who **fly midweek** or **at less trafficked hours** will pay a fraction of the full fare. If your schedule is flexible, say so, and ask if you can secure a cheaper fare by changing your flight plans.
- Search **the Internet** for cheap fares. The most popular online travel agencies are **Travelocity** (www.travelocity.com), **Expedia.com,** and **Orbitz** (www.orbitz.com). In the U.K., go to **Travelsupermarket** (© **0845/345-5708;** www.travelsupermarket.com), a flight search engine that offers flight comparisons for the budget airlines whose seats often end up in bucket-shop sales. Other websites for booking airline tickets online include **Cheapflights.com, SmarterTravel.com, Priceline.com,** and **Opodo** (www.opodo.com). Meta-search sites (which find and then direct you to airline and hotel websites for booking) include **Sidestep** (www.sidestep.com) and **Kayak** (www.kayak.com)—the latter includes fares for budget carriers like JetBlue and Spirit as well as the major airlines.

Lastminute.com is a great source for last-minute flights and getaways. In addition, most **airlines** offer online-only fares that even their phone agents know nothing about.

- Watch local newspapers for **promotional specials** or **fare wars,** when airlines lower prices on their most popular routes. Also keep an eye on price fluctuations and deals at websites such as **Airfarewatchdog.com** and **Farecast** (www.farecast.com).
- **Consolidators,** also known as bucket shops, are wholesale brokers in the airline-ticket game. Consolidators buy deeply discounted tickets ("distressed" inventories of unsold seats) from airlines and sell them to online ticket agencies, travel agents, tour operators, corporations, and, to a lesser degree, the general public. Consolidators advertise in Sunday newspaper travel sections (often in small ads with tiny type), both in the U.S. and the U.K. They can be great sources for cheap international tickets. On the downside, bucket-shop tickets are often rigged with restrictions, such as stiff cancellation penalties (as high as 50%–75% of the ticket price). And keep in mind that most of what you see advertised is of limited availability. Several reliable consolidators are worldwide and available online. **STA Travel** (www.statravel.com) has been the world's leading consolidator for students

---

Tips Don't Stow It—Ship It

Though pricey, it's sometimes worthwhile to travel luggage-free, particularly if you're toting sports equipment, meetings materials, or baby equipment. Specialists in door-to-door luggage delivery include **Virtual Bellhop** (www.virtualbellhop.com); **SkyCap International** (www.skycapinternational.com); **Luggage Express** (www.usxpluggageexpress.com); and **Sports Express** (www.sportsexpress.com).

Flying with Film & Video

Never pack film—developed or undeveloped—in checked bags, as the new, more powerful scanners in U.S. airports can fog film. The film you carry with you can be damaged by scanners as well. X-ray damage is cumulative; the faster the film, and the more times you put it through a scanner, the more likely the damage. Film under 800 ASA is usually safe for up to five scans. U.S. regulations permit you to demand hand inspections; you should do so if your film is scanned more than five times.

On international flights, store your film in transparent baggies, so you can remove it easily before you go through scanners. Keep in mind that airports are not the only places where your camera may be scanned: Highly trafficked attractions are X-raying visitors' bags with increasing frequency.

Most photo supply stores sell protective pouches designed to block damaging X-rays. The pouches fit both film and loaded cameras. They should protect your film in checked baggage, but they also may raise alarms and result in a hand inspection.

You'll have little to worry about if you are traveling with **digital cameras.** Unlike film, which is sensitive to light, the digital camera and storage cards are not affected by airport X rays, according to Nikon. Still, if you plan to travel extensively, you may want to play it safe and hand-carry your digital equipment or ask that it be inspected by hand.

Carry-on scanners will not damage **videotape** in video cameras, but the magnetic fields emitted by the walk-through security gateways and hand-held inspection wands will. Always place your loaded camcorder on the screening conveyor belt or have it hand-inspected. Be sure your batteries are charged, as you will probably be required to turn the device on to ensure that it's what it appears to be.

since purchasing Council Travel, but their fares are competitive for travelers of all ages. **Flights.com** (© **800/TRAV-800**) has excellent fares worldwide, particularly to Europe. They also have "local" websites in 12 countries. **FlyCheap** (© **800/FLY-CHEAP;** www.1800flycheap.com) has especially good fares to sunny destinations. **Air Tickets Direct** (© **800/778-3447;** www.airtickets direct.com) is based in Montreal and leverages the currently weak Canadian dollar for low fares; they also book trips to places that U.S. travel agents won't touch, such as Cuba.

• Join **frequent-flier clubs.** Frequent-flier membership doesn't cost a cent, but it does entitle you to free tickets or upgrades when you amass the airline's required number of frequent-flier points. You don't even have to fly to earn points; **frequent-flier credit cards** can earn you thousands of miles for doing your everyday shopping. Frankly, I have a ton of miles, but I can seldom find a flight on which to use them. That's because award seats are limited, especially on popular routes. *Inside tip:* Award seats are offered almost a year in advance, but seats also open up at the last minute, so if your travel plans are flexible, you may strike gold. To play the frequent-flier game to your best advantage, consult the community bulletin boards on **FlyerTalk** (www.flyertalk.com) or go to Randy Petersen's **InsideFlyer** (www.insideflyer.com). Petersen and friends review all the programs in detail and post regular updates on changes in policies and trends. *Also note:* More and more major airlines are cutting their expiration periods for mileage points—I recently saw 54,000 of my miles disappear due to expiration—so check your airline's frequent-flier program to avoid losing your miles before you use them.

BY CAR

Having your own vehicle is by far the best way to see the state.

Highway **I-95** runs north-south through Virginia between Alexandria and Emporia. From western Maryland and eastern Tennessee, the major highway is **I-81,** which runs north-south the entire length of the state through the Shenandoah Valley and Southwest Highlands. Accidents are common on both I-95 and I-81, which are heavy-duty truck routes, so be especially careful while driving on them. (So many trucks slow down as they creep side-by-side uphill and then race down the other side that I seldom get to use my cruise control on I-81!)

Major western entrance points are from West Virginia via **I-77** and **I-64.** The latter runs east-west across the state between Covington and Norfolk. In northern Virginia, **I-66** traverses the state east-west between Arlington and I-81 at Strasburg. I-66 can slow to a snail's pace during rush hours in northern Virginia.

The **Virginia Department of Transportation,** 1401 E. Broad St., Richmond, VA 23219 (© **804/786-5731;** www.virginiadot.org), publishes a free list

of road construction projects, and it maintains a 24-hour-a-day **Highway Helpline** (© **800/367-7623**) for information about road conditions and to report emergencies. It has live webcams of key northern Virginia and Hampton Roads highways and posts road condition maps online. Call © **800/792-2800** to check on conditions in Hampton Roads' often-congested tunnels.

Dial © **#77** on your cellphone to report an accident or other emergency to the state highway patrol.

The Virginia Tourism Corporation distributes a detailed **state road map** as well as one that highlights the scenic drives (see "Visitor Information & Maps," earlier in this chapter).

Most **car-rental companies** operate in Virginia's major metropolitan areas and at all but the smallest of airports.

BY TRAIN

Amtrak trains (© **800/872-7245;** www.amtrak.com) are better for getting to and from Virginia than for getting around the state. The high-speed Acela, Metroliner service, and other northeast corridor trains connect New York to Union Station in Washington, D.C., where riders can board the Metrorail subway to Alexandria. All Amtrak trains between New York and Florida stop at Washington, D.C., and Richmond; some stop at Alexandria, Quantico, and Fredericksburg. Another train follows this route from New York to Richmond, and then heads east to Newport News via Williamsburg. From Newport News, Amtrak's Thruway bus service connects to Norfolk and Virginia Beach. Some east- and westbound trains to and from Washington stop at Charlottesville, Staunton, and Clifton Forge. From Clifton Forge, a Thruway bus connects to Roanoke.

International visitors can buy a **USA Rail Pass,** good for 5, 15, or 30 days of unlimited travel on **Amtrak.** The pass is available online or through many overseas travel agents. See Amtrak's website for the cost of travel within the western, eastern, or northwestern United States. Reservations are generally required and should be made as early as possible. Regional rail passes are also available.

6 Money & Costs

As you might expect, Virginia is most expensive in its larger cities and in the Washington, D.C., suburbs of northern Virginia. It's also hard to find bargains at the beach in the summer or in the Shenandoah during the October "leaf" season. Even so, the state is not a particularly expensive destination, and is much less costly than London, New York, and other major metropolitan areas. While there are plenty of high-end restaurants, luxury hotels, and bed-and-breakfasts, smaller independent hotels and motels abound, as well as multitudinous representatives of all the major budget chains. It's possible to eat and stay well in Virginia without spending a fortune, and should you decide to splurge, you can find a lot of luxury for your money.

However much you plan to spend, it's always advisable to bring money in a variety of forms on a vacation: a mix of cash, credit cards, and traveler's checks. You should also exchange enough petty cash to cover airport incidentals, tipping, and transportation to your hotel before you leave home, or withdraw money upon arrival at an airport ATM.

ATMs

Nationwide, the easiest and best way to get cash away from home is from an ATM (automated teller machine), sometimes referred to as a "cash machine" or "cashpoint." The **Cirrus** (© **800/424-7787;** www.mastercard.com) and **PLUS** (© **800/843-7587;** www.visa.com) networks span the country; you can find them even in remote regions. Go to your bank card's website to find ATM locations at your destination. Be sure you know your daily withdrawal limit before you depart.

Don't forget your personal identification number (PIN) since all ATMs in Virginia require them to withdraw cash.

Note: Many banks impose a fee every time you use a card at another bank's ATM, and that fee is often higher for international transactions (up to $5 or more) than for domestic ones (where they're rarely more than $2). In addition, the bank from which you withdraw cash may charge its own fee. To compare banks' ATM fees within the U.S., use **www.bankrate.com**. Visitors from outside the U.S. should also find out whether their bank assesses a 1% to 3% fee on charges incurred abroad.

CREDIT CARDS & DEBIT CARDS

Credit cards are the most widely used form of payment in the United States: **Visa** (Barclaycard in Britain), **Master-Card** (EuroCard in Europe, Access in Britain, Chargex in Canada), **American Express, Diners Club,** and **Discover.** They also provide a convenient record of all your expenses, and offer relatively good exchange rates. You can withdraw cash advances from your credit cards at banks or ATMs, but high fees make these cash advances a pricey way to get cash.

I highly recommended that you travel with at least one major credit card. You must have a credit card to rent a car, and hotels and airlines usually require a credit card imprint as a deposit against expenses.

ATM cards with major credit card backing, known as **"debit cards,"** are now a commonly acceptable form of payment in most stores and restaurants. Debit cards draw money directly from your checking account. Some stores and most U.S. post offices enable you to receive cash back on your debit card purchases as well.

> **Tips Dear Visa: I'm Off to Richmond!**
>
> Some credit card companies recommend that you notify them of an impending trip or they may become suspicious and block your charges when the card is used numerous times in a destination that's not your home. If you don't call your credit card company in advance, you should carry the card's toll-free emergency number with you so that you can get in touch if a charge is refused. But perhaps the most important lesson here is to carry more than one card on your trip; a card might not work for any number of reasons, so having a backup is actually quite important.

TRAVELER'S CHECKS

Though credit cards and debit cards are more often used, traveler's checks are still widely accepted in the U.S. Foreign visitors should make sure that traveler's checks are in U.S. dollars; foreign-currency checks are often difficult to exchange.

You can buy traveler's checks at most banks. Most are offered in denominations of $20, $50, $100, $500, and sometimes $1,000. Generally, you'll pay a service charge ranging from 1% to 4%.

The most popular traveler's checks are offered by **American Express** (© **800/807-6233** or 800/221-7282 for card-holders—this number accepts collect calls, offers service in several foreign languages, and exempts Amex gold and platinum cardholders from the 1% fee) and **Visa** (© **800/732-1322;** AAA members can obtain Visa checks for a $9.95 fee for checks up to $1,500 at most AAA offices or by calling © **866/339-3378**). Call © **800/223-9920** for information on MasterCard traveler's checks.

Be sure to keep a copy of the traveler's checks serial numbers separate from your checks in the event that they are stolen or lost. You'll get a refund faster if you know the numbers.

7 Travel Insurance

The cost of travel insurance varies widely, depending on the cost and length of your trip, your age and health, and the type of trip you're taking, but expect to pay between 5% and 8% of the vacation itself. You can get estimates from various providers through **InsureMyTrip.com.** Enter your trip cost and dates, your age, and other information for prices from more than a dozen companies.

For **U.K. citizens,** insurance is always advisable when traveling in the States. Travelers or families who make more than one trip abroad per year may find an annual travel insurance policy works out cheaper. Check **www.moneysuper market.com,** which compares prices across a wide range of providers for single- and multitrip policies.

Most big travel agents offer their own insurance and will probably try to sell you their package when you book a holiday. Think before you sign. **Britain's Consumers' Association** recommends that you insist on seeing the policy and reading the fine print before buying travel insurance. **The Association of British Insurers** (© **020/7600-3333;** www.abi. org.uk) gives advice by phone and publishes *Holiday Insurance,* a free guide to policy provisions and prices. You might also shop around for better deals: Try **Columbus Direct** (© **0870/033-9988;** www.columbusdirect.net).

TRIP-CANCELLATION INSURANCE

Trip-cancellation insurance will help retrieve your money if you have to back out of a trip or depart early, or if your travel supplier goes bankrupt. Trip cancellation traditionally covers such events as sickness, natural disasters, and State Department advisories. The latest news in trip-cancellation insurance is the availability of **expanded hurricane coverage** and the **"any-reason"** cancellation coverage— which costs more but covers cancellations made for any reason. You won't get back 100% of your prepaid trip cost, but you'll be refunded a substantial portion. **Travel-Safe** (© **888/885-7233;** www.travel safe.com) offers both types of coverage. Expedia.com also offers any-reason cancellation coverage for its air-hotel packages.

For details, contact one of the following recommended insurers: **Access America** (© 866/807-3982; www.access america.com); **AIG Travel Guard** (© 800/826-4919; www.travelguard.com); **Travel Insured International** (© 800/243-3174; www.travelinsured.com); and **Travelex Insurance Services** (© 888/457-4602; www.travelex-insurance.com).

MEDICAL INSURANCE

Although it's not required of travelers, health insurance is highly recommended. Most health insurance policies cover you if you get sick away from home—but check your coverage before you leave.

International visitors should note that unlike many European countries, the United States does not usually offer free or low-cost medical care to its citizens or visitors. Doctors and hospitals are expensive, and in most cases will require advance payment or proof of coverage before they render their services. Good policies will cover the costs of an accident, repatriation, or death. Packages such as

Europ Assistance's "Worldwide Health-care Plan" are sold by European automobile clubs and travel agencies at attractive rates. **Worldwide Assistance Services, Inc.** (© **800/777-8710;** www.worldwide assistance.com) is the agent for Europ Assistance in the United States.

Though lack of health insurance may prevent you from being admitted to a hospital in nonemergencies, don't worry about being left on a street corner to die: The American way is to fix you now and bill the living daylights out of you later.

If you're ever hospitalized more than 150 miles from home, **MedjetAssist** (© **800/527-7478;** www.medjetassistance.com) will pick you up and fly you to the hospital of your choice in a medically equipped and staffed aircraft 24 hours day, 7 days a week. Annual memberships are $225 individual, $350 family; you can also purchase short-term memberships.

Canadians should check with their provincial health plan offices or call **Health Canada** (© **866/225-0709;** www.hc-sc.gc.ca) to find out the extent of their coverage and what documentation and receipts they must take home in case they are treated in the United States.

LOST-LUGGAGE INSURANCE

On flights within the U.S., checked baggage is covered up to $2,500 per ticketed passenger. On flights outside the U.S. (and on U.S. portions of international trips), baggage coverage is limited to approximately $9.07 per pound, up to approximately $635 per checked bag. If you plan to check items more valuable than what's covered by the standard liability, see if your homeowner's policy covers your valuables, get baggage insurance as part of your comprehensive travel-insurance package, or buy Travel Guard's "BagTrak" product.

If your luggage is lost, immediately file a lost-luggage claim at the airport, detailing the luggage contents. Most airlines require that you report delayed, damaged, or lost baggage within 4 hours of arrival. The airlines are required to deliver luggage, once found, directly to your house or destination free of charge.

8 Health

STAYING HEALTHY

Malaria may have been a curse of the colonists who settled Virginia, but today the state poses no unusual health threats. Although Virginia mosquitoes don't carry malaria, they are still rampant in the Tidewater during summer, especially in the marshes of Chincoteague, Assateague, and Tangier islands, so use plenty of insect repellent on the Eastern Shore.

GENERAL AVAILABILITY OF HEALTHCARE

Contact the **International Association for Medical Assistance to Travelers** (**IAMAT;** © **716/754-4883,** or 416/652-0137 in Canada; www.iamat.org) for tips on travel and health concerns in the countries you're visiting, and for lists of local, English-speaking doctors. The United States **Centers for Disease Control and Prevention** (© **800/311-3435;** www.cdc.gov) provides up-to-date information on health hazards by region or country and offers tips on food safety. The website **www.tripprep.com**, sponsored by a consortium of travel medicine practitioners, **Travel Health Online,** may also offer helpful advice on traveling abroad. You can find listings of reliable clinics overseas at the **International Society of Travel Medicine** (www.istm.org).

WHAT TO DO IF YOU GET SICK AWAY FROM HOME

Hospitals and emergency care facilities are widespread in Virginia, so unless you're deep in the backcountry, help will be close at hand. We list statewide **emergency numbers** under "Fast Facts: Virginia," later in this chapter.

In case of illness, consider asking your hotel concierge or staff to recommend a local doctor—even his or her own. Most Virginia cities and towns have hospitals, and you can try their emergency rooms for assistance. Many have walk-in clinics for cases that are not life threatening. You may not get immediate attention, but you won't pay the high price of an emergency room visit (usually a minimum of $300 just for signing your name)

If you suffer from a chronic illness, consult your doctor before your departure. Pack **prescription medications** in your carry-on luggage, and carry them in their original containers, with pharmacy labels—otherwise they won't make it through airport security. Visitors from outside the U.S. should carry generic names of prescription drugs. For U.S. travelers, most reliable healthcare plans provide coverage if you get sick away from home. Foreign visitors may have to pay all medical costs upfront and be reimbursed later. See "Medical Insurance," under "Travel Insurance," above.

9 Safety

STAYING SAFE

Most areas of Virginia are relatively free of street crime, but this is not the case in some parts of Alexandria, Richmond, Norfolk, Roanoke, and other cities. Ask your hotel staff or the local visitor information office whether neighborhoods you intend to visit are safe. Avoid deserted streets and alleys, and always be especially alert at night. Never leave anything of value visible in your parked car; it's an invitation to theft.

When heading outdoors, keep in mind that injuries often occur when people fail to follow instructions. Believe the experts who tell you to stay on the established trails. Hike in designated areas, follow the marine charts if piloting your own boat, carry rain gear, and wear a life jacket when canoeing or rafting. Watch for summer thunderstorms that can leave you drenched, send bolts of lightning your way, and suddenly flood otherwise peaceful streams. Mountain weather can be fickle any season.

10 Specialized Travel Resources

TRAVELERS WITH DISABILITIES

Most disabilities shouldn't stop anyone from traveling. There are more options and resources out there than ever before. This is especially true in Virginia, where most establishments are required to comply with the federal Americans with Disabilities Act.

The **America the Beautiful—National Park and Federal Recreational Lands Pass—Access Pass** (formerly the **Golden Access Passport**) gives visually impaired or permanently disabled persons (regardless of age) free lifetime entrance to federal recreation sites administered by the National Park Service, the Fish and Wildlife Service, the Forest Service, the Bureau of Land Management, and the Bureau of Reclamation. This includes national parks, monuments, historic sites, recreation areas, and national wildlife refuges.

The America the Beautiful Access Pass can only be obtained in person at any NPS facility that charges an entrance fee. You need to show proof of medically determined disability. Besides free entry, the pass also offers a 50% discount on some federal-use fees charged for such facilities as camping, swimming, parking, boat launching, and tours. For more information, go to www.nps.gov/fees_passes.htm or call © **888/467-2757.**

Organizations that offer a vast range of resources and assistance to disabled travelers include **MossRehab** (© **800/CALL-MOSS;** www.mossresourcenet.org); the **American Foundation for the Blind** (**AFB;** © **800/232-5463;** www.afb.org); and **SATH** (Society for Accessible Travel & Hospitality; © **212/447-7284;** www.sath.org). **AirAmbulanceCard.com** is now partnered with SATH and allows you to preselect top-notch hospitals in case of an emergency.

Access-Able Travel Source (© **303/232-2979;** www.access-able.com) offers a comprehensive database on travel agents from around the world with experience in accessible travel; destination-specific access information; and links to such resources as service animals, equipment rentals, and access guides.

Many travel agencies offer customized tours and itineraries for travelers with disabilities. Among them are **Flying Wheels Travel** (© **507/451-5005;** www.flying wheelstravel.com) and **Accessible Journeys** (© **800/846-4537** or 610/521-0339; www.disabilitytravel.com).

Flying with Disability (www.flying-with-disability.org) is a comprehensive information source on airplane travel. **Avis Rent a Car** (© **888/879-4273;** www.avis.com) has an "Avis Access" program that offers services for customers with special travel needs. These include specially outfitted vehicles with swivel seats, spinner knobs, and hand controls; mobility scooter rentals; and accessible bus service. Be sure to reserve well in advance.

Also check out the quarterly magazine *Emerging Horizons* (www.emerging horizons.com), available by subscription

($16.95 per year U.S.; $21.95 outside the U.S).

The "Accessible Travel" link at **Mobility-Advisor.com** offers a variety of travel resources to disabled persons.

British travelers should contact **Holiday Care** (℃ 0845-124-9971 in the U.K. only; www.holidaycare.org.uk) to access a wide range of travel information and resources for disabled and elderly people.

GAY & LESBIAN TRAVELERS

Virginia has its intolerant contingent, particularly in rural areas, and its Republican-controlled legislature is not about to legalize gay marriage (fornication is still technically a crime in Virginia regardless of gender!). But by and large, the state is a safe, comfortable place for gay and lesbian travelers. There are gay and lesbian communities in most cities here.

Nationally, **The International Gay and Lesbian Travel Association (IGLTA;** ℃ 800/448-8550 or 954/776-2626; www.iglta.org) is the trade association for the gay and lesbian travel industry, and offers an online directory of gay- and lesbian-friendly travel businesses and tour operators.

Many agencies offer tours and travel itineraries specifically for gay and lesbian travelers. **Above and Beyond Tours** (℃ 800/397-2681; www.abovebeyond tours.com) are gay Australia tour specialists. San Francisco–based **Now, Voyager** (℃ 800/255-6951; www.nowvoyager. com) offers worldwide trips and cruises, and **Olivia** (℃ 800/631-6277; www. olivia.com) offers lesbian cruises and resort vacations.

Gay.com Travel (℃ 800/929-2268 or 415/644-8044; www.gay.com/travel or www.outandabout.com), is an excellent online successor to the popular *Out & About* print magazine. It provides regularly updated information about gay-owned, gay-oriented, and gay-friendly lodging, dining, sightseeing, nightlife,

and shopping establishments in every important destination worldwide. British travelers should click on the "Travel" link at **www.uk.gay.com** for advice and gay-friendly trip ideas.

The Canadian website **GayTraveler** (**http://gaytraveler.ca**) offers ideas and advice for gay travel all over the world.

For gay travel guides, good options include *Spartacus International Gay Guide* (Bruno Gmünder Verlag; www. spartacusworld.com/gayguide) and the *Damron* guides (www.damron.com), with separate, annual books for gay men and lesbians.

SENIOR TRAVELERS

Mention the fact that you're a senior when you make your reservations. All major airlines, car-rental firms, and most Virginia hotels offer discounts for seniors, especially members of **AARP,** 601 E St. NW, Washington, DC 20049 (℃ 800/ 424-3410 or 202/434-2277; www.aarp. org). AARP offers members a wide range of benefits, including *AARP: The Magazine* and a monthly newsletter. Anyone over 50 can join.

A committee of deranged bureaucrats must have come up with the tongue-tying name of the **America the Beautiful— National Park and Federal Recreational Lands Pass—Senior,** which is also known as the America the Beautiful Senior Pass, or among bureaucrats as the Interagency Senior Pass. Like the National Park Service's former Golden Age Passport, which is still honored, it gives anyone 62 years or older—and passengers in their noncommercial vehicles—entrance to national parks, monuments, and historic sites, plus national recreation areas and wildlife refuges managed by the U.S. Agriculture Department. The senior pass costs a one-time fee of $10, lasts for a lifetime, and must be purchased in person at any national park, recreation area, or wildlife refuge that charges an entrance fee

(Kids) Family Travel—Virginia Is for Kids, Too

Virginia will bring history to life for your kids (and you, too) with a myriad of associations involving America's first heroes—Washington, Jefferson, Madison, Monroe, and Patrick Henry among them. Walking through old houses can bring on a case of the fidgets, but children are likely to be entertained by the living history demonstrations at **Jamestown Settlement, Yorktown Victory Center,** and the **Frontier Culture Museum** at Staunton.

Theme parks offer thrills and chills, not to mention food, fun, and entertainment, at **Paramount's Kings Dominion, Busch Gardens Europe,** and **Water Country USA.**

Virginia's family favorite is the **Virginia Aquarium & Marine Science Center** in Virginia Beach, where computers, exhibits, touch-tanks, and the museum's waterside setting help people of all ages understand the marine environment. Nearby in Norfolk, the **NAUTICUS** has interactive and "virtual adventures" featuring make-believe U.S. Navy ships. Across the harbor in Hampton, kids can see spaceships and watch IMAX movies at the **Virginia Air and Space Center.** They also will get a kick out of the **Steven F. Udvar-Hazy Center** in the Hunt Country of northern Virginia, where the National Air and Space Museum displays 200 planes, 135 spacecraft, and the spaceship model that starred in *Close Encounters of the Third Kind.*

Roanoke's **Virginia Museum of Transportation,** with its playground full of railroad cars, will keep the young and young-at-heart occupied. Richmond's **Children's Museum** and the **Science Museum of Virginia** offer activities and "touch me" exhibits.

It's not a museum, but after reading the story of *Misty of Chincoteague,* kids will adore a chance to ride a pony and see the action themselves at the **wild ponies' swim across Assateague Channel.**

To locate these and other kid-friendly attractions, accommodations, and restaurants, refer to the "Kids" icon throughout this guide.

(there are several of them in Virginia, so it can result in big savings). Besides free entry, it also offers a 50% discount on some federal-use fees charged for such facilities as camping, swimming, parking, boat launching, and tours—but not on fees charged by concessionaires. For more information, go to www.nps.gov/fees_passes.htm or call © **888/467-2757.**

Many reliable agencies and organizations target the 50-plus market. **Elderhostel** (© **800/454-5768;** www.elderhostel.org) arranges worldwide study programs for those aged 55 and over.

ElderTreks (© **800/741-7956** or 416/558-5000; www.eldertreks.com) offers small-group tours to off-the-beaten-path or adventure-travel locations, restricted to travelers 50 and older.

Publications offering travel resources and discounts for seniors include: the quarterly magazine *Travel 50 & Beyond* (www.travel50andbeyond.com) and the best-selling paperback *Unbelievably Good Deals and Great Adventures That You Absolutely Can't Get Unless You're Over 50* (McGraw-Hill), by Joann Rattner Heilman.

AFRICAN-AMERICAN TRAVELERS

Black Travel Online (www.blacktravel online.com) posts news on upcoming events and includes links to articles and travel-booking sites. **Soul of America** (www.soulofamerica.com) is a comprehensive website, with travel tips, event and family-reunion postings, and sections on historically black beach resorts and active vacations.

Agencies and organizations that provide resources for black travelers include: **Rodgers Travel** (© 800/825-1775; www.rodgerstravel.com); the **African American Association of Innkeepers International** (© 877/422-5777; www.africanamericaninns.com); and **Henderson Travel & Tours** (© 800/327-2309 or 301/650-5700; www.hendersontravel.com), which has specialized in trips to Africa since 1957.

Go Girl: The Black Woman's Guide to Travel & Adventure (Eighth Mountain Press) is a compilation of travel essays by writers including Jill Nelson and Audre Lorde. *The African-American Travel Guide* by Wayne C. Robinson (Hunter Publishing) was published in 1997, so it may be somewhat dated. The well-done *Pathfinders Magazine* (© 877/977-PATH; www.pathfinderstravel.com) includes articles on everything from Rio de Janeiro to Ghana to upcoming ski, diving, golf, and tennis trips.

STUDENT TRAVELERS

It's worthwhile to bring along your valid high school or college ID, since many museums and other Virginia attractions have discounted admissions for students.

Alcoholic beverages cannot be sold in the United States to anyone who is under 21, so if you're eligible and intend to imbibe, bring your driver's license or another photo identification with your date of birth.

The **International Student Travel Confederation** (ISTC; www.istc.org) was formed in 1949 to make travel around the world more affordable for students. Check out its website for comprehensive travel services information and details on how to get an **International Student Identity Card (ISIC),** which qualifies students for substantial savings on rail passes, plane tickets, entrance fees, and more. It also provides students with basic health and life insurance and a 24-hour help line. The card is valid for a maximum of 18 months. You can apply for the card online or in person at **STA Travel** (© 800/781-4040 in North America; www.statravel.com), the biggest student travel agency in the world; check out the website to locate STA Travel offices worldwide. If you're no longer a student but are still under 26, you can get an **International Youth Travel Card (IYTC)** from the same people, which entitles you to some discounts. **Travel CUTS** (© 800/592-2887; www.travelcuts.com) offers similar services for both Canadians and U.S. residents. Irish students may prefer to turn to **USIT** (© 01/602-1904; www.usit.ie), an Ireland-based specialist in student, youth, and independent travel.

TRAVELING WITH PETS

The **Virginia Tourism Corporation** website (www.virginia.org; see "Visitor Information & Maps," earlier in this chapter) provides information about pet-friendly events around the state and hotels and motels that accept pets. Policies vary from hotel to hotel, so call ahead to find out the rules. Many pet-friendly hotels charge an additional fee to guests who bring along their furry friends. Most B&Bs do not accept pets, but some of their owners have them, so ask before booking if you're allergic to animals.

Pets are allowed on short leashes in Virginia state parks but restricted in national parks (there are a few trails in Shenandoah National Park on which you can walk Fido). Check with each park's ranger station before setting out.

11 Sustainable Tourism/Eco-Tourism

Each time you take a flight or drive a car carbon dioxide is released into the atmosphere. You can help neutralize this danger to our planet through "carbon offsetting"—paying someone to reduce your carbon dioxide emissions by the same amount you've added. Carbon offsets can be purchased in the U.S. from companies such as **Carbonfund.org** (www.carbonfund.org) and **TerraPass** (www.terrapass.org), and from **Climate Care** (www.climatecare.org) in the U.K.

Although one could argue that any vacation that includes an airplane flight can't be truly "green," you can go on holiday and still contribute positively to the environment. In addition to purchasing carbon offsets from the companies mentioned above, you can take other steps toward responsible travel. Choose forward-looking companies who embrace responsible development practices, helping preserve destinations for the future by working alongside local people. An increasing number of sustainable tourism initiatives can help you plan a family trip and leave as small a "footprint" as possible on the places you visit.

The site **www.responsibletravel.com**, run by a spokesperson for responsible tourism in the travel industry, contains a great source of sustainable travel ideas.

You can find eco-friendly travel tips, statistics, and touring companies and associations—listed by destination under "Travel Choice"—at the International Ecotourism Society website, **www.ecotourism.org**. Also check out **Ecotravel.com,** a part online magazine and part eco-directory that lets you search for touring companies in several categories (water-based, land-based, spiritually oriented, and so on).

In the U.K., **Tourism Concern** (www.tourismconcern.org.uk) works to reduce social and environmental problems connected to tourism and find ways of improving tourism so that local benefits are increased.

The **Association of British Travel Agents** (ABTA; www.abta.com) acts as a

Frommers.com: The Complete Travel Resource

It should go without saying, but we highly recommend **Frommers.com,** voted Best Travel Site by *PC Magazine.* We think you'll find our expert advice and tips; independent reviews of hotels, restaurants, attractions, and preferred shopping and nightlife venues; vacation giveaways; and an online booking tool indispensable before, during, and after your travels. We publish the complete contents of over 128 travel guides in our **Destinations** section covering nearly 3,800 places worldwide to help you plan your trip. Each weekday, we publish original articles reporting on **Deals and News** via our free **Frommers.com Newsletter** to help you save time and money and travel smarter. We're betting you'll find our new **Events** listings (http://events.frommers.com) an invaluable resource; it's an up-to-the-minute roster of what's happening in cities everywhere—including concerts, festivals, lectures, and more. We've also added weekly **podcasts, interactive maps,** and hundreds of new images across the site. Check out our **Travel Talk** area featuring **Message Boards** where you can join in conversations with thousands of fellow Frommer's travelers and post your trip report once you return.

focal point for the U.K. travel industry and is one of the leading groups spearheading responsible tourism.

The **Association of Independent Tour Operators** (AITO; www.aito.co.uk) is a group of interesting specialist operators leading the field in making holidays sustainable.

12 Staying Connected

TELEPHONES

Generally, hotel surcharges on long-distance and local calls are astronomical, so you're better off using your **cellphone** or a **public pay telephone.** (One hotelier told me recently that he isn't making any profit on phone calls because most guests now use their own cellphones instead of making calls from their rooms.)

If you don't have a cellphone, you can buy **prepaid calling cards** in denominations up to $50 at many convenience groceries and packaging services. For international visitors these can be the least expensive way to call home. Many public pay phones at airports and elsewhere now accept American Express, MasterCard, and Visa credit cards. However you pay, **local calls** made from pay phones in Virginia cost 35¢ (no pennies, please).

Most long-distance and international calls can be dialed directly from any phone. **For calls within the United States and to Canada,** dial 1 followed by the area code and the seven-digit number. **For other international calls,** dial 011 followed by the country code, city code, and the number you are calling.

Calls to area codes **800, 888, 877,** and **866** are toll-free. However, calls to area codes **700** and **900** (chat lines, bulletin boards, "dating" services, and so on) can be very expensive—usually a charge of 95¢ to $3 or more per minute, and they sometimes have minimum charges that can run as high as $15 or more.

For **reversed-charge or collect calls,** and for person-to-person calls, dial the number 0 and then the area code and number; an operator will come on the line, and you should specify whether you are calling collect, person to person, or both. If your operator-assisted call is international, ask for the overseas operator.

For **local directory assistance** ("information"), dial 411; for long-distance information, dial 1, then the appropriate area code and 555-1212.

CELLPHONES

Just because your cellphone works at home doesn't mean it'll work everywhere in Virginia, thanks to our nation's fragmented cellphone system. My cellphone using GSM (Global System for Mobiles), which is used by much of the rest of the world, can go dead out in the country, while my CDMA (Code Division Multiple Access) model works perfectly well. It's a good bet that your phone will work in major cities whatever system it uses, and you will have near-statewide coverage with Verizon, which uses CDMA. On the other hand, AT&T, T-Mobile, and Sprint/Nextel can be weak or disappear altogether in rural areas. Take a look at your wireless company's coverage map on its website before heading out.

If you need to stay in touch at a destination where you know your phone won't work, **rent** a phone that does from **InTouch USA** (© 800/872-7626; www.intouchglobal.com) or a rental car location, but beware that you'll pay $1 a minute or more for airtime.

I find it less expensive to buy a prepaid "throwaway" cellphone, such as from **Tracfone** (www.tracfone.com) or its subsidiary **Net10** (www.net10.com). You can order from the websites in advance, or pick up a Tracfone and a prepaid card at any national drugstore chain such as CVS and Rite Aid, or at the ubiquitous Dollar General outlets (rare is the Virginia town that doesn't have a cheapo Dollar General). Wal-Mart, Target, Kmart, and Safeway are Net10 retailers.

Tracfone models cost as little as $10, with prepaid cards beginning at $20 for 60 minutes of nationwide airtime good for 60 days. Net10 phones start at $20 and include 300 minutes of nationwide airtime good for 60 days. Tracfone doubles the minutes charged if you call from out of the area code where you registered the phone, while Net 10 has no roaming fee. Neither charges extra for domestic long distance.

VOICE-OVER INTERNET PROTOCOL (VOIP)

If you have Web access while traveling, you might consider a broadband-based telephone service (in technical terms, **Voice-over Internet Protocol,** or **VoIP**) such as Skype (www.skype.com) or Vonage (www.vonage.com), which allows you to make free international calls if you use

their services from your laptop or in a cybercafe. The people you're calling must also use the service for it to work; check the sites for details.

INTERNET/E-MAIL WITHOUT YOUR OWN COMPUTER

Most **public libraries** in Virginia offer Internet access free or for a small charge. **Hotel business centers** have access, too, but often charge exorbitant rates.

To find cybercafes in your destination, check **www.cybercaptive.com** and **www. cybercafe.com**. Most major airports have **Internet kiosks** that provide basic Web access for a per-minute fee that's usually higher than cybercafe prices. Check out copy shops like **Kinko's** (FedEx Kinko's), which offers computer stations with fully loaded software (as well as Wi-Fi).

WITH YOUR OWN COMPUTER

I've been writing Frommer's guides so long that I remember when hotels competed by equipping their rooms with hair dryers and coffeemakers, which are pretty much de rigueur today. Now they try to

Online Traveler's Toolbox

Veteran travelers usually carry some essential items to make their trips easier. Following is a selection of online tools to bookmark and use.

- **Airplane Food** (www.airlinemeals.net)
- **Airplane Seating** (www.seatguru.com or www.airlinequality.com)
- **Foreign Languages for Travelers** (www.travlang.com)
- **Maps** (www.mapquest.com)
- **Subway Navigator** (www.subwaynavigator.com)
- **Time and Date** (www.timeanddate.com)
- **Travel Warnings** (http://travel.state.gov, www.fco.gov.uk/travel, www. voyage.gc.ca, or www.dfat.gov.au/consular/advice)
- **Universal Currency Converter** (www.xe.com/ucc)
- **Visa ATM Locator** (www.visa.com), **MasterCard ATM Locator** (www. mastercard.com)
- **Weather** (www.intellicast.com or www.weather.com)

one-up each other by providing high-speed Internet access for their guests' laptops. In fact, most hotels and motels in Virginia, regardless of price, offer wireless (Wi-Fi, for wireless fidelity) or high-speed dataport connections for laptops, the latter using an Ethernet network cable. The service is complimentary at many hotels, but others charge about $10 a night.

Many airports, cafes, and especially coffee shops are Wi-Fi hotspots, offering free or low-cost high-speed access. Wi-Fi is even found in some campgrounds, RV parks, and entire neighborhoods, such as King Street in Old Town Alexandria. To find public Wi-Fi hotspots, go to **www.jiwire.com**; its Hotspot Finder holds the world's largest directory of public wireless hotspots.

Most laptops sold today have built-in wireless capability, but wherever you go, bring a **connection kit** of the right power and phone adapters, a spare phone cord, and a spare Ethernet network cable—or find out whether your hotel supplies them to guests.

For information on electrical currency conversions, see "Electricity," in the "Fast Facts: Virginia" section at the end of this chapter.

13 Packages for the Independent Traveler

Virginia is not a major destination for national package tours, which are simply a way to buy the airfare, accommodations, and other elements of your trip (such as car rentals, airport transfers, and sometimes even activities) at the same time and often at discounted prices. However, a number of destinations in Virginia offer local vacation packages that combine a hotel room with an attraction, activity, or theater tickets. These packages are a good way to save money in Virginia. For example, the **Greater Williamsburg Chamber & Tourism Alliance** (www.visitwilliamsburg.com) offers a variety of multiday packages with discounted hotel and admission to Colonial Williamsburg, Busch Gardens Europe, and other local attractions (see chapter 10). Click on "Deals & Packages" at the top of the alliance's Web page.

The best place to hunt for a wide variety of local packages is at **www.virginia.org**, the Virginia Tourism Corporation's website, which collects them under its "Packages & Hot Deals" link. For example, it recently listed a package including accommodations, breakfast, and tickets to a play at Staunton's outstanding Blackfriars Playhouse (see chapter 7).

Although it caters primarily to Civil War buffs, **www.civilwartraveler.com** features money-saving packages, such as hotel, a city tour, and admission to the Museum of the Civil War in Richmond.

Most major airlines will book discounted hotels and rental cars at the same time you purchase your tickets. Those serving Virginia cities include **American** (© 800/433-7300; www.aa.com), **Continental** (© 800/525-0280; www.continental.com), **Delta** (© 800/221-1212; www.delta.com), **Northwest** (© 800/225-2525; www.nwa.com), **United** (© 800/241-6522; www.united.com), and **US Airways** (© 800/428-4322; www.usairways.com).

14 Escorted General-Interest Tours

Escorted tours are structured group tours, with a group leader. The price usually includes everything from airfare to hotels, meals, tours, admission costs, and local transportation.

Several travel companies offer escorted bus tours of historic sites in both Virginia and southeastern Pennsylvania. These 1-week or longer tours usually start in

Washington, D.C, and visit Mount Vernon, Fredericksburg, Williamsburg, Richmond, Charlottesville, and the Shenandoah National Park. From there they go on to Gettysburg and the Amish Country in Pennsylvania before ending in Philadelphia. You'll have to pay extra to get to Washington, D.C., and home from Philadelphia, but meals, lodging, and bus transportation are included in the tour prices.

Check out **Trafalgar Tours** (✆ **866/ 544-4434;** www.trafalgartours.com), **Tauck Tours** (✆ **800/788-7855;** www. tauck.com) and **Mayflower Tours** (✆ **800/323-7604;** www.mayflower tours.com) to see what they're offering when you plan to travel.

Despite the fact that escorted tours require big deposits and predetermine hotels, restaurants, and itineraries, many people derive security and peace of mind from the structure they offer. Escorted tours let you sit back and enjoy the trip without having to drive or worry about details. They take you to the maximum number of sights in the minimum amount of time with the least amount of hassle. They're particularly convenient for people with limited mobility and they can be a great way to make new friends.

On the downside, you'll have little opportunity for serendipitous interactions with locals. The tours can be jam-packed with activities, leaving little room for individual sightseeing, whim, or adventure. And they focus on the most touristy sites, so you miss out on many a lesser-known gem.

1-DAY BUS TOURS

You can also make 1-day escorted bus tours from Washington, D.C., to Williamsburg and Charlottesville with the venerable **Gray Line** (✆ **800/862-1400** or 301/386-8300; fax 301/386-2024; www.gray linedc.com). A Williamsburg historical tour costs $92 for adults, $85 for children 3 to 11 years old. A similar trip to Busch Gardens Europe costs $86 and $84, respectively. The Charlottesville trip includes a visit to Thomas Jefferson's Monticello home and costs $88 and $85, respectively.

15 Special-Interest Trips

Although Virginia is best known for its multitude of historic sites, it's also home to a host of outdoor activities. In this section I give you an overview of what I consider the best options available, where they are, and how to get statewide information. Please refer to the following chapters for detailed information.

The Virginia Tourism Corporation publishes an annual *Virginia Outdoors* magazine that gives a comprehensive rundown of the activities available, a calendar of outdoor events, and a list of the many outfitters and tour companies operating in the state. Call ✆ **800/827-3325** for a copy or see "Visitor Information & Maps," earlier in this chapter.

BICYCLING & MOUNTAIN BIKING
Bicycling is popular throughout Virginia, and with good reason. Most of the state's scenic highways are open to bicycles. My favorites are the 17-mile **George Washington Memorial Parkway** between Arlington and Mount Vernon (see chapter 4), the 105-mile **Skyline Drive** above the Shenandoah Valley (see chapter 7), the 218-mile **Blue Ridge Parkway** in the Southwest Highlands (see chapter 8), and the 22-mile **Colonial Parkway** between Jamestown and Yorktown (see chapter 10).

The state also has three excellent "rails-to-trails" parks, in which old railroad beds have been turned into biking and hiking avenues. I often use northern Virginia's **Washington & Old Dominion**

Trail, which begins in Arlington and ends 45 miles away at Purcellville in the rolling hills of the Hunt Country (see "Alexandria," in chapter 4).

In "The Great Outdoors in the Southwest Highlands" section of chapter 8, I describe two dramatic trails through some of the state's finest mountain scenery. The 34-mile **Virginia Creeper Trail,** one of the country's top bike paths, begins in the Mount Rogers National Recreation Area high up on the flanks of Whitetop Mountain, Virginia's second-highest peak, and descends to Abingdon. Near Wytheville, the 55-mile **New River Trail** follows the New River, which actually is one of the world's oldest rivers. Outfitters along both trails rent bikes and provide shuttle services so you don't have to ride both ways—particularly handy on the Virginia Creeper Trail, which drops more than 3,000 feet from Whitetop Mountain to Damascus, near Abingdon.

Down on the coast, I love pedaling along the **Virginia Beach Boardwalk,** through the natural beauty of **First Landing State Park** and **Back Bay National Wildlife Refuge,** and along all of the flat Eastern Shore roads (see chapter 11).

I've never attempted them, but Virginia is crossed by sections of three major Interstate Bicycle routes. The Maine-to-Virginia **Route 1** runs 150 miles from Arlington to Richmond and connects to 130 miles of the Virginia-to-Florida **Route 17** from Richmond to the North Carolina line at Suffolk. Some 500 miles of the **TransAmerican Bicycle Trail (Rte. 76)** runs from the Kentucky line to Yorktown, including a stretch through Mount Rogers National Recreation Area in the Southwest Highlands. For strip maps of these routes, contact **Adventure Cycling Association,** P.O. Box 8308, Missoula, MT 59802 (© **800/755-2453** or 406/721-1776; fax 406/721-8754; www.adv-cycling.org).

Mountain bikers will find plenty of trails, especially in Mount Rogers National Recreation Area and in the George Washington and Jefferson national forests, which occupy parts of the Shenandoah Valley (see chapter 7) and the Southwest Highlands (see chapter 8). For details about the latter, contact the **George Washington and Jefferson National Forests,** 210 Franklin Rd. SW, Roanoke, VA 24004 (© **540/265-6054;** www. southernregion.fs.fed.us/gwj).

Mountain Bike Virginia, by Scott Adams (Beachway Press, 1995), is a very handy atlas to Virginia's best trails, with excellent maps.

The **Virginia Department of Transportation's Bicycle Coordinator,** 1401 E. Broad St., Richmond, VA 23219 (© **800/835-1203** or 804/786-2964; www.virginiadot.org), publishes the annual *Virginia Bicycling Guide,* which describes Virginia's routes and trials and lists local bike clubs and relevant publications. Contact the department or the Virginia Tourism Corporation (see "Visitor Information & Maps," earlier in this chapter) for a free copy.

BIRD-WATCHING The big bird-watching draws in Virginia are waterfowl nesting in the flatlands and marshes along the coast on the Atlantic Flyway. Chincoteague National Wildlife Refuge on Assateague Island and Back Bay National Wildlife Refuge below Virginia Beach offer first-rate bird-watching. Chincoteague is especially good on Thanksgiving weekend, the only time the refuge's back roads are open to vehicles. See chapter 11.

BOATING The Chesapeake Bay and its many tributaries, including the Potomac, Rappahannock, York, and James rivers, are perfect for boating. In fact, you can come away from eastern Virginia with the impression that every other home has a boat and trailer sitting in the yard. Marinas abound on the Northern Neck (see chapter 5), and you can rent boats in Hampton Roads and over on the Eastern Shore, where the back bays of Chincoteague await to be explored from a fish's-eye view (see chapter 11).

A detailed map showing public access to the Chesapeake and its tributaries is available from the **Virginia Department of Conservation and Recreation,** 203 Governor St., Suite 302, Richmond, VA 23219 (*©* 804/786-1712; www.dcr.state.va.us).

CANOEING, KAYAKING & RIVER RAFTING Kayakers and canoeists will find easy, quiet paddling on the backwater creeks of the Northern Neck (see chapter 5) and in Hampton Roads and on the Eastern Shore (see chapter 11). Outfitters in Virginia Beach and Chincoteague rent both canoes and kayaks and offer guided excursions of the creeks and back bays, and you can go dolphin-watching with them off Virginia Beach.

Depending on how much rain has dropped recently, the best white-water rafting may be on the James River at Scottsville near Charlottesville (see chapter 6). White-water rafting is most likely during spring and late fall.

The best canoeing and kayaking is on the South Fork of the Shenandoah River between Front Royal Luray and Lexington (see "Rafting, Canoeing & Kayaking on the Shenandoah" on p. 161). When the water is low during summer, multitudes forget canoes and rafts and lazily float down the rivers in inner tubes.

FISHING The waters that are so great for boating are stocked with a wide array of fish. The best rivers for fishing include the South Fork of the Shenandoah near Front Royal for smallmouth bass and redbreast sunfish; the James between Richmond and Norfolk for smallmouth bass and catfish; the New near Wytheville for walleye, yellow perch, musky, and smallmouth bass; the Rappahannock from Fredericksburg to the Northern Neck for smallmouth bass and catfish; and the Chickahominy near Williamsburg for largemouth bass, chain pickerel, bluegill, white perch, and channel catfish.

The mountains have 2,800 miles of trout streams, many stocked annually. Guides are available in Lexington (see chapter 7) and Abingdon (see chapter 8).

From Virginia Beach and Chincoteague you can go deep-sea fishing on charter and party boats in search of bluefish, flounder, cobia, gray and spotted trout, sharks, and other ocean dwellers (see chapter 11).

The **Virginia Department of Game and Inland Fisheries,** 4010 W. Broad St., Richmond, VA 23230 (*©* 804/367-1000; www.dgif.state.va.us), publishes an annual freshwater-fishing guide and regulations pamphlet detailing licensing requirements and regulations. Available at most sporting-goods stores, marinas, and bait shops, licenses are required except on the first Saturday and Sunday in June, which are free fishing days.

GOLF You can play golf almost anytime and anywhere in Virginia, given the state's mild climate and more than 130 courses, but serious duffers head to **Williamsburg** and the Golden Horseshoe, Green, and Gold courses at the Williamsburg Inn, and the links at Kingsmill Resort, home of the LPGA Michelob Ultra Open in mid-May (see chapter 10). An hour's drive away, the PGA-owned Virginia Beach National Golf Club in **Virginia Beach** is one of the country's best upscale links (see chapter 11). Up in the mountains, the Homestead's beautiful course in **Hot Springs** has the nation's oldest first tee, in continuous use since 1890 (see chapter 7). Wintergreen Resort near **Charlottesville** also has an excellent course (see chapter 6), as does Lansdowne Resort near **Leesburg** (see chapter 4).

The best source for information is the Virginia Tourism Corporation's annual *Virginia Golf Guide,* which lists and describes the state's courses (see "Visitor Information & Maps," earlier in this chapter).

HIKING & BACKPACKING The same trails that make Virginia so popular with bicyclists also make it a hiker's heaven. The state's rails-to-trails paths along old railroad beds (see "Bicycling & Mountain Biking," above) are both good and easy. Some 450 miles of the **Appalachian Trail** snake through Virginia, nearly climbing Mount Rogers and paralleling the Blue Ridge Parkway and the Skyline Drive in many places. The best backcountry trails are in **Shenandoah National Park** (see chapter 7) and **Mount Rogers National Recreation Area** (see chapter 8), with less traveled trails in the George Washington and Jefferson national forests.

For information and maps of the Appalachian Trail, contact the **Appalachian Trail Conservancy,** P.O. Box 807, Harpers Ferry, WV 25425-0807 (© **304/535-6331;** www.atconf.org).

Four good books give trail-by-trail descriptions. *The Trails of Virginia: Hiking the Old Dominion,* by Allen de Hart (University of North Carolina Press, 1995), is still the most comprehensive guide. *The Hiker's Guide to Virginia,* by Randy Johnson (Falcon Press, 1992), is a slimmer, easier-to-carry volume, as is *Hiking Virginia's National Forests,* by Karin Wuertz-Schaeffer (Globe Pequot Press, 1994), which covers trails in the George Washington

and Jefferson national forests in the Shenandoah Valley and Southwest Highlands. Of more recent vintage, *Hiking Shenandoah National Park,* by Bert and Jane Gildart (Falcon Press, 2006), describes and maps the park's best trails.

HORSEBACK RIDING Equestrians will find stables with horses to rent to ride on hundreds of miles of public horse trails in Virginia, the majority of them in the Shenandoah Valley and the Southwest Highlands. The **Shenandoah National Park** has its own Skyland Stables, from which you can take guided trail rides atop the Blue Ridge (see chapter 7). The granddaddy of all trails, the **Virginia Highlands Horse Trail,** runs the length of Mount Rogers National Recreation Area, which has campgrounds especially for horse owners (see chapter 8). Horses are also permitted on the Virginia Creeper Trail and the New River Trail. You can rent horses at the Mount Rogers National Recreation Area and along the New River Trail (see chapter 8). Ironically, few stables rent horses in northern Virginia's Hunt Country, where just about everyone who rides owns a horse (see chapter 4).

The **Virginia Horse Council,** 2799 Stratford Rd., Richmond, VA 23225 (© **804/330-0345;** www.virginiahorse.com), publishes a list of public horse trails and stables statewide.

WATERSPORTS To indulge your passion for surfing, jet-skiing, wave-running, sailing, or scuba diving, head for Virginia Beach, which has it all in abundance. See chapter 11.

16 Getting Around Virginia

BY CAR

The only way I like to see Virginia is from behind the wheel of my own car. Driving your vehicle to Virginia, or renting one when you get here, will give you optimum flexibility to visit the rural beauties, including the plantations and Civil War

battlefields. And, of course, two of the state's most scenic attractions, the Skyline Drive and Blue Ridge Parkway, are motoring destinations. Only in northern Virginia, Richmond, and Hampton Roads will you encounter serious rush-hour traffic.

Virginia Driving Times & Distances

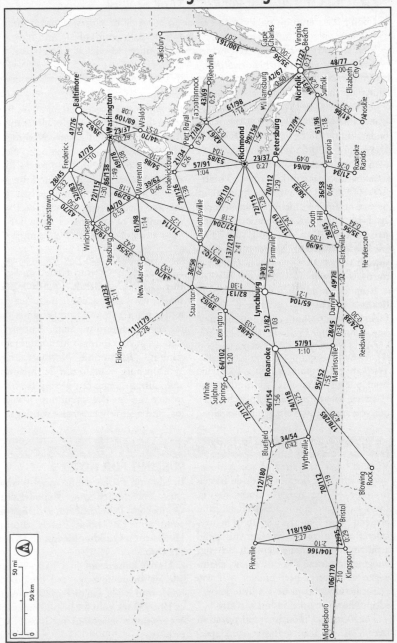

> ### *Tips* Get Out of Your Vehicle & Look Around
>
> I don't have enough pages in this book to cover all of Virginia's picturesque hamlets, villages, and towns. Don't hesitate to park your vehicle and have a look around when a charmer catches your attention. My fellow Virginians will ensure that you are richly rewarded.

Avis (© 800/331-1212; www.avis.com), **Budget** (© 800/527-0700; www.budget.com), **Dollar** (© 800/800-4000), **Hertz** (© 800/654-3131; www.hertz.com), **National** (© 800/CAR-RENT; www.nationalcar.com), and **Thrifty** (© 800/367-2277; www.thrifty.com) all operate in Virginia's metropolitan areas and at all but the smallest of airports. **Enterprise Rent-a-Car** (© 800/261-7331; www.enterprise.com) is the most widespread, with outlets in smaller cities and towns, many without airports.

Keep in mind that **foreign driver's licenses** are usually recognized in the U.S., but you should get an international one if your home license is not in English.

BY PLANE

You can get around Virginia by flying from one of its airports to another (see "Getting There," earlier in this chapter), but you are likely to change planes along the way. For example, you may have to fly through Washington Dulles International Airport, Ronald Reagan Washington National Airport, or Charlotte, North Carolina, to get from Roanoke to Richmond. As a result, flying around the state can be more time-consuming than driving, and more expensive, too. Check with the airlines or your travel agent for the most efficient, cost-effective routing.

BY TRAIN

As I noted in "Getting There," earlier in this chapter, **Amtrak** (© 800/USA-RAIL; www.amtrak.com) trains are better for getting to and from Virginia than for getting around the state. Amtrak has stations at Alexandria, Quantico, Fredericksburg, Richmond, Newport News, Williamsburg, Charlottesville, Staunton, and Clifton Forge, but getting from city to city can involve circuitous, time-eating, and relatively expensive routing.

17 Tips on Accommodations

Virginia has a vast array of accommodations, from rock-bottom roadside motels to some of the nation's finest resorts. Every national chain is present here, from low-end Super 8 all the way up to luxury-laden Ritz-Carlton. So whether you spend a pittance or a bundle depends on your budget and tastes. You can enjoy "champagne tastes on a beer budget"—if you plan carefully and possess a little knowledge of how the hotel industry works.

The Virginia Tourism Corporation (see "Visitor Information & Maps," earlier in this chapter) publishes a directory of all the state's accommodations.

SURFING FOR HOTELS

In addition to the online travel-booking sites **Travelocity.com, Expedia.com, Orbitz.com, Priceline.com,** and **Hotwire.com,** you can book hotels through **Hotels.com, Quikbook.com,** and **Travelaxe.com.**

HotelChatter.com is a daily webzine offering smart coverage and critiques of hotels worldwide. Go to **TripAdvisor.com** or **HotelShark.com** for helpful independent consumer reviews of hotels and resort properties.

After I've determined a price quoted on the general sites, I *always* go directly to

---

Tips **Driving the Civil War Trails**

One advantage of touring by car is that you can follow the state's Civil War Trails. These sign-posted driving tours follow the Shenandoah battles, the Peninsula campaign of 1862, the battles from Manassas to Fredericksburg, Lee versus Grant as the Union drove south to Richmond in 1864, and Lee's retreat from Petersburg to Appomattox in 1865. Check out **www.civilwartrails.org**.

---

my chosen hotel's site to see if it is offering an **Internet special.** Often these deals don't show up on the major travel sites.

I also always **get a confirmation number** and **printout** of any online booking transaction.

SAVING ON YOUR HOTEL ROOM

In this book, I give each hotel's **rack rate,** which is the maximum rate that it charges for a room. These price ranges are becoming meaningful only for comparative purposes since most hotels engage in "yield management," under which they change their rates almost daily—sometimes hourly—depending on how many people are booked for a particular night. In other words, you may not know the price of a room until you call the hotel or book online for a particular date.

Hardly anybody pays rack rate these days, so here are some tricks to lower the cost of your room:

- **Ask about special rates or other discounts.** Always ask whether a room less expensive than the first one quoted is available or whether any special rates apply to you. You may qualify for corporate, student, military, senior, or other discounts. Mention membership in AAA, AARP, frequent-flier programs, or trade unions, which may entitle you to special deals as well. Find out the hotel policy on children—do kids stay free in the room or is there a special rate?
- **Dial direct.** When booking a room in a chain hotel, you'll often get a better

deal by calling the individual hotel's reservation desk rather than the chain's main number.

- **Book online.** Many hotels offer Internet-only discounts, or supply rooms to Priceline.com, Hotwire.com, or Expedia.com at rates much lower than the ones you can get through the hotel itself. See "Surfing for Hotels," earlier in this section.
- **Remember the law of supply and demand.** Resort hotels are most crowded and therefore most expensive on weekends, so discounts are usually available for midweek stays. Business hotels in downtown locations are busiest during the week, so you can expect big discounts over the weekend. Many hotels have high-season and low-season prices, and booking the day after high season ends can mean big discounts.
- **Look into group or long-stay discounts.** If you come as part of a large group, you should be able to negotiate a bargain rate since the hotel can then guarantee occupancy in a number of rooms. Likewise, if you're planning a long stay (at least 5 days), you might qualify for a discount. As a general rule, expect 1 night free after a 7-night stay.
- **Sidestep excess charges and hidden costs.** When you book a room, ask whether the hotel charges for parking. Use your own cellphone, pay phones, or prepaid phone cards instead of dialing direct from hotel phones, which usually have exorbitant rates.

And don't be tempted by the room's minibar offerings: Most hotels charge through the nose for water, soda, and snacks. Finally, ask about local taxes and service charges, which can increase the cost of a room by 15% or more. If a hotel insists upon tacking on a surprise surcharge that wasn't mentioned at check-in or a "resort fee" for amenities you didn't use, you can often make a case for getting it removed.

- **Book an efficiency room.** A room with a kitchenette allows you to shop for groceries and cook meals. This is a big money saver, especially for families on long stays.
- Consider enrolling in **hotel "frequent-stay" programs,** which are upping the ante lately to win the loyalty of repeat customers. Frequent guests can now accumulate points or credits to earn free hotel nights, airline miles, in-room amenities, merchandise, tickets to concerts and events, and discounts on sporting facilities. Perks are awarded not only by many chain hotels and motels (Hilton HHonors, Marriott Rewards, Wyndham ByRequest, to name a few), but individual inns and B&Bs. Many chain hotels partner with other hotel chains, car-rental firms, airlines, and credit card companies to give consumers additional incentive to do repeat business.

LANDING THE BEST ROOM

Somebody has to get the best room in the house, and it might as well be you. You can start by joining the hotel's frequent-guest program, which may make you eligible for upgrades. A hotel-branded credit card usually gives its owner "silver" or "gold" status in frequent-guest programs for free. Always ask about a corner room. They're often larger and quieter, with more windows and light, and they often cost the same as standard rooms. When you make your reservation, ask if the hotel is renovating; if it is, request a room away from the construction. If you're a light sleeper, request a quiet room away from vending or ice machines, elevators, restaurants, bars, and discos. Ask for a room that has most recently been renovated or redecorated.

If you aren't happy with your room when you arrive, ask for another one. Most lodgings will be willing to accommodate you.

BED & BREAKFASTS

Unfortunately I have room in these pages to mention only a few standouts among Virginia's 200-plus bed-and-breakfasts. Most of them are excellent properties adorned with antiques or quality reproductions, luxurious touches like fresh flowers and top-drawer linens and toiletries, and gourmet breakfasts. Some even add whirlpool tubs to their bathrooms. All these niceties come with a price, so most bed-and-breakfasts aren't inexpensive. Nor are they for everyone, since you'll be sharing a home with strangers—with whom you might have to make small talk over breakfast. On the other hand, you don't have to go out for breakfast, and the hosts are usually fonts of current local information. In fact, B&B owners told me about many of the restaurants I recommend in these pages.

Many belong to the **Bed & Breakfast Association of Virginia,** P.O. Box 1077, Standardsville, VA 22973 (© **888/660-2228** or 540/672-6700; www.bbav.org). BBAV publishes an annual directory of its members and lists them on its website. The association inspects and approves the establishments it promotes, so you are unlikely to stay in a dump.

Regional associations with useful websites include the **Alexandria & Arlington Bed & Breakfast Network,** P.O. Box 25319, Arlington, VA 22202 (© **888/549-3415** or 703/549-3415; www.aabbn.com); the Hunt Country's **Loudoun**

County Bed & Breakfast Guild (℡ 866/ 771-2597; www.loudounbandb.com); Charlottesville's **Guesthouses Reservation Service, Inc.** (℡ 434/979-7264; www.va-guesthouses.com); **Bed and Breakfasts of the Historic Shenandoah**

Valley (www.bbhsv.org); and **Williamsburg Bed & Breakfast Network** (www.bandbwilliamsburg.com).

Most local visitor centers include bed-and-breakfasts on their websites or will send you a list of those in their area.

FAST FACTS: Virginia

American Express Call customer service (℡ **800/528-4800**) to report lost or stolen traveler's checks or for locations in Virginia. The main Virginia office is in Richmond at 1412A Starling Dr. (℡ **804/740-2030**); other locations can be found online at www.americanexpress.com.

Area Codes Virginia has several area codes. The **703** and **571** codes are both in northern Virginia and the eastern Hunt Country, where you must dial both the area code and local number even when calling locally. The **540** code runs from Fredericksburg west to Winchester and south to Roanoke. The **804** code is in Richmond, Petersburg, and the Northern Neck. The **757** code covers Williamsburg, Hampton Roads, and the Eastern Shore. The **434** code is in Charlottesville. And the **276** code is in the Southwest Highlands.

ATM Networks See "Money & Costs" on p. 31.

Automobile Organizations Auto clubs will supply maps, suggested routes, guidebooks, accident and bail-bond insurance, and emergency road service. The **American Automobile Association (AAA)** is the major auto club in the United States. If you belong to an auto club in your home country, inquire about AAA reciprocity before you leave. You may be able to join AAA even if you're not a member of a reciprocal club; to inquire, call AAA (℡ **800/222-4357**). AAA is actually an organization of regional auto clubs, so look under "AAA Automobile Club" in the White Pages of the telephone directory. AAA has a nationwide emergency road service telephone number (℡ **800/AAA-HELP**).

Business Hours Offices are usually open weekdays 9am to 5pm. Banks are open weekdays 9am to 3pm or later and sometimes Saturday mornings. Stores typically open between 9 and 10am and close between 5 and 6pm Monday through Saturday. Stores in shopping complexes or malls tend to stay open late on these days—until about 9pm—and many malls and larger department stores are open until 6pm on Sundays.

Car Rentals See "Getting Around Virginia" on p. 46, and the "Getting Around" section in the destination chapters that follow.

Cashpoints See "ATM Networks," above.

Currency The most common bills are the $1 (a "buck"), $5, $10, and $20 denominations. There are also $2 bills (seldom encountered), $50 bills, and $100 bills (the last two are usually not welcome as payment for small purchases).

Coins come in seven denominations: 1¢ (1 cent, or a penny); 5¢ (5 cents, or a nickel); 10¢ (10 cents, or a dime); 25¢ (25 cents, or a quarter); 50¢ (50 cents, or a half dollar); the gold-colored Sacagawea and presidential coins, worth $1; and the rare silver dollar.

For additional information see "Money & Costs" on p. 31.

Customs **What You Can Bring Into Virginia** Every visitor more than 21 years of age may bring in, free of duty, the following: (1) 1 liter of wine or hard liquor; (2) 200 cigarettes, 100 cigars (but not from Cuba), or 3 pounds of smoking tobacco; and (3) $100 worth of gifts. These exemptions are offered to travelers who spend at least 72 hours in the United States and who have not claimed them within the preceding 6 months. It is altogether forbidden to bring into the country foodstuffs (particularly fruit, cooked meats, and canned goods) and plants (vegetables, seeds, tropical plants, and the like). Foreign tourists may carry in or out up to $10,000 in U.S. or foreign currency with no formalities; larger sums must be declared to U.S. Customs on entering or leaving, which includes filing form CM 4790. For details regarding U.S. Customs and Border Protection, consult your nearest U.S. embassy or consulate, or **U.S. Customs** (© 202/927-1770; www.customs.ustreas.gov).

What You Can Take Home from Virginia:

Canadian Citizens: For a clear summary of Canadian rules, write for the booklet *I Declare,* issued by the **Canada Border Services Agency** (© 800/461-9999 in Canada, or 204/983-3500; www.cbsa-asfc.gc.ca).

U.K. Citizens: For information, contact **HM Customs & Excise** at © 0845/010-9000 (from outside the U.K., 020/8929-0152), or consult their website at www.hmce.gov.uk.

Australian Citizens: A helpful brochure available from Australian consulates or Customs offices is *Know Before You Go.* For more information, call the **Australian Customs Service** at © 1300/363-263, or log on to www.customs.gov.au.

New Zealand Citizens: Most questions are answered in a free pamphlet available at New Zealand consulates and Customs offices: *New Zealand Customs Guide for Travellers, Notice no. 4.* For more information, contact **New Zealand Customs,** The Customhouse, 17–21 Whitmore St., Box 2218, Wellington (© 04/473-6099 or 0800/428-786; www.customs.govt.nz).

Drinking Laws The legal age for purchase and consumption of alcoholic beverages is 21; proof of age is required and often requested at bars, nightclubs, and restaurants, so it's always a good idea to bring ID when you go out. In Virginia, many grocery and convenience stores sell beer and wine, but only state-licensed Alcoholic Beverage Control (ABC) stores are permitted to sell bottles of hard liquor. Any licensed establishment (restaurant or bar) can sell drinks by the glass. Bars must close by 2am. Do not carry open containers of alcohol in your car or any public area that isn't zoned for alcohol consumption. The police can fine you on the spot. And nothing will ruin your trip faster than getting a citation for DUI ("driving under the influence"), so don't even think about driving while intoxicated.

Driving Rules See "Getting Around Virginia," p. 46.

Electricity Like Canada, the United States uses 110–120 volts AC (60 cycles), compared to 220–240 volts AC (50 cycles) in most of Europe, Australia, and New

Zealand. Downward converters that change 220–240 volts to 110–120 volts are difficult to find in the United States, so bring one with you.

Embassies & Consulates All embassies are located in the national capital, Washington, D.C., which is just across the Potomac River from northern Virginia. Most nations have a mission to the United Nations in New York City. If your country isn't listed below, call for directory information in Washington, D.C. (🕾 202/555-1212) or log on to www.embassy.org/embassies. Some key embassies are:

The embassy of **Australia** is at 1601 Massachusetts Ave. NW, Washington, DC 20036 (🕾 202/797-3000; www.austemb.org). There are consulates in New York, Honolulu, Houston, Los Angeles, and San Francisco.

The embassy of **Canada** is at 501 Pennsylvania Ave. NW, Washington, DC 20001 (🕾 202/682-1740; www.canadianembassy.org). Other Canadian consulates are in Buffalo (New York), Detroit, Los Angeles, New York, and Seattle.

The embassy of **Ireland** is at 2234 Massachusetts Ave. NW, Washington, DC 20008 (🕾 202/462-3939; www.irelandemb.org). Irish consulates are in Boston, Chicago, New York, San Francisco, and other cities. See website for complete listing.

The embassy of **New Zealand** is at 37 Observatory Circle NW, Washington, DC 20008 (🕾 202/328-4800; www.nzemb.org). New Zealand consulates are in Los Angeles, Salt Lake City, San Francisco, and Seattle.

The embassy of the **United Kingdom** is at 3100 Massachusetts Ave. NW, Washington, DC 20008 (🕾 202/588-7800; www.britainusa.com). Other British consulates are in Atlanta, Boston, Chicago, Cleveland, Houston, Los Angeles, New York, San Francisco, and Seattle.

Emergencies Call 🕾 **911** to report a fire, call the police, or get an ambulance anywhere in the United States. This is a toll-free call (no coins are required at public telephones). Dial 🕾 **#77** on your cellphone to reach the state highway patrol.

Gasoline (Petrol) Petrol is known as gasoline (or simply "gas"), and petrol stations are known as both gas stations and service stations. While the price of gasoline has been going through the roof recently (around $3 a gallon in Virginia), it still costs about half as much in the U.S. as it does in Europe. Taxes are already included in the printed price. One U.S. gallon equals 3.8 liters or .85 imperial gallons. All but a few stations have self-service gas pumps.

Holidays Banks, government offices, post offices, and many stores, restaurants, and museums are closed on the following legal national holidays: January 1 (New Year's Day), the third Monday in January (Martin Luther King, Jr., Day), the third Monday in February (Presidents' Day/Washington and Lincoln's birthdays), the last Monday in May (Memorial Day), July 4th (Independence Day), the first Monday in September (Labor Day), the second Monday in October (Columbus Day), November 11 (Veterans Day/Armistice Day), the fourth Thursday in November (Thanksgiving Day), and December 25 (Christmas). The Tuesday after the first Monday in November is Election Day, a federal government holiday in presidential-election years (held every 4 years, and next in 2008).

For more information on holidays see "Virginia Calendar of Events," earlier in this chapter.

Internet Access See "Staying Connected" on p. 40.

Legal Aid If you are "pulled over" for a minor infraction (such as speeding), never attempt to pay the fine directly to a police officer; this could be construed as attempted bribery, a much more serious crime. Pay fines by mail, or directly into the hands of the clerk of the court. If accused of a more serious offense, say and do nothing before consulting a lawyer. Here the burden is on the state to prove a person's guilt beyond a reasonable doubt, and everyone has the right to remain silent, whether he or she is suspected of a crime or actually arrested. Once arrested, a person can make one telephone call to a party of his or her choice. International visitors should call your embassy or consulate.

Lost & Found Be sure to tell all of your credit card companies the minute you discover your wallet has been lost or stolen and file a report at the nearest police precinct. Your credit card company or insurer may require a police report number or record of the loss. Most credit card companies have an emergency toll-free number to call if your card is lost or stolen; they may be able to wire you a cash advance immediately or deliver an emergency credit card in a day or two. Visa's U.S. emergency number is ℂ **800/847-2911** or 410/581-9994. American Express cardholders and traveler's check holders should call ℂ **800/221-7282**. MasterCard holders should call ℂ **800/307-7309** or 636/722-7111. For other credit cards, call the toll-free number directory at ℂ **800/555-1212**.

If you need emergency cash over the weekend when all banks and American Express offices are closed, you can have money wired to you via **Western Union** (ℂ **800/325-6000**; www.westernunion.com).

Mail At press time, domestic postage rates were 24¢ for a postcard and 41¢ for a letter (set to rise to 42¢ in May 2008). For international mail, a first-class letter of up to 1 ounce costs 84¢ (63¢ to Canada and Mexico); a first-class postcard costs 75¢ (55¢ to Canada and Mexico); and a preprinted postal aerogramme costs 75¢. For more information go to **www.usps.com** and click on "Calculate Postage."

If you aren't sure what your address will be in the United States, mail can be sent to you, in your name, c/o General Delivery at the main post office of the city or region where you expect to be. (Call ℂ **800/275-8777** for information on the nearest post office.) The addressee must pick up mail in person and must produce proof of identity (driver's license, passport, and such). Most post offices will hold your mail for up to 1 month, and are open Monday to Friday from 8am to 6pm, and Saturday from 9am to 3pm.

Always include zip codes when mailing items in the U.S. If you don't know your zip code, visit www.usps.com/zip4.

Measurements See the chart on the inside front cover of this book for details on converting metric measurements to U.S. equivalents.

Newspapers & Magazines Each major city in Virginia has its own daily newspaper. *The Richmond Times-Dispatch* (www.timesdispatch.com), *The Roanoke Times* (www.roanoke.com), and the Norfolk *Virginian-Pilot* (www.pilot online.com) are the largest. The *Washington Post* (www.washingtonpost.com)

and *USA Today* (www.usatoday.com) are available at newsstands and coin boxes throughout the state.

Passports **For Residents of Australia:** You can pick up an application from your local post office or any branch of Passports Australia, but you must schedule an interview at the passport office to present your application materials. Call the **Australian Passport Information Service** at 🕿 **131-232,** or visit the government website at www.passports.gov.au.

For Residents of Canada: Passport applications are available at travel agencies throughout Canada or from the central **Passport Office,** Department of Foreign Affairs and International Trade, Ottawa, ON K1A 0G3 (🕿 **800/567-6868;** www.ppt.gc.ca). *Note:* Canadian children who travel must have their own passport. However, if you hold a valid Canadian passport issued before December 11, 2001, that bears the name of your child, the passport remains valid for you and your child until it expires.

For Residents of Ireland: You can apply for a 10-year passport at the **Passport Office,** Setanta Centre, Molesworth Street, Dublin 2 (🕿 **01/671-1633;** www. irlgov.ie/iveagh). Those under age 18 and over 65 must apply for a 3-year passport. You can also apply at 1A South Mall, Cork (🕿 **021/272-525**) or at most main post offices.

For Residents of New Zealand: You can pick up a passport application at any New Zealand Passports Office or download it from their website. Contact the **Passports Office** at 🕿 **0800/225-050** in New Zealand or 04/474-8100, or log on to www.passports.govt.nz.

For Residents of the United Kingdom: To pick up an application for a standard 10-year passport (5-year passport for children under 16), visit your nearest passport office, major post office, or travel agency or contact the **United Kingdom Passport Service** at 🕿 **0870/521-0410** or search its website at www.ukpa.gov.uk.

Police To reach the police in an emergency, dial 🕿 **911** from any phone (no charge).

Safety See "Safety," p. 34.

Taxes The Virginia state sales tax is 5% for most purchases plus 2% on hotel rooms. Local hotel taxes vary; in most communities it's 5%, which makes the total tax on your hotel bill at least 12%. Most local jurisdictions also add a restaurant tax, which jacks up the price of food and drink by 10% or more.

Time The continental United States is divided into **four time zones:** Eastern Standard Time (EST), Central Standard Time (CST), Mountain Standard Time (MST), and Pacific Standard Time (PST). Virginia is on **Eastern Standard Time (EST),** the same as New York and other East Coast cities. When it's noon in Virginia, it's 11am in Chicago, 10am in Denver, 9am in Los Angeles, 8am in Anchorage, and 7am in Honolulu. Daylight saving time is in effect from 2am on the second Sunday in March to the first Sunday in November. Daylight saving time moves the clock 1 hour ahead of standard time.

Tipping Tips are a very important part of certain workers' income, and gratuities are the standard way of showing appreciation for services provided. (Tipping is certainly not compulsory if the service is poor!) In hotels, tip **bellhops** at least $1 per bag ($2–$3 if you have a lot of luggage) and tip the **chamber staff** $1 to $2 per day (more if you've left a disaster area for him or her to clean up). Tip the **doorman** or **concierge** only if he or she has provided you with some specific service (for example, calling a cab for you or obtaining difficult-to-get theater tickets). Tip the **valet-parking attendant** $1 every time you get your car.

In restaurants, bars, and nightclubs, tip **service staff** 15% to 20% of the check, tip **bartenders** 10% to 15%, tip **checkroom attendants** $1 per garment, and tip **valet-parking attendants** $1 per vehicle.

As for other service personnel, tip **cabdrivers** 15% of the fare; tip **skycaps** at airports at least $1 per bag ($2–$3 if you have a lot of luggage); and tip **hairdressers** and **barbers** 15% to 20%.

Toilets You won't find public toilets or "restrooms" on the streets in most U.S. cities but they can be found in hotel lobbies, bars, restaurants, museums, department stores, railway and bus stations, and service stations. Large hotels and fast-food restaurants are often the best bet for clean facilities. If possible, avoid the toilets at parks and beaches, which tend to be dirty; some may be unsafe. Restaurants and bars in resorts or heavily visited areas may reserve their restrooms for patrons.

Useful Phone Numbers **U.S. Dept. of State Travel Advisory:** ℂ 202/647-5225, manned 24 hr. **U.S. Passport Agency:** ℂ 202/647-0518. **U.S. Centers for Disease Control International Traveler's Hot Line:** ℂ 404/332-4559. **Virginia travel, traffic and weather information:** ℂ 511. **Virginia Highway Helpline:** ℂ 800/367-7623. **Virginia Highway Patrol:** ℂ #77 (cellphones only). **Virginia Tourism Corporation:** ℂ 800/847-4822. **Hampton Roads Traffic information:** ℂ 800/792-2800.

Visas For information about U.S. visas go to **http://travel.state.gov** and click on "Visas," or go to one of the following websites.

Australian citizens can obtain up-to-date visa information from the **U.S. Embassy Canberra,** Moonah Place, Yarralumla, ACT 2600 (ℂ **02/6214-5600**) or by checking the U.S. Diplomatic Mission's website at http://usembassy-australia.state.gov/consular.

British subjects can obtain up-to-date visa information by calling the **U.S. Embassy Visa Information Line** (ℂ **0891/200-290**) or by visiting the "Visas to the U.S." section of the American Embassy London's website at www.usembassy.org.uk.

Irish citizens can obtain up-to-date visa information through the **Embassy of the USA Dublin,** 42 Elgin Rd., Dublin 4, Ireland (ℂ **353/1-668-8777;** or by checking the "Consular Services" section of the website at http://dublin.usembassy.gov.

Citizens of **New Zealand** can obtain up-to-date visa information by contacting the **U.S. Embassy New Zealand,** 29 Fitzherbert Terrace, Thorndon, Wellington (ℂ **644/472-2068**), or get the information directly from the website at http://wellington.usembassy.gov.

Weather See "When to Go," earlier this chapter, for Virginia's climate. For current conditions in northern Virginia, call ℂ **703/936-1212;** in Richmond, call ℂ **804/268-1212;** in Roanoke, call ℂ **540/982-2303.** Elsewhere, check the front pages of the telephone directory for the local number.

3

Suggested Virginia Itineraries

Virginia is a relatively large and varied state with numerous attractions across its length and breadth. Where you go and what you see will depend on your special interests—whether you're into history or into hiking, for example. Ideally you should use the "Best of Virginia" chapter to work out a route that appeals to you. I have suggested a few itineraries below that will take you throughout Virginia, to its Colonial-era attractions and its Civil War battlefields, to some of its vineyards, and up the Shenandoah with a little Shakespeare thrown in. I've also suggested how parents can travel with their children in Virginia without going stark, raving mad.

1 The Grand Tour of Virginia in 2 Weeks

This route takes you to all of Virginia's top attractions: the Shenandoah National Park, the Shenandoah Valley towns of Staunton and Lexington, Charlottesville, Richmond, Williamsburg, Jamestown, Yorktown, Virginia Beach, Fredericksburg, and George Washington's Mount Vernon home near Alexandria's historic Old Town district. You can expand any section of this route into a week's tour of one particular area of Virginia. For instance, you can spend a week in the Shenandoah Valley by staying 2 or more nights each in Winchester, Shenandoah National Park, Staunton, and Lexington. Charlottesville-Richmond-Williamsburg is another example.

This tour begins and ends at Washington Dulles International Airport in northern Virginia, the state's major air gateway, and essentially follows Interstates 66, 81, 64, and 95 to make a loop around the northern and central portions of the state. If you're driving to Virginia from the south, start in Williamsburg and work backward.

Days ❶ & ❷: The Hunt Country 𝕲𝕲

As you leave Dulles airport, first go south on Va. 28 to the National Air and Space Museum's magnificent **Steven F. Udvar-Hazy Center** (p. 94). Then head to **Leesburg,** seeing the sights in town before retiring for the night. The next morning drive to Middleburg, where you can browse its hip main street and have lunch. Spend the afternoon exploring the back roads, sampling the vintages at the nearby vineyards, and crossing the mountains to **Winchester.**

Day ❸: Winchester 𝕲 to Luray

Spend the morning seeing Winchester's sights, especially the **Museum of the Shenandoah Valley** (p. 155), which provides a fine introduction to the valley. In the afternoon, drive through **Strasburg** and **Front Royal** on your way to **Luray,** where you can go underground at **Luray Caverns** (p. 165). Spend the night in Luray or drive on up into the Shenandoah National Park.

Day ❹: The Shenandoah National Park 𝕲𝕲𝕲

From Luray, drive east on U.S. 211 to the mountaintop entrance to **Shenandoah National Park** (p. 145). Go south on the **Skyline Drive** into the park's Central District, its most scenic and best equipped.

Take in the views, hike the trails, or go horseback riding (be sure to call the stables in advance for riding reservations). Spend the night at the park's **Big Meadows Lodge** (p. 151) or **Skyland Lodge** (p. 152).

Day ❺: Staunton ✿✿✿
The next morning, take the Skyline Drive south to I-64, and then west to **Staunton,** one of Virginia's best small towns. Spend the afternoon visiting **The Woodrow Wilson Presidential Library at His Birthplace** (p. 171). See Shakespeare performed at the marvelous **Blackfriars Playhouse** (p. 170).

Day ❻: Lexington ✿✿✿
Charming **Lexington** has more attractions than any other town in the Shenandoah Valley, so arrive in time to spend at least an afternoon visiting the **George C. Marshall Museum and Research Library** and Stonewall Jackson's stuffed horse in the **Virginia Military Institute Museum** (p. 184).

Day ❼: Charlottesville ✿✿✿
I-81 and I-64 will speed you to Thomas Jefferson's hometown of **Charlottesville,** or you can take the slow but much more scenic route via the **Blue Ridge Parkway** from Buena Vista to Waynesboro, and then I-64 east. Either way, spend the afternoon touring the **University of Virginia** (p. 136) and other downtown Charlottesville attractions. The next morning, beat the crowds to Jefferson's magnificent **Monticello** (p. 135). Have lunch at nearby **Michie Tavern** (p. 134) then visit President James Monroe's **Ash Lawn–Highland** home (p. 134). When finished, take I-64 east to Richmond for the night.

Days ❽ & ❾: Richmond ✿✿
You'll have a busy 2 days seeing the sites from Richmond's days as the capital of the Confederacy. Begin at **The American Civil War Center Museum** (p. 229), which expertly explains the war's origins

from the Northern, Southern and African-American perspectives. It's next door to the **Richmond National Battlefield Park**'s own museum (p. 231). Next head to **The Museum and White House of the Confederacy** (p. 230). On the second day take in **St. John's Episcopal Church** (p. 231), where Patrick Henry made his "give me liberty, or give me death" speech, and Richmond's host of specialized museums.

Days ❿ & ⓫: Williamsburg, Jamestown & Yorktown ✿✿✿
Two days are barely enough to scratch the surface of Virginia's "Historic Triangle." Devote one of them to the lovingly restored **Colonial Williamsburg** historic district, finishing with dinner at one of the ancient taverns, or if you have children, at **Busch Gardens Europe** (p. 257). **Jamestown** will take up the next morning; **Yorktown** that afternoon. If you have a few days to spare, you can spend them relaxing at **Virginia Beach.**

Day ⓬: Fredericksburg ✿✿✿
Depart Williamsburg early and drive north via U.S. 17 to **Fredericksburg,** the boyhood home of George Washington, where you can spend the afternoon exploring **his mother's home** and the fascinating **apothecary of Hugh Mercer** (p. 104), his friend and fellow warrior. Spend the next morning at the Civil War battlefields. Then take I-95 north to Alexandria, with a stop at the **National Museum of the Marine Corps** in Triangle (p. 108).

Days ⓭ & ⓮: Alexandria & Mount Vernon ✿✿✿
George Washington, Robert E. Lee, and a host of other notables strode the cobblestone streets of **Old Town Alexandria,** the city's beautifully restored historic district beside the Potomac River. Old Town's sights will take most of a day to explore. Spend the next day south of Alexandria at Washington's home at **Mount Vernon** (p. 84). Old Town is a shuttle ride back to Dulles airport.

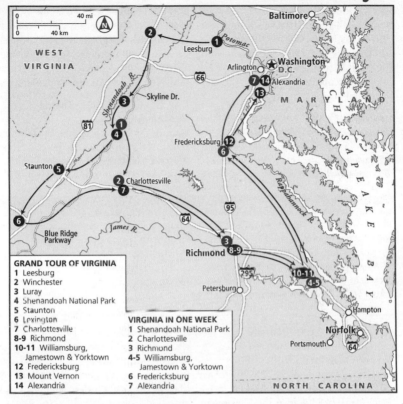

Grand Tour of Virginia

Grand Tour of Virginia

GRAND TOUR OF VIRGINIA
1 Leesburg
2 Winchester
3 Luray
4 Shenandoah National Park
5 Staunton
6 Lexington
7 Charlottesville
8-9 Richmond
10-11 Williamsburg,
    Jamestown & Yorktown
12 Fredericksburg
13 Mount Vernon
14 Alexandria

VIRGINIA IN ONE WEEK
1 Shenandoah National Park
2 Charlottesville
3 Richmond
4-5 Williamsburg,
    Jamestown & Yorktown
6 Fredericksburg
7 Alexandria

2 Virginia in 1 Week

Although you'll be pressing to see everything in Virginia in 2 weeks (Williamsburg, Jamestown, and Yorktown together can easily eat up a week), you can see the tip of the iceberg in a week if you really hurry and see only the top attractions. In devising this route, I have eliminated all but the best.

Day ❶: The Shenandoah National Park 𝒦𝒦𝒦

Drive directly to the entrance of the Central District of **Shenandoah National Park** (p. 145), on U.S. 211, at Thornton Gap. Go south on the **Skyline Drive,** take in the views, hike, or go horseback riding. Spend the night at the park's **Big Meadows Lodge** (p. 151) or **Skyland Lodge** (p. 152).

Day ❷: Charlottesville 𝒦𝒦𝒦

Drive south on the Skyline Drive to U.S. 33 east, then to U.S. 29, and then south to **Charlottesville.** Spend the afternoon touring the **University of Virginia** (p. 136) and other downtown Charlottesville attractions. The next morning beat the crowds to Jefferson's magnificent **Monticello** (p. 135). Do lunch at nearby **Michie Tavern** before visiting President James Monroe's **Ash Lawn–Highland.** When done follow I-64 east to Richmond.

Day ❸: Richmond 𝒶𝒶

It will be all you can do in a day to visit **The Museum and White House of the Confederacy** (p. 230), the **Richmond National Battlefield Park** (p. 231), **St. John's Episcopal Church** (p. 231), and the capital city's other top sights.

Days ❹ & ❺: Williamsburg, Jamestown & Yorktown 𝒶𝒶𝒶

Spend one of these days in **Colonial Williamsburg,** the next seeing **Jamestown** and **Yorktown.**

Day ❻: Fredericksburg 𝒶𝒶𝒶

Depart Williamsburg early and drive north to **Fredericksburg,** where you can spend the rest of the morning exploring George Washington's boyhood home. Tour the Civil War battlefields in the afternoon.

Day ❼: Alexandria & Mount Vernon 𝒶𝒶𝒶

Beat the crowds by spending the morning seeing the historic sights in Old Town Alexandria and the afternoon at Washington's **Mount Vernon** plantation (p. 84).

3 Virginia for Families

This 1-week route assumes you will be traveling around Virginia with children and don't want to spend most of your time cooped up with them in the same vehicle. Visiting places like George Washington's Mount Vernon and Thomas Jefferson's Monticello are great educational experiences, but the young ones won't think all that 18th-century furniture is particularly cool. Accordingly, this itinerary takes you to three areas where both you and they will be entertained.

Days ❶, ❷ & ❸: Williamsburg, Jamestown & Yorktown 𝒶𝒶𝒶

Although **Colonial Williamsburg** is a great big history lesson, it also has many activities especially for children, such as taking dancing lessons in the Governor's Mansion and marching with the local "militia." You can also keep the kids thoroughly entertained at **Busch Gardens Europe** (p. 257) and **Water Country USA** (p. 258). Costumed interpreters at **Jamestown Settlement** also will keep them occupied.

Days ❹ & ❺: Virginia Beach 𝒶

Most kids love a day or two at the beach, and **Virginia Beach** is a good place for that. There are lifeguards on duty, and the surf usually isn't threatening. On the way from Williamsburg, stop at the **Virginia**

Air & Space Center in Hampton (p. 281), where they'll love the aircraft and IMAX movie. At the beach, don't miss taking them to the **Virginia Aquarium & Marine Science Center,** with its touch tanks and "harbor seal splash" (p. 306).

Days ❻ & ❼: Chincoteague & Assateague Islands 𝒶𝒶𝒶

A drive across the 17-mile long **Chesapeake Bay Bridge-Tunnel** and up the Delmarva Peninsula will take them to **Chincoteague Island,** where Marguerite Henry based her children's book, *Misty of Chincoteague.* You and the kids can see the wild ponies grazing in the national wildlife refuge and national seashore on **Assateague Island,** and they can actually ride one during summer at the **Chincoteague Pony Centre** (p. 317).

4 Colonial Virginia in 1 Week

This route follows the progress of Virginia's Colonial settlers in 1607 from Jamestown to Williamsburg, and then through the great tobacco plantations they built along the

Colonial Virginia & Civil War Virginia

COLONIAL VIRGINIA TOUR
1 Yorktown
2 Williamsburg
3 Jamestown
4 James River Plantations
5 Fredericksburg
6 Mount Vernon
7 Alexandria

GREAT CIVIL WAR BATTLES TOUR
1 Manassas
2-3 Fredericksburg area
4-5 Richmond
6 Petersburg
7 Appomattox

state's great tidal rivers to Fredericksburg and Alexandria. See "The Grand Tour of Virginia in 2 Weeks," above, for places to stay.

Days ❶, ❷ & ❸: Williamsburg, Jamestown & Yorktown ⭑⭑⭑

As noted in the Grand Tour, above, you must hurry to see the Historic Triangle in 2 days, and you'll be busy even with 3 on your hands. Spend two of them in the beautifully restored **Colonial Williamsburg,** the other visiting the original settlement at **Jamestown** and the great battlefield at **Yorktown,** where Lord Cornwallis surrendered to George Washington.

Day ❹: The James River Plantations

This morning you can tour **Berkeley** (p. 278) and **Shirley** (p. 279), two of the great James River plantations on Va. 5 between Williamsburg and Richmond. Then head up I-295 and I-95 to Fredericksburg.

Day ❺: Fredericksburg ⭑⭑⭑

You can spend a leisurely day on the **Fredericksburg** streets tread by George Washington, Robert E. Lee, James Monroe, and Thomas Jefferson.

Days ❻ & ❼: Mount Vernon & Alexandria ⭑⭑⭑

Take I-95 north from Fredericksburg to Woodbridge, and then U.S. 1 north and

Va. 235 east to **Mount Vernon** (p. 84), Washington's magnificent plantation. It and perhaps one more Potomac plantation will take up the rest of the day. Retire to **Old Town Alexandria** via the scenic George Washington Memorial Parkway. Spend your last day exploring Old Town.

5 The Great Civil War Battles in 1 Week

This route follows the major Union attempts to capture the Confederate capital at Richmond, about 100 miles south of Washington, D.C., between 1862 and 1865. Although the Civil War raged elsewhere in Virginia, especially in the Shenandoah Valley, the last of these Union advances put an end to the nation's bloodiest conflict when Lee surrendered his sword to Grant at Appomattox Court House.

Day ❶: Manassas ✦✦

Two of the war's great battles, including its first, took place near a stream known as Bull Run, outside the town of **Manassas.** Stonewall Jackson won his nickname here when he stood his ground like a stone wall. You can spend most of a day seeing where it all took place in **Manassas National Battlefield Park** (p. 98). Plan to stay in nearby Middleburg or Leesburg in the Hunt Country.

Days ❷ & ❸: Fredericksburg ✦✦✦

Sitting beside the Rappahannock River, Fredericksburg was directly in the path of the Union advances. You will need these 2 days to explore **Fredericksburg & Spotsylvania National Military Park** (p. 112), for it includes four of the Civil War's most important battles—Fredericksburg, Chancellorsville, The Wilderness, and Spotsylvania Courthouse—plus the farmhouse where Stonewall Jackson died.

Days ❹ & ❺: Richmond ✦✦✦

Richmond withstood 4 years of war as the Confederacy's capital. Spend one of these days downtown at **The Museum and White House of the Confederacy** (p. 230) and at the **Richmond Civil War Visitor Center at Tredegar Iron Works** (p. 231). The latter serves as starting point for your second day's driving tour of the battlefields east of the city, now part of the **Richmond National Battlefield Park** (p. 231).

Day ❻: Petersburg ✦✦

The war's last great action took place as Grant laid a 10-month siege to **Petersburg,** then an important railway junction and the key to Richmond's supply line. Union forces finally broke through on April 12, 1865, forcing Lee into his final retreat. Start at downtown Petersburg's **Siege Museum** (p. 240), and then drive along the lines east of town, now part of **Petersburg National Battlefield Park** (p. 242).

Day ❼: Appomattox ✦✦✦

Lee advanced west for a week until he ran out of supplies near Appomattox Court House, about 90 miles west of Petersburg via U.S. 460, where he surrendered on April 9, 1865. The site is beautifully preserved in the **Appomattox Court House National Historical Park** (p. 140).

4

Northern Virginia

One of my northern Virginia neighbors asked me if I would omit this chapter—so you won't come here and add to our already horrific traffic. His request was in jest, but our clogged highways are anything but a joke. Officially, we have the nation's worst congestion after Los Angeles and San Francisco, and we're near the top of the road-rage list, too. It's the result of tremendous growth in the Washington, D.C., metro area over the past decade, much of it on the Virginia side of the Potomac River.

Alexandria, Arlington, and other nearby northern Virginia municipalities are no longer primarily bedroom communities for D.C. workers. Thanks to burgeoning high-tech businesses and the outsourcing of government work, we are today an economic dynamo in our own right.

Fairfax County, which wraps around Arlington and Alexandria, now has more than one million residents, making it the most populous jurisdiction in Virginia. That's twice the population of the District of Columbia. Tysons Corner, a shopping and office complex at the junction of I-495 and Va. 7, has more office space than downtown Denver, and the strip running west from there through Reston and Herndon to Washington Dulles International Airport is one of the nation's major high-tech corridors. Our metropolitan sprawl is extending its tentacles even into the bucolic Hunt Country beyond Dulles airport, where Loudoun is one of the nation's fastest-growing counties.

All that having been said, please don't let our traffic rants discourage you from coming, for it will be well worth your time. If you avoid our rush hours, you can easily get to pockets of historical charm that will take you back hundreds of years.

In Alexandria, the cobblestone streets of the 18th-century Old Town still ring with the footsteps of George Washington, James Monroe, and Robert E. Lee. Virginia's Colonial plantations begin on the Potomac south of Old Town with George Washington's Mount Vernon, one of our nation's most visited homes.

Out in the western part of Loudoun County and in most of Fauquier County, our crowded highways give way to the winding country roads, rolling hills, and picturesque horse farms and villages that make the Hunt Country a special place.

1 Alexandria ★★★

5 miles S of Washington, D.C.; 95 miles N of Richmond

Founded by a group of Scottish tobacco merchants, the riverfront town of Alexandria came into being in July 1749, when a 60-acre tract of land was auctioned off in ½-acre lots. As you stroll the brick sidewalks and cobblestone streets of highly gentrified **Old Town,** the city's official historic district, you'll see more than 2,000 buildings dating from the 18th and 19th centuries.

George Washington stood in the door of Gadsby's Tavern and reviewed his troops for the last time. Robert E. Lee spent his boyhood here. Both worshiped from the pews of Christ Church. Indeed, if they weren't instantly shocked back to death by the cars jockeying for prized parking spaces, Washington and Lee would still recognize their old haunts.

There's more than history here to explore. With its abundance of shops, boutiques, art galleries, restaurants, and tourists (not to mention hordes of older teens hanging out on Fri and Sat nights), Old Town Alexandria serves as our hip version of Georgetown over in D.C. Once you get here, you will find plenty to see, do, and eat in Old Town. Give yourself 2 days to poke around the historic district and a third to see Mount Vernon and the other Potomac plantations a short drive to the south.

ESSENTIALS
VISITOR INFORMATION

The Alexandria Convention & Visitors Association's **Ramsay House Visitor Center,** 221 King St., at Fairfax Street facing Market Square (© **800/388-9119** or 703/838-4200; 703/838-5005 for 24-hr. Alexandria events recording; fax 703/838-4683; www. funside.com), is open daily from 9am to 5pm (closed New Year's Day, Thanksgiving, and Christmas). In this 1724 house, Alexandria's oldest, you can pick up maps and brochures, find out about special events during your visit, and get information about accommodations, restaurants, sights, shopping, and whatever else. You can also get a free 1-day parking permit here (see "Getting There," below).

Be sure to pick up a free copy of *Old Town Crier* (© **703/836-9132;** www.old towncrier.com), a monthly magazine packed with information and news about special events, dining, shopping, and entertainment.

GETTING THERE

For more information about transportation see "Getting There" and "Getting Around Virginia," in chapter 2.

BY PLANE   Washington Dulles International Airport (IAD) is about 30 miles west of Alexandria (© **703/661-2700;** www.mwaa.com). **Ronald Reagan Washington National Airport (DCA)** is 2 miles north of Old Town via the George Washington Memorial Parkway (© **703/685-8000;** www.mwaa.com). Washington's **Metrorail** (see below) provides easy transport from Reagan National to Alexandria via its Blue and Yellow lines. Taxis are available at both airports, and **SuperShuttle** (© **800/BLUE-VAN;** www.supershuttle.com) operates frequent van service.

BY CAR   All the major **car-rental firms** are based at the airports. The scenic George Washington Memorial Parkway passes through Old Town as Washington Street, Alexandria's main north-south thoroughfare. I-95 crosses the Potomac River at Alexandria; take Exit 177 and go north on U.S. 1 into Old Town. Turn east on King Street off either route to reach the heart of Old Town.

If you drive here, the first item of business is to get a **free 1-day parking permit** at the Ramsay House Visitor Center (see "Visitor Information," above), which allows you to park free at any 2-hour meter, except those in Metrorail lots, for up to 24 hours. They do *not* apply to spaces without meters, especially those reserved exclusively for Old Town residents. You'll need your car's license plate number and the state in which it's registered—which could be other than Virginia if it's a rental.

BY TRAIN The **Amtrak** station (© **800/872-7245** or 703/836-4339; www.amtrak. com) is at 110 Callahan Dr., at King Street.

BY WASHINGTON METRORAIL From Arlington or Washington, take the Blue or Yellow **Metrorail** (© **202/637-7000;** www.wmata.com) lines to the King Street station (it's across the tracks from Amtrak's Alexandria station). Metrorail operates Monday to Thursday from 5:30am to midnight, Friday 5:30am to 2am, Saturday 8am to 3am, and Sunday 8am to midnight. Fares range from $1.35 to $3.90 depending on time of day and length of ride.

From the King Street Station, it's about a 15-minute walk east on King Street through Old Town's rapidly developing western section. Or you can save your shoe leather for sightseeing by boarding DASH buses numbered AT-2 or AT-5 (or the free weekend shuttle), down King Street to the corner of Fairfax Street and the door of the visitor center (see "Getting Around," below). Base fare is $1.

CITY LAYOUT

Old Town Alexandria is laid out in a simple grid. The original town grew north-south along the Potomac River, but most of what you will want to see and do today is on, or a few blocks off, King Street, the main east-west drag, between the waterfront and the King Street Metrorail station. Until a few years ago, visitors to Old Town seldom wandered west of Washington Street. But the Metro has spurred development near the station, and new stores and restaurants have sprouted up all along King Street.

Going west from the Potomac River, Union to Lee Street is the 100 block; Lee to Fairfax, the 200 block; and so on. Numbers on the cross streets (more or less going north and south) are divided north and south by King Street. King to Cameron is the 100 block north, Cameron to Queen the 200 block north, and so on; King to Prince is the 100 block south, and so on.

GETTING AROUND

As a glance at the walking tour map later in this chapter will indicate, Old Town's prime historic sites are contained within several blocks. Park your car for the day, don comfortable shoes, and start walking—it's the easiest way.

Alexandria's bus system, known as **DASH** (© **703/370-3274;** www.dashbus.com), is primarily useful for getting from the King Street Metro station to the Ramsay House Visitor Center (take buses numbered AT-2 and AT-5). On weekends from April through December, free **Dash About** shuttles run along King Street (they bear a cartoon of Mr. and Mrs. George Washington riding in a horse-drawn carriage). The free "Lunch DASH" runs along King Street weekdays from 11:30am to 2pm. Otherwise base fare is $1 with exact fare required. DASH provides service from 5:30am to 11pm weekdays, from 7am to 10pm on weekends. There's no service New Year's Day, Thanksgiving, and Christmas. The visitor center gives away route maps, as does the DASH Old Town Transit Shop, 1775-C Duke St. (© **703/299-6227**), opposite the Embassy Suites Hotel Alexandria Old Town.

For a taxi, call **Alexandria Yellow Cab Company** (© **703/549-2500**) or **Alexandria White Top Cab Company** (© **703/683-4004**).

EXPLORING OLD TOWN

Whenever you come, you're sure to run into some activity or other—a jazz festival, a tea garden or tavern gambol, a quilt exhibit, a wine tasting or an organ recital. But note that **many of Alexandria's main attractions are closed on Monday.**

Tips How to Avoid Gridlock

Traffic in the Washington, D.C., metro is so bad that a columnist for the *Washington Post* writes under the pseudonym "Dr. Gridlock." Although they start earlier and run later depending on distance from D.C., weekday rush hours generally run from 6:30 to 9:30am and from 3:30 to 6:30pm, but tie-ups can occur any time, especially in ongoing construction zones. Take the area's Metrorail or other public transportation whenever possible and try to avoid the roads altogether during rush hours. I keep my radio tuned to WTOP (103.5 FM), which gives traffic reports every 10 minutes.

THE TOP ATTRACTIONS

Carlyle House Historic Park   Patterned after Scottish-English manor houses, this architecturally impressive home was completed in 1753 by Scottish merchant John Carlyle for his bride, Sarah Fairfax, who hailed from one of the first families of Virginia. It was a social and political center visited by many great men of the time including George Washington, but its most important moment in history occurred in April 1755, when Maj. Gen. Edward Braddock, commander in chief of His Majesty's forces in North America, met five Colonial governors here and asked them to tax colonists to finance a campaign against the French and Indians. Colonial legislatures refused, one of the first instances of serious friction between America and Britain. Nevertheless, Braddock made Carlyle House his headquarters during the campaign. The house is furnished with period pieces, and the original large parlor and study have survived intact. There's seldom a wait for a tour, but if there is, you can explore the gardens or browse the gift shop, which offers jewelry, books, Colonial toys, and other items. Call or check the website for special events and lectures.

121 N. Fairfax St. (near Cameron St.). ✆ 703/549-2997. www.carlylehouse.org. Admission $4 adults, $2 children 11–17, free for children 10 and younger. Tues–Sat 10am–4pm; Sun noon–4pm. Guided 45-min. tours depart on the hour and half-hour.

Christ Church ✸   This sturdy redbrick Georgian-style church, in continuous use since 1773, would be an important national landmark even if its two most distinguished members were not George Washington and Robert E. Lee. Washington and other early members fomented revolution in the churchyard, and Lee was offered command of Virginia's army here during the Civil War. You can sit in their family pews. There have, of course, been many changes since Washington's day, but for the most part, the original structure remains, including the handblown glass in the windows. The bell tower, church bell, galleries, and organ were added by the early 1800s, the "wineglass" pulpit in 1891. The **Old Parish Hall** was restored in 1991 to its original appearance; it now houses a gift shop and an exhibit on the history of the church. Do walk in the weathered graveyard, Alexandria's first and only burial ground until 1805.

118 N. Washington St. (at Cameron St.). ✆ 703/549-1450. www.historicchristchurch.org. Free admission (donations accepted). Mon–Sat 9am–4pm; Sun 2–4pm. Gift shop Tues–Sat 10am–4pm. Services Sun 8, 9, 11:15am, and 5pm. Closed federal holidays.

Gadsby's Tavern Museum ✸   Alexandria was at the crossroads of early America, and the center of life in Alexandria was Gadsby's Tavern. Consisting of two buildings— a tavern dating from about 1785 and the City Tavern and Hotel (1792)—it's named for a memorable tavernkeeper, Englishman John Gadsby, whose establishment was renowned for elegance and comfort. The rooms have been restored to their 18th- and 19th-century appearance. The second-floor ballroom, with its musicians' gallery, was the scene of Alexandria's most lavish parties, including Thomas Jefferson's inaugural banquet in 1801. George Washington's birthnight ball and banquet have been an annual tradition here since 1797. To cap off your historical experience, you can dine at Gadsby's Tavern, which is still operating (see "Where to Dine," later in this chapter).

134 N. Royal St. (C) 703/838-4242. www.gadsbystavern.org. Admission $4 adults, $2 children 11–17, free for children 10 and younger. Museum Apr–Oct Tues–Sat 10am–5pm, Sun–Mon 1–5pm; Nov–Mar Wed–Sat 11am–4pm, Sun 1–4pm. Guided 30-min. tours begin 15 min. before and after the hour.

Lee-Fendall House *(Kids)* Revolutionary War hero Henry "Light-Horse Harry" Lee never actually lived in this house, although he was a visitor, as was his friend George Washington. Light-Horse Harry sold the original lot to Philip Richard Fendall (a Lee on his mother's side), who built the house in 1785. It was home to 37 Lees of Virginia until 1903. John L. Lewis, the American labor leader, was its last private owner; his estate sold it to the Virginia Trust for Historic Preservation, which opened it as a museum in 1974. The trust is renovating the structure today with the goal of restoring it to its 1850 appearance, right down to the paint colors. It's a treasure of Lee family furniture, heirlooms, and documents. You shouldn't have to wait long for a 30-minute guided tour, which will interpret the home as it was between 1850 and 1870 and offer insight into Victorian family life. You'll also see the award-winning garden with its magnolia and chestnut trees, roses, and boxwood-lined paths.

614 Oronoco St. (at Washington St.). (C) 703/548-1789. www.leefendallhouse.org. Admission $4 adults, $2 children 11–17, free for children 10 and younger. Tues–Sat 10am–4pm; Sun 1–4pm. Closed mid-Dec to Jan. Mandatory 30-min. tours depart on hour.

Stabler-Leadbeater Apothecary Museum Founded in 1792 by Edward Stabler, a Quaker minister and an abolitionist, The Apothecary Shop occupied these two town houses until 1933. Martha Washington ordered castor oil shortly before her death in 1802, and Robert E. Lee was shopping here in 1859 when he received orders to quash John Brown's rebellion at Harpers Ferry, West Virginia. It was more than a drugstore, however, for in addition to tinctures, elixirs, and potions such as Dragon's Blood, it also sold other products such as paint (Lee bought a few gallons for Arlington House, his mansion at what is now Arlington National Cemetery; see "A Side Trip to Arlington," later in this chapter). Although the building was renovated recently, the

---

Value **Save with a Discounted Attraction Pass**

Alexandria's Ramsay House Visitor Center usually sells money-saving **discounted attraction passes** to some of the top sights. A Block Ticket to Gadsby's Tavern, Stabler-Leadbeater Apothecary Museum, Lee-Fendall House, and Carlyle House Historic Park recently cost $9 for adults, $5 for children 11 to 17. A Very Important Patriot Pass, including the previous four museums, a guided walking or ghost tour of Old Town, and a Potomac River cruise costs $21 adults, $11 for children 11 to 17. A Potomac Pass that included two museums and a river cruise to Mount Vernon cost $30 adults, $15 for children 11 to 17. The passes change from year to year, but it will pay to ask the center what's being offered.

shop still looks like it did when the Stabler-Leadbeater family closed its doors for the last time, leaving behind a collection of more than 8,000 original objects. You'll see it all on a 30-minute guided tour.

105–107 S. Fairfax St. (between King and Prince sts.). ℭ **703/836-3713**. www.apothecarymuseum.org. Admission $4 adults, $2 children 11–17, free for children 10 and younger. Apr–Oct Tues–Sat 10am–5pm, Sun–Mon 1–5pm; Nov–Mar Wed–Sat 11am–4pm, Sun 1–4pm. Closed Jan 1, Thanksgiving, and Dec 25.

MORE ATTRACTIONS

Alexandria Black History Museum   African Americans have been part of Alexandria's history from Colonial times to the present (incumbent Mayor William D. Euile is black). The Ramsay House Visitor Center distributes a fine brochure, "A Remarkable and Courageous Journey," which describes 23 important black-history sites, with a map showing their locations. Start at this museum, in a building constructed in 1940 as the black community's first public library after a civil rights sit-in failed to integrate the Alexandria city library. It exhibits historical objects, photographs, documents, and memorabilia relating to local African Americans from the 18th century on. In addition to the permanent collection, the museum presents rotating exhibits. Optional guided tours take about 30 minutes.

902 Wythe St. ℭ **703/838-4356**. www.alexblackhistory.org. Free admission. Tues–Sat 10am–4pm. Closed Jan 1, Martin Luther King Day, Easter, July 4th, Thanksgiving, and Dec 25.

The Athenaeum   A handsome Greek Revival building with a classic portico and Doric columns, the Athenaeum is home to the Northern Virginia Fine Arts Association. Art exhibits here run the gamut from Matisse lithographs to shows of East Coast artists. The building, which dates from 1851, originally contained the Bank of the Old Dominion, whose operations were interrupted when Yankee troops used the building as their headquarters during the Civil War. Today, it hosts performances by the Alexandria Ballet and, during summer, the Alexandria Classical Guitar Festival. Guided tours are available on request.

201 Prince St. (at Lee St.). ℭ **703/548-0035**. www.nvfaa.org. Free admission (donations appreciated). Wed–Fri 11am–3pm; Sat–Sun 1–5pm. Gallery shows Apr–Nov.

Fort Ward Museum and Historic Site   Civil War buffs will enjoy taking a short drive from Old Town to this museum in a 45-acre city park on the site of one of the chain of Union forts erected to protect Washington, D.C. (yes, the Yankees occupied Alexandria during the war). It's the best preserved of the surviving forts and the only one with a museum. About 90% of the earthwork walls are preserved, and the Northwest Bastion has been restored, with six mounted guns (facing south waiting for the Confederates who never came). You can explore the fort as well as replicas of the ceremonial entrance gate and an officers' hut. The museum explains life during the occupation and shows a 12-minute orientation video. Tours are given only for groups of 12 or more. Allow about an hour.

Fun Fact **Signing Brothers**

The only brothers to sign the Declaration of Independence were Virginians Richard Henry Lee and Francis Lightfoot Lee. Their cousin, Henry "Light-Horse Harry" Lee, was both a hero of the Revolutionary War and the father of Gen. Robert E. Lee.

4301 W. Braddock Rd. ✆ 703/838-4848. www.fortward.org. Free admission. Fort daily 9am–sunset. Museum Tues–Sat 10am–5pm; Sun noon–5pm. From Old Town, follow King St. west, go right on Kenwood St., then left on W. Braddock Rd.; continue for ¾ mile to the entrance on the right.

Friendship Firehouse   Alexandria's first firefighting organization, the Friendship Fire Company, was established in 1774. As the city grew, the company attracted increasing recognition, not only for its firefighting efforts but also for its ceremonial and social presence at parades and other public occasions. Today's brick building was erected to replace an earlier one destroyed by fire in 1855. The museum not only exhibits firefighting paraphernalia dating back to the 18th century, it also documents the Friendship Company's efforts to claim George Washington as one of its own founding fathers. Tours are given by the staff on request; they take about 20 minutes.

107 S. Alfred St. (between King and Prince sts.). ✆ 703/838-3891 or 703/838-4994. http://oha.alexandriava.gov/friendship. Free admission. Fri–Sat 10am–4pm; Sun 1–4pm.

George Washington Masonic National Memorial   Visible for miles from atop Shooter's Hill, west of the King Street Metro station, this imposing neoclassical shrine is modeled after the ancient lighthouse at Alexandria, Egypt, and dedicated to American Freemasonry's most illustrious member. The heart of the memorial is the ornate hall dominated by a colossal 17-foot-tall bronze depicting Washington as lodge master. On either side are 46-foot-long murals, one depicting him laying the U.S. Capitol cornerstone in a Masonic ceremony, another showing him and his Masonic brothers attending Christ Church in Philadelphia during the Revolution. Stained-glass windows in the hall honor 16 other patriots and Freemasons associated with Washington. Be sure to see the fourth-floor museum, which displays many items, including a Washington family Bible. Other floors in the tower present information on numerous Masonic organizations and activities. On ninth floor, the observation deck offers a 360-degree view that takes in the Potomac River, all of Washington, D.C., the Maryland shore, and northern Virginia. Guided 1-hour tours are offered five times daily.

101 Callahan Dr. (at King St.). ✆ 703/683-2007. www.gwmemorial.org. Free admission. Daily 9am–5pm. Closed Jan 1, Thanksgiving, and Dec 25. Guided tours 9:30 and 11am, noon, 1, 2:15, and 3pm.

The Lyceum   The Lyceum focuses on Alexandria's history from Colonial times through the 20th century. The brick-and-stucco Lyceum itself merits a visit. Built in 1839, it was designed in the Doric temple style (with imposing white columns) to serve as a lecture, meeting, and concert hall. The first floor originally contained the Alexandria Library and natural science and historical exhibits. It was an important center of Alexandria's cultural life until the Civil War, when Union forces took it over for use as a hospital. Today it features changing exhibits and an ongoing series of lectures, concerts, and educational programs. An adjoining nonprofit shop carries books, maps, toys, and gifts.

201 S. Washington St. ✆ 703/838-4994. www.alexandriahistory.org. Free admission. Mon–Sat 10am–5pm; Sun 1–5pm.

Old Presbyterian Meeting House   Presbyterian congregations have worshiped in Virginia since Jamestown days, when the Rev. Alexander Whittaker converted the American Indian princess Pocahontas. Scottish pioneers established this congregation in 1774. Its bell tolled continuously for 4 days after George Washington's death in December 1799, and Presbyterian, Episcopal, and Methodist ministers preached memorial services from its pulpit. Among the notable Alexandrians buried in the church graveyard are John and Sara Carlyle; Dr. James Craik, who treated Washington and dressed Lafayette's wounds at Brandywine; and William Hunter, Jr., founder of the

St. Andrew's Society of Scottish descendants (bagpipers pay homage to him the first Sat of each Dec). It's also the site of the tomb of an Unknown Soldier of the Revolutionary War. The original parsonage, built in the Flounder style in 1787, is still intact. There's no guided tour, but there are recorded narratives in the church and graveyard.

321 S. Fairfax St. (at Duke St.). *C* 703/549-6670. www.opmh.org. Free admission. Mon–Fri 9am–4:30pm. Services Sun 8:30 and 11am.

TWO SPECIALIZED ATTRACTIONS

Much digging has taken place to study and preserve the past in Old Town, and some of the results are on display in the **Alexandria Archaeology Museum,** 105 N. Union St. (*C* **703/838-4399;** www.alexandriaarchaeology.org), on the third floor of the Torpedo Factory Art center. It shares space with a working laboratory. Admission is free, and it's open Tuesday to Friday 10am to 3pm, Saturday 10am to 5pm, and Sunday 1 to 5pm.

If you've ever had a clever idea for an invention you thought would revolutionize the world (and make you rich), walk into the **U.S. Patent & Trademark Office Museum,** 600 Dulaney St. (*C* **703/968-4332;** www.uspto.gov/web/offices/ac/ahrpa/opa/museum), which uses high-tech displays to explain how ideas for famous products came into being. Admission is free. The museum is open Monday to Friday 9am to 5pm, Saturday noon to 5pm. From the King Street Metro station, follow Diagonal Road south to Dulaney Street.

GUIDED TOURS

Though it's easy to see Alexandria on your own (see "Walking Tour: Old Town Alexandria," below), your experience will be enhanced by having a knowledgeable local guide. Take your pick among **Alexandria's Footsteps to the Past** (*C* **703/683-3451** or 703/850-7138; www.footstepstothepast.com), **Alexandria Tours of Old Town** (*C* **703/329-1122**), or **The Old Town Experience** (*C* **703/836-0694;** www.alexandriacitywebsite.com/OldTownExperience.htm). Even if you see everything on your own during the day, you'll enjoy spooking around Old Town after dark with **Alexandria's Original Ghost & Graveyard Tours** (*C* **703/519-1749** or 703/548-0100; www.alexcolonialtours.com). They usually explore Old Town's streets and back alleys Wednesday to Sunday nights (call for the schedule and to make reservations). The Ramsay House Visitor Center (see "Visitor Information," earlier in this section) has their schedules and will make reservations, which are required. All three tours cost $10 for adults, $5 for kids 7 to 12, free for children 6 and younger.

▐ WALKING TOUR ▐ OLD TOWN ALEXANDRIA

Start:	Ramsay House Visitor Center, King Street at Fairfax Street.
Finish:	Torpedo Factory, Waterfront at Cameron Street.
Time:	Allow approximately 2½ hours, not including museum and shopping stops.
Best Times:	Anytime Tuesday through Sunday.
Worst Times:	Monday, when many historic sites are closed.

You'll get a glimpse into the 18th century as you stroll along Alexandria's brick-paved sidewalks, lined with Colonial residences, historic houses and churches, museums, shops, and restaurants. This walk ends at the waterfront, no longer a center of commercial shipping but now home to an arts center along the Potomac riverfront.

Old Town Alexandria

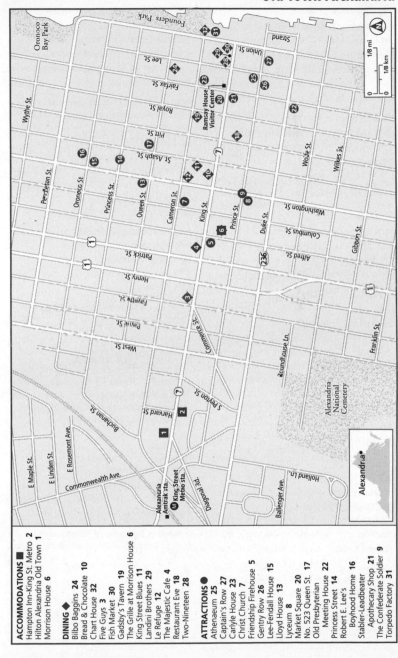

71

Begin your walk at the:

❶ Ramsay House Visitor Center

Built around 1724, the center has a Dutch barn roof and an English garden. It's located at 221 King St., at Fairfax Street, in the heart of the historic district. This is the best place to get your bearings.

Head north on Fairfax Street to:

❷ Carlyle House Historic Park

This elegant 1753 manor house is set off from the street by a low wall.

Continue north on Fairfax to the corner. Turn left on Cameron, past the back of the old city hall, to the redbrick buildings across Royal Street, known as:

❸ Gadsby's Tavern

The 18th-century tavern complex houses a museum of 18th-century antiques, while the hotel portion is an Early American–style restaurant.

TAKE A BREAK
The 18th-century atmosphere at **Gadsby's Tavern** (p. 76) is the perfect place for a sandwich or salad.

Continue west on Cameron Street and turn right on St. Asaph Street. At Queen Street, you can see:

❹ No. 523 Queen St.

At 7 feet wide, it's Alexandria's narrowest house.

Continuing north on St. Asaph, you'll come to:

❺ Princess Street

The cobble paving stones are original (and you'll see why heavy traffic is banned here).

One block farther north on St. Asaph, turn left at Oronoco Street. The house on your right at number 607 was:

❻ Robert E. Lee's Boyhood Home

Lee lived in the Federal-style mansion at 607 Oronoco St. from age 5 until he went to West Point in 1825. It's a private residence.

Across Oronoco Street, at the corner of Washington, is the:

❼ Lee-Fendall House

The gracious white-clapboard residence was home to several generations of Lees. Enter through the pretty Colonial garden.

Head south (left) on Washington, a busy commercial thoroughfare, to Queen Street and cross over to:

❽ Lloyd House

A beautiful late Georgian home (1797), the house is now part of the Alexandria Library and holds a fascinating collection of documents, books, and records on the city and state.

Proceed south on Washington Street to the quiet graveyard entrance behind:

❾ Christ Church

The Washingtons and Lees worshiped in this Episcopal church.

Leave by the front entrance, on Columbus Street, and turn left to King Street.

TAKE A BREAK
A cappuccino-and-pastry break at **Bread & Chocolate**, 611 King St. (p. 79), is guaranteed to revive flagging spirits. Sandwiches and salads are also available at this casual spot.

From King Street, turn left on Alfred Street, to the small but historic:

❿ Friendship Firehouse

You can see an extensive collection of antique fire-fighting equipment here.

Turn left at the corner of Prince Street and proceed to Washington. At the corner is the Greek Revival:

⓫ Lyceum

Built in 1839 as the city's first cultural center, today it's a city historical museum. The museum shop has a lovely selection of crafts, silver, and other gift items.

At the intersection of Washington and Prince stands:

⑫ The Confederate Soldier

The sculptor modeled the dejected bronze figure after one in the painting *Appomattox* by John A. Elder. Confederate-soldier statues in Southern towns traditionally face north (in case the Yankees return), but Alexandria's looks southward, perhaps because Union soldiers occupied the city during the war.

Continue walking east on Prince to Pitt Street, then turn left to King. Turn right and you'll see the fountain in:

⑬ Market Square

This open space along King Street from Royal to Fairfax in front of the modern but Williamsburg-style Town Hall has been used as a town market and meeting ground since 1749. Today, the market is held on Saturday mornings.

Turn right on Fairfax to the quaint:

⑭ Stabler-Leadbeater Apothecary Shop

A remarkable collection of early medical ware and handblown glass containers is on display here.

Head south on Fairfax to Duke Street, to the:

⑮ Old Presbyterian Meeting House

George Washington's funeral sermons were preached in 1799 in this 18th-century church. The graveyard has a marker commemorating the Unknown Soldier of the Revolutionary War.

Retrace your steps back to Prince Street and turn right. Between Fairfax Street and Lee Street you'll see:

⑯ Gentry Row

The local leaders who made their homes in these three-story town houses in the 18th and 19th centuries gave their name to the row. With the skyrocketing price of houses here, Old Town should be called "Gentry City."

At the corner of Prince and Lee is the:

⑰ Athenaeum

It's a handsome Greek Revival structure that now houses contemporary art shows.

Cross Lee Street to:

⑱ Captain's Row

This is a pretty cobblestone section of Prince Street. You're now in sight of the Potomac riverfront and may want to stroll down to the little waterfront park at the foot of Prince Street for a panoramic view of the river.

Continue north on Union Street, where you can begin your shopping expedition at:

⑲ Torpedo Factory

You can wander the arts-and-crafts center's studios and galleries, which are open to the public.

POTOMAC RIVER CRUISES

After you've seen Old Town's attractions on foot, you can get a fish's-eye view of the city on a cruise operated by **Potomac Riverboat Company** (© 877/502-2628 or 703/548-9000; www.potomacriverboatco.com), based at the city dock behind the Torpedo Factory Art Center at the foot of King Street. A 40-minute "Alexandria Seaport Tour" is fine for taking photos of Old Town from out on the river, and it's especially suitable if you are traveling with children. They cost $12 for adults, $10 seniors, $6 for children ages 2 to 12. Much more scenic is the 1½-hour "Washington Monuments Tour," since it goes upriver for super views of the nation's capital. They cost double but are worth the extra money. The cruises run daily from June to September and weekends during May and October. Check at the dockside booth or call for information and reservations.

The company also has cruises to Mount Vernon; see section 2 of this chapter.

OUTDOOR ACTIVITIES

This part of northern Virginia has two first-rate hiking, biking, and running trails. A 17-mile paved trail starts at Memorial Bridge and borders the **George Washington Memorial Parkway** south to Mount Vernon, passing through Old Town on the way (see "A Scenic Drive along the Potomac River," later in this chapter).

Beginning in the Shirlington area, on I-395 in neighboring Arlington, the **Washington & Old Dominion (W&OD) Trail** follows Four-mile Run Drive and Glencarlyn Park northwest to an old railroad bed, which then proceeds 45 miles through Leesburg to Purcellville (see "The Hunt Country," later in this chapter). **Big Wheel Bikes,** 2 Prince St., at The Strand (© **703/739-2300;** www.bigwheelbikes.com), rents a wide range of bikes beginning at $5 an hour. It's open Monday to Friday 11am to 7pm, Saturday 10am to 6pm, Sunday 11am to 5pm.

SHOPPING

Old Town has hundreds of boutiques, antiques stores, art galleries, and gift shops selling everything from souvenir T-shirts to 18th-century reproductions. Most of the best stores are interspersed among the multitude of restaurants and offices on King Street from the waterfront to the Metrorail station. Plan to spend a fair amount of time browsing between visits to historic sites. A guide to the city's 50-plus antiques and collectibles stores is available at the visitor center (you'll pay a premium for antiques here, so you may want to wait to buy if you're going to Fredericksburg; see chapter 5).

One essential stop is the **Torpedo Factory Art Center,** 105 N. Union St., between King and Cameron streets on the Potomac River (© **703/838-4565;** www.torpedofactory.org). This block-long, three-story waterfront structure was built by the U.S. Navy in 1918 and operated as a torpedo shell-case factory until the early 1950s, then used as storage for artifacts from the Smithsonian Institution. Today, it houses 84 working studios where artists and craftspeople create and sell their works. The shops and galleries are open daily 10am to 5pm and every second Tuesday of the month from 6 to 9pm for **Art Night.** It's closed New Year's Day, Easter, July 4th, Thanksgiving, and Christmas.

Another highlight here is the nonprofit **Winterthur Museum Store** 🌭🌭, 207 King St., between Lee and Fairfax streets (© **703/684-6092**), the only off-site venture by the renowned museum of decorative arts on the estate of horticulturist Henry Francis du Pont, in Delaware's Brandywine Valley. It's a delightful browse, including the back garden, which features all sorts of garden plants and ornaments. You'll come across fine reproductions from the Winterthur collection, including lamps, prints, ceramics, brassware, jewelry, garden furniture, and statuary. The store is open Monday to Saturday 10am to 5pm, Sunday 11am to 5pm (6pm in summer).

WHERE TO STAY

The area around the King Street Metrorail station is home to several hotels, including the Hilton Alexandria Old Town and the Hampton Inn–King Street Metro (see below). Another good bet if you want a kitchen is **Embassy Suites Hotel Old Town,** 1900 Diagonal Rd. (© **800/362-2779** or 703/684-5900; www.embassysuites.com).

In the less convenient northern end of Old Town are the **Best Western Old Colony Inn,** 1101 N. Washington St. (© **800/528-1234** or 730/739-2222; www.bestwestern. com); **Holiday Inn Hotel & Suites,** 625 First St. (© **800/465-4329** or 703/548-6300; www.holiday-inn.com); and the **Executive Club Suites** at 610 Bashford Lane

(🕿 **800/535-2582** or 703/739-2582; www.alexandria-executive-suites.com), where every unit is an apartment. Nearby, **Sheraton Suites Alexandria,** 801 N. St. Asaph St. (🕿 **800/325-3535** or 703/836-4700; www.starwoodhotels.com), provides nothing but suites, while the high-rise **Crowne Plaza Old Town Alexandria,** 901 N. Fairfax St., at Montgomery Street (🕿 **800/972-3159** or 703/683-6000; www.crowneplaza.com), stands near the river, giving some of its 258 rooms water views.

Hampton Inn–King Street Metro   Less than a block east of the Amtrak and King Street Metro stations, this six-story hotel is a bit more upscale than most of its Hampton Inn sisters. The reasonably spacious rooms are decorated in typical Hampton fashion. The best are those on the upper floors, which have views over the city. Continental breakfast is served in the lobby, which has a 24-hour coffee and juice dispenser. The outdoor pool is open during summer.

1616 King St. (at Harvard St.), Alexandria, VA 22314. 🕿 800/426-7866 or 703/299-9900. Fax 703/299-9937. www.hamptoninn.com. 80 units. $124–$249 double. Rates include continental breakfast. AE, DC, DISC, MC, V. Self-parking $10. **Amenities:** Outdoor pool; health club; business center; laundry service; coin-op washers and dryers. *In room:* A/C, TV, Wi-Fi, coffeemaker, iron.

Hilton Alexandria Old Town 🍴   Although it lacks the pampering services of Morrison House (see below), this seven-story structure nevertheless is Old Town's second-best hotel. The spacious rooms are furnished with antique reproductions. Those on the concierge level come equipped with marble bathrooms and feather beds. Off the lobby and with outdoor seating in warm weather, **Seagar's Restaurant & Piano Bar** offers seafood, prime steaks, and a little music to go with it. In addition, you can walk into its wine room and pick your vintage (couples can reserve a table for private dining).

1767 King St. (at Diagonal Rd.), Alexandria, VA 22314. 🕿 800/445-8667 or 703/837-0440. Fax 703/837-0454. www.hiltonalexandria.com. 241 units. $169–$299 double; $269–$319 suite. Rates include continental breakfast. AE, DC, DISC, MC, V. Self-parking $20. **Amenities:** Restaurant; bar; indoor pool; health club; sauna; business center; room service; laundry service; concierge-level rooms. *In room:* A/C, TV, Wi-Fi, minibar, coffeemaker, iron.

Morrison House 🍴🍴🍴   Although it was built in 1985, one of Virginia's finest boutique hotels was designed after the grand manor houses of the Federal period and thus fits right into Old Town. The enchantment begins the moment you ascend the curving staircase to its white-columned portico, where a friendly butler greets you at the door of the marble foyer. That's a fitting introduction to the inn's ask-and-it-shall-be-done service, from shining your shoes to bringing dinner to your room in the middle of the night. It's not stuffy by any means; a polite but relaxed informality reigns here. **The Grille at Morrison House,** one of Alexandria's finest restaurants, is here (p. 77), and locals and guests alike pack the lounge on Thursday, Friday, and Saturday nights to hear a resident pianist on the baby grand accompany would-be opera stars and torch singers.

Each of the spacious, luxuriously appointed guest quarters is individually decorated and furnished with Federal-period reproductions. Some have mahogany four-poster beds, brass chandeliers, and decorative fireplaces. In your room, you'll find two phones, fresh flowers, down comforters, and robes. Bathrooms are marble-lined throughout and come equipped with makeup mirrors.

116 S. Alfred St. (between King and Prince sts.), Alexandria, VA 22314. 🕿 800/367-0800 or 703/838-8000. Fax 703/684-6283. www.morrisonhouse.com. 45 units. $199–$399 double; $299–$499 suite. Spa, dining, Mount Vernon tour, and other packages available. AE, DC, MC, V. Valet parking $20. **Amenities:** Restaurant (p. 77); bar; access to nearby health club and day spa; room service; babysitting; laundry service. *In room:* A/C, TV/VCR, Wi-Fi, hair dryer, iron.

BED & BREAKFASTS

Several private Old Town homes, many of them historic properties, offer B&B accommodations under the aegis of **Alexandria & Arlington Bed & Breakfast Network,** P.O. Box 25319, Arlington, VA 22202 (© **888/549-3415** or 703/549-3415; www.aabbn.com), which also represents properties in adjoining Arlington and as far away as the Hunt Country. Check the website for a complete list and rates.

WHERE TO DINE

One of the Washington area's most popular dining destinations, Old Town has many more restaurants than it does historical attractions. You'll find cuisines from around the world offered in every price range along King Street and on Union Street south of King Street. The restaurants described below will give you a good sampling of the many tastes offered here, but don't be afraid to stroll along and pick one of your own. They all post their menus out front, and you'll know by the number of customers which restaurants get nods from the town's affluent citizenry.

King Street has two Starbucks outlets and the local branch of Bread & Chocolate (see below), but my favorite joint for morning coffee, pastries, and fresh bread is **Firehouse Bakery & Coffee Shop,** 105 S. Union St. (© **703/519-8020**), in the block south of King Street. It's open Monday to Friday 6:30am to 7pm, Saturday 7am to 7pm, and Sunday 7am to 6pm.

EXPENSIVE

Chart House ⋇ AMERICAN   One of the few Washington-area restaurants actually on the Potomac River, this member of the national Chart House chain gives you a view of the river, with alfresco patio dining in good weather. The ample, straightforward American fare includes seafood and thick, tender steaks and prime rib, supplemented by daily specials. All entrees come with freshly baked breads and unlimited trips to the salad bar, which features caviar. There's a terrific champagne Sunday brunch here, and the bar and its outdoor tables are my favorite place to cool down after walking around Old Town.

1 Cameron St. (on the Potomac River). © 703/684-5080. Reservations recommended. Sandwiches (lunch only) $9–$14; main courses $18–$32; Sun brunch $25. AE, DC, DISC, MC, V. Mon–Thurs 11:30am–3pm and 5–10pm; Fri 11:30am–3pm and 5–11pm; Sat 11:30am–3pm and 4–11pm; Sun 11am–10pm. Bar Mon–Sat 11:30am–11pm; Sun 11am–10pm.

Gadsby's Tavern ⋇⋇ AMERICAN   An essential part of the Old Town experience is to dine here, behind the portals where Washington reviewed his troops for the last time. Period furnishings, wood-plank floors, fireplace, and gaslight-style lamps re-create a Colonial atmosphere, while costumed waitstaff and balladeers make for a fun time along the lines of Colonial Williamsburg's taverns (the chow is much better here). You'll dine from the same kind of pewter and china our ancestors used, and Sally Lunn bread is baked daily. Lunch might consist of a Scottish smoked salmon and Surrey bacon club sandwich or a Virginia ham and English cheddar cheese quiche. Dinner entrees usually include one of George Washington's favorites, half a duckling stuffed with fruit and served with Madeira gravy. In winter, warm yourself with drinks like hot buttered rum and Martha's Remedy—coffee, cocoa, and brandy. The courtyard serves as an outdoor dining area during fine weather (you can smoke there, but not inside).

138 N. Royal St. (at Cameron St.). © 703/548-1288. Reservations recommended for dinner. Main courses $20–$30. AE, DISC, MC, V. Mon–Sat 11:30am–3pm and 5:30–10pm; Sun 11am–3pm and 5:30–10pm.

The Grille at Morrison House ⭐⭐⭐ (Value) INTERNATIONAL   One of Old Town's top accommodations (p. 75) also is the setting for some of its finest dining in The Grille, the inn's elegant but relaxed dining room and bar. The menu changes each evening depending what the chef and his crew have found that morning. The excellent cuisine emphasizes wild game, fish, free-range fowl, and other natural ingredients. Given the prices, this adventure in dining is a very good value. The inn also serves a scrumptious breakfast.

116 S. Alfred St. (between King and Prince sts.). (C) **703/838-8000.** Reservations highly recommended. Main courses $23–$37. AE, DC, MC, V. Mon–Fri 7–10am and 6–10pm; Sat 8–10am and 6–10pm; Sun 8–10am, 11am–2pm, and 6–10pm. Bar open until 11pm Fri–Sat.

Landini Brothers ⭐⭐ NORTHERN ITALIAN   The classic, delicate cuisine of Tuscany is consistently fine at this rustic, almost grottolike restaurant with stone walls, a flagstone floor, and rough-hewn beams overhead. It's especially charming at night by candlelight. There's additional seating in a lovely upstairs dining room. Everything is homemade—the pasta, the crusty Italian bread, and the desserts. Things might get underway with prosciutto and melon or Top Neck clams on the half shell, followed by prime aged beef tenderloin medallions sautéed with garlic, mushrooms, and rosemary in a Barolo wine sauce. Dessert choices include tiramisu and custard-filled fruit tarts. There's jazz upstairs on Friday and Saturday nights.

115 King St. (between Lee and Union sts.). (C) **703/836-8404.** Reservations recommended. Pastas $17–$19, main courses $20–$30. AE, DC, DISC, MC, V. Mon–Sat 11:30am–11pm; Sun 4–10pm.

Restaurant Eve ⭐⭐⭐ NEW AMERICAN   Old Town's finest restaurant, this exquisitely designed bistro is the creation of talented chef Cathal Armstrong and his wife, Meshelle, who named it for their young daughter, Eve. They really have two restaurants in one here. Residing under a huge skylight, their casual Bistro serves an a la carte menu for lunch and dinner. A doorway leads to The Chef's Tasting Room, a more formal venue where Cathal cooks five-course fixed-priced dinners. In either, their menus change up to 60 times a year to make use of fresh, mostly organic produce from local farms and markets. The rich bouillabaisse with cod and clams is a constant in the Bistro, where you might also find sautéed soft-shell crabs with braised fennel-and-tomato confit. To the left as you enter, an air-conditioned room holds an excellent collection of wines. A good way to sample the fare here without filing for bankruptcy is the $18 Lickity Split-Lounge Lunch Menu, offering a choice of two items such as a salad of local asparagus and Virginia ham.

110 S. Pitt St. (between King and Prince sts.) (C) **703/684-4100.** Reservations recommended. Main courses $29–$36; 5-course tasting menu $95. AE, DC, DISC, MC, V. Mon–Fri 11:30am–2:30pm and 5:30–9:30pm; Sat 5:30–9:30pm.

Two-Nineteen AMERICAN/CREOLE   Two-Nineteen is comprised of three formal Victorian-style dining rooms, a covered sidewalk patio, and the Bayou Room, a Rathskeller-like basement. Inside the main dining rooms, crystal chandeliers, rose-velvet upholstery, and a floral-patterned carpet re-create Victorian New Orleans for Creole cuisine, featured here along with less exciting Chesapeake Bay–style seafood (forget it and go to the Fish Market; see below).

219 King St. (between Fairfax and Lee sts.). (C) **703/549-1141.** Reservations recommended, especially for dinner in the formal dining rooms. Main courses $15–$30. AE, DC, DISC, MC, V. Mon–Thurs 11am–10:30pm; Fri–Sat 11am–11pm; Sun 10am–4pm (brunch) and 5–10:30pm.

MODERATE

Bilbo Baggins Global Cafe ★ *Value* INTERNATIONAL   Named for the title character in *The Hobbit,* this charming two-story restaurant offers fresh homemade fare. The downstairs has rustic wide-plank floors, wood-paneled walls, oak tables, and a brick-oven centerpiece. Upstairs is another dining room with stained-glass windows. It adjoins a skylit wine bar with windows overlooking Queen Street treetops. Candlelit at night, it becomes even cozier. The menu changes daily to reflect seasonal specialties. At dinner, you'll enjoy entrees such as a wasabi salmon filet with a ragout of fresh asparagus and wild mushrooms, and chicken breast spiced up by an andouille sausage and jalapeño-jack-cheese stuffing. An extensive wine list is available (more than 30 boutique wines are offered by the glass and another 150 by the bottle). Homemade desserts like steamed white-chocolate bread pudding topped with whipped cream provide a delightful finish. Lighter and less expensive fare is available in the bar.

208 Queen St. (between Fairfax and Lee sts.). © **703/683-0300.** Reservations accepted only for parties of 6 or more. Main courses $14–$24. AE, DC, DISC, MC, V. Mon–Thurs 11:30am–2:30pm and 5:30–10:30pm; Sat 11am–10:30pm; Sun 10am–2:30pm and 3:30–9:30pm. Closed Dec 25.

Fish Market *Value* SEAFOOD   Although the popular Fish Market has grown to include the building next door, its original corner location is a warehouse that's over 200 years old. Heavy beams, terra-cotta tile floors, exposed brick and stucco walls adorned with nautical antiques, copper pots over a fireplace, copper-topped bars, and saloon doors all lend an old-time ambience. If you're lucky, in fine weather you might get a table for two on a one-table-wide balcony above King Street. Although not exceptional, the fare is quite passable and reasonably priced Chesapeake-style (broiled, fried, or grilled) fresh fish, shrimp, oysters, and crab. A bowl of seafood stew warms me up on a cold winter's day. On weekends, there's live entertainment in the Main Dining Room and the Sunquest Room.

105 King St. (at Union St.). © **703/836-5676.** Reservations not accepted. Salads and sandwiches $6.50–$12; main courses $12–$22. AE, DC, DISC, MC, V. Sun–Thurs 11:15am–1am; Fri–Sat 11:15am–2am (kitchen closes at 12:15am).

Le Refuge ★ *Value* FRENCH   A wicker model of the Eiffel Tower sits in the bow-front window of Jean-François Chaufour's charming little restaurant, a local mainstay since 1983. Reflecting the cooking style, the intimate setting is typically French country—stucco walls adorned with wine labels and provincial ceramics, bentwood chairs, black-leather banquettes, and tables covered with beige-and-brown napery. The special three-course pre- and after-theater dinner is a great buy: It includes soup or salad; fresh catch of the day, leg of lamb, or calves' liver; and crème brûlée or peach melba for dessert. There's a lunch version for about $17. Regular house specialties include bouillabaisse, classic rack of lamb, rainbow trout amandine, and chicken Dijonnaise. Nightly specials feature produce fresh from the market.

127 N. Washington St. (at Cameron St.). © **703/548-4661.** Reservations recommended. Main courses $19–$26; fixed-price 3-course dinner $24. AE, DC, MC, V. Mon–Sat 11:30am–2:30pm and 5–10pm (early-bird dinner Mon all evening, Tues–Thurs 5–7pm and 9–10pm).

The Majestic Cafe ★★ *Finds* NEW VIRGINIAN   The bright neon sign recalls the 1950s when a small town cafe occupied this King Street storefront, but the building got a thorough makeover. Now it's one of Old Town's best bistros. The "comfort food" here is very familiar and very good: meatloaf, calves' liver, roast chicken with gravy, New York strip steaks, grilled fish. Sunday evening turns to "Nana's" family-style dinner when up to four dine for a total of $68 per table.

Tips Bags of Burgers

Everyone from panhandlers to Old Town's gentry can be seen hauling bags of juicy hamburgers, hot dogs, and seasoned french fries out of **Five Guys**, 107 N. Fayette St. (© **703/549-7991**), between King and Cameron streets. This order-at-the-counter joint harkens back to pre-McDonald's days when hamburgers weren't frozen beforehand and fresh potatoes were cut on premises. The burgers and dogs come with a choice of fixings and cost just $2.70 to $5.40. Open daily 11am to 10pm.

---

911 King St. (between Alfred and Patrick sts.). © 703/837-9117. Reservations recommended. Main courses $17–$24. AE, DC, DISC, MC, V. Tues–Fri 11:30am–2:30pm and 5:30–10pm; Sat–Sun 5:30–10pm.

INEXPENSIVE

Stalls sell inexpensive eats in the **Food Pavilion** between the Torpedo Factory, at King and Cameron streets, and the riverfront Chart House restaurant. It's open daily from 11am to 9:30pm.

Bread & Chocolate CONTINENTAL/BAKERY   Part of a successful chain, this cheerful European-style restaurant is one of Old Town's best places for fresh breads, croissants, napoleons, chocolate truffle cakes, Grand Marnier cakes, Bavarian fruit tarts, and other goodies. At breakfast, you can get a *caffè mocha* and an almond croissant, or an omelet with potatoes and a slice of melon. The rest of the day, soups, salads, sandwiches, and light main courses are available to help keep you walking.

611 King St. (between Washington and St. Asaph sts.). © 703/548-0992. Reservations not accepted. Breakfast $4–$9; sandwiches and salads $7–$8; main courses $7.50–$8. AE, DC, DISC, MC, V. Mon–Sat 7am–7pm; Sun 8am–6pm.

King Street Blues Finds Value AMERICAN/SOUTHERN   This often-noisy (especially the first-floor bar) roadhouse is one of Alexandria's most charming restaurants—and the best place in town for an inexpensive meal. It's easy to find, for it occupies all three floors of a small brick building with windows painted on its exterior brick wall. Red neon outlines the real windowpanes. Brian McCall, a local artist, has covered almost every inch of the interior walls with papier-mâché figures and murals, all done with sly tongue-in-cheek good humor. A lively crowd packs the place for the house meatloaf (with a memorable accompaniment of garlic mashed potatoes), Southern-fried catfish, chicken-fried steak, and house-smoked baby back ribs in a sweet yet spicy sauce (you can take a bottle home). For something unusual, order the Roadhouse Nachos—they come with cheese, scallions, and either chicken or pork barbecue over potato chips instead of tortilla chips.

112 N. St. Asaph St. (between King and Cameron sts.). © 703/836-8800. Reservations accepted. Salads and sandwiches $7–$9; main courses $10–$17. AE, DC, DISC, MC, V. Mon–Thurs 11:30am–10pm; Fri–Sat 11:30am–11pm; Sun 11am–10pm; bar stays open later.

ALEXANDRIA AFTER DARK

Alexandria falls under the aegis of Washington, D.C., when it comes to the performing arts. The free weekly *City Paper* (www.washingtoncitypaper.com) and the monthly magazine *Old Town Crier* (www.oldtowncrier.com) are the best sources of news about the local bar and music scene; pick up copies at the Ramsay House Visitor Center and in hotel lobbies.

King Street restaurants are the center of Alexandria's ongoing club and bar scene. Especially noteworthy are **Two-Nineteen,** 219 King St. (© **703/549-1141;** p. 77), which features live jazz Tuesday to Saturday nights in the Basin Street Lounge; the **Fish Market,** 105 King St. (© **703/836-5676;** p. 78), with either a pianist or a guitarist Thursday to Saturday nights; and **Murphy's,** 713 King St. (© **703/548-1717**), the town's best Gaelic pub with live Irish bands to accompany corned beef and cabbage on weekends.

An older crowd likes to sing along on Thursday, Friday, and Saturday evenings with the resident pianist in the cozy lounge of the **Morrison House,** 116 S. Alfred St. (© **703/838-8000;** p. 75), between King and Prince streets. You can hear wannabe professional singers belt out some fine jazz and even an aria or two.

Built about 1914 as a vaudeville house, the restored **Old Town Theater,** 815½ King St. (© **703/683-8888;** www.oldtowntheater.com), hosts movies, live music, comedy shows, and other entertainment. It serves hot dogs, burgers, pizzas, and a few main courses. Call or check the website for the schedule.

The **Birchmere,** 3901 Mount Vernon Ave., south of Glebe Road (© **703/549-5919;** www.birchmere.com), is the Washington area's prime showcase for nationally known bluegrass, country, and folk stars. Call or check the website for the schedule and reservations, which are absolutely necessary when a top performer is on stage.

A SIDE TRIP TO ARLINGTON

It's an easy excursion from Old Town to the famous **Arlington National Cemetery** ✸✸✸, a cherished shrine commemorating the lives given by members of the U.S. armed forces. Its seemingly endless rows of graves mark the mortal remains of the honored dead, both the known and the unknown, who served in conflicts from the Revolutionary War to the present.

Start at the **visitor center** (© **703/607-8052;** www.arlingtoncemetery.org), where you can get a free map—and if you have family buried here, find out where. Be sure to pick up a cemetery map, for it's easy to get lost in the maze of pathways here. Admission to the cemetery is free. It's open daily 8am to 7pm from April through September, daily 8am to 5pm October through March, with the exception of Christmas and New Year's Day. You can drive here from Old Town via U.S. 1 and Va. 110, but it's easier to ride **Metrorail's Blue Line** from the King Street Station. Parking in the cemetery lot costs $1.25 for the first 3 hours, $2 per hour thereafter.

Next door is the **Women in Military Service for America Memorial** (© **800/222-2294** or 703/533-1155; www.womensmemorial.org), honoring all women who have served in the military. Inside, there's a computerized registry of more than 250,000 women veterans.

You can spend hours looking at gravestones here, but the one you must see is the poignant **John F. Kennedy Gravesite,** marked by its eternal flame. Jacqueline Kennedy Onassis is buried next to her first husband. Nearby stands a simple white cross at the grave of brother Robert F. Kennedy. Looking north, you'll have a splendid view of the capital city across the river (during his presidency, Kennedy once remarked of this spot, "I could stay here forever").

For an even more spectacular view, walk up the ridge above the Kennedy graves to **Arlington House, The Robert E. Lee Memorial** (© **703/557-0613;** www.nps.gov/arho), a plantation manse built by George Washington Parke Custis, Martha Washington's grandson by her first marriage, after his daughter married a young Virginian named Robert E. Lee. The couple lived here for 30 years before General Lee left in

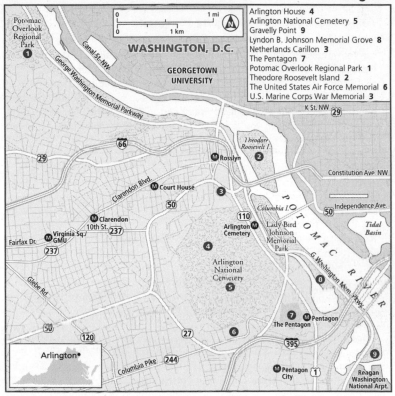

Arlington House **4**
Arlington National Cemetery **5**
Gravelly Point **9**
Lyndon B. Johnson Memorial Grove **8**
Netherlands Carillon **3**
The Pentagon **7**
Potomac Overlook Regional Park **1**
Theodore Roosevelt Island **2**
The United States Air Force Memorial **6**
U.S. Marine Corps War Memorial **3**

1861 to join the Confederate cause. He never returned. To spite him, the federal government turned his front yard into a cemetery for slain Union soldiers. The house is undergoing a massive renovation until 2010, so it is devoid of furniture. Admission is free. The mansion is open daily from 9:30am to 4:30pm (closed Christmas and New Year's Day).

Beyond the mansion, America's most distinguished honor guard slowly marches before the white-marble **Tomb of the Unknowns,** which holds the remains of unidentified combatants slain during World War I. Unknowns from World War II and the Korean War are in the crypts on the plaza in front of it. A crypt for an unknown Vietnam veteran remains vacant since modern forensic science has identified all victims of that conflict. The changing of the guard ceremony—an impressive ritual of rifle maneuvers, heel clicking, and military salutes—takes place daily every half-hour April through September, every hour on the hour the rest of the year.

Adjoining the tomb is the Greek Revival outdoor **Memorial Amphitheater,** used for holiday services, particularly on Memorial Day when the sitting president or vice president attends.

AT THE CEMETERY'S EDGES On the northern periphery of the cemetery, just off Va. 110 about 1½ miles north of the Kennedy graves, stands the famous **U.S. Marine Corps War Memorial,** better known as the Iwo Jima Memorial. The famous

> **Tips Seeing the Cemetery by Tourmobile**
>
> This quiet expanse of green is a walker's paradise, but you can ride around via the **Tourmobile** (© 888/868-7707 or 202/554-5100; www.tourmobile.com). Service is continuous daily from 8:30am to 4:30pm April through September, 9:30am to 4:30pm October through March. Tickets cost $7 for adults, $6 seniors, $3.50 for children 3 to 11. At the visitor center you can also purchase Tourmobile combination tickets that include major Washington, D.C., sights, allowing you to stop and reboard when you're ready. Tourmobiles also depart here for Mount Vernon (see below).

statue is based on news photographer Joe Rosenthal's Pulitzer Prize–winning photo of Marines raising Old Glory on Iwo Jima in February 1945. The Memorial grounds are used for military parades in summer, when there is a free shuttle from the visitor center. Call © **703/289-2500** for the schedule.

Adjacent to the Iwo Jima statue, the **Netherlands Carillon** was a gift from the people of Holland. Thousands of tulip bulbs are planted on the grounds surrounding 127-foot-high open steel tower, creating a colorful display in spring. Carillon concerts are presented on Easter Sunday and every Saturday thereafter in April, May, and September, from 2 to 4pm. Concerts are held daily from 6 to 8pm June through August. You can climb the tower after the carillonneur performs and enjoy spectacular views of Washington.

Those three shiny spires soaring dramatically into the air south of the cemetery come from **The United States Air Force Memorial** (© **703/247-5859;** www.airforcememorial.org), on Air Force Memorial Drive at Columbia Pike (Va. 244). Evoking the "bomb burst" maneuver of the Air Force's Thunderbirds precision flying team, the 270-foot-tall stainless steel spires honor the 54,000 American airmen who have died in combat. The memorial sits on a promontory with a panoramic view over the Pentagon and D.C. beyond (I watch the July 4th fireworks over the National Mall from here). Admission is free. The memorial is open daily from 8am to 11pm. Park free across Columbia Pike.

A SCENIC DRIVE ALONG THE POTOMAC RIVER

Skirting the south bank of the Potomac River for 30 miles between Mount Vernon in the south to the Capital Beltway (I-495) in the northwest, the **George Washington Memorial Parkway** ✿✿✿ is one of Virginia's most scenic drives. It's also a major commuter route, which means lots of traffic during rush hours. Other times, you can drive the entire route in about 45 minutes without stopping. The parkway runs through Old Town Alexandria via King Street; otherwise, it's a four-lane road with neither traffic signals nor stop signs. Also, with the exception of the peaceful **Lyndon B. Johnson Memorial Grove** near **The Pentagon,** you cannot make a left turn; accordingly, I drive it from south to north so I can pull off at designated areas beside or overlooking the river. My favorites are **Gravelly Point Park,** on the north side of Ronald Reagan Washington National Airport (jets roar just a few feet overhead as they take off and land), and at **Potomac Overlook Regional Park,** with a great view over Georgetown in D.C.

As noted in "Outdoor Activities," earlier in this section, you can also run, hike, or bike along part of the parkway. I enjoy hiking to a statute of the Rough Rider in the middle of **Theodore Roosevelt Island,** an 88-acre wooded preserve and bird sanctuary connected to the parkway by a footbridge just south of Rosslyn.

For more information, contact **Headquarters,** George Washington Memorial Parkway, c/o Turkey Run Park, McLean, VA 22101 (© **703/289-2500;** fax 703/289-2598; www.nps.gov/gwmp).

2 Mount Vernon & the Potomac Plantations ★★★

Mount Vernon: 9 miles S of Old Town Alexandria

Anyone with the slightest interest in early American thought, politics, sociology, art, architecture, fashion, agriculture, or the decorative arts won't want to miss the scenic drive south along the Potomac from Alexandria to Mount Vernon, the home of George and Martha Washington.

Their famous estate, one of the most visited homes in America, is on the way to two other Potomac plantations with Colonial roots. The first president gave Woodlawn, on a hilltop 3½ miles west of Mount Vernon, as a 2,000-acre gift to their adopted daughter, who was Martha's actual granddaughter via her first marriage. And at the less imposing but more fascinating Gunston Hall lived their creative neighbor and friend, George Mason, a revolutionary liberal whose words inspired Thomas Jefferson when he penned the Declaration of Independence in 1776.

Together these three great homes make a fine day trip from Alexandria or Washington, D.C.

GETTING THERE

You will need a car to get to Woodlawn, Gunston Hall, and the other attractions south of Mount Vernon, but you can get to the first president's home by public transportation.

BY CAR   It's a pleasant, picturesque drive to Mount Vernon, 8 miles south of Alexandria, via the George Washington Memorial Parkway, which in many places skirts the river's edge. After passing the traffic circle in front of Mount Vernon, the same highway becomes the Mount Vernon Memorial Parkway (Va. 235), which ends at U.S. 1.

BY SUBWAY, BUS & TAXI   It's possible to get to Mount Vernon via Metrorail and connecting bus. Take Metro's Yellow Line subway (© 202/637-7000; www.wmata.com), which stops at the King Street Station in Alexandria, to Huntington Station south of Old Town Alexandria. Exit to Huntington Avenue and catch the **Fairfax Connector** bus no. 101 (© 703/339-7200; www.fairfaxconnector.com). The bus ride from Huntington to Mount Vernon takes about 25 minutes and costs $1 each way, exact changed required. Call or check the website for the bus schedules. You can also take a **White Top Cab** (© 703/644-4500); fares are about $20 each way.

BY TOURMOBILE   The **Tourmobile** (© 202/554-5100; www.tourmobile.com) runs from Arlington National Cemetery or from the Washington Monument in Washington, D.C., to Mount Vernon from April to mid-November daily at 10am, noon, and 2pm. Tourmobile booths at the cemetery or Washington Monument sell tickets. The fare is $30 for adults, $15 for children 3 to 11, free for children 2 and younger, and it includes admission to Mount Vernon. The trip takes about 4 hours; reservations are required in person at least 30 minutes before departure.

(Fun Fact **Mother of Presidents**

Virginia is known as the "Mother of Presidents" because eight U.S. presidents were born here: George Washington, Thomas Jefferson, James Madison, James Monroe, William Henry Harrison, Benjamin Harrison, John Tyler, and Woodrow Wilson.

BY BOAT   From April to October, the **Potomac Riverboat Company,** at Union and Cameron streets behind the Torpedo Factory Art Center in Old Town Alexandria (© **703/548-9000;** www.potomacriverboatco.com), offers cruises down the river to Mount Vernon and back. They depart Tuesday to Sunday at 11am from Memorial Day to Labor Day, on weekends during May, September, and October for the 1-hour cruise to Mount Vernon. The return voyage leaves Mount Vernon at 4pm, which means you will have about 4 hours to explore the mansion and grounds (not long enough if long lines are waiting at the mansion). Weekday round-trip fares are $34 for adults, $30 for seniors, and $17 for children 6 to 11, including admission to Mount Vernon. Weekend fares are $36 for adults, $32 for seniors, and $18 for children.

THE TOP ATTRACTIONS

Gunston Hall 🏛🏛   Although he shunned public office and thus is not well known outside Virginia, George Mason (1725–92) was one of the most liberal and creative political thinkers of his time. He drafted the Virginia Declaration of Rights, upon which Thomas Jefferson drew when he wrote the Declaration of Independence in 1776. Mason also helped draft the Constitution but then refused to sign it because it didn't abolish the slave trade or initially contain a Bill of Rights.

Built between 1755 and 1759, his brick house is one of the finest examples of Colonial Georgian architecture. It is unusual hereabouts because it's only one-and-a-half stories tall (the peaked roof has gables to let light into the upstairs rooms, some of them amazingly spacious). It's also unique for the elaborate interior carvings designed by William Buckland and executed by William Bernard Sears, two indentured servants from England who went on to distinguished careers of their own. The restored formal gardens focus on the 12-foot-high English boxwood–lined walkway believed to have been planted by Mason (that's right: the shrubs could be more than 250 years old!). George and Ann Mason are buried here in the family graveyard.

At the reception center, an 11-minute film will introduce you to Mason and his estate. You must then take a 30-minute tour in order to enter the mansion. Allow 45 minutes for the total house tour, 1½ hours to see the house and gardens. En route to the house, you'll pass a small museum of Mason family memorabilia. If you have an extra hour for the round-trip stroll, you can take a nature trail down the Potomac past Mason's Deer Park and woodland area (you cannot see the river from the mansion).

10709 Gunston Rd. (Va. 242). © **703/550-9220.** www.gunstonhall.org. Admission $8 adults, $7 seniors, $4 students through 12th grade, free for children 5 and younger. Daily 9:30am–5pm (30-min. tours every half-hour 9:30am–4:30pm). Closed Jan 1, Thanksgiving, and Dec 25. From Woodlawn, drive 5½ miles south on U.S. 1, turn left on Gunston Rd. (Va. 242), then 3¾ miles to plantation entry on left.

Mount Vernon 🏛🏛🏛   You can't leave northern Virginia without visiting George and Martha Washington's magnificent home overlooking the Potomac River. Indeed, Mount Vernon has been one of America's most-visited shrines since 1858, when the

Mount Vernon & the Potomac Plantations

Gunston Hall **5**
Mount Vernon **4**
Pohick Church **1**
Pope-Leighey House **2**
Washington's Gristmill **3**
Woodlawn Plantation **2**

Mount Vernon Ladies Association purchased the estate from Washington's great-grandnephew, John Augustine Washington, Jr. The association continues to own and maintain the mansion and its grounds, and it has an ongoing effort to locate and return the estate's scattered contents and memorabilia, thus enhancing its authentic appearance (ca. 1799). About 30% of its contents belonged to the Washingtons, including a key to the Paris Bastille, which Lafayette presented to Washington in 1790 via messenger Thomas Paine; the English harpsichord of Martha Washington's grand-daughter, Nelly Custis; Martha's china tea service; and Washington's original globe, desk, and dressing table.

You will see more before reaching the mansion, thanks to the **Ford Orientation Center** and **Donald W. Reynolds Museum and Education Center,** which opened in 2006 at the estate's main gate. The latter is mostly underground, thus leaving the view of the mansion relatively undisturbed. Together their 25 galleries and theaters tell Washington's story from beginning to end. Life-size bronze statues of George, Martha, and her two grandchildren, Nelly and Washy Custis, welcome you to the orientation center, which features an 18-minute Hollywood-produced movie in which actors re-create important events in Washington's life. Likewise, the museum features lifelike wax models of Washington at three different ages; they were created with the help of forensic experts.

Tips **Don't Come Early in Spring, Summer, or Any Weekend**

You will need at least a half a day to see Mount Vernon and the nearby grist-mill and distillery. Many people show up at 8am in spring, summer, or any weekend with the idea of beating the crowds, which they inadvertently create. So I would plan to tour the mansion later in the day during these periods.

Before departing the orientation center, rent a receiver for the guided audio tour, which is broadcast throughout the estate.

Constructed of beveled pine painted to look like stone, the house is an outstanding example of Georgian architecture. You'll enter by way of the Large Dining Room, which contains many of the original chairs, Hepplewhite mahogany sideboards, and paintings. Step outside on the long front porch and enjoy the view that prompted Washington to declare, "No estate in United America is more pleasantly situated than this." Upstairs are five bedchambers, including the Lafayette Room, named for the Marquis, and George and Martha's bedroom, in which Washington died.

After leaving the house, tour the kitchen, smokehouse, overseer's and slave quarters, the Washingtons' graves, and the slave burial ground marked by two monuments to the African Americans who lived, worked, and died at the plantation. Down by the river, a 4-acre exhibition area focuses on Washington's accomplishments as an innovative farmer. He was far ahead of his time in soil conservation and crop rotation, and he switched from tobacco to wheat, which could be planted twice a year, had a more reliable market, and did not deplete the soil as quickly as the Golden Leaf.

He ground the wheat into flour at **George Washington's Gristmill,** a 1933 reconstruction 3 miles west of the plantation on Mount Vernon Memorial Parkway (Va. 235). He put the mill's byproduct to use making whiskey in a distillery. Costumed interpreters give 20-minute tours explaining how the mill operated, and they actually grind cornmeal for sale in the gift shop. They also make whiskey at the adjacent **George Washington's Distillery,** an exact reproduction of a still built in 1797–98 and burned in 1814. Note that the mill and still are near the intersection of Mount Vernon Memorial Parkway and U.S. 1, not in Gristmill Park, a county facility you'll pass on the way to Washington's mill.

There's an ongoing schedule of special activities at Mount Vernon, especially in summer, running the gamut from special garden tours to treasure hunts for children. Call or check the website to find out what's going on during your visit. Admission is free on Washington's Birthday (the federal holiday, not the actual date), when a wreath-laying ceremony is held at his tomb.

8 miles south of Old Town Alexandria and I-95. ℂ **703/780-2000.** www.mountvernon.org. Admission $13 adults, $12 seniors, $6 children 6–11. Gristmill admission $4 adults, $2 children 6–11. Combination admission $15 adults, $6.50 children 6–11. Audio mansion tour rentals $6. Mount Vernon: Apr–Aug daily 8am–5pm; Sept–Oct daily 9am–5pm; Nov–Mar daily 9am–4pm. Gristmill: Apr–Oct daily 10am–5pm.

WHERE TO DINE AT MOUNT VERNON   Plan to have lunch at Mount Vernon after touring the mansion and grounds. There's an inexpensive, mall-style **food court** in the shopping complex at the traffic circle outside the main gate that's open daily from 9:30am to 5:30pm. Next door, the charming **Mount Vernon Inn** (ℂ **703/780-0011**) serves some of the Colonial-style fare George and Martha provided their guests. It's inexpensive and the atmosphere is great—period furnishings, working fireplaces, a waitstaff in 18th-century costumes. Lunch is first-come, first-served, but reservations are highly recommended at dinner (if for no other reason than to find out if the inn is closed for a wedding reception or other event). It's open Monday through Saturday 11am to 3:30pm and 5 to 9pm, Sunday 11am to 3:30pm. Both accept American Express, Discover, MasterCard, and Visa.

Pohick Church   This "mother church of northern Virginia" was built between 1769 and 1774 under the supervision of vestrymen George Washington and George Mason. Theirs and other prominent families paid for their own box pews, laid out opposite the pulpit, which was on the side, as was prevalent in England at the time. The first president's connection led to the brick building's being known as "Washington's Church." During the Civil War, Union soldiers stabled their horses in the church and stripped the interior. They did not, however, steal the English baptismal font, which dates to the 11th or 12th century and is still used today.

9301 Richmond Hwy. (U.S. 1, at Telegraph Rd.), Lorton. ℂ 703/339-6572. www.pohick.org. Free admission (donations accepted). Mon–Fri 9am–4:30pm; Sun 12:30–4:30pm; services Sun 8 and 10am. From Woodlawn, drive 5½ miles south on U.S. 1.

Woodlawn Plantation and Pope-Leighey House ☆   On a hill overlooking the Potomac River valley (but not the river), **Woodlawn Plantation** was a 2,000-acre section of Mount Vernon, of which some 130 acres remain. George Washington gave it as a wedding gift to his adopted daughter (and Martha's granddaughter), beautiful Nelly Parke Custis, and her husband (and Washington's nephew), Maj. Lawrence Lewis, when they married in 1799. Three years later, they moved into the Georgian-style brick mansion designed by William Thornton, first architect of the U.S. Capitol, and furnished it primarily with pieces from Mount Vernon (everything you see dates to before 1840, with about 30% from the Lewis' time). Now under the auspices of the National Trust for Historic Preservation, the restored Woodlawn mansion and its elegant formal gardens reflect the lives and lifestyles of the plantation's original free and enslaved inhabitants.

On the other side of the parking lot, you leap 150 years ahead architecturally to Frank Lloyd Wright's modernistic **Pope-Leighey House,** designed in 1940 for the Loren Pope family of Falls Church. Built of cypress, brick, and glass, the flat-roofed house was created as a prototype of well-designed space for middle income people. "The house of moderate cost," said Wright in 1938 (the house and lot cost $7,000 back then), "is not only America's major architectural problem but the problem most difficult for her major architects." In 1946, the Robert A. Leigheys purchased the house. After living in it for 17 years, Mrs. Leighey donated it to the National Trust, which moved it here.

Give yourself 1½ hours to digest both houses. Normally given on the hour and half-hour, tours are only provided two times a day during March, when Woodlawn is open daily to host one of the nation's largest annual **needlework exhibits.**

Fun Fact **Our First Tippler**

Although George Washington distilled whiskey at Mount Vernon, his favorite alcoholic beverages were port, Madeira, and other sweet wines. He also liked rum punch.

9000 Richmond Hwy. © 703/780-4000. www.woodlawn1805.org or www.popeleighey1940.org. Admission to each house $7.50 adults, $3 students, free for children 4 and younger. Combination tickets $13 adults, $5 students, free for children 4 and younger. Admission may be higher during special events. Mar–Dec Tues–Sun 10am–5pm. Guided 35-min. tours twice daily in Mar, otherwise on the hour and half-hour (last tour 4:30pm). Closed Jan–Feb, Thanksgiving, and Dec 25. From Mount Vernon, drive 3 miles west on Mount Vernon Memorial Pkwy. (Va. 235) to U.S. 1. Entry is straight ahead.

3 The Hunt Country ⭑⭑

Leesburg: 35 miles NW of Washington, D.C., 115 miles NW of Richmond; Middleburg: 45 miles W of Washington, D.C., 95 miles NW of Richmond

Although horse farms extend southwestward from the Washington suburbs all the way to Charlottesville, the heart of Virginia's Hunt Country beats in the rolling hills of Loudoun and Fauquier counties, essentially between Washington Dulles International Airport and the Blue Ridge Mountains. The Colonial tradition of fox hunting still reigns out this way, and steeplechase racing is still something to do on a Saturday afternoon.

Beyond the rapid suburban development west of Dulles airport, the Hunt Country is studded with horse farms bordered by stone fences, plantations with elegant manses, picturesque villages, country inns, and fine restaurants. I enjoy exploring the scenic country roads and getting out of my vehicle in charming little hamlets like Middleburg, Aldie, Upperville, Purcellville, and Hillsboro. Don't be surprised to see rich and famous folk strolling the streets or having a bite of lunch, for some of the world's wealthiest people keep their thoroughbreds here.

The only time when you can actually visit a few of their horse farms is during the **Virginia Hunt Country Stable Tour** (© 540/592-3711; www.middleburgonline. com/stabletour), held every Memorial Day weekend.

Others with a little money have started vineyards, making the Hunt Country one of two centers of Virginia's growing wine industry. If you avoid getting tipsy in the tasting rooms, it's easy to wind your way through the farms and hamlets to Manassas, where the North and the South fought two major Civil War battles on the banks of Bull Run, including that conflict's first great contest. You will be following in the horse steps of Col. John Singleton Mosby, the famous Confederate raider who made Hunt Country life miserable for the Yankees.

ESSENTIALS
VISITOR INFORMATION

For advance information, contact the **Loudoun Convention & Visitor Association,** 222 Catoctin Circle SE, Suite 100, Leesburg, VA 20175 (© 800/752-6118 or 703/771-2170; www.visitloudoun.org). Its offices and the **Leesburg Visitor Center** are about a half-mile east of downtown on the first floor of the Jewell Building on Catoctin Circle, just south of Market Street (Va. 7 Business). The center is open daily from 9am to 5pm except New Year's Day, Thanksgiving, and Christmas. Pick up a visitor guide, a Leesburg map, a list of antiques dealers, and a guide to the county's wine trail. Also ask for a copy of the walking-tour guide to Waterford Village (see below) and a copy of "Towns & Villages of Loudoun County, Virginia," which will guide you to and through Leesburg, Middleburg, Purcellville, Lovettsville, Hamilton, Round Hill, Hillsboro, and several small hamlets.

The **Town Hall Visitors Center,** 25 W. Market St., Leesburg, VA 20178 (no phone), in the lobby of the Leesburg Town Hall, is open Saturday 9am to 5pm, Sunday noon to 5pm.

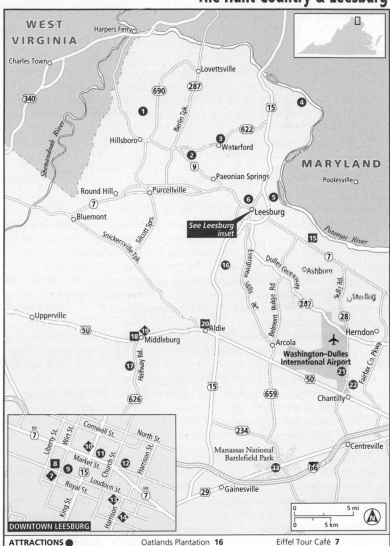

ATTRACTIONS ●
Ball's Bluff Regional Park **5**
Breaux Vineyards **1**
Dodona Manor, Home of
    George C. Marshall **12**
Loudoun County Court House **11**
Loudoun Museum **9**
Loudoun Valley Vineyards **2**
Manassas National
    Battlefield Park **23**
Morven Park **6**

Oatlands Plantation **16**
Piedmont Vineyards **17**
Sully Historic Site **22**
Steven F. Udvar-Hazy Center **21**
Tarara Vineyard & Winery **4**
Waterford Village **3**

DINING ◆
Back Street Café &
    Catering **19**
Coach Stop Restaurant **19**

Eiffel Tour Café **7**
Lightfoot Restaurant **10**
The Mighty Midget Kitchen **14**
South Street Under **13**
Tuscarora Mill **13**

ACCOMMODATIONS ■
Lansdowne Resort **15**
Little River Inn **20**
Norris House Inn **8**
Red Fox Inn **18**

Middleburg has an information center in the Pink Box, 12 Madison St., Middleburg, VA 22117 (© **540/687-8888;** www.middleburg.org). It's open Monday to Friday from 11am to 3pm, Saturday and Sunday from 11am to 4pm.

For Manassas, contact the **Prince William County/Manassas Conference and Visitors Bureau,** 8609 Sudley Rd., Suite 105, Manassas, VA 20112 (© **800/432-1792** or 703/396-7130; www.visitpwc.com). The town of Manassas has a visitor center in the Railroad Depot, 9431 West St. (© **703/361-6599**), open daily from 9am to 5pm.

For Fauquier County, contact or visit the **Warrenton-Faquier County Chamber of Commerce,** 183A Keith St., Warrenton, VA 20186 (© **540/347-4414;** fax 540/347-7510; www.fauquierchamber.org), open daily 9am to 5pm.

GETTING THERE

BY PLANE   Washington Dulles International Airport is on the eastern edge of the Hunt Country, 14 miles southeast of Leesburg and 21 miles east of Middleburg. See "Getting There" and "Getting Around Virginia," in chapter 2, for details.

BY CAR   You'll need a vehicle to explore the beautiful back roads of the Hunt Country. Washington Dulles airport has all the major rental firms. There are two routes from the Capital Beltway (I-495) to **Leesburg.** The free but slower way is Va. 7. The significantly faster route is via the Dulles Toll Road (Va. 267) between I-495 and Washington Dulles Airport; it feeds into the Dulles Greenway (© **888/707-8870;** www.dullesgreenway.com), a privately financed toll expressway connecting the airport to Leesburg. The toll from the I-495 to Leesburg is about $3.75. *Note:* The booths accept only credit cards after 9pm.

Once in downtown Leesburg, you can scout around for an on-street space or leave your vehicle in the **municipal parking garage** on Loudoun Street between King and Wirt streets, where parking is free on weekends. During the week you'll pay 50¢ an hour for the first 4 hours, $1 per hour thereafter, but no more than $5 a day.

To **Middleburg,** you can take U.S. 50 west all the way into town or follow I-66 west to Va. 28 north to U.S. 50 west. U.S. 15 south from Leesburg intersects with U.S. 50 westbound 10 miles east of Middleburg. Park anywhere you can find an on-street space in Middleburg.

LEESBURG &

Founded in 1758, Leesburg is the largest town in the Hunt Country and a good base for exploring the region. Although not as picturesque as Middleburg, it has considerable charm, with architecture ranging from pre-Revolutionary to late 19th century. The center of Leesburg and its historic district is at the intersection of Market Street (Va. 7 Business) and King Street (U.S. 15 Business), where you'll find the brick **Loudoun County Courthouse,** built in 1895, which contains a mix of Roman Revival and classical elements. Most of what you will want to see is within 2 blocks of this key crossroads, including one of the largest collections of antiques dealers in Virginia.

EXPLORING LEESBURG

An excellent way to get the scoop in Leesburg is to take a 1-hour **walking tour** offered by the Loudoun Museum (see below) Monday to Saturday at 11am and 1pm from mid-May through October (call the museum to confirm). The tours cost $10, free for children under 12.

The free **Leesburg Town Service Trolley** (© **703/777-2420;** www.transitservices. org/info_loudoun.htm) runs between the Loudoun County Government Center (on

---

⌐ Fun Fact The Gray Ghost

The Hunt Country was the stamping ground of the Confederate raider, Col. John Singleton Mosby, whose hit-and-run exploits earned him the nickname "The Gray Ghost." Today, U.S. 50 is the John S. Mosby Highway, and local residents have dubbed it the John Singleton Mosby Heritage Area. You can get a driving tour brochure explaining historic sights from local tourist info offices (see "Visitor Information," above) or directly from the **Mosby Heritage Area**, P.O. Box 1497, Middleburg, VA 20118 ((✆) **540/687-6681**; www.mosbyheritage area.org). Tour guide Dave Goetz has half-day **Mosby's Confederacy Tours** ((✆ **540/351-6073** or 540/364-9086; www.mosbystours.com), which can be combined into an all-day outing. Call for prices and reservations.

Harrison St. in downtown Leesburg) and the Leesburg Corner Premium Outlets via Market Street (Va. 7 Business) daily every 30 minutes from 7am until 6pm. It passes the Leesburg Visitor Center on Catoctin Circle.

Ball's Bluff Regional Park   On the northeastern outskirts of town, this pristine regional park is best known for a little circle of stone markers in **Ball's Bluff National Cemetery,** the nation's second smallest national cemetery. It holds the remains of 54 Union soldiers—only one identified—who fell in the Battle of Ball's Bluff, a Confederate victory in October 1861. Many more Union troops were shot dead as they scrambled down the bluff toward the Potomac River and safety in Maryland. Many of their corpses slid into the river and floated down to Washington, bringing the grim realities of the war to the nation's capital. The park has hiking trails and interpretive displays, and volunteers lead guided tours of the battlefield on weekends from May through October. *Note:* There are no public restrooms here.

Ball's Bluff Rd. (northeast Leesburg off U.S. 15 bypass). (✆) **703/737-7800**. www.nvrpa.org. Free admission. Daily dawn–dusk. Free walking tours May–Oct Sat–Sun 10am and noon. From U.S. 15 bypass, go east on Battlefield Pkwy. to Ball's Bluff Rd., turn left into parking lot.

Dodona Manor, Home of George C. Marshall 𝕱𝕱   In 1941 Gen. George C. Marshall and his wife Katherine bought Dodona Manor, an early-19th-century manse, when he planned to retire from the U.S. Army. Those plans were interrupted by World War II, when Marshall was primarily responsible for the victorious war effort. President Franklin D. Roosevelt offered to let Marshall lead the invasion of Europe, and thus get the glory that went with that job, but he also let Marshall know that he would be at a loss without him in Washington. Consequently, Marshall stayed at home as army chief of staff and recommended Gen. Dwight D. Eisenhower as commander in chief in Europe. After the war Marshall served as secretary of state (during which time he won the Nobel Peace Prize for the Marshall Plan), president of the American Red Cross, and secretary of defense. The house was in Marshall's family until 1995. It looks exactly like it did when the general spent his spare moments here in the 1940s and 1950s, with his own bed, red-leather chair, early black-and-white television, and artwork acquired in China (Generalissimo Chiang Kai-shek, Madame Chiang, and her four maids twice were houseguests). Visits begin with an 18-minute video about Marshall's career followed by a 45-minute guided tour through the house. Dodona provides a terrific view of the general's private life, while the George C. Marshall Museum in Lexington (see chapter 7) explains his outstanding public accomplishments.

212 E. Market St., near east end of Loudon St. (C) 703/777-1880. www.georgecmarshall.org. Admission $10 adults, $8 seniors, $5 students 7–17. July–Aug Sat 10am–5pm, Sun–Mon 1–5pm; Sept–June Sat 10am–5pm, Sun 1–5pm. 45-min. house tours every 30 min. Free parking at Shops at Dodona on E. Market St. (Va. 7).

Loudoun Museum This small but interesting museum houses memorabilia about the county from American Indian days to the present. It distributes free visitor information and sells helpful walking-tour booklets. A 15-minute presentation sets the scene for your tour of the county. Allow another 30 minutes to explore the museum and its gift shop.

16 W. Loudoun St., at Wirt St. (C) 703/777-7427. www.loudounmuseum.org. Admission $3 adults, $1 seniors and students 4–17, free for children 3 and younger. Mon–Sat 10am–5pm; Sun 1–5pm.

Morven Park On the northwest edge of town, this 1,200-acre estate and its mansion are don't-misses for fox hunting and horse-drawn carriage fans. The original part of Westmoreland Davis Mansion was built as a farmhouse in 1781 but was later expanded as the home of Virginia governor Westmoreland Davis. Normally home to the **Museum of Hounds and Hunting,** it is closed while undergoing a multiyear restoration. Still open, the carriage house holds the impressive **Winmill Carriage Collection.** Allow 1½ hours to take the 45-minute house tour and visit the museums.

17263 Southern Planter Lane, off Old Waterford Rd. (C) 703/777-2414. www.morvenpark.org. Estate tours $5 adults, $1 children 6–12, free for children 5 and younger; carriage collection $3 adults, $1 children 6–12, free for children 5 and younger. Fri–Mon 11am–4pm (park closes 6pm). Call for special events. Take Va. 7 Business west 1 mile from the center of town, turn right onto Morven Park Rd., left onto Old Waterford Rd. to park on right.

Oatlands Plantation George Carter, a great-grandson of legendary planter Robert "King" Carter of the Northern Neck (see "Exploring the Northern Neck," in chapter 5), built this mansion in the Federal style in 1804 but later converted it to the Greek Revival manse we see today. His formal terraced garden and its 1810 propagation greenhouse—it's considered America's second oldest—are as interesting as the mansion itself. The plantation's remaining 330 acres also contain unique tree species. Now operated by the National Trust for Historic Preservation, Oatlands hosts numerous events, such as the Antiques at Oatlands show, sanctioned sheepdog trials, a bridal fair, and an American-crafts show (call or check the website for the schedule), plus private events. From mid-November through December, the mansion is all decked out for its annual holiday candlelight tours. You must take a tour to see the house, but you can wander the gardens on your own.

20850 Oatlands Plantation Lane (on U.S. 15, 6 miles south of Leesburg). (C) 703/777-3174. www.oatlands.org. Admission $10 adults, $9 seniors and students, $1 children 5–11, free for children 4 and younger. Garden and grounds $7 per person. Mar–Dec Mon–Sat 10am–5pm, Sun 1–4pm. Guided 30- to 40-min. house tours depart on the hour. Last tour daily 4pm.

Sully Historic Site Sully Plantation, a two-and-a-half-story farmhouse, was built in 1794 by Richard Bland Lee, younger brother of Revolutionary War hero Henry "Light-Horse Harry" Lee (and thus an uncle of Robert E. Lee), who lived here with his wife, Elizabeth Collins Lee, until 1811. The original plantation had more than 3,000 acres. Washington Dulles International Airport now occupies most of the land, leaving the main house and original stone dairy, smokehouse, and kitchen building. Unlike many Virginia plantations open to the public, this one does a fine job of demonstrating the harshness of everyday life for the plantation's enslaved African-American workers on its "Forgotten Road Tours" of the reconstructed slave quarters. You must take a tour to see the house and slave quarters, but you can wander around the grounds and look into the outbuilding windows on your own. Call for a schedule of events, which include an antique car show in June and a quilt show in September.

3601 Sully Rd. (Va. 28). © 703/437-1794. www.fairfaxcounty.gov/parks/sully/index.htm. House or slave quarter tours $6 adults, $5 students, $4 seniors and children 5–15. Combination tours $8 adults, $7 students, $6 seniors and children 5–15. Grounds free. Daily 11am–4pm. Grounds open until sunset. Guided 45-min. tours depart on the hour. Call for holiday hours. Sully is on Va. 28, ¼ mile north of U.S. 50, 9 miles south of Va. 7 in Leesburg

WATERFORD VILLAGE 🌟🌟

A favorite Sunday drive for us northern Virginians is to the enchanting hamlet of **Water-ford,** with so many 18th- and 19th-century buildings that the whole village is a National Historic Landmark. Surrounded by a rolling landscape of 1,420 acres, it offers vistas of farmland and pasture that unfold behind barns and churches. You'll feel as though you've entered an English country scene. A Quaker from Pennsylvania, Amos Janney, built a mill here in the 1740s. Other Quakers followed, and by 1840, most of the buildings now on Main Street and Second Street were in place. In 1870, the railroad bypassed Waterford, and because the pace of change slowed, much of the town was preserved. Affluent professionals who work in Washington, D.C., and the bustling northern Virginia suburbs now own many of the homes. In other words, it's a real town, not a theme park like Williamsburg, so please don't traipse through their front yards.

Usually counted in the few hundreds, the population swells to the many thousands on the first full weekend in October, when local residents stage the annual **Waterford Homes Tours and Crafts Exhibit,** one of the region's best. Concerts and other events are held here throughout the year.

Be sure to get a walking-tour guide booklet at the Leesburg Visitor Center (see "Essentials," above) or from **The Waterford Foundation, Inc.,** P.O. Box 142, Waterford, VA 20197 (© **540/882-3018;** fax 540/882-3921; www.waterfordva.org). The foundation's office is in the Corner Store at Main and Second streets and is open Monday to Friday 9am to 5pm. Ask the foundation about walking tours, which are given on some Sundays.

Waterford is about 6 miles northwest of Leesburg. Don't take Old Waterford Road; it's not paved. Instead, follow Va. 7 west, turn right onto Va. 9, then right on Clark's Gap Road (C.R. 662) into Waterford.

ON THE LOUDOUN WINE TRAIL

Loudoun County has several vineyards worth visiting. Be sure to pick up a copy of "The Loudoun Wine Trail" brochure at the Leesburg Visitor Center. It's published by the **Loudoun Wine Growers Association** (www.loudounwine.com). It has a map showing the way. Most produce chardonnay, cabernet sauvignon, *norton,* merlot, and *viognier* varieties.

Rather than risk a DUI charge, you can join **Reston Limousine** (© **800/LIMO-141** or 703/478-0500; www.restonlimo.com) on one of its all-day weekend tours to four local wineries. They cost $35 per person. Reservations are required by 5pm Thursday prior to a Saturday or Sunday tour.

Driving myself, I would start at **Tarara Vineyard & Winery,** 13648 Tarara Lane (© **703/771-7100;** www.tarara.com), overlooking the Potomac River, where wines are aged in a 6,000-square-foot cave. Their 2002 *viognier* won the Virginia Governor's Cup

Kids   A Grand Home for the *Enola Gay*

When the Smithsonian Institution's magnificent National Air and Space Museum in Washington, D.C., ran out of space to house its many historic air- and spacecraft, it built the awesome **Steven F. Udvar-Hazy Center** ⍟⍟⍟, 14390 Air and Space Museum Pkwy., Chantilly, Va. (© 202/633-1000; www. nasm.si.edu/udvarhazycenter). That's off Va. 28 between U.S. 50 and the Dulles Toll Road (Va. 267), near Sully Historic Site on the southeastern edge of Washington-Dulles International Airport.

This huge Quonset hut–like hanger houses more than 200 planes and 135 spacecraft. Stars of the show are the *Enola Gay*, the B-29 Superfortress that dropped the first atomic bomb on Japan in 1945; the space shuttle *Enterprise*, which NASA used for approach and landing tests in the late 1970s; an SR-71 spy plane; and one of Air France's Concorde jetliners. The model spacecraft that starred in the movie *Close Encounters of the Third Kind* is on display, too (it's over in a corner by the *Enterprise*). It's worth going around with a retired pilot on a docent tour, beginning at 10am and 1:30pm daily from the SR-71 spy plane.

The center is open daily from 10am to 5:30pm except Christmas (the observation tower closes at 4:30pm). Admission is free, but parking costs $12 per vehicle until 4pm. The IMAX theater shows both aviation films and commercial movies (*Spiderman 3* showed here), and tickets vary. Simulator rides are $7 to $8 per person. Money-saving combination tickets are available. You'll need at least 2 hours here. There's a cafe, so you can spend half a day exploring everything.

gold medal, not that they will have any left for you to taste. It's open daily 11am to 5pm, to 6pm on weekends from June through December. Tours and tastings run continuously. From Leesburg, drive north on U.S. 15 to Lucketts, then east on C.R. 662.

Near Tarara and the river on Spinks Road is **Lost Creek Winery** (© 703/443-9836; www.lostcreekwinery.com). It's open Thursday to Monday from 11am to 5pm.

Northwest of Leesburg are **Loudoun Valley Vineyards,** on Va. 9 (© 540/882-3375; www.loudounvalleyvineyards.com), which has tours April to December Saturday and Sunday from 11am to 5pm; and **Breaux Vineyards,** north of Hillsboro on C.R. 671 (© 800/492-9961 or 540/668-6299; www.breauxvineyards.com), whose Mediterranean-style tasting room is open daily from 11am to 5pm. On C.R. 690 is **Doukénie Winery** (© 540/688-6464; www.doukeniewinery.com), formerly known as Windham Winery, which is open daily from noon to 6pm.

In the southern part of the county near Middleburg, the most interesting of the local wineries is **Piedmont Vineyards,** on Halfway Road (C.R. 626) about 3 miles south of town (© 540/687-5528; www.piedmontwines.com), a former dairy farm whose barn now houses a tasting room and gift shop. The tasting room is open daily 11am to 6pm.

Off U.S. 50 a mile east of the village, **Swedenburg Estate Vineyard,** 23595 Winery Lane (© 540/687-5219; www.swedenburgwines.com), occupies part of Valley

View Farm, founded about 1762. We can thank the late Juanita Swedenburg for bringing the lawsuit in which the U.S. Supreme Court ruled that interstate wine sales over the Internet are okay. It's open Saturday and Sunday 11am to 5pm, weekdays by appointment. Farther east on Champe Ford Road (C.R. 629), between Middleburg and Aldie, is **Chrysalis Vineyards** (© **800/235-8804** or 540/687-8222; www. chrysaliswine.com), noted for its Albariño variety from Spain. It's open daily from 10am to 5pm.

OUTDOOR ACTIVITIES
The Hunt Country's back roads and its portion of the 45-mile **Washington & Old Dominion Railroad (W&OD) Trail** (© **703/729-0596**; www.nvrpa.org/parks/ wod) bring bicyclists from all over the mid-Atlantic. The W&OD follows an old railroad bed through the heart of the area, crossing South King Street in Leesburg. I've done part of it, and believe me, it's both beautiful and an up-and-down route that can burn your thighs. You can rent wheels in downtown Leesburg from **Plum Grove Cyclery,** 217 E. Market St. (© **703/777-2252;** www.plumgrovecyclery.com), and from **Bicycle Outfitters,** 19 Catoctin Circle NE, in the Leesburg Plaza Shopping Center (© **703/777-2148;** www.bikeoutfitters.com). Both are 2 blocks north of the W&OD and charge about $25 a day.

Golfers can tee off at the Robert Trent Jones, Jr.– and Greg Norman–designed links at **Lansdowne Resort** (see "Where to Stay," below). Gary Player designed the course at **Raspberry Falls Golf & Hunt Club,** 3 miles north of Leesburg on U.S. 15 (© **703/779-2555** or 703/589-1042; www.raspberryfalls.com). Less expensive are **Goose Creek Golf Club,** 43001 Golf Club Rd. (© **703/729-2500;** www.goosecreek golf.com), and the municipal **Brambleton Regional Park Golf Course,** 42180 Ryan Rd. in nearby Ashburn (© **703/327-3403;** www.nvrpa.org).

SHOPPING
Leesburg's numerous **antiques shops** are within a block of the Market Street–King Street intersection and easy to find. The visitor center has lists of the shops, both in town and throughout the Hunt Country, or you can check the website of the **Leesburg Antiques & Collectibles Dealers Association** (www.leesburgantiques.com).

I seldom come here without browsing at **Leesburg Corner Premium Outlets,** 241 Fort Evans Rd. (© **703/737-3071;** www.premiumoutlets.com), 2 miles east of downtown at the intersection of the U.S. 15 bypass and Va. 7. It has more than 50 stores and a food court. Many well-known brands are present, including Banana Republic, Brooks Brothers, Burberry, Bass, Gap, Jockey, Liz Claiborne, Nike, Off 5th–Saks Fifth Avenue, Polo Ralph Lauren, Reebok, Tommy Hilfiger, OshKosh B'Gosh, Rockport, L'eggs/Hanes/Bali/Playtex, Mikasa, Oneida, Pfaltzgraff, and WestPoint Stevens. Leesburg Corner is open Monday to Saturday 10am to 9pm, Sunday 11am to 6pm.

WHERE TO STAY
A mansion built atop a knoll in 1773 is the centerpiece of the **Holiday Inn at Historic Carradoc Hall,** 1500 E. Market St. (Va. 7), 2 miles east of downtown (© **800/465-4329** or 703/771-9200; www.holiday-inn.com). The four suites on the mansion's second floor have country inn–like ambience. The other 122 rooms are in standard motel buildings. The most modern digs in town are at the **Hampton Inn and Suites,** 117 Fort Evans Rd. (© **800/HAMPTON** or 703/669-8640; www.leesburg.hamptoninn. com), and the **Comfort Suites Leesburg,** 80 Prosperity Ave. (© **866/533-7287** or

540/669-1650; www.comfortsuitesleesburg.com), which has some Jacuzzi-equipped units. Nearby on Va. 7 is the **Best Western Leesburg-Dulles** (© 800/528-1234 or 703/777-9400; www.guests-inc.com).

Lansdowne Resort 👭👭 Primarily a conference center, this luxurious complex between Leesburg and Dulles airport is one of Virginia's better all-around resorts. The centerpiece nine-story hotel building is surrounded by 205 acres alongside the Potomac River. Covering much of that land are 45 holes of golf on four courses, including a Greg Norman–designed 18-holer, all overseen by a clubhouse. An indoor pool off a full-service spa opens to no less than four outdoor pools with water slides and other contraptions to keep both adults and children thoroughly entertained. The four restaurants include the **Lansdowne Grill,** one of the better steakhouses in these parts. A family-style restaurant, an English pub, and a seasonal poolside snack bar round out the existing dining options. A California wine–country theme distinguishes the guest accommodations, all in the central building. Units on the top floor have marvelous views of the Potomac River Valley. My money goes for an alcove suite with bay windows. Look for ex–Washington Redskins wandering around in July during Hall of Famer Bobby Mitchell's charity golf tournament.

44050 Woodridge Pkwy. (off Va. 7), Lansdowne, VA 20176. © 800/541-4801 or 703/729-8400. Fax 703/729-6096. www.lansdowneresort.com. 296 units. $179–$349 double; $279–$349 suite. AE, DC, DISC, MC, V. Valet parking $15; free self-parking. **Amenities:** 4 restaurants; 3 bars; 4 outdoor pools; indoor pool; 3 golf courses; 4 lighted tennis courts; health club; spa; Jacuzzi; sauna; bike rental; children's programs; concierge; activities desk; business center; room service; babysitting; laundry service; concierge-level rooms. *In room:* A/C, TV, coffeemaker, hair dryer, iron.

BED & BREAKFASTS

While the Norris House Inn (below) is the only place to stay in downtown Leesburg, the county has a dozen or so other bed-and-breakfasts scattered among its rolling hills. Check them out through the **Loudoun County Bed & Breakfast Guild** (© 866/771-2597; www.loudounbandb.com).

Norris House Inn 👭 This three-story redbrick 1760 home in downtown Leesburg includes among its common rooms a parlor and a library, both with oak fireplaces. Guest-room furnishings are a charming mix of antiques, some with four-poster beds. All have private bathrooms and nonworking fireplaces. The most interesting and private accommodations are in the atticlike third floor. None of the rooms has a telephone. If the weather is good, hosts Carol and Roger Healey serve full breakfasts on the garden veranda.

108 Loudoun St. SW, Leesburg, VA 20175 (between Wirt and Liberty sts.). © 800/644-1806 or 703/777-1806. Fax 703/771-8051. www.norrishouse.com. 6 units. $125–$190 double. Rates include full breakfast. AE, DC, DISC, MC, V. No children under 8. **Amenities:** Access to nearby health club. *In room:* A/C, Wi-Fi, no phone.

WHERE TO DINE

I get my morning caffeine fix at **Market Street Coffee,** 19 W. Market St. (© 571/258-0700), and afternoon tea at **Mrs. Tate's Bake Shop & Tea Room,** 7 S. King St. (© 703/669-0912), which also serves light lunches.

Eiffel Tower Café 👭 FRENCH An elegant French country ambience reigns in this rambling clapboard house with large windows that let in plenty of sunlight. The menu is traditional French with some interesting specials such as pan-fried halibut with a spicy Szechuan pepper sauce and accompanied by lentils cooked with bacon, grilled sea bass with couscous, and scallops with mushroom risotto. Needless to say, Bastille Day (July 14) is big here.

Totaled by a Triumph

The best barbecue in Leesburg is at **The Mighty Midget Kitchen,** 202 Harrison St., at Royal Street (ℂ **703/777-6406**), one of the country's smallest restaurants at only 8 feet wide by 6 feet deep. The original building, part of a World War II bomber, was totaled in 1959 during an encounter with a Triumph sports car. The present building is made from the aluminum remnants of another B-29, rivets and all. There are a few outdoor tables; otherwise, get your barbecue, smoked kielbasa, fish sandwiches, and hot dogs to go. Open Tuesday to Thursday 11am to 7pm, Friday and Saturday noon to 8pm (to 7pm in winter), Sunday noon to 4pm—or until the barbecue runs out. Most items range from $3 to $7.

107 W. Loudon St. (between Wirt and Liberty sts.). ℂ **703/777-5242.** Reservations recommended. Main courses $20–$29. AE, DC, MC, V. Tues–Sat 11:30am–2:30pm and 5:30–9:30pm.

Lightfoot Restaurant ✴✴ ECLECTIC This fine restaurant occupies an old Romanesque Revival bank building, complete with two-story-high oak-paneled ceiling. A round mezzanine with bar underneath dominates the center of the room, which is too big and thus too noisy for intimate dining. Nevertheless, the chef puts forth an interesting mix of flavors, such as bacon-wrapped salmon over buttered grits with green pea sauce. This place and Tuscarora Mill (see below) are Leesburg's best.

11 N. King St. (north of Market St.). ℂ **703/771-2233.** Reservations recommended. Main courses $20–$32. AE, MC, V. Mon–Thurs 11:30am–11pm; Fri–Sat 11:30am–midnight; Sun 11:30am–10pm.

South Street Under DELI/BAKERY   Operated by the Tuscarora Mill (see below), this lively bakery and deli is housed in a turn-of-the-20th-century mill, one of the six historic buildings that make up the Market Station shopping and dining complex. It's the best place in town for a breakfast of gourmet coffee and hot-out-of-the-oven pastries, or a lunch of almond-and-grape chicken salad or a made-to-order sandwich on freshly baked ciabatta bread. Order at the counter, and in good weather, grab a table out in the sunny courtyard.

203 Harrison St. (in Market Station, between Loudoun and Harrison sts.). ℂ **703/771-9610.** Reservations not accepted. Most items $2–$6.50. AE, DISC, MC, V. Mon–Fri 7am–6pm; Sat 8am–6pm; Sun 8am–4pm.

Tuscarora Mill ✴✴ AMERICAN   One of Leesburg's two best restaurants, Tuskie's brings a casual, publike ambience to this 1898 mill building. High wood-beamed ceilings, grain bins, belts, pulleys, and a scale evoke the building's past in the main dining room, while plants and skylights brighten another room to the side. Delicious luncheon fare includes sandwiches and hot entrees like sautéed shrimp accompanied by cheese grits and smoked country sausage, which often appears at dinner. The dinner menu changes frequently, but other nighttime standouts might include sesame-roasted salmon.

203 Harrison St. (in Market Station, between Loudoun and Harrison sts.). ℂ **703/771-9300.** Reservations recommended, especially on weekends. Main courses $19–$43. AE, DISC, MC, V. Mon–Fri 11:30am–2:30pm and 5:30–9:30pm; Sat 11:30am–3pm and 5:30–9:30pm; Sun 11am–3pm and 5:30–9:30pm; bar serves light fare Fri–Sat until midnight.

MIDDLEBURG ✶✶✶

One of Virginia's most charming small towns, Middleburg is home to those who can afford to indulge in horses, horse breeding, steeplechase racing, and fox hunting. I am not kidding; you will see jodhpurs and riding boots worn here, although locals complain they are often on "paddock princesses"—who seldom ride but who like to look the part. Whoever's wearing it, this village is so unusual that the weekly rag calls itself the *Middleburg Eccentric.* In addition to real estate notices for farms selling for multi-millions, the paper carries ads for firms offering horse clipping and mane pulling. Keep an eye peeled because in addition to being very, very wealthy, the person walking next to you could be very, very famous, too.

Appropriately, Middleburg is home to the **National Sporting Library,** 102 The Plains Rd. (✆ **540/687-6542;** www.nsl.org), a research center housing more than 16,000 books and periodicals about horse sports and fishing, some of them dating to the 17th century. It's open Tuesday to Friday 10am to 4pm, Saturday 1 to 4pm.

Even if I do turn into a chicken when I get near a horse, I thoroughly enjoy pretending I'm filthy rich while strolling Middleburg's shady brick sidewalks—in a polo shirt and khaki trousers, quite appropriate attire here. I like poking my head into high-end shops with names like Crème de la Crème, which purveys "home embellishments," and Starbarks Cafe, which provides gourmet treats for your thoroughbred pooch. I also stop for a cone at Scruffy's Ice Cream Parlor, and grab a shot of caffeine at Cuppa Giddyup.

Middleburg is included on the National Register of Historic Villages, and with 600 residents, it's about the same size today as when it was settled in 1731. You can't get lost here, for the village occupies just 6 blocks along Washington Street (U.S. 50), with just two streets—Federal and Marshall—running parallel on either side. Start your tour at the **Pink Box Visitor Information Center,** on Madison Street a block north of the one traffic signal on Washington Street (see "Visitor Information," earlier in this section). The public pavilion next door is dedicated to the late Jacqueline Kennedy Onassis, in honor of the contributions she made "during her happy years in the village."

NEARBY ATTRACTIONS

Drive 1½ miles north of Middleburg on C.R. 626 and you'll come to **Glenwood Park** (✆ **540/687-5662**), Virginia's oldest racecourse in continuous use and home to many meets during the year, including the Virginia Fall Races in early October. Follow the gravel road uphill to the bleachers (look for the gazebo) for a gorgeous view of the Blue Ridge Mountains.

Nearby wineries are worth testing. See "On the Loudoun Wine Trail," above.

Manassas National Battlefield Park ✶✶   The first massive clash of the Civil War took place near a stream known as Bull Run on July 21, 1861. A well-equipped but poorly trained Union army of 35,000 under Gen. Irvin McDowell had marched from Washington, where cheering crowds expected them to return victorious. Most of the soldiers were 90-day volunteers who had little knowledge of what war would mean. Their goal was Richmond, but to meet the oncoming army, Gen. P. G. T. Beauregard deployed his Confederate troops along Bull Run to the north of the railroad junction of Manassas. The 10 hours of heavy fighting stunned soldiers on both sides as well as onlookers who had ridden out from Washington to watch. A Confederate victory shattered any hopes that the war would end quickly. Historians later conjectured that had the Confederates followed the fleeing Union troops, an even more decisive victory perhaps could have ended the war, with the South victorious.

Fun Fact **"Like a Stone Wall"**

Stonewall Jackson got his nickname in the first Battle of Manassas when Confederate Gen. Bernard Bee, marveling at his persistence in standing his ground, marveled: "There stands Jackson, like a stone wall!"

Union and Confederate armies met here again on August 28 through 30, 1862. The Second Battle of Manassas secured Gen. Robert E. Lee's place in history as his 55,000 men soundly defeated the Union army under Gen. John Pope.

Start your tour at the Henry Hill Visitor Center, where a museum, a 45-minute film ($3 admission; shown on the hour 9am–4pm), and a 6-minute battle map program tell the story. These hills are excellent for hiking, and there are a number of self-guided walking tours that highlight Henry Hill, Stone Bridge, and the other critical areas of the two battles. Allow about 2 hours to take in the visitor center and the First Battle walking tour (it's about 1 mile long). The tour of the entire First Battle area is 6½ miles long. The Second Battle of Manassas, which raged over a much larger area, is covered in a self-guided 12-mile driving tour that will take about 1½ hours.

6511 Sudley Rd. (Va. 234), © 703/361-1339. www.nps.gov/mana. Admission (good for 3 days) $3 adults, free for children 16 and younger. Movie $3 per person. America the Beautiful passes accepted. Battlefield daily dawn–dusk. Visitor center daily 8:30am–5pm. From Middleburg (about 11 miles), take U.S. 50 east, turn right onto U.S. 15 south, turn left at Va. 234, and continue southeast to Manassas. From I-66, take Exit 47B and go ½ mile north on Va. 234.

WHERE TO STAY

The charming **Middleburg Country Inn,** 209 E. Washington St. (© **800/262-6082** or 540/687-6082; www.middleburgcountryinn.com), serves as the town's sole bed-and-breakfast. About 5 miles north of town, **The Goldstone Inn & Estate,** 36205 Snake Hill Rd. (© **877/219-4663** or 540/687-4645), is much more luxurious—and expensive at $365 and up per night. It has 13 rooms in a restored carriage house, two cottages, and a spring house set on a 265-acre estate. If I could afford it, I would stay in its Goodwin Room.

Red Fox Inn ☆☆   The historic Red Fox Inn in the center of Middleburg maintains the romantic charm of early Virginia in its original 1728 stone structure. A later addition is the Stray Fox Inn. The Red Fox has three rooms and three suites, all with wide-plank floors and 18th-century furnishings; several have working fireplaces. Rooms in the Stray Fox also preserve a traditional character with hand-stenciled walls, canopy beds, hooked rugs, and original fireplace mantels. Continental breakfast is served in the dark, cozy **Red Fox Inn Restaurant,** which features a Colonial ambience—low-beamed ceilings, pewter dishes, and equestrian prints lining the walls. The seasonal menus feature regulars like filet mignon, crab cakes, rack of lamb and grilled fish, switching to venison, quail, and other game in autumn.

2 E. Washington St. (P.O. Box 385), Middleburg, VA 20118. © **800/223-1728** or 540/687-6301. Fax 540/687-6053. www.redfox.com. 15 units and suites. $170–$195 double; $195–$215 suite. Rates include continental breakfast. AE, DC, DISC, MC, V. **Amenities:** Restaurant (American); bar; access to nearby health club; room service; laundry service. *In room:* A/C, TV, Wi-Fi (in Red Fox only), hair dryer, iron.

A BED & BREAKFAST IN ALDIE

Little River Inn ☆ *Value*   This is no fancy, froufrou bed-and-breakfast, for friendly innkeepers Tucker and Mary Ann Withers have kept this early-19th-century farmhouse

---

⟨Tips **Grist for the Aldie Mill**

Most of the quaint hamlet of **Aldie**, 5 miles east of Middleburg on John Mosby Highway (U.S. 50), is a quintessential Hunt Country hamlet. Its centerpiece is **Aldie Mill Historic Park** (ⓒ **703/327-9777;** www.aldiemill.org), built in 1807–09 and the only gristmill in Virginia powered by twin water wheels. It has been restored to grind organic grains. The mill is open Saturday and Sunday from noon to 5pm, with milling demonstrations at 1, 2, and 3pm. Admission is $4 for adults, $2 for children 6 to 17. Aldie's antiques stores and other shops merit browsing, and a visit during the annual Aldie Mill Arts Show and Sale on weekends in June, or the Aldie Harvest Festival on the third weekend in October, will be most rewarding.

---

in Aldie simple and authentic—like grandma's house—since they opened it 1982. Staying here gives a wonderful glimpse of life in a small Virginia hamlet. Farm animals, a small garden, and a patio are out the back door, which seldom is locked, so peaceful is it here. Fresh flowers, a basket of magazines, and a few decorative pieces of china add warmth. Accommodations range from one room to a cottage of your own (none of them with telephones). The main house has five bedrooms, all charmingly furnished with antique pieces; one has a working fireplace. Or you can stay in the log cabin or the Patent House, a small late-1700s domicile, both of which have working fireplaces. Tucker comes over every morning to cook a full breakfast to order. He and Mary Ann give a 10% discount if you book 2 nights.

39307 John Mosby Hwy. (U.S. 50; P.O. Box 116), Aldie, VA 22001. ⓒ 703/327-6742. www.aldie.com. 5 units (4 with private bathroom), 2 cottages. $125–$275 double. Rates include full breakfast. AE, DC, DISC, MC, V. **Amenities:** Outdoor pool. *In room:* A/C, TV (cottages only), no phone.

WHERE TO DINE

My favorite place for tasty salads, sandwiches, or a pizza is **Back Street Cafe & Catering,** 4 E. Federal St. (ⓒ **540/687-3122**), which has outdoor tables in warm weather. The dinner menu adds pasta main courses. It's open Monday to Saturday 11:30am to 2:30pm and 5 to 9pm.

Coach Stop Restaurant *⟨Value⟩* AMERICAN   You might see a famous face or two among the locals who have been flocking to this diner-style restaurant (albeit one with racks of fine wine behind the counter and lots of horse photos on the walls) since 1958. The menu offers everything from a breakfast of Virginia country ham and eggs or creamed chipped beef on buttermilk biscuits to a dinner of honey-dipped fried chicken. Seating is at the counter or at tables and booths. Ceiling fans keep the breezes moving as you tuck into a hearty meal. Dinner entrees are above-average comfort foods like hand-cut steaks, pork chops, and roast turkey with stuffing and gravy. You can sample shad roe, a Virginia specialty, in early spring.

9 E. Washington St. ⓒ 540/687-5515. Reservations accepted. Breakfast $5–$10; sandwiches and salads $6–$12; main courses $15–$21. AE, DC, DISC, MC, V. Mon–Sat 7am–9pm; Sun 8am–9pm.

5

Fredericksburg & the Northern Neck

No journey through Virginia's storied history is complete without a stop in Fredericksburg. Sitting on the banks of the Rappahannock River, it offers both a glimpse into Colonial America and a testament to the vast amount of blood that soaked the state's soil during the Civil War.

I must admit, however, to hating the 50-mile drive on often-clogged I-95 to get here from my home in northern Virginia. All that traffic is due to rapid suburban sprawl, which is quickly absorbing Fredericksburg within the Washington, D.C., megalopolis.

But once I have arrived in Fredericksburg's remarkably preserved Historic District, I'm thrilled to walk the same streets trod by George Washington, James Monroe, Thomas Jefferson, George Mason, and other Founding Fathers who created the notion of a Bill of Rights protecting our freedoms.

And from up on Marye's Heights, my spine tingles as I look down over the killing fields where Robert E. Lee's dug-in Confederate troops literally mowed down Union forces trying to capture the town in 1862. It was the first of four great Civil War battles fought in and around Fredericksburg.

For a bit of levity, I retreat back down the hill and into two of Virginia's more entertaining historic sites, the Hugh Mercer Apothecary Shop and The Rising Sun Tavern, both survivors from Colonial times.

For a complete escape, I drive southeast from Fredericksburg onto the bucolic Northern Neck (we call it a "neck"; you call it a peninsula) between the Potomac River on one side and the Rappahannock on the other. Large and small creeks crisscross the neck, and bald eagles, blue heron, flocks of waterfowl, and an occasional wild turkey inhabit the unspoiled marshland.

Both Washington and Lee were born on the Peninsula, and their birthplaces are easy side trips from Fredericksburg. Otherwise the Northern Neck today primarily attracts weekenders from the mid-Atlantic region who—like me—come here to totally get away from it all.

At the end of the Peninsula is the fishing village of Reedville, built in the Victorian era and still making its living from the Chesapeake Bay. But the star of the Northern Neck show is Irvington, a gentrified creekside hamlet in which reside The Tides Inn and The Hope and Glory Inn, two of the state's finest retreats.

1 Fredericksburg ★★★

50 miles S of Washington, D.C.; 45 miles S of Alexandria; 50 miles N of Richmond

Fredericksburg provides a lesson in American history, especially the Colonial and Civil War eras. Its quaint downtown—a 40-square-block National Register Historic District—is well worth your time. In addition to its historical attractions, the district has a college-town ambience thanks to the University of Mary Washington, named for our first president's mother who is as revered in Fredericksburg as is her son.

The town came into being in 1728 as a 500-acre frontier settlement on the banks of the Rappahannock River. George Washington spent his formative years across the river at Ferry Farm, where he supposedly tossed a coin across the Rappahannock and never told a lie about chopping down the cherry tree. His mother lived out her life in a house he purchased for her on Charles Street, and she is buried on what was then Kenmore Plantation, home of his sister, Betty Washington Lewis.

Fredericksburg was a hotbed of revolutionary zeal in the 1770s, and many of its citizens shed both blood and treasure during the War for Independence. Thomas Jefferson, George Mason, and other founding fathers met here in 1777 to draft what later became the Virginia Statute of Religious Freedoms, the basis for the First Amendment guaranteeing separation of church and state. James Monroe practiced law here before spending his final years near Jefferson at Charlottesville.

Fredericksburg is a holy shrine for Civil War buffs. Equidistant from Richmond and Washington—the two rival capitals—the Fredericksburg area was one of the war's biggest bones of contention. The two sides fought a major battle in town and others nearby at Chancellorsville, The Wilderness, and Spotsylvania Courthouse. Stonewall Jackson was mistakenly shot by his own men at Chancellorsville; his amputated arm is buried at Ellwood Plantation. Clara Barton and Walt Whitman nursed wounded Federal soldiers in Chatham mansion, just across the river. Cannonballs embedded in the walls of some prominent buildings, as well as the graves of 17,000 Civil War soldiers, are grim reminders of that tragic era. The battlefields are now part of a national park.

ESSENTIALS
VISITOR INFORMATION

The **Fredericksburg Visitor Center,** 706 Caroline St. (at Charlotte St.), Fredericksburg, VA 22401 (© **800/678-4748** or 540/373-1776; fax 540/372-5687; www.visit fred.com), offers free maps, many restaurant menus, and walking tour brochures following the 1862 Battle of Fredericksburg and of the downtown Historic District. It also shows a 14-minute video that will get you oriented, gives out free all-day parking passes (you can leave your car in the center's lot), and sells a block ticket to the major sites (see "Money-Saving Passes," below). The center is open Memorial Day to Labor Day daily from 9am to 7pm; the rest of the year, hours are 9am to 5pm. It's closed New Year's Day, Thanksgiving, and Christmas.

On the southwestern edge of town, the **Spotsylvania County Visitor Center,** 4704 Southpointe Pkwy., Fredericksburg, VA 22407 (© **800/654-4118** or 540/891-6670), specializes in surrounding attractions. It's in the Southpoint Shopping Center on U.S. 1 at Exit 126 off I-95 and is open daily from 9am to 5pm. The county also has a visitor center in the historic district of Spotsylvania, near the battlefields (© **540/507-7996**).

There also is a **Virginia Welcome Center** at Mile 130 on southbound I-95 (see "Visitor Information & Maps," in chapter 2).

GETTING THERE

BY CAR   Depending on the volume of traffic, Fredericksburg is about an hour from Richmond or Alexandria via I-95. To reach the Historic District from I-95, take Exit 130A and follow Va. 3 east. Bear left on William Street (Va. 3 Business).

There are no parking meters in Fredericksburg but many on-street spaces are limited to 2 hours, so be sure to get a free all-day pass from the visitor center.

Value **Money-Saving Passes**

The **Fredericksburg Visitor Center** (see "Essentials," above) sells a **Pass to Historic Fredericksburg,** which includes admission to Belmont, Fredericksburg Area Museum and Cultural Center, Hugh Mercer Apothecary Shop, James Monroe Museum and Memorial Library, Kenmore, Mary Washington House, The Rising Sun Tavern, and George Washington's Ferry Farm. It's $29 for adults, $9.50 for students 6 to 18. Or you can pick any four attractions plus George Washington's Ferry Farm for $18 adults, $7 for students. Either way, those are substantial savings off individual admissions.

Note: The admission prices given in the listings below are to the individual properties without a block ticket. Most of the block-ticket attractions are closed New Year's Day, Thanksgiving, and December 24, 25, and 31.

BY PLANE   The nearest airports are Ronald Reagan Washington National, Washington Dulles International (see "Getting There" under "Alexandria" in chapter 4), and Richmond International (see chapter 9).

BY TRAIN   Fredericksburg's **Amtrak** station ((℃) **800/872-7245;** www.amtrak.com) is at Lafayette Boulevard and Princess Anne Street, on the southern edge of the Historic District, 3 blocks from the Fredericksburg Visitor Center.

Virginia Railway Express ((℃) **800/743-3843** or 703/497-7777; www.vre.org) operates early-morning, midday, and late-afternoon commuter trains between the Fredericksburg Amtrak station and Union Station in Washington, D.C., with stops at Arlington (Crystal City) and Alexandria. The one-way fare from Alexandria to Fredericksburg is about $8.50 (with discounts for children, seniors, and people with disabilities). Tickets are not sold onboard the trains. You must buy them online or at ticket vending/validating machines in the station entry area (American Express, MasterCard, and Visa cards are accepted but *not* cash). If you buy in advance, you must validate your ticket at the machine before boarding the train.

EXPLORING FREDERICKSBURG

A majority of the Historic District attractions are along Princess Anne Street within an easy walk from the visitor center, but don't miss several notable monuments along broad **Washington Avenue** north of Kenmore Plantation & Gardens. Mary Ball Washington is buried at **Meditation Rock,** a spot where she often came to pray and meditate; there's a monument there in her honor. Just across the way is the **Thomas Jefferson Religious Liberty Monument,** commemorating Jefferson's Fredericksburg meeting with George Mason, Edmond Pendleton, George Wythe, and Thomas Ludwell Lee in 1777 to draft the Virginia Statute of Religious Freedom. The **Hugh Mercer Monument,** off Fauquier Street, honors the doctor who died fighting in the Revolutionary War and whose apothecary shop is now a museum (see below).

BY WALKING TOUR   On Thursday and Friday during summer you can stroll around the Historic District and learn about the area's history and architecture with the informative **Hallowed Ground Tours** ((℃) **540/809-3918;** www.hallowedground tours.com). Held in conjunction with the Fredericksburg Area Museum and Cultural

Center (see "More Attractions," below), the 1-hour tours leave the visitor center at 10am and 1:30pm. They cost $12 for adults and $6 for children, which includes admission to the museum and cultural center. (The walking tours began in 2007, so I would call to make sure they are still operating when you're here.)

An evening option is to stroll around the historic haunts with **Ghosts of Fredericksburg Tours,** 623 Caroline St. (© **540/654-5414;** www.ghostsoffredericksburg.com). The walks depart the company's offices (diagonally across Caroline St. from the visitor center) at 8pm Thursday to Monday in July, Friday through Sunday in August, and Friday and Saturday September through December. They cost $10 per person and reservations are required.

BY TROLLEY OR HORSE-DRAWN CARRIAGE You can sit and explore the Historic District via motorized trolley or horse-drawn carriage, both of which leave from the visitor center. **Trolley Tours of Fredericksburg** (© **540/898-0737;** www.fredericksburgtrolley.com) pass 35 historic sights. The 1¼-hour narrated tours usually leave at 10:30am, noon, 1:30, and 3:30pm from June through October. They depart at 10:30am and 1:30pm the rest of the year. Fares are $15 for adults, $5 for children 17 and younger.

An alternative is to clip-clop your way around with the **Old Time Carriage Company** (© **540/371-0094**), whose 45-minute narrated rides cost $16 for adults, $10 for children younger than 10. They operate from April through December daily from 11am to 5pm. It's best to call for reservations.

THE TOP ATTRACTIONS

Belmont: The Gari Melchers Estate & Memorial Gallery ✪ Situated on 27 hillside acres overlooking the falls of the Rappahannock River, Belmont began as an 18th-century farmhouse (the central six rooms of the house date to the 1790s) and was enlarged to a 22-room estate by a later owner. Although the house has historic attributes, its fame comes from being furnished with the art treasures, family heirlooms, and European antiques of famed American artist Gari Melchers, who lived here from 1916 until his death in 1932. His wife, Corinne, gave Belmont to the Commonwealth of Virginia in 1955. In addition to Melchers's own works, there are many wonderful paintings in the house—a watercolor sketch by Jan Bruegel, 19th-century paintings by Morisot, and works by Rodin. It'll take about an hour to see the orientation video and take a guided tour of the house. You can explore the gardens and studio on your own. Call for a schedule of special exhibitions and lectures.

224 Washington St. (Va. 1001). © **540/654-1015.** www.garimelchers.org. Admission $10 adults, $5 children 6–18, free for children 5 and younger. Mar–Nov Mon–Sat 10am–5pm, Sun 1–5pm; Dec–Feb Mon–Sat 10am–4pm, Sun 1–4pm. Closed Jan 1, Thanksgiving, Dec 24–25, and Dec 31. Guided 30-min. house tours depart on hour and half-hour (last tour 30 min. before closing). From the visitor center, take U.S. 1 north across the Falmouth Bridge, turn left at the traffic light in Falmouth, and go ¼ mile up the hill; turn left on Washington St. (C.R. 1001) to Belmont.

Hugh Mercer Apothecary Shop ✪✪ *Kids* Although he was a noted physician, Dr. Hugh Mercer was better known as a warrior. Born in Scotland in 1726, he fled to Pennsylvania and became friends with George Washington when they were colonels during the French and Indian War of the 1750s. He opened this apothecary shop in 1761 and practiced here until returning to service as a brigadier-general in the American Revolution. He was with Washington during the famous crossing of the Delaware River on Christmas night of 1776. Had he not died of bayonet wounds at the Battle of Princeton a few days later, he may well have become one of our Founding Fathers.

Fredericksburg Historic District

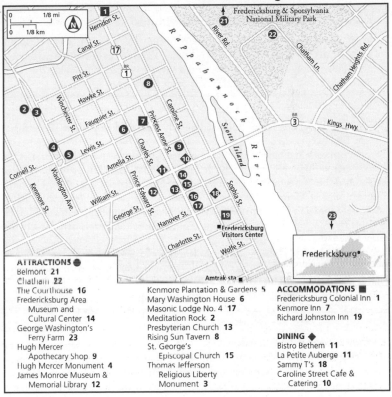

(The warrior tradition continued in his family—Gen. George S. Patton was his great-great-great-grandson.) Today this is one of the most entertaining Colonial attractions in Virginia. It's a don't-miss for children, who often let out *"Ooooos"* when hostesses in period dress show how he practiced 18th-century medicine in this little shop of horrors. Since opium, the only known anesthesia, was expensive and difficult to obtain, those waiting for treatment were often put to work holding down the screaming wretch under the knife. Even minor treatment seems ghoulish by today's standards. Optional tours run continuously, so you can join one when you get here and see what you missed on the next. A garden tour explains how plants were used as medicine in those days.

1020 Caroline St. (at Amelia St.). ☏ **800/678-4748** or 540/373-3362. www.apva.org/hughmercerapothecary. Admission $5 adults, $2 for children 6–18, free for children 5 and younger. Mar–Nov Mon–Sat 9am–5pm, Sun 11am–5pm; Dec–Feb Mon–Sat 10am–4pm, Sun noon–4pm. Half-hour tours run continuously (last tour 30 min. before closing).

James Monroe Museum and Memorial Library ⚔ Although overshadowed by George Washington, Thomas Jefferson, and James Madison, James Monroe was one of the most distinguished Americans of their time. He served as a U.S. senator; minister to France, England, and Spain; governor of Virginia; secretary of state; secretary of war; and fifth president of the United States (1817–25). As president, he promulgated the

---

Fun Fact **Giving Meaning to "Sawbones"**

In Dr. Hugh Mercer's Apothecary Shop (p.104) you can see how he used a heated cup to remove boils and carbuncles, a knife to cut out cataracts, an ominous-looking key to extract teeth, and a saw for amputating limbs. The latter instrument gave rise to the early slang term for doctors: sawbones.

Monroe Doctrine, which kept European powers from meddling in the Western Hemisphere. Monroe practiced law in Fredericksburg from 1786 until 1789, when he moved to Charlottesville and built his home, Highland (now known as Ash Lawn–Highland; see chapter 6), near his close friend Jefferson's Monticello. His great-granddaughter established this museum in 1927 on the site of his Fredericksburg office. The furnishings are original Monroe possessions. You can peruse correspondence from Jefferson (don't miss the letter written partially in code), Madison, and Benjamin Franklin. Here, too, are the gun and canteen Monroe used in the American Revolution. He and Washington were the only presidents to fight in the War of Independence. Also on display are two Rembrandt Peale portraits of Monroe and silhouettes of the Monroes by Charles Willson Peale. You must take a 30-minute guided tour, given throughout the day as demand dictates.

908 Charles St. (between William and George sts.). ℂ 540/654-1043. www.umw.edu/jamesmonroemuseum. Admission $5 adults, $1 children 6–18, free for children 5 and younger. Mar–Nov daily 10am–5pm; Dec–Feb daily 10am–4pm. Guided 30-min. tours given throughout the day (last tour 30 min. before closing).

Kenmore Plantation & Gardens 𝒶𝒶

This stately Georgian mansion was built in the 1770s for George Washington's only sister, Betty Washington, and her husband, Fielding Lewis, one of Fredericksburg's wealthiest planters and merchants. During the Revolution, Lewis financed a gun factory and built vessels for the American navy. As a result of his large expenditures in the cause of patriotism, he had to sell Kenmore to liquidate his debts. He died a few weeks after the victory at Yorktown. Today, the house sits on three of the original plantation's 1,300 acres and is being restored to its Colonial elegance. While that's going on, some of the paintings and furniture are on display in the Bissell Gallery at the visitor center. The 40-minute tours concentrate on the restoration process and the house's architectural features, especially the exquisitely molded plaster ceilings and cornices. Much of the flooring and all the woodwork and paneling are also original. Be sure to explore the famous gardens, restored and maintained according to the original plans by the Garden Club of Virginia. Also ask if any of Kenmore's many special programs are going on while you're here.

1201 Washington Ave. (between Lewis and Fauquier sts.). ℂ 540/373-3381. www.kenmore.org. Admission $8 adults, $4 children 6–17, free for children 5 and younger. Daily 10am–5pm. Mandatory 40-min. house tours depart 15 and 45 min. past the hour until 4:15pm.

Mary Washington House 𝒶

George Washington bought this white-frame house in 1772 for his mother, Mary Ball Washington, so she would be near her daughter's home at Kenmore Plantation (see above). Mary Washington was then 64 years old and had been living across the river at Ferry Farm since 1738 (see "More Attractions," below). Legend says that Lafayette found Mrs. Washington in her garden when he visited during the Revolution to pay his respects (her sundial still keeps time). Her son came in 1789 to receive her blessing before going to New York for his inauguration as president. He never saw her again, for she died later that year. You must take a 30-minute guided tour (they depart continuously) to see the indoor exhibits, including a mirror she considered to be her "best dressing glass."

1200 Charles St. (at Lewis St.). ℭ 540/373-1569. www.apva.org/marywashingtonhouse. Admission $5 adults, $2 children 6–18, free for children 5 and younger. Mar–Oct Mon–Sat 9am–5pm, Sun 11am–5pm; Nov–Feb Mon–Sat 10am–4pm, Sun noon–4pm. Guided 30-min. tours run continuously.

The Rising Sun Tavern ✿✿   The Rising Sun was originally a residence, built in 1760 by Charles Washington, George's youngest brother, but beginning in the early 1790s it served as a tavern for some 30 years. You'll be thoroughly entertained during the 30-minute tours led by a tavern wench—an indentured servant sentenced to 7 years for stealing a loaf of bread in England. The Rising Sun Tavern was a proper high-class tavern, she explains, not for riffraff. The gentlemen congregated over Madeira and cards in the Great Room or had a rollicking good time in the Taproom over multicourse meals and many tankards of ale. Meanwhile, ladies were consigned to the Retiring Room, where they would spend the entire day gossiping and doing needlework. You must take a tour, but you can join the one in progress when you get here and see what you missed on the next.

1306 Caroline St. (at Fauquier St.). ℭ 540/371-1494. www.apva.org/risingsuntavern. Admission $5 adults, $2 for children 6–18, free for children 5 and younger. Mar–Nov Mon–Sat 9am–5pm, Sun 11am–5pm; Dec–Feb Mon–Sat 10am–4pm, Sun noon–4pm. Closed Jan 1, Thanksgiving, Dec 24–25, and Dec 31. Guided 30-min. tours run continuously.

MORE ATTRACTIONS

Chatham   Across the river from downtown, this mansion was built between 1768 and 1771 by wealthy planter William Fitzhugh, a fourth-generation American who supported the Revolution politically and financially. George Washington visited twice. Now the headquarters of the Fredericksburg & Spotsylvania National Military Park (see "The Civil War Battlefields," below), during the Civil War Chatham served as headquarters for Federal commanders—Lincoln visited his generals here—and as a Union field hospital where American Red Cross founder Clara Barton and poet Walt Whitman assisted the wounded. You can tour five rooms and the grounds on your own. The dining room and parlor have exhibits on Chatham's owners and its role in the Civil War, which is explained by a 12-minute film. Also worth watching is a 30-minute video about the war's impact on Fredericksburg's civilian populace. National Park Service employees are on hand to answer questions and lead guided tours. There is a reconstructed section of a Civil War pontoon bridge as well as a picnic area on the grounds.

120 Chatham Lane. ℭ 540/371-0802. www.nps.gov/frsp. Free admission. Daily 9am–4:30pm. Closed Jan 1 and Dec 25. Take William St. (Va. 3) east across the river and follow the signs.

The Courthouse   Built in 1853, this courthouse is a fine example of Gothic Revival architecture. In fact, its architect, James Renwick, also designed St. Patrick's Cathedral in New York and the original Smithsonian "Castle" and Renwick Gallery in Washington, D.C. Exhibits in the lobby include copies of Mary Ball Washington's will and George Washington's address to the city council in 1784.

Princess Anne and George sts. ℭ 540/372-1066. Free admission. Mon–Fri 9am–4pm.

Fredericksburg Area Museum and Cultural Center   This very good local museum occupies the 1816 Town Hall in Market Square and an old bank building across the street. In existence since 1733, Market Square was the center of trade and commerce in Fredericksburg for more than a century, while Town Hall served as the

Moments   Semper Fi—The U.S. Marine Corps Museum

Rising like a beacon beside I-95 about halfway between Fredericksburg and Alexandria is the sloping steel tower atop the terrific **National Museum of the Marine Corps** ✭✭✭, 18900 Jefferson Davis Hwy. (U.S. 1) in Triangle (✆ **877/635-1775** or 703/784-6115; www.usmcmuseum.org). The shape of this stunning, modernistic building evokes the famous scene of leathernecks raising the U.S. flag over Iwo Jima during World War II—the 210-foot-tall tower slopes at the same angle as their improvised battlefield flag pole. It stands above a glass-ceiling rotunda at the museum's center, from which are suspended Marine Corps aircraft dating back to World War I. Exhibits in a labyrinth of rooms trace the corps' history since its inception in 1775. Sounds from numerous audiovisual effects can be a bit distracting, but many of the high-tech exhibits are especially good at re-creating battlefield reality. For example, a Korean War battle takes place in a chilled room to capture wintertime conditions in that conflict, while a Vietnam skirmish takes place in stifling tropical heat. You'll also feel what it was like to fly in a noisy, shaking Vietnam-era helicopter. You will need at least 3 hours to digest it all. Two cafes are present, so plan to have lunch before or after a 1½-hour tour guided by an ex-Marine docent; tours depart at 10am, noon, and 2pm. Admission is free. The museum is open from 9am to 5pm daily except Christmas. Take Exit 150 off I-95 at Triangle, go east to U.S. 1, and turn south to the museum.

city's social and legal center. Lafayette was entertained here in 1824 with lavish parties and balls, and the building continued to serve its original function until 1982. Both the first level and the 19th-century Council Chamber on the third floor host changing exhibits relating to regional and cultural history. The second floor houses permanent exhibits about the area's history. For me, the highlight is the collection of Masonic artifacts, including a Gilbert Stuart portrait of Washington and the 1668 Bible on which he took the oath when joining Masonic Lodge No. 4.

907 Princess Anne St. (at William St.). ✆ **540/371-3037**. www.famcc.org. Admission $7 adults, $2 children 6–18, free for children 5 and younger. Mar–Nov Mon–Sat 10am–5pm, Sun 1–5pm; Dec–Feb Mon–Sat 10am–4pm, Sun 1–4pm. Closed Jan 1, Dec 24–25, and Dec 31.

George Washington's Ferry Farm   The first president was 6 years old in 1738 when his family moved to this farm of about 600 acres across the river from Fredericksburg. It was here that George purportedly confessed to chopping down the cherry tree. He and his siblings took a ferry across the river to school in Fredericksburg. After their father, Augustine Washington, died in 1743, their mother Mary Ball Washington stayed on the farm until 1772, when George bought her the house in town (see above). Union soldiers camped on the farm during the Civil War. The Washington home is long gone, but you can watch archaeologists at work here during summer. Artifacts are on display in the visitor center, where interpreters will answer questions. You can take a self-guided tour of the grounds. Kenmore Plantations & Gardens manages the farm and sponsors many special programs here.

268 Kings Hwy. (Va. 3). ℭ **540/370-0732**. www.kenmore.org. Admission $5 adults, $3 children 6–17, free for children 5 and younger. Daily 10am–5pm (archaeology site May–Sept). Closed Thanksgiving, Dec 24–25, and Dec 31. Take Va. 3 east across Rappahannock River, turn right after 3rd traffic signal.

The Presbyterian Church   The local Presbyterian congregation, which dates to the early 1800s, completed this Greek Revival building in 1833. It was shelled during the Civil War, and, like St. George's Episcopal Church (below), served as a hospital where Clara Barton nursed Union wounded. Cannonballs in the front-left pillar and scars on the walls of the loft and belfry remain. The present church bell replaced one that was given to the Confederacy to be melted down for making cannons.

810 Princess Anne St. (at George St.). ℭ **540/373-7057**. Free admission. Services Labor Day to June Sun 8:30 and 11am; June–Aug Sun 8:30 and 10am (go to church office at other times).

St. George's Episcopal Church   Martha Washington's father and John Paul Jones's brother are buried in the graveyard of this church, and members of the first parish congregation included Mary Ball Washington and Revolutionary War generals Hugh Mercer and George Weedon. The original church on this site was built in 1732; the current Romanesque Revival structure, in 1849. During the Battle of Fredericksburg, the church was hit at least 25 times. It served as a Union hospital during the Battle of the Wilderness in 1864, when 10,000 wounded soldiers filled every available building in town (the New York City Police Department returned a stolen communion set in 1866). Note the three signed Tiffany windows.

905 Princess Anne St. (between George and William sts.). ℭ **540/373-4133**. www.stgeorgesepiscopal.net. Free admission. Mon–Sat 8am–10pm (unless a wedding is taking place Sat); Sun 8am–8pm, with services at 8 and 10:30am (7:45 and 10am during summer).

SHOPPING

Fredericksburg is one of Virginia's top treasure-troves for antiques and collectibles shoppers, as you will quickly note by more than 40 stores along Caroline, Sophia, and William streets. My antiques-hunting friends come here for more reasonable prices than in metropolitan areas such as Alexandria, Richmond, and Norfolk. The visitor center has brochures describing each store's specialty (see "Essentials," earlier in this chapter).

RIVER CRUISES

Operated by the same company that goes to Tangier Island from Reedville on the Northern Neck and from Onancock on the Eastern Shore, **Rappahannock River Cruises** (ℭ **804/453-2628**; www.tangiercruise.com) sends the stern-wheel *City of Fredericksburg* down the river from the city dock on Sophia Street from May through October. Most popular are the 2-hour lunch trips departing at noon Tuesday through Saturday. Fares are $26 for adults, $17 for children. The company also has dinner and Sunday brunch cruises. Call for reservations.

WHERE TO STAY

You'll find chain hotels of every ilk off I-95. Most convenient to the Historic District is the strip along Va. 3 at Exit 130. This also is Fredericksburg's major suburban shopping area, with the Spotsylvania Mall and a multitude of other centers, plus a host of national chain restaurants. Worthy motels here include the **Best Western Fredericksburg** (ℭ 800/528-1234 or 540/371-5050), **Best Western Central Plaza** (ℭ 800/528-1234 or 540/786-7404), **Hampton Inn** (ℭ 800/426-7866 or 540/371-0330),

Hilton Garden Inn (© 877/STAY-HGI or 540/786-7404), **Ramada Inn–Spotsylvania Mall** (© 800/272-6232 or 540/786-8361), and an inexpensive **Super 8** (© 800/800-8000 or 540/786-8881).

The newest properties are along U.S. 1 at Exit 126 south of town, another quickly developing commercial area known as Southpoint. These include the **Comfort Inn Southpoint** (© 800/228-5151 or 540/898-5550), **Days Inn Fredericksburg South** (© 800/325-2525 or 540/898-6800), **Fairfield Inn by Marriott** (© 228-2800 or 540/891-9100), a **Hampton Inn** (© 800/426-7866 or 540/898-5000), **Ramada Inn & Conference Center** (© 800/2-RAMADA or 540/898-1102), **Sleep Inn Southpoint** (© 877/424-6423 or 540/710-5500), and two more cheapies, the **Econo Lodge South** (© 800/800-55-ECONO or 540/898-5440) and another **Super 8** (© 800/800-8000 or 540/898-7100).

BED & BREAKFASTS

In addition to the inns listed below, the Historic District is host to **The Spooner House Bed & Breakfast,** 1300 Caroline St. (© **866/874-7422** or 540/374-5258; www.spoonerhouse.org), which has a two-room suite with private entrance in a 1794 clapboard house on land once owned by Charles Washington, the president's brother; **The Schooler House Bed & Breakfast,** 1303 Caroline St. (© **540/374-5258;** www.theschoolerhouse.com), an 1891 house with four fireplaces; and **Chez Soi Bed and Breakfast,** 114 Caroline St. (© **540/310-0036;** chezoi99@cs.com), whose Belgian-born owners speak both English and French.

Fredericksburg Colonial Inn *Value*   Located north of the Historic District, this unpretentious inn is a hub for value-conscious Civil War buffs and people participating in Civil War reenactments—don't be surprised to see musket-toting Blues and Grays in the lobby. In the breakfast room, you'll find a display of Civil War weaponry and Confederate dollars. The rooms are furnished with some reproductions but mostly with antiques, such as marble-top walnut dressers, rag rugs, and canopied beds.

1707 Princess Anne St. (at Herndon St.), Fredericksburg, VA 22401. © **540/371-5666.** Fax 540/371-5884. www.fci1. com. 30 units. $89–$149 double. Rates include light continental breakfast. AE, MC, V. *In room:* A/C, TV, Wi-Fi, fridge.

Kenmore Inn   An elegant white pediment supported by fluted columns and a front porch with wicker chairs welcome you to this late 1700s mansion in the Historic District on property originally owned by George Washington's brother-in-law, Fielding Lewis. Crystal chandeliers and Oriental rugs enhance the foyer, from whence a sweeping staircase leads to the guest rooms—a handsome assortment of both cozy and spacious accommodations furnished with a mix of antiques. Expect to find four-poster beds with lacy canopies, antique chests, and walls hung with botanical prints and engravings. The house has eight working fireplaces, four in the bedrooms. The inn serves full breakfasts to its guests in the main floor dining room, which turns into a fine-dining restaurant at dinner. The clubby pub downstairs also serves dinner as well as libation.

1200 Princess Anne St. (at Lewis St.), Fredericksburg, VA 22401. © **540/371-7622.** Fax 540/371-5480. www.kenmore inn.com. 9 units. $123–$168 double. Rates include full breakfast. AE, DC, DISC, MC, V. **Amenities:** Restaurant; bar; access to nearby health club. *In room:* A/C, TV, Wi-Fi, iron.

Richard Johnston Inn *♨♨*   Two 18th-century brick row houses are joined to form this elegantly restored inn across busy Caroline Street from the visitor center. The downstairs sitting rooms and dining room, where breakfast is served (continental during the week, full on weekends), are invitingly furnished. The Oriental rugs and

Moments Carl's Famous Frozen Custard

My sweet tooth gets satiated at the famous **Carl's,** 2200 Princess Anne St. (no phone), which has been making frozen custard with the same machines since 1947 and is listed on the National Register of Historic Places. Carl's is open daily from mid-February through mid-November.

---

mahogany furniture in the second-floor rooms in one house create a more formal atmosphere than in the others, which feature rockers and four-poster beds that lend a country charm. Third-floor dormer rooms are attractive, with low ceilings, dormer windows, and murals on their walls. The inn's original kitchen house also exudes charm, with brick floors, two queen-size beds, and a private entrance from the courtyard. The spacious Isabella's Suite also offers a private courtyard entrance as well as two queen-size beds, a kitchenette, and a separate living room. The Loft Suite apartment overlooking the courtyard also has a kitchenette and has a king-size bed in its loft. The two courtyard rooms here are pet-friendly, although you cannot leave pets unattended.

711 Caroline St. (between Hanover and Charlotte sts.), Fredericksburg, VA 22401. © 877/577-0770 or 540/899-7606. Fax 540/899-6837. www.therichardjohnstoninn.com. 9 units. $95–$190 double. Rates include breakfast. AE, MC, V. Pet fee $25. *In room:* A/C, TV, Wi-Fi, kitchenette (2 units), no phone.

WHERE TO DINE

The swankiest restaurant in town is the **Kenmore Inn Dining Room** (see "Where to Stay," above), where chef Josh Oleson presides over an excellent kitchen and extensive wine cellar. Another worthy Historic District restaurant is **Chords,** 917 Caroline St. (© **540/371-7723**), a trendy bistro with excellent food and nightly music. **Claiborne's,** 200 Lafayette Blvd. (© **540/371-7080**), in the restored train station at the southern end of Caroline Street, provides good low-country Southern chow. Top Italian is the venerable **Ristorante Renato,** 422 William St. (© **540/371-8228**).

I get my morning caffeine and pastries at **Hyperion Espresso** (© **540/373-4882**), a college-town-style coffee shop at the corner of William and Princess Anne streets. Be sure to check out the dessert case in the back room. Another Historic District relic is the old-fashioned soda fountain at **Goolrick's Pharmacy** (© **540/373-9878**), on Caroline Street at George Street.

Brock's Riverside Grill, 503 Sofia St. (© **540/370-1820**), at Lafayette Boulevard beside the river, is a pub-style joint with an outdoor bar where I slake my thirst after walking around the Historic District. In cool weather you'll find me tippling in the **Blarney Stone,** 715 Caroline St. (© **540/371-PINT**).

Bistro Bethem ★★ *Finds* SOUTHERN AMERICAN   The young husband-wife team of Blake and Aby Bethem (he's the chef) offer refined Southern cuisine at this bistro next door to La Petite Auberge (see below). An Italian restaurant once occupied the premises, and Blake uses the leftover clay pizza oven to finish off choices such as rib-eye steak with onion rings; bow-tie pasta with green peas and apple-wood-smoked bacon; and seared tuna with polenta cake and braised collard greens. His signature dish is a salad of grilled hearts of romaine lettuce with local bleu cheese, roasted red tomatoes, and pickled onions and carrots. The Bethem's wine list has won awards.

309 William St. © **540/371-9999.** Reservations recommended Fri–Sat. Main courses $23–$28. AE, MC, V. Tues–Sat 11:30am–2:30pm and 5–10pm; Sun 11:30am–2:30pm and 5–9pm.

Caroline Street Cafe & Catering *(Finds)* DELI   This bright, art-filled deli is my favorite spot for a light lunch. The smoked chicken is especially good, either sliced or as its own salad. So are the white-bean chili and a spicy summer gazpacho-style soup featuring strawberries as well as fresh local veggies. Be sure to check the daily specials on the blackboard behind the counter before placing your order.

1002 Caroline St. ℂ 540/373-1645. Reservations not accepted. Salads and sandwiches $6.50–$7. MC, V. Mon–Sat 10am–4pm; Sun 11am–4pm.

La Petite Auberge *(★)* FRENCH TRADITIONAL   Christian Etienne Reanult's delightful restaurant was designed to look like a garden, an effect enhanced by white latticework and garden furnishings. Unpainted brick walls are hung with copper pots and cheerful oil paintings, and candlelit tables are adorned with fresh flowers. A cozy lounge adjoins. Christian and his classically trained son, Raymond, change their menu daily. They might offer salade niçoise, soft-shell crab amandine, poached salmon with hollandaise sauce, and sirloin steak with béarnaise sauce. The early-bird dinner here is an attractive offering—soup, salad, a choice of seven entrees, and ice cream.

311 William St. (between Princess Anne and Charles sts.). ℂ 540/371-2727. Reservations recommended, especially at dinner. Main courses $14–$29; early-bird dinner $21. AE, DC, MC, V. Mon–Fri 11:30am–2:30pm and 5:30–10pm; Sat 11:30am–2:15pm and 5:30–10pm; early-bird dinner Mon–Thurs 5:30–7pm.

Sammy T's *(Value)* AMERICAN/VEGETARIAN   This popular, inexpensive pub offers a relaxed, tasteful setting and a creative health-food orientation. In fact, it's Fredericksburg's best option for vegetarians and vegans. It has a publike ambience, with large overhead fans, a pressed-tin ceiling, knotty-pine booths, and a long oak bar. Everything is made from scratch, with an emphasis on natural ingredients. The lunch and dinner menus offer many vegetarian and vegan items, such as vegetarian lasagna, a bean-and-grain burger, and a spicy black-bean cake. Entrees like burgers, fried oysters, and crab cakes are possibilities for meat and seafood eaters.

801 Caroline St. (at Hanover St.). ℂ 540/371-2008. Reservations not accepted. Sandwiches $4.50–$9.50; main courses $7.50–$17. AE, DISC, MC, V. Sun–Thurs 11am–9pm; Fri–Sat 11am–10pm.

2 The Civil War Battlefields ★★★

Fredericksburg has never forgotten its Civil War victories and defeats in the battles of Fredericksburg and at Chancellorsville, The Wilderness, and Spotsylvania Courthouse, 12 to 15 miles west of the city. The battles were part of three different Union attempts to advance from Washington, D.C., to Richmond between December 1862 and May 1864. Only the last one succeeded. Today, the sites are beautifully preserved in the National Park Service's **Fredericksburg & Spotsylvania National Military Park,** which also includes the Stonewall Jackson Shrine, where the great Confederate general died after being mistakenly shot by his own men.

Although park headquarters are at Chatham (p. 107), start at the **Fredericksburg Battlefield Visitor Center,** 1013 Lafayette Blvd. (U.S. 1 Business), at Sunken Road (ℂ **540/373-6122**), where you can get detailed tour brochures and watch a 22-minute video (shown on the hour and half-hour) to get you oriented. The bookstore across the parking lot rents and sells the auto-tour tapes or CDs that are essential to get the most out of your visit (see "A Battle Plan for Seeing the Battlefields," below). Be sure to pick up the park service's main brochure, which has a detailed map, and pamphlets for each of the sites. If you want more detailed information, the bookstore is packed with Civil War literature.

Tips   A Battle Plan for Seeing the Battlefields

Although you can drive around the battlefields in less than a day, you'll need 2 days to take the full 75-mile audio-guided auto tours of the Fredericksburg and Spotsylvania battlefields. Allow a minimum of 30 minutes at each of the two visitor centers and 3 hours for each of the four battlefield audio tours, plus driving times in between.

I strongly recommend the audio tour CDs available at the Fredericksburg and Chancellorsville visitor centers (there's a different recording for each battle; $4.95 to rent or $13 to purchase each CD). Renting a portable player along with them will allow you to get out of your car and still hear the informative commentary.

Although you can start at the Chancellorsville Visitor Center, I prefer to tour the battlefields in the order in which the conflicts occurred: Fredericksburg, Chancellorsville, The Wilderness, and Spotsylvania Courthouse. Spend the first day at Fredericksburg and Chancellorsville, and the second at The Wilderness and Spotsylvania Courthouse, where the battles happened within days of each other. The Stonewall Jackson Shrine at Guinea Station is 18 miles southeast of Spotsylvania Courthouse; go there last.

Admission to the battlefields is free. The Fredericksburg visitor center is open daily from 9am to 5pm with extended hours in summer and on spring and fall weekends. The actual battlefields are open daily from sunrise to sunset. You can drive through the battlefields but the visitor centers are closed New Year's Day and Christmas.

There's also a visitor center at **Chancellorsville** (see below). The Wilderness and Spotsylvania Courthouse battlefields have shelters with exhibits explaining what happened. Park rangers give **guided tours** of each battlefield daily during summer and on spring and autumn weekends. Call the visitor centers for the schedule.

For advance **information,** contact the Superintendent, Fredericksburg & Spotsylvania National Military Park, 120 Chatham Lane, Fredericksburg, VA 22405 (© **540/ 371-0802;** www.nps.gov/frsp).

BATTLE OF FREDERICKSBURG

The Battle of Fredericksburg took place from December 11 to December 13, 1862, when the Union army under Gen. Ambrose E. Burnside crossed the river into Fredericksburg via pontoon bridges. Burnside made a huge mistake when he sent the body of his 100,000 men uphill against Lee's 75,000 troops, most of them dug in behind a stone wall along Sunken Road at the base of Marye's Heights. The ground below the heights became a bloody killing field as Lee's cannon, firing from the hill, mowed down the Yankees.

Sunken Road—restored to look exactly as it did in 1862—starts at the visitor center at the base of Marye's Heights. You can examine the road and follow the gently sloping pathway up the 40-foot-high heights for the fine view that sends chills down my spine as I think of the lives lost on the fields below. Park rangers lead 35-minute guided tours of the road several times daily during the summer and on spring and fall weekends. The park also has summertime children's programs here.

BATTLE OF CHANCELLORSVILLE

President Lincoln fired Burnside after the Marye's Heights massacre. Under Gen. Joseph Hooker, Burnside's replacement, the Union forces crossed the river north of Fredericksburg in late April 1863 and advanced to Chancellorsville, a crossroads 10 miles west of Fredericksburg on the Orange Turnpike (now Va. 3). In a surprise attack, Stonewall Jackson flanked Hooker's line on May 2 and won a spectacular victory. Jackson was inadvertently shot by his own men that same night. He was taken 5 miles west to Ellwood Farm, where his left arm was amputated and buried in the family cemetery (see "Battle of the Wilderness," below). He was later moved to a farm near Guinea Station, where he died (see "Stonewall Jackson Shrine," below). By then, Lee had driven the Union army back across the Rappahannock.

Stop at the **Chancellorsville Visitor Center** (② **540/786-2880**), 12 miles west of Fredericksburg on Va. 3, to see another audiovisual orientation and related exhibits. Once again, auto-tour tapes and CDs are available at the bookstore. The center is open daily from 9am to 5pm, with extended hours in summer and on spring and autumn weekends. Be sure to get a pass here to see the gravestone over Jackson's arm at Ellwood Farm.

BATTLE OF THE WILDERNESS

A year later, under the direction of the aggressive Ulysses S. Grant, Union forces once again crossed the Rappahannock and advanced south to Wilderness Tavern, 5 miles west of Chancellorsville near what is now the junction of Va. 3 and Va. 20. Lee advanced to stop him, thus setting up the first battle between these two great generals. On May 5 and 6, 1864, the armies fought in the tangled thickets of The Wilderness. The battle was a stalemate, but instead of retreating as his predecessors had, Grant backed off and went around Lee toward his ultimate target, Richmond, via the shortest road south (now Va. 208).

The battle raged around **Ellwood Farm,** which during the Battle of Chancellorsville had served as the Confederate hospital where Stonewall Jackson's arm was amputated and buried. You can see his arm's gravestone at Ellwood Farm, which is open Saturday and Sunday during summer. At other times you must get an Ellwood pass at the Chancellorsville Visitor Center.

BATTLE OF SPOTSYLVANIA COURTHOUSE

Lee quickly regrouped and tried to stop Grant 2 days later at Spotsylvania Courthouse, about 18 miles southeast of The Wilderness. Taking advantage of thick fog and wet Confederate gunpowder, Union troops breached the Southerners' line. When Lee's reinforcements arrived, the sides spent 20 hours in the war's most intense hand-to-hand combat at a site known as Bloody Angle. During the fighting, Lee built new fortifications to the rear, which he successfully defended. Instead of pushing the fight to the finish, however, Grant again backed off, flanked his entire army around Lee's, and resumed his unrelenting march toward Richmond. It was the end of major fighting in the Fredericksburg area, as the war moved south to its ultimate conclusion 11 months later at Appomattox.

There's an exhibit shelter on Grant Drive, where park rangers lead walking tours daily during summer, weekends in spring and fall. Call the Fredericksburg or Chancellorsville visitor centers for details.

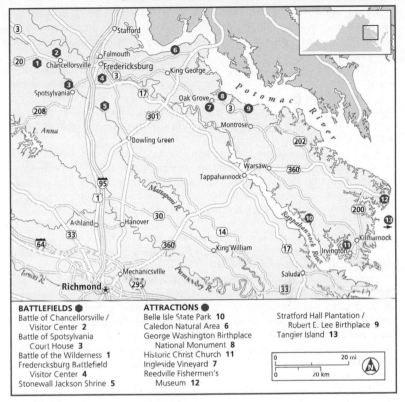

BATTLEFIELDS ●

Battle of Chancellorsville /
    Visitor Center **2**
Battle of Spotsylvania
    Court House **3**
Battle of the Wilderness **1**
Fredericksburg Battlefield
    Visitor Center **4**
Stonewall Jackson Shrine **5**

ATTRACTIONS ●

Belle Isle State Park **10**
Caledon Natural Area **6**
George Washington Birthplace
    National Monument **8**
Historic Christ Church **11**
Ingleside Vineyard **7**
Reedville Fishermen's
    Museum **12**

Stratford Hall Plantation /
    Robert E. Lee Birthplace **9**
Tangier Island **13**

0 — 20 mi
0 — 20 km

STONEWALL JACKSON SHRINE

Now part of the park, the **Stonewall Jackson Shrine** (© 804/633-6076) is in the wood-frame plantation office where the general spent the last 6 days of his life after being shot and mortally wounded by his own men at Chancellorsville. Jackson's doctors hoped that he would recover sufficiently to board a train at nearby Guinea Station for the ride to Richmond, but it was not to be. Jackson's body was taken to Lexington, where he was buried with full honors (see chapter 7). The office is the only structure remaining at the plantation and appears as it did when Jackson died. About half of its contents are original, including his deathbed.

The shrine is open 9am to 5pm daily from Memorial Day to Labor Day, Saturday to Monday the rest of the year. It's at the junction of C.R. 606 and C.R. 607, about 27 miles southeast of Chancellorsville, 18 miles southeast of Spotsylvania Courthouse. From I-95, take Exit 118 at Thornburg and follow the signs east on C.R. 606.

3 The Northern Neck ★

The peninsula between the Potomac and Rappahannock rivers known as the Northern Neck stretches 100 miles southeast from Fredericksburg to the Chesapeake Bay. A popular weekend getaway for us residents of nearby metropolitan areas, this rural land of rolling hills serrated by quiet tidal creeks is the ancestral home of the Washingtons and the Lees, who created large plantations on the riverbanks. Its hills are still punctuated by agricultural and small fishing villages (they speak in terms of counties here, not towns).

To my mind, the Northern Neck has three areas of interest. Heading east from Fredericksburg on Va. 3, you first come to George Washington's Birthplace National Monument, where the first president was born in 1732 on Pope's Creek Plantation, and Stratford Hall, the magnificently restored Lee plantation. Nearby, the Ingleside Vineyards offer tours and tastings. These three sites can easily be seen on a day trip from Fredericksburg.

A left turn on Va. 202 will take you northeast to the end of the Northern Neck, at Smith Point on the Chesapeake. Here you can explore the town of Reedville, founded as a menhaden fishing port in 1867 by Capt. Elijah Reed, a New England seafarer. Reedville soon became rich, and its captains and plant owners built magnificent Victorian-style homes. One plant still processes the small, toothless fish, which is of little use for human consumption but extremely valuable as meal, oil, and protein supplements used in everything from Pepperidge Farm cookies to Rustoleum paint. You can learn all about the menhaden at the local fishing museum. From Reedville you can depart on cruises to remote Tangier Island out in the bay.

Va. 200 will take you 20 miles south to my favorite spot on the neck, the genteel creekside hamlet of Irvington, home of Christ Church, perhaps the nation's best example of Colonial church architecture; The Tides Inn, one of Virginia's premier resorts; and The Hope and Glory Inn, one of its most romantic bed-and-breakfasts. Irvington and its neighboring villages of White Stone and Kilmarnock constitute one of Virginia's most affluent retirement communities. I stay in or near Irvington and use it as a base to explore the Northern Neck's eastern end.

ESSENTIALS

VISITOR INFORMATION   For advance information about the area, contact the **Northern Neck Tourism Council,** P.O. Box 1707, Warsaw, VA 22572 (© **800/393-6180** or 804/333-1919; www.northernneck.org). The council's offices are at 479 Main St. (Va. 3 Business) in the Regional Center. The walk-in **Virginia's Potomac Gateway Welcome Center** (© **540/633-3205**) is on U.S. 301 just south of the Potomac River Bridge. The **Reedville Fishermen's Museum** (p. 117) has information about Reedville and the Smith Point area. Information about Irvington is available at **www.townofirvington.com**.

GETTING THERE   You'll need a car to get here. From Fredericksburg, go east on Va. 3, which traverses the length of the Peninsula. From Fredericksburg, Washington's Birthplace is 40 miles; Irvington, 95 miles. The "fast" route from Fredericksburg to Reedville and Irvington is via U.S. 17 and U.S. 360. From Richmond, take U.S. 360; from Williamsburg, use U.S. 17 and Va. 3.

EXPLORING THE NORTHERN NECK

You can easily see George Washington's Birthplace, Stratford Hall Plantation, and the Ingleside Vineyards as a day trip from Fredericksburg or as stops on the way to Irvington. To do this area justice, plan on at least 3 days if you go on to Reedville and Irvington, 4 days if taking an all-day cruise to Tangier Island.

George Washington Birthplace National Monument ℱ   Although it's a re-creation of Popes Creek Plantation, where the first president was born on February 22,

1732, this national monument shows you what 18th-century farm life was like when Washington's father, Augustine, established a tobacco plantation here in 1718. George lived here until the family moved to Fredericksburg when he was 3½ years old. The manor house burned on Christmas Day in 1779 and was never rebuilt. There are no records detailing what it looked like, but the original site is outlined by oyster shells. Built in 1930–31, Memorial House and its workshop and farm are a typical plantation of that era (a guide will take you through the house). You can see the site in 1½ to 2 hours. Start at the visitor center, where a 14-minute film explains plantation life and a display case holds Washington family artifacts uncovered during archaeological digs here. Park rangers offer talks hourly and conduct guided tours from the visitor center. The graves of 32 Washington family members, including George's father, are in a small burial ground on the property.

Admission is free on the Monday of Washington's Birthday weekend in February, and a multitude of activities take place on February 22, George's actual birthday.

1732 Popes Creek Rd. (Va. 204, off Va. 3), Colonial Beach. ☎ 804/224-1732. www.nps.gov/gewa. Admission $4 adults, free for children 16 and younger (good for 7 days). National Park and American the Beautiful passes accepted. Daily 9am–5pm. Ranger talks on the hour 10am–4pm. Closed Jan 1, Thanksgiving, and Dec 25.

Historic Christ Church ✸✸✸

Elegant in its simplicity and virtually unchanged since 1735, this is the most pristine of Virginia's many Colonial-era churches. It was the gift of planter and businessman Robert "King" Carter, the richest man in the colonies at that time. His father, John Carter, four of his five wives, and two infant children are interred in the chancel (their graves are to the left as you face the Ten Commandments on the wall). King Carter's tomb is outside, on the north side of the church. Among the Carter descendants are eight governors of Virginia; two United States presidents (the Harrisons); a justice of the U.S. Supreme Court; and Gen. Robert E. Lee, who was born at Stratford Hall Plantation (see below). The Carter family still operates Shirley Plantation on the James River (p. 279).

Listed on the National Register of Historic Places, the church is cruciform in shape, its brick facade laid in a pleasing Flemish bond pattern, with a three-color design that saves the expanse of brick from monotony. Inside, the three-tiered pulpit is in excellent condition, and all 26 original pews remain (they're like box seats, with more important families occupying the larger boxes). A marble baptismal font dates to the 1660s. The building has no heat or artificial light. Its only electrical outlet is in the Carter family pew, and that's to power the organ used for services only during the summer.

Begin your visit with a 10-minute video in the museum, which displays archaeological artifacts from Corotoman, King Carter's lavish Rappahannock River plantation manse, which burned down only 4 years after he finished it in 1725. Then take a 30-minute guided tour through the church. The guides are particularly good at children's tours. Allow 30 minutes or so to wander among the gravestones.

C.R. 646, off Va. 200, 1 mile north of Irvington. ☎ 804/438-6855. www.christchurch1735.org. Free admission (suggested $5 donation). Church daily 9am–5pm; museum and 30-min. guided tours Apr–Nov Mon–Sat 10am–4pm, Sun 2–5pm. Worship services held in the church Sun at 8am from Memorial Day to Labor Day. Closed Dec.

Reedville Fishermen's Museum

Paying homage to Reedville's ancient way of earning a living, this museum consists of the 1875 William Walker House, the town's oldest building, which has been restored to appear as it did in 1900. The Covington Building houses a permanent collection and special exhibits commemorating the watermen who participate in the town's leading industry, menhaden fishing, which dates to 1874 when Capt. Elijah Reed arrived here. An 11-minute video sets the stage for a visit to the workboats out on the creek; they were refurbished in the museum's shop by volunteers, who also built the *Spirit of 1608,* a replica of the boat Capt. John Smith used to explore the Chesapeake region in 1608.

504 Main St., Reedville. ☎ **540/453-6529.** www.rfmuseum.org. Admission $5 adults, $3 seniors, free for children 12 and younger. Mid-Mar to Apr Sat–Sun 10:30am–4:30pm; May–Oct daily 10:30am–4:30pm; Nov to late Jan Fri–Mon 10:30am–4:30pm. Closed late Jan to mid-Mar. From Va. 3 east, take U.S. 360 east to Reedville.

Steamboat Era Museum   Although the building housing this interesting local museum looks like a railway station, inside it's devoted to the late-19th- and early-20th-century era when steamboats were the major means of transportation between Norfolk and Baltimore. The steamers stopped at waterside towns such as Irvington, which sported an opera house and several hotels and speak-easies in those days. An introductory video about the era sets the stage. Model ship lovers will especially enjoy master craftsman Bill Wright's four examples showing the transition from sail to steam.

156 King Carter Dr., Irvington. ☎ **804/438-6888.** www.steamboateramuseum.org. Free admission ($4 suggested donation). Thurs–Sat 10am–4pm; Sun 1–4pm.

Stratford Hall Plantation 🌟🌟🌟   This is one of the great houses of the South, magnificently set on 1,600 acres above the Potomac, renowned for its distinctive architectural style and for the illustrious members of the Lee family who lived here. Thomas Lee, a planter who served as governor of the Virginia colony, built Stratford in the 1730s. His son, Richard Henry Lee, made the motion for independence in the Continental Congress in 1776, and he and Francis Lightfoot Lee were the only brothers to sign the Declaration of Independence. Cousin Henry "Light-Horse Harry" Lee, a hero of the Revolution, coined the phrase about his friend George Washington, "First in war, first in peace, and first in the hearts of his countrymen." Light-Horse Harry and his wife, Anne Hill Carter of Shirley Plantation on the James River (see chapter 10), were the parents of Robert E. Lee, who was born here in 1807.

The H-shaped manor house, its four dependencies, coach house, and stables have been brilliantly restored. Brick chimney groupings that flank the roofline are some of the mansion's most striking features. The paneled Great Hall, one of the finest rooms to have survived from Colonial times, runs the depth of the house and has an inverted tray ceiling. On the same floor are bedrooms and a nursery, where you can see Robert E. Lee's crib. The fireplace in the nursery is trimmed with sculpted angels' heads.

Start at the visitor center, where tours begin. You can go inside the mansion and its dependencies only on 30-minute tours led by costumed guides, who will meet you at one of the outbuildings. You can easily spend another 2 hours strolling the gardens, meadows, and nature trails on this 1,600-acre estate, still operated as a working farm.

Tips **Taking a Lunch Break**

There are few places to dine in this area, so have lunch in the log cabin–style **Plantation Dining Room** at Stratford Hall Plantation. It offers worthy Virginia-style cream of crab soup, crab cake and fried oyster sandwiches, chef salads with chicken or cured ham, ham biscuits, and meals of fried chicken, crab cakes, flounder, or ham, all at reasonable prices. Open Tuesday to Sunday from 11am to 3pm.

Fun Fact **Barefoot Stomping in Irvington**

Irvington's White Fences Vineyard & Winery (© **804/438-5559**) sponsors **The Irvington Stomp** (www.irvingtonstomp.com), one of the Virginia's most unusual festivals. During the festival you can actually stomp grapes with your bare feet, just as they do in Europe. Admission is $10 for adults, $5 for children 6 to 16, free for kids under 6. The stomp is held on Saturday of Labor Day weekend.

---

483 Great House Rd. (Va. 214; 2 miles north of Va. 3), Stratford. © 804/493-8038. www.stratfordhall.org. Admission $10 adults, $9 seniors and military, $5 children 6–11, free for children 5 and younger. Grounds-only pass $5 adults, $3 children. Daily 9:30am–4pm (tours 10am–4pm). Dining room daily 11:30am–3pm. Closed Jan 1, Dec 25, and Dec 31.

ON THE WINE TRAIL

The Northern Neck has five operating vineyards and wineries that have bound together to form the **Northern Neck Wine Trail** (© **800/393-6180;** www.northern neckwinetrail.com), whose website will help you plan an inebriated tour.

The oldest, largest, and most convenient to visit from Fredericksburg is **Ingleside Vineyards,** 5872 Leedstown Rd., Oak Grove (© **804/224-8687;** www.ingleside vineyards.com), off Va. 3 on the Rappahannock River side of the Peninsula. You'll get here before arriving at Washington's birthplace and Stratford Hall, so go easy on tasting the Virginia Brut, a handcrafted sparkling wine.

Others are Irvington's **White Fences Vineyard & Winery** (© **804/438-5559;** www.whitefencesvineyard.com), a relative infant whose Meteor Bright reds and whites already have won awards; **Athena Vineyards & Winery,** 3138 Jessie Dupont Memorial Hwy., Heathsville (© **840/580-4944;** www.athenavineyards.com); **Belle Mount Vineyards,** 2570 Newland Rd., Warsaw (© **800/335-5564** or 804/333-4700; www. bellemount.com); and **Oak Crest Vineyards & Winery,** 8215 Oak Crest Dr., King George (© **540/663-2812;** www.oakcrestwinery.com), near Colonial Beach.

OUTDOOR ACTIVITIES

Country roads winding through gently rolling hills and crossing picturesque creeks make the Northern Neck a great place to ride your bicycle. One excellent route makes a loop from Reedville via U.S. 360 and C.R. 652 and 644. On C.R. 644, you'll cross the Little Wicomico River via the free Sunnybank Ferry. Some bed-and-breakfasts provide bikes for the guests, but there are no places to rent them here, so bring your own.

The Northern Neck has more than 1,100 miles of shoreline and 6,500 acres of nature preserves, making it an important stop for birds migrating along the Atlantic Flyway. It also has a substantial population of bald eagles. To see the eagles, head to the **Caledon Natural Area,** on Va. 218 near King George (© **540/663-3861;** www.dcr.virginia.gov/state_parks/cal.shtml), which has observation tours along the Potomac River and guided eagle-watching tours. Another fine place to view the migratory birds is at **Belle Isle State Park** (© **804/462-5030;** www.dcr.state.va.us/parks/ bellisle.htm), off C.R. 354 on the Rappahannock River northwest of Irvington, which has guided canoe trips as well as horseback riding on land. The **Northern Neck Audubon Society,** P.O. Box 991, Kilmarnock, VA 22482 (www.northernneckaudubon. org), organizes field trips.

Another good spot for birding and much more is **Westmoreland State Park** (© 804/493-8821; www.dcr.virginia.gov/parks/westmore.htm), off Va. 3 between George Washington's Birthplace and Stratford Hall. It's the Northern Neck's largest park and is equipped with a campground, rental cabins, hiking trails, boating, and swimming.

Golfers come here primarily to play the **Golden Eagle** course at The Tides Inn (p. 121), one of Virginia's best, and the nearby **Tartan Course** (© 804/438-6200; www.tartangolfclub.com). Be sure to ask about the Golden Eagle's money-saving lunch packages. Irvington also is home to the **King Carter Golf Course,** on Old Saint Johns Road (© 804/435-7842; www.kingcartergolfclub.com), a fine public course where you can play for less than $75. Other less challenging—and less expensive—links are **Quinton Oaks Golf Course** near Callao (© 804/529-5367; www.quinton oaks.com) and a 9-holer at **Bushfield Golf Course** on Va. 202 at Mt. Holly (© 804/472-2602).

Reedville is the jumping-off point for fishing charters on the Chesapeake Bay, where you might hook a fighting bluefish or snag a succulent rockfish (sea bass). In Reedville call Capt. Jim Hardy of *The Ranger II* (© 804/453-6635) or **Pittman's Charters** (© 804/453-3643). The latter operates the *Mystic Lady II,* a 25-passenger party boat.

You can learn to sail at **Premier Sailing School** (©/fax 804/438-9300; www. sailingschool.net), which is based at The Tides Inn.

The Tides Inn also is home to the *Miss Ann,* a 127-foot yacht that makes lunch and sunset cruises from Carter's Creek out on the Rappahannock River. A Saturday morning "whiskey run" relives pre-liquor-by-the-drink days when local residents had to cross the river to buy alcoholic beverages. Call The Tides Inn (© 800/843-3746 or 804/438-5000) for the schedule, prices, and reservations.

Another cruise option is The Hope and Glory Inn's *Faded Glory* (© 800/497-8228 or 804/438-6053), a 1952-vintage Chesapeake Bay work boat that goes on Friday night crab-feast cruises (including steamed crab, shrimp, and corn on the cob) and Saturday beach voyages. Call for details and reservations.

A CRUISE TO TANGIER ISLAND

Out in the Chesapeake Bay lies the quaint and still relatively remote **Tangier Island.** It is so remote, in fact, that you can still hear an Elizabethan brogue on the tongues of its 530 or so residents. See "A Cruise to Tangier Island," in chapter 11, for more information.

Tangier Island Cruises (© 804/453-2628; www.tangiercruise.com) leave from Buzzards Point Marina, off U.S. 360 east of Reedville at 10am daily from May to mid-October. The narrated voyages take 90 minutes each way, leaving you with 2½ hours to have lunch on Tangier and poke around the island. They return to Reedville about 3:30pm. Although you'll be stuck on the other side without a car (you can take your bike on the cruise but not a vehicle), you can go all the way across the bay by connecting with the same company's Onancock-Tangier cruise in the afternoon. Round-trip fares are $25 for adults, $12 for children 4 to 13, $5 per bicycle. Reservations are required.

WHERE TO STAY

The Northern Neck has only two chain motels. Most convenient to Irvington and Reedville is the **Holiday Inn Express,** 599 N. Main St. (Va. 3), Kilmarnock (© 800/465-4329 or 804/436-1500; www.holidayinn.com), which has an outdoor pool and high-speed Internet access throughout.

I don't speak sign language.

A hotel can close for all kinds of reasons.
Our Guarantee ensures that if your hotel's undergoing construction, we'll let you know in advance. In fact, we cover your entire travel experience. See www.travelocity.com/guarantee for details.

travelocity
You'll never roam alone.

The Hope and Glory Inn ✦✦✦   One of the most fascinating and romantic country inns I've ever had the pleasure of patronizing, this property occupies a three-story schoolhouse built in the 1890s. Unusual for its time, it was coeducational, albeit with separate front doors for boys and girls. Today, those doors lead from the front porch into a large main lounge with a comfy television nook—it's the only TV on these premises—to one side of a broad center staircase leading to seven guest rooms plus a sitting room (the latter opens to a large deck). On the other side is the cozy Detention Bar, where today's naughty students are "detained" while they sample vintages from Irvington's White Fences Vineyard & Winery.

Out back, the gardens are so lush they almost hide the six light and airy clapboard cottages, the most romantic accommodations here. The two largest cottages are town house–style; their upstairs bedrooms have Romeo-and-Juliet balconies overlooking the gardens. Although every unit has its own bathroom, guests with an exhibitionist streak can use the gardens' outdoor bathroom complete with claw-foot tub, rainmaker shower, and pedestal sink—all shaded by large trees and surrounded by a wooden privacy fence.

An eclectic mix of old furniture and lots of whimsical folk art make this seem like a visit to Great-Grandma's down on the coast (please, do not write to me complaining about the chipped paint and faded mirrors; they're part of the clever shabby-chic charm). The inn's own chef prepares gourmet breakfasts served in the school building or by a fountain in the courtyard, and you can sign up for lively Saturday night dinners at the chef's table with sharp-witted owners Dudley and Peggy Patteson ($65 for three courses, $85 for four, including wine pairings). You will have free use of bicycles and the town's two tennis courts across the street, and you can pay to use the spa and other facilities at The Tides Inn nearby (see below).

Note that other than radios with CD players, none of the on-site units have telephones, TVs, or other such modern distractions, which would interfere with romance, The Hope and Glory's raison d'être.

If you need all the comforts of home, or have a family in tow, then opt for one of the inn's Tents at Vineyard Grove, on the edge of White Fences Vineyard & Winery about a mile away. These aren't tents but modern houses, each drawing its inspiration from carpenter Gothic cottages that grew out of revival "tent meetings" in the late 18th and early 19th centuries. In addition to phones and TVs, each has three bedrooms, three bathrooms, a full kitchen, and a screened porch overlooking the headwater marshes of Carter's Creek. Your pet can stay with you in certain cottages.

65 Tavern Rd. (at King Carter Dr.; P.O. Box 425), Irvington, VA 22480. ✆ 800/497-8228 or 804/438-6053. Fax 804/438-5362. www.hopeandglory.com. 22 units (all with private bathroom). $165–$240 double; $230–$685 cottage. Rates include full breakfast. AE, DISC, MC, V. Pets accepted, $40 fee. **Amenities:** Access to nearby tennis courts and health club; free bicycles. *In room:* A/C, TV (tents only), Wi-Fi, coffeemaker (tents only).

The Tides Inn ✦✦✦   Renowned for its exceptional Golden Eagle golf course, The Tides Inn has been one of Virginia's top golf resorts since 1947. A British Raj theme dominates, with ceiling fans and Indian mahogany furniture adorning the rooms, and wooden floor-to-ceiling plantation shutters shading some rooms, all of which look out onto Carter's Creek. There's a full-service spa here, including six treatment rooms with water views and patios for cooling down with a glass of wine.

The sprawling inn consists of several low-rise buildings on the banks of Carter's Creek. In the clapboard Main Building, the dining room and Chesapeake Club lounge both have outstanding views down the creek to the Rappahannock River. The dining room serves gourmet fare, while the semicircular Chesapeake Club offers burgers and sandwiches. (Note the exquisite wood paneling in the Chesapeake Club: It includes bottle lockers left from the days before Virginia allowed liquor-by-the-drink.) The club has a pianist during the week and a band on weekends for dancing. Men must wear jackets at dinner in the main dining room (they'll lend you one), but you can partake of the same menu in the adjacent Chesapeake Club in "resort casual" attire, which is required except in the pool, marina, and tennis areas.

Rooms in the Main Building have fine views, too, but those in the cottagelike Windsor or Lancaster Houses are more spacious and feature large bathrooms, living areas, and, in some cases, balconies overlooking the creek. Other hotel-style rooms are in the East, Garden, and Terrace wings, where the preferable ground-floor units have patios. All rooms have CD and DVD players and marble bathrooms.

All facilities, including the spa, the marina, and the golf course, are open to the public. Families will especially like it here during the summer when the very good Crab Net program keeps the kids occupied. The Premier Sailing School operates here, and the 127-foot yacht *Miss Ann* takes guests cruising (see "Outdoor Activities," above). Your small pets can enjoy the luxuries, too, including a pet sitter.

480 King Carter Dr. (P.O. Box 480), Irvington, VA 22480. © **800/843-3746** or 804/438-5000. Fax 804/438-5552. www.tidesinn.com. 106 units. $160–$319 double; $185–$345 suite. $14 per room daily resort fee. Golf, spa, sailing, and other packages available. AE, DC, DISC, MC, V. Valet parking free 1st night, $5 thereafter; free self-parking. Closed Jan–Feb. From Va. 3, take Va. 200 south 2 miles to Irvington, turn right at the sign to end of King Carter Dr. Pets accepted (in some rooms), $25 per animal. **Amenities:** 4 restaurants; 3 bars; 3 heated outdoor pools; 2 golf courses; 4 tennis courts; spa; watersports equipment/rentals; bike rentals; children's programs; concierge; business center; shopping arcade; room service; babysitting; laundry service; coin-op washers and dryers. *In room:* A/C, TV, high-speed Internet, CD player, minibar, coffeemaker, iron, safe.

WHERE TO DINE

While I enjoy fine dining, in these parts I prefer to eat like a local, which means seafood fresh from the Chesapeake Bay. The steamed crabs, spiced shrimp, and broiled or fried fish don't get much fresher than at **Cockrell's Creek Seafood & Deli** (© **804/ 453-6326**), on Fleeton Road (C.R. 657) in Reedville (turn left off U.S. 360 at the curve as you enter town). It's open from 10am to 5pm Monday through Saturday.

And don't forget the Saturday night Chef's Table dinners at The Hope and Glory Inn or the dining room at The Tides Inn (see above).

The Local In the same small shopping complex as the Trick Dog Cafe (see below), this shop serves as Irvington's version of Starbucks in the morning and as a sophisticated sandwich-and-salad emporium after 11am. Breakfast sees a variety of coffees, teas, pastries and—attention New Yorkers!—bagels with lox and cream cheese. Lunch and afternoon see a variety of salads and panini sandwiches. Sweet teeth are drawn to the ice-cream bar, and laptop owners can surf the Web wirelessly here. Out-of-town newspapers are sold; you can linger over them at tables out on the patio.

4337 Irvington Rd., Irvington. © **804/438-9356.** Reservations not accepted. Breakfast $3.50–$6; sandwiches and salads $6–$8. MC, V. Summer Mon–Thurs 7:30am–5pm, Fri–Sat 7:30am–7:30pm, Sun 7:30am–3pm; off season Mon–Thurs 7:30am–3pm, Fri–Sat 7:30am–5pm, Sun 7:30am–noon.

Sandpiper Restaurant SEAFOOD This local restaurant has been serving Chesapeake Bay seafood to locals and visitors alike since 1982. Start with chargrilled bacon-wrapped shrimp and proceed to the star attraction, crab cakes made mostly of back fin meat. Other favorites include oysters fried in a delicate batter and a platter of fried or broiled seafood. Chargrilled kabobs of shrimp, scallops, filet mignon cubes, and vegetables offer variety, as does shrimp in a fresh tomato-basil sauce over linguini. Landlubbers can opt for steaks or pork chops.

Rappahannock Dr. (Va. 3), White Stone. © 804/435-6176. Reservations not accepted. Main courses $16–$25. DISC, MC, V. Tues–Thurs 5–9pm; Fri–Sat 5–10pm.

Swank's on Main ℛ *Finds* INTERNATIONAL In the middle of little Kilmarnock's 4-block-long main drag, this stylish bistro would be right at home in a large city. With a sophisticated bar at the front and chefs busy in a display kitchen to the rear, it's the Northern Neck's most urbane place to dine. The menu changes seasonally but always ranges the globe, albeit with Southern touches, such as French-style trout amandine with stone-ground grits. I topped my meal off with strawberry Pavlova.

36 Main St., Kilmarnock. © 804/435-1010. Reservations recommended. Burgers $12; main courses $16–$26. AE, MC, V. Mon–Thurs 11am–9pm; Fri–Sat 11am–10pm; Sun 11am–2pm (brunch).

Trick Dog Cafe INTERNATIONAL   This casual bistro is named for a sooty statue of a little black dog that survived the Great Irvington Fire of 1917. A local man gave the statue to his son, telling him it was a "trick dog" because he didn't need to be fed, and he would always sit and stay. The dog now resides here, where you pet it for good luck. You won't need any luck to enjoy the food here, but opt for traditional steaks and seafood instead of anything exotic. Have a green apple martini at the bar, Irvington's favorite watering hole.

4357 Irvington Rd. (Va. 200), Irvington. © 804/438-1055. Reservations recommended. Main courses $17–$25. AE, MC, V. Tues–Thurs 5–10pm; Fri–Sat 5–11pm; Sun 11am–2pm.

6

Charlottesville

Situated in the rolling foothills of the Blue Ridge Mountains, Charlottesville is one of Virginia's most fascinating places to visit, thanks in large part to its three distinct personalities.

First, it's a quintessential college town, with the University of Virginia predominating everyday life for a large portion of its 42,000 or so residents. UVA is one of the country's finest and most beautiful public universities—a fact most begrudgingly admitted by those of us who matriculated at that other fine public beauty, the University of North Carolina at Chapel Hill, one of UVA's major rivals.

Second, this vibrant cosmopolitan center is consistently ranked as one of America's best places to live. Its charm, the beauty of the surrounding countryside, and an extraordinary number of facilities for a town this size have attracted a number of rich and famous folk like rock star Dave Matthews, author John Grisham, and former pro football player-turned-broadcaster Howie Long. Indeed, you never know whose famous face you'll recognize on the streets and in the restaurants here. Most of the celebrities live on estates out in the surrounding horse country, giving them a high degree of privacy but also quick access to a town that takes them quite in stride.

That's not surprising since Charlottesville has always had more than its share of famous Americans, which brings up its third—and most important for us visitors—personality as a center of American history.

It was here that Thomas Jefferson built his famous mountaintop home, Monticello; selected the site for and helped plan the Ash Lawn–Highland home of his presidential buddy, James Monroe; designed his "academical village" at UVA; and died at home 50 years to the day after Congress adopted his Declaration of Independence. "All my wishes end where I hope my days will end," he wrote, "at Monticello."

Indeed, the third president's presence is still so much in evidence here that locals call this "Mr. Jefferson's Country."

1 Orientation & Getting Around

VISITOR INFORMATION

For information, contact the **Charlottesville/Albemarle Convention and Visitors Bureau,** P.O. Box 178, Charlottesville, VA 22902 (© **877/386-1102** or 434/977-1783; fax 434/977-6151; www.pursuecharlottesville.org). The bureau's main office is at 610 E. Market St., on the eastern end of the Downtown Mall. It also operates the **Monticello Visitors Center,** on Va. 20 at Exit 121 off I-64, near Thomas Jefferson's home. The Monticello center is open March through October daily from 9am to 5:30pm; the rest of the year, daily until 5pm. The downtown center is open Monday to Saturday from 10am to 5pm. Both are closed New Year's Day, Thanksgiving, and Christmas.

Charlottesville

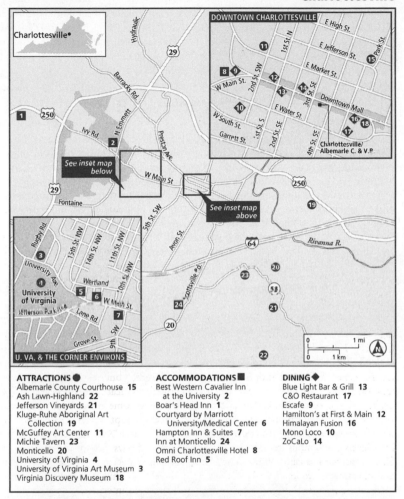

ATTRACTIONS ●
Albemarle County Courthouse **15**
Ash Lawn-Highland **22**
Jefferson Vineyards **21**
Kluge-Ruhe Aboriginal Art
    Collection **19**
McGuffey Art Center **11**
Michie Tavern **23**
Monticello **20**
University of Virginia **4**
University of Virginia Art Museum **3**
Virginia Discovery Museum **18**

ACCOMMODATIONS ■
Best Western Cavalier Inn
    at the University **2**
Boar's Head Inn **1**
Courtyard by Marriott
    University/Medical Center **6**
Hampton Inn & Suites **7**
Inn at Monticello **24**
Omni Charlottesville Hotel **8**
Red Roof Inn **5**

DINING ◆
Blue Light Bar & Grill **13**
C&O Restaurant **17**
Escafe **9**
Hamilton's at First & Main **12**
Himalayan Fusion **16**
Mono Loco **10**
ZoCaLo **14**

Be sure to pick up copies of *The Charlottesville Guide* (www.charlottesvilleguide. com), a slick, advertiser-supported booklet containing maps and information about the area's attractions, hotels, restaurants, and shops; *Charlottesville Arts & Entertainment* (www.artsmonthly.com), a monthly mini-magazine concentrating on the town's cultural life; the *Historic Downtown Dining, Entertainment and Shopping* brochure, a valuable aid in exploring the Downtown Mall; and the town's two free weekly alternative newspapers, *C-Ville Weekly* (www.c-ville.com) and *The Hook* (www.readthehook.com), both packed with restaurant listings and news about what's happening. *Bite & Sites*, a *C-Ville* supplement, reviews every restaurant in town.

GETTING THERE
BY CAR Charlottesville is on I-64 from east or west and U.S. 29 from north or south. I-64 connects with I-81 at Staunton and with I-95 at Richmond.

BY PLANE   US Airways, Delta, Northwest, and United fly commuter planes to **Charlottesville-Albemarle Airport (CHO)**, 201 Bowen Loop (© **434/973-8341;** www.gocho.com), north of town off U.S. 29. Taxis are available, and **Van on the Go** (© **877/973-7667** or 434/975-8267; www.vanonthego.com) provides shuttle service into town and shuttle service to the Washington, D.C., airports.

BY TRAIN   The **Amtrak** station is at 810 W. Main St. (© **800/872-7245;** www. amtrak.com), midway between the Downtown Mall and the university.

CITY LAYOUT

Just as it has three personalities, Charlottesville has three centers of interest to visitors. One is on the southeastern outskirts of town, where Monticello, Ash Lawn–Highland, and Michie Tavern are within 2 miles of each other. The second is the University of Virginia, at the western end of Main Street. Opposite the campus, between 13th Street and Elliewood Avenue, **The Corner** neighborhood is a typical campus enclave, with student-dominated restaurants, bookstores and clothing stores, and a dearth of parking spaces. The third area, **Historic Downtown Charlottesville,** a mile east of The Corner, is centered on the **Downtown Mall,** an 8-block, pedestrian-only strip at the eastern end of Main Street, between 2nd Street W and 7th Street E.

GETTING AROUND

The easiest way to get between the university and the Downtown Mall is on the **free trolley** operated by the Charlottesville Transit Service (CTS; © **434/296-7433**). It runs along Main Street every 10 to 15 minutes Monday to Saturday from 6:30am to midnight.

CTS also has bus service Monday through Saturday from 6:30am to 6:30pm throughout the city (but not to Monticello).

PARKING   On-street parking is extremely limited. In the Downtown Mall area, you can park free for 2 hours with merchant validation (take your ticket with you and get it stamped) in the garages on Market Street between 1st and 2nd streets NE and on Water Street between 2nd and 4th streets SE. The university's visitor parking garage is on the western side of the campus, on Emmet Street (U.S. 29 Business) a block south of University Avenue (which is the continuation of W. Main St.). On the eastern side of campus, two public garages are located opposite the University Hospital on Lee Street, off Jefferson Park Avenue. The Corner has public parking on Elliewood Avenue at 14th Street.

2 Where to Stay

The most convenient chain hotels to Monticello, Ash Lawn–Highland, and Michie Tavern are the **Holiday Inn Monticello** (© **800/465-4329** or 434/977-5100), a full-service hotel with restaurant and bar, and a **Sleep Inn and Suites** (© **800/424-6423** or 434/244-9969). Both are on 5th Street Extended just north of I-64. A few miles east, the **Comfort Inn Monticello** (© **800/424-6423** or 434/977-3300) enjoys a peaceful location on U.S. 250 at Exit 124 off I-64. The nearby **Hilton Garden Inn,** on U.S. 250 north of I-64 (© **877/STAY-HGI** or 434/979-4442), is a recent addition to Charlottesville's hotel inventory.

The traffic-signal encrusted commercial strip along U.S. 29 north of the U.S. 250 bypass (Charlottesville's major suburban growth area) is lined with an ever-expanding multitude of shopping centers, chain motels, and restaurants. Here you will find the **Doubletree Hotel Charlottesville** (© 800/494-7596 or 434/973-2121), the area's

> **Tips Avoiding the Crowds in Charlottesville**
>
> The two visitor centers operated by the **Charlottesville/Albemarle Convention and Visitors Bureau** make same-day, discounted hotel/motel reservations (see "Orientation & Getting Around," above). It's a good way to save, provided you are willing to take the risk of not having a room reserved in advance. Don't try this during University of Virginia events such as football games, graduation, and parents' weekends, when the town is packed and all accommodations are full. You may want to avoid being in Charlottesville then—or make your reservations as far in advance as possible. You will also pay premium rates at these times. Check the schedules at www.virginia.edu.

best-equipped suburban hotel, and a comfortable **Courtyard by Marriott** (© 800/321-2211 or 434/973-7100), which abuts the Fashion Square Mall. Others along U.S. 29 north include **Comfort Inn** (© 800/228-5150 or 434/293-6188), **Econo Lodge North** (© 800/553-2666 or 434/295-3185), **Hampton Inn** (© 800/426-7866 or 434/978-7888), **Holiday Inn University Area** (© 800/465-4329 or 434/293-9111), **Fairfield Inn by Marriott** (© 800/228-2800 or 434/964-9411), and **Super 8** (© 800/800-8000 or 434/973-0888).

Another good choice north of town is the **English Inn of Charlottesville,** 2000 Morton Dr. (at Emmet St.; © **800/786-5400** or 434/971-9900; www.englishinn charlottesville.com), a traditional English Tudor–style building housing a hospitable inn. It's off U.S. 29 Business just south of the U.S. 250 bypass.

EXPENSIVE

Boar's Head Inn 🏳🏳   Standing beside a picturesque lake and named for the traditional symbol of hospitality in Shakespeare's England, this university-owned property is one of the better all-around resorts in Virginia. The focal point is a 19th-century gristmill that was dismantled and brought here in the early 1960s. The place is loaded with antiques and art, and its plank flooring and huge old ceiling beams give ancient charm to the **Old Mill Room,** the resort's signature restaurant offering fine dining accompanied by an excellent selection of Virginia wines (ask about the weekend tasting events). The adjoining Bistro 1834 pub offers lighter fare and outdoor seating by the lake. The innlike guest rooms upstairs in the mill are charming and romantic, but if you want more space and a balcony, opt for a unit in one of the other lakeside structures, especially the Hunt Club building between the old mill and the resort's full-service spa. Guest quarters throughout are furnished with Colonial reproductions. Some units in the Ednam Hall, which does not face the lake, have kitchenettes. In addition to the spa and the resort's own tennis courts, guests can play at the adjacent Boar's Head Sports Club (17 tennis courts, two pools, state-of-the-art fitness center) and the university's nearby Birdwood Golf Course. The Boar's Head also is one of the best places in the region to take off on a hot-air balloon ride.

200 Ednam Dr. (P.O. Box 5307), Charlottesville, VA 22905. © **800/476-1988** or 434/296-2181. Fax 434/972-6019. www.boarsheadinn.com. 171 units. $161–$325 double; $335–$575 suite. Weekend, spa, and golf packages available. AE, DC, DISC, MC, V. U.S. 250 1 mile west of U.S. 29/250 bypass. **Amenities:** 2 restaurants; bar; 4 outdoor pools (1 heated); golf course; 6 tennis courts; health club; spa; Jacuzzi; free bicycles; children's programs; concierge; business center; shopping arcade; room service; massage; babysitting; laundry service. *In room:* A/C, TV, Wi-Fi, kitchen (11 units), fridge (stocked on request), coffeemaker, iron, safe.

MODERATE

Courtyard by Marriott University/Medical Center ⭐   Sitting at the eastern edge of the university, this modern yet Colonial-style brick building fits in with the ancient campus structures nearby. Like all Courtyards, it's designed with business travelers in mind, offering well-equipped rooms and a restaurant serving a breakfast buffet daily, dinner and libation Monday to Saturday. For the romantically inclined, six units have two-person Jacuzzi tubs almost surrounded by floor-to-ceiling mirrors.

1201 W. Main St. (at 12th St. NW), Charlottesville, VA 22903. ℭ 800/321-2211 or 434/977-1700. Fax 434/977-2600. www.courtyard.com. 137 units. $115–$199 double. AE, DC, DISC, MC, V. **Amenities:** Restaurant; bar; indoor pool; health club; Jacuzzi; room service; laundry service. *In room:* A/C, TV, Wi-Fi, fridge, coffeemaker, iron.

Hampton Inn & Suites *(Value)*   Also well-situated, this five-story brick structure is 3 blocks east of the Courtyard—far enough away from The Corner to avoid the crowds. The city's free trolley runs along Main Street, so it's easy to get from here to the campus and the Downtown Mall without having to drive. Murals of Monticello, the Rotunda, and other local scenes overlook a gas fireplace in the center of an elegant, two-story lobby. Eight of the suites here also have gas fireplaces, and all have separate bedrooms with TVs, and kitchens with microwave ovens and dishwashers. The medium-size rooms also come well equipped. Guests are treated to an extensive breakfast in a room off the lobby.

900 W. Main St. (at 10th St.), Charlottesville, VA 22903. ℭ 800/426-7866 or 434/923-8600. Fax 434/923-8601. www.hamptonsuites.com. 100 units. $124–$184 double; $159–$229 suite. Rates include full breakfast. AE, DC, DISC, MC, V. **Amenities:** Health club; coin-op washers and dryers. *In room:* A/C, TV, high-speed Internet, Wi-Fi, coffeemaker, iron.

The Omni Charlottesville Hotel ⭐⭐   You can't miss this seven-story, brick-and-glass structure with a soaring atrium lobby since its triangular shape towers above the western end of the Downtown Mall. The location is ideal since you can walk to the mall's many restaurants and shops and ride the free trolley to the university. The rooms are medium-size, and those on the upper floors have views over the city. At the street level, a fountain bubbles amid a tropical forest in the atrium lobby. With a view of the mall, a contemporary-style restaurant specializes in regional cuisine and local wines. It shares atrium space with a bistro-style sports bar. The Omni has extensive meeting space and draws more conventions and groups than most hotels here. Your small pet can share your room for a fee.

235 W. Main St. (at McIntire St.), Charlottesville, VA 22901. ℭ 800/843-6664 or 434/971-5500. Fax 434/979-4456. www.omnihotels.com. 204 units. $139–$229 double. AE, DC, DISC, MC, V. Self-parking $8. From I-64, take Exit 120 and follow Fifth Ridge St. (C.R. 631) north to McIntire St.; hotel is on the right. Small pets accepted ($50 fee). **Amenities:** Restaurant; bar; 2 pools (indoor and outdoor); health club; Jacuzzi; concierge; business center; room service; laundry service; concierge-level rooms. *In room:* A/C, TV, Wi-Fi, minibar, coffeemaker, iron.

INEXPENSIVE

Best Western Cavalier Inn at the University   Half a mile west of the Rotunda, this five-story, glass-and-steel motel is close to Scott Stadium, University Hall, and John Paul Jones Arena, the major sports venues. Although it has been around for more than 3 decades, it is maintained in top condition by the university, which owns it. The spacious motel-style rooms are entered through external walkways bordered by wrought-iron railings, which means a dearth of privacy unless you keep the drapes drawn across the floor-to-ceiling windows. A continental breakfast is served in a charming room off the lobby that doubles as the guest lounge. During summer you can cool off in a small outdoor pool. The hotel provides complimentary shuttle service to and from the airport and the Amtrak and bus stations.

105 Emmet St. (at W. Main St.; P.O. Box 5647), Charlottesville, VA 22905. ℂ 888/882-2129 or 434/296-8111. Fax 434/296-3523. www.cavalierinn.com. 118 units. $79–$119 double. Rates include continental breakfast. AE, DC, DISC, MC, V. From U.S. 29 bypass, go east on Ivy Rd. (U.S. 250 Business) 1 mile to hotel on the left. **Amenities:** Outdoor pool; business center; laundry service. *In room:* A/C, TV, Wi-Fi, coffeemaker, iron.

Red Roof Inn   In the middle of the action and a cut above most other members of this inexpensive chain, this clean, comfortable seven-story hotel is on the eastern edge of The Corner and across West Main Street from the university. Interior hallways lead to medium-size guest rooms, which contain cherrywood furniture. Despite being a bit small, the bathrooms have surprisingly ample vanity space. The Corner's many food outlets are steps away.

1309 W. Main St. (at 13th St.), Charlottesville, VA 22903. ℂ 800/843-7663 or 434/295-4333. Fax 434/295-2021. 135 units. $59–$135 double. AE, DC, DISC, MC, V. From U.S. 29 bypass, go east on Ivy Rd. (U.S. 250 Business) 1½ miles to hotel on the left. **Amenities:** Laundry service; coin-op washers and dryers. *In room:* A/C, TV, Wi-Fi.

BED & BREAKFAST ACCOMMODATIONS

Guesthouses Reservation Service, Inc., P.O. Box 5737, Charlottesville, VA 22905 (ℂ **434/979-7264;** www.va-guesthouses.com), handles bed-and-breakfast accommodations in elegant homes and private cottages. The office is open Monday through Friday from 9am to 5pm.

A block north of the Downtown Mall, the elegant **200 South Street Inn,** 200 South St. (ℂ **800/964-7008** or 434/979-0200; www.southstreetinn.com), occupies a stately 1856 house that has seen previous duty as private residence, girls finishing school, and brothel. More rooms are in an 1890-vintage house next door.

Despite its name, which in these parts conjures up images of barbecue, vegetarians and vegans will find their own hog heaven 23 miles south of town at **The White Pig Bed and Breakfast at Briar Creek Farm,** 5120 Irish Rd., Schuyler, VA 22696 (ℂ **434/ 831-1416;** www.thewhitepig.com). Norman, the owners' pet white pig, will never be over the coals, for breakfasts and Saturday dinners at this retreat are strictly vegan.

The Inn at Monticello ⓖ   The most convenient accommodations to Monticello, Ash Lawn–Highland, and Michie Tavern, this beautiful two-story stucco country house sits on 5 acres well back from Va. 20. The manicured lawn is ornamented in spring with blooming dogwood trees and azaleas. Boxwoods, tall shade and evergreen trees, shrubs, and a bubbling brook provide a lovely setting. You enter via the front porch into a sitting room with two fireplaces and a handsome collection of antiques. Guest rooms are individually decorated and have such special features as a working fireplace, private porch, or four-poster canopy bed—but no phones. Relax outdoors on the hammock or on the front veranda lined with wicker rockers. Afternoon snacks are accompanied by Virginia wine.

1188 Scottsville Rd. (Va. 20), Charlottesville, VA 22902. ℂ 877/735-2982 or 434/979-3593. Fax 434/296-1344. www.innatmonticello.com. 5 units. $135–$235 double. Rates include full breakfast. AE, MC, V. From I-64, take Va. 20 south and continue past the visitor center for about ¼ mile; the inn is on your right. **Amenities:** Access to nearby health club. *In room:* A/C, Wi-Fi, iron, no phone.

NEARBY COUNTRY INNS

Clifton ⓖⓖⓖ   You'll think you've arrived at Tara from *Gone With the Wind* when you see this stately manse, which is on the National Register of Historic Places.

Thomas Mann Randolph, husband of Thomas Jefferson's daughter, Martha, built it in 1799, originally as a trading post. Although neither as physically grand nor as well equipped as Keswick Hall at Monticello (see below), this is a more intimate retreat. In fact, a better comparison is **The Inn at Little Washington,** another outstanding restaurant with accommodations (p. 164). As there, ask and it shall be given here—from chauffeured golf outings to private tours of Monticello.

Indeed, the **Restaurant at Clifton** is among the best dining options in the Charlottesville area, providing an international a la carte menu (main courses $30) as well as fixed-priced tasting dinners (a relative bargain at $45–$75 per person). You can partake in the main dining room, which overlooks the backyard through a wall of paned windows, or at a table in the kitchen. Groups can reserve the big table for 24 in the basement wine cellar, one of Virginia's best.

Guest rooms and suites upstairs in the mansion are comfortable, but for more privacy and charm, opt for the estate's whitewashed stables, old carriage house, and Randolph's law office, which have been converted into romantic outposts. The split-level carriage house sports a grand piano and Jacuzzi, while the honeymoon cottage has a glass-walled bathroom.

1296 Clifton Inn Dr., Charlottesville, VA 22911. ⓒ **888/971-1800** or 434/971-1800. Fax 434/971-7098. www.clifton inn.net. 14 units. $255–$365 double; $340–$495 suite. Rates include full breakfast and afternoon tea. AE, DC, DISC, MC, V. Minimum 2-night stay weekends. From Charlottesville take U.S. 250 east 5 miles, turn right on N. Milton Rd. (C.R. 729), go ¼ mile to Clifton Inn Dr. on left. **Amenities:** Restaurant; bar; heated outdoor pool; clay tennis court; Jacuzzi; room service; massage; babysitting; laundry service. *In room:* A/C, TV, high-speed Internet, iron.

Keswick Hall at Monticello ✯✯✯

Although it's now owned and operated by Orient Express Hotels, this super-luxury estate was the creation of Sir Bernard Ashley, widower of famed designer Laura Ashley. Many of the 1912 vintage Italianate Crawford villa's rooms and suites have fireplaces, claw-foot tubs, and views over a golf course redesigned by Arnold Palmer, but don't expect to find these in the 14 least expensive "house rooms." All guests can roam around the vast public rooms on the main level, including a lounge with fireplace. English afternoon tea is free to guests. **Fosett's** restaurant, also espying the links, offers a mix of fine cuisine and excellent service plus special wine tastings of the estate's own vintage. Guests can also have lunch or dinner at the bistro in the adjoining Keswick Club, a private country club whose spa, fitness center, and indoor and outdoor pools are available. All these facilities make Keswick Hall more of a resort than the nearby Clifton (see above).

701 Country Club Dr., Keswick, VA 22947. ⓒ **800/274-5391** or 434/979-3440. Fax 434/977-4171. www.keswick. com. 48 units. $295–$550 double; $485–$600 suite. Rates include afternoon tea. AE, DC, MC, V. From Charlottesville take U.S. 250 or I-64 east to Shadwell (Exit 124); then Va. 22 east and follow signs to Keswick. **Amenities:** Restaurant; bar; 4 pools (1 indoor); golf course; 5 tennis courts; health club; spa; Jacuzzi; sauna; concierge; business center; room service; massage; babysitting; laundry service. *In room:* A/C, TV, high-speed Internet, Wi-Fi, iron.

Silver Thatch Inn ✯

Occupying a rambling white-clapboard Colonial-style house, a section of which dates back to Revolutionary days, this charming hostelry is located on a quiet road set on nicely landscaped grounds about 8 miles north of town. Attractively decorated with authentic 18th-century pieces, the original part of the building now serves as a cozy common room, where guests are invited for afternoon refreshments. The 1812 center part of the house is now one of the dining rooms of the **Silver Thatch Restaurant and Pub,** one of the area's most romantic dining venues. The list of Virginia and California wines is excellent. Three guest rooms are upstairs in the main house, while four others are in the President's Cottage. Named for Virginia's seven presidents, all are lovely, with down comforters on four-poster canopied beds, antique pine dressers, and carved walnut-and-mahogany armoires. Several rooms have working fireplaces. Telephones and TVs are available in the common areas.

3001 Hollymead Dr., Charlottesville, VA 22911. Ⓒ 800/261-0720 or 434/978-4686. Fax 434/973-6156. www.silver thatch.com. 7 units. $155–$190 double. Rates include full breakfast. AE, DC, DISC, MC, V. Take U.S. 29 about 8 miles north of town, turn right at traffic signal onto Hollymead Dr. to inn on the right. **Amenities:** Restaurant; bar; outdoor pool. *In room:* A/C, Wi-Fi, CD player, hair dryer, iron, no phone.

A NEARBY MOUNTAIN GETAWAY

Wintergreen Resort   With 6,700 of its 11,000 acres dedicated to the remaining undisturbed forest, this recreational real estate development offers year-round vacation activities in a Blue Ridge Mountain setting. The big draws here include skiing, golf (the short, narrow fairways of Devils Knob course follow the cool summit of a 4,000-ft.-high mountain), horseback riding, mountain biking, swimming in the lake, canoeing, and an adventure center with rock climbing, skateboarding, wintertime snow tubing, and other activities. Wintergreen also has a Nature Foundation that offers guided hikes, seminars, and camps for children. There's music in the cool air, too, since **Wintergreen Performing Arts, Inc.** (Ⓒ **434/325-8292;** www.wintergreenperformingarts.org) turns a ski slope into an amphitheater for the Wintergreen Summer Music Festival in July and weekend concerts throughout the summer.

The resort's focal point is the tastefully lodgelike Inn, which has a huge gristmill wheel occupying the two-story registration area. Most accommodations are in small enclaves scattered throughout the property, but there are also three- to seven-bedroom homes, one- to four-bedroom condos, and studios and lodge rooms. Since the homes and condos are privately owned, furnishings are highly individual, ranging from country quaint to sleek and sophisticated. Each condo is appointed with a modern kitchen, living area, bathroom for each bedroom, and balcony or patio (the mountain views are superb); most have working fireplaces.

P.O. Box 706, Wintergreen, VA 22958. Ⓒ 800/266-2444 or 434/325-2200. Fax 434/325-8004. www.wintergreen resort.com. 300 units. $139–$185 double; $159–$755 condos and homes. Recreational packages available. DISC, MC, V. Take I-64 west to Exit 107 and follow U.S. 250 west; turn left onto C.R. 151 south, and then right on C.R. 644 for 4½ miles to resort. It's about 43 miles from Charlottesville. **Amenities:** 5 restaurants; 3 bars; 5 pools (1 indoor); 3 golf courses; 24 tennis courts (3 indoor); health club; spa; watersports equipment/rentals; bike rental; children's programs; concierge (winter only); activities desk; business center; shopping arcade; babysitting; laundry service. *In room:* A/C, TV, kitchen, coffeemaker, iron.

3 Where to Dine

Charlottesville has more than 200 restaurants—so many that locals brag they have more restaurants per capita than any city in America. For a complete rundown, pick up a copy of *Bite & Sites,* a free restaurant guide supplement to *C-Ville Weekly* (www.c-ville.com), at the visitor centers (see "Visitor Information," earlier in this chapter). There are also lists and reviews in *The Hook* (www.readthehook.com), the other free newspaper found in boxes all over town.

This area's finest and most romantic dining is at Clifton, Keswick, and the Silver Thatch Inn (see "Nearby Country Inns," above).

The Corner opposite the university has several restaurants catering to the college crowd. The best are on Elliewood Avenue, a block-long, alleylike street off University Avenue. Just stroll these neighborhoods and pick your place. You can tell by the crowds which are "in" and which aren't.

I seldom go farther in search of a good meal than along Main Street on the Downtown Mall, which has restaurants to suit every taste and pocketbook. I especially enjoy strolling along the mall during warm weather when most restaurants have tables under the shade trees on Main Street, thus turning this pedestrian-only strip into a lively festival. All restaurants post their menus outside, so you can pick and choose depending on your own tastes.

For a caffeine fix, I drop into **The Mudhouse,** 213 W. Main St. (© **434/984-6833**), a quintessential college-town coffeehouse. You'll find me having a more substantial breakfast at **The Nook,** 415 E. Main St. (© **434/295-6665**), which has been serving inexpensive meals for more than half a century. Also still going strong is the soda fountain in **Timberlake Drugs,** 322 E. Main St. (© **434/295-9155**), which has been in business since 1890.

Blue Light Bar & Grill ⟨ SEAFOOD   You'll get the freshest seafood in town at this storefront restaurant on the Downtown Mall. Atop a mound of ice behind the long bar to the left as you enter wait four types of oysters—from Chincoteague; Long Island, New York; and the Pacific Northwest—waiting to be consumed raw or steamed on the half shell. If they won't do for an appetizer, order the crab cocktail with huge chunks of blue crabmeat served with drawn butter. Among the Asian-influenced main courses, many of them creative, a good bet is the monkfish coated with crushed citrus, lightly fried, and served under rice and a slightly spicy Thai-style basil sauce.

120 E. Main St. (at 2nd St.). © **434/295-1223**. Reservations recommended on weekends. Main courses $17–$20. AE, DISC, MC, V. Sun–Thurs 5–10pm; Fri–Sat 5–11pm.

C&O Restaurant ⟨⟨ INTERNATIONAL   A block south of the Downtown Mall's eastern end, this unprepossessing brick front might make you think twice, but don't be deterred, for this unusual setting has been home to acclaimed fare for more than 3 decades. From all appearances, the creaky floors in this charming old building were around in Jefferson's day. Changing monthly, the menu is basically country French but ranges across the globe—from Thailand to New Mexico and Louisiana—for additional inspiration. Many patrons stop in the downstairs Bistro, a rustic setting of exposed brick and rough-hewn barn wood, or at the outdoor patio in warm weather, while others proceed upstairs to a more formal venue or to the covered garden. All three dining areas have candlelight, tables adorned with attractive flower arrangements, and the same excellent menu choices. The C&O's list has won a *Wine Spectator* award for excellence. This is the best spot in town for a midnight snack, served daily until 1am.

515 E. Water St. (between 5th and 6th sts. SE). © **434/971-7044**. Reservations recommended (not accepted in downstairs Bistro or patio). Main courses $15–$30. AE, MC, V. Sun–Thurs 5–10pm; Fri–Sat 5–11pm. Closed 1st week in Jan, July 4th, and Dec 25.

Escafe ⟨ *Value* INTERNATIONAL   This lively bistro has been one of the town's most popular spots for an exciting meal since 1995. The constantly changing menu features salads and sandwiches, and the stellar main courses include such items as spicy Thai green- and red-chile bowl of vegetables and noodles, to which you can add the meat or seafood of your choice.

102 Old Preston Ave. (western end of the Downtown Mall). © **434/295-8668**. Reservations accepted only for groups. Sandwiches $9–$10; main courses $15–$22. AE, DC, DISC, MC, V. Tues–Wed 5:30pm–midnight; Thurs–Sat 5:30pm–2am; Sun 4:30pm–midnight.

Hamilton's at First & Main ⟨⟨ CONTEMPORARY AMERICAN   Marble-top tables, crisp linen napkins, and fresh flowers let you know you're in for some high style at this urbane bistro in the Downtown Mall. It's the kind of place you'd take a special date, but not necessarily propose marriage. The menu changes frequently, but if offered, the pan-roasted crab cakes on jasmine rice and red-pepper purée will demonstrate the chef's prowess. There is usually a dish or two with Asian influences, such as an Indian masala-style rice stir-fry with chicken and shrimp and a tomato–coconut milk sauce. The daily vegetarian blue-plate special is very tasty, too.

101 W. Main St. (at 1st St., midway along the Downtown Mall). © **434/295-6649.** Reservations recommended. Main courses $19–$32. AE, DC, DISC, MC, V. Mon–Sat 11:30am–3pm and 5:30–10pm.

Himalayan Fusion *Finds* NEPALESE/TIBETAN/VEGAN   Operated by a family of émigrés from Nepal, this casual bistro serves a mix of spicy cuisines from the Himalayans. Some dishes are familiar Indian curries, but I especially enjoyed those from Nepal, in which the ginger, coriander, and garlic flavors were strong enough not to be overwhelmed by curry. The Tibetan-style steamed *momo* dumplings were especially good; I ordered the vegetarian version but wished I had chosen them with shrimp. Vegetarians and vegans will do well here.

520 E. Main St. (east of 5th St., southeast along the Downtown Mall). © **434/293-3120.** Reservations recommended on weekends. Main courses $8–$16. AE, DISC, MC, V. Mon–Thurs 11:30am–2:30pm and 5:30–10pm; Fri 11:30am–2:30pm and 5:30–11pm; Sat noon–3pm and 5:30–11pm; Sun noon–3pm and 5:30–10pm.

Mono Loco *Finds* LATIN AMERICAN   This lively little bistro—10 tables indoors, a few more outside in warm weather—draws its inspiration from Latin America. Only names will be familiar, however, for creativity is on the loose here. I ordered a shrimp-and-bacon burrito that turned out to be a huge burrito shell from which sprang an explosion of delightful flavors. For dessert I couldn't resist bananas Castro served with sugared tortilla strips and quickly disappearing vanilla ice cream. The kitchen is tiny, so don't be in a hurry on a busy night.

200 W. Water St. (at 2nd St. SW). © **434/979-0688.** Reservations recommended on weekends. Main courses $12–$19. AE, DC, DISC, MC, V. Mon 11am–2:30pm and 5–9pm; Tues–Fri 11am–2:30pm and 5–10pm; Sat 5–10pm; Sun 5–9pm.

ZoCaLo *Finds* LATIN AMERICAN   You may see national celebrities among the local foodies dining at this high-energy bistro, whose bar draws a lively crowd of late-20s and 30-something professionals. The chef-owners draw their culinary inspiration from Latin America, offering the likes of a super-tender pork loin rubbed in Latino spices and served under a delicious pineapple mole sauce and along with Brazilian-style shredded collards and a sweet-potato cake. Smoking is permitted neither inside nor at the substantial outdoor seating until the kitchen stops serving dinner.

201 E. Main St. (in Central Plaza at 2nd St. E). © **434/977-4944.** Reservations recommended. Main courses $18–$25. AE, DISC, MC, V. Tues–Thurs 5:30–10pm; Fri–Sat 5:30–11pm; Sun 5:30–10pm; bar until 2am daily.

4 What to See & Do

The visitor centers of the Charlottesville/Albemarle Convention and Visitors Bureau (see "Visitor Information," earlier in this chapter) sell a **Presidents' Pass,** a discount block ticket combining admission to Monticello, Michie Tavern, and Ash Lawn–Highland. It costs $26 for all ages. The attractions validate the tickets when you show up, so there's no time limit on when you must use the pass. They don't advertise the fact, but the three attractions also sell the Presidents' Pass. See the box "Getting the Most out of Charlottesville," below, for advice on how best to use your time.

THE TOP ATTRACTIONS

Ash Lawn–Highland 🅐🅐   Fifth president James Monroe fought in the Revolution, was wounded in Trenton, and went on to hold more public offices than any other president. Monroe's close friendship with Thomas Jefferson brought him to Charlottesville from Fredericksburg (see chapter 5). Monroe purchased 1,000 acres adjacent to Monticello in 1793 and with Jefferson's help built an estate he called Highland. (Later owners added Ash Lawn to the name in 1838 and a two-story addition in 1882.) Before Monroe could settle in, Washington named him minister to France and sent him to Paris for 3 years. By the time he returned, he was suffering financial difficulties, and his "cabin castle" developed along more modest lines than originally intended. When Monroe left the presidency in 1825, his debts totaled $75,000, and he was forced to sell his farm. He spent his final years near Leesburg and in New York City.

Today, Monroe's 535-acre estate is owned and maintained as a working farm by his alma mater, the College of William and Mary in Williamsburg. Colonial crafts demonstrations recall the elements of daily life on the Monroe plantation. Sheep and cattle graze in the fields, while peacocks delight young visitors. The basement kitchen, the plantation office, the overseer's cottage, restored slave quarters, and the old smokehouse also remain. On a 30-minute house tour, you'll see many of the family's original furnishings and artifacts and learn a great deal about the fifth president. Allow another 30 minutes to explore the grounds and gift shop on your own.

Among many special events taking place at Ash Lawn–Highland, the outdoor **Ash Lawn Summer Opera Festival** (🕻 434/293-4500; www.ashlawnopera.org) features opera and Broadway shows and concerts.

C.R. 795. 🕻 434/293-9539. www.ashlawnhighland.org. Admission $9 adults, $8 seniors, $5 children 6–11, free for children 5 and younger. Apr–Oct daily 9am–6pm; Nov–Mar daily 11am–5pm. 30-min. house tours depart every 10–15 min. Closed Jan 1, Thanksgiving, and Dec 25. From Va. 20, follow the directions to Monticello; Ash Lawn–Highland is 2½ miles past Monticello on James Monroe Pkwy. (C.R. 795).

Michie Tavern ca. 1784 🅐🅐   In 1746, Scotsman "Scotch John" Michie (pronounced "Mickey") purchased 1,152 acres of land from Patrick Henry's father, and in 1784, Michie's son, William, built this tavern on a well-traveled stagecoach route at Earlysville, 17 miles northwest of Charlottesville. A wealthy businesswoman, Josephine Henderson, saw its value as a historic structure and in 1927 had it moved to its present location and reconstructed. Michie Tavern stands today as a tribute to early preservationists. Included in the 30-minute living-history tours are the **Virginia Wine Museum** and reproductions of the "dependencies"—log kitchen, dairy, smokehouse, icehouse, root cellar, and "necessary" (note the not-so-soft corncobs). The general store has been re-created, along with excellent crafts and clothing shops. Behind the store is a gristmill that has operated continuously since 1797.

Plan your visit to Michie Tavern to coincide with lunchtime, when a buffet is served to weary travelers in the Ordinary, a converted log cabin with original hand-hewn walls and beamed ceilings. The fare is typical Southern dishes such as fried chicken, black-eyed peas, and cornbread. They accept American Express, MasterCard, and Visa. During summer you can skip the buffet and order inexpensive barbecue sandwiches, hot dogs, ice cream, and other snacks at the Spring House, an outdoor fast-food stand behind the Ordinary.

683 Thomas Jefferson Pkwy. (Va. 683). 🕻 434/977-1234. www.michietavern.com. Admission $8 adults, $7 seniors, $3 children 6–11, free for children 5 and younger. Buffet meals $15 adults, $7.25 children; summer snack bar $3–$6

(Tips) **Getting the Most Out of Charlottesville**

Monticello, Ash Lawn–Highland, and Michie Tavern are within 2 miles of each other near the **Monticello Visitors Center,** on Va. 20 just south of I-64 (see "Visitor Information," earlier in this chapter), on the southeastern outskirts of town. You'll need a full day to fully take in all three.

The Visitors Center sells a **Presidents' Pass** ticket to the three attractions ($26 per adult, no discount for children). You should also take in the center's marvelous "Thomas Jefferson at Monticello" exhibit and see a free 30-minute video about Jefferson, which shows at 11am and 2pm daily, more frequently during summer. Both will add to your visit.

Tickets to Monticello have specific house tour times printed on them, which has reduced the long lines of people waiting to go through the mansion on spring and summer weekends and during the October "leaf season." It's a good idea to buy your tickets as early as possible so you'll have the widest choice of tour times. You can buy Monticello tickets in advance at www.monticello.org.

I would spend the morning at Monticello, then head to nearby **Michie Tavern,** where you can tour the tavern and the Virginia Wine Museum, and have lunch (expect a wait on weekends and in Oct). In the afternoon, head for Monroe's **Ash Lawn Highland,** 2½ miles away, which will take about an hour to see.

If you have time left over, head for the **University of Virginia.** Otherwise, plan to tour the campus and see the town's other sights the next day.

(most items). Daily 9am–5pm (last tour 4:20pm). Restaurant daily 11:15am–3:30pm. Snack bar mid-June to Labor Day daily 11am–4:20pm. 30-min. tavern-museum tours during dining room hours Apr–Oct; self-guided tours Nov–Mar. Closed Jan 1 and Dec 25. From the visitor center, go south on Va. 20, turn left at Thomas Jefferson Pkwy. (Va. 683); Michie Tavern is about 1 mile on right.

Monticello ✹✹✹   Pronounced "Mon-ti-*chel*-lo," the home Thomas Jefferson built over 40 years, from 1769 to 1809, is a highlight of any visit to Virginia. This architectural masterpiece was the first Virginia plantation manse to sit atop a mountain rather than beside a river. Because the Georgian architecture that characterized Jefferson's time was British, Jefferson rejected it, opting instead for the 16th-century Italian style of Andrea Palladio. Later, during his 5-year term as minister to France, he was influenced by the homes of nobles at the court of Louis XVI, and after returning home in 1789, he incorporated features of the Parisian buildings he so admired.

Today, the house has been restored as closely as possible to its appearance during Jefferson's retirement years. Jefferson or his family owned nearly all its furniture and other household objects. The vegetable garden extends to its original 1,000-foot length, and Mulberry Row—where slaves and free artisans lived and labored in light industrial shops, such as a joinery, smokehouse-dairy, blacksmith shop–nailery, and carpenter's shop—has been excavated.

Jefferson's grave is in the family burial ground, which is still in use. After visiting the graveyard, you can take a shuttle bus to the visitor parking lot or walk through the

Fun Fact The Legacy of Thomas Jefferson

The phrase "Renaissance man" might have been coined to describe Thomas Jefferson. Perhaps our most important founding father, he was a lawyer, architect, scientist, musician, writer, educator, and horticulturist.

After drafting the Declaration of Independence, Jefferson served as governor of Virginia, ambassador to France, secretary of state, and president for two terms, during which he nearly doubled the size of the United States by engineering the Louisiana Purchase from France. He sent Meriwether Lewis and William Clark on their famous exploration of the territory.

Yet despite all his achievements, Jefferson ordered that his gravestone be inscribed: "Here Was Buried Thomas Jefferson/Author Of The Declaration Of American Independence/Of The Statute Of Virginia For Religious Freedom/And Father Of The University Of Virginia."

Jefferson was 83 when he died at Monticello on July 4, 1826, 50 years to the day after his Declaration of Independence was signed at Philadelphia. Ironically, his fellow revolutionary but later heated political enemy John Adams lay on his own deathbed in Massachusetts. Unaware that Jefferson had died earlier, Adams's last words were: "Jefferson survives."

woods via a delightful path. There is a lovely wooded picnic area with tables and grills on the premises, and lunch fare can be purchased from April through October.

You must take a guided tour to enter the house. See "Getting the Most Out of Charlottesville," above, for advice about buying tickets. Optional tours of the plantation and grounds are available all year, and during summer you can send your young ones on 30-minute tours specifically designed for children.

Off Va. 53. ℂ **434/984-9822** for information, 434/984-9844 on weekends, or 434/984-9800 for recorded information. www.monticello.org. Admission $15 adults, $7 children 6–11, free for children 5 and younger. Mar–Oct daily 8am–5pm; Nov–Feb daily 9am–4:30pm. 30-min. house tours run continuously. Closed Dec 25. From the visitor center go south on Va. 20, turn left on Va. 53, and then 2 miles to entrance.

THE UNIVERSITY OF VIRGINIA 🪶🪶🪶

One of the world's most beautiful college campuses, Jefferson's **University of Virginia** is graced with spacious lawns, serpentine-walled gardens, colonnaded pavilions, and a classical Rotunda inspired by the Pantheon in Rome. Jefferson regarded its creation as one of his three greatest achievements—all the more remarkable since it was started in his 73rd year. He was, in every sense, the university's father, since he conceived it, wrote its charter, raised money for its construction, drew the plans, selected the site, laid the cornerstone in 1817, supervised construction, served as the first rector, selected the faculty, and created the curriculum. His good friends, Monroe and Madison, sat with him on the first board, and Madison succeeded him as rector, serving for 8 years.

The focal point of the university is the **Rotunda** (on University Ave. at Rugby Rd.), restored as Jefferson designed it. Enter on the ground level on the "village side"—that is, the side facing away from University Avenue. A student will be on duty at a desk to give you information, directions, and brochures. If you're up to it, be sure to climb the three stories to Jefferson's magnificent lecture room under the dome on the top floor. The Rotunda is open daily from 9am to 4:45pm except on holidays. Admission is free but donations are suggested.

Some 600 feet of tree-dotted lawn extends from the Rotunda's south portico to what is now Cabell Hall, designed at the turn of the 20th century by Stanford White. Pavilions on either side of the lawn are still used for faculty housing, each of a different architectural style "to serve as specimens for the Architectural lecturer." Behind each are a garden (originally used by faculty members to grow vegetables and keep livestock) and the original student dormitories, used—and greatly coveted—by students today. The room Edgar Allan Poe occupied is furnished as it would have been in 1826 and is open to visitors.

Paralleling the lawn are more rows of student rooms called the Ranges. Equally spaced within each of the Ranges are "hotels," originally used to accommodate student dining. Each hotel represented a different country, and students would have to both eat the food and speak the language of that country. Although a wonderful idea on Jefferson's part, it lasted only a short while since everyone wanted to eat French but not German.

When school is in session, students lead 45-minute **campus tours** daily at 10, 11am, 2, 3, and 4pm from the Rotunda. The tours are first-come, first-served, but call © **434/982-3200** to make sure there will be one when you're here. Self-guided walking tour brochures are available in the Rotunda (© **434/924-3239**) and from the university's **Visitor Information Center** (© **434/924-7166**), which is located not on campus but in the University Police Headquarters, on Ivy Road (U.S. 250 Business) just east of the U.S. 29/U.S. 250 bypass. The visitor center is open 24 hours a day. See "Getting Around," earlier in this chapter, for parking information.

Note: The university is closed 3 weeks around Christmas.

THE DOWNTOWN MALL

After I've spent a morning seeing the university, I like to have lunch and poke my head into the shops along Charlottesville's **Downtown Mall,** the pedestrian-only section of Main Street between 2nd and 7th streets. Although the strip is the country's oldest pedestrian mall, it lacks historical charm, and it may seem underwhelming during the cold winter months. But the mall changes character completely in warm weather, when restaurant tables line its entire length and it becomes the city's lively focal point. Fountains, park benches, shade trees, a tiny kiosk bar, theaters, and music-making buskers enhance it all. It's especially active when nationally known artists are in concert in the **Charlottesville Pavilion**, on the mall's eastern end (see "Charlottesville After Dark," later in this chapter).

The mall's 120 boutiques and art galleries make it the best place in Charlottesville to shop. You'll instinctively know the best stores when you pass them, but don't pass up the **Yves Delorme Outlet,** where you might find French linens at 75% off their regular prices. I usually walk the entire length in one direction just to take it all in, and then come back to specific shops and restaurants that have drawn my attention. The "Historic Downtown Dining, Entertainment and Shopping" brochure available at the visitor center is an invaluable aid. Call © **434/296-8548** for mall events.

MORE ATTRACTIONS IN TOWN

Albemarle County Courthouse   The center of village activity in Colonial days, the courthouse in the historic downtown area features a facade and portico dating from the Civil War. There's no tour offered, but you can take a glance at Jefferson's will in the County Office Building. It's easy to imagine Jefferson, Madison, and Monroe talking politics under the lawn's huge shade trees.

501 E. Jefferson St. (at 5th St. E). 🅒 **434/296-5822**. Free admission. Mon–Fri 9am–5pm.

The Kluge-Ruhe Aboriginal Art Collection 🙌   This museum, about 3 miles east of Charlottesville, houses one of the largest public collections of Australian aboriginal art in the world. It includes the gatherings of wealthy American businessman John W. Kluge, who began collecting in 1988, and of the late Professor Edward L. Ruhe of Kansas University, who began collecting while visiting Australia as a Fulbright Scholar in 1965. Kluge bought Ruhe's collection and archives and later gave it all to the University of Virginia.

400 Worrell Dr. 🅒 **434/244-0234**. www.virginia.edu/kluge-ruhe. Free admission. Tues–Sat 9am–3pm. 40-min. guided tour Sat 10:30am. Take U.S. 250 east to Pantops; take a right at the stoplight on Worrell Dr.; follow the driveway on the right to the white house at the top of the hill.

McGuffey Art Center   Local artists and craftspeople work in their studios in this early-20th-century school building a block north of the Downtown Mall. Art is also exhibited and for sale in the center's three galleries. Shows change monthly.

201 2nd St. NW (between High and Market sts.). 🅒 **434/295-7973**. www.mcguffeyartcenter.com. Free admission. Tues–Sat 10am–5pm; Sun 1–5pm.

University of Virginia Art Museum   This nationally accredited museum has permanent exhibits of American and European painting, sculpture, decorative art, and photography from the 15th to 21st centuries, ancient Mediterranean pieces, and Asian art. A highlight is its "Age of Thomas Jefferson" collection. The museum has an active temporary exhibit schedule.

Thomas H. Bayly Building, 155 Rugby Rd. 🅒 **434/924-3592**. www.virginia.edu/artmuseum. Free admission (donations welcome). Tues–Sun 1–5pm.

Virginia Discovery Museum 🅚🅘🅓🅢   The Virginia Discovery Museum is a place of enchantment, offering numerous hands-on exhibits and programs for children ages 1 through 10. Here, they can ride a miniature carousel and dress up as firefighters, soldiers, police, and other grown-ups. The Showalter Cabin, an authentic structure that once stood on a site in Mt. Crawford, Virginia, is outfitted with the simple furnishings appropriate to an early-19th-century lifestyle. An arts-and-crafts studio, an active beehive, and a changing series of traveling and made-on-site exhibits round out the fun.

524 E. Main St. (east end of Downtown Mall). 🅒 **434/977-1025**. www.vadm.org. Admission $4. Tues–Sat 10am–5pm; Sun 1–5pm. Closed Jan 1, day before Thanksgiving, and Dec 24–25.

JAMES MADISON'S MONTPELIER 🙌🙌

Set on 2,700-acre estate, facing the Blue Ridge Mountains 25 miles northeast of Charlottesville, **Montpelier** was home to President James Madison and his equally famous wife, Dolley. Madison was just 26 in 1776 when he ensured that religious freedom would be included in the Virginia Declaration of Rights, and his efforts at the federal Constitutional Convention in 1787 earned him the title "Father of the Constitution." Madison became secretary of state under his good friend Thomas Jefferson in 1801 and succeeded Jefferson as president in 1809. He and Dolley fled the White House in the face of advancing British troops during the War of 1812.

Two structures remain here from their time: the manor house and the Ice House Temple (built over a well and used to store ice). William du Pont, Sr., bought the

---

Tips **Take the Scenic Route to Montpelier**

I go between Montpelier and Charlottesville via Va. 20, one of the state's most scenic drives. This 25-mile-long **Presidents Route** more or less follows the same winding road Thomas Jefferson, James Monroe, and James Madison took when they visited each other. You'll pass near Barboursville Vineyards, Horton Cellars, and Burnley Vineyards on the way (see "On the Wine Trail," below).

---

estate in 1901 and enlarged the mansion to 55 rooms (thereby almost engulfing the Madison original); covered it in stucco; and added barns, staff houses, a sawmill, a blacksmith shop, a train station, a dairy, and greenhouses. His wife created a 2-acre formal garden, and daughter Marion du Pont Scott later built the steeplechase course in front of the mansion and initiated the **Montpelier Hunt Races,** which are still held here on the first Saturday in November.

The National Trust for Historic Preservation now owns the property and is in the process of a meticulous, multiyear restoration, which already has stripped away the du Ponts' additions to the mansion, reducing it to the 22-room brick version the Madisons occupied in 1820s. The house is open to the public during the project, with 30-minute tours explaining the near-archaeological aspects of the work.

Meanwhile, you can see the Madison's furnishings and many personal belongings (including a lock of James' hair and a bust of Dolley rendered in 1818 by John William Coffee) in the visitor center's "Treasures of Montpelier" exhibit. The center also has an exhibit showing what the house looked like during its du Pont incarnation. There's a snack bar, too, plus special children's programs during summer.

Audiotapes, included in the price of admission, guide you through the property.

You'll need 2 hours to see everything, and you'll do a bit of walking, so wear comfortable shoes. Also call ahead for a schedule of special events, such as the races in November, birthday celebrations for James (Mar 16) and Dolley (May 20), the Montpelier Wine Festival in May, and Constitution Day (Sept 17).

11407 Constitution Hwy. (Va. 20), Montpelier Station. © 540/672-2728. www.montpelier.org. Admission $12 adults, $6 children 6–14, free for children 5 and younger. Apr–Oct daily 9:30am–5:30pm; Nov–Mar daily 9:30am–4:30pm. 30-min. house tours on the hour and half-hour (last tour 30-min. before closing). Closed Jan 1, Thanksgiving, Dec 24–25, and Dec 31. Take Va. 20 north for 25 miles.

ON THE WINE TRAIL

Thomas Jefferson's dream of producing quality wines in Virginia has come true, for along with the Hunt Country in northern Virginia (see chapter 4), the Charlottesville area today is one of the state's two top winemaking regions. Be sure to pick up a brochure for the **Monticello Wine Trail** (www.monticellowinetrail.org) at one of the visitor centers; it gives information about all the nearby wineries including their business hours.

To sample all you want and not risk driving home tipsy, take a full day or afternoon excursion with **Arcady Vineyard Wine Tasting Tours** (© **434/872-9475;** www.arcadyvineyard.com). Erika and Chris Goddell, owners of Arcady Vineyard, do all the driving while taking you to and from local vineyards. They do not accept marketing or trades with the wineries, and thus are free to visit to the best, not those who pay the most. Their full-day tours cost $100 per person Monday through Thursday, $115 per person on weekends. The day trip includes a silver-service picnic lunch; the afternoon tours, a platter of appetizers. Reservations are required.

Most convenient of the local wineries to visit on your own is **Jefferson Vineyards,** 1353 Thomas Jefferson Pkwy. (Va. 53; ℭ **434/977-3042;** www.jeffersonvineyards. com), between Monticello and Ash Lawn–Highland. Thomas Jefferson and an Italian named Filippo Mazzei planted grapes on this property in 1774. Consider stopping for a taste after your day's sightseeing. From there you can drive south on C.R. 795 to the **Kluge Estate Winery** (ℭ **434/977-3895;** www.klugeestate.com), an up-and-coming vineyard whose owner, the well-heeled Patricia Kluge, has had success with her sparkling wines. You can browse her **Kluge Estate Farm Shop,** purveying the wines and other Virginia products.

If you're going to James Madison's Montpelier (see above), the award-winning **Horton Vineyards** (ℭ **800/829-4633** or 540/832-7440; www.hvwine.com) is 8 miles east of U.S. 29 on U.S. 33 near Gordonsville. Between there and U.S. 29, **Barboursville Vineyards** (ℭ **540/832-3824;** www.barboursvillewine.com), on C.R. 177 near the intersection of Va. 20 and Va. 33, was Virginia's first modern winery, having been established in 1976 by the largest family-owned Italian winemaker. Nearer to Charlottesville on C.R. 641 west of Va. 20, **Burnley Vineyards** (ℭ **540/832-2828;** www.burnley wines.com) is one of the oldest wineries in the area.

ATTRACTIONS IN THE LYNCHBURG AREA

When Jefferson wanted to get away from it all, he headed south to Poplar Forest, his country retreat near the James River town of Lynchburg, today best known as home to the late Rev. Jerry Falwell and his fundamentalist Liberty University. Lynchburg is a base from which to explore not just Poplar Forest but one of Patrick Henry's plantation homes and the village of Appomattox Court House, where Robert E. Lee surrendered to Ulysses S. Grant. Also nearby are memorials to the great African-American leader Booker T. Washington and to the D-day invasion during World War II.

Contact the **Lynchburg Convention and Visitors Bureau,** 2015 Memorial Ave., Lynchburg, VA 24501 (ℭ **800/723-5821** or 434/845-5966; www.discoverlynchburg. org), for information about the city.

Note that some of these attractions are closer to Roanoke (see chapter 8) than to Charlottesville.

Appomattox Court House National Historical Park ⌘⌘⌘   Here, in the parlor of Wilmer McLean's home 2 miles north of Appomattox, Robert E. Lee surrendered the Army of Northern Virginia to Ulysses S. Grant on April 9, 1865, thus effectively ending the bitter Civil War. Today, the 20 or so houses, stores, courthouse, and tavern that made up the village then called Appomattox Court House have been restored by the National Park Service and are an essential ingredient of any Civil War tour of Virginia. You will need at least 2 hours to visit the restored houses and walk the country lanes in the rural stillness where these events took place. Start by picking up a map of the park and a self-guided tour booklet at the visitor center in the courthouse. Upstairs, a 15-minute slide presentation and museum exhibits include excerpts from the diaries and letters of Civil War soldiers. Allow at least 2 hours to do that and visit McLean's house, Clover Hill Tavern, Meeks' Store, the Woodson Law Office, the courthouse (totally reconstructed), the jail, and Kelly House. The Confederates laid down their arms and rolled up their battle flags on the now-restored road through the village. There's a full schedule of ranger programs during the summer.

The present day town of Appomattox, 2 miles south of the park, has restaurants, budget motels, and bed-and-breakfasts. The **Appomattox Visitor Center** is in the old train station at 214 Main St. (© **877/258-4739** or 434/352-8999; www.tour appomattox.com). It's open daily from 9am to 5pm.

Va. 24 (P.O. Box 218), Appomattox. © **434/352-8987.** www.nps.gov/apco. Admission Memorial Day to Labor Day $4 adults, free for children 15 and younger (maximum $10 per vehicle); rest of year $3 adults, free for children 16 and younger (maximum $5 per vehicle). America the Beautiful and National Park Service passes accepted. Daily 8:30am–5pm. Closed Jan 1, Thanksgiving, and Dec 25. From Lynchburg take U.S. 460 east 22 miles to Va. 24 north.

Booker T. Washington National Monument

At this memorial to one of America's great African-American leaders, you can conjure up the setting of Booker T. Washington's childhood in reconstructed buildings and demonstrations of farm life and slavery in Civil War–era Virginia. Although Washington called his boyhood home a plantation, the Burroughs farm was small, at 207 acres and never with more than 11 slaves. His mother was the cook, and the cabin where he was born was also the kitchen. His family left the farm in 1865, when he was 9. He determinedly sought an education and walked most of the 500 miles from his home in West Virginia to Hampton Institute, now Hampton University (see "An Easy Excursion to Hampton & Newport News," in chapter 10). He worked his way through school and achieved prominence as an educator, founder of Tuskegee Institute in Alabama, author, and advisor to presidents. This monument was established to honor his life and work in 1956, a century after he was born. Begin at the visitor center, which offers a slide show and a map with a self-guided plantation tour and nature walks that wind through the original Burroughs property. Guided tours lasting between 30 and 45 minutes are given daily at 11am and 2pm.

12130 Booker T. Washington Hwy. (Va. 122), Hardy. © **540/721-2094.** www.nps.gov/bowa. Free admission. Daily 9am–5pm. Tours daily 11am and 2pm. Closed Jan 1, Thanksgiving, and Dec 25. From Lynchburg, take U.S. 460 west to Va. 122 south; park is 16 miles northeast of Rocky Mount.

National D-Day Memorial

On a hilltop with a splendid view of the Blue Ridge, this memorial honors the American soldiers, sailors, and airmen who fought and died in the invasion of Normandy on June 6, 1944. The town of Bedford was chosen for the monument because 19 of its young men were killed during the invasion and four more died during the Normandy campaign. The town had a population of 3,200, which meant that proportionally Bedford lost more men than any other town in the United States. Stunning in its architectural symbolism, the monument recalls the five landing beaches, the cliffs Allied soldiers climbed, and the contributions of the army, navy, and air force. Be sure to pick up a brochure or take a 45-minute guided tour, either on foot or by shuttle.

U.S. 460 at Va. 122, Bedford. © **800/352-DDAY** or 540/586-3329. www.dday.org. Admission $5 adults, $3 children 6–16, free for children 5 and younger. Walking tours $2, free for children 5 and younger. Riding tours $3 per person. Daily 10am–5pm. Closed Jan 1, Thanksgiving, and Dec 25.

Red Hill, Patrick Henry National Memorial

Fiery orator Patrick ("Give me liberty or give me death") Henry retired to Red Hill plantation, 35 miles southeast of Lynchburg, in 1794 after serving five terms as governor of Virginia. Failing health forced him to refuse numerous posts, including chief justice of the United States, secretary of state, and minister to Spain and France. He died at Red Hill on June 6, 1799, and is buried in the family graveyard. Begin your tour at the visitor center, where you can see a 15-minute video about Henry and visit the museum with the world's largest assemblage of Henry artifacts and memorabilia. The centerpiece is Peter Rothermel's famous painting *Patrick Henry before the Virginia House of Burgesses,* depicting his "If this be treason, make the most of it" speech against the Stamp Act in 1765. The site contains his actual law office, an accurate reproduction of the main house, the carriage house, and other small buildings. You can't miss the most striking feature of the landscape: Standing 64 feet high and spanning 96 feet, the Osage Orange Tree is listed in the American Forestry Hall of Fame. You'll need about an hour here.

1250 Red Hill Rd., Brookneal. (℄ **800/514-7463** or 434/376-2044. www.redhill.org. Admission $6 adults, $5 seniors, $2 students. Apr–Oct Mon–Sat 9am–4pm, Sun 1–5pm; Nov–Mar Mon–Sat 9am–4pm, Sun 1–4pm. Closed Jan 1, Thanksgiving, and Dec 25. From Lynchburg take U.S. 501 south to Brookneal, then Va. 40 east, and follow the brown signs.

Thomas Jefferson's Poplar Forest 🎯🎯   In 1806, while he was president, Jefferson himself assisted the masons in laying the foundation for this dwelling on what was then a 4,819-acre plantation and the source of much of his income. He designed the octagonal house to utilize light and airflow to the maximum in as economical a space as possible. It became his favorite place to escape from the parade of visitors at Monticello. Today, his final architectural masterpiece is again a work in progress, as it is being slowly restored to the way it looked in the early 19th century. Outside, archaeologists dig about the grounds, trying to discover how Jefferson landscaped the gardens. You can see artifacts from the buildings and grounds as they are brought to light and exhibited. During summer a pavilion covers hands-on activities representing Jefferson's time. You can tour the property on your own, but it's much more rewarding to take a 40-minute guided tour. Like James Madison's Montpelier (see above), this is a restoration in progress, not a furnished historic home.

Va. 661, Forest. (℄ **434/525-1806.** www.poplarforest.org. House tour $9 adults, $7.50 seniors, $1 children 6–16, free for children 5 and younger; self-guided grounds tour $4 per person. Apr–Nov Wed–Mon 10am–4pm (last tour begins at 4pm). 45-min. house tours depart on the hour and half-hour. Closed Thanksgiving and Dec–Mar. From Lynchburg take U.S. 221 south, go straight on Va. 811, turn left on Va. 661; entrance is about 6 miles southwest of Lynchburg.

5 Golfing, Canoeing, Ballooning & Ice-Skating

If you can afford it, the best golfing is at the Arnold Palmer–redesigned links at the private Keswick Club, which guests of Keswick Hall at Monticello can pay to play (see "Where to Stay," earlier in this chapter). The University of Virginia's 18-hole **Birdwood Golf Course** (℄ **434/293-GOLF**), adjacent to the Boar's Head Inn (p. 127), is one of the top 10 collegiate courses in the country. The 18-hole **Meadow Creek Golf Course,** 1400 Pen Park Rd. (℄ **434/977-0615**), is a short but challenging 18-holer. Call the courses to reserve tee times and get directions. Two fine courses—Devils Knob and Stoney Creek—are at Wintergreen Resort, about 43 miles away (see "A Nearby Mountain Getaway," earlier in this chapter).

You can go rafting and canoeing on the James River at Scottsville, a quaint, 19th-century town 20 miles south of Charlottesville via Va. 20. The river can run swiftly here—class I or II if it has rained recently, canoeing and tubing conditions if it hasn't. Contact **James River Runners** (℄ **434/286-2338;** www.jamesriver.com), which has been rafting the rapids, taking adventurers on overnight canoe trips, and renting canoes and inner tubes since 1979.

Charlottesville is Virginia's prime venue for hot-air ballooning, with several companies sending their craft soaring over the foothills, depending on the direction of the wind. **Bear Ballooning** (℄ **800/932-0152** or 434/971-1757; www.2comefly.com) takes off from the Boar's Head Inn (p. 127). Others include **Blue Ridge Balloon**

Company (© 434/589-6213; www.blueridgeballoon.com) and **Monticello Country Ballooning** (© 434/996-9008; www.virginiaballoon.com). Contact them well in advance of coming here.

On the Downtown Mall, the **Charlottesville Ice Park** (© 434/817-2400; www. icepark.com) offers an irregular schedule of ice-skating, skating lessons, and pickup hockey games.

6 Charlottesville After Dark

This well-heeled college town has a lot going on between sunset and the wee hours. For a complete schedule, see *Charlottesville Arts & Entertainment* (www.artsmonthly.com) and the free newspapers *C-Ville Weekly* (www.c-ville.com) and *The Hook* (www.readthe hook.com), all available at the visitor centers (see "Visitor Information," earlier).

The two top performing arts centers are on the Downtown Mall. Built in 1931 and restored in 2004 after being dark for 30 years, **The Paramount Theater,** 215 E. Main St. (© 434/979-1922; www.theparamount.net), has showcased the diverse likes of Bill Cosby, Vince Gill, Sir James Gallway, and Arlo Guthrie. At the mall's eastern end, the outdoor but covered **Charlottesville Pavilion** (© 434/817-0220; www. charlottesvillepavilion.com) hosts concerts by nationally known artists as well as community events.

You can watch local theater at **Live Arts,** 123 E. Water St. (© 434/977-4177; www.livearts.org), and **Old Michie Theatre,** 221 E. Water St. (© 434/977-3690; www.oldmichie.com), both near the Downtown Mall.

The University of Virginia has a constant and ever-changing parade of concerts, plays, lectures, and other events, most at the **Culbreth and Helms Theatres of The University of Virginia** and the **Heritage Repertory Theatre,** all at 109 Culbreth Rd. (© 434/924-3376; www.virginia.edu/drama/hrt.htm).

Like most college towns, Charlottesville sees numerous bands blasting away, especially on weekends. Even if you're hard of hearing, you can feel the music coming from the student-oriented bars around The Corner. The largest venue is **Starr Hill Brewery,** 709 W. Main St. (© 434/977-0017; www.starrhill.com), a restaurant, music hall, and brewery west of the Downtown Mall. On the mall, there's nighttime jazz or blues at **Miller's,** 109 W. Main St. (© 434/971-8511).

7

The Shenandoah Valley

Those of us who live in or near the Shenandoah Valley are fortunate indeed, for this is one of the most beautiful areas of the eastern United States. All we have to do is take a Sunday drive in the rolling hills dotted with picturesque small towns and well-tended farms with old stone homesteads to appreciate its grandeur.

If you're like me, you'll come here to see the view from the magnificent Shenandoah National Park atop the Blue Ridge Mountains. The park offers spectacular landscapes and a plethora of hiking and riding trails, including a portion of the Maine-to-Georgia Appalachian Trial. The Skyline Drive—one of America's great scenic routes—runs the full length of the park and connects directly with the Blue Ridge Parkway, which continues south to North Carolina's Great Smoky Mountains.

Outdoor enthusiasts can ride horses and go tubing, canoeing, or rafting down on the valley floor.

As it is throughout Virginia, history is a major reason to come here. You can see where George Washington carved his initials at Natural Bridge while surveying the valley and examine the Winchester office he used during the French and Indian War.

Union and Confederate armies seesawed up and down the valley during the Civil War, when the North tired to cut off Robert E. Lee's supplies from this "Breadbasket of the Confederacy." Stonewall Jackson left Virginia Military Institute at Lexington to become a great Confederate general. The entire VMI Corps of Cadets fought heroically in the legendary Battle of New Market. After the war, Lee settled in Lexington as president of what is now Washington and Lee University, and both he and Jackson are buried there. As it surely must have been in their time, Lexington is one of the country's most charming college towns.

Woodrow Wilson was born in Staunton in 1856, and a museum adjoining his birthplace pays tribute to this president's peace-loving ideals. Today his hometown is renowned for performing Shakespeare in its exact replica of the Bard's indoor theater.

Across the mountains you can take the waters in the same Warm Springs frequented by Thomas Jefferson and relax at one of the nation's premiere mountain resorts at Hot Springs.

Indeed, this 150-mile long valley and the mountains bordering it have something for everyone.

EXPLORING THE VALLEY

VISITOR INFORMATION For information about attractions, accommodations, restaurants, and services in the entire region, contact the **Shenandoah Valley Travel Association (SVTA),** 277 W. Old Cross Rd. (P.O. Box 1040), New Market, VA 22844 (✆ 877/847-4878 or 540/740-3132; fax 540/740-3100; www.visitshenandoah.org). The SVTA operates a visitor center in New Market, just off I-81 at U.S. 211 (Exit

---

> ### Tips   Snow, Ice & Fog
>
> Major highways in the Shenandoah Valley are kept open during winter, but snow, ice, and fog can close secondary roads, especially the Skyline Drive and other mountain roads during winter. Check with the **Virginia Department of Transportation** (© **800/367-7623**; www.virginiadot.org) or the **Weather Channel** (www.weather.com) for present conditions.

---

264). The center, open daily from 9am to 5pm, has a free phone line for making hotel reservations.

GETTING THERE & GETTING AROUND   The gorgeous scenery of the Shenandoah Valley is best seen by private vehicle, so bring your own or rent one at the airport. At least part of your trip should include the park's spectacular Skyline Drive (see below).

The fastest way to and through the region is via I-81, which runs the entire length of the valley floor and has been designated one of America's 10 most scenic interstates. It's also a very busy truck route. Since the big rigs constantly change speed as they go up and down hill, drive defensively at all times.

Alongside I-81, the legendary Valley Pike (U.S. 11) is much more peaceful and is like a trip back in time at least 50 years, with its small towns and villages, old-fashioned gas stations, ancient motels, shops, and restaurants. Likewise, the old U.S. 340 follows the scenic western foothills of the Blue Ridge.

I-66 enters the valley from Washington, D.C., before ending at Strasburg. I-64 comes into the valley's southern end from both east and west, running contiguous with I-81 between Staunton and Lexington. Other major east-west highways crossing the valley are Va. 7 and U.S. 50, 211, 33, 250, and 60.

US Airways Express (© **800/428-4322**) has commuter flights to and from **Shenandoah Valley Regional Airport (SHD)** off I-81 between Harrisonburg and Staunton (© **540/234-8304;** www.flyshd.com). Avis, Hertz, and Enterprise have rental cars at the airport. Call © **540/234-8304** for airport shuttle service. The nearest major airport is Washington Dulles International, 50 miles east of Front Royal (see "Getting There" and "Getting Around Virginia," in chapter 2). There are also airports in Charlottesville (see chapter 6) and Roanoke (see chapter 8).

Amtrak (© **800/872-7245;** www.amtrak.com) offers direct service to Staunton.

1 Shenandoah National Park & the Skyline Drive ★★★

Running for 105 miles atop the spine of the Blue Ridge Mountains, Shenandoah National Park is a haven for plants and wildlife. Although long and skinny, the park encompasses some 300 square miles of mountains, forests, waterfalls, and rock formations. It has more than 60 mountain peaks higher than 2,000 feet, with Hawksbill and Stony Man exceeding 4,000 feet. Unfortunately high humidity and ozone levels frequently create obscuring smog during the summer, so spring and fall are the best seasons to catch the panoramic views from overlooks from the Skyline Drive over the Piedmont to the east and the Shenandoah Valley to the west. The drive gives you access to the park's visitor facilities and to more than 500 miles of hiking and horse trails, including the Appalachian Trail.

Today, over two-fifths of the park is considered wilderness. Animals such as deer, bear, bobcat, and turkey have returned, and sightings of deer and smaller animals are frequent; the park also boasts more than 100 species of trees.

Europeans began settling these slopes and hollows in the early 18th century. The national park came into being 200 years later, when President Franklin D. Roosevelt's Depression-era Civilian Conservation Corps built the recreational facilities, guard walls, cabins, and many hiking trails. The corps completed the Skyline Drive in 1939.

To me, the park is most interesting and beautiful in the **Central District,** between U.S. 211 at Thornton Gap and U.S. 33 at Swift Run Gap. Unless I'm just passing through, I spend most of my time in this 35-mile strip.

JUST THE FACTS

ACCESS POINTS & ORIENTATION   The park and its Skyline Drive have four entrances. Northernmost is at **Front Royal** on U.S. 340 near the junction of I-81 and I-66, about 1 mile south of Front Royal and 75 miles west of Washington, D.C. The entrances to the Central District are at **Thornton Gap,** 33 miles south of Front Royal on U.S. 211 between Sperryville and Luray, and at **Swift Run Gap,** 68 miles south of Front Royal on U.S. 33 between Standardsville and Elkton. The southern gate is at **Rockfish Gap,** 105 miles south of Front Royal at I-64 and U.S. 250, some 21 miles west of Charlottesville and 18 miles east of Staunton.

The Skyline Drive is marked with **mile posts,** starting at zero at the Front Royal entrance and increasing as you go south, with Rockfish Gap on the southern end at Mile 105.

DISTRICTS   The access roads divide the park into three areas: **Northern District,** between Front Royal and U.S. 211 at Thornton Gap (Mile 0 to Mile 31.5); **Central District,** between Thornton Gap and U.S. 33 at Swift Run Gap (Mile 31.5 to Mile 65.7); and **Southern District,** between Swift Run Gap and I-64 at Rockfish Gap (Mile 65.7 to Mile 105).

INFORMATION   For free information, call or write to Superintendent, Shenandoah National Park, 3655 U.S. Hwy., 211 East, Luray, VA 22835 (© **540/999-3500;** www.nps.gov/shen). The headquarters is 4 miles west of Thornton Gap and 5 miles east of Luray on U.S. 211.

Aramark Virginia Sky-Line Co., the park's major concessionaire (© **888/896-3833;** www.visitshenandoah.com), maintains an informative website on which you can book accommodations at the park's lodges and cabins.

American Park Network (www.americanparknetwork.com) publishes a helpful advertiser-supported guide to the park, and it has bountiful information on its website.

The **Shenandoah National Park Association** (© **540/999-3582;** www.snpbooks. org), is the best source of maps, guidebooks, and other publications about the park's cultural and natural history. It has a bookstore at park headquarters, and many of its publications are available at the visitor centers.

For guidebooks and detailed topographic maps of the park's three districts, write or call the **Potomac Appalachian Trail Club (PATC),** 118 Park St., Vienna, VA 22180 (© **703/242-0315,** or 703/242-0965 for a recording of the club's activities; www.patc. net). The PATC helps build and maintain the park's portion of the Appalachian Trail, including trail cabins (see "Hiking & Other Sports," below). The PATC is part of the **Appalachian Trail Conservancy,** P.O. Box 807, Harpers Ferry, WV 25425-0807

⌐Tips⌐ Your Indispensable Guide

In addition to the magnificent map brochure the ranger will hand you, be sure to get a copy of *Shenandoah Overlook* when you enter the park or stop by a visitor center. This tabloid newspaper will be your bible during your visit since it tells you about ranger programs and everything else that's going on during your visit.

(© **304/535-6331;** www.appalachiantrail.org), which covers the entire trail from Maine to Georgia.

The **National Geographic** (www.nationalgeographic.com) publishes a terrific topographic map of the park's hiking trails, showing them all on one weatherproof sheet (map no. 228). One of the best trail guidebooks is the third edition of *Hiking Shenandoah National Park* by Bert and Jane Gildart (Globe Pequot, 2006).

EMERGENCIES   In case of emergencies, call the park headquarters (© **540/999-3500**).

FEES, REGULATIONS & BACKCOUNTRY PERMITS   Entrance permits good for 7 consecutive days are $15 per car, $10 per motorcycle, $8 for each pedestrian or bicyclist from March through November. These fees are $10, $10, and $5, respectively, from December through February. An annual pass ($30) is good for 1 year. Park entrance is free to holders of America the Beautiful—National Parks and Federal Recreational Lands Passes and the National Park Service's Golden Eagle, Golden Access, and Golden Age passports.

The **speed limit** on the Skyline Drive is 35 mph, although given the number of camper vans and rubberneckers creeping along this winding, two-lane road, you'll be lucky to go that fast. This is no place to have a fit of road rage.

Plants and animals are protected; so all hunting is prohibited. Pets must be kept on a leash at all times and are not allowed on some trails. Wood fires are permitted only in fireplaces in developed areas. The Skyline Drive is a great bike route, but neither bicycles nor motor vehicles of any sort are allowed on the hiking trails.

Most of the park is open to backcountry camping. Permits, which are free, are required; get them at the entrance gates, visitor centers, or by mail from park headquarters (see "Information," above). Campers are required to leave no trace of their presence. No permits are necessary for backcountry hiking, but the same "no-trace" rule applies.

VISITOR CENTERS   There are two park visitor centers, **Dickey Ridge Visitor Center,** at Mile 4.6 in the Northern District, and **Byrd Visitor Center,** in the Central District at Mile 51 in Big Meadows. Both are open daily 8:30am to 5pm from mid-April through October (to 6pm on weekends from July through Labor Day) and on an intermittent schedule through Thanksgiving weekend in late November. Both provide information, maps of nearby hiking trails, interpretive exhibits, films, slide shows, and nature walks.

Operated by the town of Waynesboro, the **Rockfish Gap Information Center,** on U.S. 211 (at Exit 99 off I-64) at the park's southern gate (© **540/943-5187**) has a terrific room-size topographical map of the region (and a life-size statue of Robert E. Lee). Daily hours are 9am to 5pm (closed Thanksgiving, Christmas, and New Year's Day).

SEASONS   The park's high season is from mid- to late October, when the fall foliage peaks, and weekend traffic on the Skyline Drive can be bumper-to-bumper. Days also tend to be more clear in fall than in summer, when lingering haze can obscure the views. In spring, the green of leafing trees moves up the ridge at the rate of about 100 feet a day. Wildflowers begin to bloom in April, and by late May, the azaleas are brilliant and the dogwood is putting on a show. Nesting birds abound, and the normally modest waterfalls are at their highest during spring, when warm rains melt the highland snows. You'll find the clearest views across the distant mountains during winter, but many facilities are closed then, and snow and ice can shut down the Skyline Drive. Also, parts of the drive are closed at night during Virginia's hunting season from mid-November to early January.

RANGER PROGRAMS   The park offers a wide variety of ranger-led activities—nature walks, interpretive programs, cultural and history lectures, and campfire talks. Most are held at or near Dickey Ridge Visitor Center in the north; Byrd Visitor Center and the Big Meadows and Skyland lodges and campground in the center; and Loft Mountain campground in the south. Schedules are published seasonally in the *Shenandoah Overlook,* available at the entrance gates, visitor centers, and from park headquarters.

SEEING THE HIGHLIGHTS

As I said at the outset of this section, I spend most if not all of my time in the **Central District,** between U.S. 211 at Thornton Gap and U.S. 33 at Swift Run Gap (that is, between Mile 31.5 and Mile 65.7). To my eye, this is the best part of the park. It has the highest mountains, best views, nearly half of the park's 500 miles of hiking trails, and its only stables and overnight accommodations: Big Meadows and Skyland lodges. You can see the views in a day, but give it at least 2 nights if you're doing any hiking, riding, or fishing. Make your reservations for Big Meadows or Skyland as early as possible (see "Accommodations," below). If you can't get a room in one of them, Luray has the nearest accommodations to the Central District (see section 5, later in this chapter).

SCENIC OVERLOOKS   My favorite of the 75 designated overlooks in the Central District are **Stony Man Overlook** (Mile 38.6), offering panoramas of Stony Man Cliffs, the valley, and the Alleghenies; **Thoroughfare Mountain Overlook** (Mile 40.5; elevation 3,595 ft.), one of the highest overlooks, with views from Hogback Mountain south to cone-shaped Robertson Mountain and the rocky face of Old Rag Mountain; **Old Rag View Overlook** (Mile 46.5), dominated by Old Rag, sitting by itself in an eastern extremity of the park; and **Franklin Cliffs Overlook** (Mile 49), offering a view of the cliffs and the Shenandoah Valley and Massanutten Mountain beyond. You'll need only 10 minutes or so at each overlook, so plan to pull off at all of these. Assuming you're not smogged in, it'll be 40 minutes well spent.

Tips **Avoiding the Crowds**

With its proximity to the Washington and Baltimore metropolitan areas, the park is at its busiest on summer and fall weekends and holidays. The fall-foliage season in October is the busiest time, and reservations for October accommodations in or near the park should be made as much as a year in advance. The best time to visit is during the spring and on weekdays from June through October.

Tips **Slow Down, You Move Too Fast . . .**

Unless you're caught in heavy traffic on fall foliage weekends, you can drive the entire length of the **Skyline Drive** in about 3 hours without stopping. But why rush? Give yourself at least a day, so lovely are the views from its scenic overlooks. Stop for lunch at a wayside snack bar, lodge, or one of seven official picnic grounds (or any of the overlooks will do for an impromptu picnic). Better yet, get out of your car and take at least a short hike down one of the hollows to a waterfall.

If you're in the Northern District, pull off at the **Shenandoah Valley Overlook** (Mile 2.8), with views west to the Signal Knob of Massanutten Mountain across the south fork of the river; and **Range View Overlook** (Mile 17.1; elevation 2,800 ft.), providing fine views of the central section of the park, looking south. In the Southern District, **Big Run Overlook** (Mile 81.2) looks down on rocky peaks and the largest watershed in the park.

WATERFALLS   Only one waterfall is visible from the Skyline Drive, at Mile 1.4, and it's dry part of the year. On the other hand, 15 other falls are accessible via hiking trails (see "Hiking," below).

HIKING & OTHER SPORTS

HIKING   The number-one outdoor activity here is hiking. The park's 112 trails total more than 500 miles, varying in length from short walks to a 101-mile segment of the Appalachian Trail running the entire length of the park. Access to the trails is marked along the Skyline Drive. There are parking lots at the major trail heads, but they fill quickly on weekends.

I strongly recommend that you get maps and trail descriptions before setting out—even before leaving home, if possible. Free maps of many trails are available at the visitor centers, which also sell the topographic maps, published by the Potomac Appalachian Trail Conference, as well as a one-sheet map of all of the park's walks published by the National Geographic. See "Information," above, for contact information.

An alternative to doing it yourself is to take a guided outdoor adventure organized by **Aramark Virginia Sky-Line Co.** (© 888/896-3833; www.visitshenandoah.com). Led by mountain guides, they include short hikes from the park lodges ($10 per person), 1-day hikes ($89–$178 per person), 2-day excursions ($178 per person), and rock-climbing expeditions ($99 per person). Call or check Aramark's website for schedules and reservations.

At a minimum, take one of the short hikes on trails at Dickey Ridge Visitor Center (Mile 4.6) and the Byrd Visitor Center/Big Meadows (Mile 51). There's an excellent 1.6-mile hike at Stony Man (Mile 41.7).

My gimpy knees don't necessarily agree, but I've concluded that these are the best trails in the Central District:

- **Limberlost Accessible Trail:** At Mile 43 south of Skyland, Limberlost is accessible to visitors in wheelchairs. The 1.3-mile loop runs through an old-growth forest of ancient hemlocks. The trail has a 5-foot-wide, hard-packed surface; crosses a 65-foot bridge; and includes a 150-foot boardwalk.

- **White Oak Canyon** ⚘⚘⚘: Everyone's favorite trail (especially when linked to the Cedar Run Falls trail; see below) begins at Mile 42.6 just south of Skyland and descends into a steep gorge that is the park's scenic gem. The 7.3-mile trail goes through an area of wild beauty, passing no less than six waterfalls and cascades. The upper reaches to the first falls are relatively easy, but farther down the track can be rough and rocky. This not an easy trail, especially coming back up the 2,160-foot climb, a brutal ascent if you're out of shape. In other words, allow all day.
- **Cedar Run Falls:** Several trails begin at Hawksbill Gap (Mile 45.6). A short but steep trail leads 1.7 miles round-trip to the summit of Hawksbill Mountain, the park's highest at 4,050 feet. Another is a moderately difficult 3.5-mile round-trip hike to Cedar Falls and back. You can also connect from Cedar Run to White Oak Canyon, a 7.3-mile loop that will take all day.
- **Dark Hollow Falls** ⚘: The park's most popular short hike is the 1.4-mile walk to Dark Hollow Falls, the closest cascade to the Skyline Drive. The trail begins at Mile 50.7 near the Byrd Visitor Center. Allow 1¼ hours for the round-trip.
- **Camp Hoover/Mill Prong** ⚘: Starting at the Milam Gap parking area (Mile 52.8), this 4-mile round-trip hike drops down the Mill Prong to the Rapidan River, where President Herbert Hoover, an avid fisherman, had a camp during his administration (sort of the Camp David of his day). The total climb is 850 feet; allow 4 hours.

Access points to the **Appalachian Trail** are well marked at overlooks on the Skyline Drive. Along the trail, five backcountry shelters for day use each offer only a table, fireplace, pit toilet, and water. The **Potomac Appalachian Trail Club,** 118 Park St. SE, Vienna, VA 22180 (© **703/242-0315;** www.patc.net), maintains huts and fully enclosed cabins that can accommodate up to 12 people. Use of the huts is free, but they are intended for long-distance hikers only. Cabins cost $10 to $20 on weekdays, $15 to $40 on weekends. You can reserve cabins by calling PATC Monday to Thursday between 7 and 9pm, Thursday and Friday from noon to 2pm (*only* during these hours). You'll have to submit a signed form (available on PATC's website), so you'll want to start the process as early as possible. PATC's website also shows cabin availabilities.

FISHING   The park's streams are short, with limited fishing, so it's hardly worth the time and effort. The park publishes a free recreational fishing brochure and an annual list of streams open for fishing, available at the Big Meadows and Loft Mountain waysides or at sporting-goods stores outside the park.

HORSEBACK RIDING   Horses are allowed only on trails marked with yellow, and only via guided expeditions with **Skyland Stables** (© **540/999-2211;** www.visit shenandoah.com), on the Skyland Lodge grounds (Mile 41.8). Rides cost $30 per hour. Pony rides for children are $5 for 15 minutes, $10 for 30 minutes. Children must be 4 feet, 10 inches tall to ride the horses (otherwise they can take a pony ride); an adult must accompany those younger than 12. The stables operate from April through November. Call for reservations at least 1 day in advance.

CAMPING

The park has four campgrounds with tent and trailer sites (but no hookups anywhere). In the middle of the park's Central District, **Big Meadows** (Mile 51.2) has the best location and sites equipped for campers with disabilities. You can reserve Big Meadows sites in advance by calling © **800/365-2267** daily between 10am and

---

Tips It Gets Chilly up Here

It was a stifling 93°F (34°C) as I drove through Luray one recent summer afternoon. An hour later I arrived at Big Meadows Lodge atop the Blue Ridge—where the temperature was 58°F (14°C). My traveling companion Ann Barnard and I immediately pulled out our sweaters and long pants! In other words, it's always much cooler on the mountaintops than down in the valley, especially at night. So bring suitable clothing, including comfortable walking shoes.

10pm, or on the park service's reservation website at http://reservations.nps.gov. They cost $20 per night. Big Meadows is open from early April to the end of October.

Sites at **Mathews Arm** (Mile 22.2), **Lewis Mountain** (Mile 57.5), and **Loft Mountain** (Mile 79.5) are on a first-come, first-served basis at $15 per site per night. They are open from mid-May to late October. Lewis Mountain has only 31 sites and is often full during summer and early fall. Mathews Arm and Loft Mountain have 100 and 200 sites, respectively, and usually only fill on summer and fall weekends.

ACCOMMODATIONS

Situated on the Skyline Drive in the Central District, **Big Meadows Lodge** and **Skyland Lodge** (see below) are the only hotels in the park. They are 9½ miles apart. Lodge reservations should be made well in advance—up to a year ahead for the peak fall season. You can make them through the **National Park Reservations** (© 866/875-8456; www.nationalparkreservations.com) or directly through **Aramark Virginia Sky-Line Co.** (© 888/896-3833; www.visitshenandoah.com), the concessionaire that operates both.

Aramark also manages **Lewis Mountain Cabins,** adjacent to the Lewis Mountain Campground at Mile 57.5 in the Central District. These simple abodes range from $27 for a "tent cabin" to $123 for connecting rooms. They all have private bathrooms and are supplied with towels and linens.

Although I prefer the historical ambience of Big Meadows and its convenience to many activities, I'll stay at either if it means I can get room with a view of the Shenandoah Valley.

The sections that follow later in this chapter describe accommodations in other Shenandoah Valley towns. Luray is nearest to the Central District (see section 5).

Big Meadows Lodge *Value* Big Meadows is what you expect a historic mountain lodge to be. Built of stone and timber, the rustic main building sports a large guest lounge with a roaring fireplace, and its window walls present a spectacular view over the Shenandoah Valley. Accommodations consist of small, rustic rooms in the main lodge, in cabins, and multi-unit lodges with suites spread out over the premises. Not all units have the valley view, however, so request a "terrace" room in the main lodge building. The view is worth paying extra for, but make sure the reservation clerk understands that you don't want just any room. Whichever unit you get, you'll have plain but comfortable furnishings and a private bathroom. "Deluxe" units in the Rapidan and Doubletop buildings have air-conditioning and TVs; otherwise, you won't have such modern amenities. No unit has a phone, but your cellphone should work out on the lodge terrace overlooking Luray, and there's wireless Internet access in public areas of the main lodge. The main-lodge dining room features traditional fare such as prime rib, fried chicken, mountain trout, and pastas. Wine, beer, and cocktails are available. Live entertainment keeps the taproom busy during the season. Big Meadows is a major recreational center. Many hiking trails start here, and it's also the site of the Byrd Visitor Center.

P.O. Box 727, Luray, VA 22835 (on Skyline Dr. at Mile 51.2). ℂ **800/999-4714** or 540/999-2221. Fax 540/999-2011. www.visitshenandoah.com. 97 units. $72–$135 double main lodge; $87–$127 double motel; $130–$165 suite; $92–$103 cabin room. Highest rates charged weekends and in Oct. AE, DISC, MC, V. Closed Nov to early May. **Amenities:** Restaurant; bar. *In room:* A/C (some units), TV (some units), coffeemaker, no phone.

Skyland Lodge   Skyland was built by naturalist George Freeman Pollock in 1894 as a summer retreat almost atop Stony Man Mountain, the highest point on the Skyline Drive at 3,680 feet. The main building is smaller and less charming than Big Meadow Lodge's. The resort offers rooms in the main lodge as well as in rustic wood-paneled cabins and motel-type accommodations spread out over its 52 acres. Some of the buildings are dark-brown clapboard, others are fieldstone, and all nestle among the trees. More rooms have wonderful views than at Big Meadow, but again, tell the reservations clerk you want a view. The most panoramic views are from the Shenandoah building, whose air-conditioned rooms have TVs. More rooms also have air-conditioning and TVs here, too. The main building's dining room has a view, and it offers the same fare as at Big Meadows. There's a fully stocked taproom here, too, and the park's only stables are nearby.

P.O. Box 727, Luray, VA 22835 (on Skyline Dr. at Mile 41.7). ℂ **800/999-4714** or 540/999-2211. Fax 540/999-2231. www.visitshenandoah.com. 177 units. $87–$131 double lodge; $122–$189 suite; $66–$124 double cabin room; $223–$275 family cabin. Highest rates charged weekends and in Oct. Packages available. AE, DISC, MC, V. Closed Nov to early May. **Amenities:** Restaurant; bar. *In room:* A/C (some units), TV (some units), coffeemaker, no phone.

WHERE TO DINE

In addition to the lodges at Big Meadows and Skyland, there are daytime restaurants and snack bars at Big Meadows (Mile 51), Elkwallow Wayside (Mile 24.1), Panorama-Thornton Gap (Mile 31.5), and Loft Mountain (Mile 79.5).

Picnic areas with tables, fireplaces, water fountains, and restrooms are at Dickey Ridge (Mile 4.6) and Elkwallow (Mile 24.1) in the Northern District; Pinnacles (Mile 36.7), Big Meadows (Mile 51), and Lewis Mountain (Mile 57.5) in the Central District; and South River (Mile 62.8) and Loft Mountain (Mile 79.5) in the Southern District. Since the areas are far apart, pick the one nearest to you. Big Meadows is most convenient to park activities.

2 Winchester: A Fitting Introduction ✦

76 miles W of Washington, D.C.; 189 miles NW of Richmond

To paraphrase Abraham Lincoln's Gettysburg Address, it is altogether fitting that Winchester comes first in my descriptions of the valley's towns, for its excellent Museum of the Shenandoah Valley provides an altogether fitting introduction to this area. Especially if you're arriving by car from the north or from Washington Dulles International Airport, Winchester should be your first stop.

Prior to the museum's opening in 2005, Winchester was best known as Virginia's "Apple Capital," so-called because of the number of apple orchards in the northern end of the valley. The **Shenandoah Apple Blossom Festival** in May is one of the region's most popular events.

Winchester

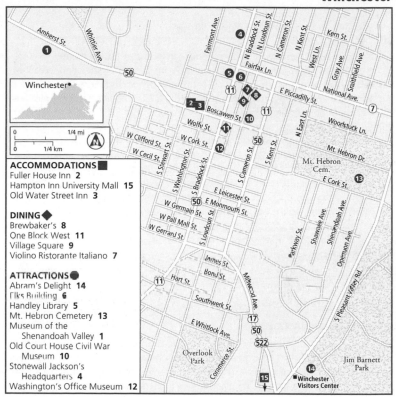

ACCOMMODATIONS ■
Fuller House Inn **2**
Hampton Inn University Mall **15**
Old Water Street Inn **3**

DINING ◆
Brewbaker's **8**
One Block West **11**
Village Square **9**
Violino Ristorante Italiano **7**

ATTRACTIONS ●
Abram's Delight **14**
Elks Building **6**
Handley Library **5**
Mt. Hebron Cemetery **13**
Museum of the
    Shenandoah Valley **1**
Old Court House Civil War
    Museum **10**
Stonewall Jackson's
    Headquarters **4**
Washington's Office Museum **12**

What is now Winchester was the site of a Shawnee Indian campground before Pennsylvania Quakers settled here in 1732. George Washington set up shop in town during the French and Indian War 20 years later, and his office is still here. Thanks to its strategic location, Winchester changed hands no fewer than 72 times during the Civil War. Both Confederate Gen. Stonewall Jackson and Union Gen. Philip Sheridan made their headquarters here at one time or another.

Give yourself at least a morning or afternoon here to visit the Museum of the Shenandoah Valley, Washington's office, and Stonewall Jackson's headquarters. If you're a country music fan, you can drive by Winchester native Patsy Cline's old haunts and visit her gravesite on the edge of town.

ESSENTIALS
VISITOR INFORMATION   The **Winchester/Frederick County Visitors Center,** 1360 S. Pleasant Valley Rd., Winchester, VA 22601 (© **540/542-1326;** fax 540/450-0099; www.visitwinchesterva.com), is open daily from 9am to 5pm (closed New Year's Day, Easter, Thanksgiving, and Christmas). The center shows an 18-minute video about the area and has a small exhibit about Patsy Cline, Winchester's contribution to country music (see "'Crazy' for Patsy Cline," above). Take Exit 313 off I-81, go west on U.S. 50, and follow the signs.

Fun Fact   **"Crazy" for Patsy Cline**

Only die-hard country music fans know a Winchester native named Virginia Hensley by her real name, for it was as Patsy Cline that she sang "Walkin' After Midnight" on the nationally televised *Arthur Godfrey's Talent Scouts* in the 1950s. The record of that song sold a million copies. Other tunes like "Crazy," "Leavin' on Your Mind," and "Imagine That" will forever be linked to Patsy Cline.

She was only 30 years old when she, Hawkshaw Hawkins, and Cowboy Copas died in a plane crash in March 1963. Her body was brought home and buried in Shenandoah Memorial Park, 3 miles south of town on U.S. 522.

The Winchester/Frederick County Visitors Center (see "Essentials," below) has a Patsy Cline Corner that includes her very own jukebox. Pick up a brochure that points the way to her home, Gaunt's Drug Store where she worked, the high school she attended, GNM Music where she cut her first record, the house where she married second husband Charlie Dick, and her grave.

GETTING THERE   Winchester is on I-81, U.S. 11, U.S. 522, U.S. 50, and Va. 7.

EXPLORING THE TOWN

The visitor center distributes free maps, walking-tour brochures of the Old Town historic district, and Patsy Cline driving-tour maps (www.patsycline.com). Most helpful is a 90-minute **Follow the Apple Trail** audio driving tour ($5 for a tape, $8 for a CD), which will guide you around Winchester and Frederick County. Other driving tours highlight Winchester's African-American heritage and the Civil War Battle of Third Winchester.

The heart of Winchester's historic area is the **Old Town Mall,** a 4-block-long pedestrian mall along Loudon Street between Piccadilly and Cork streets. I enjoy strolling the mall, exploring a number of boutiques and enjoying refreshment at coffeehouses, pastry shops, and several restaurants, some of which offer outdoor seating under shade trees in warm weather (see "Where to Dine," below). Facing the mall, the imposing **Frederick County Court House** was built in 1840 and is now home to the Old Court House Civil War Museum (see below).

While walking between the George Washington and Stonewall Jackson museums (see below), you can't miss the elaborate, Beaux Arts–style **Handley Library,** at the corner of Braddock and Piccadilly streets (© **540/662-9041**). Built between 1907 and 1912, it's adorned with a full panoply of Classic Revival statues. A copper-covered dome covers the rotunda, which symbolizes the spine of a book, with the two flanking wings representing its open pages.

Across the street from the library is the white-columned **Elks Building,** headquarters of Union Gen. Philip Sheridan from 1864 to 1865.

Any doubt that this northern end of the valley was fought over during the Civil War will be dispelled at **Mt. Hebron Cemetery,** on Woodstock Lane, east of downtown. Some 8,000 men killed in the battles are buried here—the Rebels in Stonewall

Confederate Cemetery on the south side of the street, the Yankees in the National Cemetery on the north side.

Abram's Delight If you're here between April and October, walk across the lot from the visitor center to this native-limestone residence built beside a lake in 1754 by Quaker Isaac Hollingsworth. The oldest house in Winchester, it served as the town's first Quaker Meeting House. Today, it's fully restored and furnished with 18th- and 19th-century pieces. Guided tours are available.

1340 S. Pleasant Valley Rd. (C) **540/662-6519.** www.winchesterhistory.org. Admission (without block ticket) $12 family, $5 adults, $4.50 seniors, $2.50 students 7–18, free for children 6 and younger. Apr–Oct Mon–Sat 10am–4pm, Sun noon–4pm. 45-min. house tours depart when a guide is available. Closed Nov–Mar.

Museum of the Shenandoah Valley ✸✸✸ A visit to this terrific museum will enrich your tour of the valley by explaining in a nutshell its geography and history. The museum opened on the western side of town in 2005 at the site of **Glen Burnie,** a lovingly restored, redbrick plantation home standing on the original homestead of Winchester founder James Wood. With sections dating to 1755, Glen Burnie is surrounded by magnificent formal gardens, which shouldn't be missed (many couples have held weddings among the flowers). You should allot at least 2 hours to see the museum, the Glen Burnie manse, and the gardens. Begin in the modern museum building, where a 9-minute video (shown every 15 min.) will set the stage for your tour of the complex. A huge topographic map of the entire valley then introduces exhibits tracking the Shenandoah's development from prehistoric times to the present. The museum also houses the remarkable collection of 18th-century furniture and art— including paintings by Rembrandt Peale and Gilbert Stuart—amassed by the late Julian Wood Glass, Jr., the last descendant of James Wood to live at Glen Burnie. Also not to be missed is an extraordinary miniature house collection. The museum's tearoom serves soups, salads, and sandwiches from 11am to 4pm.

801 Amherst St. (U.S. 50 W.). (C) **888/556-5799** or 540/662-1473. www.shenandoahmuseum.org. Admission to museum $8 adults, $6 seniors and students 7–18; gardens $6 adults, $5 seniors and students 7–18; museum and gardens $10 adults, $9 seniors and students 7–18; Glen Burnie and gardens $12 adults, $10 seniors and students 7–18, free for children 6 and younger. Tues–Sun 10am–4pm. Closed Jan 1, Thanksgiving, and Dec 25.

Old Court House Civil War Museum Housed in the 1840 Frederick County Court House, this new museum tells of Winchester's role in the Civil War, when it see-sawed between Union and Confederate hands. Both sides used the courthouse as a hospital and prison. The museum's most interesting exhibit is upstairs where upwards of 500 prisoners were detained. Many of them carved graffiti into the walls, which you can see through windows.

20 N. Loudon St. (on Old Town Mall). (C) **540/542-1145.** www.civilwarmuseum.org. Admission $3 per person, free for children 5 and younger. Wed–Sat 10am–5pm; Sun 1–5pm.

(Value Saving with a Block Ticket

You can buy a **block ticket** to visit Abram's Delight, Washington's Office Museum, and Stonewall Jackson's Headquarters for $20 for a family, $10 adults, $9 seniors, and $4 students 7 to 18 (free for children 6 and younger). Tickets are available at the museums or at the Winchester/Frederick County Visitors Center (see "Essentials," above).

Stonewall Jackson's Headquarters ⭐ Stonewall Jackson used this Victorian home, once owned by a great-grandfather of actress Mary Tyler Moore, as his headquarters in the winter of 1861 to 1862. It's filled with maps, photos, and memorabilia. As you aren't allowed to just walk through, plan on taking a guided tour. Two guides are usually on hand, so there's seldom a wait.

415 N. Braddock St. (between Peyton St. and North Ave.). © 540/667-3242. www.winchesterhistory.org. Admission (without block ticket) $12 family, $5 adults, $4.50 seniors, $2.50 students 7–18, free for children 6 and younger. Apr–Oct Mon–Sat 10am–4pm, Sun noon–4pm. Mandatory 30-min. house tours depart as needed. Closed Nov–Mar.

Washington's Office Museum ⭐⭐ George Washington used this small log cabin (since covered with clapboard) as his office in 1755 and 1756 when he was a colonel in the Virginia militia, charged with building a fort to protect the colony's frontier from the French and the Indians. The building itself is the highlight of this charming little museum, whose exhibits explain Washington's career from 1748 to 1758. You can see it all in 30 minutes. Informative staff members are on hand to answer questions and lead guided tours.

32 W. Cork St. (at Braddock St.). © 540/662-4412. www.winchesterhistory.org. Admission (without block ticket) $12 family, $5 adults, $4.50 seniors, $2.50 students 7–18, free for children 6 and younger. Apr–Oct Mon–Sat 10am–4pm, Sun noon–4pm. Closed Nov–Mar.

WHERE TO STAY

If you decide to stay over, the area along Millwood Avenue (U.S. 50) at I-81 (Exit 313), on the southeast side of town, has Winchester's major shopping mall and several chain restaurants and motels. About half the rooms at the **Holiday Inn** (© 800/465-4329 or 540/667-3300) face a courtyard with outdoor pool; the hotel's restaurant is one of the town's more popular lunch spots. Also nearby are the venerable **Best Western Lee-Jackson Motor Inn** (© 800/528-1234 or 540/662-4154), the **Comfort Inn Winchester** (© 800/228-5150 or 540/667-5000), a **Fairfield Inn & Suites** (© 800/228-2800 or 540/665-8881), the **Hampton Inn University Mall** (© 800/426-7866 or 540/667-8011), a **Wingate Inn** (© 800/676-4283), and an inexpensive **Red Roof Inn** (© 866/386-4682 or 540/667-5000).

Among the local bed-and-breakfasts, **Fuller House Inn,** 229 W. Boscowen St. (© 877/722-3976 or 540/722-3976; www.fullerhouseinn.com), and **Old Water Street Inn,** 217 W. Boscowen St. (© 866/665-6770 or 540/665-6777) are both in the historic district. Nearby are **Brownstone Cottage Bed & Breakfast,** 162 McCarty Lane (© 540/662-1962; www.brownstonecottage.com), and **Long Hill Bed & Breakfast,** 547 Apple Pie Ridge Rd. (© 866/265-8390 or 540/450-0341; www. longhillbb.com).

A NEARBY COUNTRY INN WITH A FRENCH FLAVOR

L'Auberge Provençale ⭐⭐ (Value) Executive chef Alain Borel and his vivacious wife, Celeste, have re-created the look, feel, and cuisine of Provence in a 1750s fieldstone farmhouse set on a hilltop with a view of the Blue Ridge. In the original main house are three intimate dining rooms and a parlor to which guests are invited for predinner drinks in front of the fireplace. Three of the 11 guest rooms are in this building; antiques and beautiful fabrics complement the Colonial farmhouse's fine features. The remaining cozy accommodations, in an adjoining gray-clapboard addition, are individually decorated with Victorian and European pieces and lovely French Provincial–print fabrics. Exceptional works of fine art—including prints by renowned artists and a unique selection of carved wooden animals and small handcrafted bird sculptures—adorn the guest rooms. Alain uses the finest-quality ingredients, many from his own garden or local farmers, to create his superb five-course prix-fixe dinners (reservations required). Even breakfast is a splendid repast, and Alain will provide a gourmet picnic lunch on request. No children younger than 10 need apply for a room here. Although not as luxurious as The Inn at Little Washington (see section 4, later in this chapter), the accommodations here are larger, making this very good value for what you pay.

U.S. 340 (P.O. Box 190), White Post, VA 22663. ℂ **800/638-1702** or 540/837-1375. Fax 703/837-2004. www. laubergeprovencale.com. 14 units. $155–$325 double. Rates include full breakfast. AE, DC, MC, V. From I-81, take U.S. 50 east 7 miles, turn right on U.S. 340; the inn is 1 mile on the right. No children younger than 10. **Amenities:** Restaurant; heated outdoor pool; Jacuzzi. *In room:* A/C, CD player, coffeemaker.

WHERE TO DINE

The Old Town Mall along Loudon Street in the heart of downtown has a number of coffeehouses, bakeries, and restaurants, most between Boscawen and Piccadilly streets. Best for fine dining is **Village Square** (ℂ **540/667-8961**), which has a sophisticated piano bar and excellent wine shop adjacent. The cuisine is *nouveau americain,* such as a roast chicken and grits casserole. I've met people in Leesburg who will drive over for lunch or dinner at **Violino Ristorante Italiano** (ℂ **540/667-8006**). For informal fare, there's the publike **Brewbaker's** (ℂ **540/667-0429**). All three offer outdoor seating in good weather.

One Block West ⊛ ECLECTIC   You'll find some of Winchester's most refined dining in this small brick building almost hidden on Indian Alley, which runs north-south 1 block west of the Loudon Street mall (hence, the name of the restaurant). Although he changes the menu daily, owner Ed Matthews puts the grill to excellent use on steaks, tuna, lamb chops, pork loin, and bison. Wednesday was tapas night during my recent visit.

25 S. Indian Alley (between Boscawen and Cork sts.). ℂ **540/662-1455**. Reservations recommended. Main courses $20–$36. AE, MC, V. Tues–Sat 11am–2pm and 5–10pm.

3 Middletown & Strasburg: Antiques Galore ⊛

Middletown: 13 miles S of Winchester, 174 miles NW of Richmond, 76 miles W of Washington, D.C.; Strasburg: 6 miles S of Middletown

On U.S. 11, essentially flanking the intersection of I-81 and I-66 south of Winchester, the hamlet of Middletown and the small town of Strasburg are collectively one of the best places in Virginia to browse for antiques and collectibles. This is especially true of Strasburg, which justifiably calls itself the "Antiques Capital of Virginia." The sprawling **Great Strasburg Antiques Emporium** is one of the state's largest collections of dealers. Both towns have exceptional country inns offering antiques-filled accommodations and fine dining, and Middletown's Wayside Theatre will entertain anyone who loves live theater.

In between Middletown and Strasburg stands Belle Grove Plantation, the 18th-century home of President James Madison's sister and later the site of a fierce Civil War battle. The house and battlefield now comprise a national historic site. Also in the Civil War, Gen. Stonewall Jackson rolled the railroad locomotives he stole from the Union during his daring Great Train Raid on Martinsburg, West Virginia, down the Valley Pike to the existing station at Strasburg, which is now a local museum.

Except for Belle Grove Plantation, the museums here are not as interesting as are others in the valley. Consequently, I would stop in Middletown and Strasburg either to hunt for antiques and collectibles or to stay in one of two inns in order to catch a show at the Wayside Theatre.

ESSENTIALS

VISITOR INFORMATION   The **Winchester/Frederick County Visitors Center** (see "Winchester: A Fitting Introduction," above) has in-depth information about Middletown.

GETTING THERE   From I-81, take Exit 302 west to U.S. 11 into Middletown. Take exits 298 or 300 into Strasburg.

THE TOP ATTRACTIONS

Cedar Creek and Belle Grove National Historical Park 🏛️🏛️   One of the finest homes in the Shenandoah Valley, the beautiful Belle Grove stone mansion was built in 1797 by Maj. Isaac Hite, whose grandfather, Joist Hite, first settled here in 1732. Major Hite's wife was Nelly Madison Hite, sister of President James Madison. At Madison's request, Thomas Jefferson was actively involved in Belle Grove's design. The columns and Palladian-style front windows are just two examples of Jefferson's influence. Although now part of Cedar Creek and Belle Grove National Historical Park, P.O. Box 700, Middletown, VA 22645 (© **540/868-9176;** www.nps.gov/cebe), the mansion is owned and operated by the National Trust for Historic Preservation. The interior is furnished with period antiques. You must take a guided 45-minute tour to go inside, but you can tour the grounds on your own.

Belle Grove was at the epicenter of the decisive Civil War Battle of Cedar Creek, fought on 4,000 acres surrounding the manor house on October 19, 1864. Across U.S. 11, the **Cedar Creek Battlefield Foundation Visitors Center** (© **888/628-1864** or 540/869-2064; www.cedarcreekbattlefield.org) explains what happened and distributes the National Park Service's battlefield brochure. The battle is reenacted each year on the weekend closest to October 19.

336 Belle Grove Rd. (off U.S. 11), Middletown. © 540/869-2028. www.bellegrove.org. Admission $8 adults, $7 seniors, $4 children 6–12, free for children 5 and younger. Belle Grove Apr–Oct Mon–Sat 10am–4pm, Sun 1–5pm; Nov Sat 10am–3pm, Sun 1–4pm. Closed Dec to mid-Mar except tours at Thanksgiving and Dec 25. Cedar Creek Battlefield Apr–Oct Mon–Sat 10–4pm; Nov–Mar by appointment only. Guided 45-min. house tours depart 15 min. past the hour (last tour 3:15pm). From Winchester, take U.S. 11 south or I-81 south to Exit 302 at Middletown, then U.S. 11 south 1 mile.

The Museum of American Presidents   This small Strasburg museum displays the monumental collection of presidential memorabilia of Leo M. Bernstein, a former Washington, D.C., lawyer and banker who restored the Wayside Inn (see "Where to Stay & Dine," below). Among the highlights are a lock of George Washington's hair and James Madison's writing desk from his bedroom at Montpelier. Next door, the **Jeanne Dixon Museum and Library** contains many papers and personal possessions belonging to the late astrologer and psychic, Bernstein's friend and business associate. Its hours and admission prices are the same as at the presidents' museum. I haven't been in Strasburg on a weekend since it opened, so I have no opinion of the Dixon museum. Note they both are open only on summer weekends.

130 N. Massanutten St. (U.S. 11), Strasburg. © 540/465-5999. www.waysideofva.com. Admission $5 adults, $4 seniors and students, $3 children 6–16, free for children 5 and younger. Combination tickets available with Stonewall Jackson Museum at Hupp's Hill and Crystal Caverns. Memorial Day to Labor Day Sat–Sun 10am–5pm.

Stonewall Jackson Museum at Hupp's Hill and Crystal Caverns   Although not on the same level as the Stonewall Jackson House in Lexington (p. 183), this small museum does a good job of explaining the nine valley battles Stonewall Jackson commanded. It does so from the common soldier's perspective, using Civil War photographs, excerpts from diaries of local residents, and videos. Brochures outline a walking tour of the battlefield. Also on-site, Crystal Caverns are less commercialized than most others in the valley, with tours concentrating on the geology and history of the cave.

33229 Old Valley Pike (U.S. 11), Strasburg. (C) 540/465-5884. www.waysideofva.com. Museum or caverns admission $5 adults, $4 seniors and students, $3 children 6–16, free for children 5 and younger. Combination museum-cavern tickets $9 adults, $7 seniors and children 6–12, free for children 5 and younger. Combination tickets with Museum of American Presidents available. Daily 10am–4pm. Call for cavern tour times.

ANTIQUING

Antiques lovers will want to hunt in nearby Strasburg, which has a bevy of fine outlets at the intersection of U.S. 11 and Va. 55. The **Great Strasburg Antiques Emporium** ★★, 110 N. Massanutten St. ((C) **540/465-3711;** www.strasburgemporium. com), is one of the state's largest shops, an enormous warehouse with vendors selling both antiques and a plethora of collectibles (I have become quite lost wandering around this labyrinth). It's open Sunday to Thursday from 10am to 5pm, Friday and Saturday from 10am to 7pm. A coffee shop at the front serves sandwiches and salads for lunch.

You can't buy them, but there are plenty of antiques at the **Strasburg Museum,** 440 E. King St. (Va. 55; (C) **540/465-3175**), just 2 blocks east of the emporium. It occupies the old train station where Stonewall Jackson brought his stolen locomotives. Admission is $3 for adults, $1 for teenagers, 50¢ for children younger than 12. The museum is open May through October daily from 10am to 4pm.

WHERE TO STAY & DINE

Out in the hills northwest of Middletown, the serene **Inn at Vaucluse Springs,** 231 Vaucluse Spring Lane, Stephens City, VA 22655 ((C) **800/869-0525** or 540/869-0200; www.vauclusespring.com), offers a romantic retreat from life's pressures. It has 15 guest rooms in six buildings, including cottages and a Federal-style mansion house, the inn's centerpiece.

Hotel Strasburg ★   Built as a hospital in 1902, this restored Victorian hotel is furnished with an impressive collection of period pieces. Most units are in the main building, but three suites and a room are in the Chandler House, while the Taylor House holds four suites. Ten rooms have Jacuzzis. Known for excellent international fare, the dining room is Strasburg's best place for breakfast, lunch, or dinner. A first-floor pub offers friendly conversation and libation.

213 Holliday St., Strasburg, VA 22657. (C) **800/348-8327** or 540/465-9191. Fax 540/465-4788. www.hotelstrasburg. com. 29 units. $83–$105 double; $119–$180 suite. Weekend and other packages available. AE, DC, DISC, MC, V. From I-81, take Exit 298 and go south on U.S. 11 1½ miles to the first traffic light; turn right 1 block, left at the light onto Holliday St. **Amenities:** Restaurant; bar; Wi-Fi. *In room:* A/C, TV.

Wayside Inn ★★   This rambling roadside inn first offered libation to Shenandoah Valley travelers in 1724, and it has continued to function ever since. In the 1960s, Washington financier and antiques collector Leo M. Bernstein restored it, and today, rooms are beautifully decorated with an assortment of 18th- and 19th-century pieces. Each room's decor reflects a period style, from Colonial to elaborate Victorian Renaissance Revival. Expect to find canopied beds, armoires, highboys, writing desks, antique clocks, and stenciled or papered walls adorned with fine prints and oil paintings. Southern-style home cooking is served in seven antiques-filled dining rooms. Cocktails and light fare are served in **Larrick's Tavern.**

7783 Main St., Middletown, VA 22645. (C) **877/869-1797** or 540/869-1797. Fax 540/869-6038. www.alongthe wayside.com. 24 units. $99–$159 double. Weekend and theater packages available. AE, DC, DISC, MC, V. From I-81, take Exit 302 to U.S. 11 (Main St.). **Amenities:** Restaurant; bar. *In room:* A/C, TV.

MIDDLETOWN AFTER DARK

Since 1961, the **Wayside Theatre,** 7853 Main St. (U.S. 11) in Middletown ((C) **540/ 869-1776;** www.waysidetheatre.org), has staged fine productions by contemporary dramatists. Actor Peter Boyle and actresses Susan Sarandon and Donna McKechnie began their careers here. Tickets range from $12 to $28. The box office is open Monday to Friday from 10am to 5pm.

4 Front Royal: A Spy's Home

20 miles SE of Strasburg; 174 miles NW of Richmond; 70 miles W of Washington, D.C.

At the northern end of the Skyline Drive, Front Royal has the valley's widest array of outdoor activities: golfing; horseback riding; and canoeing, rafting, kayaking, and inner tubing on the sometimes lazy, sometimes rapid South Fork of the Shenandoah River (see "Rafting, Canoeing & Kayaking on the Shenandoah," below). And if you didn't disappear into the caverns in Luray, you can go underground here. If you're not headed into the great outdoors, you can see the town's sights in half a day.

Strategically located on a plain near a pass in the Blue Ridge and at the juncture of the north and south forks of the Shenandoah River, Front Royal was named for a royal oak that stood in the town square during the Revolutionary War. In those days, it was a wild and woolly frontier way station at the junction of the two trails that later became U.S. 340 and Va. 55. During the Civil War, it was home to the infamous Confederate spy Belle Boyd, whose close contact—to say the least—with Union officers led to Stonewall Jackson's surprise victory at the Battle of Front Royal in 1862.

Across the mountains to the east are two wineries and the nationally famous inn and restaurant in "Little Washington."

ESSENTIALS

VISITOR INFORMATION   Contact the **Front Royal/Warren County Visitors Center,** 414 E. Main St., Front Royal, VA 22630 ((C) **800/338-2576** or 540/635-5788; fax 540/622-2644; www.ci.front-royal.va.us). It's located in the old train station and is open daily from 9am to 5pm except New Year's, Thanksgiving, and Christmas days. From I-66, follow U.S. 340 into town and turn left on Main Street at the Warren County Courthouse.

GETTING THERE   From I-66, take Exit 6, U.S. 340/U.S. 522 south; it's 5 minutes to town. Front Royal is also easily reached from I-81 by taking I-66 east to Exit 6.

EXPLORING THE TOWN & THE CAVERNS

Civil War enthusiasts should pick up a free "Brother Against Brother" driving tour brochure from the visitor center (see "Essentials," above). It will lead you to the key sites of the Battle of Front Royal, which Stonewall Jackson won in May 1862. He directed his troops from atop a knoll in **Prospect Hill Cemetery,** on Prospect Street, where the remains of 276 soldiers from all 13 Confederate states are buried.

Rafting, Canoeing & Kayaking on the Shenandoah

The streams flowing west down from Shenandoah National Park end up in the South Fork of the Shenandoah River, which winds its way through a narrow valley between the Blue Ridge and Massanutten mountains. The switchbacks between Front Royal and Luray are the region's main center for river rafting, canoeing, and kayaking from mid-March to mid-November. The amount of recent rain will determine whether you go white-water rafting, canoeing, kayaking, or just lazily floating downstream in an inner tube.

About 5½ miles of the river skirts the **Raymond R. "Andy" Guest Jr. Shenandoah River State Park,** 8 miles south of Front Royal on U.S. 340 (℃ 540/622-6840; www.dcr.state.va.us/parks/andygues.htm). The park has 5½ miles of river frontage, 13 miles of hiking trails, fishing, horseback riding, picnic areas, and a primitive campground (℃ 800/933-PARK or 804/225-8367 to reserve a site). The park is open daily from 8am to dusk. Admission is $3 per vehicle weekdays, $4 on weekends and holidays.

Several rafting and canoe outfitters are based along U.S. 340, which parallels the river between Front Royal and Luray. All require advance reservations, and all are closed from November through April.

- **Front Royal Canoe Company** (℃ 800/270-8808 or 540/635-5440; www. frontroyalcanoe.com) provides equipment and guides from its location on U.S. 340 south of Front Royal.
- In Bentonville, a small village about 8 miles south of Front Royal, you'll find **Downriver Canoe Company** (℃ 800/338-1963 or 540/635-5526; www. downriver.com).
- Near Luray, you can go with **Shenandoah River Outfitters** (℃ 800/622-6632 or 540/743-4159; www.shenandoah-river.com).

In downtown, you'll find two mildly fascinating Civil War attractions on Chester Street, 1 block north of the visitor center. You should be able to see them both in 1½ hours.

Operated by the United Daughters of the Confederacy, the **Warren Rifles Confederate Museum** (℃ 540/636-6982; http://users.erols.com/va-udc/museum.html) memorializes the great conflict with a collection of Civil War firearms, battle flags, uniforms, letters, diaries, and other personal items. Admission is $3 for adults, free for students and children accompanied by adults. It's open April 15 through November 1 Monday to Saturday from 9am to 4pm, Sunday noon to 4pm, and by appointment the rest of the year.

Next door behind the **Warren Heritage Society** (℃ 540/636-1446; www.warrenhs. org) is the restored **Belle Boyd Cottage,** in which the Confederate spy pillow-talked with her unsuspecting Union lovers. The white, house-size cottage now houses the society's archives. It's open from May through August Monday to Saturday from noon to 4pm; September through April Monday to Friday noon to 4pm. Admission is $3 per person, free for children under 10. Or you can buy a combination ticket for $5 and visit the **Balthis House,** built in 1788 and the oldest remaining house on Chester Street. It was just opening during my recent visit, so call the society for details.

Skyline Caverns *Kids* Although not as varied as those in Luray Caverns (see section 5, below), the highlights here are rock formations called anthodites—delicate white spikes that spread in all directions from their positions on the cave ceiling. Their growth rate is about 1 inch every 7,000 years. A sophisticated lighting system enhances formations like the Capitol Dome, Rainbow Trail, and Painted Desert. A miniature train covering about a half-mile is a popular attraction for kids. The cave temperature is a cool 54°F (12°C) year-round, and the tours take an hour, so bring a sweater, even in summer.

10344 Stonewall Jackson Hwy. (U.S. 340). ℂ 800/296-4545 or 540/635-4545. www.skylinecaverns.com. Admission $16 adults, $8 children 7–13, free for children 6 and younger. Train rides $3 adults, free for children under 6. June 15 to Labor Day daily 9am–6:30pm; Mar 15–June 14 and day after Labor Day to Nov 14 Mon–Fri 9am–5pm, Sat–Sun 9am–6pm; Nov 15–Mar 14 daily 9am–4pm. Mandatory 1-hr. tours run continuously. Entry is 2 miles south of downtown Front Royal, 1 mile south of the Shenandoah National Park's northern entrance.

SPORTS & OUTDOOR ACTIVITIES

GOLF Front Royal has more golf courses than any other valley town. Duffers are welcome at the 27-hole **Shenandoah Valley Golf Club** (ℂ 540/635-3588; www.svgcgolf.com), the 36-hole **Bowling Green Country Club** (ℂ 540/635-2095; www.bowlinggreencc.net), the 18-hole **Jackson's Chase** (ℂ 540/635-7814; www.jacksonschase.com), the 18-hole **Blue Ridge Shadows** (ℂ 866/631-9661 or 540/631-9661; www.blueridgeshadows.com), and the 9-hole **Front Royal Country Club** (ℂ 540/636-9062). Call for directions, starting times, and greens fees.

HORSEBACK RIDING The Front Royal area also offers more horseback riding than anywhere else in the valley. The 4,500-acre **Marriott Ranch,** 5305 Marriott Lane, Hume, VA 22639 (ℂ 877/278-4574 or 540/364-2627; www.marriottranch.com), offers 1½-hour guided trail rides, buggy rides, summer sunset rides, and full-moon rides. Serious equestrians can stay over in **The Inn at Fairfield Farm,** the ranch's bed-and-breakfast inn (ℂ 540/364-3221), which has 10 rooms (7 with bathrooms). Hume is on the eastern side of the Blue Ridge, about 15 minutes from Front Royal via U.S. 522, C.R. 635, and C.R. 726.

   Highlander Horses, 5297 Reliance Rd., Front Royal (ℂ 540/636-4523; www.highlanderhorses.com), is another stable.

WHERE TO STAY

The newest motel here is a **Hampton Inn** (ℂ 800/426-7866 or 540/635-1822), on U.S. 340 south of I-66. The **Quality Inn Skyline Drive** (ℂ 800/228-5151 or 540/635-3161), on U.S. 522 east of U.S. 340, is the largest and best-equipped motel; it's also within walking distance of the visitor center and museums. An inexpensive **Super 8** (ℂ 800/800-8000 or 540/636-4888) is at the junction of U.S. 340 and Va. 55.

   My favorite bed-and-breakfast here is **Killahevlin,** 1401 N. Royal Ave. (ℂ 800/847-6132 or 540/636-7335; www.vairish.com), occupying a hilltop mansion built by William Edward Carson, an Irishman who came to the United States in 1885 when he was 15 years old and amassed a fortune in the limestone business. The house is listed on the National Register of Historic Places. Among its luxurious amenities is an Irish pub just for guests.

   Another good choice is the cozy **Woodward House on Manor Grade,** 413 S. Royal Ave./U.S. 340 South (ℂ 800/635-7011; www.acountryhome.com), 7 blocks south of the visitor center.

WHERE TO DINE

Main Street Mill Restaurant and Pub AMERICAN   Occupying a picturesque 1922 mill building next door to the visitor center, this establishment has massive supporting columns and ceiling beams of chestnut. Local artist Patricia Windrow executed the distinctive *trompe l'oeil* murals representing Front Royal's pioneer and 19th-century eras. Lunch fare includes soups, spicy chili, salads, and overstuffed deli sandwiches. Main courses range from pastas to bacon-wrapped filet mignon to a Virginia ham dinner.

500 E Main St. (next to visitor center) ℂ 540/636-3123. Reservations not needed. Sandwiches $5–$6.50; main courses $10–$18. AE, MC, V. Sun–Thurs 10:30am–9pm; Fri–Sat 10:30am–10pm.

Soul Mountain Café *(finds)* INTERNATIONAL   A porcelain Buddha oversees this lively storefront bistro, where a crew of young chefs turn out wide-ranging fare. The mesclun salad with roasted tomato and tossed with pesto was very good and large enough for a light meal. Andouille sausage sautéed with peppers over penne pasta was almost too cayenne-laden to eat, but the slow-roasted Jamaican jerk chicken with coconut cream treated my tropically inspired tongue with the utmost respect.

300 E. Main St. (at Chester St.). ℂ 540/636-0070. Reservations accepted. Main courses $11–$25. MC, V. Mon–Sat noon–9pm; Sun noon–4pm.

OVER THE MOUNTAINS TO "LITTLE WASHINGTON"

A more scenic alternative to taking the short route via U.S. 340 south from Front Royal to Luray is U.S. 522 across the Blue Ridge, then U.S. 211 west across Thornton Gap. This route takes you into the eastern Blue Ridge foothills, which are a southern extension of the Hunt Country described in chapter 4. The northern entry to the Shenandoah National Park's Central District is on U.S. 211.

Going this way will give you a chance to tipple the vintages at two reasonably good wineries, both on Hume Road (C.R. 635) between U.S. 522 and the village of Hume. You come first to **Rappahannock Cellars** (ℂ 540/635-9398; www.rappahannock cellars.com), whose owners moved their winery here from California. It's open Sunday through Friday 11:30am to 5pm, Saturday 11:30am to 6pm. Next is the acclaimed **Oasis Winery** (ℂ 540/635-7627; www.oasiswine.com), whose Cuvée D'or brut has won international accolades. It's open Monday to Friday 11am to 5pm, Saturday and Sunday 11am to 6pm.

Just off U.S. 211 you'll come to the two-street village of **Washington,** better known in these parts as "Little Washington." Then–surveyor's assistant George Washington helped lay it out in 1749. Today it's dominated by The Inn at Little Washington (see below), but we common folk can walk across the street and grab a bite at the plain and inexpensive **Country Cafe** (ℂ 540/675-1066). It's open Monday to Thursday 8am to 8pm, Friday and Saturday 8am to 9pm. We can also catch chamber music, jazz, drama, or a film at **The Theatre at Washington** (ℂ 540/675-1253; www.theatre-washington-va.com) and at **Ki Theatre** (ℂ 540/987-3164; www.kitheatre.org).

Rather than forking over a king's ransom to stay at The Inn at Little Washington, we can retire at the **Heritage House Bed and Breakfast** (ℂ 888/819-8280; www.heritagehousebb.com) or the more expensive **Foster Harris House Bed and Breakfast** (ℂ 800/874-1036 or 540/675-3757; www.fosterharris.com). Both are on Washington's Main Street.

Caledonia Farm–1812 *(★★)*   This 1812 Federal-style stone farmhouse, listed on the National Register of Historic Places, is a delightful country retreat set on a 115-acre working cattle farm adjacent to the Shenandoah National Park. A scenic old barn, livestock, and open pastureland make for a bucolic setting. The common rooms are furnished with country charm. The upstairs suite has two bedrooms and a private bathroom. A breezeway connects the main house with the romantic two-and-a-half-room guesthouse. Both suites offer working fireplaces and views of the Blue Ridge. TVs, VCRs, coffeemakers, and irons are available on request. There are bikes and a hot tub for guests' use. Host Phil Irwin, a retired broadcaster (as his deep voice will attest), is the county tourism coordinator and will arrange hayrides and many other activities. Phil has stables for your pet horse. You can drive into the hamlet of Flint Hill and have dinner Wednesday through Saturday at the fine **Four & Twenty Black-birds** (© 540/675-1111).

47 Dearing Rd., Flint Hill, VA 22627. © 800/262-1812 or 540/675-3693. www.bnb1812.com. 2 units. $140 double. Rates include full breakfast. DISC, MC, V. From Front Royal, take U.S. 522 south 12 miles to Flint Hill and turn right onto C.R. 641, to C.R. 606 and then to C.R. 628; look for a sign indicating a right turn to the farm. No children under 13. **Amenities:** Bikes; hot tub. *In room:* A/C, TV/VCR (on request), fridge, coffeemaker (on request).

The Inn at Little Washington ★★★ One of America's finest country inns, this marvelous establishment is not so much an outstanding inn with a restaurant as it is an outstanding restaurant with outstanding rooms. Owner/chef Patrick O'Connell makes inventive use of regional products—trout, Chesapeake Bay seafood, wild ducks, local cheeses—for his fabulous fixed-price dinners (if you have to ask how much, your credit limit likely isn't high enough). For a real treat, reserve one of the two fireside tables back in the kitchen, where you can watch the master and his crew at work. The extraordinary 14,000-bottle wine cellar may leave you pondering before selecting from its 40-page list (trust the waiters; they know what they're doing even if you don't). Dinner reservations are essential. They begin taking them 30 days in advance, and Saturdays are often fully booked within 2 days.

English decorator Joyce Evans magnificently appointed the inn's rooms, and her orig-inal sketches are framed and hanging in the upstairs hallways. The two bi-level suites have loft bedrooms, balconies overlooking the courtyard garden, and bathrooms with Jacuzzi tubs. Antiques and Oriental rugs add warmth to the rooms, distinguished by extravagantly canopied beds and hand-painted ceiling borders. Some rooms are across the street atop the inn's shops: The old Mayor's House has been turned into a suite with its own garden, and three other houses provide accommodations, including the Rose Cottage, which has hosted former Vice President Al Gore and his wife, Tipper.

Middle and Main sts. (P.O. Box 300), Washington, VA 22747. © 540/675-3800. Fax 540/675-3100. www.theinnatlittle washington.com. 15 units. $400–$970 double; $745–$1,255 suite. Rates include continental breakfast and afternoon tea. MC, V. From Front Royal, take U.S. 522 south 16 miles, then west on U.S. 211 to Washington. **Amenities:** Restau-rant; bar; Jacuzzi; room service; in-room massage; babysitting; laundry service. *In room:* A/C, safe.

5 Luray: An Underground Organ

6 miles W of Shenandoah National Park; 91 miles SW of Washington, D.C.; 135 miles NW of Richmond

Established in 1812, this small town is home to the famous Luray Caverns, the most visited caves in the eastern United States. Although Luray has little else in the way of attractions, its accommodations are the closest to the Shenandoah National Park's popular Central District. Thus, it is the most convenient base in the valley if you can't get a room at one of the park's inns. The park headquarters and the Thornton Gap entry are up U.S. 211 a few miles east of town.

Luray also is near the South Fork of the Shenandoah River, making it a center of watersports (see "Rafting, Canoeing & Kayaking on the Shenandoah," above). You can also go horseback riding at a charming country inn nearby.

ESSENTIALS

VISITOR INFORMATION The **Luray–Page County Chamber of Commerce,** 46 E. Main St., Luray, VA 22835 (✆ **888/743-3915** or 540/743-3915; fax 540/743-3944; www.luraypage.com), is open daily 9am to 5pm. The chamber's visitor center is a good source of information about Shenandoah National Park.

GETTING THERE From Shenandoah National Park, take U.S. 211 west. From I-81, follow U.S. 211 East (this scenic road goes up and over Massanutten Mountain; see "A Mountain Resort with Golf & Skiing," below). From Front Royal, take U.S. 340 south.

EXPLORING THE CAVERNS

Luray Caverns ★ This U.S. Registered Natural Landmark is the Shenandoah Valley's most interesting and entertaining cave. In addition to monumental columns in rooms more than 140 feet high, you'll see beautiful cascades of natural colors on the interior walls. The works of man and nature are combined into an unusual organ that produces music when rubber-tipped plungers tap the stalactites. Guided 1-hour tours depart every 20 minutes and follow a system of brick-and-concrete walkways. It's about 55°F (13°C) down here all the time, so bring a jacket or sweater.

You get more for your money here, for admission to the caverns includes the **Car and Carriage Caravan Museum,** a collection of antique carriages, coaches, and cars—including actor Rudolph Valentino's 1925 Rolls-Royce. The complex also contains a snack bar, gift shop, and fudge kitchen. Separate admission is charged to get thoroughly confused in the outdoor **Garden Maze.**

Across U.S. 211 stands the **Luray Singing Tower,** a stone carillon with 47 bells. It was given to the town of Luray in 1937 as a memorial to one of its residents. Free concerts are given spring through autumn (pick up a schedule at the Luray visitor center or at the caverns).

U.S. 211 west (2 miles west of downtown). ✆ **540/743-6551.** www.luraycaverns.com. Admission to caverns and car museum $19 adults, $16 seniors, $9 children 6–12, free for children 5 and younger; Garden Maze $5 adults, $4 children. Apr–June 14 daily 9am–6pm; June 15 to Labor Day daily 9am–7pm; day after Labor Day to Oct daily 9am–6pm; Nov–Mar Mon–Fri 9am–4pm, Sat–Sun 9am–5pm. Guided 1-hr. tours of caverns depart every 20 min. Self-guided tour of car museum.

Luray Zoo *(Kids)* Various "wild animal parks" and even a "Dinosaur Land" vie for your attention in the Shenandoah. If you're traveling with children, this small zoo is worth a stop. It's a rescue facility, which means owners Kilby and Jennifer Westhoff take in unwanted or abused exotic animals, including crocodiles and alligators. The snake collection is one of the largest on the East Coast. Best times to visit are the 11:30am animal encounter show or the 3:30pm venomous snake demonstration from Memorial Day to Labor Day.

1087 U.S. Hwy. 211 W. (2 miles west of downtown). ✆ **540/743-4113.** www.lurayzoo.com. Admission $10 adults, $5 children 3–12, free for children 2 and younger. Apr–Oct daily 10am–5pm; Nov–Mar Sat–Sun 10am–5pm.

WHERE TO STAY

Just as bed-and-breakfasts proliferated during the 1980s and early 1990s, **mountain cabins** are the latest trend around Luray. One worthy example is **Shadow Mountain**

Escape, 1132 Jewell Hollow Rd. (© **540/843-0584;** www.shadowmountainescape. com), with three timber-frame cabins set on 15 acres bordering Shenandoah National Park. The visitor center (see "Essentials," above) can provide information about others.

The **Days Inn,** on U.S. 211 northeast of town (© **800/325-2525** or 540/743-4521), is surrounded by acres of farmland, giving most rooms mountain views. The **Best Western,** on West Main Street/U.S. 211 Business (© **800/528-1234** or 540/743-6511), is an older motel in town. Both have outdoor swimming pools.

The Cabins at Brookside 🐾   Owners Bob and Cece Castle remodeled this 1940s service station/motel into a collection of log-look cabins with comfortable Williamsburg-style furnishings throughout. These are the closest accommodations to the Shenandoah National Park's Central District. Although located along busy U.S. 211, the rear of the cabins open to decks or sunrooms overlooking a bubbling brook, and road noise dies down after dark. Four "honeymoon" units have whirlpool tubs or hot tubs, four have gas fireplaces, and one has a kitchen (the others, refrigerators only). None has a TV or phone, but three newer cabins about 2 miles away do. Open for breakfast, lunch, and dinner, the **Brookside Restaurant** on the premises serves inexpensive Southern-style home cooking.

2978 U.S. 211 E., Luray, VA 22835. © 800/299-2655 or 540/743-5698. Fax 540/743-2413. www.brooksidecabins. com. 12 cabins. $85–$195 double. AE, DC, DISC, MC, V. From Luray, go east 4½ miles on U.S. 211. From Shenandoah National Park Headquarters, go west ½ mile on U.S. 211. **Amenities:** Restaurant. *In room:* A/C, fridge, coffeemaker, no phone.

Luray Caverns Motel West *Value*   Sitting opposite Luray Caverns, which owns and spotlessly maintains it, this older one-story motel with a plantation facade is dated, but the spacious rooms have pleasant views across pastureland to the Blue Ridge Mountains. The choice unit is an apartment with full kitchen. A sister establishment, the equally clean **Luray Caverns Motel East** (© **540/743-4531**), is a short distance east on U.S. 211 Business. Many of its 44 units are small but comfortable stone cottages. Rates are the same at both motels.

U.S. 211 W. (P.O. Box 748), Luray, VA 22835. © 540/743-4536. 19 units. $68–$90 double; $168 apt. Rates include continental breakfast. AE, DISC, MC, V. **Amenities:** Outdoor pool. *In room:* A/C, TV, coffeemaker.

BED & BREAKFASTS

Woodruff Inns 🐾🐾   Owners Lucas and Deborah Woodruff have converted three Victorian houses into charming B&Bs. Their star is **The Victorian Inn,** on Main Street, which has three romantic, Jacuzzi-equipped suites. The suites have sun-filled sitting rooms and balconies with private entries so you don't have to go through the house to get to your room. The master suite also has a fireplace—in the bathroom, of all places. Less expensive but nonetheless charming are rooms in the nearby **Woodruff House** and **The Victorian Rose.** They both have hot tubs in their gardens. All three houses are furnished with mid- to late-19th-century antiques. The Woodruffs also have riverside cottages for rent.

138 E. Main St., Luray, VA 22835. © 866/937-3466 or 540/743-1494. Fax 540/743-1722. www.woodruffinns.com. 9 units. $129–$219 double; $239–$325 suite. Rates include breakfast, afternoon tea. DISC, MC, V. **Amenities:** Jacuzzi; massage. *In room:* A/C, coffeemaker.

A NEARBY EQUESTRIAN INN

Jordan Hollow Inn 🐾🐾   Horse lovers and hikers have been enjoying this working farm and inn since 1980. It has a stable of horses and ponies and 5 picturesque miles of hiking trails at the base of Hawksbill Mountain. They rent horses and have 1½-hour

New Market: Students at War

Between Luray and Staunton at the intersection of I-81 and U.S. 211, the village of **New Market** holds a hallowed place in Civil War history, for it was here that 257 Virginia Military Institute cadets charged the veteran Union lines on May 15, 1864, won the day, and returned to campus victorious. A descendant of Thomas Jefferson and nine other students were killed and 47 were wounded. Hearing of the battle, Union Gen. Ulysses S. Grant exclaimed, "The South is robbing the cradle and the grave."

Today the cadets are honored by the **New Market Battlefield State Historical Park** and the **Hall of Valor Museum** ✪✪, 8895 Collins Dr. ((©️ 540/740-3101; www4.vmi.edu/museum/nm). The Hall of Valor is one of Virginia's finest Civil War museums. Two films, including the award-winning "Field of Lost Shoes" (45 min.), tell the story. Explaining the military strategies, the museum's circular display of photos and newspaper headlines is the best chronological account of the war in Virginia I've seen. It begins with a wall-size painting of Richmond before the war and ends with a photo of the burned-out city in 1865.

Outside on the rolling, grassy fields, students lead 1-hour tours at 1 and 3pm daily during summer, or you can take a self-guided 1-mile walking tour along the final Confederate assault on the Union line. The Bushong farmhouse, which served as a battlefield hospital, is now a museum of 19th-century valley life.

Admission is $9 for adults, $8 seniors and active-duty military, $5 for children 6 to 17, free for kids under 6. The museum is open daily 9am to 5pm except New Year's Day, Thanksgiving, and Christmas. The battle is reenacted in mid-May.

While here you can explore New Market's many antique and collectibles stores along Congress Street (U.S. 11) and sample good home cooking at the inexpensive **Southern Kitchen,** 9576 Congress St. ((©️ **540/740-3514**), ½ mile south of the I-81 interchange. It's open daily 7am to 9pm.

guided trail rides of the property ($38 per person). The inn has been undergoing improvements of late, including the installation of log veneers on the buildings to add a rustic touch. A spa and tennis courts were on the drawing board. Three types of guest quarters are offered. Those in the vine-entangled Arbor View are suites with separate living rooms and spacious, romantic bedrooms with a two-person whirlpool tub in one corner, a realistic-looking electric fireplace in another. The bedrooms open to a long porch with high-backed rockers suitable for taking in the mountain view. The units in the log-sided, cabinlike Mare Meadow Lodge sport oversize rustic furniture. Most luxurious of all are six log cabins recently built atop a hill with great views of Hawksbill Mountain. These have two-person hot tubs, flatscreen TVs with DVD players, and small fireplaces.

The Farmhouse Restaurant, in the original clapboard homestead with wrap-around porches upstairs and down, offers very good cuisine, much of it with an Indian flare, along with Virginia wine. It's open for dinner daily from 5 to 9:30pm. Reservations recommended.

326 Hawksbill Park Rd., Stanley, VA 22851. © **888/418-7000** or 540/778-2285. Fax 540/778-1759. www.jordan hollow.com. 14 units. $190–$250 double; $300 cabin. Rates include full breakfast. AE, DC, DISC, MC, V. Closed 1–3 weeks in Jan. From Luray, take U.S. 340 south 6 miles, turn left on Hawksbill Park Dr. (C.R. 624), left on Marksville Rd. (C.R. 689), right on Hawksbill Park Rd. (C.R. 629). **Amenities:** Restaurant (American/Indian); business center; in-room massage. *In room:* A/C, TV, coffeemaker, iron.

WHERE TO DINE

The **Farmhouse Restaurant,** at Jordan Hollow Inn (see "A Nearby Equestrian Inn," above), serves some of the best cuisine in this area. For inexpensive country cooking, drive out to the **Brookside Restaurant,** at The Cabins at Brookside (p. 166).

A Moment to Remember Espresso Bar & Cafe AMERICAN   Across Main Street from the visitor center, this converted Victorian-era hardware store still has its pressed-tin ceiling, oak counter, nail and screw drawers, and shelves, which now hold books and knickknacks. It's the business district's favorite place for morning coffee, bagels, and croissants, or for a lunch of freshly made salads and sandwiches ranging from a simple BLT to a tasty Thai chicken wrap. Dinner is served Friday and Saturday nights, with the likes of curried salmon and chile-rubbed pork tenderloin.

55 E. Main St. © **540/743-1121.** Reservations not accepted. Breakfast $3.50–$6; sandwiches $6–$8; main courses $12–$16 (Fri–Sat only). MC, V. Mon–Thurs 8am–4pm; Fri–Sat 8am–9pm.

The Victorian Inn 🎯🎯 REGIONAL   At night the first floor of this romantic member of the Woodruff Inns (see "Where to Stay," above) turns into Luray's only fine-dining venue. The menu varies by season and availability of local produce. One autumn evening saw pork tenderloin with a spiced pear sauce and Cornish hen with an apple cider sauce. Summer might see salmon baked in a garlic-wine sauce. Barboursville Vineyards provides the house wines.

138 E. Main St. © **540/743-1494.** Reservations requested on weekends. Main courses $18–$30. AE, DISC, MC, V. Wed–Sun 5–9pm.

A MOUNTAIN RESORT WITH GOLF & SKIING

Primarily a timeshare operation, **Massanutten Resort,** P.O. Box 1227, Harrisonburg, VA 22801 (© **800/207-6277** or 540/289-9441; www.massresort.com), offers year-round outdoor activities. The property has 27 holes of golf, tennis courts, indoor and outdoor swimming pools, a half-dozen downhill ski slopes, and areas for snowboarding and snow tubing (riding inner tubes down a gentle slope). The 140 hotel rooms have a queen-size or two double beds, sitting areas, and balconies. Most of the 800-plus timeshare units are equipped with kitchens, fireplaces, and decks, and many have whirlpools. There's a full-service restaurant, a pizzeria, bar, and grocery store on-site. From I-81, take Exit 247A and follow U.S. 33 east 10 miles to the resort entrance on the left.

6 Staunton: A Presidential Birthplace & the Bard's Playhouse 🎯🎯🎯

42 miles S of New Market; 142 miles SW of Washington, D.C.; 92 miles NW of Richmond

The birthplace of Woodrow Wilson, our 28th president, Staunton (pronounced "*Stanton*") is equally proud today of its Blackfriars Playhouse, a stunning replica of one of Shakespeare's theaters, which has brought the Bard to the Shenandoah and made Staunton the valley's prime performing-arts center. Along with Wilson's first home,

Staunton

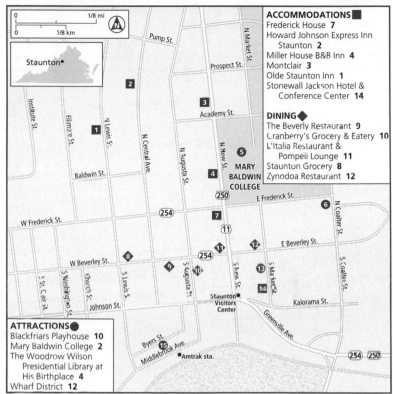

ACCOMMODATIONS ■
Frederick House **7**
Howard Johnson Express Inn
   Staunton **2**
Miller House B&B Inn **4**
Montclair **3**
Olde Staunton Inn **1**
Stonewall Jackson Hotel &
   Conference Center **14**

DINING ◆
The Beverly Restaurant **9**
Cranberry's Grocery & Eatery **10**
L'Italia Restaurant &
   Pompeii Lounge **11**
Staunton Grocery **8**
Zynodoa Restaurant **12**

ATTRACTIONS ●
Blackfriars Playhouse **10**
Mary Baldwin College **2**
The Woodrow Wilson
   Presidential Library at
   His Birthplace **4**
Wharf District **12**

many 19th-century downtown buildings in Staunton's revitalized historic district have been refurbished, including the train station and its adjacent **Wharf District,** now a shopping and dining complex. **Mary Baldwin College,** whose pastoral campus lies across the street from the Wilson birthplace, lends a university atmosphere to this downtown in renaissance.

Settled well before the Revolution, Staunton was a major stop for pioneers on the way west. The Frontier Culture Museum on the outskirts of town explains the origins of the unique Shenandoah Valley farming communities. In the early 1800s, this was the eastern terminus of the Staunton-Parkersburg Turnpike (now U.S. 250), a major mountain road linking the Shenandoah Valley and the Ohio River. When the Central Virginia Railroad arrived in 1854, Staunton became even more of a regional center.

Plan to spend at least a full day exploring one of Virginia's best small towns and an evening at the theater.

ESSENTIALS
VISITOR INFORMATION   The **Staunton Visitors Center,** 35 S. New St. (at Johnson St.), Staunton, VA 24401 (© **540/332-3971;** www.stauntonva.org), provides information, free maps, and walking-tour brochures to the historic district. It's open from May through December daily 9am to 6:30pm, January through March daily 9:30am to 5:30pm.

Fun Fact **Mr. Jefferson on the Run**

Staunton served as Virginia's capital for 17 days during June 1781, when then-Governor Thomas Jefferson fled Richmond to avoid advancing British troops.

You can get general information from the **Staunton/Augusta County Travel Information Center** (© 800/332-5219 or 540/332-3972) at the Frontier Culture Museum, on U.S. 250 west of Exit 222 off I-81. It is open daily from 9am to 5pm except New Year's Day, Thanksgiving, and Christmas.

GETTING THERE   Staunton is at the junctions of I-64 and I-81 and U.S. 11 and U.S. 250. **Amtrak** trains serve Staunton's station at 1 Middlebrook Ave. (© 800/872-7245; www.amtrak.com).

GETTING AROUND   The free **Downtown Staunton Trolley** runs around town approximately every 25 minutes. The Green Line covers downtown and nearby areas, while the Silver Line goes farther afield. The Red Line runs around downtown on Friday and Saturday evenings. Their hours change seasonally, so pick up a schedule at the Staunton Visitors Center, the trolley's first stop (see "Visitor Information," above). Riding the Green Line will give you an informative 25-minute tour of the town.

EXPLORING THE TOWN

Downtown Staunton is a treasure-trove of Victorian architecture, from stately residences to the commercial buildings downtown and in the adjacent Wharf District (actually along the railroad, not a river). Pick up a walking-tour brochure from the visitor center (see "Essentials," above), and set out on your own. The brochure describes five tours, but be sure to take the "Beverly" and "Wharf" tours, which cover all of historic downtown.

Free 2-hour **guided tours** of downtown depart from in front of The Woodrow Wilson Presidential Library at His Birthplace at 10am on Saturday from May through October. Whether you do it yourself or take the guided tour, be prepared to work up a sweat: Staunton is built on the side of a steep hill, a la San Francisco.

Blackfriars Playhouse ✦✦✦ *Finds*   Home to the **American Shakespeare Center,** this stunning re-creation of the first indoor theater in the English-speaking world, which William Shakespeare and his colleagues built on part of London's Blackfriars Monastery in 1642, is, in itself, a reason to visit Staunton. As in the Bard's time, the audience sits on three sides of the stage, most on benches (don't worry; you can rent cushions and seat backs). Members of the theater's acclaimed resident company as well as touring troupes perform Shakespeare's masterpieces, but the theater also hosts other classic plays and performances by modern-day musicians. Be sure to take an actor-led guided tour, which sheds light not only on this theater but how plays were performed in the Bard's day. *Note:* The theater is dark Monday and Tuesday.

10 S. Market St. (between Beverley and Johnson sts.). Box office at 35 S. New St. (at Johnson St.). © 877/682-4235 or 540/851-1733. www.americanshakespearecenter.com/blackfriars-playhouse. Tours $5; tickets $18–$36. Box office Mon–Sat 10am–5pm. 1-hr. tours usually Mon–Fri 11am and 2pm, Sat 11am (call for current schedule).

Frontier Culture Museum *Kids*   In light of its history as a major stopping point for pioneers, Staunton is a logical location for this museum, which consists of 17th-, 18th-, and 19th-century working farmsteads representing the origins of the Shenandoah's early settlers—Northern Irish, English, and German—and explaining how aspects of each were blended into a fourth farm, a typical Colonial American homestead. Staff members in period costumes plant fields, tend livestock, and do domestic chores. A 15-minute film will set the stage for your self-guided exploration, which will take about 2 hours to thoroughly cover. Children will love seeing the animals, but bring them in warm weather since many exhibits are outdoors. The museum store sells fudge freshly made by the dairy farm.

Richmond Rd. (U.S. 250), ½ mile west of I-81. ☎ 540/332-7850. www.frontiermuseum.org. Admission $10 adults, $9.50 seniors, $9 students, $6 children 6–12, free for children 5 and younger. Mid-Mar to Dec daily 9am–5pm; Jan to mid-Mar daily 10am–4pm. Closed Jan 1, Thanksgiving, and Dec 25.

The Woodrow Wilson Presidential Library at His Birthplace ✺✺✺ A National Historic Landmark, this handsome home, built in 1846 by a Presbyterian congregation as a manse for their ministers, stands beside an excellent library and museum detailing Wilson's life. The future president was born here on December 28, 1856, but as a minister, Wilson's father had to move often, and so the family left Staunton when he was only 2. The house is furnished with many family items, including the crib Wilson slept in and the chair in which his mother rocked him. The galleries of the museum next door trace Wilson's Scotch-Irish roots, his academic career as a professor and president at Princeton University, and, of course, his 8 presidential years (1913–21). America's entry into World War I and Wilson's unsuccessful efforts to convince the U.S. Senate to participate in the League of Nations are also explored. Don't overlook the beautiful Victorian garden or Wilson's presidential limousine, a shiny Pierce-Arrow, in the museum. You must take the 40-minute guided tour of the house, but you can wander through the museum and gardens on your own. About 1½ hours will be required to see it all.

24 N. Coalter St. (at Frederick St.). ☎ 888/496-6376 or 540/885-0897. www.woodrowwilson.org. Admission $8 adults, $5 students, $3 children 6–12, free for children 5 and younger. Mar–Oct Mon–Sat 9am–5pm, Sun noon–5pm; Nov–Feb Mon–Sat 10am–4pm, Sun noon–4pm. 40-min. guided house tours depart every 45 min.

SHOPPING

Beverley Street between Lewis and Market streets—downtown Staunton's main drag—is a fine place to browse a number of art galleries and antiques stores. More than 40 antiques and collectibles dealers rent space in **The Staunton Antique Market,** 19 W. Beverley St. (☎ **540/886-7277;** www.stauntonantiques.com). I'm always left astounded by the vast collection of old stuff crammed into **Worthington Hardware Co.,** 26 W. Beverley St. (☎ **540/885-0891**), which once was a hardware store. The **Wharf District,** along Middlebrook Avenue and Byers Street, has more antiques shops.

Fans of the singing Statler Brothers, who grew up here, can buy their albums and souvenirs at their **Statler Brothers Gift Shop,** 1409 N. August St. (☎ **540/885-7297;** www.statlerbrothers.com).

The town of Waynesboro, 15 miles east of Staunton on I-64, is home to the **Artisans Center of Virginia,** 801 W. Broad St. (U.S. 340; ☎ **877/508-6069** or 540/946-3294; www.artisanscenterofvirginia.org), which represents more than 200 skilled artisans from throughout the Virginia, each chosen by a jury. You can both browse and buy their work in the center's gallery. Also in Waynesville is the **P. Buckley Moss Museum,** 150 P. Buckley Moss Dr. (☎ **800/343-8643** or 540/949-6473; www. pbuckleymoss.com), which displays her endearing paintings, many inspired by the valley's Amish and Mennonite communities. She has been a full- or part-time resident of Waynesboro since 1964.

WHERE TO STAY

The budget-priced **Howard Johnson Express Inn,** 268 N. Central Ave. (© **800/ 446-4656** or 540/886-5330; www.hojo.com), is downtown's only chain motel. The four-story building faces a parking lot, but the rooms are moderately spacious and reasonably comfortable. Three rooms have Jacuzzi tubs, and there's an outdoor pool.

Near Exit 225 off I-85 (Woodrow Wilson Pkwy.) north of town, the **Holiday Inn Golf & Conference Center** (© 800/465-4329 or 540/248-6020) is adjacent to the Country Club of Staunton, where guests can play. Staunton's largest concentration of motels is on U.S. 250 at Exit 222 off I-81, where you'll find the **Best Western Staunton Inn** (© 800/528-1234 or 540/885-1112), a **Comfort Inn** (© 800/228-5150 or 540/886-5000), an above-average **EconoLodge** (© 800/446-6900 or 540/ 885-5158), a **Hampton Inn** (© 800/426-7866 or 540/886-7000), and a **Super 8** (© 800/800-8000 or 540/886-2888).

Frederick House ★★   I always stay in one of these seven historic town houses dating from 1810 and now a cross between an inn and a bed-and-breakfast. The rooms and suites are individually decorated with authentic antiques and reproductions from the Victorian era. Most have gleaming hardwood floors below Oriental rugs, and seven units have fireplaces. All suites have separate living rooms, and three of them have two bedrooms. If you don't mind bright light at the crack of dawn, my favorite unit here is the Harmon Suite, whose bedroom once was a sun porch extending across the rear of one of the houses. With an oversize king-size bed, it's understandably the honeymoon suite. Frederick House is across the street from Mary Baldwin College and just 2 blocks from Woodrow Wilson's birthplace and the Blackfriars Playhouse. Hosts Karen Cooksey and Denny Eister serve gourmet breakfasts including delicious whole-grain waffles.

28 N. New St., Staunton, VA 24401. © **800/334-5575** or 540/885-4220. Fax 540/885-5180. www.frederickhouse. com. 23 units. $99–$169 double; $149–$249 suite. Rates include full breakfast. Theater and other packages available. AE, DISC, MC, V. **Amenities:** Access to nearby health club; laundry service. *In room:* A/C, TV, Wi-Fi.

Stonewall Jackson Hotel & Conference Center   Next door to the Blackfriars Playhouse, this classic downtown hotel first opened in 1924 and served as Staunton's special-occasions center until the 1960s, when it fell on hard times and was turned into an assisted-living facility. Thanks to a recent $21-million restoration, it's back in business as the town's prime commercial hotel and conference center. Be sure to walk up on the mezzanine and check out the 1924 Wurlitzer piano-organ. It overlooks the bright lobby whose walls showcase some of the hotel's original silverware, dishes, and other 1920s mementos. A restaurant off the lobby was serving breakfast daily and dinner Friday through Saturday nights during my visit. Rooms in the original building were expanded and updated but are still a tad smaller than those in a new wing added during the restoration. They all have antique-look furniture, writing desks, two phones, and bathrooms with ample granite vanities. There's an indoor pool here.

24 S. Market St., Staunton, VA 24401. © **866/880-0024** or 540/885-4848. Fax 540/885-4840. www.stonewall jacksonhotel.com. 124 units. $89–$179 double; $200–$400 suite. AE, DC, DISC, MC, V. **Amenities:** Restaurant (American); bar; indoor pool; Jacuzzi; exercise room; business center; room service; laundry service. *In room:* A/C, TV, Wi-Fi, high-speed Internet, coffeemaker, iron.

Fun Fact **The 1950s Live**

The 1950s are still very much alive at **Wright's Dairy Rite,** 346 Greenville Ave. (U.S. 11), a block south of Richmond Road (© **540/886-0435**), a classic drive-in that has had carhop service since it opened in 1952. Even if you dine inside this brick building or outside on the patio, you must lift a phone to place your order, and wait for it to be delivered to your leatherette booth. Nothing here costs more than $8. MasterCard and Visa are accepted. Sunday through Thursday from 10am to 10pm, Friday and Saturday from 10am to 11pm (to 9 and 10pm, respectively, during winter).

BED & BREAKFASTS

Bed-and-breakfasts in Staunton include **Miller House Bed & Breakfast Inn,** 210 N. New St. (© **877/996-3186** or 540/886-3186; www.millerhousebandb.com), a large Victorian with wraparound porch; **Olde Staunton Inn,** 260 N. Lewis St. (© **866/653-3786** or 540/886-0193; www.oldestauntoninn.com), a 1910-vintage home; and **Montclair,** 320 N. New St. (© **877/885-8823** or 540/885-8832; www.bbonline.com/va/montclair).

WHERE TO DINE

Staunton probably runs second only to Charlottesville in restaurants per capita, and it keeps adding more as the town's renaissance continues. In fact, there are so many that I wonder if the local residents know how to cook for themselves.

Staunton Station, the town's old railway depot on Middlebrook Avenue between Augusta and Lewis streets in the Wharf District, is now a dining/entertainment complex. Here you'll find **The Depot Grille** (© **540/885-7332**) and **The Pullman Restaurant** (© **540/885-6612**), both publike establishments. The Pullman has better food and outdoor seating, while The Depot Grille is more family oriented. Nearby in the Wharf District, **Byers Street Bistro** (© **540/887-8100**) is a lively restaurant-bar with warm-weather outdoor tables fronting a municipal parking lot on Byers Street at Central Avenue. All are moderately priced.

A nearby pub I like for both food and ambience is **Mill Street Grill,** 1 Mill St. (© **540/886-0656**), south of Johnson Street. Occupying the basement of the old White Star mill, which produced Melrose flour from 1890 to 1963, it offers barbecue ribs, steaks, prime rib, and seafood as well as vegetarian dishes. Heavy beams and backlit stained-glass windows portraying chefs at work contribute to a warm and cozy ambience.

On Beverly Street, in the heart of downtown, **Baja Bean & Co. Restaurant & Cantina,** 9 W. Beverly St. (© **540/885-9988**), uses fresh ingredients in its Southern California–influenced Mexican cuisine. Local young folk hang out at the **Clock Tower Tavern,** 27 W. Beverly St. (© **540/213-2403**), which serves American fare and provides live music after 9pm on weekends. It gets its name from the clock tower atop the building. For daytime soups, salads, and sandwiches, head for **The Pampered Palate Café,** 26–28 E. Beverly St. (© **540/886-9463**), which is open Monday, Tuesday, and Saturday 9am to 5:30pm, Wednesday through Friday 9am to 7:30pm.

The Beverly Restaurant *Value* AMERICAN   Family-owned and -operated since 1961, this storefront eatery in the heart of the business district hearkens back to that nearly bygone era when even hash-house cooks made everything from scratch. The fresh fare is typically small-town Southern: rib-eye steaks, fried shrimp or fish, veal cutlets, and roast beef. I think the old-fashioned cooked breakfasts are the best in downtown. English tea is served from 3 to 5pm.

12 E. Beverly St. (℃) **540/886-4317.** Reservations not accepted. Breakfast $2–$6; sandwiches $4.50–$7.50; main courses $5.50–$8. MC, V. Mon–Fri 7am–7pm; Sat 8am–3pm.

Cranberry's Grocery & Eatery *Value* HEALTH/VEGETARIAN   Walk through this gourmet natural-foods grocery to the counter in the rear, where you can order the healthiest breakfast or lunch in Staunton. Fresh fruit, freshly baked muffins, and yeast waffles lead the morning list. Lunch brings sandwiches, salads, and huge wraps, some with meat or chicken but most vegetarian. Wash it down with a freshly squeezed veggie juice.

75 New St. (℃) **540/885-4755.** Reservations not accepted. Breakfast $3–$6; salads and sandwiches $4.50–$8. MC, V. Mon–Sat 7:30am–4:30pm.

L'Italia Restaurant and Pompeii Lounge ✹ ITALIAN   This pleasant establishment is run by accomplished cooks who moved here from Italy. You'll enter through a nondescript foyer in front of a small bar, but French doors lead to sophisticated L'Italia, with modern art hung in lighted alcoves. Ceiling spotlights highlight the black tables and chairs set far apart for privacy. Upstairs, the Pompeii Lounge presents outdoor dining on its rooftop patio, which hosts live music Friday and Saturday nights during summer. The well-prepared offerings at both institutions range from Sicilian-style veal parmigiana to northern Italian veal piccata in a sauce of white wine, lemon, and capers.

23 E. Beverly St. (℃) **540/885-0102.** Reservations recommended. Main courses $11–$20. AE, DISC, MC, V. Tues–Thurs 11am–10pm; Fri–Sat 11am–11pm; Sun 11am–9pm. Pompeii Lounge open later Fri–Sat.

Mrs. Rowe's Restaurant and Bakery ✹✹ *Value* SOUTHERN   Opened in 1947 by the late Mrs. Mildred Rowe and still run by her family, this is one of the better home-style restaurants in Virginia. Made from recipes from Mrs. Rowe's own cookbook, dishes here are very much in the Southern tradition but lighter than the usual fare cooked elsewhere with ample portions of salt and lard. Grilled steaks, country ham, and pork chops lead the regular items, and you can also choose from daily specials such as meatloaf and gravy or fried flounder filet, but this is not the best place for fried chicken. I often order a vegetable plate, so good are they here (corn pudding, spoon bread, baked tomatoes, and cucumber-and-onion salads are notable). The fresh pies are so tasty that locals order slices along with their main courses, just to make sure they get their favorite flavors. And the cookies are fabulous: Mrs. Fields should have learned how to cook her chocolate chip cookies from Mrs. Rowe.

74 Rowe Rd. (U.S. 250, just east of I-81). (℃) **540/886-1833.** Reservations not accepted. Sandwiches $5.50–$7.50; main courses $8–$14. DC, DISC, MC, V. Mon–Sat 7am–8pm; Sun 7am–7pm. Breakfast daily 7–10:45am.

Staunton Grocery ✹✹ *Finds* NEW AMERICAN   Until another establishment opens and robs it of its perch, this is Staunton's top restaurant. Although bistro-style, it's more formal and intimate than its main competitor, Zynodoa Restaurant (see below), as its candles and white-linen table cloths attest. The menu, which changes frequently depending on what the chef has corraled from local farms, is expressed for foodies. One recent offering: "Roasted monk fish + house cured bacon + hominy stew + fried pork belly + garlic kale." That's a lot of olde Virginny ingredients, but it was anything but down-home cooking. Yummy!

105 W. Beverly St. ℂ 540/886-6880. Reservations recommended. Main courses $24–$29. AE, MC, V. Tues–Sat 5:30–10pm; Sun 5:30–8:30pm.

Zynodoa Restaurant ★★ (Finds) ECLECTIC This casual bistro in a converted storefront takes its name from the American Indian pronunciation of "Shenandoah." You can converse with local professionals at the friendly bar before retiring to a booth or table to pick from an eclectic menu that changes seasonally. Appetizers such as seared sea scallops with steamed asparagus and shaved Romano cheese are smallish though artistically presented, whereas the main courses are more substantial. Lamb, duck, and filet mignon are constants but I like the spicy Thai shrimp as well as the meatloaf served with a mango-tinged barbecue sauce.

115 E. Beverley St. ℂ 540/885-7775. Reservations recommended. Main courses $14–$20. AE, MC, V. Daily 4pm–midnight.

STAUNTON AFTER DARK

Staunton's showpiece is the **Blackfriars Playhouse** (see above), where you can see performances of Shakespeare's plays as well as concerts. For art-house movie fans, the restored **Visulite Cinemas,** 12 N. Augusta St. (ℂ 540/885-9958), showcases offbeat films such as Michael Moore's *Sicko*, which won't hit the mall cinemas in these Republican-leaning parts. The Visulite dates from 1937.

The pubs in and around **Staunton Station,** the old railway depot on Millwood Avenue, as well as the Clock Tower Tavern and the Pompeii Lounge on East Beverly Street (see "Where to Dine," above), have live bands playing on weekend nights. The city has a summertime program of free outdoor concerts in Gypsy Hill Park and the Wharf District. Check with the visitor center for a schedule.

STAUNTON-TO-LEXINGTON VIA RAPHINE

The rural area around the tiny hamlet of Raphine, about halfway between Staunton and Lexington, is quintessential Shenandoah Valley, with country roads winding among farms blanketing steep hills. This gorgeous area makes an easy excursion from either of the two towns or as a stop when traveling between them. The quick way is via I-81, but Va. 252 is much more scenic. However you get here, follow Raphine Road (C.R. 606) between the Interstate and Va. 252.

Starting at Exit 205 off I-81, take Va. 56 east toward Steele's Tavern and follow the signs to the picturesque **Cyrus McCormick Farm** (ℂ 540/377-2255; www.vaes.vt. edu/steeles/mccormick/mccormick.html). Now part of a Virginia Tech agricultural research facility, it's in a lovely rural setting with a small blacksmith shop, a gristmill, and other log cabins, where exhibits include a model of Cyrus McCormick's 1831 invention, the first reaper, which revolutionized American agriculture and made him a fortune. This is an excellent place to spread out a picnic and take a half-mile walk along Mad Creek to the mill pond. It's open daily from 8:30am to 5pm; admission is free.

Now backtrack west on Va. 56, go under I-81, and follow C.R. 606 for 1 mile through Raphine to the award-winning **Rockbridge Vineyard** (ℂ 888/511-9463 or 540/377-6204; www.rockbridgevineyard.com). The tasting room is open Sunday and Monday from noon to 5pm, Tuesday through Saturday 10am to 6pm.

Four miles west of I-81 is the 1882-vintage **Wade's Mill** (ℂ 540/348-1400; www.wadesmill.com), which grinds whole grains into flour, cornmeal, polenta, semolina, and an herb beer mix for pancakes (the mill supplies the area's top restaurants).

The shop sells high-quality kitchen gear, and occasional cooking events feature guest chefs. The mill is open from April to the Sunday before Christmas Wednesday to Saturday 10am to 5pm, and on Sunday from 1 to 5pm during summer.

Next to the mill stands **Buffalo Springs Herb Farm** (© 540/348-1083; www. buffaloherbs.com), where those of you with green thumbs will enjoy exploring the herb gardens and browsing the retail shop in a huge barn, which purveys gardening equipment and supplies. The farm is open Wednesday to Saturday 10am to 5pm year-round, and Sunday 1 to 5pm during April, May, and September to December.

Most of this area is in northern Rockbridge County, so contact the **Lexington & Rockbridge Area Visitor Center** for more information (see section 8, later in this chapter).

A COUNTRY B&B WITH A FINE VIEW

Fox Hill Bed & Breakfast ♣   On rolling pastureland with a fine view of the Blue Ridge, this modern B&B is the perfect place to relax before or after touring the Raphine area. It's near the hamlet of Fairfield, making Lexington an easy 13 miles south via on U.S. 11. Fox Hill is no Victorian home full of frilly lace and antiques, for it was built during the 1990s as an equestrian inn. The architecture is more German than Virginian, with lots of knotty pine and a big stone fireplace in the guest lounge. Most of the spacious guest rooms are in the main building. Five open to patios or balconies, and three have heat-and-glow fireplaces. Innkeepers Sue and Mark Erwin rent out the barns and pastureland to a horse trainer, so you will see horses here but you won't be able to ride them. On the other hand, there's a nature trail to a stream on the 38 acres. Mark also is a clockmaker by trade, as evidenced by numerous antique timepieces hanging in the guest lounge. Some outlying units here have kitchens but not daily maid service. Your dog can stay with you here.

4383 Borden Grant Trail, Fairfield, VA 24435. © **800/869-8005** or 540/377-9922. www.foxhillbb.com. 6 units. $125–$165 double. Rates include full breakfast. DISC, MC, V. Dogs accepted ($13 pet fee). *In room:* A/C, TV, Wi-Fi, kitchen (some units), no phone.

STAUNTON–TO–WARM SPRINGS VIA MONTEREY

Another scenic alternative to I-81 from Staunton to Lexington is via U.S. 250 West across the mountains into Highland County, whose rugged beauty has given it the nickname "Virginia's Switzerland." In fact, U.S. 250 from Staunton to the town of **Monterey** is one of the state's most scenic excursions. Carved out of the rocks in the early 1800s as the Staunton-Parkersburg (W.Va.) Turnpike, the two-lane highway climbs (and I do mean *climbs*) over four mountains on its way to Monterey. Don't be in a hurry: the 50-mile drive will take 1½ hours.

On the way you'll pass through the village of McDowell, site of a Civil War battle, which is explained in the **Highland Museum and Heritage Center** (© 540/396-4478). The museum is behind the local funeral home on U.S. 250 and is open Wednesday to Saturday 11am to 4pm, Sunday 1 to 4pm. Admission is free. Next door, members of the local Mennonite community sell homemade maple syrup and candy in the **Sugar Tree Country Store & Sugar House** (© 540/396-3469), which still has its pot-belly stove.

Seen from U.S. 250 as it descends into the valley, Monterey's white clapboard churches and Victorian homes conjure up images of New England hamlets. At more than 2,500 feet elevation, it enjoys a refreshing, springlike climate during summer. Information is available in the Highland Inn on Main Street (see below). Pick up a walking-tour brochure and stroll along picturesque Main Street (U.S. 250) past the likes of **H&H Cash Store,** a holdover from the days when general stores sold a little bit of everything. You can also poke your head into good arts-and-crafts stores, including a 1797 **Log Cabin,** which now serves at the local SPCA thrift shop (© **540/ 468-3504**).

The best (and most crowded) time to be here is on the second and third full weekends in March, when Monterey hosts the **Highland Maple Festival,** one of Virginia's top annual events (see "Virginia Calendar of Events," in chapter 2). A smaller version, the **Hands and Harvest Festival,** is held on the second weekend in October.

Accommodations are available at the charming **Highland Inn,** on Main Street (© **888/466-4682** or 540/468-2143; fax 540/468-3143; www.highland-inn.com), a 16-unit, veranda-fronted hotel built in 1904, renovated and improved in the 1990s. You can have dinner here Tuesday through Sunday, or brunch on Sunday. **High's Restaurant** on Main Street (© **540/468-1600**) serves inexpensive, down-home Southern fare Monday to Saturday from 6am to 8pm, Sunday from 7am to 6pm.

For more information contact the **Highland County Chamber of Commerce,** P.O. Box 223, Monterey, VA 24465 (© **540/468-2550;** fax 540/468-2551; www.highlandcounty.org). It's open Monday through Friday from 10am to 5pm.

From Monterey, U.S. 220 takes you 30 miles south through the scenic Jackson River Valley to Warm Springs (see below). From there, you can drive 42 miles across the mountains to Lexington via Va. 39 and the Goshen Pass, a marvelously scenic drive in itself.

7 Warm Springs & Hot Springs: Taking the Waters ⊙★

Hot Springs: 220 miles SW of Washington, D.C., 160 miles W of Richmond; Warm Springs: 5 miles N of Hot Springs

At temperatures from 94°F to 104°F (35°C–40°C), thermal springs rise in appropriately named Bath County. This little valley—that's correct, Bath County is not in the Shenandoah Valley—has been a retreat since the 18th century, when Thomas Jefferson and other notables stopped at Warm Springs to "take the waters." The Homestead was founded in 1766 and is still one of the nation's premier spas and golf resorts (the nation's oldest tee is here). After you've soaked in the waters, played the links, and had your pedicure, you can hear small ensembles making music at the Garth Newel Music Center.

Warm Springs today is a charming little hamlet that serves as the Bath County seat. The even smaller village of Hot Springs, 5 miles to the south, is virtually a company town: It lives to serve The Homestead. Hot Springs' Main Street begins where U.S. 220 circles around the resort and runs for 2 blocks south; here you'll find a country grocery store and several upscale art and clothing dealers, some in the old train depot.

Granted, there is a whole lot of money visiting and living in this valley, including the Rev. Pat Robertson, who has a mansion up on the mountaintop. Fortunately we of the tax-paying classes don't have to spend a fortune to enjoy it for a day or two, since there are relatively inexpensive places to stay and eat here.

ESSENTIALS

VISITOR INFORMATION The **Bath County Chamber of Commerce,** 169 Main St. (P.O. Box 718), Hot Springs, VA 24445 (© **800/628-8092** or 540/839-5409; www.discoverbath.com), operates a visitor center on Main Street south of The Homestead. It's open Monday to Saturday 9am to 5pm. There's an information kiosk on U.S. 220 just south of the Va. 39 junction in Warm Springs. It usually has copies of a walking-tour brochure to the little village.

GETTING THERE   U.S. 220 runs north and south through Hot Springs and Warm Springs, with access to I-64 at Covington, 20 miles of winding mountain road south of Hot Springs. The scenic route is via Va. 39 from Lexington, a 42-mile drive that follows the Maury River through the canyonlike Goshen Pass. You can also take the scenic route via Monterey, described at the end of the "Staunton: A Presidential Birthplace & the Bard's Playhouse" section, earlier in this chapter.

The nearest regular air service is at **Roanoke Regional Airport.** Clifton Forge has an **Amtrak** station (© 800/872-7245; www.amtrak.com).

TAKING THE WATERS IN THE JEFFERSON POOLS ✸✸✸

The most famous of the thermal springs are the **Jefferson Pools,** in a grove of trees in Warm Springs, just south of the intersection of U.S. 220 and Va. 39 (© **540/839-5346**). The crystal-clear, 98°F (37°C) waters of these natural rock pools circulate gently and offer a wonderfully relaxing experience. The octagonal white clapboard bathhouse covering the men's pool was built in 1761, and the women's building dates to 1836, and they've been little changed since. The only luxuries you'll get at the pools are a clean towel and a rudimentary changing room. The Homestead owns them, however, and provides massages in an adjacent building ($70–$130 per session). Use of the pools costs $15 an hour. Reservations aren't taken for the pools—just walk in. They are open June to October daily from 10am to 7pm. Call for winter weekend hours.

There's music in the mountain air on summer weekends at the **Garth Newel Music Center** ✸✸ on U.S. 220 between Warm Springs and Hot Springs (© **877/558-1689** or 540/839-5018; fax 540/839-3154; www.garthnewel.org). The center's summer-long music festival has been drawing critical acclaim since the 1970s, and concerts now go into the autumn months. Long known for classical music, it now features jazz, blues, and other varieties—all performed by small ensembles. Garth Newel also sponsors a series of Music Holiday Weekend Retreats in spring, fall, and winter. Accommodations and dining at the on-site **Manor House** are part of the package. Call, write, or check the website for details.

WHERE TO STAY

The Homestead ✸✸✸   With a prodigious reputation dating back to 1766, this famous spa and golf resort has hosted presidents since Thomas Jefferson, plus social elites like the Henry Fords, John D. Rockefeller, the Vanderbilts, and Lord and Lady Astor. Two mountains flank its main building, which is built of red Kentucky brick with white-limestone trim. Guests enter across a porch adorned with white rockers into the Great Hall, lined with 16 Corinthian columns and a 211-foot floral carpet. Two fireplaces, wing chairs, Chippendale-reproduction tables with reading lamps, and deep sofas create a warm atmosphere. Afternoon tea is served daily to the classical music of the piano in the background.

Guests have a variety of accommodations in rooms and suites with a Virginia country-manor ambience and custom-designed mahogany furniture. Most units offer spectacular mountain views. Best are the suites in the South Wing, which have working fireplaces, private bars, sun porches, two TVs, and two phones.

In addition to its three outstanding golf courses and 12 tennis courts, diversions include bowling, fishing, hiking, horseback and carriage rides, ice-skating on an Olympic-size rink, lawn bowling and croquet, billiards, sporting clays and skeet trap, and downhill and cross-country skiing mid-December to March. Then you can ease the aches and pains in the springs-fed indoor pool or the full-service spa.

Under the supervision of European-trained chefs, the historic **Dining Room** is a lush palm court, in which an orchestra performs every evening during six-course dinners and for dancing afterward (coat and ties required after 6pm). The Homestead's signature restaurant, **The 1766 Grille,** is more casual, as is the **Casino Club.** It's all a bit rich for my plastic, but I do dine across Main Street at **Sam Snead's Tavern,** a casual pub serving traditional American fare (open for dinner only). Or you can dine at the golf clubs or at the ski slopes.

Although this large property primarily hosts conventions and other group meetings, it's still a very good family resort.

P.O. Box 2000, Hot Springs, VA 24445. © 800/838-1766 or 540/839-1776. Fax 540/839-7670. www.thehomestead. com. 483 units. $270–$550 double; $450–$900 suite. 15% resort service fee added to bill. Rates include breakfast, afternoon tea, and dinner. Weekend, golf, and other packages available. AE, DC, DISC, MC, V. Main entrance is off U.S. 220 south of Main St. **Amenities:** 5 restaurants; 3 bars; indoor and outdoor pools; 3 golf courses; 12 tennis courts; health club; spa; bike rentals; children's programs; game room; concierge; shopping arcade; salon; room service; massage; babysitting; laundry service. In room: A/C, TV, high-speed Internet, iron, safe.

Inn at Gristmill Square ⭐ (Value   Five restored 19th-century buildings, including an old mill, make this unique hostelry in Warm Springs seem like a small village. It includes the Blacksmith Shop, which houses a country store; the Hardware Store, with seven guest units; the Steel House, with four units; the Miller's House, with four rooms; and the old silo, with two rooms. (I love the silo rooms with their curving walls.) Furnishings are period pieces, with comfortable upholstered chairs, brass chandeliers, four-poster beds, and marble-top side tables, and many units have working fireplaces. Breakfast is served in your room in a picnic basket. Other facilities include an outdoor pool and three tennis courts, and you can wade in the warm stream winding through the property.

The rustic **Waterwheel Restaurant** (see "Where to Dine," below) and **Simon Kenton Pub** are cozy spots in the old mill building.

C.R. 645 (Box 359), Warm Springs, VA 24484. © 540/839-2231. Fax 540/839-5770. www.gristmillsquare.com. 16 units, 1 suite. $95–$160 double. Rates include continental breakfast. DISC, MC, V. From U.S. 220 N., turn left onto C.R. 619 and right onto C.R. 645. **Amenities:** Restaurant; bar; outdoor pool; 3 tennis courts; health club; sauna; room service; massage; babysitting. In room: A/C, TV, fridge, iron.

BED & BREAKFASTS

Other bed-and-breakfasts include **Warm Springs Inn** (© 540/839-5351), a converted courthouse across the road from the Jefferson Pools. In Hot Springs, **Vine Cottage Inn** (© 800/410-9755 or 540/839-2422; www.vinecottageinn.com) is a block from The Homestead.

Anderson Cottage Bed & Breakfast ⭐⭐ (Value   One of Bath County's oldest buildings, this log-and-white-clapboard charmer has been in owner Jean Randolph Bruns' family since the 1870s. She has welcomed guests since 1983 and still operates it as "private home B&B" (in contrast to the more commercial operations that number in the hundreds throughout Virginia). Out back across an expansive lawn, a warm stream flows through the property in the heart of the picturesque village (Jean supplies special towels for taking a warm dip). The house is packed with wide-board floors, Oriental rugs, working fireplaces, loaded bookcases, and so many Randolph family heirlooms and photos that it seems like you're staying in a museum. Accommodations are individually decorated and exceptionally spacious. Originally an 1820s brick kitchen, the Guest Cottage is ideal for families, with two bedrooms, two bathrooms, a full kitchen/dining/sitting room with fireplace, and a living room. The rooms are not air-conditioned (seldom needed at this altitude), nor do they have TVs, phones, or other such amenities.

208 Old Germantown Rd. (P.O. Box 176), Warm Springs, VA 24484. © **540/839-2975.** www.bbonline.com/va/ anderson. 4 units (all with private bathroom). $90–$135 double. Rates include full breakfast. No credit cards. From Va. 39, turn left onto Old Germantown Rd. (C.R. 692), to 4th house on the left. *In room:* Fridge (some units), no phones.

AN UNUSUAL COUNTRY INN

Fort Lewis Plantation & Lodge 🐸🐸 *Kids*   You'll discover one of Virginia's most unusual country inns at John and Caryl Cowden's farm beside the Cowpasture River, which cuts a north-south valley over the mountain from Warm Springs. About half their guest quarters are in a reconstructed barn, from which an outside spiral staircase leads to three rooms inside the silo—I do love those round walls in old silos. One end of the rough-look barn is now a comfortable lounge with stone fireplace and large windows looking out over a Jacuzzi-equipped deck to the farmland and mountains beyond. Other guests stay in hand-hewn log cabins, each with a fireplace, or in a restored farmhouse.

The Cowdens' summertime garden supplies vegetables for excellent meals served in the old Lewis Mill, whose upstairs has been turned into a game room. A screened porch to one side shelters **Buck's Bar,** which serves beer and wine. Activities include mountain biking, hiking, and taking a cool dip in one of Virginia's best swimming holes (it has a rock wall on one side). You can fish for trout in the Cowpasture River, but don't count on eating your catch; you must throw it back into the river. Fort Lewis Lodge is popular with families getting away from Washington, D.C., and other nearby cities, so book early.

H.C.R. 3, Box 21A, Millboro, VA 24460. © **540/925-2314.** Fax 540/925-2352. www.fortlewislodge.com. 19 units. $190–$210 double; $245–$295 cabin. Rates include breakfast and dinner. MC, V. From Warm Springs, go 14 miles east on Va. 39, turn left on Indian Draft Rd. (C.R. 678) and drive north 11 miles, then turn left on River Rd. (C.R. 625) to entrance. **Amenities:** Restaurant; bar; swimming hole; Jacuzzi; bike rental; game room. *In room:* A/C.

WHERE TO DINE

Part of a gasoline station 3½ miles north of Hot Springs, the clean and modern **Varsity Grill** (© **540/839-4000)** provides inexpensive breakfasts, salads, and deli sandwiches. It's open daily from 7am to 10pm.

Country Cafe AMERICAN   I've seen the Rev. Pat Robertson munching on fried chicken here at Hot Springs' favorite country restaurant. It's good Southern fare like my mother used to cook. All is not fried, however, including the broiled, sautéed, or chargrilled mountain trout, the best meal here. Finish it off with a slice of cream pie. Beer and wine are served but not spirits.

U.S. 220 S. (1 mile south of The Homestead). © **540/839-2111.** Reservations not accepted. Main courses $8–$15. MC, V. Tues–Sat 7am–9pm; Sun 8am–2pm.

The Waterwheel Restaurant 🐸 INTERNATIONAL   The finest dining here outside The Homestead, this charmer occupies the old mill building at the Inn at Gristmill Square in Warm Springs (see "Where to Stay," above), thus is its name derived from the huge water wheel that once powered the grist. The signature dish here is mountain trout lightly breaded with cornmeal and walnuts; it's a tasty twist on Southern cooking. The crispy roasted duck is another favorite. There's an extensive wine cellar, from which you can partake pre- or après-meal in the tiny, one-table pub.

C.R. 645 (in Inn at Gristmill Square), Warm Springs. ✆ **540/839-2231**. Reservations highly recommended. Main courses $20–$25. MC, V. May–Nov Sun–Thurs 6–9pm, Fri–Sat 6–9:30pm; Nov–Apr Sun–Thurs 6–8:30pm, Fri–Sat 6–9pm. Sun brunch year-round 11am–2pm.

8 Lexington: A College Town with a Slice of American History ★★★

36 miles S of Staunton; 180 miles SW of Washington, D.C.; 138 miles W of Richmond

A college atmosphere prevails in Lexington, one of America's most charming small towns. Fine old homes line tree-shaded streets, among them the house where Stonewall Jackson lived when he taught at Virginia Military Institute. A beautifully restored downtown looks so much like it did in the 1800s that scenes for the movie *Sommersby* were filmed on Main Street (Richard Gere's character was hanged behind Stonewall's house). After the Civil War, Robert E. Lee came to Lexington to serve as president of what was then Washington College; he and his horse, Traveller, are buried here. And Gen. George C. Marshall, winner of the Nobel Peace Prize for his post–World War II plan to rebuild Europe, graduated from VMI, which has a fine museum in his memory.

Washington and Lee University has one of the oldest and most beautiful campuses in the country. Built in 1824, Washington Hall is topped by a replica of an American folk art masterpiece, an 1840 carved-wood statue of George Washington, Lee reputedly planted some of the massive trees dotting the campus.

Sometimes called the West Point of the South, VMI opened in 1839 on the site of a state arsenal, abutting the Washington and Lee campus (W&L's buildings are like brick Southern manses; VMI's look like stone fortresses). The most dramatic episode in VMI's history took place during the Civil War at the Battle of New Market on May 15, 1864, when the corps of cadets helped turn back a larger Union army. A month later, Union Gen. David Hunter got even, bombarding Lexington and burning down VMI.

ESSENTIALS

VISITOR INFORMATION   The **Lexington & Rockbridge Area Visitor Center,** 106 E. Washington St., Lexington, VA 24450 (✆ **877/453-9822** or 540/463-3777; fax 540/463-1105; www.lexingtonvirginia.com), is a block east of Main Street. Begin your tour of Lexington at this excellent source of information, for it offers museum-like displays about the town's history, has an accommodations gallery for making same-day hotel reservations, and distributes free walking-tour brochures (you can park in the center's lot while touring the town). The center is open daily from 8:30am to 6pm June through August, from 9am to 5pm the rest of the year. It's closed New Year's Day, Thanksgiving, and Christmas.

GETTING THERE   Lexington is at the junction of I-81 and I-64. U.S. 60 and U.S. 11 go directly into town.

EXPLORING THE TOWN

Be sure to pick up a free **walking tour** brochure at the visitor center. It explains Lexington's historic buildings and contains one of the best maps of downtown.

For a good overview, take a ride with **Lexington Carriage Company** (✆ **540/463-5647**), whose horse-drawn carriages depart from the visitor center for 45-minute narrated tours daily from 10am to 6pm during the summer, from 11am to 5pm during April, May, September, and October. Fares are $16 for adults, $14 for seniors, $7 for children ages 7 to 13, free for kids under 7.

(*Fun Fact* **Presidential Prototype**

The George C. Marshall Museum and Research Library served as the prototype for modern presidential libraries, starting with President Truman's in Independence, Missouri.

Haunting Tales of Historic Lexington (© 540/464-2250) conducts 1¼-hour nighttime walks through the streets, back alleys, and Stonewall Jackson Cemetery from Memorial Day weekend to Halloween. The cost is $10 for adults, $6 for children 4 to 10, and free for children younger than 4. Reservations are strongly recommended, so call ahead.

George C. Marshall Museum and Research Library 🞛🞛   Facing the VMI parade ground, this impressive stone structure houses the personal archives of General of the Army George C. Marshall, a 1901 graduate of VMI. As army chief of staff in World War II, Marshall virtually directed that conflict (he chose Gen. Dwight D. Eisenhower to command all Allied forces in Europe). After the war he served as secretary of state and secretary of defense under President Truman. He is best remembered for the Marshall Plan, which fostered the economic recovery of western Europe after the war. For his role in promoting postwar peace, he became the first career soldier to be awarded the Nobel Peace Prize, in 1956. His Nobel medal is on display. An electronic map charts the war and Marshall's decisions, and films explain his extraordinary life. Allow an hour to explore the museum on your own.

VMI Parade Grounds. © 540/463-7103. www.marshallfoundation.org. Admission to museum $5 adults, $4 seniors, free for students and children; free admission to research library. Museum daily 9am–5pm; research library Mon–Fri 9am–4:30pm.

Lee Chapel and Museum 🞛🞛🞛   This magnificent Victorian-Gothic chapel on the Washington and Lee campus was built of brick and native limestone in 1867 at the request of General Lee. Begin by walking up on the auditorium stage and taking a look at Edward Valentine's striking white-marble sculpture *Lee Recumbent.* A docent will explain the history of the building and the intricacies of the statue, which Valentine carved between 1871 and 1875, shortly after Lee's death. The chapel was due for renovations in late 2007, so Charles Willson Peale's 1772 portrait of George Washington wearing the uniform of a colonel in the Virginia militia and Theodore Pine's painting of Lee in Confederate uniform, which usually flank the statue, may be elsewhere. Assuming renovations are complete, climb down the narrow rear steps to the basement, where the remains of the general and many other members of the Lee clan (including "Light-Horse Harry" Lee of Revolutionary War fame) are entombed. Robert E. Lee's beloved horse, Traveller, is buried in a plot outside the museum. Across the vestibule, Lee's office remains just as he left it when he died on October 12, 1870. The museum is devoted to the history of the university and its two namesakes and includes the impressive Washington-Custis-Lee collection of American portraits. Allow 30 minutes to see the statue, the crypt, and Lee's office, another 30 in the museum.

Washington and Lee University. © 540/458-8768. http://leechapel.wlu.edu. Free admission (donations suggested). Apr–Oct Mon–Sat 9am–5pm, Sun 1–5pm; Nov–Mar Mon–Sat 9am–4pm, Sun 1–5pm. Limited free parking on Jefferson St. opposite west end of Henry St. Follow signs from parking lot.

Lexington

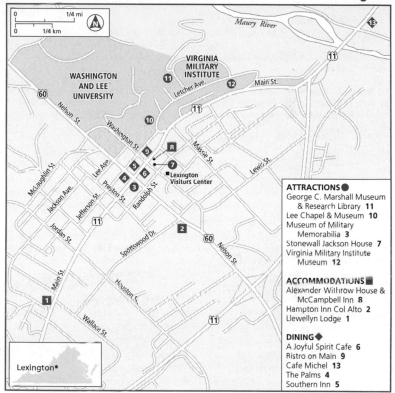

ATTRACTIONS ●
George C. Marshall Museum
& Research Library **11**
Lee Chapel & Museum **10**
Museum of Military
Memorabilia **3**
Stonewall Jackson House **7**
Virginia Military Institute
Museum **12**

ACCOMMODATIONS ■
Alexander Withrow House &
McCampbell Inn **8**
Hampton Inn Col Alto **2**
Llewellyn Lodge **1**

DINING ◆
A Joyful Spirit Cafe **6**
Bistro on Main **9**
Cafe Michel **13**
The Palms **4**
Southern Inn **5**

Museum of Military Memorabilia   This small but fascinating museum displays a collection of military uniforms and various bits of soldiers' gear, with the oldest dating from 1740 in Prussia and the newest from the 1991 Persian Gulf War. The uniforms come from several different countries and represent a number of conflicts. You'll also see insignia, flags, a few weapons, trench art from World War I, and a piece of the Berlin Wall. If you miss the beginning, you can join the 45-minute guided tours in progress.

122½ S. Main St. (in the driveway next to the Presbyterian Church). ☎ **540/464-3041.** Admission $3 per person. Apr–Oct Wed–Fri noon–5pm, Sat 9am–5pm; rest of year by appointment. 45-min. tours run continuously.

Stonewall Jackson House ★★   Maj. Thomas Jonathan Jackson came to Lexington in 1851 to take a post as teacher of natural philosophy (physics) and artillery tactics at VMI. Jackson lived here with his wife, Mary Anna Morrison, from early 1859 until he was summoned to Richmond in 1861; it was the only house he ever owned. Exhibits tell the story of the Jacksons' stay here, and many of the Jacksons' personal effects duplicate the items on the inventory of Jackson's estate made shortly after he died near Chancellorsville in 1863. His body was returned to Lexington and buried in **Stonewall Jackson Memorial Cemetery** on South Main Street. Also have a look at the backyard vegetable garden and the carriage house, which protects a Rockaway model Jackson owned.

Impressions

Let us cross the river and rest under the shade of the trees.
—Stonewall Jackson's last words, May 10, 1863

8 E. Washington St. (between Main and Randolph sts.). ℂ 540/463-2552. www.stonewalljackson.org. Admission $6 adults, $3 children 6–17, free for children 5 and younger. Mon–Sat 9am–6pm; Sun 1–6pm. Guided 30-min. tours depart on the hour and half-hour (last tour 30 min. prior to closing). Closed Jan 1, Easter, Thanksgiving, and Dec 25.

Virginia Horse Center   Sprawling across nearly 400 acres, the Virginia Horse Center offers educational seminars and sales of fine horses, and it has a coliseum for concerts as well as horse shows. Annual events include draft pulls, rodeos, various competitions, and competitive breed shows. Call or check the website for the schedule. It's not worth driving out here to see, but a corner of the main concourse is devoted to the **American Work Horse Museum,** displaying carriages, wagons, plows, and other horse-drawn farm implements.

Va. 39, 1 mile west of U.S. 11 and north of I-64. ℂ 540/463-7060. www.horsecenter.org. Admission varies by event; most are free. Open year-round. From downtown, take U.S. 11 north, turn left on Va. 39 ¹⁄₁₀ mile north of I-64; the center is 1 mile on the left.

Virginia Military Institute Museum 🎖🎖   This museum tracing VMI's history is well worth a visit, especially to see the raincoat Stonewall Jackson was wearing when his own men accidentally shot him at Chancellorsville (the bullet hole is in the upper left shoulder) and—thanks to taxidermy—Jackson's unflappable war horse, Little Sorrel. Also here are one of Gen. George S. Patton's shiny helmet liners. Patton graduated from VMI in 1907. The museum resides in the basement of **Jackson Memorial Hall,** the school's auditorium built in 1915 with federal funds paid in partial compensation for the Union army's burning the school after its cadets helped defeat Federal troops at the Battle of New Market in May 1864. Be sure to step into the auditorium, where B. West Clinedinst's oversize oil painting of the cadets' heroic Civil War charge looms over the stage.

Letcher Ave., VMI Parade (in Jackson Memorial Hall). ℂ 540/464-7232. www4.vmi.edu/museum. Free admission ($3 donation suggested). Daily 9am–5pm. Closed Jan 1, Thanksgiving, and Christmas week.

THE NATURAL BRIDGE 🎖

Thomas Jefferson called this hugely impressive limestone formation "the most sublime of nature's works . . . so beautiful an arch, so elevated, so light and springing, as it were, up to heaven." The bridge was part of a 157-acre estate Jefferson acquired in 1774 from King George III. In the early 1750s it was included in the survey of western Virginia carried out by George Washington, who carved his initials into the face of the sheer stone wall and beside Cedar Creek at the base of the gorge. This geological oddity dramatically rises 215 feet above the creek; its span is 90 feet long and spreads at its widest to 150 feet. The Monacan Indian tribes worshiped it as "the bridge of God." Today, it is also the bridge of man, as U.S. 11 passes over it.

The bridge itself and its **Monacan Indian Living History Village** definitely are worth seeing, but to my mind they are surrounded by a borderline tourist trap. That's not to say you and the children can't eat up a day here, or that the youngsters won't thoroughly enjoy themselves at the caverns (45-min. tours depart every 30 min.) and the toy, haunted house, and wax museums. There's a small, independently operated zoo up the road, but you, the kids, and especially the animals will have more fun at the nearby Virginia Safari Park (see "On Safari in Virginia," below). Also here: a department store–size souvenir shop, a restaurant, and a hotel.

There are no guided tours, but there are interpreters under the bridge and in the Monacan village. The bridge is a steep ¼-mile downhill walk from the visitor center (passing the remains of a 1,500-year-old arbor vitae tree), but shuttle buses will take you down and back up. From there, the 1-mile-long **Cedar Creek Trail** descends past a cave and a waterfall. During summer, a 45-minute sound-and-light show begins at dusk beneath the bridge.

Admission to the bridge, Monacan village, and show is $12 for adults, $6 for children 5 to 12. Tickets to the wax or toy museum or caverns cost $10 for adults, $5 for children 5 to 15. Combination tickets to any two of the attractions are $18 adults, $9 children 5 to 15. Any three attractions cost $23 adults, $12 for kids 5 to 15. The bridge is open daily from 8am to dusk. The attractions are open during summer daily from 8am to sunset; the rest of the year, daily from 8am to 5pm.

The bridge is 12 miles south of Lexington on U.S. 11 (take Exit 175 off I-81). For more information, or to book a hotel room or campsite here, contact Natural Bridge, P.O. Box 57, Natural Bridge, VA 24578 (© **800/533-1410** or 540/291-2121; fax 540/291-1896; www.naturalbridgeva.com).

OUTDOOR ACTIVITIES

The Lexington & Rockbridge Area Visitor Center (see "Essentials," above) publishes a useful guide, *Rockbridge Outdoors,* which gives a complete rundown of the area's active pursuits.

An avid outdoorsman, co-host John Roberts at **Llewellyn Lodge** organizes fly-fishing trips and hiking expeditions into the nearby hills and mountains (see "Where to Stay," below).

CANOEING, KAYAKING & RAFTING   The Maury River, which runs through Lexington, provides some of Virginia's best white-water rafting and kayaking, especially through the Goshen Pass, on Va. 39 northwest of town. The visitor center has information about several put-in spots, or you can rent equipment or go on expeditions on the Maury and James rivers with **Twin River Outfitters,** 917 Rockbridge Rd. (P.O. Box 99), Glasgow, VA 24455 (© **540/258-1999;** www.canoevirginia.com). Call, write, or check the website for schedules and reservations.

Kids On Safari in Virginia

It's a far cry from the real Serengeti Plain, but the **Virginia Safari Park** (*Kids Kids*, at Exit 180 off I-81 (© 540/291-3205; www.virginiasafaripark.com), has zebras, giraffes, antelopes, monkeys, emus, deer, elk, and bison among more than 700 animals roaming the hills between Lexington and Natural Bridge. There's even a petting area with goats, lambs, and pigs. The best way to see the beasts is on a 90-minute wagon ride at 1 and 3pm on Saturday and Sunday. At other times you merely drive your own vehicle through the park. Admission is $12 for adults, $11 for seniors, and $8 for children 3 to 12. The park is open from mid-March to Thanksgiving weekend daily 9am to 5pm.

HIKING   Two linear parks connect to offer hikers and joggers nearly 10 miles of gorgeous trail between Lexington and Buena Vista, a railroad town 7 miles to the southeast. The major link is the **Chessie Nature Trail,** which follows an old railroad bed along the Maury River between Lexington and Buena Vista. No vehicles (including bicycles) are allowed, but you can cross-country ski the trail during winter. The Chessie trail connects with a walking path in **Woods Creek Park,** which starts at the Waddell School on Jordan Street and runs down to the banks of the Maury. Both trails are open from dawn to dusk. The visitor center has maps and brochures.

There are excellent hiking, mountain-biking, horseback-riding, and all-terrain-vehicle trails in the **George Washington National Forest,** which encompasses much of the Blue Ridge Mountains east of Lexington. Small children might not be able to make it, but the rest of the family will enjoy the 3-mile trail up to **Crabtree Falls,** a series of cascades tumbling 1,200 feet down the mountain (it's the highest waterfall in Virginia). Heartier hikers can scale up to the Appalachian Trail on the mountaintop. Crabtree Falls is on Va. 56 east of the Blue Ridge Parkway; from Lexington, go north on I-81 to Steeles Tavern (Exit 205), then east on Va. 56.

SHOPPING

Lexington's charming 19th-century downtown offers more than a dozen interesting shops and art galleries, most of them on Main Street and on the blocks of Washington and Nelson streets between Main and Jefferson streets. Among the best is **Artists in Cahoots,** a cooperative venture run by local artists and craftspeople in the Alexander-Witherow House, at the corner of Main and Washington streets (① **540/464-1147**). It features an outstanding selection of paintings, sculptures, wood and metal crafts, hand-painted silk scarves, handblown glass, Shaker-style furniture, photographs, prints, decoys, stained glass, and jewelry. **Virginia Born & Bred,** 16 W. Washington St. (① **540/463-1832**), has made-in-Virginia gifts. Collectibles hunters will find an amazing array of old and not-so-old stuff literally stuffed into **The Second Hand Shop,** 7 S. Jefferson St. (① **540/463-7559**), between Washington and Nelson streets.

WHERE TO STAY

Lexington has several chain motels, especially at the intersection of U.S. 11 and I-64 (Exit 55), 1½ miles north of downtown. The 100-unit **Best Western Inn at Hunt Ridge,** 25 Willow Springs Rd./Va. 39 (① **800/464-1501** or 540/464-1500; www.dominionlodging.com), is the only full-service hotel among them, offering a restaurant, bar, limited room service, indoor-outdoor pool, and fine mountain views. Try to get one of its six rooms with balconies.

Other nearby motels are **Comfort Inn** (① 800/628-1956 or 540/463-7311), **Country Inn & Suites** (① 800/456-4000 or 540/464-9000), **EconoLodge** (① 800/446-6900 or 540/463-7371), **Holiday Inn Express** (① 800/465-4329 or 540/463-7351), and **Super 8** (① 800/800-8000 or 540/463-7858).

Hampton Inn Col Alto ⟨★★⟩   This is no ordinary Hampton Inn: Col Alto is an 1827 manor house built on a plantation then on the outskirts of town. The carefully renovated mansion now houses 10 bedrooms comparable to deluxe country inns or B&Bs. An interior designer individually decorated these luxurious quarters with made-in-Virginia linens, reproduction antiques, and bright, vivid paints and fabrics. Accommodations range in size from huge, light-filled rooms on the front of the house to smaller, more private ones in the rear. One unit even has a semi-round "fan" window of the style favored by Thomas Jefferson. Manor house guests can choose to have breakfast and the morning newspaper delivered to their rooms. Rooms in the new, L-shaped motel wing next door are somewhat larger than average and have microwave ovens, coffeemakers, robes, and irons and ironing boards; some have balconies overlooking a courtyard with outdoor swimming pool and whirlpool. Guests in both wings get complimentary continental breakfasts in the original dining room, but it's standard Hampton Inn fare, not a fancy breakfast like those served at most bed-and-breakfasts.

401 E. Nelson St., Lexington, VA 24450. ℭ 800/426-7866 or 540/463-2223. Fax 540/463-9707. www.hampton innlexington.com. 86 units. $134–$169 double motel room; $215–$265 double manor house. Rates include continental breakfast. AE, DC, DISC, MC, V. **Amenities:** Outdoor pool; health club; Jacuzzi; concierge; laundry service. *In room:* A/C, TV, Wi-Fi, coffeemaker, iron.

HISTORIC COUNTRY INNS

Make reservations for Alexander-Witherow House, McCampbell Inn, and Maple Hall through **Historic Country Inns of Lexington,** 11 N. Main St., Lexington, VA 24450 (ℭ **877/283-9680** or 540/463-2044; fax 540/463-7262; www.lexingtonhistoric inns.com).

Alexander-Witherow House and McCampbell Inn 𝒢   The Alexander-Witherow House is a lovely late Georgian town house built in 1789 as a family residence over a store. Artists in Cahoots (see "Shopping," above) occupies the ground floor. Accommodations are all homey suites with separate living rooms and small kitchens. Comfortable furnishings include wing chairs, four-poster beds, and hooked rugs on wide-board floors. The McCampbell Inn, across Main Street, houses the main office for Historic Country Inns; guests at both hostelries eat breakfast here. Begun in 1809, with later additions in 1816 and 1857, it occupies a rambling building, with rooms facing both Main Street and the quieter back courtyard. Furnishings are a pleasant mix of antiques and reproductions; all units have wet bars and refrigerators, and one of the suites has a Jacuzzi.

11 N. Main St. ℭ 877/283-9680 or 540/463-2044. Fax 540/463-7262. www.lexingtonhistoricinns.com. 15 units, 8 suites. $105–$150 double; $165–$190 suite. Rates include extensive continental breakfast. DISC, MC, V. *In room:* A/C, TV, high-speed Internet, fridge, coffeemaker, iron.

Maple Hall 𝒢   Set on 56 rolling acres 6 miles north of Lexington, this handsome redbrick, white-columned 1850 plantation house offers a restful retreat. Old boxwoods surround the inn, which consists of a main house, the restored Guest House, and the Pond House. Rooms are individually furnished—many with antiques, Oriental rugs, and massive Victorian pieces; 10 units have gas fireplaces. The Guest House has a living room, kitchen, and three bedrooms with bathrooms. The Pond House, added in 1990, contains four suites and two mini-suites. Guests relax on the shaded patio, on porches with rocking chairs, and on back verandas overlooking the fishing pond and nearby hills. A pool, tennis court, and 3-mile hiking trail are on-site. Elegant dining in pretty gardenlike surroundings attracts a good following to the fine-dining **Maple Hall Restaurant,** which is open daily for dinner.

3111 N. Lee Hwy. (U.S. 11), Lexington, VA 24450. ℭ 877/283-9680 or 540/463-6693. Fax 540/463-2114. www. lexingtonhistoricinns.com. 21 units. $105–$150 double; $165–$185 suite/Guest House. Rates include breakfast. DISC, MC, V. Take U.S. 11 for 6 miles north of town; house is near Exit 195 of I-81. **Amenities:** Restaurant; outdoor pool; golf course; tennis court. *In room:* A/C, TV, kitchen (in Guest House).

BED & BREAKFASTS

In addition to the one mentioned below, Lexington has several other B&Bs; the visitor center offers a complete list.

Llewellyn Lodge *(Value* A brick Colonial-style house, John and Ellen Roberts' Llewellyn Lodge is within easy walking distance of all of Lexington's historic sites. On the first floor are a cozy sitting room with working fireplace and a TV room. Guest rooms are decorated in exceptionally attractive color schemes. All rooms have ceiling fans, and four have TVs. A screened gazebo out back has a fan, too. Co-host John has hiked just about every trail and fished every stream in the Blue Ridge Mountains; he organizes fly-fishing and hiking expeditions (see "Outdoor Activities," above).

603 S. Main St., Lexington, VA 24450. *©* 800/882-1145 or 540/463-3235. Fax 540/463-3235. www.llodge.com. 6 units. $79–$179 double. Rates include full breakfast. AE, DISC, MC, V. **Amenities:** Laundry service. *In room:* A/C, TV (in 4 rooms), Wi-Fi, coffeemaker (in 2 rooms), iron.

WHERE TO DINE

If your sweet tooth starts aching while you're walking around town, stop in at Lexington's famous **Sweet Things,** 106 W. Washington St., between Jefferson Street and Lee Avenue (*©* **540/463-6055**), for a cone or cup of "designer" ice cream or frozen yogurt. It's open Monday through Thursday noon to 9:30pm, Friday and Saturday noon to 10pm, and Sunday 2 to 9:30pm.

Get your caffeine fix at **Lexington Coffee Shop,** 9 W. Washington St. (*©* **540/ 464-6586**), a quintessential, college-town coffeehouse with a selection of exotic brews plus bagels and pastries. It's open Monday through Friday 7:30am to 5pm, Saturday 8am to 5pm, and Sunday 9 to 3pm.

Bistro on Main *(Finds* ECLECTIC High-quality photographs—all for sale—decorate the walls of this storefront bistro offering a mix of cuisines. A light-fare list ranging from burgers to a vegetarian ratatouille is available until 11pm, while the wide-ranging regular dinner menu offers shrimp and grits in a low-country wine-and-cream sauce, chicken or steak fajitas, grilled New York steak, and vegetarian grilled portobello mushrooms with tomato, spinach, and Monterrey jack with a roasted pepper sauce. I was not impressed by the crab cakes.

8 N. Main St. *©* 540/464-4888. Reservations recommended. Main courses $13–$21; light fare $8–$11. MC, V. Tues–Sat 11:30am–2:30pm and 5–9pm (light fare to 11pm).

Cafe Michel *(©©* FRENCH/AMERICAN French-born Michel Galand came to this country as a chef at The Homestead (p. 178) and operated a restaurant in Clifton Forge before moving to Lexington and opening this fine establishment. Peach-colored walls, faux Roman columns, and lots of plants make it seem like a south-of-France outpost on a hill north of downtown. A relaxed atmosphere prevails, even though it's one of Lexington's favorite special-event restaurants. (The Rev. Pat Robertson was fine dining down here the night after I saw him gnawing on a chicken leg at the Country Cafe in Hot Springs.) The meat or seafood mixed grills are very good, as is Michel's seafood Provençal.

640 N. Lee Hwy. *©* 540/464-4119. Reservations recommended. Main courses $17–$24. AE, DISC, MC, V. Mon–Thurs 5–9pm; Fri–Sat 5–10pm.

A Joyful Spirit Cafe *(Finds* DELI This bright, lively, order-at-the-counter restaurant is the best place in town for hot coffee and pastries for breakfast and creative sandwiches with a joyful combination of flavors for lunch. Bagels with salmon, cream cheese, and capers are available all day. If you're lucky you can claim one of the two tables out on the sidewalk.

26 S. Main St. ℂ **540/463-4191**. Reservations not accepted. Breakfast $2–$4; sandwiches and salads $3.50–$7. AE, DISC, MC, V. Mon–Fri 8:30am–5pm; Sat 10am–5pm; Sun 11am–4pm.

The Palms AMERICAN/PUB FARE   With neon palms in its storefront window, this popular pub draws town and gown alike with its substantial (if uninspired) fare, sports TVs, and friendly bar. At lunch or dinner, the hearty burgers will not disappoint. Deli sandwiches run the gamut from roast beef to smoked turkey. Dinner entrees include choices like baby back ribs, in-house cut steaks, steamed shrimp, and pastas. The building was constructed in 1836 as a debating hall and public library. You can still get into lively debates at the friendly bar.

101 W. Nelson St. ℂ **540/463-7911**. Reservations not accepted. Sandwiches, burgers, and salads $5.50–$8.50; main courses $7.50–$17. AE, DISC, MC, V. Mon–Sat 11:30am–1am; Sun noon–11pm.

Southern Inn ⭐ REGIONAL   Crisp linen adorns the plain wooden booths at this former down-home-style Southern restaurant (note the brass coat hooks between the booths and the 1950s neon sign out front). You can order excellent sandwiches such as Dijon and tarragon chicken salad, and the regular menu features comfort food such as an excellent rendition of Mom's meatloaf, but the real stars here are specials like sea scallops sautéed with garlic and herb butter, and braised lamb shanks with herb risotto. There's an excellent wine list featuring Virginia vintages. The small but lively pub next door serves the same fare and attracts a more affluent crowd than The Palms (see above).

37 S. Main St. ℂ **540/463-3612**. Reservations recommended. Sandwiches $11–$13; main courses $13–$30. AE, MC, V. Mon–Tues 5–10pm; Wed–Sat 11:30am–10pm; Sun 11:30am–9pm.

LEXINGTON AFTER DARK

The ruins of an old limestone kiln provide the backdrop for the open-air **Theater at Lime Kiln** ⭐⭐ on Borden Road off U.S. 60 W. (ℂ **800/594-TIXX** or 540/436-7088; www.theateratlimekiln.com), which presents musicals, plays, and concerts from March through September. My friend Ann Barnard and I recently saw Leon Redbone in concert here.

You can joint W&L students and faculty for famous visiting artists in concerts, plays, and recitals in the **Lenfest Center for the Performing Arts,** on the W&L campus (ℂ **540/458-8000;** http://lenfest.wlu.edu). The schedule is released prior to each school year.

If you're here during the summer, catch a free **Friday Alive** concert in Davidson Park on East Nelson Street. Rock, reggae, and other bands make outdoor music on Fridays from 5:30 to 8:30pm. You can also relive the 1950s at **Hull's Drive-In,** 4 miles north of downtown on U.S. 11 (ℂ **540/436-2621;** www.hullsdrivein.com), one of the nation's few remaining outdoor movie theaters. It shows double features Friday, Saturday, and Sunday nights from April through October.

8

Roanoke & the
Southwest Highlands

You soon notice after leaving the vibrant, railroad-oriented city of Roanoke that I-81 begins climbing into the mountains as it heads into the Southwest Highlands, Virginia's increasingly narrow "tail" hemmed in by West Virginia, Kentucky, Tennessee, and North Carolina. You don't come down on the other side of the mountains, however, for I-81 will deposit you instead in the Great Valley of Virginia, whose floor averages 2,000 feet in altitude. Just as they delineate the Shenandoah Valley, the Blue Ridge Mountains form the eastern boundary of the Southwest Highlands. But while peaks above 4,000 feet are rare in the Shenandoah, here they regularly exceed that altitude, with Mount Rogers reaching 5,729 feet, the highest point in Virginia.

Thousands of acres of this beautiful country are preserved in the Jefferson National Forest and in Mount Rogers National Recreation Area, which rivals the Shenandoah National Park with 300 miles of hiking and riding trails, including a stretch of the Appalachian Trail. Two other major routes, the Virginia Creeper and New River trails, lure hikers and bikers along old railroad beds by riverbanks.

The Highlanders are justly proud of their history, which includes Daniel Boone's following the Wilderness Road through the mountains, plateaus, and hollows to Cumberland Gap and on into Kentucky. Gorgeous Abingdon and other small towns still have log cabins from those frontier days.

The Highlanders have also preserved their traditional arts, crafts, and renowned mountain music. Abingdon hosts both Virginia's official state theater and the Highlands Festival, one of America's top annual arts-and-crafts shows. The famous Carter family makes mountain music at tiny Maces Spring, and fiddlers from around the world gather every August for their old-time convention at Galax.

Whether you love history, drama, music, arts, crafts, the great outdoors, or all of the above, you will be enchanted with Virginia's beautiful Southwest Highlands.

EXPLORING THE SOUTHWEST HIGHLANDS

VISITOR INFORMATION   A one-stop source for regional information is the **Regional Visitor Center,** 975 Tazewell St., Wytheville, VA 24382 (© **800/446-9670** or 276/619-5003; www.virginiablueridge.org), which shares space with the Wytheville Convention and Visitors Bureau. It offers brochures from all towns in the region. The center is open daily from 8am to 5pm. Take Exit 70 off I-81 and follow the signs.

GETTING THERE & GETTING AROUND   As is true in most parts of Virginia, traveling by **car** is the only way to go. Truck-infested I-81 runs the entire length of the highlands and is its major thoroughfare. U.S. 11 follows I-81, and the Blue Ridge

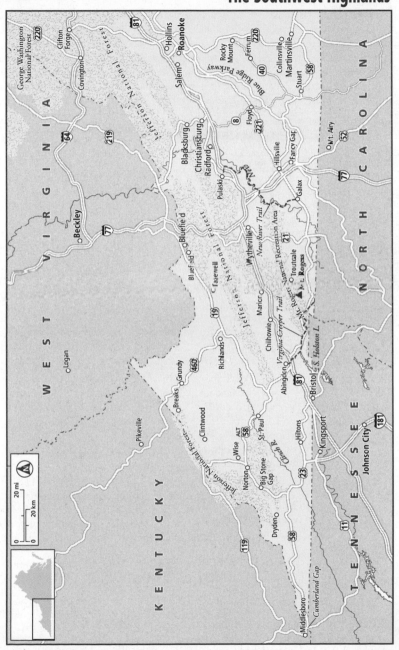

The Southwest Highlands

Parkway parallels it to the east. I-77 cuts north-south through the center of the region (the section from Wytheville north to Bluefield, West Virginia, is one of America's most scenic interstates). Otherwise, most byways in the region are mountain roads—narrow, winding, and sometimes steep—so give yourself ample time to reach your destination.

The area's air gateway is Roanoke Regional Airport (see "Getting There," below). The nearest **Amtrak** (© **800/872-7245;** www.amtrak.com) stations are in Lynchburg and Clifton Forge, each about 50 miles from Roanoke.

1 The Blue Ridge Parkway ⭐

Maintained by the National Park Service, the Blue Ridge Parkway, in effect, is a continuation of the 105-mile-long Skyline Drive in the Shenandoah National Park, running another 469 miles southwest through the Blue Ridge Mountains to the Great Smoky Mountains National Park in North Carolina. Magnificent vistas and the natural beauty of the forests, wildlife, and wildflowers combine with pioneer history to make this a scenic and fascinating route.

Unlike the Skyline Drive, which is surrounded by a national park, the parkway runs through mountain meadows, farmland, and forests (some, but not all, national forests) for most of its route. Nature hikes, camping, and other activities are largely confined to the visitor centers and to more than 200 overlooks. There are about 100 **hiking trails** along the route, including the Appalachian Trail, which follows the parkway from Mile 0 to about Mile 103.

In Virginia, the 62-mile stretch between Otter Creek and Roanoke Mountain is the most scenic part. It crosses the James River Gorge and climbs Apple Orchard Mountain, the highest parkway point in Virginia (elevation 3,950 ft.). At times, the road here follows the ridgeline, rendering spectacular views down both sides of the mountains at once. It also passes the peaceful Peaks of Otter Lodge, the only hotel actually on the parkway (p. 194).

South of Roanoke, the parkway runs through lower country, with more meadows and less mountain scenery.

JUST THE FACTS

ACCESS POINTS & ORIENTATION   The northern parkway entrance is near Waynesboro at the southern end of the Skyline Drive, on U.S. 250 at Exit 99 off I-64. The major access points in Virginia are U.S. 60 east of Buena Vista; U.S. 501 between Buena Vista and Lynchburg (Otter Creek and the James River Gorge); U.S. 460, Va. 24, U.S. 220, and the Mill Mountain Spur near Roanoke; U.S. 58 at Meadows of Dan; and I-77 at Fancy Gap. You can also get up here from Buchanan or Bedford via Va. 43, but note that trucks are not permitted on Va. 43 between Buchanan and the parkway.

Mile Posts on the west side of the parkway begin with Mile 0 at the northern Rockfish Gap entry and increase as you head south. The North Carolina border is at Mile 218.

INFORMATION   For general information, contact the **National Park Service (NPS),** 199 Hemphill Knob Rd., Asheville, NC 28801 (© **828/298-0398;** www.nps. gov/blri). Ask for a copy of the NPS's brochure with an excellent map of the parkway and the *Parkway Milepost,* a quarterly tabloid newspaper with articles about the parkway and a schedule of events. Both are available at the visitor centers, which also sell books about the parkway.

You can also get an information packet, including a copy of the indispensable *Blue Ridge Parkway Directory & Travel Planner,* from the **Blue Ridge Parkway Association,** P.O. Box 2136, Asheville, NC 28802-2136 (© **828/298-0398;** www.blueridge parkway.org).

EMERGENCIES   Call the National Park Service at © **800/727-5928** in case of emergencies anywhere along the parkway.

FEES, REGULATIONS & BACKCOUNTRY PERMITS   There is no fee for using the parkway. The maximum speed limit is 45 mph in rural areas, 35 mph in built-up zones. Bicycles are allowed on paved roads and parking areas, not on any trails. Camping is permitted in designated areas (see "Camping," below). Fires are permitted in campgrounds and picnic areas only. Hunting is prohibited. Pets must be kept on a leash. No swimming is allowed in parkway ponds and lakes.

VISITOR CENTERS   Several visitor centers along the parkway are the focal points of most visitor activities, including ranger programs. The **Rockfish Gap Visitor Center,** at the northern end (Mile 0), is open year-round. Others are closed from November to March. Hours for all are 9am to 5pm daily. Here's a rundown heading south:

Humpback Rocks Visitor Center (Mile 5.8) has picnic tables, restrooms, and a self-guiding trail to a reconstructed mountain homestead.

James River Visitor Center (Mile 63.6), near U.S. 501 northwest of Lynchburg, is worth a stop. It has a footbridge that crosses the river to the restored canal locks, exhibits, and a nature trail. The nearby Otter Creek wayside has a daytime restaurant and campground.

Peaks of Otter (★★ (Mile 85.9), at Va. 43 northwest of Bedford, is the most picturesque visitor center. It has a 2-mile hike to the site of a historic farm, wildlife and Native American exhibits, restrooms, and the Peaks of Otter Lodge (p. 194), which sits beside a gorgeous lake wedged between two cone-shaped mountains—the Peaks of Otter. A trail leads to the top of Sharp Top, the taller of the two at 3,875 feet. Weather permitting, a **shuttle bus** runs to within 1,500 feet of the peak. It's a strenuous 1.6-mile hike to the summit, so allow 3 hours for the total excursion. Needless to say, wear comfortable walking shoes and bring water. The bus runs May through August daily every hour on the hour from 10am to 4pm; September and October, from 10am to 5pm. Buy your tickets and water at the camp store (© **540/586-1614**) beside the visitor center. One-way fares are $5 for adults, $4 for children younger than 13.

Virginia's Explore Park (Mile 115) is on the grounds of the living history museum on the outskirts of Roanoke.

Rocky Knob (Mile 167.1), southeast of Va. 8, has some 15 miles of hiking trails (including the Rock Castle Gorge National Recreational Trail), a comfort station, and a picnic area.

Mabry Mill (Mile 176), between Va. 8 and U.S. 58, has a picturesque gristmill with a giant wheel spanning a little stream. Displays of pioneer life, including crafts demonstrations, are featured and the restored mill still grinds flour. A restaurant, open May through October, adjoins it.

SEASONS   The parkway is at its best during spring, when the wildflowers bloom and leaves are multihued green, and during mid-October, when changing leaves are at their blazing best (and traffic is at its heaviest). Winter is not a good time since most facilities are closed, and snow, ice, and fog can close the road.

ON THE WINE TRAIL At Mile 171.5, between Va. 8 and U.S. 58 north of Mabry Mill, you can turn off on C.R. 726 and follow the signs to **Chateau Morrisette** (© 540/593-2865; www.chateaumorrisette.com), one of the three largest vineyards in Virginia. It produces Black Dog and Our Dog Blue, two of the state's best-known red wines. It's open for tastings and sales Monday through Thursday 10am to 5pm, Friday and Saturday 10am to 6pm, and Sunday 11am to 5pm. A restaurant is open for lunch Wednesday through Sunday from April through December, Friday and Saturday from January through March. It serves dinner on Friday and Saturday all year.

CAMPING

The visitor centers at **Otter Creek,** Mile 60.8 (© **804/299-5125**); **Peaks of Otter,** Mile 86 (© **540/586-4357**); **Roanoke Mountain,** Mile 120.4 (© **540/982-9242**); and **Rocky Knob,** Mile 174.1 (© **540/745-9664**) all have campgrounds. The **Roanoke Mountain campground** is actually on Mill Mountain, about 1 mile west of the parkway above Roanoke (see section 2, below).

Campgrounds are open from about May 1 to early November, depending on weather conditions. Drinking water and restrooms are available, but shower and laundry facilities are not. There are tent and trailer sites, but none have utility connections. Sites cost $16 a night. America the Beautiful senior pass holders get a 50% discount. Daily permits are valid only at the campground where purchased.

Cabins are available at **Rocky Knob Cabins,** Meadows of Dan, VA 24120 (© **540/ 593-3903**).

ACCOMMODATIONS

Peaks of Otter Lodge *(Value* Split-rail fences and small footbridges add to the picturesque beauty of this serene, lakeside lodge nestled in a gorgeous valley between two mountain peaks. The main lodge building has a restaurant, a crafts and gift shop, and a game and TV room with a view of the lake. On a grassy slope overlooking the lake, accommodations are in motel-like units a 600- to 900-foot walk from the main building (bring an umbrella and insect repellent). Virtually identical, the rooms have private balconies or terraces to maximize the splendid view. Only the lodge rooms equipped for guests with disabilities have TVs or phones (Roanoke folk come up here to literally get away from it all). Reservations are accepted beginning October 1 for the *following* year's fall foliage season. Winter and early spring are not overly crowded, but reservations should be made weeks ahead for all good-weather months. The casual, family-style Lakeview Restaurant is open daily from 7:30am to 8:30pm. The parkway's Peaks of Otter visitor center, with its ranger programs and shuttle bus up Sharp Top Mountain, is within walking distance (see "Just the Facts," above).

Milepost 86 (P.O. Box 489), Bedford, VA 24523. © **800/542-5927** (in Virginia and North Carolina) or 540/586-1081. Fax 540/586-4420. www.peaksofotter.com. 63 units. $99–$119 double. MC, V. **Amenities:** Restaurant; bar. *In room:* A/C, no phone (except disable-equipped units).

2 Roanoke: City below a Star *(*

54 miles SW of Lexington; 74 miles NE of Wytheville; 193 miles SW of Richmond; 251 miles SW of Washington, D.C.

Sprawling across the floor of the Roanoke Valley, Virginia's largest metropolitan area west of Richmond likes to call itself the "Capital of the Blue Ridge." It's also known as "Star City," for the huge lighted star overlooking the city from Mill Mountain, which stands between it and the Blue Ridge Parkway.

Roanoke

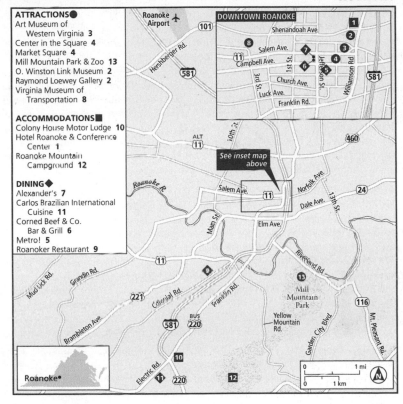

ATTRACTIONS●
Art Museum of
  Western Virginia **3**
Center in the Square **4**
Market Square **4**
Mill Mountain Park & Zoo **13**
O. Winston Link Museum **2**
Raymond Loewey Gallery **2**
Virginia Museum of
  Transportation **8**

ACCOMMODATIONS■
Colony House Motor Lodge **10**
Hotel Roanoke & Conference
  Center **1**
Roanoke Mountain
  Campground **12**

DINING◆
Alexander's **7**
Carlos Brazilian International
  Cuisine **11**
Corned Beef & Co.
  Bar & Grill **6**
Metro! **5**
Roanoker Restaurant **9**

There was no star on the mountain when Colonial explorers followed the Roanoke River gorge through the Blue Ridge Mountains in the 17th century. They established several settlements in the Roanoke Valley, including one named Big Lick. When the Norfolk and Western Railroad arrived in the 1880s and laid out a town for future development, it decided that *Roanoke*—a Native American word for "shell money"— was a more prosperous-sounding name for the new city.

Roanoke is still a major railroad junction, as the many tracks running through downtown will attest, but it's also a lively regional center of business and the arts. Roanoke launched itself on a renaissance long before Norfolk and other Virginia cities undertook to rebuild their downtown areas. Most notable to us visitors is the restored **Market Square** area around the Historic City Market. With its museums, theater, and trendy restaurants, Market Square serves as the focal point for both daytime activities and lively after-dark entertainment.

With its zoo, museums, restaurants, and a fine theater, Roanoke makes a great place to overnight if you're traveling the Blue Ridge Parkway. If you're just touring the state, you can easily spend a day and more exploring its sights.

ESSENTIALS

VISITOR INFORMATION

Contact the **Roanoke Valley Convention and Visitors Bureau,** 101 Shenandoah Ave. NE, Roanoke, VA 24016 (© **800/635-5535** or 540/342-6025; fax 540/342-7119; www.visitroanokeva.com), in the restored Norfolk & Western Railway Passenger Station (which it shares with the O. Winston Link Museum; p. 197). The station sits across the tracks from Market Square in front of the Hotel Roanoke & Conference Center. The bureau's visitor center is the best place to pick up maps and brochures for walking and biking tours before starting to explore Roanoke, and you can make same-day hotel reservations here. Be sure to watch the 8-minute video about the valley and go behind the staff desk for a look at a one-eighth-scale model of steam locomotive No. 1218. The center is open daily from 9am to 5pm.

GETTING THERE

BY PLANE **Roanoke Regional Airport** (ROA; © **540/362-1999;** www.roanoke regionalairport.com), 5½ miles northwest of downtown off Hershberger Road (Exit 3E off I-581), is served by Allegiant, Delta, Northwest, United, and US Airways. The major car-rental units have booths on-site. **Roanoke Airport Transportation Service** (© **800/228-1958** or 540/345-7710) runs vans to downtown and to Blacksburg and to other highland points as far away as Abingdon (see section 4, later in this chapter) and throughout the Shenandoah Valley (see chapter 7). If you're not in a hurry, you can catch the **Smartway Bus** (© **800/388-7005** or 540/982-6622; www.smartwaybus. com), an express service that stops at the airport nine times a day Monday through Saturday on its way between Roanoke and Blacksburg. One-way fare to downtown is $3.

BY CAR From I-81, take I-581 (Exit 143) south into the heart of Roanoke. I-581 becomes U.S. 220; together, they form an expressway that passes all the way through town. The Blue Ridge Parkway runs along the top of the mountains east of the city; the major Roanoke exits are at U.S. 460, Va. 24, the Mill Mountain Spur Road (at Mile 120), and U.S. 220.

BY TRAIN The nearest **Amtrak** (© **800/872-7245;** www.amtrak.com) stations are at Lynchburg and Clifton Forge, each about 50 miles from Roanoke.

GETTING AROUND

Yellow Cab (© **540/345-7711**) is the largest taxi company here. **Valley Metro** (© **540/982-2222;** www.valleymetro.com) provides public bus service Monday through Saturday from 5:45am to 8:45pm. The downtown transfer point is Campbell Court, 17 W. Campbell Ave. The visitor center distributes free Ride Guide route maps.

EXPLORING DOWNTOWN

Market Square , in the center of downtown at Market Street and Campbell Avenue, is Roanoke's answer to Alexandria's Old Town and Richmond's Shockoe Slip. As they have for more than a century, stands and shops at the **Historic City Market** display plants, flowers, fresh fruits and vegetables, dairy and eggs, and farm-cured meats (Sat morning is the best time to visit). Nearby, restored Victorian-era storefronts house an eclectic mix of trendy restaurants, gift shops, art galleries, antiques dealers, an Orvis outdoor-wear, and pawnshops. Of special note is **Agnew Seed Store,** which still uses its old-fashioned oak drawers.

Built of red brick in 1922, the **Market Building** now houses a food court offering the downtown lunch crowd an inexpensive international menu, from Chinese egg rolls to North Carolina–style barbecue. The market and food court are open Monday through Saturday.

Center in the Square, the big modern building on Market Square at Campbell Avenue (© **540/342-5700;** www.centerinthesquare.org), is home to the History Museum of Western Virginia, the Science Museum of Western Virginia, and the Art Museum of Western Virginia (until the latter opens a new facility in 2008; see below), as well as the Mill Mountain Theatre (see "Roanoke After Dark," later in this chapter).

An enclosed walkway leads over the railroad tracks from Market Square to the visitor center and the O. Winston Link Museum, both in the city's restored train station. It sits in front of the Hotel Roanoke & Conference Center, itself a sightseeing attraction (p. 200).

Also from Market Square, you can follow the **David S. and Susan S. Goode Railwalk** beside the tracks to the Virginia Museum of Transportation.

Art Museum of Western Virginia

This fine regional museum focusing on 19th- and 20th-century American art and decorative arts, including works by artists from throughout the South, will get even better in the fall of 2008 when it opens a magnificent gallery building on Salem Avenue at Williamson Road. Even if it hasn't opened when you visit, you can't help but admire the new building's steel-and-zinc roofline, which evokes its Blue Ridge Mountains backdrop. Meanwhile, the museum occupies space in Center in the Square. Call or check the website for special exhibits and events.

1 Market Sq., in Center in the Square. © 540/342-5760. www.artmuseumroanoke.org. Admission $3 adults, free for children under 12 (docent-led tours available for a fee). Tues–Sat 10am–5pm; Sun 1–5pm.

History Museum of Western Virginia

Tools, costumes, and weapons tell the story of Roanoke and southwestern Virginia from American Indian days 10,000 years ago through pioneer days 2 centuries ago to the present. The museum carries books, maps, and prints for sale. Joint tickets are available with the O. Winston Link Museum (see below).

1 Market Sq., in Center in the Square. © 540/342-5770. www.history-museum.org. Admission $3 adults, $2 seniors and children 6–12, free for children 5 and younger. Tues–Fri 10am–4pm; Sat 10am–5pm; Sun 1–5pm.

O. Winston Link Museum ✫✫✫

In the restored Norfolk & Western railway station, this marvelous museum is devoted to the extraordinary black-and-white railroad photography of the late O. Winston Link. Born in Brooklyn, New York, in 1914 of parents who hailed from Virginia and West Virginia, Link took his first photos of N&W locomotives in 1955 while on another assignment in Staunton. For the next 5 years, he traced the railroad's tracks, taking thousands of pictures of smoking locomotives just before diesel-powered models put an end to the era of steam. His most dramatic shots came at night. The museum, which he helped design, is both art gallery and railroad museum, for many items such as an original 1930s gasoline pump and parts of a country store are on display in front of the photos in which they appear. This juxtaposition of art and history makes this one of the most fascinating museums in Virginia and the best railway museum I've ever seen. It's a must-see for railroad buffs—and everyone else with an interest in photography. You'll need 30 minutes to watch a video about Link's life and at least another hour to tour the exhibits. Come here first, then follow the David S. and Susan S. Goode Railwalk along the tracks to the actual locomotives and railway cars on display at the Virginia Museum of Transportation (see below).

Fun Fact **"The Father of Industrial Design"**

Built in 1905, Roanoke's Norfolk & Western train station not only houses of the visitor center and the O. Winston Link Museum, it's also home to the **Raymond Loewy Gallery.** Known as "the father of industrial design," Loewy remodeled the station in 1947 but is better known for the slenderized Coca-Cola bottle, the Studebaker Avanti automobile, and logos for Exxon, Shell, and Nabisco, all displayed here. Free admission; open daily 9am to 5pm.

---

101 Shenandoah Ave. (in old train station). ✆ **540/982-5465.** www.linkmuseum.org. Admission $5 adults, $4.50 seniors, $4 children 3–11, free for children 2 and younger. Includes admission to History Museum of Western Virginia. Combination tickets with Virginia Museum of Transportation $10 adults, $8 seniors, $6 children 3–11, free for children 2 and younger. Daily 10am–5pm.

Science Museum of Western Virginia/Hopkins Planetarium *(Kids)*   Children will be intrigued with the high-tech interactive exhibits here. A weather gallery features a tornado simulator and a Weather Channel–like studio. Other permanent galleries have hands-on exhibits in physics, geology (including a moon rock), and the human body ("Big Mouth" is a walk-in human mouth). The Hopkins Planetarium offers programs related to the stars, planets, and galaxies; the MegaDome Theatre shows big-screen films. The museum store on the ground level offers a fascinating collection of educational toys.

1 Market Sq., in Center in the Square. ✆ **540/342-5710.** www.smwv.org. Exhibits admission $8 adults, $7 seniors, $6 children 3–12, free for children 2 and younger. Combination exhibits, planetarium, and IMAX shows $13 adults, $12 seniors, $11 children 3–12, free for children 2 and younger. Tues–Sat 10am–5pm; Sun 1–5pm.

Virginia Museum of Transportation *(star star) (Kids)*   In a restored freight depot 5 blocks west of Market Square, this wide-ranging museum has aviation and automotive exhibits, but its best feature is an extraordinary collection of vintage locomotives, passenger and mail cars, and cabooses on display under the Claytor Pavilion's big roof out back. You can climb aboard some of them, get up close and personal with others, but the best way to see them is on a guided tour of the rail yard (call for times). Also out back, a playground will keep the kids occupied riding in model trains, cars, and a helicopter. Inside, they will get a kick out of a gargantuan and very real model railroad, and can learn about the effects of motion in the Star Station, which the museum best describes as "a petting zoo of transportation artifacts." The oral history exhibit featuring African Americans talking about working on the railroad is worth an adult stop. You'll need 1 to 2½ hours to thoroughly digest all the exhibits.

303 Norfolk Ave. (at 3rd St.). ✆ **540/342-5670.** www.vmt.org. Admission $8 adults, $7 seniors, $6 children 3–11, free for children 2 and younger. Combination tickets with O. Winston Link Museum $10 adults, $8 seniors, $6 children 3–11, free for children 2 and younger. Mon–Sat 10am–5pm; Sun 1–5pm. Rail yard closes 30 min. earlier.

ATTRACTIONS ON OR NEAR MILL MOUNTAIN

Situated between the city and the Blue Ridge Parkway, Mill Mountain offers panoramic views over Roanoke Valley. The two main attractions are in **Mill Mountain Park,** on the Mill Mountain Parkway Spur, a winding road that leaves the Blue Ridge Parkway at Mile 120. Local citizens know they're home when they see the white neon **Roanoke Star on the Mountain.** Erected in 1949 as a civic project, it stands

89 feet tall, uses 2,000 feet of neon tubing, and is visible from most parts of the city. Stop at the base for a magnificent view over the city and valley.

Also here is the **Discovery Center** (✆ 540/853-1236; www.roanokeva.gov/ outdoors), which explains the wildlife, geology, and history of the mountain. Its honeybee exhibit is worth seeing. Admission is free. It's open from April through October Monday through Saturday 10am to 6pm, Sunday 1 to 5pm; November through March Monday through Friday 10am to 4pm, Saturday noon to 5pm, Sunday 1 to 5pm.

From the city, take Walnut Avenue, which becomes the J.P. Fishburn Parkway and intersects the Mill Mountain Parkway Spur at the entry to Mill Mountain Park.

Mill Mountain Zoo *(Kids)*   This small zoo is home to more than 50 animal species, including snow leopards, monkeys, prairie dogs, hawks, red pandas, Japanese macaques, and a bald eagle. The animals are caged, so don't come up here if that bothers you. The future was a bit uncertain for the open-air, narrow gauge train that runs around the periphery, giving access to red wolves and deer (unconfirmed rumor said it could be moved to the Virginia Transportation Museum). You'll need about 1½ hours up here.

Mill Mountain Pkwy. Spur (in Mill Mountain Park). ✆ 540/343-3241. www.mmzoo.org. Admission $6.75 adults, $6.40 seniors, $4.50 children 2–12, free for children 1 and younger. Train rides $2. Daily 10am–4:30pm. Closed Dec 25.

Virginia's Explore Park   It's a 7-mile drive on the Blue Ridge Parkway from Mill Mountain to this a 1,100-acre reserve astride the gorge cut by the Roanoke River on its way through the Blue Ridge. You can hike or mountain bike on 8½ miles of trails and canoe or fish on the river. On-site bike rentals are available. Like the Frontier Culture Museum in Staunton (p. 170), the historical areas of the park feature reconstructed settlements with costumed reenactors who explain what life was like in these parts around 1671, 1757, and 1850. This is more of an adventure, however, for these settlements are not farms but on the forested slopes of the steep gorge. If you and your small children are not up to the strenuous, 1.8-mile walk, staff-driven golf carts will take you. Begin at Blue Ridge Parkway Visitors Center and allow about 2 hours for a self-guided tour of the historic areas. You can take a break at the moderately priced Brugh Tavern (appropriately pronounced "Brew"), which serves lunch Wednesday through Sunday.

Note: Government officials have negotiated a lease-option agreement with a developer, who has until mid-2008 to decide if he will expand the park. Meanwhile, the park is operating normally, and guest comments have been favorable.

Mile Post 115, Blue Ridge Pkwy. ✆ 800/842-9163 or 540/427-1800. www.explorepark.org. Museum admission $9 adults, $7 seniors, $5 children 4–15, free for children 3 and younger. Grounds year-round daily 8am–sunset; historic areas Apr to mid-Nov Wed–Sat 10am–5pm, Sun noon–5pm; Brugh Tavern May–Oct Wed–Sun 11am–4pm. From Mill Mountain, take Mill Mountain Pkwy. Spur to Blue Ridge Pkwy., turn left, go to Mile Post 115, turn right on Roanoke River Pkwy. to park.

WHERE TO STAY

If you're coming off the Blue Ridge Parkway, convenient choices include the **Holiday Inn Tanglewood** (✆ 800/465-4329 or 540/774-4400) and a **Sleep Inn** (✆ 800/628-1929 or 540/772-1500). Near the airport, Hershberger Road (Exit 3 off I-581) has the **Holiday Inn Roanoke Valley View** (✆ 888/465-4329 or 540/362-4500) and the **Best Western at Valley View** (✆ 800/362-2410 or 540/362-2400). Farther out, Peters Creek Road (Exit 2 off I-581) has a **Courtyard by Marriott** (✆ 800/321-2211 or 540/563-5002), a **Hampton Inn** (© 800/426-7866 or 540/265-2600), and an inexpensive **Super 8 Roanoke** (© 800/800-8000 or 540/563-8888).

Colony House Motor Lodge ☆   The same family has owned and operated this clean, well-maintained motel since it was built in 1959 (yes, it's authentically "retro"). A series of peaked roofs creates cathedral ceilings in some of the spacious rooms, all of which have louvered screen doors that let in fresh air without sacrificing privacy. About half the units are at the rear of the property; they face a steep hillside and get less light but also less traffic noise. About three-quarters have refrigerators and microwave ovens, and two suites have whirlpool tubs. A roadside outdoor swimming pool has a view of the Kmart across Franklin Road. Continental breakfast is served here, and Carlos Brazilian International Cuisine (p. 203) and other restaurants are nearby.

3560 Franklin Rd. (U.S. 220 Business), Roanoke, VA 24014. © **866/203-5850** or 540/345-0411. Fax 540/345-1137. www.colonyhousemotorlodge.com. 72 units. $63 double. Rates include continental breakfast. AE, DC, DISC, MC, V. From I-581/U.S. 220, exit at Franklin Rd. (U.S. 220 Business), turn left at traffic signal to motel on right. From Blue Ridge Pkwy., take U.S. 220 Business west, exit on Franklin Rd. north to motel on right. **Amenities:** Outdoor pool; exercise room; business center; coin-op washers and dryers. *In room:* A/C, TV, Wi-Fi (1 building), fridge (some units).

Hotel Roanoke & Conference Center—A Doubletree Hotel ☆☆☆   The Norfolk and Western Railroad built this grand Tudor-style hotel in 1882 on a hill overlooking its new town, even before it changed the name from Big Lick to Roanoke. Heated by steam from the railroad's maintenance shops and cooled by America's first hotel air-conditioning system (which cooled the rooms with circulating ice water), it became a resort as well as a stopover. Some 26 passenger trains a day rolled into the station (now the visitor center and the O. Winston Link Museum) at the foot of the hill, and virtually every celebrity passing though Roanoke stayed here, among them Elvis Presley and five presidents. For the locals, it was *the* place for wedding receptions, reunions, beauty pageants, and other special events.

The hotel fell on hard times and was closed from 1989 to 1995, when it reopened after a magnificent restoration financed in part by Virginia Tech and local residents who dug into their pockets to save the venerable property. Now managed by Doubletree Hotels, it's recognized as a Historic Hotel of America, and Roanokers—who call it simply The Hotel—again celebrate very special occasions in the elegant **Regency Room** (p. 202). Pub fare is available in the knotty **Pine Room Pub,** which has a large bar, sports TV, and billiard table, and you can dance the weekend nights away at **Club a.k.a.** in the basement.

The building was gutted and rebuilt above the public areas, so all the rooms and suites are completely modern. Given the odd shape of the structure, there are now 92 room configurations, many with sloping ceilings and gable windows. Some have windows on two sides, while a few others seem like small cottages.

⌒Tips Worth a Look

Even if you don't stay at the **Hotel Roanoke & Conference Center,** come inside after visiting the O. Winston Link Museum across the street to see the hotel's rich, black walnut–paneled lobby with its Oriental rugs and leather lounge furniture. To the right, as you enter, is the oval-shaped Palm Court lounge with its four lovingly restored murals of Colonial and Victorian Virginians dancing the reel, waltz, minuet, and quadrille.

---

110 Shenandoah Ave., Roanoke, VA 24016. ℃ **800/222-8733** or 540/985-5900. Fax 540/853-8264. www.hotel roanoke.com. 332 units. $129–$209 double; $258–$458 suite. Packages available. AE, DC, DISC, MC, V. Self-parking $7; valet parking $10. From I-581 south, take Exit 5, cross Wells Ave. into parking lot. **Amenities:** 2 restaurants; 2 bars; outdoor pool; health club; concierge; business center; room service; laundry service; concierge-level rooms. *In room:* A/C, TV, Wi-Fi, coffeemaker, iron.

A NEARBY MOUNTAIN RESORT

Mountain Lake Hotel   Surrounded by 2,600 acres, this rustic mountaintop resort consists of a stately, rough-cut-stone lodge with clusters of small, white-clapboard summer cottages nearby. The lobby has a massive fireplace. A stone archway separates the lobby from the adjoining bar and lounge. The spacious, stone-walled dining room has large windows offering panoramic lake views—a romantic evening setting. More than 20 types of accommodations are available in the main hotel, cottages, and the Blueberry Ridge Complex (units in the latter are more sizeable and modern, and they're open year-round). The popular parlor suites have Jacuzzis and fireplaces, and some rooms offer lake views. Dark-wood Chippendale-reproduction furnishings give the decor a traditional look. Cottages are more simply furnished, although guests enjoy kitchens and porches with rockers. Chestnut Lodge is a three-story gray-clapboard building set on the side of a hill. Rooms here are decorated in country style, with fireplaces and balconies. Your unit will not have a TV, but there's plenty of swimming, boating, fishing, hiking, and tennis to keep you busy.

> **(Fun Fact Dirty Dancing**
>
> Mountain Lake played the part of the Catskills resort in the movie *Dirty Dancing,* starring Patrick Swayze and Jennifer Grey.

Pembroke, VA 24136. ℃ **800/346-3334** or 540/626-7121. Fax 540/626-7172. www.mountainlakehotel.com. 101 units, including 22 cottages. $195–$300 double; $295–$365 suite; $220–$920 cabin. Rates include breakfast and dinner. AE, DC, DISC, MC, V. Hotel closed Nov–Apr. From I-81, take Exit 118B, U.S. 460 west; turn right onto C.R. 700 and go 7 miles to Mountain Lake. **Amenities:** Restaurant; bar; outdoor pool; tennis court; Jacuzzi; sauna; watersports equipment/rentals; bike rentals; children's programs; game room; shopping arcade; massage; coin-op washers and dryers. *In room:* Wi-Fi, kitchen (10 cottages only), coffeemaker.

WHERE TO DINE

Roanoke is one of Virginia's more interesting dining scenes. While you can still get good country cooking here (including my favorite biscuits), young chefs are using flavors their Southern ancestors never imagined, much less tasted.

DOWNTOWN RESTAURANTS

Market Square (see "Exploring Downtown," earlier in this chapter) is Roanoke's dining center, with the 3 blocks of Campbell Avenue between Williamson Road and Jefferson Street, and the contiguous block of Jefferson Street, offering a host of restaurants catering to many tastes and all pocketbooks. Take a stroll and see what's happening (most post their menus outside).

Behind the stalls on Market Street, **Wertz's Country Restaurant & Wine Bar** (℃ **540/342-5133**) uses gourmet produce in sandwiches and salads at lunch, while tender, 21-day-aged steaks appear along with seafood and pasta dishes at dinner. Its wine cellar is one of the city's best. **202 Market,** 2 Market Square (℃ **540/343-6644**), a *très* cool bistro and wine bar, competes head-to-head with Metro! (see below) as coolest downtown restaurant. **Billy's Ritz,** 102 Salem Ave. (℃ **540/342-3937**), specializes in steaks and grilled seafood, and it's open on Sunday evening. The Market

Square branch of **Awful Arthur's Seafood Company,** 108 Campbell St. (© **540/344-2997**), also is open on Sunday, and it has sidewalk tables during warm weather. For a bite to your tongue, **Tong's Thai,** 19 Salem Ave. (© **540/344-7732**), serves spicy Siamese cuisine. A block to the west, **Frankie Rowland's Steakhouse,** 104 S. Jefferson St. (© **540/527-2333**), is Roanoke's swankiest purveyor of tender beef. It's across the street from Alexander's (see below).

I check my e-mail and get my caffeine fix at **Mill Mountain Coffee & Tea Co.,** 112 Campbell Ave. (© **540/342-9404**), and order my cooked breakfasts at **Ernie's,** 210 Market St. (© **540/342-7100**), which opens at 6am Monday through Saturday.

Alexander's ⭐⭐ NEW AMERICAN   In operation since 1979, Alexander's was the first trendy restaurant to open during downtown's Renaissance, and it's still one of the best. The pinkish lighting, widely spaced tables, and extraordinarily attentive waitstaff make this a great place for special occasions. Using organic meats, vegetables, and cheeses, the New American menu blends the classics with flavors from Louisiana, Asia, and the Mediterranean. Veal Alexander, with lump crabmeat and a hollandaise sauce, is a regular, as is shrimp étouffée with grits cakes, which will exercise your taste buds.

105 S. Jefferson St. © **540/982-6983**. Reservations recommended. Main courses $20–$36. AE, MC, V. Wed 11am–2pm; Tues–Thurs 5–9pm; Fri–Sat 5–10pm.

Corned Beef & Co. Bar and Grill AMERICAN   A block west of Market Square, this lively sports-bar emporium—the largest one of its kind I've ever seen—occupies half a city block. There's a sophisticated billiard parlor and beaucoup TV screens for watching every game being televised at the moment. You can even watch from a rooftop patio during warm weather. Having a good time may be the main reason to come here (it literally overflows with young folk on weekend nights), but the chow is better than average pub fare: deli sandwiches (including the namesake corned beef), salads, wood-fired pizzas, and main courses such as chicken *diablo* (a breast piqued with Texas Pete hot sauce). I'm particularly fond of the shrimp and asparagus quesadillas.

107 Jefferson St. © **540/342-3354**. Reservations accepted. Salads, sandwiches, burgers $6.50–$9; pizzas $9–$12; main courses $10–$22. AE, DC, DISC, MC, V. Mon–Sat 11:30am–midnight (bar open to 2am).

Metro! ⭐⭐ *Finds* ECLECTIC   This sophisticated, high-energy bistro and lounge brings the big city to Roanoke. You can watch the chefs scurrying around the open kitchen through the big storefront windows on Campbell Avenue, but wander on in for a drink and some sushi at the large martini bar, which dominates the main dining room. Most of the city's well-heeled young professionals will be here, especially on weekend nights when Metro! turns into a South Beach–style lounge. Beforehand, the kitchen provides a wide range of exciting fare, from sushi and sashimi to curry-brushed lamb shank and line-caught wahoo with a Mexican accent.

14 Campbell Ave. © **540/345-6645**. Reservations recommended, especially on weekends. Sushi $9–$16; main courses $26–$39. Tasting menus $60–$75 per person. AE, DISC, MC, V. Mon 5–10pm; Tues–Sat 11am–2pm and 5–10pm (bar to 2am).

The Regency Room ⭐⭐⭐ INTERNATIONAL   The Hotel Roanoke & Conference Center's main dining room has long been Roanokers' favorite place for a special dinner, and with good reason. Fresh flowers adorn the widely spaced tables, and the waitstaff provides the best service in town. The food lives up to the setting, too. The signature peanut soup has been around since 1940, and it provides a fitting—if fattening—entree to the crab cakes, which hold a half-pound of back-fin lumps, the best part of these tasty crustaceans. The chef makes some unusual uses of other Virginia fare as well, such as his Corn Cake Chesapeake, a cornbread cake topped with crab-meat, shrimp, oysters, and scallops simmered in a Smithfield ham sauce. There's live music for dancing on Friday and Saturday nights.

In Hotel Roanoke & Conference Center, 110 Shenandoah Ave. (© 540/985-5900. Reservations recommended. Break-fast $7–$14; main courses $24–$38. AE, DC, DISC, MC, V. Sun–Thurs 7–10:30am, 11:30am–2pm, and 5–9pm; Fri–Sat 7–10:30am, 11:30am–2pm, and 5–10pm.

OTHER RESTAURANTS

Carlos Brazilian International Cuisine ★★ BRAZILIAN/INTERNATIONAL

It's worth taking a ride out to Brazilian-born chef Carlos Amaral's fine restaurant, across from the Tanglewood Mall, not only for the excellent food but for the view over the Roanoke Valley. Most dining rooms here have no view at all, but reserve as soon as possible for a table in the semicircular Olinda Room, whose window walls offer an unimpeded vista (and be sure to tell them you want the Olinda Room). The food highlights are obviously Brazilian, and include *moquca mineira,* a blend of shrimp, clams, and fish in a slightly spicy tomato sauce and served over rice and thinly sliced onions and green peppers. Chicken sautéed with pineapple, papaya, and apples is another winner. Vegetarians can pick from pastas, Brazilian black beans served with collard greens, or a meatless version of paella Valenciana (there's regular paella, too).

4167 Electric Rd. (U.S. 220 Business; south of I-581/U.S. 220), (© 540/342-6455. Reservations recommended. Main courses $12–$30. AE, MC, V. Mon–Fri 5–10pm; Sat 4–10pm. From downtown, take I-581/U.S. 220 south to 1st Franklin Rd. exit, turn right, go uphill on Electric Rd., make U-turn after Ogden Rd; restaurant is up hill on right. From Blue Ridge Pkwy., take U.S. 220 west to 1st Franklin Rd. exit, turn left, go uphill on Franklin Rd., which becomes Elec-tric Rd., make U-turn after Ogden Rd.; restaurant is up hill on right.

Roanoker Restaurant ★ Value SOUTHERN A popular local restaurant since

1941, the Roanoker occupies a Colonial-style building surrounded by much-needed parking lots. Several dining rooms offer booth seating arranged to provide privacy. Antique signs from Roanoke businesses adorn the walls. At breakfast, the fluffy bis-cuits are the best I've ever eaten, either plain, sandwiching country ham or sausage, or covered in sausage gravy. Lunch and dinner specials change daily, depending on avail-able produce. If you're lucky, the fresh vegetables will include skillet-fried yellow squash and onions, a mouthwatering Southern favorite.

2522 Colonial Ave. (south of Wonju St.). (© 540/344-7746. Reservations not accepted. Breakfast $4–$7; sandwiches $5–$8; main courses $7.50–$13. MC, V. Tues–Sat 7am–9pm; Sun 8am–9pm. From downtown, go south on Franklin Rd., turn right on Brandon Ave., left on Colonial Ave. From I-581, go south to Colonial Ave. exit, turn left at traffic light on Colonial Ave. to restaurant on left.

ROANOKE AFTER DARK

Available at the visitor center (see "Essentials," earlier in this chapter) and at many hotels and restaurants, the free *City Magazine* has a rundown of what's going on around town.

Mill Mountain Theatre, in the Center in the Square building on Campbell Avenue (© **800/317-6455** or 540/342-5740; www.millmountain.org), offers children's pro-ductions, free lunchtime readings (Oct–May), and year-round matinee and evening performances on two stages. Productions range from Shakespeare to minstrels. Recent performances have included *Lord of the Flies* and *Misery.* Ticket prices range from $5 to $30, depending on performance and venue.

The **Roanoke Civic Center,** 710 Williamson Rd. NE (© **540/981-1201;** www. roanokeciviccenter.com), hosts visiting performers and concerts by **The Roanoke Symphony** (© **540/343-9127;** www.rso.com).

Baseball fans can see the Class A **Salem Avalanche** (© **540/389-3333;** www.salem avalanche.com), an affiliate of the big-league Houston Astros, play in Salem, Roanoke's sister city.

The Market Square area running along Campbell Avenue to Jefferson Street is Roanoke's pub-crawling scene, especially on weekends when many restaurants and pubs have music and dancing. **Metro!** attracts the well-heeled young professional set, while **Corned Beef & Company** gets the sometimes rowdy masses (don't be surprised to see a cop or two across Jefferson St.). **The Regency Room,** the **Pine Room,** and the **a.k.a. Club** in the Hotel Roanoke & Conference Center have live music and dancing on weekends.

3 The Great Outdoors in the Southwest Highlands

The Southwest Highlands are great for getting outdoors and experiencing nature, especially if you're into hiking, biking, and horseback riding. Mount Rogers National Recreation Area (NRA), one of Virginia's prime locales for backcountry activities, runs for 60 miles along the mountaintops south of I-81 between Wytheville and Abingdon. Adding to the allure are two old railroad beds turned into excellent biking-and-hiking trails on its northern and southern flanks: the New River Trail State Park to the north and the Virginia Creeper Trail to the south.

MOUNT ROGERS NATIONAL RECREATION AREA

Noted for its 400 miles of hiking, mountain biking, cross-country skiing, and horse trails, including part of the Appalachian Trail, Mount Rogers NRA includes 117,000 forested acres. Included is its namesake, Virginia's highest peak at 5,729 feet. Nearby White Top is the state's second-highest point at 5,520 feet. Most of the land, however, flanks Iron Mountain, a long ridge running the area's length. Ranging the extensive upland meadows are wild ponies, introduced to keep the grasses mowed.

Not all of this expanse is pristine; as part of the George Washington and Jefferson National Forest, it's subject to multiple uses such as hunting and logging. Nevertheless, you'll find three preserved wilderness areas and plenty of backcountry to explore, with mountain scenery that's some of the best in Virginia.

JUST THE FACTS

ACCESS POINTS & ORIENTATION   Access roads from I-81 are U.S. 21 from Wytheville; Va. 16 from Marion; S.R. 600 from Chilehowie; Va. 91 from Glades Spring; and U.S. 58 from Damascus and Abingdon. S.R. 603 runs 13 miles lengthwise through beautiful highland meadows from Troutdale (on Va. 16) to Konnarock (on U.S. 58).

INFORMATION   Since the area is so vast and most facilities widespread, it's a good idea to get as much information in advance as possible. Contact the **Mount Rogers National Recreation Area,** 3714 Hwy. 16, Marion, VA 24354 (© **800/628-7202** or 276/783-5196; www.fs.fed.us/r8/gwj/mr).

FEES, REGULATIONS & BACKCOUNTRY PERMITS   There is no charge to drive through the area, but parking fees of $3 per vehicle apply to specific recreational areas, payable on the honor system. Except for the Appalachian Trail and some others reserved for hikers, mountain bikes are permitted but must give way to horses. Bikers and horseback riders must walk across all bridges and trestles. Hikers must not spook the horses. Fishing requires a Virginia license. The "leave no trace" ethic applies: Leave nothing behind, and take away only photographs and memories.

VISITOR CENTER   The area headquarters is at 3714 Va. 16, about 6 miles south of Marion (take Exit 45 off I-81 and go south on Va. 16). Exhibits describe the area, and there's a bookstore with maps and other publications for sale. The center is open Memorial Day to October Monday through Friday from 8am to 4:30pm, Saturday from 9am to 4pm. Off season, it's open Monday through Friday from 8am to 4:30pm. It's closed on federal holidays.

SEASONS   The area gets the most visitors on summer and fall weekends and holidays. Spring is punctuated by wildflowers in bloom (the calendars published by the Blue Ridge Parkway are generally applicable here), while fall foliage is at its brilliant best in mid-October. Cross-country skiers use the trails during winter. Summer thunderstorms, winter blizzards, and fog any time of the year can pose threats in the high country, so caution is advised.

SEEING THE HIGHLIGHTS

You can enjoy the scenery without getting out of your car. From Marion on I-81, take Va. 16 south 16 miles to the country store at Troutdale. Turn right on S.R. 603 and drive 13 miles southwest to U.S. 58. Turn right there and drive 20 miles down Straight Branch—a misnomer if ever there was one—through Damascus to I-81 at Abingdon.

An alternative route is to continue on Va. 16 south past Troutdale and turn west on U.S. 58. This will take you past **Grayson Highlands State Park.** After you pass the park, turn right on S.R. 600 north. This road climbs almost to the summit of White Top Mountain. Up there, a dirt track known as Spur 89 branches off for 3 miles to the actual summit; it's the highest point in Virginia to which you can drive a vehicle and has great views. S.R. 600 then descends to a dead-end at S.R. 603; turn right there and drive down to U.S. 58, then west to Damascus and Abingdon, as described above.

OUTDOOR PURSUITS

CAMPING   In addition to the horse camps mentioned below, the recreation area has several other campgrounds, all open from mid-April through December. A limited number of sites can be reserved in advance by calling © **877/444-6777** or going to www.recreation.gov.

On S.R. 603 between Troutdale and Konnarock, **Grindstone** serves as a base camp for hikers heading up Mount Rogers. It has 109 sites with campfires, drinking water, a .5-mile nature trail, and weekend ranger programs during summer. **Beartree Recreation Area,** a popular site 7 miles east of Damascus on U.S. 58, features a sand beach on a 12-acre lake stocked with trout for fishing. Both Grindstone and Beartree have flush toilets and warm showers. Grindstone has electric and water hookups; Beartree does not. Fees range from $7.50 to $19 per night.

HIGH-COUNTRY HIKING   Almost two-thirds of the area's 400 miles of trails are on these routes: the local stretch of the **Appalachian Trail** (64 miles), the **Virginia Highlands Horse Trail** (66 miles), and the **Iron Mountain Trail** (51 miles). Many of the other 67 trails connect to these main routes, and many can be linked into circuit hikes.

You can walk for days on the white-blaze Appalachian Trail without crossing a paved road, especially on the central stretch up and down the flanks of Mount Rogers between S.R. 603 and S.R. 600. A spur goes to the top of the mountain. The blue-blaze

Mount Rogers Trail, a very popular alternate route, leaves C.R. 603 near Grindstone Campground; a spur from that track heads down into the pristine Lewis Fork Wilderness before rejoining the Appalachian Trail.

Running across the southern end of the area, the **Virginia Creeper Trail** offers a much easier, but no less beautiful, hike (and bike ride). This 34-mile route follows an old railroad bed from Abingdon to White Top Mountain (see "The Virginia Creeper Trail," below).

HORSEBACK RIDING   Riders can use 150 miles of the area's trails, including Iron Mountain, New River, and the Virginia Highlands Horse Trail, which connects Elk Garden to Va. 94. Horse camps are at Fox Creek, on Va. 603; Hussy Mountain, near Speedwell; and Collins Cove, about 4 miles east of Cripple Creek. They have toilets, and drinking water for horses (but no water for humans).

THE VIRGINIA CREEPER TRAIL ✿✿✿

The fabulously beautiful **Virginia Creeper Trail** is a 34-mile hiking, biking, and horseback-riding route that follows an old railroad bed between Abingdon and White Top Station, at the North Carolina line on the southern flank of White Top Mountain, just inside Mount Rogers National Recreation Area. The name comes from the fact that steam locomotives had such a slow time on the grade that they became known collectively as the Virginia Creeper. If you can ride a bike, this is one of Virginia's top outdoor excursions.

The trail starts at an elevation of 2,065 feet in Abingdon, drops to 2,000 feet at Damascus (11 miles east on U.S. 58), then climbs to 3,675 feet at White Top. No one I know is about to ride a bike *up* that mountain, so the idea is to stay in Abingdon, take a shuttle bus to the top, and mostly coast for 17 of the 23 gorgeous miles downhill to Damascus.

Beginning 2 miles east of Damascus, the stretch between Green Cove Station and Iron Bridge crosses High Trestle (about 100 ft. high) and has swimming holes in the adjacent stream. Green Cove is a seasonal Forest Service information post with portable toilets and a snack bar. It was at Green Cove that O. Winston Link took one of his most famous photographs, of a mare bowing her head as the Creeper crawled past. It's on display at the O. Winston Link Museum in Roanoke and the Abingdon Passenger Train Station in Abingdon (see sections 2 and 4, respectively, in this chapter).

Outfitters in Damascus renting bikes and operating shuttles to the top of the trail include **Blue Blaze Bike & Shuttle Service** (✆ 800/475-5905 or 276/475-5095; www.blueblazebikeandshuttle.com); **Adventure Damascus Bicycles** (✆ 888/595-2453; www.adventuredamascus.com); and **The Bike Station,** 501 E. 3rd St. (✆ 276/475-3629; www.thebike-station.com). They are on Laurel Avenue (U.S. 58) in Damascus. In Abingdon, **Virginia Creeper Trail Bike Shop** (✆ 888/245-3648 or 276/676-2552; www.vacreepertrailbikeshop.com) is on Pecan Street near the trail head. All charge about $12 adults, $7 children for the shuttle; or $23 adults, $21 children for both shuttle and rental. Reservations are advised, so call ahead.

You can get a bird's-eye view of the highlands from the basket under a hot-air balloon. **Balloon Virginia** (✆ 276/628-6353) in Abingdon flies just-after-sunrise and just-before-dusk rides. Call for prices and reservations, which are essential.

For more information contact the Abingdon Convention & Visitors Bureau (see "Essentials" in section 4, below) or the website of the **Virginia Creeper Trail Club,** P.O. Box 2382, Abingdon, VA 24212 (**www.vacreepertrail.org**).

(*Fun Fact* **Trail Town, USA**

The village of **Damascus** (www.damascus.org) makes so much of its living off the Virginia Creeper that it calls itself "Trail Town, USA." Its **Trail Days** festival in mid-May draws hikers and cyclists from far and wide (**www.traildays.info**).

NEW RIVER TRAIL STATE PARK 🏍🏍

The exceptional **New River Trail** runs for 57 miles between Galax and Pulaski. The trail follows an old railroad bed beside the New River, which, despite its name, is in geologic terms one of the oldest rivers in the United States (it predates the Appalachian Mountains). The river flows toward the Mississippi River, on its way carving the New River Gorge in southeastern West Virginia, the best white-water rafting spot in the eastern U.S.

The park's headquarters are at **Foster Falls State Park,** a restored mining hamlet on Foster Falls Road (C.R. 608), about 20 miles northeast of Wytheville, or 2 miles north of U.S. 52 (take Exit 24 off I-77 and follow the signs). From April through November you can enter the trail here daily from 8am to 10pm. Parking costs $2 per vehicle during the week, $3 on weekends.

Other entries to the trail are at **Shot Tower Historical State Park** (see below); **Draper,** near Exit 92 off I-81; **Allisonia** and **Hiwassee,** both on C.R. 693; **Barren Springs,** on Va. 100; **Austinville,** on Va. 69; **Ivanhoe,** on Va. 94; **Byllesby Dam,** on C.R. 602; and **Galax,** on U.S. 58. There's also a branch trail to **Fries,** on Va. 94.

Foster Falls River Company (© **276/699-1034,** or 276/228-8311 in Wytheville) rents bicycles, canoes, kayaks, inner tubes, and horses at Foster Falls. Bikes cost $6 per hour or $20 per day. Canoes and kayaks start at $7 an hour or $30 per day. Tubes go for $10 per day. The adjacent stables (© **276/699-2460**) rent horses and have guided horse and pony rides along the trail (call for prices and reservations). The livery is open from Memorial Day to Labor Day daily from 8am to 5pm. The company also provides shuttle service between the key points along the trail, so you don't have to walk, ride, or paddle back to your car.

For more information, write or call **New River Trail State Park,** 176 Orphanage Rd., Foster Falls, VA 24360 (© **276/699-6778;** www.dcr.state.va.us/parks/newriver.htm). The office is open Monday through Friday 8am to 4:30pm.

While in this area, you can stop at **Shot Tower Historical State Park,** on U.S. 52 near Exit 5 off I-77, which features a stone shot tower built about 1791. Molten lead, poured from the top of the tower, fell 150 feet into a kettle, thus cooling and turning into round shot. The lead was mined at nearby Austinville, birthplace of Stephen Austin, the "Father of Texas." (There's a monument to Austin at the New River Trail State Park in Austinville.) Admission to the park is free, but parking costs $2 per vehicle during the week, $3 on weekends. The park is open daily from 8am to dusk.

WHERE TO STAY

There are no accommodations within Mount Rogers National Recreation Area. The closest is **Fox Hill Inn,** a bed-and-breakfast off Va. 16 near Troutdale (© **800/874-3313** or 540/677-3313; www.bbonline.com/va/foxhill).

The Virginia Creeper Trail ends in Abingdon, which has several hotels and bed-and-breakfasts (see "Where to Stay" in "Abingdon," below).

Country Music's Crooked Road

Southwestern Virginia has been central to the evolution of country music since the first European settlers arrived in these hills and valleys with few possessions other than their mandolins and fiddles. Some of the great country artists hail from here—the Carter Family, Ralph Stanley, and the Stonemans to name a few—and numerous music festivals such as the famous Old Time Fiddlers Convention in Galax take place in this area.

The area's music heritage is formally recognized by **The Crooked Road: Virginia's Heritage Music Trail,** P.O. Box 268, Big Stone Gap, VA 24219 (© **866/676-6847;** www.thecrookedroad.org). This official route follows U.S. 23, U.S. 421, U.S. 58, U.S. 221, Va. 8, and Va. 40 for more than 200 miles from Breaks in the west to Rocky Mount in the east. Along the way it passes such country music shrines as the **Ralph Stanley Museum & Traditional Music Center** in Clintwood; the **Carter Family Fold** in Hiltons; the **Birthplace of Country Music Museum** in Bristol; the **Blue Ridge Music Center** on the Blue Ridge Parkway; the **Rex Theater** in Galax; the **Floyd Country Store** in Floyd; and the **Blue Ridge Music Institute** in Ferrum.

Marion is the closest town to the area's center. Tops there is the **General Francis Marion Hotel** (© 877/783-4802 or 276/793-4800; www.gfmhotel.com), a lovingly restored 1927 commercial hotel on Main Street (U.S. 11) in the center of Marion's business district. On U.S. 11 north of downtown are the **Best Western Marion** (© 800/528-1234 or 540/783-3193), the **EconoLodge Marion** (© 800/553-2666 or 540/783-6031), and **Rodeway Inn** (© 877/424-6423 or 276/783-5112). The latter is a vintage one-story motel built in 1952 but still in good shape.

At the strategic intersection of I-81 and I-77 close to New River Trail State Park, Wytheville has more than 1,200 motel rooms, most in national chain establishments along the interstates. The largest concentration is at Exit 73 off I-81 (U.S. 11), where the **Holiday Inn Wytheville** (© 800/465-4329 or 276/228-5483) has its own restaurant. Also at Exit 73 is a **Days Inn** (© 800/325-2525 or 276/228-5500), **Motel 6** (© 800/446-8356 or 276/228-7988), and **Red Carpet Inn** (© 800/251-1962 or 276/228-5525). Some rooms in the Days Inn, Motel 6, and Red Carpet Inn are virtually beside I-81 and are subject to traffic noise. You can also take Exit 73 to reach a parking lot–surrounded **EconoLodge** (© 800/424-4777 or 276/228-5517), about 1 mile to the south on U.S. 11.

4 Abingdon: A Show-Stopping Town ★★★

49 miles SW of Wytheville; 133 miles SW of Roanoke; 315 miles SW of Richmond; 437 miles SW of Washington, D.C.

While on his first expedition to Kentucky in 1760, Daniel Boone tramped across the 2,000-foot-high Holston Valley and camped at the base of a hill near a small settlement known as Black's Fort. When wolves emerged from a cave and attacked his dogs, Boone named the place Wolf Hill. Boone and other pioneers opened the area for settlement, and by 1778, a thriving community named Abingdon had grown up around Black's Fort and Wolf Hill. The Washington County Courthouse has replaced the fort,

Abingdon

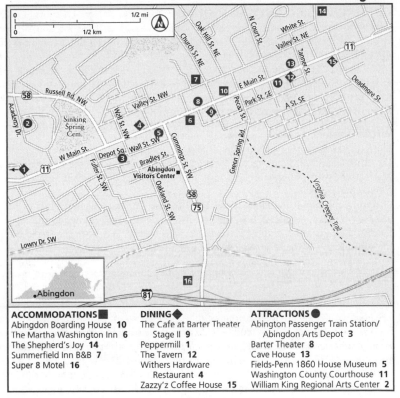

ACCOMMODATIONS ■	DINING ◆	ATTRACTIONS ●
Abingdon Boarding House **10**	The Cafe at Barter Theater	Abington Passenger Train Station/
The Martha Washington Inn **6**	Stage II **9**	Abingdon Arts Depot **3**
The Shepherd's Joy **14**	Peppermill **1**	Barter Theater **8**
Summerfield Inn B&B **7**	The Tavern **12**	Cave House **13**
Super 8 Motel **16**	Withers Hardware	Fields-Penn 1860 House Museum **5**
	Restaurant **4**	Washington County Courthouse **11**
	Zazzy'z Coffee House **15**	William King Regional Arts Center **2**

but Boone's cave is still there, behind one of the historic buildings on tree-shaded Main Street.

Indeed, Abingdon today looks much as it did in those early years, making it one of Virginia's most picturesque small towns and one of my favorites to visit. Its beauty and historical charm have attracted more than its share of actors, artists, craftspeople, and even a few writers. Visitors drive hundreds of miles to attend shows at the Barter, Virginia's official state theater, and the town is crowded the first 2 weeks of August for the popular Virginia Highlands Festival, a display of the region's best arts and crafts.

You can spend a fascinating few days walking around this beautiful town, seeing a couple of plays, and literally coasting on your bike down White Top Mountain on the Virginia Creeper Trail, one of the country's great bicycle paths (see "The Virginia Creeper Trail," above).

ESSENTIALS

VISITOR INFORMATION   Contact the **Abingdon Convention & Visitors Bureau,** 335 Cummings St., Abingdon, VA 24210 (✆ **800/435-3440** or 276/676-2282; fax 276/676-3076; www.abingdon.com). Located in a gorgeous Victorian house, the **Abingdon Visitors Center** is on the left as you drive into town on U.S. 58. It's open daily from 9am to 5pm. Stop here to pick up a map and walking tour brochure.

GETTING THERE & GETTING AROUND **Tri-Cities Regional Airport** (© 423/ 325-6000; www.triflight.com) is about 30 miles southwest of Abingdon between Bristol and Kingsport, Tennessee. You can rent a car there or call **Bob's Limo Service** (© 423/325-6379).

Abingdon is at the junction of I-81 and U.S. 11, U.S. 19, and U.S. 58. From I-81, take Exit 17 and follow U.S. 58 West directly into town. U.S. 11 runs east-west along Main Street (which has a phenomenal amount of traffic for such a small town). The local **taxi depot** is at 495 W. Main St. (© 276/628-4409).

WHAT TO SEE & DO

Using the walking tour brochure and map you picked up at the visitor center (see "Essentials," above), head out on the brick sidewalks to explore the historic part of Main Street, which runs for about ¾ mile. It goes up and down two hills, so wear comfortable walking shoes.

Begin your tour at the **Fields-Penn 1860 House Museum,** at the corner of Main and Cummings streets (© 276/676-0216), which depicts how Abingdon's upper class lived in the mid–19th century (James Fields, who built it, was a bricklayer and building contractor; George Penn, who bought it in the 1890s, was a lawyer). The museum is open from April to December Wednesday from 11am to 4pm and Thursday through Saturday from 1 to 4pm. Admission is $3 adults, $2 children 6 to 12, free for kids under 6.

From there, you'll head west on Main Street through Abingdon's 3-block-long business district. Several antiques and collectibles emporia will vie for your attention, but keep going to Depot Square. Turn left there to the **Abingdon Passenger Train Station,** which has been restored as home to the **Historical Society of Washington County** (© 276/628-8761). Don't miss the dramatic railway photographs of O. Winston Link, whose work is also showcased in his museum in Roanoke (p. 197). The station is open April to October Monday through Friday 10am to 4pm, Saturday 10am to 2pm (weekdays only Nov–Mar). The old freight depot next door is now the **Abingdon Arts Depot** ☆ (© 276/628-9091; www.abingdonartsdepot.org), where you can watch artists at work in their studios April to October Thursday through Saturday 11am to 3pm.

Now backtrack east along Main Street, where The Martha Washington Inn, the Barter Theatre, and 30 other buildings and homes—with birthdates ranging from 1779 to 1925—wait to be observed. At the bottom of the hill, a right turn on Pecan Street will take you to the western head of the **Virginia Creeper Trail** (see section 3, above). Parked under a shed there is "Abingdon's Mollie," or officially Norfolk & Western Engine No. 433, similar to the steam locomotives that had such a tough time with the grade that they became facetiously known as the "Virginia Creeper."

Back on Main Street, turn right and walk to the top of the next hill. Stop there to look up at the Tiffany stained-glass windows in the **Washington County Courthouse,** built in 1869 to replace an earlier version burned during the Civil War. The Tiffany windows were added as a memorial to World War I veterans. From here you'll head downhill again past **The Tavern,** considered the oldest building in town. Built around 1779 and used as a stagecoach inn and tavern, it's now home to one of the town's better restaurants (see "Where to Dine," below). You can still see the mail slot in the original post office in an addition on the east side of the building.

On the west side of town, art lovers can visit the **William King Regional Arts Center,** 415 Academy Dr. (© 276/628-5005; www.wkrac.org), where three galleries

---

Fun Fact **The Wolves & Daniel Boone's Dogs**

After walking over Abingdon's second hill—where the 1869 Washington County Courthouse stands—you'll come to the **Cave House,** now home to the Cave House Crafts Shop (see "Shopping," below). Behind the house is the cave from whence emerged the wolves that attacked Daniel Boone's dogs. It's not marked, but to find it, take the alley to the left of the house to a stop sign, and turn right. You can peer through lattice into the mouth of the cave, which is below a rickety old barn.

---

host rotating exhibits showcasing regional and world art. One gallery focuses on regional heritage. There's also a good museum shop. Admission is free. The center is open Tuesday 10am to 9pm; Wednesday to Saturday 10am to 5pm; Sunday 1 to 5pm. The center is in a refurbished school building (turn uphill off West Main St. on Academy Dr. at the Chevron station and follow the signs for arts-center parking).

TWO NEARBY GRISTMILLS & A WINERY

A scenic 4¼-mile drive leads from Valley Street in Abingdon through a picturesque valley to **White's Mill** ((C) 276/628-2960), built in 1790 and now on the National Register of Historic Places. It's owned by a nonprofit foundation, which is slowly restoring its 22-foot diameter steel wheel and original grinding stone. Admission is by donation, and it's open Wednesday through Sunday 10am to 6pm. You can buy meal from the mill's electric grinders. A shop across the road sells local handcrafts.

About 4 miles south of town via Va. 75, **Parks Mill** (ca. 1780; (C) **276/628-9191; www.parksmill.com**) is another restoration in progress. There's a general store and restaurant serving ice cream and vinegary North Carolina barbecue ($4 for a sandwich, $9 for a plate). In other words, you can drive out here, see the mill, and have lunch or refreshment. The mill and store are open Tuesday through Sunday 11:30am to 9pm. From I-81 follow Va. 75 for 3¼ miles south to a left turn on Parks Mill Road. The mill is another 1½ miles on the left.

In rolling hills about 7½ miles east of town, **Abingdon Vineyard & Winery** ((C) **276/623-1255; www.abingdonwinery.com**) is open for tasting its reds and whites from mid-March to mid-December, Tuesday to Saturday 10am to 6pm, Sunday noon to 6pm. Follow U.S. 58 east 5 miles past I-81, turn right on Oseola Road (S.R. 722), and follow the grape cluster signs 2½ miles to the winery.

SHOPPING

Mountain arts and crafts are for sale in the **Cave House Crafts Shop** 𝕱𝕱, 279 E. Main St. ((C) **276/628-7721**), a 130-member cooperative in the 1858 Victorian home built in front of the famous wolf cave. The handmade quilts here are extraordinary. The shop is open January and February Thursday through Saturday 10am to 5:30pm and March to December Monday through Saturday 10am to 5:30pm; mid-April through December it's also open Sunday 1 to 5pm.

Main Street has no fewer than 10 **antiques shops,** which you will pass during your walking tour. Note that most are closed on Sunday, some on Monday.

Put your hunter-gatherer instincts into high gear at **Dixie Pottery** ((C) **276/676-3550; www.dixiepottery.com**) about 5 miles south of Abingdon on U.S. 11 (½ mile south of Exit 13 off I-81). This warehouse-style store sells decorative objects and housewares from around the world. You'll find both cheap and high-quality china, porcelain figurines, candles, dried and artificial flower arrangements, baskets, brass, copper, pewter, enamel, and cookware. It's open Monday through Saturday 9:30am to 6pm, Sunday 1 to 6pm.

WHERE TO STAY

Abingdon has six chain motels adjacent to I-81. **Hampton Inn** (✆ 800/426-7866 or 276/619-4600) and **Super 8** (✆ 800/800-8000 or 276/676-3310) are most convenient to downtown at Exit 17. **Quality Inn & Suites** (✆ 877/676-9090 or 276/676-9090) and **Holiday Inn Express** (✆ 800/465-4329 or 276/676-2929) are at Exit 19, at the north end of town. **Best Western Abingdon Inn & Suites** (✆ 800/800-8000 or 276/676-3310) and **Comfort Inn** (✆ 800/221-2222 or 276/676-2222) are at Exit 14, between downtown and Dixie Pottery.

The Martha Washington Inn   Across Main Street from the Barter Theatre in the heart of the historic district, this is one of Virginia's best in-town country inns. The stately Greek Revival portico creates a formal facade for this two-and-a-half-story red-brick hotel. Its center portion was built as a private residence in 1832 and later served as a girls school. White-wicker chairs give the front porch the look of an old-time resort. With loudly creaking floors, the lobby and adjoining parlors are elegantly decorated, with original marble fireplaces and crystal chandeliers. Choose from regular or deluxe rooms, the latter larger and more lavishly appointed with rich fabrics and fine antiques. Two premium suites have museum-quality furnishings, two fireplaces, whirlpool tubs, and steam showers. Another suite has a small private balcony off the anteroom between its sleeping and living parlors. The elegant **dining room** serves good American fare amid Victorian elegance at breakfast and dinner, and **Martha's Gourmet Market** offers excellent made-to-order sandwiches and salads weekdays from 10am to 3pm. You can pamper yourself in the full spa and swim all year in the indoor pool.

150 W. Main St., Abingdon, VA 24210. ✆ **888/999-8078** or 276/628-3161. Fax 276/628-8885. www.marthawashington inn.com. 61 units. $225–$245 double; $265–$285 suite. $10 per unit resort fee. AE, DC, DISC, MC, V. **Amenities:** 2 restaurants (American); bar; indoor pool; health club; spa; business center; room service; babysitting; laundry service; concierge-level rooms. *In room:* A/C, TV, Wi-Fi, iron.

BED & BREAKFASTS

In addition to the Summerfield Inn listed below, Abingdon has more than 15 B&B accommodations. Among them, **The Shepherd's Joy** (✆ **276/628-3273**; www.shepherdsjoy.com) is a working sheep farm, while **Abingdon Boarding House** (✆ **276/628-9344** or 276/608-1263; www.abingdonboardinghouse.com) is the oldest operating boardinghouse in the area.

Summerfield Inn Bed & Breakfast   Just 1 block from Main Street and the Barter Theatre, this ideally located 1920s Colonial Revival residence is where I stay when I'm in Abingdon. Wicker rockers and an old-fashioned swing on the wraparound front porch invite one to sit a spell. The living room is furnished with a player piano and plush Regency-style sofas flanking the fireplace. The guest rooms offer both the ambience of a private home and the luxurious comfort of a fine hotel; each is elegantly furnished with antiques and reproductions. I am particularly fond of the three private units in the Carriage House next to the main building, especially the Rose Room with its two-person hot tub and walk-in shower. In fact, five of the seven units here have jetted tubs. Friendly hosts Janice and Jim Cowan serve full breakfasts in the formal dining room or, in warm weather, on the porch.

101 W. Valley St., Abingdon, VA 24210. © 800/668-5905 or 276/628-5905. Fax 276/628-7515. www.summerfield-inn.com. 7 units. $155–$185 double. Rates include full breakfast. AE, MC, V. *In room:* A/C, TV, Wi-Fi, iron.

WHERE TO DINE

Don't forget the dining room and Martha's Gourmet Market in The Martha Washington Inn (see above). The dining room is Abingdon's most elegant place to dine, while the daytime market provides excellent salads and sandwiches.

Other choices include the eclectic **Peppermill,** 967 W. Main St. (© **276/623-0530**), about a mile west of downtown, and **Withers Hardware Restaurant,** 260 W. Main St. (© **276/628-1111**), which occupies an old hardware store and has a non-smoking bar.

The Cafe at Barter Theater Stage II DELI   Big window walls let lots of light into this delightful, gardenlike room attached to the Barter Theater's Stage II. Theater posters add an artsy touch, while easy chairs and sofas make this seem like a coffeehouse. In fact, you can get your morning latte or espresso here, plus high-cholesterol pastries. Big deli sandwiches, paninis, and wraps are both lunchtime and evening specialties. Everything is made from scratch, so don't be in a rush. Order at the counter and they'll call an actor's name when your order is ready (I did love being called Harrison Ford). Notice the *Book of Fantasies* sculpture out front.

110 Main St. (actually on Church St.). © 276/619-5462. Reservations not accepted. Salads and sandwiches $5–$6.50. AE, DISC, MC, V. Mon–Tues 11am–4pm; Wed–Sat 11am–11pm; Sun 11am–10pm.

The Tavern ✸✸ INTERNATIONAL   Set aside a night for The Tavern, for having dinner in the town's oldest building is an essential part of the Abingdon experience. The Tavern was built in 1779 as an inn for stagecoach travelers. Exposed brick and stone walls, log beams, and hand-forged locks and hinges make it seem little changed since then. Despite the indoor charm, choice warm-weather tables are on an upstairs porch or on the brick terrace under a canopy of towering trees. The menu reflects gregarious German-born owner Max Hermann's well-traveled background, with Wiener schnitzel, baked salmon sprinkled with Thai spices, chicken saltimbocca, and medallions of beef with a French influence.

222 E. Main St. © 276/628-1118. Reservations recommended for outdoor seating. Main courses $21–$35. AE, MC, V. Mon–Sat 5–10pm. Closed Jan 1, Thanksgiving, and Dec 25.

Wildflour Bakery & Cafe ✸✸ (Value BAKERY/AMERICAN   Housed in the Campbell House, a Victorian-era farmstead now adjacent to I-81, this restaurant is really two establishments. It's a coffeehouse in the mornings, with freshly baked pastries to accompany your caffeine. The lunch menu of sandwiches, soups, and salads changes daily; you might find Jamaican-style jerk chicken with a mango salsa. An accomplished chef takes over at night and brings a touch of fine dining. He might offer fried green tomatoes with a basil rémoulade for starters, and salmon crusted with roasted garlic and pastrami and served with a Creole mustard sauce. Side dishes such as smoked Gouda and scallion grits put a new twist on old Southern favorites. A tasty vegetarian choice always is offered.

2444 Lee Hwy. (U.S. 11, north of I-81). © 276/676-4221. Reservations recommended at dinner. Lunch $5–$10; main courses $12–$26. AE, MC, V. Mon 8am–3pm; Tues 8am–6pm; Wed–Sat 8am–9pm (dinner 5–9pm). From downtown, take Main St. (U.S. 11) north; restaurant is 1st building on left after I-81.

> **Fun Fact Hams for Hamlet**
>
> The career of an aspiring, Virginia-born actor named Robert Porterfield came to a halt during the Great Depression. Giving up on Broadway, he and 22 other unemployed actors came to Abingdon in the summer of 1933 and began putting on plays and shows. Their first production was John Golden's *After Tomorrow,* for which they charged an admission of 40¢, or the equivalent in farm produce—thus did their little operation become known as the Barter Theatre.
>
> Playwrights who contributed—among them Noel Coward, Thornton Wilder, Robert Sherwood, Maxwell Anderson, and George Bernard Shaw—were paid with a Virginia ham. Shaw, a vegetarian, returned the smoked delicacy and requested spinach instead; Porterfield and his crew obliged.

Zazzy'z Coffee House ★ (Finds) COFFEE SHOP/DELI   When failing eyesight made Dr. Ramsey White stop filling cavities, he converted this Victorian house from dental offices into this charming coffee shop. One room contains Abingdon's only bookstore (you can buy the *New York Times* here), while another is set aside for Internet access (two computer terminals plus wireless access, all complimentary). In addition to house-ground coffee, the snack bar in the rear serves breakfast and lunches of deli-style sandwiches, salads, and soups.

380 E Main St. © 276/698-3333. Reservations not accepted. Most items $2.50–$5. AE, DISC, MC, V. Mon–Thurs 7am–7pm; Fri 7am–9pm; Sat 8am–7pm; Sun 8am–5pm.

ABINGDON AFTER DARK

During summer you can take in a movie at the **Moonlite Drive-in,** on U.S. 11 South next to Dixie Pottery (© **276/628-7881**). It's one of a handful of drive-in movie theaters left in Virginia.

Barter Theatre ★★★   Official policy still permits barter for admission (with prior notice), but theatergoers now pay cash to attend the State Theater of Virginia, America's longest-running professional repertory theater. The building was built around 1832 as a Presbyterian church and later served as a meeting hall for the Sons of Temperance. It functioned as the town hall and opera house when Robert Porterfield brought his unemployed actors here in 1933 (see "Hams for Hamlet," above). Recent productions, now performed by a professional company, have included *Baby: A Musical* and *Singing in the Rain.* The theater's alumni include Hume Cronyn, Patricia Neal, Fritz Weaver, Ernest Borgnine, Gregory Peck, and Ned Beatty. Across Main Street, the **Barter's Stage II** specializes in the classics. The season for both stages runs from February through December. The main stage is dark Monday and Tuesday. 127 W. Main St. (at College St.). © 276/628-3991. www.bartertheatre.com. Tickets $20–$40, depending on show and time.

The Carter Family Fold Music Shows ★★   Anyone with the slightest interest in country or traditional mountain music will make the 78-mile round-trip from Abingdon to Maces Spring, a hamlet in the Poor Valley, where you will see and hear established and aspiring artists every Saturday night at the Carter Family Memorial Music

Center. This is the ancestral home of country music royalty A. P. Carter, wife Sara, and Maybelle Addington Carter (Maybelle was Sara's cousin, A. P.'s sister-in-law, and mother of June Carter, who married Johnny Cash). Their descendants won't allow today's performers to use any electric equipment, so the music is as pure as it was when the Carters cut their first record in 1927. These are no formal concerts, for local residents buck dance and clog in front of the stage. Come early to visit the log cabin in which A. P. Carter was born in 1891 and to see the Carter Family Museum in the country store he operated from 1943 until his death in 1960. An annual music festival during the first weekend in August (the same time as the Virginia Highlands Festival in Abingdon) draws well-known singers and music groups, clog-dance performers, and local artisans who sell crafts. C.R. 614, Maces Spring. (✆ 276/386-9480. www.carterfamily fold.org. Music show tickets $5 adults, $1 children 6–12, free for children 5 and younger. Museum and cabin admission 50¢ per person. Shows Sat 7:30pm; doors and museum open 6pm. From Abingdon take I-81 south 17 miles to Bristol, U.S. 58 west 19 miles to Hiltons, then C.R. 614 east 3 miles to auditorium.

9

Richmond

Now a sprawling metropolitan area flanking the James River in the center of the state, Richmond has been Virginia's capital since 1780 and has been the stage for much history. It was in Richmond's St. John's Church that Patrick Henry concluded his address to the second Virginia Convention with the stirring words "Give me liberty, or give me death!" During the Revolution, turncoat Gen. Benedict Arnold led British troops down what is now Main Street in 1781 and set fire to many buildings, including tobacco warehouses—in those days, the equivalent of banks. Cornwallis briefly occupied the town, and Lafayette came to the rescue.

But it was in the role as capital of the Confederate States of America that Richmond left an indelible mark on American history. Jefferson Davis lived in the Confederate White House here while presiding over the rebel government, and it was in the mansion that Robert E. Lee accepted command of the Army of Northern Virginia. For 4 years, the Union army tried unsuccessfully to capture the city. Troops often battled on its outskirts; its tobacco warehouses overflowed with prisoners of war, its hospitals with the wounded, and its cemeteries with the dead. Richmond didn't fall into Union hands until Lee abandoned Petersburg—an easy excursion to the south—a week before surrendering at Appomattox.

The city has a host of other attractions, including splendid old homes, an excellent fine arts museum, a hands-on science museum with state-of-the-art planetarium, and a botanical garden. But its prime attractions are the monuments, battlefields, and museums that recall the nation's bloodiest conflict. If you have any interest at all in the Civil War, Richmond is an essential stop.

1 Orientation & Getting Around

VISITOR INFORMATION
The **Richmond Visitors Center,** 401 N. 3rd St. (between Clay and Marshall sts.), Richmond, VA 23219 (© **888/742-4666;** www.visit.richmond.com), provides information and operates a same-day discounted hotel reservation service. It also shows a 10-minute orientation video. The center is in the Greater Richmond Convention Center and is open Monday through Friday from 9am to 5pm (to 6pm from Memorial Day weekend through Labor Day). There are free 20-minute parking in spaces by the serpentine brick wall on 3rd Street between Clay and Marshall streets.

In addition, the **Richmond International Airport Visitors Center** (© **804/236-3260**) is open Monday through Friday 9:30am to 4:30pm.

The state operates a visitor information center in the **Bell Tower** (© **804/786-4485**) on the State Capitol grounds, off 9th Street between Grace and Marshall streets. It's open Monday through Friday 9am to 5pm. The small gift shop is a good place to stock up on "Virginia Is for Lovers" gear.

Another comprehensive source of information is **www.discoverrichmond.com**, a community site operated by the *Richmond Times-Dispatch* newspaper.

As soon as you see one, grab a copy of Richmond's free alternative newspaper, *Style Weekly* (www.styleweekly.com), available in boxes throughout town. It is a very good source of what's going on while you're here.

GETTING THERE

BY PLANE   **Richmond International Airport (RIC)**, Airport Drive off I-64, I-295, and Williamsburg Road (U.S. 60; (C) **804/226-3052**; www.flyrichmond.com), known locally as Byrd Field, is about 15 minutes east of downtown. American, Continental, Delta, Northwest, JetBlue, Skybus, TWA, United, and US Airways fly there. The major car-rental companies have desks at the airport, and taxis are available. **Groome Transportation** ((C) **800/552-7911** or 804/222-7222; www.groometransportation.com) offers 24-hour van service to Richmond, Petersburg, Fredericksburg, and Williamsburg. One-person fares range from $11 to downtown Richmond to $40 to Williamsburg. Public bus service is available during weekday morning and evening rush hours, but frankly, if I could afford to fly into Richmond, I would forget the local bus system.

BY CAR   Richmond is at the junction of **I-64**, traveling east-west, and **I-95**, traveling north-south. **I-295** bypasses both Richmond and Petersburg on their east sides. **U.S. 60** (east-west) and **U.S. 1** and **U.S. 301** (north-south) cross here.

BY TRAIN & BUS   Several daily **Amtrak** ((C) **800/872-7245**; www.amtrak.com) trains pull into two stations here. The main terminal is at 7519 Staples Mill Rd. (U.S. 33), north of I-64. There is no shuttle service from the Staples Mill Road station into tourist areas, so a better choice is the **Main Street Station** at 1500 E. Main St. in Shockoe Bottom. This restored French Renaissance–style building served as the city's transportation hub from 1901 until 1959 and is itself worth a look.

The **Greyhound/Trailways** bus terminal is at 2910 N. Boulevard ((C) **800/231-2222**; www.greyhound.com).

CITY LAYOUT

Richmond is located at the fall line of the James River. Instead of growing away from the river, the original city spread westward along the north shore. Thus, the main streets run east-west for several miles from the original settlement, in today's Shockoe Bottom. Although Richmond now has suburbs sprawling across the surrounding countryside, most of the hotels, restaurants, and historic sites of interest to visitors are in the old part of the city.

Several bridges cross the river, and there's access to Brown's Island and Belle Isle from the **Richmond Riverfront Canal Walk,** a promenade extending along the

---

Impressions

Broad-streeted Richmond . . . The trees in the streets are old trees used to living with people. Family trees that remember your grandfather's name.
　　　　　　　　　　　　　　　　　　　—Stephen Vincent Benet, *John Brown's Body*

downtown riverfront beside the **James River & Kanawha Canal** (see "What to See & Do," later in this chapter).

Foushee Street divides street numbers east and west, while **Main Street** divides them north and south. **Broad Street** is the major east-west thoroughfare, and it's one of the few downtown streets with two-way traffic.

THE NEIGHBORHOODS IN BRIEF

As you explore the neighborhoods described below (moving from east to west), you'll get a good sense of Richmond's history.

Church Hill Named for St. John's Church, its major landmark, this east Richmond neighborhood is largely residential, with many 19th-century Greek Revival residences.

Tobacco Row Bordering Church Hill and paralleling the James River for some 15 blocks between 20th and Pear streets, this is the latest urban redevelopment area. Handsome redbrick warehouses are being turned into apartment houses. The Edgar Allan Poe and Virginia Holocaust museums are here.

Shockoe Bottom Shockoe Bottom is roughly bounded by Dock and Broad streets and 15th and 20th streets, with the heart at the 17th Street Farmer's Market between East Main and East Franklin streets. Richmond's first business district, it once encompassed tobacco factories, produce markets (farmers still sell produce at stands on N. 17th St.), slave auction houses, warehouses, and shops, and it retains much of its original character. Today, old-fashioned groceries with signs in their windows for fresh chitterlings stand alongside trendy shops, restaurants, and noisy nightclubs aimed primarily at 20-somethings.

Shockoe Slip Bordering downtown roughly between 10th and 14th streets and Main and Canal streets, this warehouse and commercial area was reduced to rubble in 1865 and rebuilt as a manufacturing center after the war. Today it's the city's most urbane dining and entertainment section. With its cobblestones restored and old-fashioned street lamps providing light, East Cary Street features renovated warehouses containing restaurants, galleries, nightspots, shops, and two major hotels. The Richmond Riverfront Canal Walk boat rides begin here.

Downtown West and north of Shockoe Slip, downtown is Richmond's governmental and financial center. It includes the old and new city halls, the state capitol, and government buildings of **Capitol Square;** and the historic homes and museums of the **Court End** area, notably the Valentine Richmond History Center, Museum and White House of the Confederacy, and John Marshall House. It also encompasses the Coliseum, the city's convention center, and the Carpenter Center for the Performing Arts.

Jackson Ward Home to many free African Americans before the Civil War ended slavery, Jackson Ward, north of Broad Street, is a National Historic District. Its famous residents have included the first woman bank president in the United States, Maggie Walker, and legendary dancer Bill "Bojangles" Robinson, who donated a stoplight for the safety of children crossing the intersection of Leigh Street and Chamberlayne Avenue (where a monument to him stands today). Notable, too, is the fine ornamental

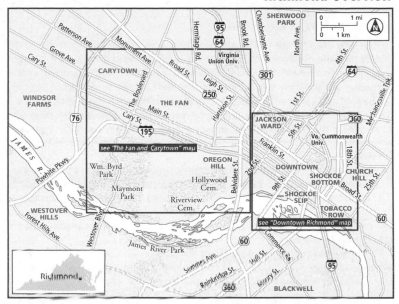

ironwork gracing the facades of many Jackson Ward residences.

The Fan Just west of downtown, The Fan is named for the shape of the streets, which more or less "fan" out from downtown. Bordered by West Broad, Boulevard, West Main, and Belvidere, this gentrified area of turn-of-the-20th-century town houses includes Virginia Commonwealth University and many restaurants and galleries. Monument Avenue's most scenic blocks, with the Civil War statues—and one of African-American tennis star Arthur Ashe—down its median strip, are in The Fan.

Carytown Just west of Boulevard, affluent Carytown has been called Richmond's answer to Georgetown. Cafes, restaurants, boutiques, antiques shops, and the Byrd Theater, a restored movie palace, bring Saturday-afternoon crowds to West Cary Street between Boulevard and Nasemond Street.

GETTING AROUND

BY PUBLIC TRANSPORTATION   The Greater Richmond Transit Company (GRTC; ✆ **804/358-GRTC;** www.ridegrtc.com) operates the **public bus** system throughout the metropolitan area. Base bus fare is $1.25 (exact change only). Service on most bus routes begins at 5am and ends at midnight. GRTC also has express bus service from Richmond to both Petersburg and Fredericksburg.

BY TAXI   Call **Yellow Cab Service Inc. (**✆ **804/222-7300)** or **Veterans Cab Association (**✆ **804/329-1414).** Fares are approximately $1.50 per mile.

Tips **Safety in Richmond**

As in any city, it's wise to stay alert and be aware of your surroundings, whatever the time of day. Ask at the visitor centers or at your hotel desk if a neighborhood you intend to visit is safe. Most neighborhoods described in this chapter are generally safe during the day, and Shockoe Slip, Shockoe Bottom, The Fan, and Carytown are safe during the evening when their restaurants are open. Nevertheless, avoid all deserted streets after dark. Most hotels have free shuttles in the downtown area, so take them when going out in the evening.

---

2 Where to Stay

The **Richmond Visitors Center** (© **888/742-4666**) makes same-day reservations for walk-in visitors, often at a discount. See "Visitor Information," above. Note that rooms can be scarce here on NASCAR weekends at Richmond International Raceway (see "Sports & Outdoor Activities," later in this chapter).

Chain motels are scattered throughout the suburbs. The Executive Center area, on West Broad Street (U.S. 33/250) at I-64 (Exit 183), about 5 miles west of downtown, is a campuslike area convenient to the major attractions. The best of its hotels is the California-style **Sheraton Richmond West** (© 800/325-3535 or 804/285-1234), which provides a free shuttle to downtown. Nearby are the Colonial-look **Comfort Inn Executive Center** (© 800/228-5150 or 804/672-1108), a **Courtyard by Marriott** (© 800/321-2211 or 804/282-1881), a **Days Inn** (© 800/329-7466 or 804/282-3300), an **EconoLodge** (© 800/553-2666 or 804/672-8621), the **Hampton Inn West** (© 800/426-7866 or 804/747-7777), the **Holiday Inn West** (© 800/465-4329 or 804/285-9951), a **Shoney's Inn** (© 800/222-2222 or 804/672-7007), and a **Super 8** (© 800/800-8000 or 804/672-8128).

All of the hotels listed below provide **free shuttle service** to attractions and restaurants within a 3-mile radius, which covers all of downtown.

The Berkeley Hotel 🏛🏛   At this elegant inn, on the border of downtown and Shockoe Slip, a handsome redbrick facade opens into a seemingly old-world interior. Although established in 1988, the hotel creates the illusion that it was built long ago. A cozy ambience and attentive service prevail. The luxuriously appointed guest quarters—some with whirlpool tubs—are decorated in a French country theme. The Berkeley has one of Richmond's finest hotel dining rooms. **Nightingale's Lounge** adjoins.

1200 E. Cary St. (at 12th St.), Richmond, VA 23219. © **888/780-4422** or 804/780-1300. Fax 804/648-4728. www.berkeleyhotel.com. 55 units. $205–$225 double; $675 suite. Weekend and other packages available. AE, DC, DISC, MC, V. Valet parking $15. **Amenities:** Restaurant; bar; access to nearby health club; laundry service. *In room:* A/C, TV, Wi-Fi, coffeemaker, iron, safe.

Crowne Plaza Hotel   You won't mistake this Crowne Plaza for any other building in town—it's a starkly modern, triangular 16-story high-rise with reflecting glass windows. Most of the rooms offer stunning river and city views, especially the Point Suites in the sharp corners of the building (their windows render 270-degree views). Some suites are bi-level, with sleeping lofts upstairs. It's less expensive than The Berkeley and the Omni Richmond, and it's only a few blocks to Shockoe Slip. The mezzanine-level **Pavilion Cafe** serves all three meals, while the **Great Room** off the lobby offers Starbucks coffee, drinks, and light fare with a view of Canal Walk.

Downtown Richmond

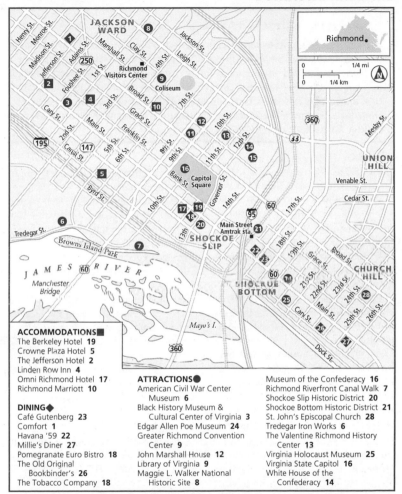

ACCOMMODATIONS ■
The Berkeley Hotel **19**
Crowne Plaza Hotel **5**
The Jefferson Hotel **2**
Linden Row Inn **4**
Omni Richmond Hotel **17**
Richmond Marriott **10**

DINING ◆
Café Gutenberg **23**
Comfort **1**
Havana '59 **22**
Millie's Diner **27**
Pomegranate Euro Bistro **18**
The Old Original
   Bookbinder's **26**
The Tobacco Company **18**

ATTRACTIONS ●
American Civil War Center
   Museum **6**
Black History Museum &
   Cultural Center of Virginia **3**
Edgar Allen Poe Museum **24**
Greater Richmond Convention
   Center **9**
John Marshall House **12**
Library of Virginia **9**
Maggie L. Walker National
   Historic Site **8**

Museum of the Confederacy **16**
Richmond Riverfront Canal Walk **7**
Shockoe Slip Historic District **20**
Shockoe Bottom Historic District **21**
St. John's Episcopal Church **28**
Tredegar Iron Works **6**
The Valentine Richmond History
   Center **13**
Virginia Holocaust Museum **25**
Virginia State Capitol **16**
White House of the
   Confederacy **14**

---

555 E. Canal St. (at 6th St.), Richmond, VA 23219. ℃ **800/227-6963** or 804/788-0900. Fax 804/788-7087. www. crowneplaza.com/ric-downtown. 299 units. $99–$229 double; $250–$880 suite. AE, DC, DISC, MC, V. Self-parking $10; valet parking $14. **Amenities:** Restaurant; bar; indoor pool; exercise room; Jacuzzi; sauna; business center; room service; laundry service; concierge-level rooms. *In room:* A/C, TV, high-speed Internet, coffeemaker, iron.

The Jefferson Hotel ⸙⸙⸙ This stunning six-story Beaux Arts building is the creation of Maj. Lewis Ginter, a founder of the American Tobacco Company who in addition founded the Lewis Ginter Botanical Garden (see "What to See & Do," later in this chapter). The magnificent limestone-and-brick facade is adorned with Renaissance-style balconies, arched porticos, and an Italian clock tower. Two-story faux-marble columns, embellished with gold leaf, encircle the soaring rotunda—the original lobby—which has a small museum explaining the hotel's history. From there, the marble grand staircase, wide and red-carpeted, leads up to reception in the Palm Court

---

Fun Fact   Mr. Jefferson's Ascot

With its Rotunda, grand marble staircase, skylit Palm Court, and small museum dedicated to itself, The Jefferson Hotel is an attraction in its own right. Take a close look at Edward Valentine's stunning statue of Thomas Jefferson standing in the middle of the Palm Court. In an effort to save it during a 1902 fire, Valentine and others lassoed the statue and pulled it down on some mattresses. Unfortunately the fall decapitated Mr. Jefferson. Valentine added the ascot to conceal T.J.'s scar.

---

lobby. There Edward Valentine's statue of Thomas Jefferson stands directly under a stained-glass domed skylight, 9 of its 12 panes original Tiffany glass.

Furnished with custom-made 18th-century reproduction pieces, the well-equipped rooms come in 57 different configurations, including two-room suites with a multitude of phones (politicians make good use of them when the state legislature is in session). It's worth an extra $20 or so a night to get one of the Deluxe rooms, which have more space and charm—some have their original fireplace mantels—than the Superior models. Despite the building's ornate balconies, only the Presidential suite opens to one of them.

Formerly known as **Lemaire,** the hotel's formal dining room was being renovated and switched from French during my recent visit. The **Rotunda** (as in the University of Virginia) is put to use for outstanding Sunday brunches (about $40 for adults, $25 for children, including champagne; reservations are required). Off the Rotunda, **T.J.'s** (as in Thomas Jefferson, who else?) offers good Mediterranean-inspired fare in a relaxed setting. The hotel's bar is almost hidden behind the Rotunda's original reception windows. Across the way, the gift shop serves freshly brewed coffees and teas. Other notable amenities include a state-of-the-art health club and a resortlike indoor pool under a skylight.

Your pets can enjoy the luxuries here, too.

101 W. Franklin St. (at Adams St.), Richmond, VA 23220. ℂ 800/484-8014 or 804/788-8000. Fax 804/225-0334. www.jeffersonhotel.com. 264 units, including 36 suites. $310–$340 double; $395–$2,100 suite. Weekend and other packages available. AE, DC, DISC, MC, V. Self-parking $10; valet parking $15. Pets accepted ($35 per-day fee). **Amenities:** 2 restaurants; bar; indoor pool; health club; access to nearby YMCA; concierge; business center; salon; room service; massage; babysitting; laundry service. *In room:* A/C, TV, Wi-Fi, minibar, iron, safe.

Linden Row Inn ⭐ 〈Value   Not only the facades of this row of seven mid-19th-century Greek Revival town houses, but their garden dependencies (small, separate buildings) have remained intact. Original interior features, such as fireplaces, marble mantels, and crystal chandeliers, grace the town houses, which the National Trust for Historic Preservation has officially designated a Historic Hotel of America. Rooms in the houses, all with windows nearly reaching the 12-foot ceilings, have a mix of late-Empire and early-Victorian pieces, with marble-top dressers. Garden rooms overlook a walled garden and patio, and the garden dependencies of the town houses offer accommodations with private entrances and contemporary-look furniture.

100 E. Franklin St. (at 1st St.), Richmond, VA 23219. ℂ 800/348-7424 or 804/783-7000. Fax 804/648-7504. www.lindenrowinn.com. 70 units. $89–$129 double; $169–$249 suite. Rates include continental breakfast. AE, DC, MC, V. Valet parking $11. **Amenities:** Access to nearby YMCA; room service; laundry service. *In room:* A/C, TV, high-speed Internet, coffeemaker, iron, safe.

Omni Richmond Hotel 🍴 Along with The Berkeley Hotel (see above) across the street, the Omni enjoys a terrific location next to Shockoe Slip's boutiques, restaurants, and clubs. It boasts a handsome pink-marble lobby, with green velvet–upholstered chairs and sofas around a working fireplace. Rooms are decorated in soft pastels, and some have spectacular views of the nearby James River. Club-floor rooms offer access to a private lounge, where a complimentary continental breakfast and afternoon refreshments are served on weekdays. **Barlow's Terrace,** the hotel's casual restaurant, opens to the James Center office tower's atrium. Note that self-parking here is on an hourly in-out rate, so if you're going to use your vehicle, the valet service is less expensive.

100 S. 12th St. (at E. Cary St.), Richmond, VA 23219. 📞 **800/843-6664** or 804/344-7000. Fax 804/648-6704. www. omnihotels.com. 361 units. $159–$199 double; $350–$750 suite. Weekend and other packages available. AE, DC, DISC, MC, V. Self-parking $18 (in-out hourly rate applies); valet parking $19. **Amenities:** Restaurant; bar; indoor/outdoor pool; access to nearby health club; concierge; room service; babysitting; laundry service; concierge-level rooms. *In room:* A/C, TV, high-speed Internet, minibar, coffeemaker, iron.

Richmond Marriott This Marriott is ideally located for conventioneers since it sits next door to the Greater Richmond Convention Center (including the Richmond Visitors Center) in a downtown area formerly populated by wig and nail shops, but which is being rapidly redeveloped. In fact, the hotel has extensive meeting space of its own. Many of the spacious accommodations offer panoramic city views, and those on the top three floors add their own concierge lounge offering breakfast and afternoon refreshments. A bar, coffee shop, and steakhouse restaurant are off the lobby. Other amenities include a health club with a shallow indoor swimming pool.

500 E. Broad St. (at 5th St.), Richmond, VA 23219. 📞 **800/228-9290** or 804/643-3400. Fax 804/788-1230. www. marriott.com. 402 units. $129–$259 double; $300–$600 suite. Weekend and other packages available. AE, DC, DISC, MC, V. Self-parking $9; valet parking $12. **Amenities:** Restaurant; bar; indoor pool; health club; concierge; business center; room service; coin-op washers and dryers; concierge-level rooms. *In room:* A/C, TV, Wi-Fi, coffeemaker, iron.

3 Where to Dine

The city has hundreds of restaurants, of which I have room to mention only a few. You won't go wrong following the "Critics' Picks" in Richmond's free alternative newspaper, *Style Weekly* (www.styleweekly.com), available in boxes throughout town.

I've arranged the restaurants by neighborhood, running from east to west across the city in the order they're described in "Neighborhoods in Brief," above.

CHURCH HILL

Millie's Diner 🍴🍴 ECLECTIC Once Millie's really was a diner, and although it's been renovated, the counter, booths with jukeboxes, and open kitchen from those days are still here. It hasn't been a diner since 1989; since then talented young chefs have worked at the gas stove, turning out a variety of tasty dishes. My favorite, the spicy Thai shrimp, is usually on the menu, which changes every few weeks. Whatever you order, it will be made from scratch—as you watch, if you grab a counter seat. Excellent fare, an entertaining waitstaff, and hearty portions make this noisy eatery highly popular among Richmond's young professionals, especially for Sunday brunch. You can dine outside at lunch or brunch during warm weather but not at dinner.

2603 E. Main St. (at 26th St.). 📞 **804/643-5512.** Reservations accepted only for seating before 6:30pm. Main courses $19–$32. AE, DC, DISC, MC, V. Tues–Fri 11am–2:30pm and 5:30–10:30pm; Sat 10am–3pm (brunch) and 5:30–10:30pm; Sun 9am–3pm (brunch) and 5:30–9:30pm.

TOBACCO ROW

The Old Original Bookbinder's ✸✸ SEAFOOD/STEAKS   On the first floor of River Lofts, one of the old Tobacco Row warehouses converted into condos, this branch of the Philadelphia institution is Richmond's best place for seafood. The warehouse's brick walls and the exposed air ducts overhead add a certain rustic charm to this chic but casual spot, which is so popular you should book as soon as possible. The chef takes his own approach to crab imperial and other traditional Chesapeake dishes and adds more inventive fare such as wasabi-crusted salmon with sautéed lump crabmeat and an orange ginger sauce. For landlubbers, steaks range from 8 to 24 ounces. There's validated parking in the lot across the street, plus valet parking Friday and Saturday evenings.

2306 E. Cary St. (between 23rd and 24th sts.). © **804/643-6900.** Reservations highly recommended. Main courses $18–$43. AE, MC, V. Mon–Sat 5–10pm; Sun 5–9pm.

SHOCKOE BOTTOM

Café Gutenberg INTERNATIONAL   Next to Richmond's ancient Farmer's Market, this bookstore, wine shop, and cafe is the kind of place "where artsy people like to wallow in their misery," to quote a longtime local resident. The rest of us can enjoy some reasonably good food at very reasonable prices. Every day sees a lunch-plate special, while main courses range from miso-crusted rainbow trout to grilled bratwurst with German potato salad. Lunch or dinner, the filet mignon sandwich is my choice. You can watch the Bottom scene from sidewalk tables in warm weather.

1700 E. Main St. (at 17th St.). © **804/497-5000.** Reservations recommended. Lunch plates $8–$10; main courses $10–$29. AE, MC, V. Mon–Fri 11am–11pm; Sat–Sat 8am–11pm.

Havana '59 CUBAN   This lively theme restaurant presents a strange sight across the street from the covered stalls of the Farmer's Market, especially during warm weather when its big, garage-style storefront windows roll up to let fresh air in—and cigar smoke out. Then you might swear you're in Havana in 1959 when Fidel Castro marched into town. Fake palms, ceiling fans, string lights, Cuban music, and adobe walls with gaping holes (where plaster ought to be) set a festive scene. The Cuban-accented cuisine lives up to the ambience. The menu changes frequently, so you never know what will be marching into Havana any given day. There's validated parking in the lot at Franklin and 17th streets.

16 N. 17th St. (between Main and Franklin sts.). © **804/649-2822.** Reservations recommended. Main courses $18–$26. AE, DC, DISC, MC, V. Mon–Thurs 5–10pm; Fri–Sat 5–11pm.

SHOCKOE SLIP

East Cary Street between 12th and 15th streets is Richmond's premier dining mecca, with a bevy of good-to-excellent restaurants. On-street **parking** is always at a premium in this busy area, but you can resort to the municipal garage on East Cary Street at 14th Street.

In addition to the eateries listed below, you can get fresh sushi at **Ninanohena,** 1309 E. Cary St. (© 804/225-8801); excellent Italian at **La Grotta Restaurant,** 1218 E. Cary St. (© 804/644-2466); Chinese at the venerable **Peking Pavilion,** 1302 E. Cary St. (© 804/649-8888); Chesapeake Bay seafood at the **Hard Shell,** 1411 E. Cary St. (© 804/643-2333); upscale American at **Sam Miller's Warehouse,** 1210 E. Cary St. (© 804/643-1301); and Spanish tapas and paella at **Europa,** 1409 E. Cary St.

Steak lovers with extra cash can grill it at a branch of **Morton's of Chicago** at 111 Virginia St. (© **804/648-1662**), a block south of East Cary Street (© **804/643-0911**).

Consistently popular with young professionals as a watering hole, **Siné Irish Pub & Restaurant,** 1327 E. Cary St. (© **804/649-7767**), is anything but a typical Irish pub, offering a wide selection of seafood, steaks, and chicken in addition to the usual corned beef and cabbage. In warm weather you can dine and drink on the deck out back.

My top spot for morning coffee, tea, and breakfast is **Shockoe Espresso & Roastery,** 105 Shockoe Slip (© **804/648-3734**), which is actually on the cul-de-sac at the end of 13th Street south of East Cary Street.

Pomegranate Euro Bistro ✸ INTERNATIONAL   Chef Kevin LaCivita provides the Slip's best and most romantic dining at his European-style bistro with an exposed brick wall on one side, a wine rack holding excellent vintages on the other. His menu changes seasonally. In May, for example, he may offer fresh Chesapeake Bay striped bass (we locals call it a "rock fish") encrusted with sea salt and thyme, then roasted over potatoes with Swiss chard.

1209 E. Cary St. (between 12th and 13th sts.). © 804/643-9354. Reservations recommended. Main courses $24–$28. AE, DISC, MC, V. Mon noon–2pm; Tues–Fri noon–2pm and 5:30–11pm; Sat 5:30–10pm.

The Tobacco Company AMERICAN   Appropriately, this dining-entertainment complex is in a former tobacco warehouse that's been converted to a sunny, plant-filled three-story atrium. It was a pioneer in Shockoe Slip's renaissance and still draws so many tourists and expense-account types that locals consider it a tourist trap. It's a fun place, nonetheless. An antique elevator carries you from the first-floor cocktail lounge to the two dining floors above. Nostalgic touches abound—brass chandeliers, Tiffany-style lamps, a cigar-store Indian, even an old ticket booth that now serves as the hostess desk. Exposed-brick walls are festooned with antique collectors' items. Contemporary American cuisine is featured. Lunch specialties could be as light as a vegetarian burger or as hearty as crab cakes. At dinner, you might begin with crab croquets, and then move on to slow-roasted prime rib with seconds on the house. There's live music in The Club downstairs Tuesday through Saturday nights, with dancing Thursday through Saturday.

1201 E. Cary St. (at 12th St.). © 804/782-9431. Reservations accepted. Main courses $21–$30. AE, DISC, MC, V. Mon–Thurs 11:30am–2:30pm and 5:30–10pm; Fri–Sat 11:30am–2:30pm and 5–10:30pm; Sun 10:30am–2:30pm and 5–9:30pm.

DOWNTOWN

Although much of West Broad Street is still down on its heels, the area around the Empire Theatre, between North Adams and North Jefferson streets, has seen a renaissance with the opening of art galleries and restaurants. In addition to Comfort, reviewed below, you can dine at the more refined **Bistro Twenty Seven,** 27 W. Broad St. (© **804/780-0086**), and at **Popkin Tavern,** 123 W. Broad St. (© **804/343-1909**), a hip, high-energy sports bar.

Comfort ✸ AMERICAN   This old storefront with pressed-tin ceiling is home to Richmond's best comfort food, which one local wag described as "soul food for white folks." Very good versions of meatloaf, fried catfish, and pulled pork barbecue appear, all in substantial portions, but I opted for a smoky pork tenderloin in a bourbon-and-molasses sauce served with braised collard greens and cheese grits. My Southern mother never cooked anything that good.

200 W. Broad St. (at N. Jefferson St.). © 804/780-0004. Reservations recommended. Main courses $16–$26. AE, MC, V. Mon–Fri 11:30am–2:30pm and 5:30–10:30pm; Sat 5:30–10:30pm.

Tips **A Sobering Experience**

Richmond's favorite spot for cooked breakfasts and after-the-bars-close sobering-up meals is the **3rd Street Diner**, 218 E. Main St., at 3rd Street (☎ **804/788-4750**), which stays open 24 hours Friday and Saturday. It's a noisy diner with less-than-lightning-fast service, but nothing on the menu costs more than $10.

THE FAN

You pay a premium in the Shockoes for ambience and location. You get equally as good but less expensive fare by driving out to The Fan, where the two neighborhood restaurants below have been feeding the locals for years. You'll get a good look at The Fan's gentrified row houses, too, as you drive around hunting for a parking space.

Joe's Inn *Value* ITALIAN   This popular neighborhood hangout has been serving inexpensive Greek-accented Italian fare since 1952, including veal parmigiana, fish, pizzas, and pasta. The house specialty is gargantuan portions of spaghetti. Two can easily share an order of somewhat rubbery spaghetti a la Joe, which is served steaming hot *en casserole,* bubbling with a layer of baked provolone between the pasta and heaps of rich meat sauce. Soups, salads, omelets, and sandwiches are also options. Stop by anytime for a mouthwatering stack of hotcakes or French toast. Joe's occupies two storefronts: a dining room side and a bar side with sleek mahogany booths and ornate brass-trimmed ceiling fans.

205 N. Shields Ave. (between Grove and Hanover sts.). ☎ **804/355-2282**. Reservations not accepted. Breakfast $4–$13; sandwiches $4.50–$7; main courses $7–$14. AE, MC, V. Mon–Thurs 9am–midnight; Fri–Sat 8am–2am; Sun 8am–midnight.

Strawberry Street Café *⊛ Value* AMERICAN   This casual cafe is decorated in turn-of-the-20th-century style, with a beautiful oak bar and a gorgeous stained-glass room divider. At lunch or dinner, you can help yourself to unlimited offerings from an extensive salad bar partially nestled in a claw-foot bathtub. The dinner menu offers pastas plus steaks, pork chops, and homemade chicken potpie with a flaky crust. The weekend brunch bar lets you create a memorable meal from an assortment of fresh fruits, yogurt, baked ham, pastries, hot breakfast foods, salads, homemade muffins, and beverages.

421 N. Strawberry St. (between Park and Stuart aves.). ☎ **804/353-6860**. Reservations needed only for large groups. Sandwiches and burgers $6–$11; main courses $8–$17; weekend brunch buffet $11. AE, MC, V. Mon–Thurs 11am–3pm and 5–10:30pm; Fri 11am–2:30pm and 5–11pm; Sat 11am–11pm; Sun 10am–10:30pm.

CARYTOWN

While tourists and other visitors head for Shockoe Slip, the locals are more likely to go in search of a good meal in Carytown. Indeed, you'll find a great variety of cuisine along the 7 blocks of West Cary Street between Boulevard and Nasemond Street.

Can Can Brasserie FRENCH   This chic Parisian-style bistro and wine bar would be right at home on the Avenue des Champs-Elysées. Lots of dark wood and etched room dividers carry out the theme, and a long steel-topped bar to one side is a good place to sample both wine and *fruits de mer crus* (that is, a raw bar). It's a lively, fun joint, but I had received mixed reviews about the cuisine. My roasted red snapper atop chick pea polenta and Swiss chard proved the point; the fish was so-so but the

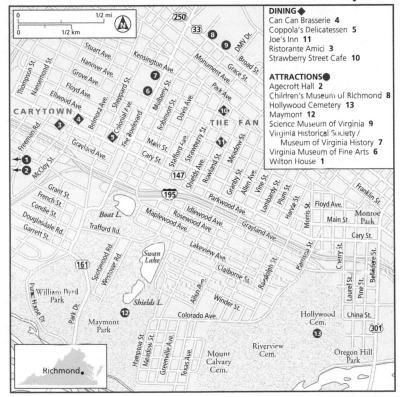

DINING ◆
Can Can Brasserie **4**
Coppola's Delicatessen **5**
Joe's Inn **11**
Ristorante Amici **3**
Strawberry Street Cafe **10**

ATTRACTIONS ●
Agecroft Hall **2**
Children's Museum of Richmond **8**
Hollywood Cemetery **13**
Maymont **12**
Science Museum of Virginia **9**
Virginia Historical Society /
Museum of Virginia History **7**
Virginia Museum of Fine Arts **6**
Wilton House **1**

vegetables were terrific. Next time I'll stick to steak and fries, sole *meunière,* and the reportedly very good burgers.

3120 W. Cary St. (between Belmont and McCloy sts.). © **804/358-7274.** Reservations recommended. Burgers $10–$11; main courses $21–$24. AE, MC, V. Mon–Sat 11:30am–midnight; Sun 9am–3pm and 5:30–10pm. Coffee bar opens daily 7am.

Ristorante Amici ⭐ NORTHERN ITALIAN   This delightful restaurant has been serving some of Richmond's best northern Italian cuisine since 1991. On the street floor is a small bar and seating at several additional tables for dinner, and during good weather, patrons vie for seats on a covered sidewalk patio. The owners of Amici (which means "friends" in Italian) hail from Cervinia, a resort in the Italian Alps, where they perfected their craft. Their menu changes seasonally, but you might begin with grilled portobello mushroom caps with garlic, basil, and olive oil; and thin slices of veal loin with delicate tuna sauce. Among the entree highlights is a Black Angus tenderloin steak with a Gorgonzola cheese sauce. From the grill also come fresh salmon, Boston sole, jumbo shrimp and scallops, chicken breast, lamb chops, and bison. Stunning desserts include a wicked tiramisu. The wine list, with many Italian vintages, is surprisingly affordable.

3343 W. Cary St. (between Freeman Rd. and S. Dooley St.). © **804/353-4700.** Reservations recommended. Main courses $14–$30. AE, DISC, MC, V. Mon–Thurs 11:30am–2:30pm and 5:30–10pm; Fri–Sat 11:30am–4pm and 5:30–11pm; Sun 5:30–10pm.

PICNIC FARE

In Carytown, **Coppola's Delicatessen,** 2900 W. Cary St., at South Colonial Avenue (© **804/359-NYNY**), evokes New York's Little Italy with an aromatic clutter of cheeses, sausages, olives, pickles, and things marinated. Behind-the-counter temptations include pasta salads, antipasti, cannoli, specialty sandwiches, and pasta dinners. Prices are low; this is a down-to-earth deli, not a pretentious gourmet emporium, though the fare is as good as any the latter might offer. Hours are Monday through Wednesday from 10am to 8pm, Thursday through Saturday from 10am to 9pm, Sunday from 11am to 4pm. There's a branch a block north of Shockoe Slip at Main and 12th streets (© **804/ 225-0454**), which is open Monday through Friday from 10am to 4pm.

4 What to See & Do

Well worth taking is a 2-hour walking tour of downtown given by **Historic Richmond Tours** (© **804/649-0711**, option 4; www.richmondhistorycenter.com), a service of the Valentine Richmond History Center (see "Top Historical Attractions," below). They depart from the Richmond Visitors Center during the summer daily at 10:30am and cost $10 per person. The history center also has special-theme weekend bus tours of the city, ranging from its vital role in the Civil War to a modern baseball game, plus Sunday walking tours. These are given seasonally, so call or check the website to see what will take place during your visit and to make reservations, which are required.

Although the best way to see the downtown sights is on foot, a narrated trip with **Richmond Tours** (© **877/913-0151** or 804/213-0151; www.richmondtours.com) will give you the lay of the land before striking out on your own. The 3-hour "Discover Richmond" tour departs daily at 9:45am and gives an overview of the city. Fares are $29. The 2-hour "Richmond at a Glance" tour hits the highlights. It runs from April through October daily at 2pm and costs $27. Children younger than 12 get a $2 discount on all tours. They'll pick you up at your hotel if you book at least a day in advance.

RICHMOND RIVERFRONT CANAL WALK ⑥

George Washington envisioned a system of canals that would link America's eastern seaboard with the Ohio and Mississippi rivers in the west. In Richmond, construction began in 1789 on the James River & Kanawha Canal, which was to run alongside the James River and connect it to the Kanawha River. It reached as far as Buchanan, Virginia, before the railroads made canal transportation obsolete in the early 19th century (its towpath was later sold to the Richmond and Allegheny Railroad, which laid tracks along it).

The city has restored more than 1 mile of the canal between Tobacco Row and the Tredegar Iron Works, at the foot of 5th Street, and turned it into the **Richmond Riverfront Canal Walk** (© **804/648-6549;** www.richmondriverfront.com). Brochures are available at the city's visitor centers (see "Orientation & Getting Around," earlier in this chapter).

The ends of the walk are the most interesting parts. Near the eastern end, at the foot of Virginia Street in Shockoe Slip, you can take a 35-minute ride on the canal in a bateau operated by **Richmond Canal Cruises** (© **804/648-6549**). Weather permitting, the motorized passenger boats run from mid-June to mid-August Wednesday through Saturday from noon to 7pm, Sunday from noon to 5pm. Spring and fall schedules are usually Thursday through Saturday from noon to 7pm, Sunday from noon to 5pm, but call to confirm. Rides are $5 for adults, $4 seniors and children 5 to 12, free for kids younger than 5. Buy tickets at the booth at the foot of Virginia Street.

At the western end of the walk, at the foot of 5th Street, the **Tredegar Iron Works** on Brown's Island was the South's largest industrial complex during the Civil War, producing about half of the Confederacy's armaments. The restored brick building now houses the National Park Services' **Richmond Civil War Visitor Center at Tredegar Iron Works** (see the review for Richmond National Battlefield Park, below). Opposite the visitor center, **Brown's Island** is the scene of festivals and free outdoor concerts and movies sponsored by Venture Richmond (see "Fun Freebies," later in this chapter).

TOP HISTORICAL ATTRACTIONS

The American Civil War Center Museum ⟨★★⟩

Before visiting Richmond's other Civil War sites, I would go through this museum, next door to the Richmond National Battlefield's visitor center and own museum (see below). Using films, photos, contemporary quotations, and other sources, it explains the buildup to the war (1775–1860), its causes, and its legacies from three perspectives: the North, the South, and the African-American. At the end you'll have a chance to vote on what you think it was all about. The museum occupies an 1861 foundry building. More than 150 artifacts are on display, including life masks of Abraham Lincoln and Robert E. Lee.

500 Tredegar St. ⓒ 804/780-1865. www.tredegar.org. Admission $8 adults, $6 seniors and students, $2 children 7–12, free for children under 7. Parking $3 per hour. Daily 9am–5pm.

John Marshall House ⟨★⟩

This historic property is the restored home of John Marshall, a giant in American judicial history, serving as chief justice of the U.S. Supreme Court from 1801 to 1835. In 1803, Marshall ruled in *Marbury v. Madison* that federal courts can overturn acts of Congress, thus establishing the power of the doctrine of judicial review. Earlier, Marshall served in the Revolutionary Army, argued cases for his close friend George Washington, served as ambassador to France under John Adams, and had a brief term as secretary of state. He was a political foe of his cousin, Thomas Jefferson. Largely intact, the house he built between 1788 and 1790 is remarkable for many original architectural features—exterior brick lintels, interior wide-plank pine floors, wainscoting, and paneling. Period antiques and reproductions supplement Marshall's own furnishings and personal artifacts. You must take a guided tour to see the house. If you have to wait, spend the time checking out the museum shop and the gardens.

818 E. Marshall St. (at 9th St.). ⓒ 804/648-7998. www.apva.org/marshall. Admission $10 adults, $7 seniors, $5 students, free for children under 4. Admission includes Valentine Richmond History Center and 1812 Wickham House. Tues–Sat 10am–4:30pm; Sun noon–5pm. Guided 1-hr. house tours run as necessary Tues–Fri, on the hour and half-hour Sat–Sun.

Maggie L. Walker National Historic Site ⟨Finds⟩

The daughter of a former slave, Maggie L. Walker was a gifted woman who achieved success in the world of finance and business and rose to become the first woman bank president in the country. Originally a teacher, Walker, after her marriage in 1886, became involved in the affairs of a black fraternal organization, the Independent Order of St. Luke, which grew under her guidance into an insurance company, then into a full-fledged bank, the St. Luke Penny Savings Bank. The bank continues today as the Consolidated Bank and Trust, the oldest surviving African-American-operated bank in the United States. Walker also became editor of a newspaper and created and developed a department store. Her residence from 1904 until her death in 1934, this house remained in her family until 1979. The National Park Service has restored it to its 1930 appearance. Park rangers lead 30-minute guided tours.

600 N. 2nd St. (between Lee and Jackson sts.). © 804/771-2017. www.nps.gov/malw. Free admission. Mon–Sat 9am–5pm. Closed Jan 1, Thanksgiving, and Dec 25. 30-min. tours depart as necessary.

The Museum and White House of the Confederacy 🐾🐾🐾 A required stop for Civil War buffs, this excellent museum houses the largest Confederate collection in the country, much contributed by veterans and their descendants. All the war's major events and campaigns are documented, and exhibits include period clothing and uniforms, a replica of Lee's headquarters, the role of African Americans in the Civil War, Confederate memorabilia, weapons, and art. When the rebels moved their capital to Richmond, the city government leased the 1818 mansion next door as a temporary home for President Jefferson Davis. As the White House of the Confederacy, it was the center of wartime social and political activity in Richmond. Formal dinners, luncheons, and occasional cabinet meetings were held in the dining room, a Victorian chamber with ornate ceiling decoration; some of the furniture in this room is original to the Davis family. The entrance hall is notable for its classical Comedy and Tragedy figures holding exquisite gas lamps. Guests were received in the center parlor, interesting now for its knickknacks produced by captured Confederate soldiers and for an 1863 portrait of Davis. Upstairs are the bedrooms and the office in which Davis conducted the business of war. You can explore the museum on your own, but you must take a guided tour to see the house (tours depart from the museum lobby). Allow at least 2 hours to see both. There is validated parking in Virginia Commonwealth University's medical center parking deck next door.

Note: The VCU hospital and other buildings have nearly surrounded the museum, leaving it in what its officials call a "state of siege." Consequently, they have been examining options of relocating the museum (the White House of the Confederacy isn't going anywhere). It's not likely to happen before 2010, but I suggest calling ahead or checking the website before visiting in 2009.

1201 E. Clay St. (at 12th St.). © 804/649-1861. www.moc.org. Museum admission $8 adults, $7 seniors, $4 children 7–18, free for children 6 and younger. White House admission $8 adults, $7 seniors, $4 children 7–18, free for children 6 and younger. Combination ticket (White House and museum) $11 adults, $10 seniors, $6 children 7–18, free for children 6 and younger. Mon–Sat 10am–5pm (tours 11:30am–4pm); Sun noon–5pm (tours 12:30–4pm). 45-min. White House tours depart continuously. Closed Jan 1, Thanksgiving, and Dec 25.

Poe Museum 🐾 The poet Edgar Allan Poe was orphaned at age 2 and taken into the home of John and Frances Valentine Allan, thus his middle name. As a young man, Poe worked as an editor, critic, and writer for the *Southern Literary Messenger.* The desk and chair he used are among the memorabilia, photographs, portraits, and documents that tell the story of his rather sad life and career. Consisting of four buildings, the museum complex centers on the Old Stone House, the oldest building in Richmond; it dates to about 1736. Poe didn't live here, but as a 15-year-old he was part of a junior honor guard that escorted Lafayette here when the aging general visited in 1824. The other buildings were added to house the collection of Poe artifacts and publications, the largest in existence. Most fascinating is the Raven Room's illustrations of "The Raven" by Edouard Manet and James Carling. You can take a guided tour or see the house and its Enchanted Garden containing evergreens and flowers on your own. (The Poe Museum is only a block from the Virginia Holocaust Museum, so park once to see both attractions.)

Tips Keep Going

It's convenient to combine a tour of the Civil War battlefields east of Richmond with the James River plantations (see chapter 10), since the Fort Harrison and Glendale/Malvern Hill visitor centers are near Va. 5, the Plantation Route.

1914–1916 E. Main St. © 888/213-2763 or 804/648-5523. www.poemuseum.org. Admission $6 adults, $5 seniors and students, free for children under 9. Tues–Sat 10am–5pm; Sun 11am–5pm. 50 min. tours depart on the hour (last tour departs 4pm).

Richmond National Battlefield Park 😊😊😊   As the political, medical, and manufacturing center of the South and the primary supply depot for Lee's Army of Northern Virginia, Richmond was a prime Union target throughout the Civil War. In 1862 Gen. George McClellan's Peninsula Campaign attacked from the southeast, and in 1864 Gen. Ulysses S. Grant advanced from the north. Neither succeeded in capturing Richmond, but Grant won the war by laying siege to Petersburg, thus cutting off Richmond's supplies from the south. The bloody battlefields of those campaigns ring Richmond's eastern side, now mostly suburbs, for some 80 miles.

Stop first at the **Richmond Civil War Visitor Center at Tredegar Iron Works**, at the foot of 5th Street on the Richmond Riverfront Canal Walk (see above). Here, a 22-minute video about the battles will get you oriented. Upstairs, the "Richmond Speaks" exhibit poignantly tells the city's story with photos, artifacts, and readings from letters soldiers wrote to their families. Outside stands a touching statue of President Abraham Lincoln and son Todd, a depiction of their visit to Richmond shortly after it fell in 1865. The visitor center and Chimborazo Medical Museum (see below) are open daily 9am to 5pm; they are closed New Year's Day, Thanksgiving, and Christmas.

Before driving around the battlefields, be sure to get the free park service brochure, which has an excellent map outlining the route, and buy an audiotape or CD tour at the bookshop ($10 tape, $16 CD), which also carries a wide array of Civil War books. You will need at least an hour at the visitor center and another 3 to complete the battlefield tour without stops, so give yourself at least half a day, more to do it in comfort.

Your first stop heading out of town will be the **Chimborazo Medical Museum,** on East Broad Street at 33rd Street. This was the site of one of the Confederacy's largest hospitals (about 76,000 patients were treated here). Park headquarters are located here.

There are visitor centers at **Cold Harbor** to the northeast and at **Fort Harrison** and **Glendale/Malvern Hill** to the southeast. Cold Harbor was the scene of a particularly bloody 1864 encounter during which 7,000 of Grant's men were killed or injured in just 30 minutes. Programs with costumed Union and Confederate soldiers reenacting life in the Civil War era take place during the summer. The Cold Harbor Visitor Center is open daily 9am to 5pm, and rangers lead walking tours of the battlefield during summer. The Fort Harrison and Glendale/Malvern Hill visitor centers are open daily 9am to 5pm in summer.

For more information, contact the park at 3215 E. Broad St. at 33rd St., Richmond, VA 23223. © 804/226-1981. www.nps.gov/rich. Admission to all visitor centers is free. Parking (in the Tredegar Iron Works lot) $3 per hour.

St. John's Episcopal Church 😊😊   Originally known simply as the "church on Richmond Hill," St. John's dates to 1741, but its congregation was established in

1611. Alexander Whitaker, the first rector, instructed Pocahontas in Christianity, baptized her, and married her to John Rolfe. The building is best known as the 1775 meeting place of the second Virginia Convention. In attendance were Thomas Jefferson, George Wythe, George Mason, Benjamin Harrison, George Washington, Richard Henry Lee, and many other historic personages. In support of a bill to assemble and train a militia to oppose Great Britain, Patrick Henry stood up and delivered his incendiary speech: "Is life so dear, or peace so sweet, as to be purchased at the price of chains or slavery? Forbid it, Almighty God! I know not what course others may take; but as for me, give me liberty, or give me death!"

You'll see the original 1741 entrance and pulpit, the stained-glass windows, and the pew where Patrick Henry sat during the convention. Henry's speech is reenacted on Sunday at 2pm from Memorial Day through Labor Day (admission is free but donation plates are passed). Purchase tour tickets at the gift shop behind the church.

2401 E. Broad St. (at 24th St.). ℂ 804/648-5015. www.historicstjohnschurch.org. Free admission (donations accepted). Tours $6 adults, $5 seniors, $4 children 7–18, free for children 6 and younger. 20-min. tours given Mon–Sat 10am–3:30pm and Sun 1–3:30pm (to 4:30pm in summer); services Sun 8:30 and 11am.

The Valentine Richmond History Center ⊛ This museum takes its name from Mann S. Valentine II, a 19th-century businessman and patron of the arts whose fortune was based on a patent medicine called Valentine's Meat Juice, and his brother, the noted sculptor Edward Valentine, whose extraordinary image of Thomas Jefferson adorns The Jefferson Hotel. Documenting the history of Richmond from the 17th to the 20th centuries, it includes the Federal-style **1812 Wickham House,** built in 1812 by attorney John Wickham, Richmond's wealthiest citizen, who helped defend Aaron Burr against treason charges in 1807. Wickham assembled the finest talents of his day to design and decorate his mansion and entertained Richmond's social elite here, along with such visiting notables as Daniel Webster, Zachary Taylor, John Calhoun, Henry Clay, and William Thackeray. Highlights include spectacular wall paintings, perhaps the rarest and most complete set in the nation; the Oval Parlor, surely one of the 100 most beautiful rooms in America; and the circular Palette Staircase.

Even more interesting to art lovers is the **Edward Valentine Sculpture Studio,** in a carriage house behind the Wickham House. It contains Edward Valentine's personal effects and plaster models of his work, including an early version of *Lee Recumbent,* his magnificent statue of Robert E. Lee now at the Lee Chapel and Museum in Lexington (p. 182).

Wickham's Garden Café is a good place to refresh during your walking tour. It's open Monday through Friday from 8am to 3pm.

1015 E. Clay St. ℂ 804/649-0711. www.richmondhistorycenter.com. Admission $10 adults, $7 seniors, $5 students, free for children under 4. Admission includes John Marshall House and 1812 Wickham House. Tues–Sat 10am–5pm; Sun noon–5pm. 30-min. Wickham House tours depart on the hour 11am–4pm.

Virginia State Capitol ⊛⊛ Thomas Jefferson was minister to France when he was commissioned to work on a capitol building for Virginia. He patterned the Classical Revival building on the Maison Carrée, a Roman temple built in Nîmes during the 1st century A.D., which he greatly admired. The colonnaded wings were added between 1904 and 1906. Today the building is the second-oldest working capitol in the United States, in continuous use since 1788.

As he did in so many of his designs, Jefferson made the central portion a magnificent rotunda, its domed skylight ceiling ornamented in Renaissance style. The room's dramatic focal point is Houdon's life-size statue of George Washington, said to be a

> *Fun Fact* **A Lifelike Washington**
>
> The Houdon statue of George Washington in the rotunda of the Virginia State Capitol is the only one ever made of the first president from life. "That is the man, himself," said Lafayette. "I can almost realize he is going to move."

perfect likeness. A Carrara-marble bust of Lafayette by Houdon is also displayed in the rotunda, along with busts of the seven other Virginia-born presidents.

Washington Irving took notes in 1807 while John Marshall tried and acquitted Aaron Burr of treason in the old Hall of the House of Delegates, where Virginia's legislators met from 1788 to 1906. The Confederate Congress also met in the room, which resembles an open courtyard.

Visitors enter a very different environment, for the capitol's modern welcome center was added under the south lawn as part of a massive restoration of the building completed in 2007. From there you can wander through the building, but I highly recommend a 1-hour guided tour, given on the hour until 4pm.

To the east is the **Executive Mansion,** official residence of governors of Virginia since 1813. Another historic building is the old **Bell Tower,** built in 1824, which now houses a state visitor center.

1000 Bank St. (at 10th St.). ✆ **804/698-1788.** http://legis.state.va.us. Free admission. Mon–Sat 9am–5pm; Sun 1–4pm. 1-hr. guided tours depart on the hour (last tour 4pm).

THE "BOULEVARD MUSEUMS"

The following museums are either on or near Boulevard, a major north-south avenue. While they're interesting and informative, they are not on a par with major museums in such cities as New York, Washington, and Chicago.

Virginia Historical Society/Museum of Virginia History *☆*   Housed in the neoclassical Battle Abbey, built in 1913 as a shrine to the state's Civil War dead, the South's oldest historical society (founded in 1831) has the world's largest collection of Virginia artifacts. Touring the major exhibit, "The Story of Virginia, an American Experience," is like rummaging through the state's attic: You'll see gold buttons from Pocahontas's hat, Patrick Henry's eyeglasses, and much more. Long-term and changing exhibits cover a range of subjects, from Colonial armaments to archaeologists solving Virginia historical mysteries. Genealogists will find a treasure-trove of family histories in the library of some 125,000 volumes and 7 million manuscripts.

428 N. Boulevard (at Kensington Ave.). ✆ **804/358-4901.** www.vahistorical.org. Admission $5 adults, $4 seniors, free for anyone under 18. Free admission to galleries on Sun. Mon–Sat 10am–5pm; Sun 1–5pm. Closed Jan 1, Easter, July 4th, Thanksgiving, and Dec 24–25.

Virginia Museum of Fine Arts *☆☆*   One of the most splendid art museums for a city this size, the VMFA possesses more than 20,000 works of art, so many that it is undergoing a multiyear expansion that will add nearly 50% to its exhibition space. Among its gems is the largest public Fabergé collection outside Russia—more than 300 objets d'art created at the turn of the 20th century for tsars Alexander III and Nicholas II. The imperial jewel-encrusted Easter eggs evoke what art historian Parker Lesley calls the "dazzling, idolatrous realm of the last czars." Other highlights include the Goya portrait *General Nicholas Guye,* a life-size marble statue of Roman emperor Caligula, Monet's *Iris by the Pond,* and six magnificent Gobelin *Don Quixote* tapestries. That's not

Kids Cool Richmond Stuff for Kids

There are few DO NOT TOUCH signs in the **Science Museum of Virginia**, 2500 W. Broad St. (© **800/659-1727** or 804/864-1400; www.smv.org), with tons of hands-on educational exhibits aimed at children. Even adults will enjoy seeing a movie in the 250-seat Ethyl Corporation IMAX Dome & Planetarium, which shows IMAX films as well as sophisticated special-effects multimedia planetarium shows. The building itself merits attention: It's the Beaux Arts former Broad Street Station, designed in 1919 by John Russell Pope (architect of the Jefferson Memorial, the National Archives, and the National Gallery of Art) as the city's train station. Admission is $10 adults, $9 seniors and children 4 to 12. Tickets to films cost $8.50 to $10 depending on the movie. The exhibits are open Monday to Saturday 9:30am to 5pm and Sunday 11:30am to 5pm. Call or check the website for IMAX showtimes.

Nearby the **Children's Museum of Richmond**, 2626 W. Broad St. (© **877/295-2667** or 804/424-2667; www.c-mor.org), has more innovative hands-on exhibits for kids age 6 months to 12 years. Admission is $7 per person, $4 after 4pm. It's open Tuesday through Saturday (Mon–Sat in summer) from 9:30am to 5pm, Sunday from noon to 5pm.

---

to mention the works of de Kooning, Gauguin, van Gogh, Delacroix, Matisse, Degas, Picasso, Gainsborough, and others; antiquities from China, Japan, Egypt, Greece, Byzantium, Africa, and South America; art from India, Nepal, and Tibet; and an impressive collection of contemporary American art. The museum also has an inexpensive cafeteria.

200 N. Boulevard (at Grove Ave.). © **804/340-1400**. www.vmfa.state.va.us. Free admission ($5 donation suggested). Wed–Sun 11am–5pm. Closed Jan 1, July 4th, Thanksgiving, and Dec 25.

HOUSES, GARDENS & CEMETERIES

Agecroft Hall   In an elegant neighborhood overlooking the James River, Agecroft Hall is a late-15th-century Tudor manor house built in Lancashire, England, brought here piece by piece in the 1920s. Today it serves as a museum portraying the social history and material culture of an English-gentry family of the late-Tudor and early-Stuart eras. Typical of its period, the house has ornate plaster ceilings, massive fireplaces, rich oak paneling, leaded and stained-glass windows, and a two-story great hall with a mullioned window 25 feet long. Furnishings authentically represent the period. Adjoining the mansion are a formal sunken garden, resembling one at Hampton Court Palace, and a formal flower garden, an Elizabethan knot garden, and an herb garden. Visitors see a brief video about the estate before taking the tour. Plan some time to explore the gardens as well. Appropriately, the **Richmond Shakespeare Festival** (© **804/323-4000;** www.richmondshakespeare.com) plays here each June and July.

4305 Sulgrave Rd. © **804/353-4241**. www.agecrofthall.com. Admission $7 adults, $6 seniors, $4 students; half price for gardens only. Tues–Sat 10am–4pm; Sun 12:30–5pm. Guided 30-min. house tours depart on hour and half-hour.

Hollywood Cemetery   Perched on the bluffs overlooking the James River not far from Maymont (see below), Hollywood Cemetery is the serenely beautiful resting place of presidents Monroe and Tyler, Confederate president Jefferson Davis, six Virginia governors, and 18,000 Confederate soldiers, including James Ewell Brown (Jeb) Stuart and 21 other Confederate generals. Designed in 1847, it was conceived as a place where nature would remain undisturbed. A 90-foot granite pyramid, a monument constructed in 1869, marks the Confederate section. A 20-minute film about the cemetery is shown in the office. The best way to see it from April through October is on a 90-minute walking tour by **Historic Richmond Tours** (© **804/649-0711**, option 4; www.richmondhistorycenter.com), Monday through Saturday at 10am and once a month on Sunday. The tours cost $7 per person. Reservations are required.

412 S. Cherry (at Albemarle St.). © 804/648-8501. www.hollywoodcemetery.org. Free admission. Cemetery daily 8am–5pm (to 6pm during daylight saving time); office Mon–Fri 8:30am–4:30pm.

Lewis Ginter Botanical Garden 🏵🏵   In the 1880s, self-made Richmond millionaire, philanthropist, and amateur horticulturist Lewis Ginter (a founder of the American Tobacco Company and creator of The Jefferson Hotel) built the Lakeside Wheel Club as a playground for the city's elite. The resort boasted a lake, a 9-hole golf course, cycling paths, and a zoo. At Ginter's death in 1897, his niece, Grace Arents, converted the property to a hospice for sick children. An ardent horticulturist herself, she imported rare trees and shrubs and constructed greenhouses. Grace died in 1926, leaving her estate to the city to be maintained as a botanical garden and public park. Today it's one of the finest botanical gardens in the state, and its **Conservatory** is the only such classical, domed facility in Virginia. Start at the visitor center and give yourself plenty of time to walk through the 40 acres of gardens. In addition, you can tour the Bloemendall House (named for Ginter's ancestral home in the Netherlands), visit the conservatory and library-education complex, have lunch at the **Garden Cafe** or refreshments in the **Robins Tea House,** and browse the garden shop. Anyone with a green thumb will love it all.

1800 Lakeside Ave. (at Hilliard Rd) © 804/262-9887. www.lewisginter.org. Admission $10 adults, $9 seniors, $6 children 3–12, free for children 2 and younger. Daily 9am–5pm (to 9pm Thurs in Apr and July–Sept). Take I-95 N. to Exit 80 (Parham Rd.) and turn left on Parham Rd., right on Lakeside.

Maymont 🏵 🏵ids   In 1886, Maj. James Henry Dooley, another of Richmond's many self-made millionaires, purchased a 100-acre dairy farm and built this 33-room Romanesque Revival–style mansion surrounded by beautifully landscaped grounds. The house has a colonnaded sandstone facade, turrets, and towers. The details of the formal rooms reflect various periods, most notably 18th-century French. Maymont is elaborately furnished with pieces from many periods chosen by the Dooleys—Oriental carpets, an Art Nouveau swan-shaped bed, marble and bronze sculpture, porcelains, tapestries, and Tiffany vases.

The Dooleys lavished the same care on the grounds. They laid out Italian and Japanese gardens, and planted horticultural specimens and exotic trees culled from the world over. The **Nature & Visitor Center** has interactive exhibits interpreting the James River. There are outdoor animal habitats for birds, bison, beaver, deer, elk, and bear. At the **Children's Farm,** youngsters can feed chickens, piglets, goats, peacocks, cows, donkeys, and sheep. A collection of late-19th- and early-20th-century horse-drawn carriages—surreys, phaetons, hunting vehicles—is on display at the **Carriage House.** Carriage and hayrides are a weekend afternoon option during summer.

You can see everything else on your own, but you must take a guided tour in order to visit Maymont House Museum's upstairs rooms. There are parking lots at the Nature & Visitor Center on Shields Lake Drive, off Spottswood Road near the

Children's Farm, and at Hampton Street and Pennsylvania Avenue near the mansion and gardens.

2201 Shields Dr. (north of the James River between Va. 161 and Meadow St.). © 804/358-7166. www.maymont.org. Free admission ($5 donation suggested). Carriage, tram, and hay wagon rides $3 adults, $2 children. Tues–Sun noon–5pm (last house tour 4:30pm). Guided 25-min. house tours depart every half-hour. Go south to the end of Boulevard; follow signs to the parking area.

Wilton House   Originally built on the James River about 14 miles below Richmond, this 1753 Georgian mansion was painstakingly dismantled and reconstructed on this bluff overlooking the river in 1933. Most of the original brick, flooring, and paneling were saved. Wilton's design has been attributed to Williamsburg architect Richard Taliaferro. It was part of a 2,000-acre plantation where William Randolph III entertained many of the leading figures of the day, including George Washington, Thomas Jefferson, and Lafayette. The house has a fine collection of period furnishings based on an 1815 inventory. All rooms feature pine paneling, some with fluted pilasters and denticulate cornices.

215 S. Wilton Rd. (off W. Cary St.). © 804/282-5936. www.wiltonhousemuseum.org. Admission $6 adults, $5 seniors and students, free for children 5 and younger. Tues–Fri 1–4:30pm, Sat 10am–4pm, Sun 1:30–4:30pm; Feb by appointment only. Tours depart continuously every 45 min. Closed national holidays. Take Va. 147 (W. Cary St.) west and turn south on Wilton Rd.

SPECIAL-INTEREST MUSEUMS

Built by Richmond's Jewish community, one of the oldest in the United States, the **Virginia Holocaust Museum,** 2000 E. Cary St. (© **804/257-5400;** www.va-holocaust. com), in Tobacco Row between 20th and 21st streets, honors those who died in or lived through the Holocaust. Local survivors tell their stories in the moving Survivors' Room. There's also a mock ghetto surrounded by barbed wire and a model of an underground hiding place. Admission is free, but donations are encouraged. The museum is open Monday through Friday 9am to 5pm, Saturday and Sunday 11am to 5pm.

In Jackson Ward, the **Black History Museum & Cultural Center of Virginia,** 00 Clay St. (yes, that's the address), at Foushee Street (© **804/780-9093;** www.black historymuseum.org), houses documents, limited editions, prints, art, and photos emphasizing the history of the state's African-American community. It's in a Federal–Greek Revival–style house built in 1832 and purchased a century later by the Council of Colored Women under the leadership of Maggie L. Walker. Admission is $5 adults, $4 seniors, $3 for children under 12. It's open Tuesday through Saturday 10am to 5pm.

The lobby of the **Library of Virginia,** 800 Broad St., between 8th and 9th streets (© **804/692-3919;** www.lva.lib.va.us), has changing exhibits of state documents and published works, some of them more than 400 years old. Containing papers going back to the 1600s, the library's records are a treasure-trove for genealogists. It's open Monday through Saturday from 9am to 5pm; admission is free.

Although it is minuscule when compared to the National Air and Space Museum's monstrous Steven F. Udvar-Hazy Center in the Hunt Country (see chapter 4) or the fine Virginia Air & Space Center in Hampton (see chapter 10), the **Virginia Aviation Museum,** 5701 Huntsman Rd. (© **804/236-3622;** www.vam.smv.org), on the grounds of Richmond International Airport, does have some beautifully restored craft dating from 1916 to 1946 plus a SR-71 Blackbird spy plane. The museum is a division of the Science Museum of Virginia (see "Cool Richmond Stuff for Kids," above).

Admission is $9 adults, $5 seniors, $4 for kids 4 to 12. It's open Monday through Saturday 9:30am to 5pm, Sunday noon to 5pm (closed Thanksgiving and Christmas).

NEARBY ATTRACTIONS

About 14 miles north of Richmond on I-95, the communities of **Ashland** and **Hanover** have deep historical roots. Patrick Henry once tended bar at Hanover Tavern, built in 1723, and argued cases in the Hanover County Courthouse, dating from 1735. For more information contact the **Ashland/Hanover Visitor Center,** 112 N. Railroad Ave. in Hanover (© **800/897-1479** or 804/752-6766; www.town.ashland.va.us). Hours are daily 9am to 5pm except major holidays.

Paramount's Kings Dominion *(Kids*   This 400-acre fanciful facility is one of the most popular theme parks on the East Coast. Although it offers a wide variety of attractions, many with themes from Paramount movies and TV shows, it's principally known for its thrill rides and water park. It's especially famous for having one of the largest roller coaster collections on the East Coast (you can spend all day here just being jolted up and down). The shows change from year to year so as not to bore the locals, but you can count on several from the Nickelodeon and Country Music Television cable channels, both Paramount properties. Almost like its own theme park, the splash-happy **WaterWorks** features two monstrous wave pools and White Water Canyon, a wet and-wild ride simulating white-water rafting. **Best Western Kings Quarters** offers accommodations on-site (© **804/876-3321;** www.bestwesternkings quarters.com).

Doswell, VA. © **804/876-5000.** www.kingsdominion.com. Admission changes annually, usually about $45 ($30 after 4pm) ages 3–61 and over 48 in. tall, $25 seniors and anyone else under 48 in. tall, free for children under 3. Season passes available. Hours generally Memorial Day to Labor Day daily 10:30am to 9 or 10pm; Apr–May and day after Labor Day to early Oct Sat–Sun 10:30am–8pm. Take Va. 30 (Exit 98) off I-95.

Scotchtown *(Kids*   One of Virginia's oldest plantation houses, Scotchtown is a charming one-story white-clapboard home in a parklike setting of small dependencies and gardens. Charles Chiswell of Williamsburg built the house around 1719, but it's best known as a residence of Patrick Henry, who bought it in 1770 and lived here from 1771 to 1778 with his wife, Sarah, and their six children. Henry served as governor of Virginia during those years, but sadly, Sarah was mentally ill during much of that time and eventually confined to a room in the basement. Although Henry last lived at Red Hill near Lynchburg (see chapter 6), this is the only house he ever occupied that is still standing. It has been beautifully restored and furnished with 18th-century antiques, some associated with the Henry family. In the study, Henry's mahogany desk-table still bears his ink stains, and bookshelves hold his law books. Scotchtown has associations with another historical figure, Dolley Madison, whose mother was a first cousin to Patrick Henry. Dolley and her mother lived here while their family moved back to this area from North Carolina. Unlike so many historic houses, none of the rooms here are roped off, so you can go into all of them during the leisurely and informative guided tours, which give an overview of 18th-century plantation life in Virginia, in addition to the specific Henry story.

16120 Chiswell Lane, Beaverdam. © **804/227-3500.** www.apva.org/scotchtown. Admission $7 adults, $5 seniors, $4 students 6–18, free for children 5 and younger; grounds only $3 per person. Apr–Oct Thurs–Sat 10am–4:30pm, Sun 1:30–4:30pm; Nov–Mar by appointment only. 1-hr. house tours depart on demand. Closed Easter, Mother's Day, July 4th. From Ashland follow Va. 54 west, turn right on Scotchtown Road (C.R. 671) north, take right fork on C.R. 685.

5 Sports & Outdoor Activities

SPECTATOR SPORTS

AUTO RACING   See NASCAR racing at **Richmond International Raceway,** between Laburnum Avenue and the Henrico Turnpike/Meadowbridge Road (© **804/ 329-6796;** www.rir.com). The raceway is Virginia's largest sports facility, attracting crowds of 70,000 or more. Unless you're a NASCAR fan, check the website and avoid being in Richmond on race weekends, when accommodations are scarce.

BASEBALL   The **Richmond Braves** (© **804/359-4444;** www.rbraves.com), the top minor league club in the Atlanta Braves' organization, compete in the AAA International League from April to mid-September. All home games are played at the 12,500-seat Diamond, 3001 N. Boulevard.

COLLEGE SPORTS   The **University of Richmond**'s Spiders play football and basketball in the **Colonial Athletic Association** (© **804/289-8388;** www.richmond spiders.com). **Virginia Commonwealth University**'s Rams play basketball at the **Coliseum** (© **804/282-7267;** www.vcurams.vcu.edu).

HORSE RACING   Virginia's only parimutuel racetrack, **Colonial Downs,** is on Va. 155, between I-64 (Exit 205) and U.S. 60 in New Kent County, 25 miles east of Richmond (© **888/482-8722** or 804/966-7223; www.colonialdowns.com). Call or check the website for schedules and ticket prices.

OUTDOOR ACTIVITIES

GOLF   Golf courses abound in the Richmond area. Among them are the public **Belmont Park Recreation Center,** 1800 Hilliard Rd. (© **804/266-4929;** www.vrps. com), and semi-private **Glenwood Golf Club,** Creighton Road (© **804/226-1793**).

6 Shopping

Richmond's neighborhoods have a number of specialty shops, including those mentioned below. The visitor centers provide brochures that cover these and many other stores around the city and out in the suburbs.

For distinctive souvenirs, don't forget museum gift shops, especially those at the Science Museum, Art Museum, Museum and White House of the Confederacy, Valentine Richmond History Museum, and the Virginia Children's Museum.

There are upscale shops along East Cary Street in Shockoe Slip, but the best place in town for a pleasant shopping stroll is in **Carytown,** the 7 blocks of West Cary Street between Boulevard and Nasemond Street that are lined with a mix of small stores and interesting cafes. Antiques hunting is good here, especially at **Thomas-Hines Antiques,** 3027 W. Cary St. (© **804/355-2782**), and **Mariah Robinson Antiques and Fine Art,** 3455 W. Cary St. (© **804/355-1996**). **Ten Thousand Villages,** 3201 W. Cary St. (© **804/358-5170**), carries international handcrafts, with lots of baskets and primitive pottery.

You'll also find gourmet food shops, ethnic restaurants, secondhand clothing stores, and the landmark **Byrd Theater,** which shows second-run films at discount prices.

7 Richmond After Dark

Richmond is no New York or London, so you won't be attending internationally recognized theaters and music halls. Nevertheless, you might be able to catch visiting productions and artists at several venues. The city has its own ballet company and theater groups, and pierced-set bands rock Shockoe Bottom.

Current entertainment schedules can be found in the Thursday "Weekend" section of the *Richmond Times-Dispatch* (www.timesdispatch.com), the city's daily newspaper. The free tabloid *Style Weekly* (www.styleweekly.com) has details on theater, concerts, dance performances, and other happenings. It's widely available at the visitor centers and in hotel lobbies.

MAJOR CONCERT HALLS & ALL-PURPOSE AUDITORIUMS

Although it was closed for major renovations during my recent visit, the **Carpenter Center for the Performing Arts,** 600 E. Grace St., at 6th Street (© 804/782-3900; www.vapaf.com), was scheduled to reopen its doors again in late 2009. Built in 1928 as a lavish cinema, it will host national touring companies for dance, orchestra, and theater performances. The Richmond Ballet, the Virginia Opera, and the Richmond Symphony usually perform here as well (see "The Performing Arts," below).

Next to the Greater Richmond Convention Center, the **Richmond Coliseum,** 601 E. Leigh St. (© 804/780-4970; www.richmondcoliseum.net), hosts everything from the Ringling Bros. and Barnum & Bailey circus to rock concerts. It seats about 12,000. Major sporting events—wrestling, ice hockey, and basketball—are also scheduled.

In the summer months, Richmond goes outdoors to **Dogwood Dell Festival of the Arts** in Byrd Park, at Boulevard and Idlewild Avenue (© 804/646-3355; www.ci.richmond.va.us/parks/dogwood.aspx), for free music and drama under the stars in this tiered grassy amphitheater. Bring the family, spread a blanket, and enjoy a picnic.

THE PERFORMING ARTS

You can catch family plays and musicals at **Theatre IV,** 114 W. Broad St. (© 804/344-8040; www.theatreiv.org), which stages family-oriented performances in the **Empire Theater,** at Broad and Jefferson streets.

The **Richmond Ballet** (© 804/359-0906; www.richmondballet.com), the official State Ballet of Virginia, performs from mid-October to May. Their productions run the gamut from classical to modern, from *The Nutcracker* to commissioned world premieres. The ballet, the **Virginia Opera** (© 804/643-6004; www.vaopera.org), and the **Richmond Symphony** (© 804/788-1212; www.richmondsymphony.com) all perform in the Carpenter Center for Performing Arts.

Tickets for most events are available through **Ticketmaster** (© 804/262-8003; www.ticketmaster.com).

THE CLUB & MUSIC SCENE

Shockoe Bottom is the city's funky nightlife district, although the usual weekend revelers are more likely to have pierced eyebrows than packed wallets. It occupies the square block beginning with the 17th Street Farmer's Market going east along East

---

Tips Fun Freebies

A nonprofit organization called **Venture Richmond** (© 804/788-6466; www.venturerichmond.com) keeps Richmond hopping with a series of free outdoor concerts, beer blasts, and street festivals from May through September. Check the website for what's happening.

Main and East Franklin streets to 18th Street. Its joints attract the "let's see your ID" crowd, and they go up and down in popularity. If you can find a parking space, you can see for yourself what's going on by barhopping around Shockoe Bottom's busy block (but *do not* wander off onto deserted streets). *Note:* Many Shockoe Bottom establishments are closed on Sunday and Monday.

Up Cary Street in the more affluent (and well-behaved) Shockoe Slip, several restaurants and pubs have live music, including **The Tobacco Company,** 1201 E. Cary St. (© **804/782-9555**), which has acoustic jazz upstairs Tuesday through Saturday and dancing downstairs Wednesday through Saturday from 8pm to 1am.

8 An Easy Excursion to Petersburg ⨉⨉

After his frontal assaults failed to capture Richmond in 1864, Gen. Ulysses S. Grant recognized that the key to victory was Petersburg, a vital rail junction on the Appomattox River 23 miles south of the Confederate capital. Moving his troops south across the James River at Hopewell east of Richmond, he advanced on Petersburg, hoping thus to cut off Gen. Robert E. Lee's supplies and starve him into submission. The ever-wily Lee quickly countered, however, and the tragic 10-month Siege of Petersburg ensued. Finally, on April 2, 1865, a Union assault smashed through Lee's right flank, at what is now a fine privately funded memorial park. Lee retreated west that very night and surrendered a week later at Appomattox Court House (see "Attractions in the Lynchburg Area," in chapter 6).

Sitting at the strategic junction of interstates 95 and 85, Petersburg today is a quiet Southern city. Although much of its downtown business district has a down-on-its-heels appearance, the Old Town section near the river is undergoing a restoration and has several antiques stores and restaurants to go with the city's visitor center and two Civil War–era museums. The major sights, however, are on Petersburg's eastern and southern outskirts, where the battle lines were drawn.

VISITOR INFORMATION   When you arrive, take Washington Street (Exit 52) west and follow the Petersburg Tour signs to the **Petersburg Visitor Center,** 425 Cockade Alley, Petersburg, VA 23804 (© **800/368-3595** or 804/733-2400; www. petersburg-va.org), where you can get maps and literature and buy a block ticket to local museums (see below). The center is open daily from 9am to 5pm.

There's also a visitor information center at the **Carson Rest Area** on I-95 northbound (© **434/246-2145**), 18 miles south of the city. It's open daily from 9am to 5pm.

EXPLORING OLD TOWN PETERSBURG

Begin at the visitor center, in the basement of the 1815 McIlwaine House at the heart of revitalizing Old Town. From here, you can stroll the nearby streets—some still paved with cobblestones—past the Old Farmers Market and other Victorian-era buildings, many of which now house antiques shops and art galleries.

Old Town's top attraction is the **Siege Museum,** 15 W. Bank St. (© **804/733-2404;** www.craterroad.com/siegemuseum.html), occupying the old Merchant Exchange, a magnificent Greek Revival temple-fronted building. It tells the story of everyday life in Petersburg up to and during the siege in displays and an interesting 18-minute film narrated by the late actor Joseph Cotten, a Virginia native whose ancestors lived in Petersburg during the Civil War. The film is shown on the hour and half-hour. Give yourself another 30 minutes to see the museum.

⌒Moments The First Memorial Day

After the Civil War, a group of Petersburg schoolgirls and their teacher came to Old Blandford Church to decorate the graves of the soldiers buried in the churchyard. The ceremony inspired Mary Logan, wife of Union Gen. John A. Logan, who was head of the major organization of Union army veterans, to campaign for a national Memorial Day, which was first observed in 1868.

Centre Hill Mansion, 1 Centre Hill Circle (© **804/733-2401**), between Adams and Tabb streets, is a nicely restored 1823 mansion furnished with Victorian pieces. You'll have to take a 30-minute tour (departing every hour 10:30am–4:30pm).

Both the Seige Museum and Centre Hill Mansion are open daily 10am to 5pm.

The visitor center sells **block tickets** to the Siege Museum, Centre Hill Mansion, and Old Blandford Church (see below) for $11 adults, $9 seniors and children 7 to 12. Otherwise, admission to each is $5 adults, $4 seniors and children. Active-duty military personnel pay the seniors/children rate.

THE CIVIL WAR BATTLEFIELDS

Together, the sites below will take most of a day to tour. After a look around Old Town, drive out to the national battlefield's visitor center east of the city and follow the one-way tour to The Crater. You'll come out of the national battlefield at Crater Road (U.S. 301); Old Blandford Church is a quarter-mile north. Have lunch at King's Barbecue No. 2, which is on Crater Road south of I-95 (see "Where to Stay & Dine," below). Spend the afternoon at Pamplin Historical Park.

Old Blandford Church ⓐ   About 2 miles south of downtown, this ancient church boasts one of the largest collections of Tiffany-glass windows in existence and is noted for the first observance of Memorial Day. The church was constructed in 1735 of imported English brick but abandoned in the early 1800s. During the Civil War, the building became a hospital for wounded soldiers. Many were later buried in the 189-acre graveyard, whose oldest gravestone dates from 1702. The 13 Confederate and border states each sponsored one of the Tiffany windows as a memorial to its Confederate dead. The local Ladies Memorial Association commissioned the 14th window. The artist himself, Louis Comfort Tiffany, gave the church the 15th window, a magnificent "Cross of Jewels" that is thrillingly illuminated at sunset. You can visit the parklike graveyard on your own, but the only way to see inside the church is on a 45-minute guided tour.

319 S. Crater Rd. (U.S. 301; at Rochelle Lane). © **804/733-2396**. Admission $5 adults, $4 seniors and children. Daily 10am–5pm. 30-min. tours depart every 45 min. 10am–4pm. From downtown take Bank St. east and turn right on Crater Rd. (U.S. 301).

Pamplin Historical Park & The National Museum of the Civil War Soldier ⓐ
The Petersburg Breakthrough Battle, where Union troops actually broke through the Confederate lines on April 2, 1865, to end the siege, occurred on the grounds of this fine, privately owned park, where more than a mile of interpretive trails lead through some of Virginia's best-preserved Confederate earthwork fortifications. There's a re-created Military Encampment with costumed interpreters and a Battlefield Center with artifacts and "War So Terrible," a film about Civil War combat. Guides lead 30- to 45-minute walking tours of the battlefield at least once a day; call for times since

the tours will add immeasurably to your visit. The nearby **Banks House** served as Grant's headquarters. One of Virginia's few remaining slave dwellings is behind the house. You start all this at **The National Museum of the Civil War Soldier,** which is dedicated to the common foot soldier (no famous generals need apply). The Field Quarter interprets what slave life was like in the 19th century. Allow 1 hour in the main museum, at least another 2 to see the battlefield and historic homes. The Hardtack & Coffee Cafe offers snacks and Southern-style lunch fare.

6125 Boydton Plank Rd. (U.S. 1). © 877/726-7546 or 804/861-2408. www.pamplinpark.org. Admission $15 adults, $14 seniors, $9 children 6–11, free for children 5 and younger. Daily 9am–5pm (to 6pm in summer). Closed Jan 1, Thanksgiving, and Dec 25. Park is 6 miles south of downtown, 1 mile south of I-85.

Petersburg National Battlefield Park ★★★   Encompassing some 2,646 acres along the city's eastern and southern flanks, this park preserves the key sites of the siege that lasted from mid-June 1864 to early April 1865. The main visitor center (on Va. 36) displays exhibits and artifacts, while a one-way 4-mile battlefield driving tour has wayside exhibits; some stops have short walking trails. The last and most fascinating is the site of The Crater, literally a huge depression blown into the ground when a group of Pennsylvania volunteer infantry, including many miners, dug a passage beneath Confederate lines and exploded 4 tons of powder, creating the 170- by 60-foot crater. The explosion killed 278 Confederates, and, during the ensuing battle, thousands more men on both sides were killed or wounded. Stop at the Taylor Home before you get there for a view down over The Crater. To get a fuller perspective, follow the entire siege line from the Eastern Front visitor center 26 miles to Five Forks Battlefield in Dinwiddie County.

Also part of the park is **Grant's Headquarters at City Point,** at present-day Hopewell, 26 miles to the east via Va. 36. City Point was the largest Union supply base during the war. Abraham Lincoln spent 2 of the last 3 weeks of his life there.

5001 Siege Rd. (Va. 36; 2½ miles east of downtown via E. Washington St.). © 804/732-3531. www.nps.gov/pete. Admission $5 per vehicle, $3 per pedestrian or bicyclist. Daily 9am–5pm. Closed Jan 1, Dr. Martin Luther King Jr. Day, Thanksgiving, and Dec 25.

ATTRACTIONS AT FORT LEE

Fort Lee is home to the U.S. Army Quartermaster Corps and its **Quartermaster Museum** (© 804/734-4203; www.qmmuseum.lee.army.mil), which has uniforms and equipment from all of America's wars. Stars of the show are the World War II jeep with a Mercedes car seat specially installed for Gen. George S. Patton and one of the armored "Circus Wagons" in which Gen. Dwight D. Eisenhower lived when on the road in Europe during the war. The museum is open Tuesday through Friday 10am to 5pm, Saturday and Sunday 11am to 5pm. Admission is free.

Next door, the **U.S. Army Women's Museum** (© 804/734-4327; www.awm. lee.army.mil) is the only facility in the world dedicated to army women. It traces their contributions from the Revolution to the present. If you, a relative, or another woman you know was in the army, especially during World War II, then this is a poignant stop. It's open Tuesday through Friday from 10am to 5pm and Saturday, Sunday, and federal holidays from 11am to 4:30pm. Admission is free.

The gate into Fort Lee is a mile east of the national battlefield visitor center on Va. 36. This is an active U.S. army post, so you must show valid photo identification, and you and your vehicle also are subject to being searched. Tell the guards at the gate that you want to visit the Quartermaster Museum and the U.S. Army Women's Museum, and they'll tell you how to get there.

WHERE TO STAY & DINE

National chain motels near I-95 and Washington Street (Exit 52) include **Best Western** (𝄐 800/528-1234 or 804/733-1776), **Howard Johnson** (𝄐 800/654-2000 or 804/732-5950), **Ramada Inn** (𝄐 800/272-6232 or 804/733-0730), **Super 8** (𝄐 800/800-8000 or 804/861-0793), and **Travelodge** (𝄐 800/578-7878 or 804/733-0000).

As you tour Old Town, you can fuel up on pastries and caffeine at **Java Mio,** 322 N. Sycamore St. (𝄐 **804/861-1646**), a trendy coffeehouse offering sandwiches and salads for lunch plus dinner and live music on Friday night.

King's Barbecue 🌟 (Value AMERICAN   Open since 1946, this Petersburg institution supplies some of the best barbecue in the South. The setting is a pine-paneled room adorned with an extraordinary collection of pig dolls and figurines. Pork, beef, ribs, and chicken smoke constantly in an open pit right in the dining room. Unlike most other barbecue emporia, the meat is served just as it comes from the pit. Aficionados can enjoy the smoked flavor *au naturel* or apply vinegary sauce from squeeze bottles. The menu also offers such Southern standbys as crispy fried chicken, ham steak, and seafood items like salmon cakes and fried oysters.

Near The Crater and Old Blandford Church, **King's Barbecue No. 2,** 2910 S. Crater Rd. (𝄐 **804/732-0975**), has the same offerings.

3221 W. Washington St. (U.S. 1 South). 𝄐 **804/732-5861.** Main courses $8–$17. AE, MC, V. Tues–Sun 7am–9pm. Follow U.S. 1 south to the city limits, 3 miles from downtown.

10

Williamsburg, Jamestown & Yorktown

In many respects a visit to Virginia is a great big history lesson, and nowhere is that more true than on the Peninsula, stretching southeast from Richmond between the James and York rivers.

This area saw not only the establishment of English-speaking Colonial America at Jamestown in 1607, it watched as its citizens gathered in Williamsburg to help foment the Revolution, which ended here with the deciding Battle of Yorktown. Today that history comes alive in the "Historic Triangle" of Williamsburg, Jamestown, and Yorktown.

You will learn all you can absorb at Colonial Williamsburg's beautifully restored Historic Area. At Jamestown you will see where the first English settlers landed, examine archaeological artifacts uncovered from their first fort, and visit re-creations of the ships they came in and the village they built. At Yorktown you will walk the ramparts from which Washington bombarded Cornwallis into submission, thus turning the colonists'

dream of a new nation into a reality. Along the James River you will tour the tobacco plantations that created Virginia's first great wealth.

At the eastern end of the Peninsula, where it meets the Chesapeake Bay, Hampton is America's oldest continuously English-speaking town, but it also has a modern air-and-space museum. In the shipbuilding city of Newport News, one of the country's finest maritime museums displays part of the USS *Monitor,* whose Civil War battle with the CSS *Merrimac* out on Hampton Roads was the world's first engagement between ironclad ships.

As soon as the kids become bored with all that history, you can take them to the Busch Gardens Europe theme park and the thoroughly wet Water Country USA, which help make this one of America's family vacation meccas.

It's also a bargain-hunter's paradise, with numerous outlet stores west of Williamsburg. And golfers can play some of the country's finest courses.

GETTING THERE & GETTING AROUND

BY PLANE **Newport News/Williamsburg International Airport (PHF),** 14 miles east of Williamsburg (© **757/877-0221;** www.nnwairport.com), is served by AirTran, Delta, and US Airways. **Avis** (© 800/331-1212), **Budget** (© 800/527-0700), **Enterprise** (© 800/261-7331), **Hertz** (© 800/654-3131), and **National** (© 800/328-4567) have desks at the airport, and taxis await each incoming flight.

More flights arrive at **Richmond International Airport** (see chapter 9), about 45 miles west of town via I-64. **Norfolk International Airport** (see chapter 11) is about the same distance to the east, but traffic on I-64 can cause delays in ground transport to Williamsburg during rush hours, especially on summer weekends when beach traffic funnels through the Hampton Roads Bridge Tunnel.

BY CAR   The main drag is **I-64,** which runs down the center of the Peninsula between Richmond and Hampton. When traffic on I-64 comes to a standstill (as it can on summer weekends), you can take the mostly four-lane **U.S. 60,** which parallels it. The two-lane John Tyler Highway (Va. 5) also runs between Richmond and Williamsburg, passing the James River plantations (see section 4, later in this chapter). The scenic **Colonial Parkway** connects Williamsburg, Jamestown, and Yorktown. Va. 199 runs around the southern side of Williamsburg, and when combined with I-64 forms a beltway around the town.

BY TRAIN & BUS   Both **Amtrak** trains (© 800/872-7245; www.amtrak.com) and **Greyhound** buses (© 800/231-2222; www.greyhound.com) arrive at the local **Transportation Center** (© 757/229-8750), at Boundary and Lafayette streets within walking distance of Williamsburg's Historic Area.

Other than driving, the easiest way to get from Williamsburg to Jamestown and Yorktown from March 1 through October 31 is via the **Historic Triangle Shuttle** (© 757/898-2410), which follows the Colonial Parkway. The buses depart the Colonial Williamsburg Visitor Center daily every 30 minutes from 9am to 3:30pm, with the final return trips departing Jamestown and Yorktown at 5:15pm. The rides cost $2 each way but are free with admission to Historic Jamestowne and Yorktown Battlefield (see sections 2 and 3, respectively, later in this chapter). Save your admission tickets.

1 Williamsburg (★(★(★

150 miles S of Washington, D.C.; 50 miles E of Richmond

"I know of no way of judging the future," said Patrick Henry, "but by the past." That particular quotation couldn't be more fitting as an introduction to Williamsburg, since Henry played an important role here when, as a 29-year-old backcountry lawyer, he spoke out against the Stamp Act in the House of Burgesses in 1765. Many considered him an upstart and called the speech traitorous; others were inspired to revolution.

You'll never have a better opportunity to examine the past than in Colonial Williamsburg, as the town's restored Historic Area is known. Unlike most other historical attractions in Virginia, Williamsburg has not just been meticulously re-created to look exactly as it did in the 1770s, when the town served as Virginia's capital. Today, Williamsburg's Historic Area is, for all practical purposes, one of the world's largest and best living-history museums.

Here the British flag flies most of the year over the Capitol building. Women wear long dresses and ruffled caps, and men don powdered wigs. Taverns serve Colonial fare, blacksmiths and harness makers use 18th-century methods, and the local militia drills on Market Square. Clip-clopping horses draw carriages just as their ancestors did when George Washington rode these streets. Your impromptu banter with "Thomas Jefferson" in the King's Arms Tavern will seem so authentic you won't even notice it's Bill Barker, an actor who has been bringing Jefferson to life since 1976.

Youngsters will enjoy watching a musket being fired and being locked up in the town's stocks, but they might otherwise become a bit bored with all the talk about history and start badgering you to get on to Busch Gardens Europe. But it's worth the effort, for both you and they will come away with an understanding and appreciation of life in 18th-century Virginia, before the advent of running water and video games.

ESSENTIALS

VISITOR INFORMATION

For advance information specific to the Historic Area, contact the **Colonial Williamsburg Foundation,** P.O. Box 1776, Williamsburg, VA 23187 (© **800/447-8679** or 757/220-7645; www.colonialwilliamsburg.com). Open 365 days a year, the foundation's visitor center is both a font of information and the beginning of any visit here (see "Exploring the Historic Area," below). There also is a regional information desk in the visitor center.

The next-best source for general information about the hotels, restaurants, and activities is the **Greater Williamsburg Chamber & Tourism Alliance,** 421 N. Boundary St., Williamsburg, VA 23187 (© **800/368-6511** or 757/229-6511; fax 757/253-1397; www.visitwilliamsburg.com), between Lafayette and Scotland streets, 2 blocks north of the Historic Area. The alliance sells one of the best maps of the area, and you can reserve hotel rooms, buy tickets, and search for money-saving package deals on its website. The office is open Monday through Friday 8:30am to 5pm.

The **Williamsburg Hotel and Motel Association** (© **800/446-9244**) publishes *Williamsburg Great Entertainer Magazine,* a visitors guide. It also operates a hotel and motel reservation service in conjunction with the Greater Williamsburg Chamber & Tourism Alliance.

ARRIVING

Amtrak Trains and Greyhound buses arrive at the **Transportation Center** (© **757/229-8750**), at Boundary and Lafayette streets. See "Getting There & Getting Around," above, for air, train, and bus links to Williamsburg.

Williamsburg is on I-64 about halfway between Richmond and Norfolk. For the Historic Area, take Exit 238 (Va. 143) off I-64 and follow the signs south to Va. 132 and Colonial Williamsburg. The visitor center will be on your left as you approach the town. Va. 199, which forms a beltway around the southern side of the city, joins I-64 at Exit 242 east of town; this is the quickest way to get to Busch Gardens Europe and Water Country USA. The scenic Colonial Parkway runs through a tunnel under the Historic Area; you can get on and off at the Colonial Williamsburg Visitor Center.

ORIENTATION & GETTING AROUND

CITY LAYOUT   The 1-mile-long-by-half-mile-wide restored **Historic Area** is at the center of Williamsburg. The 99-foot-wide **Duke of Gloucester Street** is this area's principal east-west artery, with the Capitol building at the eastern end and the Wren building of The College of William and Mary at the west end. **Merchants Square** shops and services are on the western end of Duke of Gloucester Street, next to the college. The visitor center is north of the Historic Area.

Richmond Road (U.S. 60 W.) runs northwest from the Historic Area and is Williamsburg's main commercial strip, with numerous motels, restaurants, and shopping centers, including the area's outlet malls. On the east side of town, **York Street/Pocahontas Trail** (U.S. 60 E.) goes out to Busch Gardens Europe. **Bypass Road** joins these two highways on the north side of the Historic Area.

GETTING AROUND   Since cars are not allowed into the Historic Area between 8am and 10pm, you must park elsewhere. The Colonial Williamsburg Visitor Center (see "Exploring the Historic Area," below) has ample free parking. Once you have bought your tickets, you can use them to ride Colonial Williamsburg's shuttle buses from the visitor center to and around the Historic Area (only ticket holders are

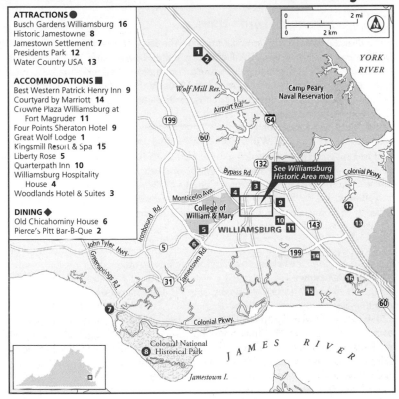

ATTRACTIONS ●
Busch Gardens Williamsburg **16**
Historic Jamestowne **8**
Jamestown Settlement **7**
Presidents Park **12**
Water Country USA **13**

ACCOMMODATIONS ■
Best Western Patrick Henry Inn **9**
Courtyard by Marriott **14**
Crowne Plaza Williamsburg at
    Fort Magruder **11**
Four Points Sheraton Hotel **9**
Great Wolf Lodge **1**
Kingsmill Resort & Spa **15**
Liberty Rose **5**
Quarterpath Inn **10**
Williamsburg Hospitality
    House **4**
Woodlands Hotel & Suites **3**

DINING ◆
Old Chicahominy House **6**
Pierce's Pitt Bar-B-Que **2**

allowed on these buses). The **Red Line** bus will take you between the visitor center and the **Gateway Building,** behind the Governor's Palace, where guides conduct a 30-minute Orientation Walk. It's a good way to get an overview of the village. From there, **Blue Line** buses make a circle around the circumference of the Historic Area. The buses begin operating at 8:50am, with frequent departures until 10pm. The two lines merge after 5pm, forming one loop around the area.

You can also walk from the visitor center to the Historic Area, a 20-minute stroll via a footpath.

The easiest way to get around outside the Historic Area is by public buses operated by **Williamsburg Area Transport** (✆ **757/259-4093;** www.williamsburgtransport. com). Not to be confused with Colonial Williamsburg's shuttle buses, they run Monday through Saturday about every hour from 6am to 8pm, to 10pm during the summer months. Fare is $1.25. Exact fare is required. The **Blue Line** runs west from the Transportation Center and passes a majority of the area's motels, chain restaurants, and shopping centers on Richmond Road (U.S. 60 W.). The **Gray Line** operates east from the Transportation Center to Busch Gardens via Lafayette Street and Pocahontas Trail (U.S. 60 E.). The **Yellow Line** links the Colonial Williamsburg Visitor Center to the Transportation Center and Busch Gardens from Memorial Day to Labor Day.

Fun Fact **Learning Lord's Lines**

You'll see a familiar face in *Williamsburg—the Story of a Patriot,* the 35-minute film shown at the Colonial Williamsburg Visitor Center—and on TVs in hotels operated by the Colonial Williamsburg Foundation. It's Jack Lord, who later became famous as the detective in the 1970s TV show *Hawaii 5-0.* Students at the College of William and Mary consider the 1950s film so campy that they learn every one of Lord's lines by heart.

The land is flat here, so getting around via bicycle is a great idea. **Bike and stroller rentals** are available from Easter through October at the **Woodlands Hotel & Suites,** at the Colonial Williamsburg Visitor Center (© **757/229-1000;** p. 249).

Yellow Cab (© **757/722-1111**) and **Williamsburg Taxi** (© **757/566-3009**) are based at the Transportation Center (see "Arriving," above).

HISTORY & BACKGROUND

In 1699, after nearly a century of famine, fevers, and battles with neighboring American Indian tribes, the beleaguered Virginia Colony abandoned the mosquito-infested swamp at Jamestown for a planned city 6 miles inland and about halfway to Yorktown, which had developed as a major seaport. They named it Williamsburg for the reigning British monarch, William of Orange.

Royal Gov. Francis Nicholson laid out the new capital on a grid with public greens and a half-acre of land for every house on the main street. People used their lots to grow vegetables and raise livestock. Most houses were whitewashed wood frame (trees being more abundant than brick), and kitchens were in separate structures to keep the houses from burning down. A "palace" for the governor was finished in 1720.

The town prospered and became the major cultural and political center of Virginia. The government met here four times a year during "Publick Times," when rich planters and politicos (one and the same, mostly) converged on Williamsburg and the population, normally about 1,800, doubled. Shops displayed their finest wares, and there were balls, horse races, fairs, and auctions.

Williamsburg played a major role as a seat of royal government and later as a hotbed of revolution until the government was moved to Richmond in 1780 to be safer from British attack. Many of the seminal events leading up to the Declaration of Independence occurred here. Thomas Jefferson and James Monroe studied at the College of William and Mary, the nation's second-oldest university behind Harvard. Jefferson was the second state governor and last occupant of the Governor's Palace before the capital moved to Richmond (Patrick Henry was the first). During the Revolution, Williamsburg was the headquarters of Washington (he planned the siege of Yorktown in George Wythe's house), Rochambeau, and Cornwallis.

A REVEREND, A ROCKEFELLER & A REBIRTH

Williamsburg ceased to be an important political center after 1780 but remained a charming Virginia town for another 150 years or so. As late as 1926, the Colonial town plan was virtually intact, including numerous original buildings. Then the Reverend W. A. R. Goodwin, rector of **Bruton Parish Church** (and no known relation to yours truly), envisioned restoring the entire town to its Colonial appearance as a symbol of our early history. He inspired John D. Rockefeller, Jr., who during his lifetime contributed some $68 million to the project and set up an endowment to help provide for permanent restoration and educational programs. Today gifts and bequests by thousands of Americans sustain the project Goodwin and Rockefeller began.

Today, the Historic Area covers 301 acres of the original town. A mile long, it encompasses 88 original buildings and several hundred reconstructed houses, shops, taverns, public buildings, and outbuildings, most on their original foundations after extensive archaeological, architectural, and historical research.

Williamsburg set a very high standard for other Virginia restorations. Researchers investigated international archives, libraries, and museums and sought out old wills, diaries, court records, inventories, letters, and other documents. The architects studied every aspect of 18th-century buildings, from paint chemistry to brickwork. Archaeologists recovered millions of artifacts excavating 18th-century sites to reveal original foundations. The Historic Area also includes 90 acres of gardens and greens, and 3,000 surrounding acres serve as a "greenbelt" against commercial encroachment.

The Colonial Williamsburg Foundation, a nonprofit organization, owns most of the Historic Area, conducts the ongoing restoration, and operates the Historic Area and its visitor center. A profit-making subsidiary owns and operates the foundation's hotels and taverns. Needless to say, "CW" exerts enormous influence over tourism, the town's main income earner.

EXPLORING THE HISTORIC AREA
FIRST STOP: THE VISITOR CENTER

Begin your visit at the **Colonial Williamsburg Visitor Center,** on Va. 132 south of U.S. 60 Bypass (© **800/447-8679** or 757/220-7645; www.colonialwilliamsburg.com). You can't miss it; bright green signs point the way from all access roads to Williamsburg. The center and Historic Area attractions are open daily 9am to 5pm (to 9pm in summer). Some attractions are closed on specific days, and hours can vary, so check the *This Week* brochure for current information.

The visitor center has a bookstore, a coffee shop, a regional information desk, and two **reservations services:** one for Colonial Williamsburg Foundation **hotels** (© **800/ 447-8679** or 757/220-7645; www.colonialwilliamsburg.com), the other for two of its four Colonial **taverns** (© **800/828-3767** or 757/229-2141). It's advisable to make tavern reservations well in advance anytime, and it's essential every day during the summer and on weekends during spring and fall (see "The Early Bird Gets the Reservation," later in this chapter).

The center continuously shows a free 8-minute video about Williamsburg, and once you've bought your ticket, you can watch the 35-minute orientation film, *Williamsburg—The Story of a Patriot,* which also runs throughout the day.

Parking at the visitor center is free. You can park for an hour for free, and then pay, in the public lots and garages near **Merchants Square** at the western end of Duke of Gloucester Street. But be careful: Spaces labeled "P2" are restricted to 2 hours; those marked "P1" and "P6" are long-term.

Tickets

It costs nothing to stroll the streets of the Historic Area and perhaps debate revolutionary politics with the actors playing Thomas Jefferson or Patrick Henry, but you will need a **ticket** to enter the key buildings and the museums, see the 35-minute orientation film at the visitor center, use the Historic Area shuttle buses, and take a 30-minute Orientation Walk through the restored village.

Tips **Planning Your Time in Williamsburg**

There is so much to see and do in the Historic Triangle that you can easily spend a week in this area and still not see everything. Colonial Williamsburg itself requires a minimum of 2 days to explore, preferably 3. It will take at least another day to see Jamestown and Yorktown. If you have kids in tow, they'll want to spend a day at Busch Gardens Europe or Water Country USA, although you can satisfy them by visiting the parks after dark during the summer months.

Spend ample time planning your visit at the Colonial Williamsburg Visitor Center. Historic Area programs change frequently, so it's imperative to pick up a copy of *This Week*, the single most valuable tool in planning the best use of your time. It gives the hours the attractions are open and the times and places of the week's presentations, exhibits, plays, and events. It also has a detailed map.

The Colonial Williamsburg Foundation changes its system of tickets and passes so frequently that I'm almost wasting ink telling you what they were at press time. You should *definitely* call the visitor center or check the Colonial Williamsburg website (www.colonialwilliamsburg.com) for the latest information. With that caveat, this was the pass structure as it existed when we went to press.

A 1-day **Capital City Pass** ticket allowed access to most Historic Area attractions, but not the Governor's Palace or the walking tours. It cost $36 for adults, $18 for children 6 to 14, free for children 5 and younger. You could add the Governor's Palace for $9 adults, $4.50 children. It is good for the day you buy it, regardless of the time you purchased it.

Much more useful is the **Governor's Key-to-the-City Pass,** which includes everything you're likely to see and is good for 2 days. At press time it was going for $49 adults, $24 children 6 to 17.

For longer stays, it's worth paying $59 per adult, $29 for children 6 to 17 for a **Freedom Pass,** which is good for 1 year and includes a 50% discount on the nighttime performances.

Tickets are available at the Colonial Williamsburg Visitor Center, a **ticket booth** at the Merchants Square shops on Henry Street at Duke of Gloucester Street, and **Lumber House** on Duke of Gloucester Street opposite the Palace Green.

American Express, Diners Club, MasterCard, and Visa credit cards are accepted at Colonial Williamsburg ticket outlets, attractions, hotels, and taverns.

THE COLONIAL BUILDINGS
Bassett Hall
Built between 1753 and 1766, Bassett Hall was the mid-1930s residence of Mr. and Mrs. John D. Rockefeller, Jr., and it is restored and furnished to reflect their era. The mansion's name derives from the ownership of Martha Washington's nephew Burwell Bassett, who lived here from 1800 to 1839. In spite of changes the Rockefellers made, much of the interior is original, including woodwork, paneling, mantels,

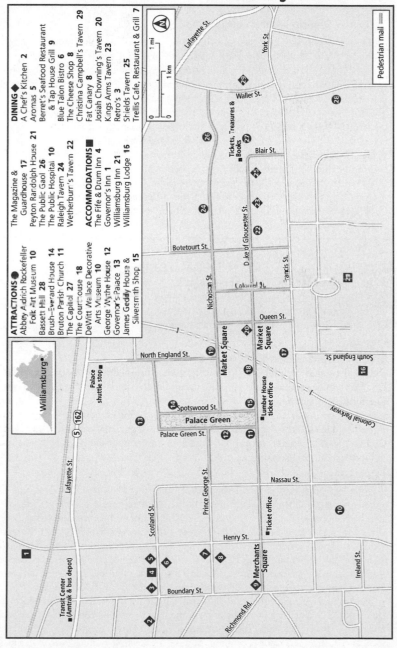

ATTRACTIONS

Abbey Aldrich Rockefeller Folk Art Museum **10**
Bassett Hall **28**
Brush-Everard House **14**
Bruton Parish Church **11**
The Capitol **27**
The Courthouse **18**
DeWitt Wallace Decorative Arts Museum **10**
George Wythe House **12**
Governor's Palace **13**
James Geddy House & Silversmith Shop **15**
The Magazine & Guardhouse **17**
Peyton Randolph House **21**
The Public Gaol **26**
The Public Hospital **10**
Raleigh Tavern **24**
Wetherburn's Tavern **22**

ACCOMMODATIONS

The Fife & Drum Inn **4**
Governor's Inn **1**
Williamsburg Inn **21**
Williamsburg Lodge **16**

DINING ◆

A Chef's Kitchen **2**
Aromas **5**
Berret's Seafood Restaurant & Tap House Grill **9**
Blue Talon Bistro **6**
The Cheese Shop **8**
Christina Campbell's Tavern **29**
Fat Canary **8**
Josiah Chowning's Tavern **20**
Kings Arms Tavern **23**
Retro's **3**
Shields Tavern **25**
Trellis Cafe, Restaurant & Grill **7**

Pedestrian mall

Williamsburg

Transit Center (Amtrak & bus depot)

Palace shuttle stop

Palace Green

Lumber House ticket office

Merchants Square

Ticket office

Lafayette St.
York St.
Waller St.
Blair St.
Botetourt St.
Duke of Gloucester St.
Francis St.
Colonial St.
Nicholson St.
Queen St.
Market Square
South England St.
North England St.
Spotswood St.
Palace Green St.
Prince George St.
Nassau St.
Scotland St.
Henry St.
Boundary St.
Ireland St.
Richmond Rd.
Colonial Parkway
Tickets, Treasures & Books
Lafayette St.

1 mi
1 km

(Value Saving Money on Tickets

You can buy tickets to Colonial Williamsburg, Busch Gardens Europe, Water Country USA, Colonial Historical National Park, and other Historic Triangle attractions separately and pay full price, or you can do some shopping and come up with money-saving combination deals. For example, as I write this the **Historic Triangle Pass** included admission to Colonial Williamsburg, Historic Jamestowne, Jamestown Settlement, Yorktown Battlefield, and the Yorktown Victory Center for $68 per person, regardless of age, good for 5 days. Be sure to check out **Flex Tickets,** which combine several area attractions for one price. They are available at the Colonial Williamsburg Visitor Center. Some hotels and motels offer discounted ticket prices to local attractions if you stay with them; it's worth asking when you call to make your reservation. The Williamsburg Hotel & Motel Association sponsors **"I Am a Williamsburg Vacation"** (© 800/ **211-7164;** www.gowilliamsburg.com), which lets you combine tickets and hotels into a one-price Flex Vacation Package.

and yellow-pine flooring. Much of the furniture is 18th- and 19th-century American in the Chippendale, Federal, and Empire styles. There are beautifully executed needle-work rugs made by Mrs. Rockefeller, and early-19th-century prayer rugs adorn the morning room. Hundreds of examples of ceramics and china are on display, as are collections of 18th- and 19th-century American and English glass, Canton enamelware, and folk art.

Brush-Everard House *

One of the oldest buildings in Williamsburg, the Brush-Everard House was built in 1717 as a residence-cum-shop by public armorer and master gunsmith John Brush. The most distinguished owner was Thomas Everard, two-time mayor of Williamsburg. Though not as wealthy as George Wythe and John Randolph, he was in their elite circle. He enlarged the house, adding the two wings that create a U shape. Today, the home is restored and furnished to its Everard-era appearance. The smokehouse and kitchen out back are original.

The Capitol ***

Virginia legislators met in the H-shaped Capitol from 1704 to 1780. America's first representative assembly, it had an upper house, His Majesty's Council of State, of 12 members appointed for life by the king. Freeholders of each county elected members of the lower House of Burgesses (there were 128 burgesses by 1776). The Burgesses became a training ground for patriots such as George Washington, Thomas Jefferson, Richard Henry Lee, and Patrick Henry. As 1776 approached, the Burgesses passed resolutions against Parliament's Stamp Act and levy on tea—in Henry's immortal words, "taxation without representation," which became a motto of the Revolution.

The Capitol burned down in 1747, was rebuilt in 1753, and succumbed to fire again in 1832. This reconstruction is of the 1704 version, complete with Queen Anne's coat of arms adorning the tower and the Great Union flag flying overhead. The Secretary's Office next door is original. You must take a 30-minute **tour** to get inside the Capitol.

The Courthouse ✪✪✪

An intriguing window on Colonial life's criminal justice division is offered in the courthouse, which dominates Market Square. An original building, the courthouse was the scene of proceedings ranging from criminal trials to the issuance of licenses. Wife beating, pig stealing, and debtor and creditor disputes were among the cases tried here. You can participate in the administration of Colonial justice at the courthouse by sitting on a jury or acting as a defendant. In Colonial times, convicted offenders were usually punished immediately after the verdict. Punishments included public flogging at the whipping post (conveniently located just outside the courthouse) or being locked in the stocks or pillory, where the offenders were subjected to public ridicule. Jail sentences were very unusual—punishment was swift and drastic, and the offenders then returned to the community, often bearing lifelong evidence of their conviction.

George Wythe House ✪

On the west side of the Palace Green is the elegant restored brick home of George Wythe (pronounced "with"), classics scholar, noted lawyer and teacher (Thomas Jefferson, Henry Clay, and John Marshall were his students), and member of the House of Burgesses. A close friend of royal governors, Wythe nevertheless was the first Virginia signer of the Declaration of Independence. Wythe did not sign the Constitution, however, because it did not contain a Bill of Rights or antislavery provisions. His house was Washington's headquarters prior to the siege of Yorktown and Rochambeau's after the surrender of Cornwallis. Open-hearth cooking is demonstrated in the outbuilding.

Governor's Palace ✪✪✪

This meticulous reconstruction is of the Georgian mansion that was the residence and official headquarters of royal governors from 1714 until Lord Dunmore fled before dawn in the face of armed resistance in 1775, thus ending British rule in Virginia. The palace now portrays the final 5 years of British rule. Though the sumptuous surroundings, nobly proportioned halls and rooms, 10 acres of formal gardens and greens, and vast wine cellars all evoke splendor, the king's representative was, by that time, little more than a functionary of great prestige but limited power. He was more apt to behave like a diplomat in a foreign land than an autocratic Colonial ruler.

Tours, given continuously through the day, end in the gardens, where you can explore the elaborate geometric parterres, topiary work, bowling green, pleached *allées,* and a holly maze patterned after the one at Hampton Court. Plan at least 30 minutes to wander the stunning grounds and visit the kitchen and stable yards.

James Geddy House & Foundry ✪

This two-story L-shaped 1762 home (with attached shops) is an original building where you can see how a comfortably situated middle-class family lived in the 18th

---

⎛Fun Fact Hang 'Em High

In Colonial times, all civil and criminal cases (the latter punishable by mutilation or death) were tried in the General Court. Since juries were sent to deliberate in a third-floor room without heat, light, or food, there were few hung juries. Thirteen of Blackbeard the Pirate's crew were tried here and sentenced to hang.

Fun Fact　**The College of William & Mary**

Standing at the western end of Duke of Gloucester Street, the stately **Sir Christopher Wren Building** may not be part of Colonial Williamsburg, but it is the oldest restored structure here. It's also America's oldest college building. Constructed between 1695 and 1699, even before there was a Williamsburg, it's the campus centerpiece of **The College of William and Mary,** the country's second-oldest college behind only Harvard University. King William III and Queen Mary II chartered the school in 1693, and over the next century it was the alma mater of many of the country's early leaders, including Thomas Jefferson. (Its most famous modern alumni are actresses Glenn Close and Linda Lavin and comedian Jon Stewart of *The Daily Show*.) Fire gutted the Wren building in 1705, 1859, and 1862. Its exterior walls remained intact, and in 1928 John D. Rockefeller, Jr., restored it to its Colonial appearance. The college still uses its upstairs classrooms and offices, but the first-floor Grammar School, Great Hall, and Wren Chapel (site of many a campus marriage) are open to the public Monday through Friday from 10am to 5pm, Saturday 9am to 5pm, and Sunday from noon to 5pm. Admission is free. The college's **visitor information office** in the rear of the building (© **757/221-4000;** www.wm.edu/visitors/index.php) has campus maps.

century. Unlike the fancier abodes, the Geddy House has no wallpaper or oil paintings; a mirror and spinet from England, however, indicate relative affluence.

James Geddy, Sr., was a gunsmith and brass founder who advertised in the *Virginia Gazette* of July 8, 1737, that he had "a great Choice of Guns and Fowling Pieces, of several Sorts and Sizes, true bored, which he will warrant to be good; and will sell them as cheap as they are usually sold in England." A younger son, James, Jr., became the town's foremost silversmith and was a member of the city's Common Council involved in furthering the patriot cause. Craftsmen cast silver, pewter, bronze, and brass items at a foundry here.

The Magazine & Guardhouse ☆☆

Another original building, this octagonal brick structure was constructed in 1715 to house ammunition and arms for the defense of the colony. In Colonial Williamsburg, every able-bodied freeman belonged to the militia from the ages of 16 to 60 and did his part in protecting hearth and home from attack by local tribes, riots, slave uprisings, and pirate raids. The high wall and guardhouse were built during the French and Indian War to protect the magazine's 60,000 pounds of gunpowder. Today the building is stocked with 18th-century equipment—flintlock muskets, cannons, barrels of powder, bayonets, and drums, the latter for communication purposes. Children can join the militia here during the summer (see "Especially for Kids," below).

Peyton Randolph House ☆

The Randolphs were one of the most prominent and wealthy families in Colonial Virginia. Sir John Randolph was a respected lawyer, Speaker of the House of Burgesses, and Virginia's representative to London, where he was the only Colonial-born Virginian ever to be knighted. When he died he left his library to 16-year-old Peyton, "hoping he will betake himself to the study of law." When Peyton Randolph died in 1775, his cousin, Thomas Jefferson, purchased his books at auction; they eventually became the nucleus of the Library of Congress. Peyton Randolph followed in his father's footsteps, studying law in London after attending the College of William and Mary. Known as the great mediator, he was unanimously elected president of 1774's First Continental Congress in Philadelphia, and though he believed in nonviolence and hoped the colonies could amicably settle their differences with England, he was a firm patriot.

The house (actually, two connected homes) dates to 1715. It is today restored to reflect the period around 1770. The house is open to the public for self-guided tours with period-costumed interpreters in selected rooms.

The Public Gaol 𝕲

As noted above, imprisonment was not the usual punishment for crime in Colonial times, but persons awaiting trial and runaway slaves sometimes spent months in the Public Gaol. In winter, the cells were bitterly cold; in summer, they were stifling. Beds were piles of straw; leg irons, shackles, and chains were used frequently; and the daily diet consisted of "salt beef damaged, and Indian meal." In its early days, the gaol doubled as a madhouse, and during the Revolution redcoats, spies, traitors, and deserters swelled its population.

The gaol opened in 1704. Debtors' cells were added in 1711 (though the imprisoning of debtors was virtually eliminated after a 1772 law made creditors responsible for their upkeep), and keeper's quarters were built in 1722. The thick-walled redbrick building served as the Williamsburg city jail through 1910. The building today is restored to its 1720s appearance.

The Public Hospital 𝕲

Opened in 1773, the "Public Hospital for Persons of Insane and Disordered Minds" was America's first mental asylum. From 1773 to about 1820, "treatment" involved solitary confinement and a grisly course of action designed to "encourage" patients to "choose" rational behavior (it was assumed back then that patients willfully chose a life of insanity). So-called therapeutic techniques included the use of drugs, submersion in cold water for extended periods, bleeding, blistering salves, and an array of restraining devices. On a self-guided tour, you'll see a 1773 cell, with a straw-filled mattress on the floor, ragged blanket, and manacles. The hospital also is the entry for Colonial Williamsburg's museums (see below).

Raleigh Tavern 𝕲𝕲

This most famous of Williamsburg taverns was named for Sir Walter Raleigh, who launched the "Lost Colony" that disappeared in North Carolina some 20 years before Jamestown was settled. After the Governor's Palace, it was the social and political hub of the town, especially during Publick Times. Regulars included George Washington and Thomas Jefferson, who met here in 1774 with Patrick Henry, Richard Henry Lee,

---

Tips Carriage Rides

A fun way to see the Historic Area is on horse-drawn carriage rides, which depart from a horse post in front of the magazine and guardhouse (see above). Check with the visitor center for schedules and prices.

(*Fun Fact* **Stocks & Bondage**

The punishments meted out in 18th-century Williamsburg included public ridicule. The convicted had their neck, arms, and legs bound in stocks and pillories. Passersby added to the ridicule by tossing rotten tomatoes at the convicts. Modern visitors are more likely to have a laugh; in fact, millions of us have had our photos taken with our heads and hands dangling from the stocks.

---

and Francis Lightfoot Lee to discuss revolution. Patrick Henry's troops gave their commander a farewell dinner here in 1776.

The original tavern was destroyed by fire in 1859. Reconstructed on the original site in 1932, its facilities include two dining rooms; the Apollo ballroom, scene of elegant soirees; a clubroom that could be rented for private meetings; and a bar where ale and hot rum punch were the favored drinks. In the tavern bakery, you can buy 18th-century confections like gingerbread and Shrewsbury cake as well as cider to wash them down.

Wetherburn's Tavern

Though less important than the Raleigh, Wetherburn's also played an important role in Colonial Williamsburg. George Washington occasionally favored the tavern with his patronage. And, like the Raleigh, it was mobbed during Publick Times and frequently served as a center of sedition and a rendezvous of Revolutionary patriots. The heart-of-yellow-pine floors are original, so you can actually walk in Washington's footsteps. Windows, trim, and weatherboarding are a mixture of old and new; and the outbuildings, except for the dairy, are reconstructions. **Tours** lasting 25 minutes are given throughout the day.

THE COLONIAL WILLIAMSBURG MUSEUMS 🐾🐾

From the central hallway of the Public Hospital (see above), an elevator descends underground to Colonial Williamsburg's two fine museums.

The 62,000-square-foot **DeWitt Wallace Decorative Arts Museum** houses some 10,000 objects representing the highest achievement of American and English artisans from the 1640s to 1800. You'll see period furnishings, ceramics, textiles, paintings, prints, silver, pewter, clocks, scientific instruments, mechanical devices, and weapons. Don't miss Charles Willson Peale's 1780 portrait of George Washington, which he patterned after the coronation portrait of George III of England, in the Masterworks Gallery.

Go through the Weldon Gallery on the upper level to the **Abby Aldrich Rockefeller Folk Art Museum** with more than 2,600 folk-art paintings, sculptures, and art objects. Mrs. Rockefeller was a pioneer in this branch of collecting in the 1920s and 1930s. Her collection includes household ornaments and useful wares (hand-stenciled bed covers, butter molds, pottery, utensils, painted furniture, boxes), mourning pictures (embroideries honoring departed relatives and national heroes), family and individual portraits, shop signs, carvings, whittled toys, calligraphic drawings, weavings, quilts, and paintings of scenes from daily life.

A cafe here offers light fare, beverages, and a limited luncheon menu.

SHOPS, CRAFTS & TRADE EXHIBITS

Numerous 18th-century crafts demonstrations occur throughout the Historic Area. Such goings-on were a facet of everyday life in the preindustrial era. Dozens of crafts are practiced by more than 100 master craftspeople. They're an extremely skilled group, many having served up to 7-year apprenticeships both here and abroad. The program is part of Williamsburg's efforts to present an accurate picture of Colonial society, portraying the average man and woman as well as more illustrious citizens.

You can see a cabinetmaker, a wig maker, a silversmith, a printer and bookbinder, a maker of saddles and harnesses, a blacksmith, a shoemaker, a gunsmith, a milliner, a wheelwright, and house-wrights—all carrying on, and explaining, their trades in the 18th-century fashion.

ESPECIALLY FOR KIDS

In addition to Busch Gardens Europe and Water Country USA (see below), families can enjoy many hands-on activities in the Historic Area. A fun activity is at the **Governor's Palace,** where the dancing master gives lessons. During the summer kids can "enlist" in the militia and practice marching and drilling at the **Magazine and Guardhouse** (I still have a snapshot of myself holding a flintlock when I was a boy). If they get unruly, you can lock them in the stocks in front of the **Courthouse.** Inquire at the visitor center for special themed tours in areas of your children's specific interests.

THE THEME PARKS

Busch Gardens Europe *(Kids)*   At some point you may need a break from early American history, especially if you have kids in tow, so head over to Busch Gardens Europe, a 360-acre family entertainment park. Here you can get a peek at European history, albeit fanciful, in authentically detailed 17th-century hamlets from England, Ireland, Scotland, France, Germany, and Italy. Little mental effort is required to enjoy the villages, shows, festivities, and more than 50 rides, including the world-class roller coasters Apollo's Chariot and Alpengeist.

The usual starting place is Elizabethan **England,** where you can watch "Pirates," a 3-D movie with sound effects. From there, you proceed to **Scotland,** home of the famous Anheuser-Busch Clydesdale horses and the serpentine Loch Ness Monster, a terrifying roller coaster with two interlocking 360-degree loops and a 130-foot drop. Back on ground, proceed to **Ireland,** where you can go to Budweiser beer school and see animals at Jack Hanna's Wild Reserve.

Next comes **France,** where you and the kids can lose whatever cookies you have left on the Griffin Dive Coaster. The Royal Theatre is the venue for the park's nighttime entertainment and special events. In an odd juxtaposition, New France is home to Trappers Smokehouse, a Southern-style barbecue joint. Now it's on to **Germany,** where Land of the Dragons lets the kids explore a three-story treehouse and ride a flume and a dragon-themed Ferris wheel. Both you and kids can drop your hearts on the Alpengeist inverted roller coaster. Dancers and an oompah band entertain in Das Festhaus, a 2,000-seat festival hall where Oktoberfest never ends. It's the best place to take a break, cool off, and have a cold drink.

Tips Coin of the Realm

Rather than have your children walking around with real loot, you can purchase "Colonial Currency" at the Colonial Williamsburg Visitor Center. The scrip looks like 18th-century money and can only be spent at Historic Area shops and restaurants.

From Germany, a 300-foot bridge crosses the "Rhine River" to **Italy,** where the water ride Escape from Pompeii will whisk you to the smoldering ruins of the ancient Italian city destroyed by a volcano, and Roman Rapids will speed you to a splash in front of the ruins. Also here is Apollo's Chariot, a "hypercoaster" with nine vertical drops of up to 210 feet. Tamer rides pay tribute to Leonardo da Vinci's inventions.

During October, the park switches to a "Howl-O-Scream" theme after 6pm on weekends, with bloodcurdling screams splitting the artificial fog, which fills the night air. It's a fun time for young ghouls to be out and about.

1 Busch Gardens Blvd. (3 miles east of Williamsburg on U.S. 60). © 800/343-9746. www.buschgardens.com. Admission and hours vary, so call ahead, check website, or get brochure at visitor centers. Admission about $55 adults, $48 children 3–6, free for children 2 and younger for unlimited rides, shows, and attractions. Mid-May to Labor Day daily; Mar–May and Sept–Oct Fri–Sun. Closed Nov to late Mar.

Presidents Park *(Overrated)*   This outdoor facility across Va. 199 from Water Country USA boasts 20-foot-high busts of all 43 U.S. presidents—which caused one wag to describe it as "Mt. Rushmore East." Standing as they do in the middle of a garden, they also remind me a bit of those mysterious stone statues on Easter Island. They're the result of 5 year's work by sculptor David Adicks. Self-guided tours explain each president's accomplishments, complete with music from his day. It's a quick refresher course in American history, but I don't think it's interesting enough to keep children's attention, especially after they've visited the Historic Area.

211 Water Country Pkwy. (off Va. 199). © 800/588-4327 or 757/259-1121. www.presidentspark.org. Admission $12 adults, $12 seniors, $9 children 4–17. Apr–Aug daily 9am–8pm; Sept–Mar daily 9am–5pm.

Water Country USA *(Kids)*   Virginia's largest water-oriented amusement park features exciting water slides, rides, and entertainment set to a 1950s and 1960s surf theme. The largest ride—Big Daddy Falls—takes the entire family on a colossal river-rafting adventure. Or, you can twist and turn on giant inner tubes through flumes, tunnels, water "explosions," and down a waterfall to "splashdown." And there's much more, all of it wet and sometimes wild. It's a perfect place to chill out after a hot summer's day in the Historic Area.

176 Water Country USA Pkwy. (off Va. 199, north of Exit 242 off I-64). © 800/343-7946. www.watercountryusa. com. Admission and hours vary, so call ahead, check website, or get brochure at visitor centers. Admission about $39 adults, $32 children 3–6, free for children 2 and younger. Mid-May to late May Fri–Sun; late May to Labor Day daily. Closed day after Labor Day to mid-May. Take Va. 199 north of I-64 and follow signs.

OUTDOOR ACTIVITIES

BICYCLING   Not only is a bike the easiest way to get around the Historic Area, the 23-mile-long **Colonial Parkway** between Jamestown and Yorktown is one of Virginia's most scenic bike routes. There is no dedicated bike path, but vehicular traffic usually is light enough that you'll have the road virtually to yourself. You'll pedal along the banks of the James and York rivers (where there are picnic areas) and through a tunnel under Colonial Williamsburg. The 7 miles between Williamsburg and Jamestown are flat, but you'll have more car traffic to contend with than on the rolling 13-mile journey to Yorktown. Rentals are available at the Woodlands Hotel & Suites (p. 262).

GOLF   The Williamsburg area is *the* place to play golf in Virginia—if you can afford it, since a round here can cost $100 and up during the prime summer months. It all started in 1947 with the noted Golden Horseshoe course at the **Williamsburg Inn** (© 757/229-1000), which has two additional 18-holers to play. On the James River, **Kingsmill Resort** (© 800/832-5665 or 757/253-3998) has three top-flight 18-hole courses of its own, including the world-famous River Course, home of the LPGA Michelob Ultra Open in May. See "Where to Stay," below, for more about the Williamsburg Inn and Kingsmill Resort.

Ford's Colony (© **800/334-6033** or 757/258-4130; www.fordscolony.com) has two Dan Maples–designed courses, the challenging Blue-Gold (12 of 18 holes bordered by water) and the more forgiving White-Red. Another Maples-designed course is in the works. Golf carts here have satellite global positioning equipment, so you know exactly how long you have to hit your next shot. **Williamsburg National Golf Club** (© **800/826-5732** or 757/258-9642; www.wngc.com) has Virginia's only Jack Nicklaus–designed course, which *Golf Digest* magazine considers one of the state's top 10 links.

Royal New Kent Golf Club (© **888/253-4363** or 804/966-7023) has "a succession of you've-never-seen-this-before holes," according to *Golf Digest*. Its sister course at **Stonehouse Golf Club** (© **888/253-4363** or 757/566-1138) is more like a mountain course, with great vistas to please your eyes and deep bunkers to test your skills. Also pleasing to the eye, **Kiskiack Golf Club** (© **800/989-4728** or 757/566-2200) has two lakes nestled among its rolling hills.

Call the courses for current greens fees, directions, and tee times.

HORSEBACK RIDING   One- and 3-hour rail rides are available at **Stonehouse Stables** (© **757/566-9633**; www.stonehousestables.com) in Toano, off U.S. 60 west of Williamsburg. Call for prices and reservations, which are required.

SHOPPING
IN THE HISTORIC AREA

Duke of Gloucester Street is the center for 18th-century wares created by craftspeople plying the trades of our forefathers. The goods include hand-wrought silver jewelry from the Sign of the Golden Ball, hats from the Mary Dickenson shop, pomanders to ward off the plague from McKenzie's Apothecary, hand-woven linens from Prentis Store, books bound in leather and hand-printed newspapers from the post office, gingerbread cakes from the Raleigh Tavern Bake Shop, and everything from foods to fishhooks at Greenhow and Tarpley's, a general store. In fine weather, check out the outdoor market next to the Magazine.

Not to be missed is the **Craft House,** on Duke of Gloucester Street at Henry Street in Merchants Square. Run by the Colonial Williamsburg Foundation, it features exquisite works by master craftspeople and authentic reproductions of Colonial furnishings. There are also reproduction china, toys, games, maps, books, prints, and souvenirs aplenty.

Other "shoppes" in **Merchants Square** offer a wide range of merchandise: antiques, antiquarian books and prints, 18th-century-style floral arrangements, candy, toys, handcrafted pewter and silver items, needlework supplies, country quilts, Oriental rugs, and everything Virginian, including hams and peanuts. It's not all of the "ye olde" variety, however, for national chains such as Chico's, Williams-Sonoma, and Barnes & Noble (disguised as the William and Mary Bookstore) are here, too. Merchants Square has free 2-hour parking for its customers.

ON RICHMOND ROAD

Shopping in the Historic Area is fun, but the biggest draws are along Richmond Road (U.S. 60) between Williamsburg and Lightfoot, an area 5 to 7 miles west of the Historic Area. If you like outlet shopping, Richmond Road is for you.

Most of the action is at **Prime Outlets Williamsburg** 🕊🕊, between Airport and Lightfoot roads (℗ **877/466-8853** or 757/565-0702; www.primeoutlets.com). The largest and best outlet mall here, it eclipses its competition by a mile, which is about how far you will walk from one side to the other. I always drive through it first and spot my favorite shops before hunting down a parking space. You'll find an ever-growing array of shops including Bass, Bose, Brooks Brothers, Coach Leather, Crabtree & Evelyn, Eddie Bauer, Etienne Aigner, Harvé Bernard, J. Crew, Jones New York, Jos. A. Bank, L'eggs/Hanes/Bali, Maidenform, Mikasa, Naturalizer, Nike, Reebok/Rockport, Royal Doulton, Seiko, Van Heusen, and Waterford Wedgwood. They are open Monday through Saturday 10am to 9pm, Sunday 10am to 7pm.

Before getting there you'll pass **Patriot Plaza Premium Outlets** (℗ **757/258-0767**), between Ironbound and Airport roads. It's a small, upmarket mall with Orvis, WestPoint Stevens, and Plow & Hearth. Shops here are open Monday through Saturday 10am to 9pm, Sunday 10am to 6pm.

Among the major stores in residence at **The Williamsburg Outlet Mall** (℗ **888/746-7333** or 757/565-3378), at the intersection of U.S. 60 and Lightfoot Road (C.R. 646), are Bass, Bon Worth, Dockers, Dress Barn, Farberware, L'eggs, and Big Dogs. It's enclosed in an air-conditioned mall, a saving grace on sweltering summer days. It's open Monday through Saturday 10am to 9pm, Sunday 10am to 6pm.

Across the highway you can browse for collectibles and perhaps find a priceless piece of antiquity at the **Williamsburg Antique Mall,** 500 Lightfoot Rd. (℗ **757/565-3422;** www.antiqueswilliamsburg.com), with 45,000 square feet of dealer space. It's open Monday through Saturday 10am to 6pm, Sunday noon to 5pm.

Farther west is the famous **Williamsburg Pottery Factory** (℗ **757/564-3326;** www.williamsburgpottery.com), a 200-acre shopping complex with over 31 tin buildings selling an eclectic collection of merchandise from all over the world. Shops sell Christmas decorations, garden furnishings, lamps, art prints, dried and silk flowers, luggage, linens, baskets, hardware, glassware, cookware, candles, wine, toys, crafts, clothing, food, jewelry, plants (there's a greenhouse and nursery)—even pottery. There's plenty of quality and plenty of kitsch. It even has its own **Pottery Factory Outlets,** but do your major discount shopping at Prime Outlets. Summer hours are Monday through Friday 9am to 7pm, Sunday 9am to 6:30pm; it's open daily 9am to 5pm the rest of the year.

Continue west 1½ miles on U.S. 60, and you'll come to the **Williamsburg Doll Factory** (℗ **757/564-9703;** www.dollfactory.com), with limited-edition porcelain collector's dolls. You can observe the doll-making process and buy parts to make your own. Other items available are stuffed animals, dollhouses and miniatures, clowns, and books on dolls. It's open Monday through Saturday 9am to 5pm, Sunday 10am to 5pm.

ON THE WINE TRAIL

In 1623, the Jamestown settlers were required to plant "20 vines for every male in the family above the age of 20." By doing so, it was thought, the fledgling colony would develop a profitable wine industry. As it turned out, the profitable industry was tobacco, not grapes, and winemaking never took off.

Until the 1980s, that is, when the **Williamsburg Winery,** 5800 Wessex Hundred (℗ **757/229-0999;** www.williamsburgwinery.com), Virginia's first modern vineyard, proved that good grapes could be grown on the Peninsula. *Wine Spectator* magazine's critics have twice cited its vintages for excellence. Its Governor's White is the most

(*Value* **Just for Guests**

There are advantages to staying at one of the Colonial Williamsburg Foundation's hotels. For example, you can purchase discounted Colonial Williamsburg admission tickets valid for the length of your stay (recently $29 adults, $15 children 6–17). You also get breaks on other fees and can use your room keys to charge Historic Area expenses to your hotel bill.

Like most hotels these days, room rates at the foundation's accommodations vary widely depending on the season and how many guests may be booked on a given night. Try to reserve as far in advance as possible for the busy summer season and for spring and fall weekends. You might get a bargain during other times, especially if business is slow. You also can make walk-in reservations at the Colonial Williamsburg Visitor Center—at discounted rates if the hotels have rooms to spare (don't expect to get a deal on weekends and holidays). Also be sure to ask about holiday, golf, family, and other package deals.

---

widely purchased of Virginia's wine, although you'll find the John Adlum blended chardonnay much better. Tastings and 45-minute tours cost $8 per person.

Time your visit to have a bite of lunch along with your Two Shilling Red in the winery's **Gabriel Archer Tavern.** Freshly baked French bread accompanies interesting salads and sandwiches (turkey with cranberry chutney presents a terrific combination of flavors). It's reasonably priced, too, with lunch items running $7 to $12, dinner main courses $10 to $20.

The winery is open Monday through Saturday 10am to 5pm, Sunday 11am to 5pm (Apr–Oct daily to 6pm). The tavern serves lunch Monday to Friday, dinner Thursday through Monday. From the Historic Area, take Henry Street (Va. 132) south, turn right on Va. 199, left on Brookwood Drive, and another left on Lake Powell Road to the winery.

WHERE TO STAY
COLONIAL WILLIAMSBURG FOUNDATION HOTELS

The Colonial Williamsburg Foundation operates four hotels in all price categories: Williamsburg Inn (very expensive), Williamsburg Lodge (expensive), Woodlands Hotel & Suites (moderate), and the Governors Inn (inexpensive), plus a collection of tavern rooms and houses known as the Colonial Houses. Guests at all except the Governors Inn can use most of the sports and dining facilities at the Williamsburg Inn and Williamsburg Lodge, including Colonial Williamsburg's full-service spa.

For advance reservations, call the **visitor center reservations service** (© 800/447-8679; www.colonialwilliamsburg.com). You also can make walk-in reservations at the Colonial Williamsburg Visitor Center.

Governors Inn   Least expensive of the foundation's hotels, the Governors Inn is a two- and three-story, 1960s-vintage brick motel, most of whose rooms open to outdoor walkways. Natural wood furniture brightens the standard rooms, and Williamsburg posters on the walls remind you where you are. There's an outdoor pool for cooling off. It's on the northwestern edge of the Historic Area near the Transportation Center, which means that trains come by during the night. *Note:* Pets are no longer accepted.

506 Henry St. (Va. 132), at Lafayette St., Williamsburg, VA 23185. © 800/447-8679 or 757/229-1000. Fax 757/220-7480. www.colonialwilliamsburg.com. 200 units. $49–$109 double. Rates include continental breakfast. AE, DC, DISC, MC, V. **Amenities:** Outdoor pool; access to nearby health club; babysitting; laundry service. *In room:* A/C, TV, iron.

Williamsburg Inn *ϐϐϐ*   One of the nation's most distinguished hotels, this rambling white-brick Regency-style inn has played host to heads of state from 17 countries including Queen Elizabeth II (both in 1957 for Jamestown's 350th anniversary and in 2007 for the 400th); U.S. presidents Truman, Eisenhower, Nixon, Ford, Reagan, and Clinton; and lesser lights such as Shirley Temple. With giant floor-to-ceiling windows overlooking the renowned Golden Horseshoe golf course, the **Regency Dining Room** features classic American cuisine (coats and ties are still required after 6pm). There are better restaurants here now, but the champagne Sunday brunch is worth a go (reservations are required). All of the spacious accommodations (suites range up to 600 sq. ft.) have lavish marble bathrooms with double hand basins and separate tubs and showers. All are exquisitely furnished with reproductions, books, and photos of famous prior guests. Rooms in a modern building called **Providence Hall,** adjacent to the inn, are furnished in a contemporary blend of 18th-century and Oriental styles, with balconies or patios overlooking tennis courts and a beautiful wooded area. The inn's fitness center is in Providence Hall, whose guests enjoy the same privileges at those in the main inn. This is also a great golf resort, with three top-flight courses to play, including the noted Golden Horseshoe (see "Outdoor Activities," above). Colonial Williamsburg's full-service spa is between here and the Williamsburg Lodge (below).

136 Francis St., Williamsburg, VA 23187. © 800/447-8679 or 757/229-1000. Fax 757/220-7096. www.colonial williamsburg.com. 62 units. Main inn $319–$579 double, $439–$799 suite; Providence Hall $300–$359 double. AE, DC, DISC, MC, V. **Amenities:** Restaurant; bar; outdoor pool; 3 golf courses; 8 tennis courts; health club; spa; bike rentals; children's programs; concierge; business center; room service; babysitting; laundry service. *In room:* A/C, TV, Wi-Fi, fridge, iron, safe.

Williamsburg Lodge *ϐϐ*   Across the street from the Williamsburg Inn, the foundation's second-best hotel recently underwent a massive renovation that restored most of it to its original 1930s appearance, albeit with modern conveniences. The original structures were gutted, and Colonial Williamsburg's state-of-the-art conference center was added. Only the existing Tazewell Wing, a 1970s-vintage structure whose rooms have balconies facing landscaped courtyards, escaped serious surgery. The other more luxurious rooms are in five Colonial-style "Guest Houses" linked to the main building by covered brick walkways. The new units are notable for their Colonial Williamsburg–designed furniture and their retro 1930s bathrooms. Guests here share all of the Williamsburg Inn's facilities, including the luxurious spa across the street. Large suites occupy the second floor of the main building, which houses a restaurant and comfy bar.

310 S. England St., Williamsburg, VA 23185. © 800/447-8679 or 757/229-1000. Fax 757/229-7685. www.colonial williamsburg.com. 323 units. $129–$239 double; $249–$359 suite. AE, DC, DISC, MC, V. **Amenities:** 2 restaurants; bar; 2 outdoor pools; 8 tennis courts; health club; spa; bike rentals; children's programs; game room; concierge; business center; room service; babysitting; laundry service; coin-op washers and dryers. *In room:* A/C, TV, Wi-Fi, stocked fridge, coffeemaker, iron, safe.

Woodlands Hotel & Suites *ϐ* *Kids*   Located beside the visitor center, this is the foundation's third-best hotel. A separate building with a peaked roof and skylights holds the lodgelike lobby, where guests are treated to continental breakfast in a room with a fireplace. Interior corridors lead to the guest quarters in a U-shaped building around a courtyard. The more expensive suites have separate living and sleeping rooms divided by the bathroom and a wet bar with coffeemaker, fridge, and microwave oven (you won't have a fridge or microwave in the moderately spacious rooms). All units have Colonial-style pine furniture and photos of the Historic Area on their walls. The Huzzah! family restaurant (think Applebee's) is on the premises. There's plenty to keep kids occupied around the complex. Couple that with the pullout sofa beds in the suites, and it's a good choice for families of moderate means.

105 Visitors Center Dr. (P.O. Box 1776), Williamsburg, VA 23187. ℂ 800/447-8679 or 757/229-1000. Fax 757/229-7079. www.colonialwilliamsburg.com. 300 units. $69–$159 double; $119–$209 suite. Rates include continental breakfast. AE, DC, DISC, MC, V. **Amenities:** Restaurant; bar; outdoor pool; access to nearby health club; bike rentals; children's programs; concierge; babysitting; coin-op washers and dryers. *In room:* A/C, TV, Wi-Fi, fridge (suites only), coffeemaker (most units), iron.

COLONIAL HOUSES 🐾🐾

My favorite way to experience Colonial Williamsburg up close and personal is to stay in one of the foundation's **Colonial Houses.** In fact, they are the only way to actually stay in the Historic Area mere steps from the main attractions. Scattered throughout the Historic Area, the Colonial Houses are former laundries, workshops, small homes, and stand-alone kitchens that have been converted into one- and two-bedroom bungalows. Others are rooms in taverns, some of which have as many as 16 units. Some rooms are tiny; tell the reservation clerk precisely what size room and what bed configuration you want. For example, I have stayed in the Robert Carter Kitchen, a two-story converted cookhouse just off the Palace Green. It has a downstairs living room and Pullman kitchen, and a winding staircase leads to a bedroom and bathroom. The sloping upstairs ceiling under a dormer roof was head-knockingly low on the sides.

Tastefully furnished with 18th-century antiques and reproductions, all the houses are variously equipped with kitchens, living rooms, and fireplaces—and in some cases, sizable gardens. They all have air-conditioning, TVs, phones with dial-up dataports, and coffeemakers. The Williamsburg Inn, which manages the houses, provides room service, and guests here can use the facilities there. Each house has its own parking space. Tavern rooms range from $159 to $269, while houses go for $199 to $459 per night. Reserve through the visitor center's reservations service (ℂ **800/447-8679;** www.colonialwilliamsburg.com).

OTHER HOTELS & MOTELS

I have room in these pages to mention but a few of this area's more than 80 chain hotels and motels. You can book rooms, buy tickets, and search for money-saving package deals on **www.visitwilliamsburg.com,** operated jointly by the Greater Williamsburg Chamber & Tourism Alliance and the Williamsburg Hotel and Motel Association (see "Visitor Information" under "Essentials," above). Or you can call the association's reservations service at ℂ **800/446-9244.**

The majority of hotels and motels are west of the Historic Area on Richmond and Bypass roads. None of them is within walking distance of the Historic Area, but you can take the local buses (see "Orientation & Getting Around," earlier in this chapter).

You can walk to the Historic Area from the **Best Western Patrick Henry Inn,** at York and Page streets (ℂ **800/446-9228** or 757/229-9540), and the nearby **Four Points Sheraton Hotel,** 351 York St. (ℂ **800/962-4743** or 757/229-1400), both on the eastern edge of the area. They also are within an easy drive or short bus ride to Busch Gardens.

Closest to Busch Gardens are the **Marriott Williamsburg,** 50 Kingsmill Rd. (ℂ **800/442-3654** or 757/220-1500), the **Courtyard by Marriott,** 470 McLaws

Circle (© **800/321-2211** or 757/221-0700), and the **Quality Inn at Kingsmill** (© **877/424-6423** or 757/220-1100). All are in an office park off U.S. 60 East at the entry to the Kingsmill complex.

Sitting on U.S. 60 between the Historic Area and Busch Gardens, the **Crowne Plaza Williamsburg at Fort Magruder,** 6545 Pocahontas Trail (© **800/333-3333** or 757/220-2250), draws lots of conventions and meetings but is also a good choice for families with children.

Great Wolf Lodge 𝄞 *Kids*   About 7 miles west of the Historic Area, near the intersection of I-64 and Va. 199, this theme hotel built of logs to resemble a rustic Rocky Mountain lodge is geared to families with children. A whimsical theme prevails (the two cafeteria-style restaurants are named Bear Claw Cafe and Camp Critter Bar & Grille), but despite the rusticity, the star of the show is a monstrous indoor water park featuring a plethora of pools and water slides. You may have to pry your kids away from this aqua wonderland to see the Historic Area, but you won't need to take them to Water Country USA if you stay here. On the other hand, you can spend your leisure adult hours being pampered in the full-service spa. While a few guest rooms have hot tubs and fireplaces geared to grownups, most carry on the family theme, with log cabin–like areas set aside for bunk beds (the kids get their own flatscreen TVs). A few larger units have kitchens. Only the hotel's guests can use the water park, whose admission is included in the room rates—thus explaining why they appear so expensive.

549 E. Rochambeau Dr., Williamsburg, VA 23188. © **800/551-9653** or 757/229-9700. Fax 757/227-9780. www. greatwolflodge.com. 301 units. $139–$419 double. AE, DC, DISC, MC, V. **Amenities:** 3 restaurants (regional, pizza); 2 bars; indoor and outdoor pools; health club; spa; children's programs; game room; activities desk; business center; room service; massage; babysitting; laundry service; coin-op washers and dryers. *In room:* A/C, TV, high-speed Internet, fridge, coffeemaker, iron, safe.

Quarterpath Inn *Value*   Built in the 1960s and owned and operated by the same family since 1982, this clean, well-maintained motel is the best inexpensive property in the area. On the eastern side of town, you can walk to the Historic Area, and Busch Gardens is 2 miles away. Its rooms are in two-story buildings facing a parking lot, across which is an outdoor swimming pool. The relatively spacious rooms have king-size beds or two doubles plus tub/shower combination bathrooms. Four of the king-size-bed rooms have whirlpool tubs. Coffee is available in the lobby.

620 York St. (U.S. 60 E.), Williamsburg, VA 23185. © **800/446-9222** or 757/220-0960. Fax 757/220-1531. www.quarter pathinn.com. 130 units. $45–$99 double. Packages available. AE, MC, V. **Amenities:** Outdoor pool. *In room:* A/C, TV.

Williamsburg Hospitality House   On Richmond Road about a half-mile west of the Historic Area and opposite the College of William and Mary's football stadium, this four-story brick hotel is as convenient to the major sights as any large nonfoundation, nonchain hotel. It's built around a central courtyard with flowering trees, plants, and umbrella tables. Spacious guest rooms and public areas are appointed with a gracious blend of 18th-century reproductions. You can open the windows in some units, thus letting in fresh air. Meetings rather than families make up the bulk of the business here, but couples will fit right in.

415 Richmond Rd., Williamsburg, VA 23185. © **800/932-9192** or 757/229-4020. Fax 757/220-1560. www.williamsburg hosphouse.com. 295 units. $99–$200 double; $275–$475 suite. AE, DC, DISC, MC, V. **Amenities:** 2 restaurants; bar; outdoor pool; fitness room; game room; concierge; room service. *In room:* A/C, TV, Wi-Fi, coffeemaker, iron.

BED & BREAKFASTS

Williamsburg has more than 20 B&Bs, including **Williamsburg Sampler,** 922 Jamestown Rd., Williamsburg, VA 23185 (© **800/722-1169** or 757/253-0399; www.williamsburgsampler.com), a 1976-vintage replica of an 18th-century plantation manse. For more choices, go to **www.bandbwilliamsburg.com,** official site of the Williamsburg Bed & Breakfast Network (no phone). You can book online.

The Fife & Drum Inn ☆☆ Finds   Occupying upstairs quarters in one of the Merchants Square buildings, this relaxed and interesting charmer is the only privately owned inn in the Historic Area. "Colonial Williamsburg is your front yard," say owners Billy and Sharon Scruggs. Their guests gather under the cathedral ceiling of the common room complete with fireplace, big TV with DVD player, and a small library of books about Williamsburg. Sharon and Billy, who grew up here, put out a full breakfast every morning, including Virginia country ham biscuits. A sky-lit hallway with faux-brick floor and clapboard siding (you will swear it's a street) leads to the seven medium-size rooms and two suites, some of which have dormer windows. The suites open to a narrow porch out back. Collages of old Williamsburg postcards hanging on the walls overlook an eclectic mix of furniture with whimsical features such as birdhouses hiding a few of the TVs. The Conservancy Room is the most romantic, with a canopied double bed and a claw-foot bathtub. The inn does not have an elevator, but you can opt for a street-level Colonial cottage around the corner and avoid the 17 steps in the main building. The cottage can sleep up to six.

441 Prince George St., Williamsburg, VA 23185. © 888/838-1783 or 757/345-1776. Fax 757/345-3433. www.fife anddruminn.com. 9 units. $165–$190 double; $285–$295 cottage. Rates include full breakfast. AE, DISC, MC, V. Free parking. *In room:* A/C, TV, Wi-Fi, iron.

Liberty Rose ☆☆   Williamsburg's most romantic B&B, Brad and Sandra Hirz's 1920s two-story white-clapboard home enjoys a premier location on a wooded hilltop 1¼ miles from the Historic Area. An overall feeling of graciousness makes it a refuge from the rigors of sightseeing. Throughout you'll find Victorian, French- and English-country, and 18th-century antiques and reproductions, as well as fresh roses in every room. The elegant parlor, complete with grand piano that guests may play, has a working fireplace and comfortable chairs for relaxing. The accommodations are luxurious, each distinctively decorated. Bathrobes and a bowl of chocolates are de rigueur, as are telephones in each room. A full breakfast is served on the morning porch or in the courtyard. Children are not accepted here.

1022 Jamestown Rd., Williamsburg, VA 23185. © 800/545-1825 or 757/253-1260. www.libertyrose.com. 4 units. $185–$275 double. Rates include full breakfast. AE, MC, V. No children accepted. *In room:* A/C, TV, Wi-Fi.

A NEARBY RESORT WITH CHAMPIONSHIP GOLF

Kingsmill Resort & Spa ☆☆☆   Nestled in a peaceful setting on beautifully landscaped grounds beside the James River, this luxurious, country club–like resort is the centerpiece of a 2,900-acre residential development. It's one of Virginia's most complete resorts, offering three golf courses, a sports complex with 15 tennis courts, and a full-service spa. The highlight is the world-famous River Course, home of the LPGA Michelob Ultra Open golf championship. Accommodations consist of guest rooms and one-, two-, and three-bedroom suites in gray clapboard buildings overlooking the James River (most expensive), golf-course fairways, or tennis courts. The suites have complete kitchens and living rooms with fireplaces. Daily housekeeping service,

---

Tips **The Early Bird Gets the Reservation**

Advance reservations for dinner at Christiana Campbell's and King's Arms taverns are essential during the summer and on weekends during spring and fall. You can book tables up to 60 days in advance by dropping by or calling the visitor center (ℂ **800/447-8679** or **757/229-2141**). Lunch reservations are only accepted for major holidays.

---

including fresh linens, is included. Kingsmill's main dining room offers fine cuisine with a terrific view of the James, while the golf club's steakhouse overlooks the River Course. You can have a snack and sip an Anheuser-Busch cold one down at the marina. Guests can take a complimentary shuttle to Colonial Williamsburg and Busch Gardens Europe.

1010 Kingsmill Rd., Williamsburg, VA 23185. ℂ **800/832-5665** or 757/253-1703. Fax 757/253-3993. www.kingsmill. com. 425 units. $239–$299 double; $349–$699 suite. Golf, tennis, and spa packages available. AE, DC, DISC, MC, V. From I-64 take Exit 242 and follow Va. 199 west past U.S. 60 to sign for Kingsmill on the James. **Amenities:** 5 restaurants; 6 bars; indoor and outdoor pools; 3 golf courses; 15 tennis courts; health club; spa; Jacuzzi; sauna; bike rentals; children's programs; concierge; business center; room service; babysitting. *In room:* A/C, TV, Wi-Fi, kitchen (suites only), coffeemaker, iron.

WHERE TO DINE

Williamsburg abounds in restaurants catering to tourists. Most national chain, fast-food, and family restaurants have outlets on Richmond Road (U.S. 60) west of town.

COLONIAL WILLIAMSBURG FOUNDATION TAVERNS 🐾🐾

The Colonial Williamsburg Foundation runs four reconstructed 18th-century "ordinaries" or taverns. They aim at authenticity in fare, ambience, costuming of the staff, and entertainment by wandering balladeers. Dinner at one of the taverns is a necessary ingredient of the Williamsburg experience. Their seasonal hours and menus change often, so what I write here may be inaccurate by the time you arrive. Current offerings are posted out front and at the ticket booth on Henry Street at Duke of Gloucester Street, and are available at the visitor center, so you can see what's being served before making your reservations.

Christiana Campbell's Tavern One block behind the Capitol, Christiana Campbell's Tavern is "where all the best people resorted" around 1765. George Washington recorded in his diary that he dined here 10 times over a 22-month period. After the capital moved to Richmond, business declined and operations ceased. In its heyday, the tavern was famous for seafood, and today that is once again the specialty. Campbell's is an authentic reproduction with 18th-century furnishings, blazing fireplaces, and flutists and balladeers to entertain diners. Dinner here is a sit-down affair with reservations highly recommended. The menu leans toward fish and fowl, in contrast to the meat-oriented King's Arms Tavern (see below).

302B Waller St. ℂ **800/447-8679** or 757/229-2141. Reservations highly recommended. Main courses $24–$37. AE, DC, DISC, MC, V. Tues–Sat 5–9pm.

Josiah Chowning's Tavern In 1766, Josiah Chowning announced the opening of a tavern "where all who please to favour me with their custom may depend upon the best of entertainment for themselves, servants, and horses, and good pasturage." It's charming, with low-beamed ceilings, raw pine floors, and country-made furnishings.

There are two working fireplaces, and at night you dine by candlelight. These days it's once again operated like a boisterous 18th-century pub, with plenty of ale and light fare such as pit-cooked Virginia-style barbecue sandwiches, Brunswick stew, and country ham biscuits. One of the best things to do here after 5pm is to take in the 18th-century music, magic, and games.

Duke of Gloucester St. ℂ **800/447-8679** or 757/229-2141. Reservations not accepted. Most items $5–$14. AE, DC, DISC, MC, V. Mon–Sat 11am–10pm.

King's Arms Tavern　On the site of a 1772 establishment, King's Arms Tavern is a re-creation of the tavern and an adjoining home. Stables, a barbershop, laundry, smokehouse, kitchen, and other outbuildings have also been reconstructed. The original proprietress, Mrs. Jane Vobe, was famous for her fine cooking, and her establishment's proximity to the Capitol made it a natural meeting place during Publick Times. Today the 11 dining rooms (8 with fireplaces) are painted and furnished following early Virginia precedent. The Queen Anne and Chippendale pieces are typical appointments of this class of tavern, and the prints, maps, engravings, aquatints, and mezzotints lining the walls are genuine examples of period interior decorations. Balladeers wander the rooms during dinner. There's outdoor dining in the garden during warm weather. Like at Christiana Campbell's, reservations are required for dinner here.

409 E. Duke of Gloucester St. ℂ **800/447-8679** or 757/229-2141. Reservations required at dinner. Lunch $9.50–$13; main courses $24–$36. AE, DC, DISC, MC, V. Lunch daily 11:30am–2:30pm; dinner seating daily 5–9pm.

Shields Tavern _Value_　With 11 dining rooms and a garden under a trumpet-vine-covered arbor that seats 200, Shields is the largest of the Historic Area's tavern/restaurants. It's named for James Shields who, with his wife, Anne, and family, ran a much-frequented hostelry on this site in the mid-1700s. Based on a room-by-room inventory of Shields' personal effects, the tavern has been furnished with items similar to those used in the mid–18th century, and many rooms have working fireplaces. One side of the building operates as an 18th-century coffeehouse, where you can pop in for breakfast of scones and Danish. The other side proffers a modern bill of fare such as roast beef sandwiches and chicken salad wraps.

422 E. Duke of Gloucester St. ℂ **800/447-8679** or 757/229-2141. Reservations not accepted. Most items $4–$9. AE, DC, DISC, MC, V. Daily 8:30am–9pm.

RESTAURANTS IN MERCHANTS SQUARE

Berret's Seafood Restaurant & Tap House Grill ℱ SEAFOOD　A congenial, casual place, Berret's has a popular outdoor Tap House Grill, where you will find me quenching my thirst after schlepping around the Historic Area all day. It has heaters, so you can sit out here well into autumn. In the adjoining restaurant, canvas sailcloth shades, blue-trimmed china, and marine artifacts on the walls make an appropriate backdrop for the excellent seafood. Oysters or clams raw or steamed on the half shell do nicely as starters. For a main course, the crab cakes are pan-fried and served over a thin slice of Virginia ham—a pleasant combination of flavors. The Tap House serves sandwiches at night. There's a good selection of Virginia microbrews and wines by the glass.

199 S. Boundary St. (at Francis St.). ℂ **757/253-1847.** Reservations recommended for dinner. Sandwiches and salads (Tap House Grille only) $8.50–$14; main courses $25–$30. AE, DISC, MC, V. Restaurant daily 11:30am–3:30pm and 5:30–10pm; Tap House Grill daily 4–10pm.

Blue Talon Bistro ℱℱ _Value_ FRENCH/AMERICAN　"Serious comfort food" is the motto at this lively bistro, although much of the comfort food has a decidedly

---

(*Value* **Where to Eat Cheap**

Attracting both a town and gown crowd, **Aromas,** 431 Prince George St. ((C) **757/221-6676**), is both Williamsburg's favorite coffeehouse and one of its best choices for light, inexpensive meals. The barbecue sandwiches at **Retro's,** two doors away at 435 Prince George St. ((C) **757/235-8816**), are better than Pierce's (p. 269), and it serves tasty hot dogs, too.

French flair. The menu ranges from American-style rotisserie chicken and cedar-roasted salmon to French *choucroute*. You can also order a fat hamburger here anytime. With most main courses priced less than $20 and a glass of house wine at $4, the value here is as good as the food. Order-at-the-bar breakfast here is *très* French, with hot-out-of-the-oven croissants and other pastries.

420 Prince George St. (between Henry and Boundary sts.). (C) 757/476-2583. Reservations recommended. Burgers $9.50; main courses $17–$22. DISC, MC, V. Daily 8am–9pm.

The Cheese Shop *Value* DELI   This gourmet deli is the best place in Williamsburg for takeout salads, sandwiches, and other fixings. Head to the rear counter and place your order for ham, roast beef, turkey, chicken, and barbecue sandwiches on a choice of fresh bread. The cheese counter has a wide selection of domestic and imported brands plus fresh salads. You can eat your meal at wrought-iron umbrella tables out front. The marvelous Fat Canary adjoins (see below).

410 Duke of Gloucester St. (between Henry and Boundary sts.). (C) 757/220-0298. Most items $4.50–$6. AE, DISC, MC, V. Mon–Sat 10am–8pm; Sun 11am–6pm.

A Chef's Kitchen 🌟🌟🌟 *Finds* ECLECTIC   Veteran chef John Gonzales, who has authored two cookbooks and appeared on several TV shows, says he started this fascinating cooking school–cum–restaurant because he "felt sorry for the audiences on the Food Network" who never get to eat the meals they watch being prepared. Here you not only will watch this entertaining chef at work, you will enjoy the fruits of his labors over the course of a 3-hour evening. The restaurant is designed like a culinary classroom, with 25 seats at three tables arranged stadium-style so all can watch him at the kitchen up front. The one nightly seating begins at 6:30pm with champagne and hors d'oeuvres. Then John prepares and serves at least four courses, each paired with an inexpensive "great find" wine (the $10-a-bottle vintages are available in the gourmet store at the front of the building). The menu changes completely every few weeks but is announced in advance on the restaurant's website. The fixed price includes wine and the tip, making this a good value. Make your reservations as early as possible. John also teaches hands-on daytime classes.

501 Prince George St. (between Boundary and Armistead sts.). (C) 757/564-8500. www.achefskitchen.biz. Reservations required. Fixed-price menu $80 per person, including tip. DISC, MC, V. Wed–Sat 6:30pm seating.

Fat Canary 🌟🌟🌟 CREATIVE AMERICAN   This high-energy bistro is consistently Williamsburg's best restaurant. The sophisticated but relaxed dining room sports a long bar down one side—a favorite local watering hole—and an open kitchen that uses fresh local and other ingredients for its creative American fare. Both the full and more limited and less expensive menus are offered on the patio out front during warm weather. Reservations are not accepted at the outdoor tables, but it's worth the wait. Everything is excellent here. Served as a side dish, the house version of "hopping john" left me wishing for an entire plate of this tasty blend of black-eyed peas, shrimp, *tasso* ham, and rice. The restaurant's name comes from Colonial-era poet John Lyly's line, "Oh for a bowl of fat Canary, rich Palermo, sparkling sherry." By that he meant wines from the Canary Islands as well as Italy. Today's wine list is very good, with more than a dozen vintages available by the glass.

410 Duke of Gloucester St. (between Henry and Boundary sts.). (C) **757/229-3333.** Reservations recommended indoors, not accepted outdoors. Main courses $22–$25; outdoor light menu $15–$18. AE, DISC, MC, V. Daily 5–10pm.

Trellis Cafe, Restaurant & Grill AMERICAN   Executive chef Marcel Desaulniers has brought national recognition to this restaurant, whose decor evokes delightful establishments in California's wine country. He is best known for his *Death by Chocolate* dessert cookbook, whose namesake is the finest item offered here these days. Marcel changes the menu every season to take advantage of local produce, which his staff combines with the best in foods from different regions of the United States. The fixed-price dinner, which includes a salad or a bowl of soup, a main course, and ice cream or sorbet, is a money-saver, but I always upgrade the dessert to Marcel's sinful Death by Chocolate. If weather is fine, you can dine out on the brick terrace.

Duke of Gloucester St. (between Henry and Boundary sts.). (C) **757/229-8610.** Reservations recommended at dinner. Main courses $16–$32; fixed-price dinners $29. AE, DC, DISC, MC, V. Daily 11am–3pm and 5–9:30pm.

NEARBY COUNTRY-STYLE DINING

Old Chickahominy House ☞☞ TRADITIONAL SOUTHERN   One of the great places to sample traditional, down-home Virginia cooking, the Old Chickahominy House is a reconstructed 18th-century house with mantels from old Gloucester homes and wainscoting from Carter's Grove Plantation. Floors are bare oak, and walls, painted in traditional Colonial colors, are hung with gilt-framed 17th- and 18th-century oil paintings. Three adjoining rooms house an antiques/gift shop. The entire effect is cozy and charming. Before making my rounds, I always opt for the plantation breakfast of real Virginia ham with two eggs, biscuits, cured country bacon and sausage, grits, and coffee or tea. At lunch, Miss Melinda's special is a cup of Brunswick stew with Virginia ham on hot biscuits, fruit salad, homemade pie, and tea or coffee. Also check out the Shirley Pewter Shop next door.

1211 Jamestown Rd., at Va. 199. (C) **757/229-4689.** Reservations not accepted. Most items $4–$9. MC, V. Daily 8:30–10:15am and 11:30am–2:30pm. Closed 2 weeks in Jan, July 4th, Thanksgiving, and Dec 25.

Pierce's Pitt Bar-B-Que BARBECUE   Visible from I-64, this gaudy yellow-and-orange barbecue joint has been dishing up pulled pork, chicken, and smoked ribs since 1961, as the walls hung with old photos of the owners and their family and staff will attest. The pulled pork is better than the ribs here, but unlike the unadulterated version at King's Barbecue in Petersburg (p. 243), here it comes soaked in a smoky-flavored, tomato-based sauce. Order at the counter and take your meal (served in plastic containers) to a table inside or outdoors under cover. No alcoholic beverages are served here.

447 E. Rochambeau Dr., Lightfoot (beside I-64). (C) **757/565-2955.** Reservations not accepted. Sandwiches $3.50–$4.50; main courses $6–$19. MC, V. Daily 10am–9pm. From Historic Area go west on Richmond Rd. (U.S. 60), right on Airport Rd. (C.R. 645) 2 miles toward I-64, follow signs to restaurant on Rochambeau Dr., about 2 miles.

WILLIAMSBURG AFTER DARK

You should spend at least one evening taking in a little 18th-century nightlife in Colonial Williamsburg. The Colonial taverns have evening entertainment, but don't miss an **18th-Century Play** staged in and around the historic buildings.

Colonial Williamsburg also conducts nighttime tours and other activities in the Historic Area. Check the schedule in *This Week,* the weekly brochure. Copies are available at the visitor center (see "Exploring the Historic Area," earlier in this chapter).

Another fun way to spend a warm-weather evening is spooking around the Historic Area, either with one of Colonial Williamsburg's official tours or with the **Original Ghosts of Williamsburg Tours** ✦✦ (© **877/62-GHOST** or 757/565-4821; www. theghosttour.com), which entertainingly blends ghost stories and local folklore with historical fact. Children will enjoy them, too. The candlelight tours are based on L. B. Taylor's best-selling 1983 book, *The Ghosts of Williamsburg.* The tours cost $10 per person (free for kids younger than 6) and take place nightly March through December, Saturdays in January and February. Call for reservations, which are essential.

The **Kimball Theatre,** on Duke of Gloucester Street in Merchants Square (© **757/ 565-8588;** www.kimballtheatre.com), hosts concerts, special lectures by W&M professors, puppet shows, second-run movies, and other events. Call or drop by the theater to see what's going on. William and Mary drama department students refine their skills in the **William and Mary Theater** (© 757/221-2676; www.wm.edu). The college also has an active calendar of concerts and lectures. W&M's athletic teams participate in a full schedule of intercollegiate contests (© **757/221-3340;** www.tribe athletics.com).

For more ideas pick up a copy of *Williamsburg* magazine or check its website at www.williamsburgmag.com.

2 Jamestown: The First Colony ✦✦

9 miles SW of Williamsburg

The story of Jamestown, the first permanent English settlement in the New World, is documented here in a national park on the Jamestown Island site where they landed. Here you'll learn the exploits of Capt. John Smith, the colony's leader, rescued from execution by the American Indian princess Pocahontas; the arrival of the first African-American slaves; and how life was lived in 17th-century Virginia. Archaeologists have excavated more than 100 building frames, evidence of manufacturing ventures (pottery, winemaking, brick making, and glass blowing), wells, and roads. Opened prior to Jamestown's big 400th-anniversary bash in 2007, the fascinating Archaearium museum displays hundreds of thousands of artifacts of everyday life—tools, utensils, ceramic dishes, armor, keys, and the like—uncovered during the digs.

Next door at Jamestown Settlement, a state-run living-history museum complex, you can see re-creations of the three ships in which the settlers arrived in 1607, the colony they built, and a typical American Indian village of the time.

Allow at least half a day for your visit and consider packing a lunch. There is a cafe at Jamestown Settlement, but you may want to take advantage of the picnic areas at the National Park Service site.

GETTING THERE & GETTING AROUND   The scenic way here from Williamsburg is via the picturesque Colonial Parkway, or you can take Jamestown Road (Va. 31).

An alternative to driving from Williamsburg from March through October is the **Historic Triangle Shuttle** (see "Getting There & Getting Around," earlier in this chapter). Once you're here, the free **Jamestown Area Shuttle** (© 757/898-2410) runs continuously between Historic Jamestowne and Jamestown Settlement.

Fun Fact **A Shiny Hand**

The statue of Pocahontas standing beside the old church at Historic Jamestowne is green, well-weathered brass—except her outstretched right hand. Legend says you'll have good luck if you shake her hand, which hundreds of people do every day, thus keeping it perpetually bright and shiny.

Historic Jamestowne 𝒶𝒶𝒶   Now part of the Colonial National Historical Park and jointly administered by the National Park Service and the Association for the Preservation of Virginia Antiquities (APVA; www.apva.org), this is the site of the actual colony. It was an island then; now an isthmus separates it from the mainland. After entering the park, stop first at the reconstructed **Glasshouse,** where costumed interpreters make glass in the ancient way used by the colonists in 1608 during their first attempt to create an industry (it failed). Remains of the original glass furnaces are nearby. Then proceed to the visitor center, where a museum and a 15-minute film telling the story of Jamestown from its earliest days to 1699, when the capital of Virginia moved to Williamsburg, will get you oriented. Inquire at the reception desk about audiotape tours and ranger-led walking tours, costumed interpretive programs, and other programs offered during your visit.

Spend at least 30 minutes in the visitor center, which stands near the actual site of **"James Cittie,"** as the colonists called their new village. The center's exhibits and 18-minute film put Jamestown in perspective with the rest of the world in 1607 and explain how the colonist lived. A pathway leads from the center over a marsh to the actual settlement. The brick foundations outside aren't original, but they do stand on the actual locations of the 17th-century homes as determined by extensive and very much ongoing archaeological work. You're welcome to view the digging, and APVA archaeologists and volunteers will answer your questions. Most of what's left of James Cittie is now about 18 inches below ground, but the tower of one of the first brick churches in Virginia (1639) still stands. Behind the tower, **Memorial Church** is a 1907 re-creation built by the Colonial Dames of America on the site of the structure (note the glass panels along the sides of the floor, which show some of the original foundation). In 1619, the church housed the first legislative assembly in English-speaking North America. A wooden stockade fence stands above the triangular borders of the 1607 **James Fort,** part of which has eroded into the James River.

A short walk along the seawall past Confederate breastworks—built during the Civil War to protect this narrow part of the river—will take you to the fascinating **Archaearium,** which artfully displays the results of the archaeological digs, including the skeleton of one of the settlers and a resin cast reproduction of another belonging to a young man who apparently died of a musket shot to the right knee, giving rise to the theme of the interactive display: "Who Shot J. R.?"

A fascinating **5-mile loop drive** begins at the visitor center parking lot and winds through 1,500 wilderness acres of woodland and marsh that have been allowed to return to their natural state in order to approximate the landscape as 17th-century settlers found it. Illustrative markers interpret aspects of daily activities and industries of the colonists—tobacco growing, lumbering, silk and wine production, pottery making, farming, and so on.

Allow at least 2 hours for this special attraction.

Southern end of Colonial Pkwy., at Jamestown Rd. (Va. 31). *C* **757/898-2410** or 757/229-1773. www.nps.gov/colo. Admission $10 adults, free for children 15 and younger. Includes admission to Yorktown Battlefield, good for 7 days. American the Beautiful and National Park Service passports accepted. Main gate daily 8:30am–4:30pm; visitor center daily 9am–5pm. Closed Jan 1 and Dec 25.

Jamestown Settlement *Kids* Built in 1957 by the Commonwealth of Virginia to celebrate Jamestown's 350th anniversary, this living-history museum shows you what the settlers' three ships, their colony, and a typical Powhatan Indian village looked like, and costumed interpreters demonstrate how they lived back then.

The entrance building shows a 20-minute film, *1607: A Nation Takes Root,* about Jamestown and has museum galleries featuring artifacts, documents, decorative objects, dioramas, and graphics relating to the Jamestown period. Don't miss the exact reproduction of the deerskin-and-seashells cape worn by Powhatan, father of Pocahontas (the Ashmolean Museum in Oxford, England, has the original).

Leaving the museum complex, you'll come directly into the **Powhatan Indian Village,** representing the culture and technology of a highly organized chiefdom of 32 tribes that inhabited coastal Virginia in the early 17th century. There are several mat-covered lodges, which are furnished as dwellings, as well as a vegetable garden and a circle of carved ceremonial posts. Historical interpreters tend crop, tan animal hides, and make bone and stone tools and pottery. The exhibits are interactive, assigning such activities as having you use a shell to scrape the fur off deerskin. Children are more likely to enjoy a visit here than to Historic Jamestowne.

Triangular **James Fort** is a re-creation of the one constructed by the Jamestown colonists in the spring of 1607. Inside the wooden stockade are primitive wattle-and-daub structures with thatched roofs representing Jamestown's earliest buildings. Interpreters are engaged in activities typical of early-17th-century life, such as agriculture, military activities (including firing muskets), carpentry, blacksmithing, and meal preparation.

A short walk from James Fort are reproductions of the three **ships,** the *Susan Constant, Godspeed,* and *Discovery,* that transported the 104 colonists to Virginia. Boarding and exploring the ships will give you an appreciation of the hardships they endured even before they reached the hostile New World.

A guided 1½-hour tour is the best way to take all this in. They are given several times a day.

Jamestown Rd. (Va. 31), at James River. *C* **888/593-4682** or 757/253-4838. www.historyisfun.org. Admission $14 adults, $6.25 children 6–12, free for children 5 and younger. Combination ticket with Yorktown Victory Center $19 adults, $9.25 children 6–12, free for children 5 and younger. Daily 9am–5pm (to 6pm June 15–Aug 15). Closed Jan 1 and Dec 25.

3 Yorktown: Revolutionary Victory ★★★

14 miles NE of Williamsburg

Although the 13 American colonies declared their independence from England on July 4, 1776, their dream of freedom from King George III came to fruition here at Yorktown in October 1781, when Gen. George Washington won the last major battle of the American Revolution. "I have the Honor to inform Congress that a Reduction of the British Army under the Command of Lord Cornwallis is most happily effected," Washington wrote to the Continental Congress on October 19, 1781. Though sporadic fighting would continue for 2 years before a treaty was signed, the Revolutionary War, for all intents and purposes, was over.

Today the decisive battlefield is a national park, and the Commonwealth of Virginia has built the Yorktown Victory Center, an interpretive museum explaining the road to revolution, the war itself, and the building of a new nation afterward.

Predating the Revolution and overlooking the picturesque York River, the old town of Yorktown itself is worth a visit, especially its re-created a Colonial-era seaport village at **Yorktown Riverwalk Landing,** on Water Street almost beneath the Coleman Bridge, which carries U.S. 17 over the York River. Here you'll find shops, a restaurant, and a museum dedicated to the Chesapeake Bay's famous "watermen."

You'll need at least half a day to digest all this history. Plan to spend a morning or afternoon seeing the sights and having lunch.

ESSENTIALS

VISITOR INFORMATION   For advance information contact **York County Tourism and Events,** P.O. Box 523, Yorktown, VA 23690 (© **757/890-3300;** www. yorkcounty.gov/tourism).

GETTING THERE & GETTING AROUND   The easiest and most scenic way here from Williamsburg is via the picturesque Colonial Parkway. From Norfolk or Virginia Beach, take I-64 West to U.S. 17 North and follow the signs to Yorktown. Park free in the garage at the Yorktown Riverwalk Landing on Water Street.

A good alternative to driving here from Williamsburg during the summer is the **Historic Triangle Shuttle** (see "Getting There & Getting Around," earlier in this chapter). Once you're here, the free **Yorktown Trolley** makes nine stops along the waterfront and in the village from March 1 to October 31, every 20 to 25 minutes daily from 10am to 6pm Memorial Day through Labor Day weekends; weekends during April, May, September, and October.

HISTORY

Yorktown's history dates to 1691, when the General Assembly at Jamestown passed the Port Act creating a new town on the York River, which unlike the James River, has a shoal-free, deepwater channel to the Chesapeake Bay. Yorktown quickly became a principal mid-Atlantic port and a center of tobacco trade. By the time of the American Revolution, it was a thriving town with several thousand planters, innkeepers, seamen, merchants, craftsmen, indentured servants, and slaves. Water Street, paralleling the river, was lined with shops, inns, and loading docks.

THE VICTORY AT YORKTOWN   After a rather fruitless and exhausting march through the Carolinas, Cornwallis brought his army to Yorktown in hopes of being moved to New York by the British navy. Marching quickly from the north, George Washington's army of 17,600 American troops and their French allies laid siege to Yorktown on September 28, 1781. Meanwhile, a French fleet sailed up from the Caribbean and drove the British navy away from the Virginia Capes, thereby cutting off Cornwallis' escape route.

On October 9, the allies began bombarding the British positions. Washington personally fired the first American round. At 8pm on October 14, the French stormed Redoubt 9 while the Americans made short work of Redoubt 10.

Just 2 days later, a desperate Cornwallis tried to escape with his troops across the York River to Gloucester Point, but a violent storm scattered his boats. On October 17 at 10am, a British drummer appeared on the rampart and beat out a signal indicating a desire to discuss terms with the enemy. A cease-fire was called, and a British

---

(Tips Best Battlefield Strategies

You'll enjoy the 90-minute audio driving-tour tape or CD of the Yorktown bat-tlefield. Narrated by "British and American colonels" whose polite hostilities to each other are most amusing, the taped commentary further elucidates the battlefield sites. Listen to the introduction in the parking lot; it will tell you when to depart. Tape or not, drive the Battlefield Route first; then if time per-mits, the Encampment Route.

---

officer was led to American lines where he requested an armistice. On October 18, commissioners met at the house of Augustine Moore and worked out the terms of sur-render.

At 2pm on October 19, 1781, the French and Continental armies lined Surrender Road, each stretching for over a mile on either side. About 5,000 British soldiers and seamen, clad in new uniforms, marched out of Yorktown to a large field, where they laid down their weapons and battle flags. Gen. Charles O'Hara of the British Guards represented Cornwallis who, pleading illness, did not surrender in person.

THE TOP ATTRACTIONS

Yorktown Battlefield 𝕲𝕲𝕲   Today, most of Yorktown and the surrounding bat-tlefield areas are included in this 4,300-acre section of the Colonial National Histori-cal Park. You can drive around the key battle sites, which have interpretive markers, but begin at the visitor center, where the 16-minute documentary film *Siege at York-town* is shown on the hour and half-hour. Not to be missed among the museum dis-plays is Washington's actual sleeping and dining tent, now preserved in a hermetically sealed room (it's really cool to actually walk into his tent without entering the glass-enclosed room). There's also a replica (which you can board and explore) of the quar-terdeck of HMS *Charon;* additional objects recovered during excavations; exhibits about Cornwallis's surrender and the events leading up to it; and dioramas detailing the siege. Upstairs, an "on-the-scene" account of the Battle of Yorktown is given by a 13-year-old soldier in the Revolutionary army, his taped narrative accompanied by a sound-and-light show.

National Park Service Rangers are on hand to answer questions. They give free **tours** of the British inner defense line seasonally (call the visitor center for times).

To make it easy to follow what happened, the park is divided into two routes. You won't stay in your car the whole time; it's frequently necessary to park, get out, and walk to redoubts and earthworks. A lot of the drive is very scenic, winding through woods and fields abundant with bird life. The Encampment Route is especially beautiful.

On the 7-mile **Battlefield Route,** you'll see the **Grand French Battery,** where French soldiers manning cannons, mortars, and howitzers fired on British and Ger-man mercenary troops; the **Moore House,** where British and American representa-tives hammered out the surrender on October 18, 1781; and **Surrender Field,** where the British laid down their arms at the end of the siege.

Note that the Moore House usually is open daily 10am to 4:30pm during sum-mer, weekends 1 to 4pm in spring and autumn, but check with the visitor center to be sure. The 10-mile **Encampment Route** takes you to the sites of Washington's and Rochambeau's headquarters, the French cemetery and Artillery Park, and allied encampment sites.

North end of Colonial Pkwy. (C) **757/898-2410** or 757/898-3400. www.nps.gov/colo. Admission $10 adults, free for children 15 and younger. Includes admission to Yorktown Battlefield, good for 7 days. American the Beautiful and National Park Service passports accepted. Audiotape tours $3.95; CDs $4.95. National Park Service passports accepted. Battlefield daily 8:30am–dusk. Visitor center daily 9am–5pm (closed Dec 25).

Yorktown Victory Center 🐾   This state-operated multimedia museum offers an excellent orientation to Yorktown, and coming here first will prepare you for your battlefield tour. You'll start with an open-air timeline walkway known as the "Road to Revolution," which illustrates the relationship between the colonies and Great Britain beginning in 1750. Aspects of the American Revolution are explored in its gallery exhibits. "Witnesses to Revolution" focuses on ordinary individuals who recorded their observances of the war and its impact on their lives. The "Converging on Yorktown" gallery and *A Time of Revolution* film focus on the military campaign. "Yorktown's Sunken Fleet" uses artifacts recovered from British ships sunk during the siege of Yorktown to describe shipboard life. "The Legacy of Yorktown: Virginia Beckons" examines how people from many different cultures shaped a new American society.

Outdoors, costumed interpreters in the Continental Army encampment re-create the lives of men and women who took part in the American Revolution. There are presentations on weaponry, military drills and tactics, medicine, and cookery. Nearby, an 18th-century farm site demonstrates how "middling" farmers—no wealthy plantation owners here—lived and worked.

Colonial Pkwy., ½ mile west of Yorktown. (C) **888/593-4682** or 757/253-4838. www.historyisfun.org. Admission $9.25 adults, $5 children 6–12, free for children 5 and younger. Combination ticket with Jamestown Settlement $19 adults, $9.25 children 6–12, free for children 5 and younger. Daily 9am–5pm (to 6pm June 15–Aug 15). Closed Jan 1 and Dec 25.

TOURING THE TOWN

Though it is doubtful that Yorktown would have recovered from the destruction and waste that accompanied the Siege of 1781, it received the coup de grâce in the "Great Fire" of 1814 and declined steadily over the years, becoming a quiet rural village. Although it remains the seat of York County, it never regained its prominence as a seaport and has, like Williamsburg, changed so little that many of its picturesque old streets and buildings (whose walls escaped the fire) have survived intact to this day.

Self-guided or ranger-led walking tours of historic Yorktown—which includes some places of interest not related to the famed battle—are available at the Yorktown Battlefield visitor center (call for times; see listing above). From the visitor center, take the path to:

The Victory Monument   News of the allied victory at Yorktown reached Philadelphia on October 24, 1781. Five days later, Congress resolved "that the United States . . . will cause to be erected at York, in Virginia, a marble column, adorned with emblems of the alliance between the United States and his Most Christian Majesty; and inscribed with a succinct narrative of the surrender of Earl Cornwallis to his excellency General Washington, Commander in Chief of the combined forces of America and France."

So much for government intentions: The cornerstone of the symbolic 98-foot marble shaft with Lady Liberty atop was laid a century later to open the Yorktown Centennial Celebration. The podium is adorned with 13 female figures hand in hand in a solemn dance to denote the unity of the 13 colonies; beneath their feet is the inscription "One Country, One Constitution, One Destiny"—a moving post–Civil War sentiment.

Of Bug-Eyes & Skipjacks

On Water Street adjacent to the Yorktown Riverwalk Landing, the **Watermen's Museum** (② **757/887-2641**) displays a bug-eye, a skipjack, a dug-out canoe, and other working boats unique to the Chesapeake Bay, plus oyster harvesting tools and other equipment used by the region's famous "watermen" to earn their livings. Admission is $4 for adults, $1 for students, free for kids younger than 6. It's open April through November, Tuesday to Saturday 10am to 4pm, Sunday 1 to 5pm; weekends only in winter.

A footpath leads from the monument into town, where you can explore:

Cornwallis Cave According to legend, Cornwallis lived here in two tiny "rooms" during the final days of the siege when he hoped to cross the river and escape overland to New York. Various occupants of the cave—which may at one time have included the pirate Blackbeard—carved out the two rooms. Confederate soldiers later enlarged the shelter and added a roof. The cave is at the foot of Great Valley Road, right on the river.

From here you can follow Water Street along the river and Yorktown's white-sand beach (locals like to sunbathe and swim here) to **Yorktown Riverwalk Landing,** the town's waterfront dining-and-shopping complex.

The Dudley Digges House This 18th-century weather-board house on Main Street at Smith Street is the only wood-frame house to survive the siege. Owner Dudley Digges was a Revolutionary patriot who served with Patrick Henry, Benjamin Harrison, and Thomas Jefferson on the Committee of Correspondence. After the war, he was rector of the College of William and Mary. It's still a private residence, not open to the public.

The Nelson House Scottish merchant Thomas Nelson made three voyages between Great Britain and Virginia before deciding to settle in Yorktown in 1705. He became co-operator of a ferry, charter member of a trading company, builder of the Swan Tavern, and a large-scale planter. In 1729, he built this house, at Main and Nelson streets, which is considered one of the finest examples of Georgian architecture in Virginia. His grandson, Thomas Nelson, Jr., signed the Declaration of Independence, served as governor of Virginia during the war, and marched the 3,500-man state militia to Yorktown to help Washington win the victory. The Revolution ruined his health and fortune, however, and he died in 1789.

Though damaged (cannonballs remain embedded in the brickwork), the house survived the Battle of Yorktown, and the Nelson family continued to live in it until 1907. The National Park Service acquired the house in 1968 and restored it to its original appearance.

It's open daily 10am to 4:30pm in summer, daily 1 to 4pm the rest of the year.

The Sessions House Just across from the Nelson House, this is the oldest house in Yorktown, built in 1692 by Thomas Sessions. At least five U.S. presidents have visited the house, today a private residence.

The Custom House Dating to 1720, this brick building at the corner of Main and Read was originally the private storehouse of Richard Ambler, collector of ports. It became Gen. J. B. Magruder's headquarters during the Civil War. The Daughters of the American Revolution maintains it today as a museum.

Grace Episcopal Church   On Church Street near the river, Grace Church dates to 1697 and has been an active house of worship since then. Its first rector, the Rev. Anthony Panton, was dismissed for calling the secretary of the colony a jackanapes. Gunpowder and ammunition were stored here during the siege of Yorktown. During the Civil War, the church served as a hospital. It's open to visitors daily 9am to 5pm. The communion silver, made in England in 1649, is still in use. Thomas Nelson, Jr., is buried in the adjacent graveyard.

The Swan Tavern   For over a century the Swan Tavern, at the corner of Main and Ballard streets (C **757/898-3033**), was Yorktown's leading hostelry. Originally owned by Thomas Nelson, it was in operation 20 years before Williamsburg's famous Raleigh Tavern. The Swan was demolished in 1863 by an ammunition explosion at the courthouse across the street, rebuilt, and destroyed again by fire in 1915. Today it is reconstructed as per historical research, and the premises house a fine 18th-century antiques shop. It's open Tuesday to Saturday 10am to 5pm, Sunday noon to 5pm.

The Poor Potter   Constructed on the site of Yorktown's original pottery factory on Read Street, inland from the Custom House, this reconstruction shows how the locals produced pottery of better quality than their English cousins were making back home.

WHERE TO DINE

Carrot Tree SANDWICHES/SALADS   Occupying the Cole Diggs House, Yorktown's oldest brick residence (ca. 1720), this sandwich shop is a good place for refreshment during your walking tour of town. The house was restored by the National Park Service, which won't allow a stove inside for safety reasons. Consequently, many items are prepared in Williamsburg and heated in a microwave oven here. It's good stuff nevertheless. Check out the pastries in the chiller box by the front door; they make a fine snack. Lunch sees salads, barbecue, Brunswick stew, and made-to-order sandwiches.

411 Main St. (at Read St.). C **757/246-9559.** Reservations recommended. Most items $5–$12. AE, DISC, MC, V. Sun–Thurs 11am–3:30pm; Fri–Sat 11am–3:30pm and 4:30–8:30pm.

Nick's Riverwalk Restaurant ✔ AMERICAN   The main tenant in Yorktown Riverwalk Landing, this interesting if not gourmet restaurant stretches across the waterfront side of the complex, affording excellent views of the river and the Coleman Bridge almost overhead. It really is two restaurants, each with its own kitchen. On the one hand is the more refined **Dining Room;** on the other, the casual and less expensive **Rivah Café.** The latter has outdoor seating in fine weather. Both feature all-American fare, with names to match: Nebraska pork chops, Hawaii seared yellowfin tuna, San Francisco cioppino stew, Louisiana crawfish cakes, and, of course, Maine lobster. The wine list is more far ranging, with vintages from as far away as Chile and South Africa. This is the top spot in town for lunch or dinner after you've toured the battlefields.

323 Water St. (in Yorktown Riverwalk Landing). C **757/875-1522.** Reservations recommended in Dining Room. Dining Room main courses $16–$22; Rivah Café sandwiches $8.50–$10. AE, DISC, MC, V. Dining Room Sun–Thurs 11:30am–2:30pm and 5–9pm; Rivah Café daily 11:30am–3:30pm and 4:30–9pm.

4 James River Plantations

While Williamsburg was the political capital of Virginia during the 18th century, its economic livelihood depended on the great tobacco plantations beside the James River. Several of the mansions built during that period of wealthy landowners still stand today between Williamsburg and Richmond, some occupied to this day by the same families that have produced generals, governors, and two presidents. Two of them are open to the public, providing an authentic feel for 18th-century plantation life.

SEEING THE PLANTATIONS

Plantations are on both sides of the James River, but the easiest to visit are on John Tyler Highway (Va. 5) between Williamsburg and Richmond. From Williamsburg, take Jamestown Road and bear right on Va. 5. From Richmond, take Main Street east, which becomes Va. 5. This so-called Plantation Route covers a distance of 55 miles between Williamsburg and Richmond and makes an excellent scenic driving tour between the two cities. You can easily see them in half a day.

Berkeley Plantation *&*   The aristocratic Harrison family bought Berkeley in 1691. Benjamin Harrison III made it a prosperous operation, and in 1726 his son, Benjamin Harrison IV, built the three-story Georgian mansion. Benjamin Harrison V was a signer of the Declaration of Independence and thrice governor of Virginia. The next generation produced William Henry Harrison, the frontier fighter whose nickname "Old Tippecanoe" helped him get elected as our ninth president. His grandson, another Benjamin Harrison, took the presidential oath 47 years later. George Washington was a frequent guest, and every president through Tyler enjoyed Berkeley's gracious hospitality.

Berkeley was twice occupied by invading troops. A British army under Benedict Arnold burned the family portraits, practiced target shooting on the cows, and went off with 40 slaves. Gen. George McClellan's Union army trampled the gardens and chopped up the elegant furnishings for firewood. After the war, the Harrisons never returned to live at Berkeley.

John Jamieson, a Scottish-born New Yorker who had served as a drummer in McClellan's army, purchased the disfigured manor house and 1,400 acres in 1907. His son, Malcolm, completely restored the house and grounds to their appearance in the early days of the Harrisons' tenure. The plantation is now owned by the Malcolm E. Jamieson family. Allow 1½ hours to see a 10-minute audiovisual presentation, take a 45-minute guided tour of the house, and explore the magnificent grounds and gardens.

12602 Harrison Landing Rd. (off Va. 5), 30 miles west of Williamsburg. ℭ **888/466-6018** or 804/829-6018. www. berkeleyplantation.com. Admission $11 adults, $7.50 children 13–16, $6 children 6–12, free for children 5 and younger. Grounds only $7.50 adults, $6 children 13–16, $5 children 6–12, free for children 5 and younger. Daily 9am–5pm (last tour 4:30pm). Closed Thanksgiving and Dec 25.

(Moments **Virginia Is for Gardens**

Garden Week in Virginia, during the last week in April, is the ideal time to visit the plantations. All the grounds are at their magnificent, full-bloom best then. It's also the only time that the manor house at **Westover,** which shares Berkeley's lane off Va. 5 (ℭ **804/829-2882**), is open to the public. Richmond's founder, William Byrd II, built this beautiful Georgian manor house in the 1730s directly on the banks of the James. You can walk around the grounds and gardens year-round, daily 9am to 6pm. Admission is an honorary $2. The grounds at **Sherwood Forrest Plantation,** 14501 John Tyler Hwy./Va. 5 (ℭ **804/282-1441;** www. sherwoodforest.org), also are open to the public daily 9am to 5pm. Admission is $5. Sherwood Forrest was home of U.S. President John Tyler.

Fun Fact **The First Thanksgiving**

On December 4, 1619, 38 English settlers sent by the Berkeley Company put ashore after a 3-month voyage. They fell on their knees in a prayer of thanksgiving. If you're here the first Sunday of November, you can participate in the annual commemoration of that first Thanksgiving in the New World.

Shirley Plantation ✶✶✶ Described by one architectural historian as "the most intact 18th-century estate in Virginia," Shirley was founded beside the James River in 1613, making it Virginia's oldest plantation. It's also America's oldest family-owned business, begun in 1638. The plantation manse was built between 1723 and 1738 by Shirley heiress Elizabeth Hill and her husband, John Carter, eldest son of Robert "King" Carter, the richest man in the colonies (it was King Carter who financed Historic Christ Church in Irvington on the Northern Neck; p. 117). Their granddaughter, Anne Hill Carter, was born, grew up, and married Virginia governor and Revolutionary War hero Henry "Light-Horse Harry" Lee here. Their son, Robert E. Lee, made his own place in history. The extraordinarily well-preserved mansion is noted for its carved "flying staircase"—it rises three stories with no visible means of support—and Queen Anne forecourt flanked by the kitchen and other dependent buildings, both the only remaining examples of this architectural style in America. Now in its 11th generation, the Carter family continues to operate Shirley as a working plantation. After the 30-minute tour, allow at least another 30 minutes to explore the grounds and dependencies of this National Historic Landmark.

501 Shirley Plantation Rd. (off Va. 5), Charles City, 35 miles west of Williamsburg. © **800/232-1613** or 804/829-5121. www.shirleyplantation.com. Admission $11 adults, $7.50 children 6–18, free for children 5 and younger. Daily 9am–5pm (last tour 4:30pm). 30-min. house tours depart every half-hour. Closed Thanksgiving and Dec 25.

5 An Easy Excursion to Hampton & Newport News

Jamestown was barely 2 years old when Capt. John Smith sent a contingent of men to build a fort on the Hampton River, strategically located on the western shore of Hampton Roads. The colony's first seaport, there's been a town here since 1610, making Hampton the nation's oldest continuously English-speaking settlement. It was here in 1718 that British troops displayed the head of Edward Teach, better known as Blackbeard the Pirate, whom they killed during a furious battle on North Carolina's Outer Banks. His captured crew was dispatched to the gallows in Williamsburg.

Unfortunately, there are few remaining structures from those early days other than the U.S. Army's **Fort Monroe,** for during the Civil War a Confederate general ordered the town burned to the ground rather than permit Union forces holding the fort to quarter troops and former slaves here. You can visit the Fort Monroe room where Confederate president Jefferson Davis was imprisoned after the war, the fine museum at Hampton University, and the very modern Virginia Air and Space Center, a smaller but excellent rendition of the Smithsonian Institution's National Air and Space Museum in Washington, D.C.

Named for Christopher Newport, skipper of the *Discovery,* one of the three ships that brought the Jamestown settlers to Virginia, Newport News also dates back to the early 1600s and has a long maritime tradition. The city is home to the Mariners'

Museum, the largest maritime museum in the Western Hemisphere, and home to the remains of the USS *Monitor.*

Hampton has enough interesting sights to take up most of a day trip from Williamsburg. The Mariners' Museum is on the way to Hampton, so you can spend part of the morning there on the way. You can also visit both cities on day excursions from Norfolk and Virginia Beach (see chapter 11).

ESSENTIALS

VISITOR INFORMATION   For advance information contact the **Hampton Convention and Visitor Bureau,** 1919 Commerce Dr., Hampton, VA 23666 (© 800/ 800-2202 or 757/727-1102; fax 757/727-6712; www.hamptoncvb.com). The bureau's visitor center shares quarters with the **Hampton History Museum,** where you can learn of the city's past. The visitor center is open daily 9am to 5pm; the museum, Monday to Saturday 10am to 5pm, Sunday 1 to 5pm. Both are closed New Year's Day, Thanksgiving, and Christmas. Admission to the museum is $5 adults, $4 seniors and children 4 to 12, free for kids under 4.

For information about Newport News, contact the **Newport News Tourism Development Office,** 700 Town Center Dr., Suite 320, Newport News, VA 23606 (© **888/493-7386** or 757/926-1400; fax 757/926-1441; www.newport-news.org). The walk-in **Newport News Visitor Center** is in Newport News Park, 13560 Jefferson Ave., west of Fort Eustis Boulevard near Exit 250 off I-64 (© **888/493-7386** or 757/886-7777). It's open daily from 9am to 5pm except Thanksgiving and Christmas.

Newport News Park, 13560 Jefferson Ave. (© **757/888-3333;** www.nnparks. com), is the largest municipal park east of the Mississippi River and has one of the best campgrounds in Virginia.

GETTING THERE   From Williamsburg, take I-64 East. To reach downtown Hampton, take Exit 267 and turn right on Settlers Landing Road and cross the Hampton River to the visitor center (a left turn at the exit will take you to Fort Monroe and the Casemate Museum via the village of Poquoson). To reach the Mariners' Museum, take Exit 258 and follow J. Clyde Morris Boulevard (U.S. 17) south; the museum is at the southern end of the boulevard. From Norfolk and Virginia Beach, take I-64 West through the Hampton Roads Bridge Tunnel to these exits.

Amtrak (© **800/872-7245;** www.amtrak.com) has daily service to its station in Newport News.

ATTRACTIONS IN HAMPTON

The Casemate Museum ✦   The Casemate Museum is a must-see for Civil War buffs, for Confederate president Jefferson Davis was imprisoned in the bowels of this stone fort in 1865 after being captured in Georgia. The accusation that he had participated in Lincoln's assassination was disproved, and Davis was released in 1867. Located at the tip of a peninsula and surrounded by a moat, the fort was built between 1819 and 1834. Robert E. Lee served as second in command of the construction detachment in 1831 when he was a young officer in the Army Corps of Engineers, and Edgar Allen Poe spent 16 months here in 1828 and 1829 as an enlisted man. The dungeonlike casemates were designed as storage for seacoast artillery. After 1861, they were modified to serve as living quarters for soldiers and their families. You'll need about 45 minutes in the museum to view displays of military memorabilia and Davis's sparsely furnished quarters (his intricately carved pipe—an egg-shaped bowl clenched in an eagle's claw—is outside the door). **Tours** can be arranged in advance by contacting the museum. Note that you'll need to show a picture ID in order to get into Fort Monroe.

Fort Monroe. ℂ **757/788-3391.** http://fort.monroe.army.mil/museum. Free admission. Daily 10:30am–4:30pm. Closed Jan 1, Thanksgiving, and Dec 25. From I-64 take Exit 267. From downtown Hampton, take Settlers Landing Rd. east across Hampton River bridge and under I-64 into Phoebus, take right fork onto County St., turn right on Mallory St., left on Mellen St., straight into Fort Monroe. Follow signs to museum.

Hampton University Museum ⍟

Across the river from downtown, Hampton University was founded in 1868 to provide an education for newly freed African Americans. Its graduates include Booker T. Washington, who founded Tuskegee Institute in Alabama and whose birthplace is preserved near Lynchburg (see chapter 6). Near the campus entrance stand the Emancipation Oak Trees, where the Emancipation Proclamation was read to the people of Hampton for the first time in 1863. Four other landmarks are nearby, including the imposing Memorial Chapel (1886). The museum is noted for its fine collection of African-American art, including a significant number of Harlem Renaissance paintings. Don't miss the works by Henry O. Tanner, including his renowned *The Banjo Lesson*. It also has notable holdings of African art, including one of the world's first collections of Kuba art from the Democratic Republic of the Congo. Rivaling the African collection is the Native American collection, which includes works from 93 tribes; it was established in 1878, when the federal government began sending Native Americans from reservations in the West to be educated at Hampton.

Huntington Building, Hampton University. ℂ 757/727-5308. www.hamptonu.edu/museum. Free admission. Mon–Fri 8am–5pm; Sat noon–4pm. Closed major holidays. From downtown Hampton, take Settlers Landing Rd. across the Hampton River and follow signs to the university and museum.

Virginia Air & Space Center ⍟⍟ (Kids)

A stunning glass-fronted futuristic structure on the edge of Hampton's riverfront, this museum chronicles the history of aviation and space travel and also serves as the official visitor center for NASA's Langley Research Center and Langley Air Force Base. There's a 3-billion-year-old rock brought back from the moon by Apollo 17. In the main gallery, about 10 air vehicles are suspended from the 94-foot vaulted ceiling, and below sits the *Apollo 12* command module—complete with reentry burn marks. A 3-D IMAX theater shows 45-minute films about flying and space as well as full-length features. There are no guided tours; allow at least 2 hours to explore it all on your own, more if you see a movie.

600 Settlers Landing Rd. (at King St.). ℂ **757/727-0900.** www.vasc.org. Admission $9 adults, $8 seniors and military, $7 children 3–11, free for children 2 and younger. Combination tickets including IMAX films available. Memorial Day to Labor Day Mon–Wed 10am–5pm, Thurs–Sun 10am–7pm; off season Mon–Sat 10am–5pm, Sun noon–5pm.

HARBOR CRUISES

The most popular harbor cruises in Virginia are on the *Miss Hampton II,* 764 Settlers Landing Rd. (ℂ **888/757-2628** or 757/722-9102; www.misshamptoncruises.com), a 65-foot passenger boat that sails from downtown across Hampton Roads and within sight of the huge U.S. naval base at Norfolk. You'll pass the landing site of the Jamestown settlers and Blackbeard's Point, where the pirate's head was displayed in 1718, and the pre–Civil War **Fort Wool,** on a 15-acre island out in the Chesapeake. The narrated 3-hour cruises depart from the town dock, on Settlers Landing Road beside the Radisson Hampton hotel. Departures usually are daily at 10am and 2pm

Memorial Day to Labor Day; Tuesday through Saturday at 10am in April, May, September, and October; but call ahead to be sure. Fares are $21 for adults, $19 for seniors and military, $9 for children 6 to 12, free for kids younger than 6.

A MARITIME MUSEUM IN NEWPORT NEWS

The Mariners' Museum ✦✦✦   My parents brought my sister Jean and I to this outstanding museum when I was about 12 years, which may have influenced me to later become an officer in the United States Navy, so well does it tell the story of men who have gone down to the sea in ships. Dedicated to preserving the culture of the sea and its tributaries, it's the largest maritime museum in the Western Hemisphere, and it became larger in 2007 with the opening of the **USS *Monitor* Center,** which houses the remains of the famous Union ironclad. The *Monitor* sank off Cape Hatteras after her stalemate battle with the CSS *Merrimac* on Hampton Roads in 1862. Divers located her in the 1990s and later recovered her round, one-gun turret, which is kept here in a perpetual bath of salt water to prevent it from rusting. You can actually walk into a remarkable, full-size reproduction of the turret exactly as it was found, lying upside down, on the floor of the Atlantic Ocean, a crewman's skeleton clearly visible. Hundreds of other artifacts—including handwritten letters—also are on display.

Elsewhere in the museum, handcrafted ship models, scrimshaw, maritime paintings, decorative arts, working steam engines, and more are displayed in spacious galleries. Shown on the hour and half-hour, an 18-minute film narrated by James Earl Jones discusses maritime activity the world over. There usually are two guided tours per day Monday to Friday (call for schedule). Docents lead guided tours on request. The museum is in a pleasant 550-acre park setting, with a lake, picnic areas, and walking trails. There's a cafe, and the gift shop sells quality nautical items.

100 Museum Dr. ⓒ **757/596-2222.** www.mariner.org. Admission $13 adults, $12 seniors, $7.50 children 6–17, free for children 5 and younger. Mon–Sat 10am–5pm; Sun noon–5pm. Closed Thanksgiving and Dec 25. From I-64, take Exit 258A, follow J. Clyde Morris Blvd. (U.S. 17) south to intersection with Warwick Blvd. (U.S. 60), go straight on Museum Dr.

Norfolk, Virginia Beach & the Eastern Shore

The Jamestown colonists first set foot in the New World at Cape Henry on April 26, 1607. Although they stayed just long enough to plant a cross in the sand and give thanks for their safe passage from England, later generations did decide to live here—lots of them, including some of my close relatives.

Today, the cities of Norfolk, Virginia Beach, Portsmouth, and Chesapeake comprise a megalopolis of nearly a million people sprawling along the southern shores of Hampton Roads, one of the world's largest natural harbors.

Norfolk and Portsmouth have been important seaports since being founded in 1682 and 1752, respectively. They were fought over often during the Civil War, including the famous battle between the first ironclads, USS *Monitor* and CSS *Merrimac,* out on Hampton Roads.

Indeed, the navy still rules here, for this area has America's largest concentration of naval bases, which are its economic backbone.

The sailors once made Norfolk a bawdy seaport, but the city has rebuilt its downtown into a vibrant center of shopping, dining, and sightseeing. Norfolk's attractions include Virginia's best art museum, a marvelous botanical garden, and the state zoo.

A brief ferry ride across the Elizabeth River takes you on an easy excursion to Portsmouth's gentrified Olde Town, whose rich architecture may remind you of Charleston and Savannah.

Virginia Beach's population more than doubles during the summer, when 20 miles of uninterrupted sand and surf draw vacationers from around the globe. With a host of outdoor activities, a multitude of hotels, and close proximity to the other cities, it's no mystery why most visitors make "VaBeach" (as locals refer to the oceanfront area) their base for exploring this area.

From Virginia Beach, the 17-mile engineering marvel known as the Chesapeake Bay Bridge-Tunnel will whisk you north to a different world: Virginia's rural Eastern Shore. Here you will visit Chincoteague Island, home of an ancient fishing village, and its neighbor, Assateague Island, site of a magnificent national seashore and a wildlife refuge teeming with birds and the famous wild ponies of Assateague.

1 Norfolk ✶

190 miles SE of Washington, D.C.; 93 miles E of Richmond; 17 miles W of Virginia Beach

Downtown Norfolk was notorious for its sailor bars when I was growing up about 75 miles south of here. For many years, in fact, we didn't go into downtown Norfolk. All that has now changed, for the city has put itself through a notable renaissance. Today the rowdy joints are out in suburban strip malls, replaced by a vibrant, modern downtown of high-rise offices, condominiums, marinas, museums, shops, nightspots, and a 12,000-seat minor league baseball park. The MacArthur Center, a shopping mall just a few blocks from the riverfront, now dominates downtown. More condos and office buildings are going up as I write, as is Norfolk's new downtown cruise-ship terminal.

Also here are Virginia's finest art museum, its official zoo, and a botanical garden that comes ablaze with springtime azaleas. After dark, the state's symphony, opera, and stage company add highbrow culture. And if you're a foodie, hot restaurants bring exciting tastes to downtown and the hip residential neighborhood known as Ghent. Interspersed among the modern ingredients are reminders of Norfolk's past, such as historic houses and the old City Hall, now a museum and memorial to World War II hero Gen. Douglas MacArthur.

Indeed, this rising Southern star—dubbed by the local tourist bureau as "The New Norfolk"—is one of the more diverse and fascinating Virginia cities in which to spend a day or two.

ESSENTIALS
VISITOR INFORMATION

For advance information, contact the **Norfolk Convention & Visitors Bureau,** 232 E. Main St., Norfolk, VA 23510 (℗ **800/368-3097** or 757/441-1852; fax 757/622-3663). The bureau dispenses walking-tour brochures and other information at its offices (Mon–Fri 8:30am–5pm), which are across Main Street from the Norfolk Marriott. The main downtown walk-in information center, however, is at NAUTICUS (p. 289).

Arriving from the west via I-64, there's a **Norfolk Visitor Center** on Fourth View Street at Exit 273 in the Ocean View section (℗ **757/441-1852**). It's open daily 9am to 5pm.

The **Freemason Street Reception Center,** 401 E. Freemason St. (℗ **757/441-1526**), next to the Moses Myers House (p. 289) also has visitor information.

GETTING THERE

BY PLANE   Norfolk International Airport (ORF), on Norview Avenue 1½ miles north of I-64 (℗ **757/857-3351;** www.norfolkairport.com), is served by American, Continental, Delta, Northwest, Southwest, United, and US Airways. The major car-rental firms have desks here. Taxis await all flights, and **Carey VIP Chauffeured Services** (℗ **877/422-1105** or 757/963-0433; www.careyvip.net) runs limousines and vans to points between Williamsburg and Virginia Beach.

BY CAR   From the west, I-64 runs from Richmond to Norfolk, then swings around the eastern and southern suburbs, where it meets I-664 to form the Hampton Roads Beltway around the area. U.S. 460 also runs the length of Virginia to Norfolk and is a good way to avoid the backups that often plague the bridge-tunnels on I-64 and I-664, especially on summer weekends. U.S. 13 and U.S. 17 also pass through the area. From Virginia Beach, I-264 goes through downtown and Portsmouth.

BY TRAIN & BUS   Amtrak (℗ **800/872-7245;** www.amtrak.com) trains stop in Newport News, the nearest station. **Greyhound** (℗ **800/231-2222;** www.greyhound.com) has bus service to downtown Norfolk.

CITY LAYOUT   Norfolk occupies two peninsulas formed by the Chesapeake Bay and the Elizabeth and Lafayette rivers. **Downtown** is on the southern side of the city, on the north bank of the Elizabeth River. Within walking distance to the northwest, **Freemason** is Norfolk's oldest residential neighborhood, with most of its 18th- and

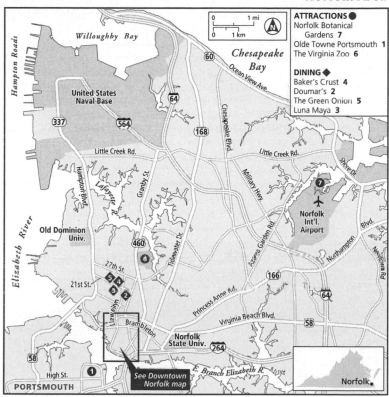

19th-century town houses restored as private homes, businesses, and restaurants. You'll still find a few cobblestone streets here.

Northwest of Freemason, across a semicircular inlet known as The Hague, **Ghent** was the city's first subdivision and is now its trendiest enclave. Most houses in "old" Ghent, near The Hague and The Chrysler Museum of Art (p. 288), were built between 1892 and 1912. Now thoroughly gentrified, it's home to everyone from well-heeled professionals to writers, artists, and college students. The heart of Ghent's business district runs along **Colley Avenue** between Baldwin Avenue and 21st Street, and along **21st Street** from Colley Avenue east to Granby Street. Here you'll find antiques shops, restaurants, and the artsy NARO Cinema.

GETTING AROUND

A car is the easiest way to get around this spread-out area. **Parking** is available downtown at the MacArthur Center and in municipal garages (the most convenient is on Atlantic Ave. between Waterside Dr. and Main St.). The city posts a downtown map showing its parking garages at **www.norfolk.gov/parking**. Visitors to the Douglas MacArthur Memorial (p. 288) can have their tickets validated for 3 hours free parking.

Once you're downtown, the free **Norfolk Electric Transit** (**NET;** www.norfolk. gov/visitors/net.asp) trolleys are the easiest way to get around Monday through Friday 6:30am to 11pm, Saturday noon to midnight, Sunday noon to 8pm. The weekday

---

Tips Avoiding Gridlock

Hampton Roads has some of Virginia's most congested traffic. Lengthy backups can occur anytime on I-64 at the Hampton Roads Bridge-Tunnel, and especially during weekday rush hour and all day on summer weekends. I take U.S. 460 from Petersburg to Norfolk on summer weekends, thus avoiding both the Hampton Roads and Monitor-Merrimac bridge-tunnels. U.S. 13 is another alternate route if you're coming from the northeast. If you're approaching on I-64 from the west, an alternative is to take I-664 and the Monitor-Merrimac Bridge-Tunnel, then Va. 164 east to Portsmouth and the Midtown Tunnel (U.S. 58) into Norfolk. Tune your radio to 610 AM or call © **800/792-2800** on your cellphone to check on current conditions.

---

route runs from Harbor Park across downtown on Main Street and north via Granby Street to Virginia Beach Boulevard and the Harrison Opera House. The weekend route makes a loop around the downtown shopping-and-dining area and then north along Granby Street to Virginia Beach Boulevard. The routes are shown on NET's website and on city maps distributed at the visitor centers (see "Essentials," above).

Hampton Roads Transit (**HRT;** © **757/222-6100;** www.gohrt.com) provides public bus service throughout the region. Although it can take as long as 2 hours each way, the Route 20 bus goes from Monticello Avenue and Charlotte Street to the Virginia Beach oceanfront. Fares are $1.50 for adults, 75¢ for seniors and persons with disabilities, $1 for children younger than 19, free for kids shorter than 38 inches tall. Exact change is required.

For taxis, call **Yellow Cab** (© **757/622-3232**), **Black and White Cabs** (© **757/855-4444**), or **Green & White Taxis** (© **757/855-3333**).

SEEING THE SIGHTS

Downtown Norfolk's centerpiece is the **MacArthur Center,** a 1-million-square-foot shopping mall covering the 9 square blocks bordered by Monticello and City Hall avenues, Freemason Street, and St. Paul's Boulevard (© **757/627-6000;** www.shop macarthur.com). The main entrance is on Monticello Avenue at Market Street. Anchored by Nordstrom and Dillard's department stores, it has most of the mall regulars, an 18-screen cinema, a food court, and full-service restaurants.

Built in 1983 between Waterside Drive and the Elizabeth River, the **Waterside Festival Marketplace** (© **757/627-3300;** www.watersidemarketplace.com), which everyone calls simply The Waterside, was the catalyst for downtown Norfolk's revitalization, like Baltimore's Inner Harbor, Boston's Faneuil Hall, and New York's South Street Seaport. The Elizabeth River Ferry and harbor cruises leave from the dock outside this glass-and-steel pavilion. With so much of its shopping business now going to the MacArthur Center, The Waterside now is primarily a dining and entertainment center (see "Norfolk After Dark," later in this chapter).

In **Town Point Park,** to the west of The Waterside, don't miss *The Homecomer,* a statue of a returning sailor greeted by his wife and child, and the moving **Armed Forces Memorial,** where bronze letters written home by sailors litter the ground. The park's amphitheater features a full schedule of free events all year—concerts, children's theater, magic shows, puppetry, and more. Beyond the park stand the riverfront's most

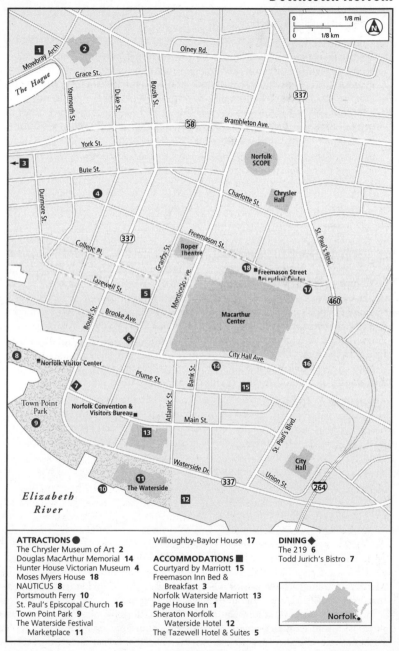

0   1/8 mi
0   1/8 km

Mowbray Arch
Olney Rd.
The Hague
Grace St.
Yarmouth St.
Duke St.
Boush St.
337
58
Bramhleton Ave.
York St.
Dunmore St.
Bute St.
Norfolk SCOPE
Charlotte St.
Chrysler Hall
College Pl.
337
Grandy St.
Freemason St.
Roper Theatre
Monticello Ave.
St. Paul's Blvd
Freemason Street Reception Center
Tazewell St.
5
Brooke Ave.
Boush St.
460
Macarthur Center
6
City Hall Ave.
16
Norfolk Visitor Center
8
Plume St.
Bank St.
14
7
Atlantic St.
15
Norfolk Convention & Visitors Bureau
Town Point Park
9
Main St.
13
St. Paul's Blvd
City Hall
Waterside Dr.
11
The Waterside
337
Union St.
264
Elizabeth River
10
12

ATTRACTIONS ●
The Chrysler Museum of Art **2**
Douglas MacArthur Memorial **14**
Hunter House Victorian Museum **4**
Moses Myers House **18**
NAUTICUS **8**
Portsmouth Ferry **10**
St. Paul's Episcopal Church **16**
Town Point Park **9**
The Waterside Festival
   Marketplace **11**

Willoughby-Baylor House **17**

ACCOMMODATIONS ■
Courtyard by Marriott **15**
Freemason Inn Bed &
   Breakfast **3**
Norfolk Waterside Marriott **13**
Page House Inn **1**
Sheraton Norfolk
   Waterside Hotel **12**
The Tazewell Hotel & Suites **5**

DINING ◆
The 219 **6**
Todd Jurich's Bistro **7**

Norfolk

Tips **Norfolk's Cannonball & Civil War Trails**

Two self-guided walking tours of downtown will take you through 400 years of Norfolk's history. Beginning at the Freemason Street Reception Center, 401 E. Freemason St., sidewalk inlays and medallions mark the route of the **Cannonball Trail** through downtown, along the waterfront, and through the historic Freemason neighborhood. The local version of Virginia's **Civil War Trails** follows much the same route but with an emphasis on Norfolk in 1862. Pick up maps and brochures at the visitor centers.

conspicuous buildings, the huge gray **NAUTICUS, The National Maritime Center** and the glass-enclosed, semicircular **Half Moone Cruise and Celebration Center,** the city's modern cruise-ship terminal (www.cruisenorfolk.org).

East of the Elizabeth River bridges and I-264, **Harbor Park,** a 12,000-seat stadium, is home to the **Norfolk Tides,** a Class AAA International League baseball team affiliated with the Baltimore Orioles (© **757/622-2222;** www.norfolktides.com).

THE TOP ATTRACTIONS

The Chrysler Museum of Art 🌟🌟🌟   Built in 1932 as the Norfolk Museum of Arts & Sciences, this imposing Italian Renaissance building on The Hague inlet was renamed in 1971 when Walter P. Chrysler, Jr., gave a large portion of his collection to the city. Today it's Virginia's finest art museum, spanning artistic periods from ancient Egypt to the present and including one of the finest and most comprehensive glass collections in the world. Adjoining is an outstanding collection of Art Nouveau furniture. Other first-floor galleries exhibit ancient Indian, Islamic, Asian, African, and pre-Columbian art. Most second-floor galleries are devoted to painting and sculpture, particularly Italian baroque and French, including works by Monet, Renoir, Matisse, Braque, Bernini, and Rouault. American art holdings include 18th- and 19th-century paintings by Charles Willson Peale, Benjamin West, John Singleton Copley, and Thomas Cole; and 20th-century works by Thomas Hart Benton, Calder, Kline, Warhol, Rauschenberg, and Rosenquist. A permanent gallery is devoted solely to photography, showcasing everyone from Walker Evans to Diane Arbus.

Pick up a free audio tour at the information desk, which will explain some of the key items as you see them. Allow at least 2 hours here, half a day to do it complete justice.

The museum administers the Moses Myers House (see below).

245 W. Olney Rd. © **757/664-6200.** www.chrysler.org. Admission Thurs–Sun $7 adults, $5 seniors and students, free for children 11 and younger; Wed free (donations encouraged). Wed 10am–9pm; Thurs–Sat 10am–5pm; Sun 1–5pm. Closed Jan 1, July 4th, Thanksgiving, and Dec 25.

Douglas MacArthur Memorial 🌟🌟   General of the Army Douglas MacArthur's immortal words "I shall return" are engraved on a bronze plaque, along with excerpts from his other speeches, at his final resting place in Norfolk's old city hall, an imposing domed structure with a columned front portico. In a scene a bit reminiscent of the Taj Mahal in India, the dome towers over the side-by-side marble crypts of the general and his wife, Jean. Shown every half-hour in a theater next door, a 25-minute film will give you a perspective on MacArthur's life and help you understand the exhibits. Filled with his personal memorabilia, the chronologically arranged galleries trace U.S.

history during MacArthur's life and his role in events up to his ringing "Old Soldiers Never Die" speech to Congress after President Truman fired him during the Korean War. Of particular interest: MacArthur's famous corncob pipe, his omnipresent sunglasses, his field cap with its sides rolled down, and a replica of the plaque marking the spot on the USS *Missouri* where MacArthur presided over the surrender of Japan. The memorial will validate your city garage tickets for 3 hours free parking.

MacArthur Sq. (between City Hall Ave. and Plume St., at Bank St.). (℃ 757/441-2965. www.macarthurmemorial.org. Free admission (donations encouraged). Mon–Sat 10am–5pm; Sun 11am–5pm. Closed Jan 1, Thanksgiving, and Dec 25.

Hunter House Victorian Museum   This redbrick and stone-trimmed Romanesque Revival–style house was built by prominent banker and merchant James Wilson Hunter in 1894 from plans designed by Boston architect W. P. Wentworth. Hunter and his wife, Lizzie Barnes Hunter, had three children, none of whom ever married and all of whom spent their entire lives here. They bequeathed the house as a museum of Victorian architecture and decorative arts, the role it plays today. Their original furnishings and decorative arts are still here, along with pieces donated by others. It's a fascinating look at how life was lived in Victorian Norfolk. You must take a tour, which departs on the hour and half hour.

240 W. Freemason St. (℃ 757/623-9814. www.hunterhousemuseum.org. Admission $5 adults, $4 seniors, $1 children. Wed–Sat 10am–3:30pm; Sun 12.30–3.30pm. Tours on the hour and half-hour (last tour 3:30pm).

Moses Myers House   It has the MacArthur Center looming over its backyard these days, but this handsome early-Federal brick town house was in Norfolk's oldest residential neighborhood when it was built by Moses Myers and his wife, Eliza, who came to Norfolk in 1787. They were the first Jews to settle here, and programs in observance of Jewish holidays are among the museum's annual events. Some 70% of the furniture and decorative arts displayed are original to the first generation of the family, who lived here until 1930. Two Gilbert Stuart portraits of Mr. and Mrs. Myers hang in the drawing room, which contains some distinctive Empire pieces. The fireplace surround has unusual carvings depicting a sun god—with the features of George Washington. Tours lasting 1 hour and covering both houses depart from the **Freemason Street Reception Center** at 401 E. Freemason St. (℃ 757/441-1526).

Also administered by The Chrysler Museum of Art, the 1794 **Willoughby-Baylor House,** a block away at 601 E. Freemason St., is now known as the **Norfolk History Museum.**

331 Bank St. (℃ 757/441-1526. www.chrysler.org. Free admission (donations recommended). Wed–Sat 10am–4pm. Last tour daily 3pm. Guided 1-hr. tours of both houses depart on the hour. Closed Jan 1, Memorial Day, July 4th, Thanksgiving, and Dec 25.

NAUTICUS, The National Maritime Centre *(Kids*   The large gray waterfront building designed like an artist's rendering of a futuristic battleship is a multifaceted facility dedicated to the U.S. Navy and the sea over which it rules. It's actually three

---

(*Tips* **Safety in Norfolk**

In downtown Norfolk stick to the busy main streets between the MacArthur Center and The Waterside, and don't take unnecessary risks like wandering off into deserted or ill-lit side streets. Volunteer **Public Safety Ambassadors** now patrol the streets and will escort you back to your car (℃ 757/478-7233).

Tips Stop, Look & Listen

Take a few minutes before going on board the USS *Wisconsin* to view the Hampton Roads Naval Museum's multimedia presentation in which seamen reminisce about their experiences aboard the battleship. Then rent a 45-minute audiotape tour. Although docents, many of them veterans of the ship, are on duty to explain what's what, the tape is the best way to see the Goliath. Otherwise, you'll be staring at a lot of gray steel and teak decking.

---

attractions in one. You must pay to enter the third-floor **NAUTICUS,** a very good children's museum with a plethora of movies and hands-on interactive exhibits aimed at families with kids ages 8 to 14. After a morning here, your school-age kids may be ready to enlist.

Admission is free to the second-floor **Hampton Roads Naval Museum** ✴ (✆ 757/ **444-8921;** www.hrnm.navy.mil), in which the U.S. Navy tells the story of its presence here. The exhibit describing the Civil War battle between the ironclads USS *Monitor* and CSS *Merrimac* out on Hampton Roads is worth seeing.

The star of this show, however, is the real battleship **USS *Wisconsin* ✴✴✴.** Berthed alongside on the Elizabeth River, the mighty 888-foot ship was built in 1943 and saw duty in the Pacific during World War II. It was recalled from mothballs to fight in the Korean and Gulf wars. It is once again on inactive reserve status, meaning it can be recalled to duty within 3 months. You cannot go inside, since the innards are hermetically sealed, but you can walk on board and stare up at the enormous 16-inch guns overhanging its teak main deck. It's quite a sight. (There's a spectacular view of the bow framed by a tile archway on Boush St. at the end of Plume St.)

Save a pill for the *Victory Rover* cruises to the naval station, which leave from here (see "Harbor Cruises to Where the Ironclads Fought," below). You can buy tickets combining admission to NAUTICUS and a cruise.

1 Waterside Dr. ✆ **800/664-1080** or 757/664-1000. www.nauticus.org. Free admission to 1st deck, naval museum, and battleship; admission to NAUTICUS exhibits and theaters $9.95 adults, $8.95 seniors, $7.50 children 4–12, free for children 3 and younger. Combination NAUTICUS/Victory Rover cruise, $23 adults, $16 children 4–12, free for children 3 and younger. Battleship audiotape tour $5 ($3 with NAUTICUS admission). NAUTICUS and Naval Museum Memorial Day to Labor Day daily 10am–6pm; rest of year Tues–Sat 10am–5pm, Sun noon–5pm. Entire complex closed Thanksgiving and Dec 25.

Norfolk Botanical Garden ✴✴   The grounds of this botanical garden, on Lake Whitehurst about 4 miles northeast of downtown, are brilliantly abloom from early April to mid-June with one of the East Coast's largest display of azaleas—the best time to visit. This quiet beauty can be seen by 25-minute tram tour, by 45-minute canalboat tour, or by foot over more than 12 miles of floral pathways. The Statuary Vista is a beautiful setting for Moses Ezekiel's heroic-size statues of great painters and sculptors— Rembrandt, Rubens, Dürer, and da Vinci, among others. Notable, too, are the rose garden, with more than 450 varieties among its 3,000 bushes; a classic Japanese hill-and-pond garden; a fragrance garden; an Italian Renaissance garden with terraces, statuary, a fountain, and a reflecting pool; and a children's garden designed especially for kids. Behind the pool is the Hofheimer Camellia Garden and Renaissance Court, where April's Azalea Festival queen is crowned. Garden lovers can easily spend half a day here. You can grab a bite at the Azalea Café and browse for gifts in the garden shop.

6700 Azalea Garden Rd. (off Norview Ave., near airport). ℂ 757/441-5385. www.nbgs.org. Admission $7 adults, $6 seniors, $5 children 6–16, free for children 5 and younger. Boat tours $4 adults, $3 children 4–12, free for children under 4. Gardens Apr to mid-Oct daily 9am–7pm; mid-Oct to Mar daily 9am–5pm. Tram tours Apr to mid-Oct daily 10am–4pm; mid-Oct to Mar Mon–Fri 1–4pm, Sat–Sun 10am–4pm. Boat tours Apr to mid-Oct Mon–Fri 11:45am–1:45pm, Sat–Sun 11:45am–3:45pm; mid-Oct to Mar Sat–Sun 11:45am–3:45pm. Cafe Mon–Sat 9am–3pm, Sun 10am–4pm. Take I-64 to Exit 279 (Norview/Airport), go east on Norview Ave., turn left on Azalea Garden Rd.

St. Paul's Episcopal Church ⓖ

Although severely damaged when the British shelled Norfolk on January 1, 1776, this lovely brick Anglican church survived and is the only pre-Revolution building left in downtown. A cannonball from one of Lord Dunmore's ships remains lodged in the southwest wall. The main chapel was constructed in 1739 to serve a parish that had been in existence since about 1636. The tower was added in 1902, and the interior was restored to its Colonial Revival form in 1913. This is a serene respite in the middle of bustling downtown, so take a moment to reflect inside the church, and then examine the ancient tombstones in the shady churchyard, Norfolk's first burial ground. Graves date to the 1600s, although the earliest original stone is from 1748; three others dating from 1673, 1687, and 1681 were brought here.

201 St. Paul's Blvd. ℂ 757/627-4353. Free admission (donations suggested). Mon–Fri 9am–5pm. Services Wed noon, Sun 8 and 10:30am.

The Virginia Zoo ⓖ (Kids)

Your children will be entertained and educated at Virginia's state zoo, on 53 acres adjacent to Norfolk's Lafayette Park and bordered by the Lafayette River. You can take them on a boardwalk safari and see rhinos, giraffes, and baboons in the noted African plains exhibit. Tigers, monkeys, elephants, reptiles, and colorful birds also are among the nearly 400 animals here.

3500 Granby St. (at 35th St.). ℂ 757/441-2374. www.virginiazoo.org. Admission $7 adults, $6 seniors, $5 children 2–11. Daily 10am–5pm. Closed Jan 1, Thanksgiving, and Dec 25. From downtown, go north on Monticello Ave., which merges with Granby St., to the zoo on the right.

HARBOR CRUISES TO WHERE THE IRONCLADS FOUGHT

Three cruise boats docked at The Waterside or NAUTICUS offer cruises on the Elizabeth River, Hampton Roads, and the Chesapeake Bay. You will pass the naval base with nuclear subs and aircraft carriers and cross the site of the Civil War battle between the *Monitor* and the *Merrimac.*

The best for the money is the 2-hour *Victory Rover* (ℂ 757/627-7406; www. navalbasecruises.com) cruise from NAUTICUS to the Norfolk Naval Station—or as close thereto as security will permit. It has summertime trips departing at 11am, 2pm,

---

Tips **Tours of the Naval Station**

In these days of tight security at military bases, the **Naval Station Norfolk Tour** operated by Hampton Roads Transit (HRT; ℂ 757/222-6100; www.gohrt.com) is the only way to go ashore in the huge complex and see the aircraft carriers and other ships. The tours depart from the Naval Station Tour Center, 9079 Hampton Blvd., every 30 minutes or every hour, depending on time of year. Fares are $7.50 for adults; $5 for seniors, children younger than 12, and persons with disabilities. All persons 16 and older will need a picture ID to get on the base. Backpacks are not permitted on the base. Call for reservations.

and 5:30pm, and at least one trip a day (usually departing at 2pm) the rest of the year. Fares are $16 adults, $10 for children. Combination tickets with admission to NAU-TICUS cost $23 adults, $16 for children.

From April to October, there are cruises on the *American Rover* (© 757/627-7245; www.americanrover.com), a graceful schooner modeled after 19th-century Chesapeake Bay schooners. Prices for the 1½-hour midday cruise and the 2-hour 3pm cruises along the Elizabeth River are $14 and $16 for adults, $8 to $10 for children younger than 12, respectively. It also goes on sunset voyages and adults-only Saturday night party cruises. Call for exact times and reservations.

From mid-April to October, the *Carrie B* (© 757/393-4735; www.carrieb cruises.com), a reproduction of a 19th-century Mississippi riverboat, offers daily 1½- and 2½-hour cruises departing at noon and 2pm, respectively, from The Waterside. They pick up passengers at Portsmouth's North Landing 10 minutes later. Fares start at $18 for adults, $9 for children. There's also a 2½-hour sunset cruise. Call for the schedule and reservations.

Also departing from The Waterside, the sleek *Spirit of Norfolk* (© 866/211-3803 or 757/625-3866; www.spiritofnorfolk.com) is like an oceangoing cruise ship, complete with dancing, good food, and entertainment. Offerings include lunch cruises starting $25 per person, dinner cruises from $43, and moonlight party cruises with cocktails from $24. Call for the schedule and to make reservations.

SHOPPING FOR ANTIQUES 🅐🅐

Norfolk is one of the better places in Virginia to search for antiques, with at least 32 shops selling a range of furniture, decorative arts, glassware, jewelry, and other items from both home and overseas. The best place to look is in Ghent, where several shops sit along the 4 blocks of West 21st Street between Granby Street and Colonial Avenue, especially at the corner of Llewellyn Avenue. Granby Street has more than a dozen shops of its own. The visitor centers have a complete list and description of the shops.

WHERE TO STAY
DOWNTOWN

Courtyard by Marriott 🅐 *Value*   Compared to its suburban sisters, this breed of city-center Courtyards has a larger lobby with fireplace, a bar open nightly, and a restaurant serving both breakfast and dinner. Dark-wood trim and thick carpets also help give it an upscale ambience. The comfortable rooms and suites are typical Courtyard, with big desks, high-speed Internet, and other amenities aimed at business travelers. Unlike the other downtown hotels, here you can open the windows to let in fresh air. This is downtown's best moderately priced hotel.

520 Plume St. (between Court St. and St. Paul Blvd.), Norfolk, VA 23510. © 800/321-2211 or 757/963-6000. Fax 757/963-6001. www.courtyard.com. 140 units. $100–$159 double; $159–$179 suite. AE, DC, DISC, MC, V. Valet parking $15; no self-parking. **Amenities:** Restaurant; bar; heated indoor pool; health club; Jacuzzi; business center; room service (dinner only); laundry service; coin-op washers and dryers. *In room:* A/C, TV, high-speed Internet, fridge, coffeemaker, iron.

Norfolk Waterside Marriott 🅐🅐   One of Norfolk's two convention hotels (the Sheraton, below, is the other) and its most elegant, this 24-story high-rise is connected to The Waterside via a covered skywalk. Its mahogany-paneled lobby is a masterpiece of 18th-century European style, with fine paintings, a crystal chandelier, potted palm trees, comfortable seating areas with gleaming lamps, and one-of-a-kind antiques. A magnificent staircase leads to a breakfast-only restaurant, a piano lounge, and meeting

A Ferry Ride to Olde Towne Portsmouth

Across the Elizabeth River from downtown Norfolk, Portsmouth's **Olde Towne** section traces its roots back to 1752. Like those in Charleston and Savannah, its homes present a kaleidoscope of architectural styles: Colonial, Federal, Greek Revival, Georgian, and Victorian. Plaques mounted on imported English street lamps point out their architectural and historical significance.

Ferries were the main means of getting across the river until the 1950s, and the paddlewheel **Elizabeth River Ferry** (© 757/222-6100; www.hrtransit. org) still makes the short but picturesque trip. During summer it departs The Waterside marina every 30 minutes daily 7am to 11:45pm. Off-season service ends at 9:45pm Sunday through Thursday, 11:45pm Friday and Saturday. Fare is $1 for adults; 50¢ for children, seniors, and passengers with disabilities (exact change required). There is no ferry service on Thanksgiving and Christmas Day.

Get off at the second stop, Portsmouth's **North Landing Visitor Center**, on Harbor Court (© 800/767-8782 or 757/393-5111; www.visitportsva.com), and pick up a walking tour brochure and map. The center is open daily 9am to 5pm.

Guided **Olde Towne Trolley Tours** (© 757/393-5111) depart the visitor center at 10am and noon on Wednesdays and Saturdays during summer. Fares are $13 adults, $12 for children.

Worth seeing is the **Lightship Museum**, in Riverfront Park at the foot of London Boulevard (© 757/393-8741), which is the lightship *Portsmouth*, built in 1915 and anchored offshore until the 1980s to warn mariners of the dangerous shoals on the approach to Hampton Roads. Also in the park is the **Portsmouth Naval Shipyard Museum** (© 757/393-8591).

Tree-lined High Street, the main drag running inland from the harbor, has several restaurants and coffee shops, including the **Bier Garden** (© 757/393-6022) and **Cafe Europa** (© 757/399-6652). Best of all is **Fusion 440**, 447 Dinwiddie St. (© 757/398-0888).

rooms on the second floor. There's a branch of Don Shula's Steakhouse and sports bar downstairs off the lobby. Guest rooms are sumptuously furnished with dark-wood pieces. Although the rooms do not have balconies, odd-numbered upper-floor units do have a river view. The indoor pool here opens to a sun deck overlooking the river.

235 E. Main St. (between Atlantic St. and Martins Lane), Norfolk, VA 23510. © 800/228-9290 or 757/627-4200. Fax 757/628-6452. www.marriott.com. 405 units. $169–$259 double; $250–$700 suite. AE, DC, DISC, MC, V. Valet parking $26; self-parking $19. **Amenities:** 2 restaurants; 2 bars; heated indoor pool; health club; concierge; business center; room service; laundry service; coin-op washers and dryers; concierge-level rooms. *In room:* A/C, TV, Wi-Fi, coffeemaker.

Sheraton Norfolk Waterside Hotel ⑁⑁   Next door to The Waterside and overlooking busy Norfolk Harbor, this contemporary 10-story hotel has a more modern ambience than its main competition, the traditionally styled Marriott 2 blocks away.

A three-story, light-filled atrium lobby gives way to two restaurants with outdoor seating and a bar with 30-foot windows overlooking the river. About a third of the spacious units facing the river have small balconies (they're allotted on a first-come, first-served basis). Although the Sheraton draws groups and conventions, its location and facilities also make it a good choice for individuals, couples, and families.

777 Waterside Dr., Norfolk, VA 23510. © **800/325-3535** or 757/622-6664. Fax 757/625-8271. 445 units. $139–$169 double; $159–$189 suite. AE, DC, DISC, MC, V. Valet parking $20; self-parking $12. Small pets accepted free. **Amenities:** Restaurant; bar; outdoor heated pool; health club; concierge; business center; babysitting; laundry service; concierge-level rooms. *In room:* A/C, TV, Wi-Fi, coffeemaker, iron.

The Tazewell Hotel & Suites Built in 1906, this hotel underwent a renovation a few years ago that was intended to restore it to boutique-hotel status. The two-story lobby with floor-to-ceiling paned windows and the brass elevator doors were repaired to their former grand-hotel status, and the rooms were improved, but the project stopped short of luxury status. As is the case with most hotels built back then, some of the rooms are tiny by today's standards. The best feature: It's in the midst of Granby Street's restaurant row.

245 Granby St., Norfolk, VA 23510. © **757/623-6200.** Fax 757/623-6123. www.thetazewell.com. 58 units. $109–$199 double. Rates include continental breakfast. AE, DISC, MC, V. Parking $15. **Amenities:** Access to nearby health club; exercise room; laundry service. *In room:* A/C, TV, Wi-Fi (some floors), coffeemaker, iron.

BED & BREAKFASTS

Freemason Inn Bed and Breakfast ✦ Although this three-story, 1897-vintage Victorian is technically on York Street, the house actually faces Brambleton Avenue in the historic Freemason neighborhood, a few blocks walk to downtown. Tall windows and white walls brighten the entire house during the day, while working gas fireplaces in the antiques-laden guest quarters add coziness at night. Three of the four rooms also have two-person Jacuzzi tubs. Two have king-size beds, including the Wishing Oak Bridal Suite, named for an ancient oak tree under which many a Norfolk knot was tied. A back porch with wicker furniture overlooks a landscaped courtyard. Breakfasts are served in bed if you wish, wine and cheese are put out each evening, and bicycles are available for guests to ride.

411 W. York St. (west of Boutetort St., facing Brambleton Ave.), Norfolk, VA 23510. © **866/388-1897** or 757/963-7000. Fax 757/233-1897. www.freemasoninn.com. 4 units. $145–$265 double. Rates include full breakfast. Honeymoon and other packages available. AE, MC, V. Free parking. **Amenities:** Free bicycles; room service (breakfast only). *In room:* A/C, TV, Wi-Fi.

Page House Inn ✦ Across the street from The Chrysler Museum of Art in the Ghent district, this grand three-story brick Colonial Revival mansion with an expansive veranda was built in 1899. You will find a plethora of golden oak here—paneling, sliding doors, and moldings, plus a hand-carved fireplace in the living room and a soaring staircase ascending to the rooms upstairs. In the basement, a billiards room boasts a big-screen TV. Guest quarters are beautifully furnished with four-poster beds and one-of-a-kind antiques. Five units have gas-log fireplaces. The grandest also sports a sunken hot tub and a walk-in steam room/shower big enough for two. Host Carl Albero serves a gourmet breakfast (served in your room if you like) and afternoon sherry and port, and he will provide lunches to go. His Yorkshire terrier, Stormi, provides company for your own small pooch.

323 Fairfax Ave. (at Mowbray Arch), Norfolk, VA 23507. © **800/599-7659** or 757/625-5033. Fax 757/623-9451. www.pagehouseinn.com. 7 units. $140–$225 double. Rates include full breakfast. AE, MC, V. Free parking. Small dogs accepted ($25 fee). **Amenities:** Health club; free bicycles; laundry service. *In room:* A/C, TV, Wi-Fi, iron.

WHERE TO DINE
DOWNTOWN

The downtown renaissance has turned **Granby Street** from Main to Charlotte streets into Norfolk's Restaurant Row, as hip new dining rooms open all the time (and a few disappear). Here you'll find The 219 (see below) plus a wide range of other restaurants and pubs.

The best seafood restaurant is **456 Fish,** 456 Granby St. (© 757/625-4444), while the swanky **Byrd & Baldwin Brothers Steakhouse,** 116 Brooke Ave. (© 757/222-9191), in a restored 1906 building half a block west of Granby Street, has the best steaks. A sister of these two, **Bodega,** 422 Granby St. (© 757/622-8577), serves tapas along with the street's best Spanish and Italian fare. The fast-paced **Empire Little Bar & Bistro,** 245 Granby St. (© 757/626-3100), specializes in tapas and is open daily until 2am. **Domo Sushi,** 273 Granby St. (© 757/628-8282), serves just that, plus other Japanese offerings. **Havana,** 255 Granby St. (© 757/627-5800), serves Cuban-influenced fare.

To catch the games and woof a burger, head to **Baxter's,** 500 Granby St. (© 757/622-9837), a monstrous sports bar with pool tables and good pub fare (open daily 11am–2am, Baxter's cures my late-night hunger pangs). The pierced set hangs out after dark at **Hell's Kitchen,** 124 Granby St. (© 757/624-1910), but the office crowd gathers for excellent lunchtime sandwiches and salads.

The MacArthur Center, on Monticello Avenue at Market Street, has a branch of the elegant but informal **Kincaid's Fish, Chop & Steak House** (© 757/622-8000), offering exactly what its name says (but not necessarily speedy service), and a very good and inexpensive **food court** up on the third floor. The Waterside also has a food court plus branches of Joe's Crab Shack, Outback Steakhouse, and Hooters. See "Norfolk After Dark," below.

My favorite downtown breakfast spot is **D'Egg,** 404 E. Main St. (© 757/626-3447), opposite the Norfolk Marriott, an inexpensive diner where you can get eggs, waffles, pancakes, and other traditional day-starters. It's open daily from 7am to 3pm.

Todd Jurich's Bistro 🏶🏶🏶 CREATIVE AMERICAN   Todd Jurich's urbane bistro is the finest restaurant in Hampton Roads. You'll see why when you partake of Todd's creative twists on Southern traditions, such as his all-lump-meat crab cakes—a far cry, indeed, from the fried cakes dispensed at many Chesapeake Bay seafood shacks. Todd uses only fresh produce, drawn whenever possible from local farms that practice "eco-logically sound agriculture." For lunch, you can choose from salads, sandwiches, or smaller portions of the nighttime mains. Vintages from the award-winning wine list go on sale during cocktail hour (4:30–6:30pm) at the wine bar.

150 Main St. (entry on Boush St., opposite NAUTICUS). © 757/622-3210. Reservations recommended. Main courses $21–$35. AE, DC, DISC, MC, V. Mon–Fri 11:30am–2pm and 5:30–10pm; Sat 5:30–10pm.

The 219 🏶🏶 *Value* PIZZA/ECLECTIC   This casual storefront cafe was a pioneer in downtown's renaissance, and it's still one of Granby Street's top restaurants. In fact, its crab cakes are among the best in all of Norfolk. Asian flavors crop up here, as in the Napa snapper—red snapper with Napa cabbage in a lemon-grass broth. You also can opt for one-person pizzas with usual and unusual toppings. There's always a vegetarian selection such as tofu fried in a spicy chile-and-garlic sauce.

219 Granby St. (at Brooke Ave.). © 757/627-2896. Reservations recommended. Pizzas $11; main courses $14–$21. AE, DISC, MC, V. Mon–Thurs 11:30am–2:30pm and 5–10pm; Fri 11:30am–2:30pm and 5–11pm; Sat 5–11pm; Sun 11am–9pm (brunch 11am–3pm).

Fun Fact Cones & Carhops

Some of the wafflelike ice-cream cones made at **Doumar's,** an old-fashioned drive-in with carhops and curb service at 19th Street and Monticello Avenue (© **757/627-4163**), come from the original cone-making machine invented by Abe Doumar at the St. Louis Exposition in 1904. Abe's descendants keep his invention oiled and working, and descendants of his North Carolina–style barbecue sandwiches (a steal at $2 apiece), burgers, hot dogs, sundaes, and milkshakes round out the extremely inexpensive menu. Doumar's has been around since the 1930s, which makes it a hip historical attraction. Open Monday through Thursday 8am to 11pm, Friday and Saturday 8am to 12:30am.

IN GHENT

The heart of Ghent lies along Colley Avenue between Maury and Spotswood avenues, flanking the artsy Naro Theatre. I love to stroll these 3 short blocks and take in the busy scene, especially on warm weekend evenings when the restaurants are busy and their sidewalk tables are packed. In addition to The Green Onion (below), several good restaurants satisfy a variety of tastes. **San Antonio Sam's** (© **757/623-0233**) and **Colley Cantina** (© **757/622-0033**) both serve Tex-Mex fare; **Zio's** (© **757/624-1400**) has the best Italian. **Kelley's Tavern** (© **757/623-3216**) dishes up reasonably good pub fare. Around the corner on Spotswood Avenue, **No Frills Bar & Grill** (© **757/627-4262**) has creative American cuisine.

The neighborhood branch of **Baker's Crust,** 330 W. 21st St. (© **757/625-3600**), in the Palace Shops between Llewellyn and DeBree streets, is both the best place in town for breakfast and one of the better values for lunch and dinner. The bakery provides fresh pastries to start your day and bread for a variety of sandwiches at lunch and dinner.

The Green Onion ASIAN/INTERNATIONAL   This bistro-style storefront restaurant with a display kitchen in the rear isn't the fanciest place to dine, but the chef mixes flavors in exciting combinations, such as pan-seared scallops finished with a sweet-chile glaze and coconut sticky rice, and rare sashimi-grade tuna crusted with macadamia nuts and sesame seeds. Meat lovers can opt for a rib-eye steak topped with tempura onion rings. Vegetarians always have a choice here.

1603 Colley Ave. (between Spotswood Ave. and 21st St.). © **757/963-6100.** Reservations recommended. Main courses $16–$22. AE, DISC, MC, V. Tues–Thurs 5–10pm; Fri–Sat 5–11pm; Sun 10am–2pm and 5–9pm.

Luna Maya *Value* LATIN AMERICAN/VEGETARIAN   This little creation of Bolivian-born sisters Karla and Vivian Montano brings the delightful flavors of Latin America to Ghent. Although burritos and tamales outnumber dishes from Bolivia and Argentina, this is no refried-bean joint. Try a shrimp or chorizo burrito, and you'll see what I mean. Vegetarians get at least four choices here daily. You won't get linens and silver, but the food is interesting and very good.

2000 Colonial Ave. (at 21st St. in Corner Shops). © **757/622-6986.** Reservations not accepted. Main courses $10–$18. AE, MC, V. Tues–Sat 5:30–9:30pm.

NORFOLK AFTER DARK

For a rundown on events, pick up a copy of *Port Folio* (**www.portfolioweekly.com**), a weekly paper free at the visitor information offices, most hotel lobbies, and The

Waterside. The "Daily Break" section in the local rag, *The Virginian-Pilot* (www.pilot online.com), is also a good source.

THE PERFORMING ARTS

From opera to riverside rock concerts, Norfolk has a wider array of performing arts than any city in the state, and the choices keep growing.

If your brow is high, the **Virginia Stage Company** (© 757/627-1234; www.va stage.com) puts on dramas and musicals from October through April in the **Wells Theatre,** 110 Tazewell St. (© 757/627-6988), at Monticello Avenue opposite the MacArthur Center. Built in 1913, this restored Beaux Arts gem is on the National Register of Historic Places. The **Virginia Symphony** (© 757/892-6366; www.virginia symphony.org) often plays at **Chrysler Hall,** Charlotte Street and St. Paul's Boulevard, and the **Virginia Opera** (www.vaopera.org) sings at the **Harrison Opera House,** 160 E. Virginia Beach Blvd. at Llewellyn Avenue (© 757/623-1223).

Chrysler Hall and the Harrison Opera House are part of the **Norfolk SCOPE** complex (© 757/664-6464; www.sevenvenues.com), which also includes the futuristic **Norfolk SCOPE Arena,** Brambleton Avenue and St. Paul's Boulevard, which seats 12,000 for the circus, ice shows, sports, concerts, and other events.

Norfolk SCOPE also manages the restored **Attucks Theater,** on Church Street at Virginia Beach Boulevard (© 757/664-6464; www.attuckstheatre.org), which was built by African-American entrepreneurs in 1919 and named for Crispus Attucks, a black man who was the first American patriot to die in the Revolutionary War. Duke Ellington, Cab Calloway, Count Basie, and many other famous musicians performed here from the 1920s through the early 1950s, when it was among a row of nightclubs, restaurants, and stores on Church Street that comprised one of the liveliest African-American neighborhoods in the segregated South. Today you might hear the Preservation Hall Jazz Band or Jerry "The Iceman" Butler.

Town Park, between The Waterside and NAUTICUS on the Elizabeth River, is the scene of constant outdoor entertainment during the warm months, most sponsored by **Norfolk Festevents** (© 757/441-2345; www.festeventsva.org). These include Friday night concerts, the annual Norfolk Harborfest in June, Cingular Norfolk Jazz Festival in July, and the Cingular Town Point Virginia Wine Festival in October.

THE BAR & CLUB SCENE

Most grownup club action these days is found along Granby Street between Main and Charlotte streets, where some of the many restaurants and bars have live music (see "Where to Dine," above). Take a stroll any night, especially on weekends, and you're bound to hear tunes to your liking. Check out **Scotty Quixx,** 436 Granby St.

Tips The Best Time to Be Entertained

The best time to be entertained in Norfolk—or anywhere in Hampton Roads, for that matter—is during the **Virginia Arts Festival** (www.vaartsfest.com) from mid-April through mid-May. That's when the likes of Itzhak Perlman, the Martha Graham Dance Company, and the Tokyo String Quartet appear at venues from Williamsburg to Virginia Beach. Call © 877/741-2787 or 757/282-2800 for information, 757/671-8100 for tickets. Adding to the fun, the arts festival coincides with Norfolk's International Azalea Festival.

(© 757/625-0008), and **Hell's Kitchen,** 124 Granby St. (© 757/624-1906). Since the scene changes significantly from night to night depending on which bands are playing where, don't forget to pick up a copy of the local alternative newspaper, *Port Folio* (www.portfolioweekly.com), which will give a good rundown of what's going on when you're here.

A block to the east, opposite the MacArthur Center, the **Norva Theater,** 317 Monticello Ave. (© 757/627-4547; www.thenorva.com), hosts rock, reggae, and other bands. With lounges overlooking the stage from three levels, it's more a big club than a theater these days.

Once the center of Norfolk nightlife, the **Waterside Festival Marketplace** (see "Seeing the Sights," earlier in this chapter) attracts a mostly young after-dark crowd these days. Here you'll find **Jillian's** (© 757/624-9100), a noisy emporium with a restaurant, sports bar, billiards and electronic games, and a dance club with music to thrill the soul of any 18-year-old. A bit more refined are the dueling pianos at **Crocodile Rocks** (© 757/478-1138). I like to stroll through The Waterside to see what's going on, then head over to Granby Street.

2 Virginia Beach (★)

20 miles E of Norfolk; 110 miles E of Richmond; 207 miles S of Washington, D.C.

Just as Norfolk has given itself a major face-lift in recent years, so has Virginia Beach had a bit of cosmetic surgery. The city's 20 miles of unbroken sand and surf have always lured families from throughout the region to take their annual beach vacations here. Many of them are of modest means, and traditionally the beach takes on a certain "Redneck Riviera" flavor from Memorial Day to Labor Day. But that image is changing as new hotels and surfside parks add luster to the oceanfront area.

Although resorts line the beachfront and obscure ocean views from everywhere except their own rooms, the 59-block-long Boardwalk (it's actually concrete) boasts immaculate landscaping, wood benches, small parks, a bike-skating path, public restrooms, and attractive white Colonial-style street lamps. And during the summer, the Boardwalk hosts free live entertainment most evenings.

There is more to do in Virginia Beach than lying on the sand, swimming, kayaking, fishing, and chasing dolphins offshore. Nature lovers can drive a few miles south to the **Back Bay National Wildlife Refuge,** which attracts migrating birds and protects several miles of beach and marshlands from development, and to the deserted beaches of **False Cape State Park** down by the North Carolina border. Here also is the **Virginia Aquarium & Marine Science Center,** the most popular museum in the state and a terrific place to take the kids even if it isn't raining. History lovers will find several sites of interest, including the **First Landing Cross,** where the Jamestown settlers planted their own cross on April 26, 1607.

ESSENTIALS
VISITOR INFORMATION

For information on planning your trip or assistance while you're here, contact the **Visitor Information Center,** 2100 Parks Ave., Virginia Beach, VA 23451 (© 800/822-3224; www.vbfun.com). A large board has phones connected to the reservations desks of major hotels and resorts. Particularly helpful are the center's annual "Vacation Guide" and a free **map** showing public restrooms and municipal parking lots in the

Virginia Beach

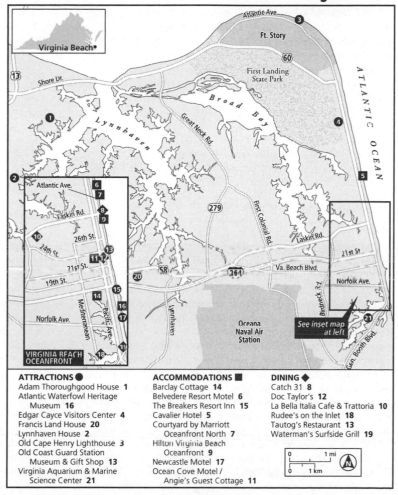

ATTRACTIONS ●
Adam Thoroughgood House **1**
Atlantic Waterfowl Heritage
 Museum **16**
Edgar Cayce Visitors Center **4**
Francis Land House **20**
Lynnhaven House **2**
Old Cape Henry Lighthouse **3**
Old Coast Guard Station
 Museum & Gift Shop **13**
Virginia Aquarium & Marine
 Science Center **21**

ACCOMMODATIONS ■
Barclay Cottage **14**
Belvedere Resort Motel **6**
The Breakers Resort Inn **15**
Cavalier Hotel **5**
Courtyard by Marriott
 Oceanfront North **7**
Hilton Virginia Beach
 Oceanfront **9**
Newcastle Motel **17**
Ocean Cove Motel /
 Angie's Guest Cottage **11**

DINING ◆
Catch 31 **8**
Doc Taylor's **12**
La Bella Italia Cafe & Trattoria **10**
Rudee's on the Inlet **18**
Tautog's Restaurant **13**
Waterman's Surfside Grill **19**

resort area. The center is at the eastern end of I-264. It's open daily from 9am to 5pm, to 8pm from Father's Day through Labor Day weekend.

A satellite office is in First Landing State Park's **Chesapeake Bay Center,** 2500 Shore Dr. (U.S. 60; © **757/412-2316**). It's open daily from 9am to 5pm.

There are **information kiosks** at the beach on Atlantic Avenue at 17th and 24th streets from late spring through October. *Note:* These are the only official visitor information booths at the beach; most others with "tourist information" signs are come-ons for the many timeshare sales operations here.

Racks at the visitor information center and elsewhere contain several slick give-away tourist publications packed with information and money-saving coupons.

GETTING THERE

BY PLANE   Virginia Beach is served by **Norfolk International Airport (ORF),** about 15 miles west of the oceanfront resort area (see "Essentials" in "Norfolk," earlier in this chapter).

BY CAR   Follow I-64 to I-264 East. I-264 ends near the heart of the oceanfront resort area. Also from the west, U.S. 60 becomes the scenic Shore Drive, which dead-ends at Pacific Avenue on the northern end of the ocean beach; a right turn takes you along this main north-south drag through the resort area. From the north or south, U.S. 13 and 17 will take you to I-64.

CITY LAYOUT

The city of Virginia Beach covers a huge geographic area between the Chesapeake Bay and the North Carolina line. There's no downtown; instead, it's like one giant suburb. Most municipal offices are at the southeastern end of Princess Anne Road. The largest commercial district is known as **Pembroke,** off I-64 at the intersection of Independence and Virginia Beach boulevards, where the up-and-coming **Virginia Beach Town Center** houses many national restaurants and retailers.

You can forget about all that if you're here on vacation, for the fun is at the **Oceanfront,** the prime resort area. Here you will find a solid line of big hotels, restaurants, beachwear and souvenir shops, and video-game arcades. The famous **Boardwalk** and its adjacent bike/skating path run along the beach from 1st Street at Rudee Inlet north to 39th Street. Behind the beachfront hotels, **Atlantic Avenue** takes you north-south between Rudee Inlet all the way north to Cape Henry. A block inland, the four-lane **Pacific Avenue** goes from the inlet north to 42nd Street (it's a much speedier way through the resort area than Atlantic Ave.). At Rudee Inlet, Pacific Avenue gives way to **General Booth Boulevard,** which takes you southwest past the Virginia Aquarium & Marine Science Center.

To the north, Chesapeake Bay and the Atlantic Ocean meet at Cape Henry, home to **Cape Henry Lighthouse, Fort Story,** and the **First Landing State Park.**

Some 12 miles south of the resort area, **Sandbridge** is an oceanfront enclave of cottages and condos. Sandbridge is aptly named, for it constitutes a "sand bridge" connecting the Virginia mainland to North Carolina's magnificent Outer Banks chain of barrier islands, which stretch for hundreds of miles to the south of here. To the east is the Atlantic Ocean. To the west, a maze of "back bay" marshes and waterways makes this a natural jewel comparable to Assateague Island on the Eastern Shore (see section 3, later in this chapter). You can't drive from Sandbridge to the Outer Banks because of **Back Bay National Wildlife Refuge** and **False Cape State Park,** which protect the Peninsula and offer undisturbed beach and marshland for hikers, bikers, bird-watchers, and sun worshipers.

GETTING AROUND

Between mid-June and Labor Day, especially on weekends, parking spaces near the beach can be as scarce as hen's teeth. Try the **municipal parking garages** on Atlantic Avenue at 3rd, 9th, 19th, and 26th streets or a few private pay lots along Pacific Avenue (the visitor information center has free maps that show them).

I usually leave my car at my hotel and get around on the **VB Wave Trolley** (**www.vbwave.com**), whose Route 30 runs from May through September, about every 15 minutes from 8am to 2am along Atlantic Avenue between Rudee Inlet and 42nd

Street. You can transfer at 40th Street to the regular Route 33 bus for First Landing State Park and other points to the north.

Memorial Day through Labor Day weekends, the **Aquarium Trolley** (Rte. 31) runs daily, about every 15 minutes from 8am to 2am between Atlantic Avenue at 40th Street and the Virginia Aquarium & Marine Science Center on General Booth Boulevard. And the **Shoppers Express** (Rte. 32) goes from Atlantic Avenue to Laskin Road past the Hilltop Shopping Center to Lynnhaven Mall.

Fare on any VB Wave Trolley is $1 per ride except for children shorter than 38 inches tall, who ride free. It's more economical to buy a 1-, 3-, and 5-day **Discount Fare Card** for $3, $5, and $8, respectively. All permit unlimited rides. Buy them at the automated blue-and-yellow dispensing machines at the trolley stops or at the transit kiosk on Atlantic Avenue at 24th Street.

The trolleys are operated by **Hampton Roads Transit** (**HRT;** © 757/222-6100; www.gohrt.com), which also provides public bus service in the region. HRT's **oceanfront terminal** is on Pacific Avenue between 19th and 20th streets. From there, the Route 20 bus goes to downtown Norfolk (it takes up to 2 hr. each way). Regular bus fares are $1.20 for adults, $1 for children younger than 19, free for kids shorter than 38 inches tall. Exact change is required.

For a taxi, call **Andy's Cab Co.** (© 757/495-3300).

OUTDOOR ACTIVITIES

Virginia Beach offers a wonderful variety of watersports, starting, of course, with its fine-sand beach for swimming. But note that between Memorial Day and Labor Day, no ball playing, fishing, or other sports are allowed on the beach between 2nd Street and 42nd Street from 10am to 5pm.

BIKING, JOGGING & SKATING   You can walk, jog, or run on the Boardwalk, or bike and skate on its adjoining bike path. There are biking and hiking trails in **First Landing State Park** (which rents bikes) and in **Back Bay National Wildlife Refuge** (see "Parks & Wildlife Refuges," below).

You can rent wheels from early March to October from **Cherie's Bicycle & Blade Rental** (© 757/437-8888) and **Bonnie's Beach Bikes** (© 757/460-9051), which have stations every couple of blocks along the Boardwalk. Rentals start at $6 an hour, $59 a week.

FISHING   Deep-sea fishing aboard a party boat can be an exciting day's entertainment for novices and dedicated fishermen alike. Headquarters for both party and private charter boats is the **Virginia Beach Fishing Center,** 200 Winston-Salem Ave. (© 757/422-5700; www.virginiafishing.com), on Rudee Inlet. Make reservations at the center at least a day in advance.

You can also drop a line from the **Virginia Beach Fishing Pier,** between 14th and 15th streets, oceanfront (© 757/428-2333), open April through October. It has bait for sale and rods for rent. On the Chesapeake Bay, **Lynnhaven Inlet Fishing Pier,** Starfish Road off Shore Drive (© 757/481-7071), open 24 hours a day in summer, rents rods and reels and sells crab cages.

GOLF   Next to Williamsburg, Virginia Beach offers more golf holes per capita than any other Virginia destination. Sand, water, and wind make up for the area's flat terrain to provide plenty of challenges at the **Virginia Beach National Golf Club** (© 877/484-3872 or 757/563-9440; www.vbnational.com), designed by Pete Dye

---

Tips Good Golf Packages

You don't have to be Tiger Woods to take advantage of golf packages organized by **Virginia Beach Golf Getaways** (© 866/482-4653; www.vbgolf.com). Check the website or ask the visitor center for a copy of its annual golf guide.

---

and Curtis Strange and formerly known as the Tournament Players Club of Virginia Beach.

Elevated tees and strategically placed water and bunkers pose problems at **Heron Ridge Golf Club** (© 757/426-3800; www.heronridge.com), designed by Fred Couples and Gene Bates. Sharp fairway angles at the Rees Jones-designed **Hell's Point Golf Course** (© 757/721-3400; www.hellspoint.com) have been described as "devilish." Another Rees Jones project, **Honey Bee Golf Course** (© 757/471-2768) is shorter (par 70) but presents challenges for beginners and experts alike. The city has several public links, including **Red Wing Lake Municipal Golf Course** (© 757/437-4845; www.vbgov.com/dept/parks).

Call the courses for greens fees, tee times, and directions.

KAYAKING Even if you've never settled your stern into a kayak, you're sure to enjoy a paddling excursion in this area's quiet backwaters or a dolphin-watching adventure on the high seas. As the popularity of kayaking has increased, so has the number of operators here. The local convention and visitor bureau (see "Essentials," above) publishes a "Virginia Beach Adventure Getaways" brochure listing all of them and some hotels that have outdoor packages.

Kayak Nature Tours (© 888/669-8368 or 757/480-1999; www.tidewateradventures.com) has been around the longest and is still one of the best. It has 2½-hour dolphin-watching trips from May through October. The guides also lead tours of the Back Bay National Wildlife Refuge and to other nearby locations. Tour prices range from $45 to $80, with a 25% discount for children accompanied by an adult. Reservations are required.

If Kayak Adventures doesn't have space, contact **Wild River Outfitters** (© 877/431-8566 or 757/431-8566; wildriveroutfitters.com), **Back Bay Getaways** (© 757/721-4484; www.backbaygetaways.com), or **Ocean Rentals Ltd.** (© 800/695-4212 or 757/721-6210; www.oceanrentalsltd.com). The latter two are in Sandbridge and specialize in touring the nearby Back Bay National Wildlife Refuge.

SCUBA DIVING The Atlantic Ocean off Virginia Beach is colder and less clear than it is below Cape Hatteras, North Carolina, but that's not to say you can't dive here. **Lynnhaven Dive Center** (© 757/481-7949; www.ldcscuba.com) sends its two dive boats out to more than 20 nearby wrecks and other sites year-round, and it has trips to warmer waters in North Carolina. It also teaches diving and rents equipment.

SURFING Unlike the huge breakers on the north shore of Oahu, the waves here usually are gentle enough during summer for novices to learn to stay up on a surfboard—and probably not break a leg in the process (don't sue me if you do!). If you've never been on a board and would like to test your balance, take a 2-hour lesson from **Ocean Rentals Ltd.** (© 800/695-4212 or 757/721-6210; oceanrentalsltd.com) in Sandbridge for $45 per person. Reservations are required.

SWIMMING   During the summer season, lifeguards are on duty along the resort strip from 2nd to 42nd streets; they also handle raft, umbrella, and beach-chair rentals. Despite their presence, you should always be careful when swimming in the surf, particularly if a northeast wind is kicking up a dangerous undertow. When in doubt, ask the lifeguard.

You can get away from the summer crowds—and the lifeguards—by driving 12 miles south of Rudee Inlet to **Little Island City Park,** in the residential beach area of Sandbridge. To really escape the crowds, take the tram from there to **False Cape State Park** (see "Parks & Wildlife Refuges," below).

WAVE RUNNING & PARASAILING   You can rent exciting WaveRunners from **Rudee Inlet Jet Ski Rentals** next to the Virginia Beach Fishing Center at Rudee Inlet (© 757/428-4614).

PARKS & WILDLIFE REFUGES

One of the best things about Virginia Beach is that you don't have to go far from the busy resort to find open spaces for hiking, biking, camping, and bird-watching.

Back Bay & False Cape ✿✿✿   Especially inviting for bird-watchers, canoeists, and kayakers is **Back Bay National Wildlife Refuge,** in the southeastern corner of Virginia near the North Carolina line. Actually on the northern end of North Carolina's Outer Banks, its 9,200 acres of beaches, dunes, marshes, and backwaters are typical of the barrier island environment. It also is on the main Atlantic Flyway for migratory birds, and a wide range of wildlife lives here all year. No swimming, surfing, or sunbathing is allowed on the pristine beach, but you can collect shells, surf-cast for fish, and bird-watch. There are also nature trails and a canoe launching spot with marked trails through the marshes. Daily admission April through October is $5 per vehicle, $2 per pedestrian or biker; it's free November through March. The refuge is open daily from sunup to sundown all year. The **visitor contact station** (© 757/721-2412) is open Monday through Friday 8am to 4pm, weekends 9am to 4pm. It offers nature and environmental education programs by reservation only. Note that pets are permitted, on leashes, October through March only. From Rudee Inlet, go south on General Booth Boulevard and follow the signs 12 miles to Sandbridge and the refuge. For more information, contact the Refuge Manager, 4005 Sandpiper Rd., Virginia Beach, VA 23456 (© 757/721-2412; www.fws.gov/backbay).

The kayak outfitters mentioned under "Outdoor Activities," above, will take you paddling in the refuge.

Swimming and sunbathing are permitted on the beach in **False Cape State Park,** 4 miles south of the Back Bay visitor contact station via a hiking and biking trail. You'll find 6 miles of beachfront (to the North Carolina line), an interpretive trail, and more than 3 miles of hiking trails. Primitive camping is by permit only, which you can get by calling © 800/933-7275. The park has no other visitor facilities, so bring everything you will need, including drinking water. It's open daily sunrise to sunset.

You can't park in the national wildlife refuge lot while visiting False Cape State Park, so leave your vehicle at Little Island City Park in Sandbridge. From there, you can either hike or bike the 6 miles to False Cape or take the refuge's specially built **tram** that inches its way along the trails daily from Memorial Day through Labor Day weekends, Friday through Sunday in April, May, September, and October. It departs at 9am and returns at 12:45pm and stops for about 2 hours at the False Cape. It's first-come, first-served, but call ℭ **800/426-3643** to make sure it's running. Fares are $8 adults, $6 seniors and children under 12.

For more information, contact the park at 4001 Sandpiper Rd., Virginia Beach, VA 23456 (ℭ **757/426-7128;** www.dcr.state.va.us/parks/falscape.htm).

First Landing State Park 🎯🎯 The Virginia Company, which went on to settle Jamestown, made its first landing in the New World on April 16, 1607, in what is now this fine state park, whose 2,888 preserved acres run between the Lynnhaven River and the Chesapeake Bay to within 2 blocks of the oceanfront. Rabbits, squirrels, and raccoons are among the many species in this urban park, which boasts 19 miles of hiking trails. The main entrance is on Shore Drive (U.S. 60), where the visitor information center is open daily 9am to 5pm. The grounds and trails are open daily 8am to sunset. The 64th Street entry, off Atlantic Avenue, leads to a quiet-water beach on Broad Bay. Admission to the park during summer is $3 per vehicle on weekdays, $4 on weekends. Bikes are prohibited except on the gravel, 6-mile Cape Henry Trail, which runs between the 64th Street entrance and the trail center.

There are 20 two-bedroom cabins that can be rented here. Rates vary by season, and bookings are essential, so call the state park reservations center (ℭ **800/933-7275**). Open from March through November, a bayside campground in a wooded area beside a fine beach has 222 sites for tents and RVs for $22 to $28 a night plus tax. The park store (ℭ **757/412-2302**) rents bicycles and beach equipment and supplies.

For more information, contact the park at 2500 Shore Dr., Virginia Beach, VA 23451 (ℭ **757/412-2320;** www.dcr.state.va.us/parks/1stland.htm).

Next to the campground, the **Chesapeake Bay Center** (ℭ **727/412-2316**) has an exhibit about the Jamestown settlers' landing here in 1607. It also shows a short video and has an exhibit about the local ecology, both put together by the Virginia Aquarium & Marine Science Center; it's interesting but not as good as the main museum (p. 306). There's a visitor information desk here. A beachside amphitheater hosts concerts during the summer (call for a schedule). The center is open daily 9am to 5pm.

THE TOP ATTRACTIONS

Atlantic Wildfowl Heritage Museum 🎯🎯 This small but excellent museum displays a collection of carved decoys—some of them more than a century old—and decorative wildlife, plus paintings of ducks, geese, and other wildfowl. It occupies the white-brick-and-clapboard DeWitt beach cottage built in 1895 by Virginia Beach's first mayor. The oldest structure on the waterfront, the cottage alone is worth a stop as you stroll along the Boardwalk. It's operated by the Back Bay Wildfowl Guild, which applies the donations and profits from the gift shop (which carries excellent decoys) to its conservation efforts.

1113 Atlantic Ave. (at 12th St.). ℭ **757/437-8432.** www.awhm.org. Free admission (donations encouraged). Summer Mon–Sat 10am–5pm, Sun noon–5pm; off season Tues–Sat 10am–5pm, Sun noon–5pm. Closed Jan 1, Thanksgiving, Dec 25, and Dec 31.

Edgar Cayce Visitors Center You don't have to be the least bit psychic to visit this center carrying on the work of the late Edgar Cayce, whose own psychic talent manifested itself when he found he could enter into an altered state of consciousness and answer questions on any topic. His answers, or "discourses," now called "readings," number some 14,305. If you don't know about Cayce, show up at 2pm for a 30-minute movie about his life, followed by a 30-minute guided tour. The A.R.E. Bookstore has

Tips **The Sound of Freedom**

The **Naval Air Station Oceana** (www.nasoceana.navy.mil) is home to those low-flying U.S. Navy F-14 Tomcat and F/A-18 Hornet fighter planes whose thundering jets disturb the peace over the beach. That's the "sound of freedom" to patriotic locals; the "sound of money" to wags who emphasize that Oceana is the city's largest employer. Other than when they roar over at a 600-foot altitude, the best way for us civilians to see them up close is on a **Naval Air Station Oceana Tour** offered by Hampton Roads Transit (℮ 757/222-6100; www.hrtransit.org). The tours depart from the HRT kiosk at Atlantic Avenue and 24th Street during the summer, Monday through Friday at 9:30 and 11:30am. Fares are $7.50 for adults; $5 for seniors, children younger than 12, and persons with disabilities. Everyone older than 18 years old will need a picture ID to get on the base. Do not bring backpacks.

an excellent selection of books and videos about holistic health, parapsychology, life after death, dreams, and even cooking. The Meditation Room on the third floor offers a spectacular view of the ocean and is painted with colors chosen because Cayce's readings suggested they can help attain higher consciousness. Outside the center is the Meditation Garden. Inside, the health center and spa offer steam baths, facials, and massages to the public.

215 67th St. (at Atlantic Ave.). ℮ 757/428-3588. www.edgarcayce.org. Free admission. Mon–Sat 9am–8pm; Sun noon–8pm. 30-min. film daily 2pm. 30-min. guided tours depart daily 2:30pm. Closed Thanksgiving and Dec 25.

Old Cape Henry Lighthouse ⋒⋒   Built in 1791–92, this picturesque brick structure was the first lighthouse authorized by the U.S. Congress. It marked the southern entrance to Chesapeake Bay until 1881, when a new lighthouse nearby took over. If you're in shape, you can climb the 191 steps to the top for a spectacular view over Cape Henry, the bay, and the ocean. The gift shop carries a plethora of lighthouse-themed items.

Across the road, the Jamestown colonists' **First Landing Site** is marked by a cross and plaque where they "set up a Crosse at Chesapeake Bay and named that place Cape Henry" for Henry, Prince of Wales. Also here are a monumental relief map showing the French and British naval engagement off Cape Henry during the Revolutionary War and a statue of the French commander. Now known as the **Battle Off the Capes,** this decisive battle effectively trapped Cornwallis at Yorktown and helped end British dominion in America.

Note: You must be more than 4 feet tall to climb the lighthouse. This is all part of the U.S. Army's Fort Story, so everyone 18 and over will need a photo ID to access the fort's historic area.

583 Atlantic Ave. (in Fort Story). ℮ 757/422-9421. www.apva.org. Admission $4 adults, $2 children 3–12, free for children younger than 3. Mar 16–Oct 31 daily 10am–5pm; Nov 1–Mar 15 daily 10am–4pm. Closed Thanksgiving and Dec 5–Jan 4.

Old Coast Guard Station Museum and Gift Shop ⋒   In the heart of the oceanfront resort area, this small museum is housed in the white-clapboard building constructed in 1903 as a lifesaving station. Its exhibits recall rescue missions and

Dolphin-Watching & Splashing with the Seals

Provided you're not overly prone to seasickness, one of the most interesting things to do here is to take an offshore **dolphin-watching cruise** ☆☆☆ given by the Virginia Aquarium & Marine Science Center (daily June–Sept, Sat–Sun in spring and fall). The center also has **whale-watching cruises** in winter (also offshore) and **sea life–collecting trips** in summer. The trips cost $18 to $30 for adults, $14 to $25 for children younger than 12. The boats leave from Rudee Inlet. Call the aquarium or check its website for schedules (✆ **757/425-3474;** www.virginiaaquarium.com). To make reservations, which are required, call (✆ **757/385-3474**).

Another marvelous experience at the center, especially for children 8 and older, is its **Harbor Seal Splash** ☆☆☆. Accompanied by an animal-care specialist, you actually get into a pool and splash around with the resident harbor seals and participate in a training session. The 2-hour sessions take place April through September. If you can afford it, the $125 per person is worth it. Call ✆ **757/385-0300** for reservations, which are required.

shipwrecks along the coast. Not all is old here, for you can manipulate a video cam atop the building to get a bird's-eye view of the beach. You can see it all in 45 minutes. An excellent gift shop carries clocks, drawings, books, and other things nautical.

24th St. and Atlantic Ave. ✆ 757/422-1587. www.oldcoastguardstation.com. Admission $4 adults, $3 seniors, $2 children 6–18, free for children under 6. Summer Mon–Sat 10am–5pm, Sun noon–5pm; off season Tues–Sat 10am–5pm, Sun noon–5pm. Closed Jan 1, Thanksgiving, Dec 25, and Dec 31.

Virginia Aquarium & Marine Science Center ☆☆☆ *Kids*　　This entertaining, educational facility focusing on Virginia's marine environment is a wonderful place to take the kids. Its 45 acres are beside Owl Creek salt marsh, a wildlife habitat. You can easily spend half a day here, a full day to see—and learn—it all. Plan to spend at least half of your time in the main building, where touch tanks will fascinate you and the kids (bet you don't know a horseshoe crab's mouth feels like a toothbrush). Rays willingly swim over in one tank to have their leathery hides petted. Kids will love playing with the switches and dials in a dark room designed like a submarine, complete with sonar "pings." The sub looks out into one of several room-size aquariums holding a myriad of sea turtles, sharks, rays, and other species found in Virginia waters. Movies in the center's 3-D IMAX theater feature animals leaping off the screen at you.

As you leave the main building, take a look at the salt marsh room, which will prepare you for a .3-mile nature hike along the creek, or to take an informative 35-minute cruise in a 50-passenger pontoon boat on Owl Creek and through Virginia Beach's last undeveloped salt marsh. There's an observation tower from which you might see some of the wild animals living on an island across the creek. The boardwalk nature trail leads to the smaller Owl Creek Marsh Pavilion, were river otters play in an outdoor tank and more than 50 species of birds fly about an aviary (the big noisy birds passing overhead are fighters taking off and landing at nearby Oceana Naval Air Station). It also houses the fascinating "Macro Marsh" display in which everything is enlarged 10 times normal size to give you a crab's eye view of the world.

The Aquarium Trolley stops at both buildings, so you can get on at the pavilion; otherwise, you'll have to walk back to your car outside the main building.

717 General Booth Blvd. (southwest of Rudee Inlet). ✆ 757/385-3474. www.virginiaaquarium.com. Admission $12 adults, $11 seniors, $7.95 children 4–11, free for children 3 and younger. IMAX tickets $7.50 adults, $6 seniors, $6.50 children 3–11, free for children under 3. Owl Creek Cruise $5 per person, $3.50 with combination ticket. Combination museum and IMAX tickets $17 adults, $16 seniors, $14 children 3–11, free for children under 3. Combination museum and Owl Creek Cruise tickets $15 adults, $14 seniors, $11 children 3–11, free for children under 3. Memorial Day to Labor Day daily 9am–7pm; Sept–May daily 9am–5pm. Owl Creek cruises Apr–Sept. Closed Thanksgiving and Dec 25.

HISTORIC HOMES

While the oceanfront resort area is a modern development, settlers carved out inland homesteads and plantations starting in the 1600s. Dating to around 1680 and 1725, respectively, the Adam Thoroughgood and Lynnhaven houses are interesting because they were both built in the fashion of English farm cottages of Elizabethan times, 150 years before the Georgian architecture prevalent elsewhere in Colonial Virginia. Allow half a day to see them all, including driving times.

Adam Thoroughgood House 🐾 One of the oldest homes in Virginia and the most interesting of the trio discussed in this section, this medieval English-style cottage sits on 4½ acres of lawn and garden overlooking the Lynnhaven River. It was built around 1680 by one of Adam Thoroughgood's grandsons (historians believe its namesake didn't live in the house). The interior has exposed wood beams and whitewashed walls, and though the furnishings did not belong to the Thoroughgoods, they are original to the period and reflect the family's English ancestry.

1636 Parish Rd. (at Thoroughgood Lane). ✆ 757/460-0007. www.vbgov.com. Admission $4 adults, $3 seniors and children 13–18, $2 children 6–12, free for children 5 and younger. Tues–Sat 9am–5pm; Sun 11am–5pm. Guided 30-min. tours available by request (last tour 4:30pm). From oceanfront, take I-264 W. to Exit 3, go north on Independence Blvd. (Va. 225), turn right on Pleasure House Rd., right on Thoroughgood Sq., left on Thoroughgood Dr., and follow the very small signs to the house.

Francis Land House Built as a plantation manor in the mid–18th century (now beside one of the region's busiest highways), this Georgian-style brick house is a restoration work in progress. Some rooms are furnished with antiques and reproductions. The highlights here are 7 acres of herb, vegetable, and pleasure gardens and a .1-mile wetlands nature trail.

3131 Virginia Beach Blvd. (just west of Kings Grant Rd.). ✆ 757/431-4000. www.vbgov.com. Admission $4 adults, $3 seniors and children 13–18, $2 children 6–12, free for children 5 and younger. Tues–Sat 9am–5pm; Sun 11am–5pm. Guided 30-min. house tours depart by request (last tour 4:30pm).

Lynnhaven House Built in 1725, this medieval-style cottage still doesn't have running water or electricity. When the Association for the Preservation of Virginia Antiquities took the house over in 1971, it stripped away plaster and discovered the Champford ceiling beams in their original condition (note the chalk marks carpenters made in 1725). Tours led by costumed docents explain the house and interpret Colonial lifestyles. We moderns won't find Lynnhaven oysters as gigantic as the shells excavated from the trash pit and displayed in the kitchen.

4405 Wishart Rd. (off Independence Blvd.). ✆ 757/460-1688. www.apva.org. Admission $4 adults, $3 seniors, $2 children 5–16, free for children 4 and younger. Tues–Sat 10am–4pm; Sun noon–4pm. Guided 45-min. tours depart by request. From the beach, take I-264 W. to Exit 3, head north on Independence Blvd. (Va. 225), take a right, and drive ⅓ mile on Wishart Rd.

WHERE TO STAY

The hotels and B&Bs listed below are just the tip of the more than 11,000 hotel rooms in Virginia Beach. Even with that many places to stay, you should reserve as far in advance as possible from mid-June through Labor Day, and especially on weekends when room rates are at their highest. Late spring and early fall are good times to visit; both have warm weather and lower rates. Least expensive prices are in the cold winter months, when few come here.

With so many hotels offering so many rooms, choosing the right one can be a daunting task. The Virginia Beach visitor information center (see "Essentials," earlier in this chapter) maintains a **reservations service** (© **800/822-3224**) that will help you find accommodations in any price range. The center's annual "Vacation Guide" lists all the local hotels and their current rates. It also distributes an annual accommodations directory published by the **Virginia Beach Hotel/Motel Association** (www. va-beach-hotels.com). The association's website has links to many of the hotels, most of which give their current room rates.

HOTELS

Belvedere Resort Motel *&& Value* This five-story building is the crown jewel of the few less expensive, family-operated oceanfront hotels left on the Oceanfront here. It justifiably attracts lots of repeat guests, so book early. Like the nearby Courtyard by Marriott Oceanfront North (see below), it's far enough north to avoid the rowdy crowds. The motel-style rooms have screen doors that swing open to balconies facing the ocean. The combo tub/shower bathrooms are small but compensate with separate sinks and vanities. A few rooms have king-size beds (most have two doubles). The 10 units on the ends of the building are somewhat larger and have cooking facilities. There's a small swimming pool, sun deck, and the **Belvedere Coffee Shop** (see "Where to Dine," below). Guests also get free use of bicycles.

Oceanfront at 36th St. (P.O. Box 451), Virginia Beach, VA 23458. © **800/425-0612** or 757/425-0612. Fax 757/ 425-1397. 50 units. $64–$156 double. AE, MC, V. Free parking. Closed late Oct to Mar. **Amenities:** Coffee shop; outdoor pool; free bicycles; room service. *In room:* A/C, TV, kitchen (in efficiencies), fridge, coffeemaker (in efficiencies).

The Breakers Resort Inn Another reasonably priced, family-operated oceanfront hotel, The Breakers occupies a yellow boxlike nine-story building. Its rooms are comfortably furnished with contemporary pieces. All have oceanfront balconies; some rooms with king-size beds contain hot tubs. Efficiency apartments have a bedroom with two queen-size beds, a living room with a Murphy bed, and kitchenette with two-burner stove (but no oven). Additional amenities include free bicycles. The onsite cafe serves breakfast and lunch.

1503 Atlantic Ave. (oceanfront at 16th St.), Virginia Beach, VA 23451. © **800/237-7532** or 757/428-1821. Fax 757/ 422-9602. www.breakersresort.com. 57 units. $55–$270 double. Packages available. AE, DC, DISC, MC, V. Free parking. **Amenities:** Restaurant (breakfast and lunch); heated outdoor pool; free bicycles; coin-op washers and dryers. *In room:* A/C, TV, high-speed Internet, kitchen (in efficiencies), fridge, coffeemaker, iron.

Cavalier Hotel *&&* Virginia Beach's best-equipped resort actually consists of two hotels—the original Cavalier on the Hill, built in 1927 across Atlantic Avenue from the beach, and the Cavalier on the Ocean, which has been kept up-to-date since it opened in 1973. Although it's not directly on the beach, and it's open only during the summer and is mainly used for overflow guests, the original building has all the charm. Its enclosed veranda with white-wicker furnishings, potted plants, and great ocean views evoke images of the days when F. Scott and Zelda Fitzgerald danced here and lunches were black tie. Some of its guest rooms have Williamsburg-quality Chippendale reproductions, Colonial-print fabrics, gilt-framed artwork, and museum-quality decorative objects. Some feature European-style bathrooms with black-and-white tile, pedestal sinks, whirlpools, lighted makeup mirrors, and bidets. The heated indoor Olympic-size pool is magnificently tiled and illuminated by a skylight. Open all year, the newer beachside building has nicely decorated contemporary-style rooms, all with oceanfront balconies. A shuttle connects the two wings when both are open. The boardwalk stops just short of the Cavalier, so unlike all other hotels here, its lawn fronts directly on the beach.

Oceanfront at 42nd St., Virginia Beach, VA 23451. (©) **800/446-8199** or 757/425-8555. Fax 757/428-7957. www. cavalierhotel.com. 425 units. $89–$289 double; $199–$499 suite. Weekend and other packages available. AE, DC, DISC, MC, V. Parking $7.50. **Amenities:** 5 restaurants; 3 bars; 1 indoor pool; 2 outdoor pools (full-size, children's); 3 tennis courts; health club; watersports equipment/rentals; bike rentals; children's programs; concierge; activities desk; business center; room service; laundry service; concierge-level rooms. *In room:* A/C, TV, Wi-Fi (in beach wing), minibar (in suites and oceanfront rooms), coffeemaker, iron.

Courtyard by Marriott Oceanfront North (*Value*) This 11-story oceanfront hotel was one of the first Courtyards designed as much as a resort as for business travelers. Making this a good family choice is the oceanfront's largest outdoor pool, with waterfalls, bridges, a lifeguard on duty, and its own bar. Here the beach substitutes for an actual courtyard, and big window walls look out to the Boardwalk from the plush lobby and bright, casual dining room, which provides good hotel fare for breakfast, lunch, and dinner (you can dine outside in fine weather). Marriott's standard furniture prevails in the spacious guest quarters, all of which have balconies overlooking the ocean. Ten units have whirlpool tubs. The eight huge suites have bedrooms and living rooms, which come equipped with wet bars, microwave ovens, and refrigerators. A small indoor pool and a fitness room look out to the beach.

Its slightly older sister, the **Courtyard by Marriott Oceanfront South,** 2501 Atlantic Ave., at 25th Street (© **800/321-2211** or 757/491-6222; www.courtyard oceanfront.com), lacks an outdoor pool, but otherwise is identical.

3737 Atlantic Ave. (oceanfront at 37th St.), Virginia Beach, VA 23451. (©) **800/321-2211** or 757/437-0098. Fax 757/437-4272. www.courtyardoceanfrontnorth.com. 160 units. $99–$329 double. AE, DC, DISC, MC, V. Free parking. **Amenities:** Restaurant; bar; outdoor and indoor pools; health club; Jacuzzi; room service (dinner only); coin-op washers and dryers. *In room:* A/C, TV, high-speed Internet, fridge, coffeemaker, iron.

Hilton Virginia Beach Oceanfront This 21-story tower opened on the oceanfront in 2005 and immediately raised the stakes for all other hotels here. You'll see what I mean upon entering the grand lobby, where a huge water wall shaped like a Neptune's shell changes its colors every few minutes. The hotel's most unique feature is its rooftop recreation area, featuring a heated indoor pool, snack restaurant, bar, and an outdoor pool whose horizon seemingly meets the sea. You can see all the way to Norfolk from up here on a clear day. On the ground level, the casual but sophisticated **Catch 31** fishhouse is one of the beach's better restaurants (p. 311), and part of it becomes the fine-dining **Salacia** at night. The spacious rooms and suites come equipped with modern amenities such as 32- or 42-inch flatscreen TVs and high-speed Internet access. Parlor suites add Murphy beds and kitchenettes. Empyrean Club units on the top three floors have the best views and their own 24-hour concierge lounge serving continental breakfast, evening hors d'oeuvres, and cocktails. All units except the City View rooms have balconies. This Hilton and the Cavalier (see above) are the two best resorts here.

3001 Atlantic Ave., Virginia Beach, VA 23451. ℂ **800/445-8667** or 757/213-3001. Fax 757/213-3019. www. hiltonvb.com. 291 units. $209–$429 double; $270–$389 suite. AE, DC, DISC, MC, V. Valet parking $8. **Amenities:** 3 restaurants; 2 bars; outdoor and indoor pools; health club; watersports equipment/rentals; concierge; activities desk; business center; shopping arcade; limited room service; spa; massage; babysitting; laundry service; concierge-level rooms. *In room:* A/C, TV, high-speed Internet, kitchen (in parlor suites), coffeemaker, iron, safe.

Newcastle Motel   Situated beside the Atlantic Wildfowl Heritage Museum (p. 304), the 10-story, family-operated Newcastle offers the most unusual mix of rooms on the beach, ranging from standard motel units to romantic deluxe models with canopy beds, gas fireplaces, his-and-her shower heads, and wooden Venetian blinds to keep passersby from watching you frolic in big whirlpool tubs. All units have balconies, refrigerators, microwave ovens, and spa tubs. Guests get free access to bicycles in summer. The seasonal **Cabana Cafe** to one side offers reasonably priced meals under a big, beachside awning.

1201 Atlantic Ave. (oceanfront at 12th St.), Virginia Beach, VA 23451. ℂ **800/346-3176** or 757/428-3981. www. newcastlehotelvb.com. Fax 757/491-4394. 83 units. $60–$240 double. Rates include continental breakfast off season. Packages available. AE, DC, DISC, MC, V. Free parking. **Amenities:** Restaurant; indoor pool; health club; room service; coin-op washers and dryers. *In room:* A/C, TV, Wi-Fi, kitchen (2 units), fridge, coffeemaker, iron, safe.

Ocean Cove Motel/Angie's Guest Cottage ℝ (*Value*   Once a terrific bed-and-breakfast known simply as Angie's Guest Cottage, this establishment has been spiffed up in recent years, but it no longer serves breakfast. It does, however, still house one of Virginia's few official Hostelling International hostels, offering men's, women's, and coed dorm rooms plus a communal kitchen. Consequently, you'll find a delightful mix of American and international folks here. The original cottage, built in 1918 as family housing for the nearby lifesaving station (now the Old Coast Guard Station Museum and Gift Shop; p. 305), houses two simple but comfortable units. Next door are two kitchen-equipped apartments, each with porch and deck. Across the yard are three one-story cottages, each with three bedrooms, two bathrooms, and full kitchens; they are rented by the week and are the only units here with telephones.

302 24th St. (between Pacific and Arctic aves.), Virginia Beach, VA 23451. ℂ **757/491-1830.** www.oceancovemotel. com or www.angiescottage.com. 9 units (all with bathroom), 34 dorm beds. $64–$158 double room; $14–$21 dorm bed; $600–$1,250 cottage (per week). MC, V. Free on-street parking with $20 refundable deposit for permit. *In room:* A/C, TV (duplex units and cottages), fridge (upstairs, duplex, and cottage units), kitchen (duplex and cottage units).

A BED & BREAKFAST NEAR THE BEACH

Barclay Cottage ℝ (*Value*   This two-story, white-clapboard Victorian with wrap-around verandas is *very* coastal Southern, with rocking chairs on the porches and green shutters trimming tall windows hung with lace curtains. It was used as a boarding-house and school for many years before being converted into this charming B&B. The guest rooms are adorned with Victorian pieces, including feather beds, and the two downstairs rooms have jetted bathtubs. Innkeepers Stephen and Marie-Louise LaFond serve a full family-style breakfast in the lounge promptly at 9am. They also provide beach buggies to haul your complimentary umbrellas, chairs, and boogie boards to the beach, a 2-block walk away. Their "business center" is a computer squirreled away in an armoire in the upstairs hallway, and their "fitness center" consists of a basket full of barbells.

400 16th St. (at Arctic Ave.), Virginia Beach, VA 23451. ℂ **757/422-1956.** www.barclaycottage.com. 5 units (3 with private bathroom). $78–$195 double. Rates include full breakfast. AE, DISC, MC, V. Free parking. *In room:* A/C, Wi-Fi.

WHERE TO DINE

Until Doc Taylor's opened (see below), my favorite spot for breakfast was the **Belvedere Coffee Shop,** an old-fashioned diner at the Belvedere Motel, Oceanfront at 36th Street (© **757/425-1397**). It's still the best for a beachside breakfast, especially the two-person booth whose one bench faces the ocean. Prices range from $3 to $10. It's open daily 7am to 3pm, to 2:30pm off season.

The relatively inexpensive **Big Sam's Inlet Cafe & Raw Bar,** 300 Winston-Salem Ave. (© **757/428-4858**), overlooking the WaveRunner docks on Rudee Inlet, is another fine early-morning choice. It's open daily from 7am to 2am, making it a good place for a late-night snack, too.

For excellent picnic fare, head to the beach branch of **Taste Unlimited,** 213 36th St. (© **757/243-3011**), at Pacific Avenue. Sandwiches and salads are served on the premises at lunch. It's open daily 9am to 7pm (to 6pm off season).

Catch 31 🍴🍴 INTERNATIONAL   This modernistic restaurant serves seafood almost as good as its spectacular setting on the ground floor of the Hilton Virginia Beach Oceanfront. Floor-to-ceiling windows look out on the ocean in one direction, to the city's lively Neptune Park on the other. Reserve an outdoor table in summer to be treated to the park's nightly life entertainment. You can fill up at the raw bar with steamed shellfish or with a "seafood tower," Catch 31's signature dish—two or three plates stacked high with chilled crabmeat, Maine lobster, Chesapeake Bay crab legs, and a few other items with accompanying sauces. The menu changes as soon as fresh catch is delivered, so keep your eye on the ever-changing specials board for the latest arrivals. Meat lovers can opt for high-quality steaks, ribs, and chops, and there's a nightly pasta for vegetarians. At night part of the restaurant becomes the fine-dining **Salacia** (like, $60 for a Kobe steak).

3001 Atlantic Ave. (in Hilton Virginia Beach Oceanfront). © **757/213-3472**. Reservations highly recommended. Main courses $19–$30. AE, DC, DISC, MC, V. Mon–Fri 6:30am–11pm; Sat–Sun 7am–11pm (to 10pm daily off season). Bar daily 11am–2am.

Doc Taylor's 🄥𝘢𝘭𝘶𝘦 AMERICAN   Occupying its own vintage beach cottage, this is the breakfast and lunch operation of Tautog's Restaurant (see below), with which it shares owners and a parking lot. It's really a charming version of a diner, with a kitchen with counter seating in the old living room. The choice seats are on the enclosed porch. Breakfast provides the usual grilled items plus toasted bagels and my favorite, the "Old South," with diced country ham, eggs, and cheese grits combined. You can wash it down with a bloody mary or mimosa.

207 23rd St. (between Atlantic and Pacific aves.). © **757/425-1960**. Reservations not accepted. Breakfast $3–$15; lunch $3.50–$8. AE, DISC, MC, V. Daily 7am–3pm.

La Bella Italia Cafe & Trattoria 🍴 𝘝𝘢𝘭𝘶𝘦 ITALIAN   This deli is an excellent place to pick up sandwiches or Italian breads, pastries, and cookies for a day at the beach. After dark, you had best reserve a table, for a mesquite-fired oven produces the area's best pizzas, and locals flock here for bowls of homemade pasta. You'll recognize a few southern Italian favorites such as spaghetti Bolognese, but others are more creative. For starters, try the bruschetta, fried calamari, or in summer when the tomatoes are ripe and sweet, the *caprese* salad with homemade mozzarella.

1065 Laskin Rd. (in Laskin Center, 1 block east of Birdneck Rd.). © **757/422-8536**. Reservations highly recommended for dinner. Pizza $8–$13; main courses $14–$19. AE, DISC, MC, V. Mon–Thurs 11:30am–2:30pm and 5–10pm; Fri–Sat 11:30am–2:30pm and 5–11pm.

Rudee's on the Inlet ℛ SEAFOOD/STEAKS   This popular restaurant, occupying a replica of an old Coast Guard station, is dark and cozy on the inside, with big louvered windows overlooking Rudee Inlet. But that's not where you want to dine in good weather. Instead, walk across the parking lot to the marina-side sun deck and grab one of the gliding booths (that's right: you, the booth, and its green canopy actually slide back and forth). They serve a full menu out here until 5pm, and then light fare and raw-bar items, for the deck is one of the most popular after-work watering holes for the locals. Although steaks and other fare are offered, seafood is the highlight. Everything is prepared to order, so kick back and enjoy the waterside setting while the chef fries or broils your fish, shrimp, scallops, above-average crab cakes, and oysters (best when they are being harvested during months spelled with an "r": Sept–Apr). Many fresh-off-the-boat items are market priced. Valet parking is available.

277 Mediterranean Ave. (at Rudee Inlet). ℂ 757/425-1777. Reservations not accepted, but call ahead for preferred seating. Sandwiches $6–$11; main courses $13–$24. AE, DC, DISC, MC, V. Mon–Sat 11am–10pm; Sun 9am–10pm (bar later depending on business).

Tautog's Restaurant ℛℛ *Finds* SEAFOOD   Occupying one of the few remaining Victorian-era beach cottages still standing in the heart of the resort area, this is the most charming restaurant here and one of the most popular with locals, many of whom ride their bikes here in summer to avoid the beach's parking nightmare. You can dine inside, but opt instead for a table under ceiling fans out on the front porch. Seafood predominates, with "Wesley's world-famous crab cakes" leading the list. Another winner is the flounder with crab-and-shrimp filling poached in parchment. It's all very good value. You might find a space in the small parking lot in the rear (take the alley between here and Doc Taylor's).

205 23rd St. (between Atlantic and Pacific aves.). ℂ 757/422-0081. Reservations recommended. Sandwiches $7–$8; main courses $11–$19. AE, DISC, MC, V. Sun–Wed 5:30–10pm; Thurs–Sat 5:30–11pm.

Waterman's Surfside Grille *Value* SEAFOOD   Many hotels have dining rooms beside the Boardwalk here, but this big coastal-style building is the last stand-alone, family-owned restaurant right on the beach. Surfers started the business as a hot dog stand in the 1960s, although the present full-service restaurant—now a certified city landmark—dates to 1982, with a thorough renovation in 2006. Traditional Chesapeake-style seafood stars here and all of it is fresh, not frozen. I think the crab cakes are the best on the oceanfront, and you can order one of them as a money-saving sandwich. Given the higher prices you pay for inferior quality elsewhere, the value-for-money is good here.

415 Atlantic Ave. (at 5th St.). ℂ 757/428-3644. Reservations recommended. Sandwiches and burgers $7.50–$14; main courses $15–$24. AE, DISC, MC, V. Daily 11am–11pm (bar later).

VIRGINIA BEACH AFTER DARK

The prime performing arts venue is the 20,000-seat, open-air **Verizon Wireless Virginia Beach Amphitheater,** inland at Princess Anne and Dam Neck roads (ℂ 757/368-8888 for schedule, 757/671-8100 for tickets). Big-name singers and bands appear here as well as more highbrow acts like the Virginia Symphony. About 7,500 seats are under cover, with some 12,500 spaces out on the lawn. Big TV screens and a state-of-the-art sound system let everyone see and hear what's going on. The season runs April through October.

During summer, there is nightly entertainment in **Neptune Park,** on the oceanfront at 30th Street, and frequent outdoor concerts on stages at 7th, 17th, and 24th streets along the Boardwalk (the visitor information center can tell you when and where). The biggest is the annual **Verizon Wireless American Music Festival** (© 757/425-3111; www.beachstreetusa.com) over Labor Day weekend on the beach at 5th Street. You might catch the KC & the Sunshine Band on one stage, the Steve Miller Band on another.

Hotels and restaurants all along the beach have live music for nighttime dancing during the summer. Just follow your ears along the Boardwalk—but remember, some pubs along Atlantic Avenue can get rough late at night.

3 Chincoteague & Assateague Islands ★★★

83 miles N of Virginia Beach and Norfolk; 185 miles SE of Washington, D.C.

Winding waterways, abundant wildlife, and down-home cooking and hospitality will welcome you to Virginia's tranquil Eastern Shore. The Atlantic Ocean and the Chesapeake Bay border the state's 70-mile-long end of the Delmarva Peninsula—so-called because it's shared by Delaware, Maryland, and Virginia. A map of the Peninsula may lead you to think that innumerable beaches wait to be explored on the string of barrier islands. Yes, there are beaches out there, but most of them are preserved in their natural state by the government, the Nature Conservancy, and other organizations, which keep them off-limits to members of the general public like us.

But we can visit two of Virginia's jewels: Chincoteague and Assateague islands. Back when I had a regular job, I used to spend my summer weekends relaxing at these two remote islands, which are unlike anything else in Virginia.

Wonderful Assateague is home to the Chincoteague National Wildlife Refuge and Assateague Island National Seashore, which together prevent any development and thus protect hordes of wildlife and 37 miles of pristine beach. In addition to Assateague's famed herds of wild ponies, it is on the main Atlantic Flyway, and its population of both migratory and resident birds is simply astounding. Indeed, it's one of the top places in Virginia to see wildlife. What you will *not* see is a single hotel or condo as you laze away your days on Assateague's remarkably undisturbed beach.

Protected from the ocean by Assateague, Chincoteague Island is surrounded by bays full of flounder, oyster beds, and clam shoals. Settled by the English in the late 1600s, it is famous as the setting of Marguerite Henry's children's book, *Misty of Chincoteague*. Later made into a film, the book aroused wide interest in the annual pony penning and swim on the last Wednesday in July, when pony-size wild horses are rounded up on Assateague, forced to swim across to Chincoteague, and sold to benefit the local fire department.

While Chincoteague is beginning to come out of its self-induced doze and experience a modern building boom (condos are replacing my favorite waterside bars, I report with profound sorrow), it retains much of its scruffy fishing-village charm. Rickety old piers still jut out into the water next to modern motels, and except for busy summer weekends, watermen in work boats still outnumber tourists on jet skis.

ESSENTIALS
VISITOR INFORMATION
The **Chincoteague Chamber of Commerce,** 6733 Maddox Blvd., Chincoteague Island, VA 23336 (© 757/336-6161; fax 757/336-1242; www.chincoteaguechamber. com), operates a visitor center in the traffic circle on Maddox Boulevard, about a mile before the Assateague Bridge. It's open Monday through Saturday 9am to 4:30pm.

There's a **Virginia Welcome Center** on U.S. 13 just south of the Maryland state line (see "Visitor Information & Maps," in chapter 2).

GETTING THERE

There is neither airport nor public transportation on the Eastern Shore, so you'll need a **car.** From Norfolk and Virginia Beach take U.S. 13 north across the **Chesapeake Bay Bridge-Tunnel** (www.cbbt.com), a beautiful 18-mile drive over and under the bay ($12 toll per car). U.S. 13 runs north-south down the center of the Eastern Shore. To reach Chincoteague, turn east on Va. 175, about 65 miles north of the bridge-tunnel and 5 miles south of the Maryland line.

AREA LAYOUT

Va. 175 crosses several miles of salt marshes and the Chincoteague Channel before dead-ending in the old village at **Main Street,** which runs north-south along the Chincoteague's western shore. Turn right at the stoplight to reach the motels, marinas, and bait shops that line Main Street south of the bridge. Turn left on Main Street and then right at the light for **Maddox Boulevard,** 9 blocks north of the bridge, which heads east to Assateague Island. Maddox Boulevard is Chincoteague's prime commercial strip, with an abundance of shops, restaurants, and motels. **Church Street** goes east 2 blocks north of the bridge and turns into **East Side Drive,** which runs along the island's Eastern Shore. **Ridge Road** and **Chicken City Road** (yes, it's really named Chicken City) together run north-south down the middle of the island. On Assateague, there's only one road other than a wildlife drive, and it goes directly to the beach.

GETTING AROUND

These flat islands are great for biking. Although there are no bike paths per se on Chincoteague, there are lanes set aside on some of the streets, particularly Maddox Boulevard as it approaches the Assateague Bridge. Bikes are allowed on the trails and paths on Assateague, so you can ride all the way to the beach. Several shops on Maddox Boulevard rent bikes of various sizes. The **Bike Depot,** at the Refuge Inn (© 757/336-5511; p. 321), and **Jus' Bikes,** 6727 Maddox Blvd. (© 757/336-6700), are closest to Assateague Island. Rates start at $3 an hour at both, $14 a day.

Another easy way to get around after dark during summer is on the **Pony Express Trolley** (© 757/336-6519), which circles Chincoteague Island every 30 minutes Sunday through Thursday 5 to 11pm, Friday and Saturday 5pm to midnight. The fare is 25¢ per ride, exact change required. The trolley also has summertime narrated **tours** of Chincoteague, usually on Wednesday at 2:30 and 3:30pm, but call ahead for a current schedule. Tickets go on sale the same day for these first-come, first-served tours, which depart from the Chincoteague Community Center, 6155 Community Drive, off Deep Hole near Maddox Boulevard. Fares are $3 for adults, $2 for children younger than 13.

ASSATEAGUE ISLAND 🌟🌟🌟

You and I own all of Assateague Island, which is completely occupied by the **Chincoteague National Wildlife Refuge** and the **Assateague Island National Seashore,** and thus jointly administered by the U.S. Fish and Wildlife Service and the National Park Service. Of the island's 37 miles, 12 are in Virginia. Wildlife on this end is afforded a higher degree of protection than in the Maryland sector. In fact, a fence at the state line keeps Maryland's wild horses and other critters away from the Virginia side.

The Eastern Shore

MARYLAND

Smith I.

Assateague I.

New Church

Chinco-teague I.

Cedar I.

2

175 Chincoteague **3**

Saxis

4

Tangier
Sound

Pocomoke

Hallwood

Assateague I.
Wildlife
Refuge

from Reedville

Sound

316

5

Wallops I.

Bloxom

Tangier **1**

Tangier I.

Watts I.

13

Assawoman I

Parksley

Onancock-
Tangier Island cruise

Metompkin I.

Onancock **6**

Accomac

Onley

C

Melfa

H

178

E

Cedar I.

S

Wachapreague

A

Painter

182

P

Belle Haven

Parramore I.

E

183

Exmore

A

K

Nassawadox

E

Hog Island
Bay

7 Machipongo

Hog I.

B

13

A

T

L

A

N

T

I

C

A

Cobb I.

Y

Cheriton

Wreck I.

O

C

E

A

N

Cape
Charles

South
Bay

Ship Shoal I.

Myrtle I.

Smith I.

Fishermans I.

| | 0 | 10 mi |
| 0 | 10 km | |

60

Virginia Beach

Assateague Island National Seashore **5**
Barrier Island Center & Museum **7**
Chincoteague National Wildlife Refuge **3**
NASA Wallops Flight Facility **2**
Onancock **6**
Oyster and Maritime Museum **4**
Refuge Waterfowl Museum **4**
Tangier Island **1**

Tips Book Early for the "Pony Penning"

The famous **wild ponies**—they're actually small horses—have lived on Assateague since the 1600s. Legend says their ancestors swam ashore from a shipwrecked Spanish galleon, but most likely English settlers put the first horses on Assateague, which formed a natural corral. Separated by a fence from their cousins in Maryland, the Virginia horses are now owned by the Chincoteague Volunteer Fire Department, which rounds them up and sells the foals at auction during its famous **Pony Penning** on the last Wednesday in July. Make your hotel reservations well in advance of this extremely popular event.

Bird-watchers know Assateague Island as a prime Atlantic Flyway habitat where sightings of peregrine falcons, snow geese, great blue heron, and snowy egrets have been made. The annual Waterfowl Week, generally held around Thanksgiving, takes place when a large number of migratory birds use the refuge.

THE WILDLIFE REFUGE

You first enter the **Chincoteague National Wildlife Refuge,** which is open May through September daily 5am to 10pm, April and October daily 6am to 8pm, November through March daily 6am to 6pm. The refuge accepts the America the Beautiful entrance passes issued by federal agencies; otherwise, admission is $10 per car for 1 week, free for pedestrians and bikers. (*Note:* Don't be surprised if the national seashore has added a fee to fund repairs to its parking lots.)

Unless you're here just for the beach, start your visit at the refuge's **Herbert H. Bateman Education and Administrative Center** (© 757/336-3696), on the left, ¼-mile east of the bridge, where you can watch a video about the refuge and its wildlife. It has wildlife and birding programs, which are great for kids. The center is open daily 9am to 5pm during summer, to 4pm off season (closed New Year's Day and Christmas).

You may see some of the wild ponies while driving to the beach, but the best place to see them—your chance is greatest at dawn—is on the paved **Wildlife Drive,** which runs for 3¼ miles through the marshes. This one-lane, one-way road is open to pedestrians and bicyclists all day, to motorized vehicles after 3pm. The **Woodland Trail,** a 1.6-mile hiking loop, is another good place to spot the wild ponies grazing out in the marshes. But be advised: This area is infested with mosquitoes, so bring and use insect repellent.

The most informative way to see the multitudinous wildlife is on a **Wildlife Tour** (© 757/336-3696) in an air-conditioned bus. The 1¾-hour narrated rides depart the visitor center at 10am, 1, and 4pm daily Memorial Day weekend through Labor Day, and on weekends in March, April, September, and October. The tour costs $12 for adults, $10 seniors, $5 for children 2 to 12. Buy your tickets at the visitor center.

If your heart's up to it, you can climb the 198 steps for a terrific view from atop **Assateague Island Lighthouse,** built in 1867 to warn ships of the shoals offshore. It is open to the public from March to Thanksgiving Friday, Saturday, and Sunday from 9am to 3pm. Admission is $4 adults, $2 children 2 to 12.

For **information** about the refuge and visitor-center seasons and programs, contact the Refuge Manager, Chincoteague National Wildlife Refuge, P.O. Box 62, Chincoteague Island, VA 23336 (© 757/336-6122; www.fws.gov/northeast/chinco).

THE NATIONAL SEASHORE

The beach itself is in the **Assateague Island National Seashore,** operated by the National Park Service. You'll find a visitor center, bathhouses, and summertime lifeguards. In addition to swimming and sunning, activities at the beach include shell collecting (most productive at the tip of the Tom's Cove spit of land, on the island's southern tip) and hiking. You can ride a bike here from Chincoteague on the paved bike path beside the main road (or make a detour along Wildlife Dr.) to the **Tom's Cove Visitor Center,** which has a splendid view over the marshes. Rangers give summertime programs such as wildlife viewing, aquarium talks, nighttime hikes, and campfires. Pick up a copy of the *Assateague Island Times* for the schedule. The visitor center is open daily 9am to 6pm in summer, 9am to 5pm spring and autumn, 9am to 4pm in winter. It is closed Thanksgiving and Christmas.

Several **regulations** apply. Pets and alcoholic beverages are prohibited, even in your vehicle. In-line skating is not allowed, nor are off-road vehicles. Surf fishing with a Virginia state license is allowed except on the lifeguard beach at Tom's Cove. Climbing and digging in the sand dunes is illegal. No overnight sleeping is allowed anywhere (backcountry camping is permitted on the Maryland end, a 12-mile hike from the Virginia-side visitor centers). And finally, thou shalt not feed the horses.

For information about the national seashore, contact the Superintendent, Assateague Island National Seashore, 8586 Beach Rd. (P.O. Box 38), Chincoteague Island, VA 23336 (© **757/336-6577;** www.nps.gov/asis).

OUTDOOR ACTIVITIES

CRUISES   While most visitors head for the beach on Assateague, don't overlook the broad bays and creeks that surround Chincoteague. A good way to get out on them is with **Captain Barry's Back Bay Cruises** 𝒜𝒜 (© **757/336-6508;** www.captainbarry. bigstep.com). Barry Frishman moved from New York to Chincoteague and set about learning everything he could about the water and what's in it. Now he shares his knowledge by taking guests out on his pontoon boat for 1½-hour early-morning bird-watching expeditions ($25 per person); 2-hour afternoon "Sea Life Expeditions" ($25 per person); 4-hour morning or afternoon "Back Bay Expeditions" in search of crabs, fish, shells, and clams ($45 per person); champagne sunset cruises ($35); and romantic dinner cruises ($225 per couple). Call for Barry's schedule and reservations, which are required.

Another excellent option is Chincoteague native Mark Colburn's *Assateague Explorer* 𝒜𝒜 (© **866/PONY-SWIM** or 757/990-1795; www.assateagueisland.com/ explorer.htm). His 1½-hour Pony Express Nature Tours ($20 per person) go up along

---

(Kids Pony Rides

You can't bring a child to Chincoteague without letting him or her ride a pony—perhaps one of Misty's descendants—at the **Chincoteague Pony Centre,** 6417 Carriage Dr. (© **757/336-2776;** www.chincoteague.com/ponycentre), off Chicken City Road south of Maddox Boulevard. This small-scale equestrian center is open Memorial Day weekend through Labor Day daily 9am to 10pm, with pony rides ($6) 9am to 1pm and 3:30 to 6pm, with a pony show Monday through Saturday at 8pm. Spring and fall hours are Friday and Saturday from 9am to 6pm, with the pony show Saturday at 8pm. Admission is $8 adults, $5 for children. The gift shop sells all things pony, and you can even buy a pony.

A Cruise to Tangier Island

Barely above sea level and short on dry land (many deceased are buried in their loved ones' front yards), **Tangier Island** ⍟ was discovered by Capt. John Smith in 1608 and permanently settled in 1686. In fact, the local accent hearkens back to the Elizabethan English. It's not a Nantucket or a Martha's Vineyard, however, for Tangier's charm is in visiting a remote and authentic fishing village—the "Soft Shell Capital of the World," as evidenced by the many crab pens lining the channel into the harbor.

Local citizens await your arrival to take you on a 10-minute island tour by oversize golf cart; the tour is worth $5 to get an overview. You can bring your own bike or rent a golf cart at the wharf, although you can walk to almost every place worth seeing within 30 minutes.

Most day-trippers head to **Hilda Crockett's Chesapeake House** (② 757/ 891-2331), where $19 fetches an all-you-can-eat family-style lunch. **Fisherman's Corner** (② 757/891-2900) serves soft shell crabs, and **Waterfront Restaurant,** at the dock (② 757/891-2248), serves sandwiches at picnic tables under tin pavilions. After lunch walk up Main Street to **Wanda's Gift Shop** (② 757/891-2255), and see how soft shell crabs are harvested.

You can stay overnight at Hilda Crockett's, although I would opt for **Shirley's Bay View Inn** (② 757/891-2396; www.tangierisland.net) or **Sunset Inn Bed & Breakfast** (② 757/891-2535), both on the island's western side, which has a beach and terrific sunsets. All three charge about $120 for a double and accept MasterCard and Visa.

Weather permitting, **Tangier-Onancock Cruises** (② 804/453-4434; www. tangierislandcruises.com) leave Onancock May 15 to October 15 daily at 10am. The voyage takes 90 minutes. The return trip leaves Tangier at 2pm. Round-trip fare is $25 for adults, $12 for children 6 to 11, free for children 5 and younger, and $5 for bicycles. Reservations are not accepted. You can also get here from Reedville on the Northern Neck (see chapter 5).

Plan to look around genteel **Onancock** (www.onancock.com), which dates to 1680 and whose gourmet market, boutiques, and art galleries stand in marked contrast to Chincoteague's fishing-town image. The cruise boat docks behind **Hopkins & Bro. General Store,** built in 1842 and now home to **Mallards at the Wharf** (② 757/787-8558), a good restaurant (daily 11:30am–9pm). Look in the store side of the building for walking tour brochures and other information about Onancock. Also worth a peek is **Kerr Place,** on Market Street (Va. 179), a stately Federal mansion built about 1800 and now home to the Eastern Shore of Virginia Historical Society (② 757/787-8012; www.easternshorehistory.org).

The best place to stay is the **Charlotte Hotel & Restaurant,** 7 North St. (② 757/787-7400; www.thecharlottehotel.com), which has eight rooms upstairs over a very good restaurant serving breakfast and dinner. For lunch I head to **Stella's,** 57 Market St. (② 757/789-5045), for salads, sandwiches, and tasty pizza.

the calm backwaters off Assateague in search of ponies and other wildlife to observe. He also has a 3-hour cruise around Chincoteague Island, flounder fishing trips, and sunset cruises (all $35 adults, $25 children under 12). He will also do private fishing and hunting charters off season. Mark's grandfather, by the way, had a role in the movie version of *Misty of Chincoteague.*

FISHING Before it became a tourist mecca, Chincoteague was a fishing village for centuries—and it still is. Both work and pleasure boats prowl the back bays and ocean for flounder, croaker, spot, kingfish, drum, striped bass, bluefish, and sharks, to name a few species.

You can go flounder fishing with Mark Colburn's *Assateague Explorer* (see above).

You can get to it yourself, either from a rented boat or by throwing your line from a dock. For charter boats, equipment, supplies, free tide tables, and advice, check in at **Barnacle Bill's Bait & Tackle** (© 757/336-5188) or **Capt. Bob's** (© 757/336-6654), both on South Main Street.

KAYAKING & SURFING The waters around Chincoteague are ideal for sea kayaking, and **Oyster Bay Outfitters,** 6429 Maddox Blvd. (© 888/732-7108 or 757/336-0700; www.oysterbayoutfitters.com), has half- and full-day trips. The company also rents kayaks, and it teaches surfboarding on Assateague Island. Call for prices and reservations.

MUSEUMS

The large airstrip you pass on the way to Chincoteague on Va. 175 is part of NASA's **Wallops Flight Facility,** a research and testing center for rockets, balloons, and aircraft. The facility also tracks NASA's spacecraft and satellites, including the space shuttles. Across the highway is the **NASA Visitor Center** (© 757/824-2298; www.wff.nasa.gov), one of the best places to park the kids on a rainy day. The center's exhibits and entertaining 20-minute film explain the role of astronauts in the space program. Kids will get a kick out of seeing a practice space suit from Apollo 9. Admission is free. The visitor center is open July 4th through Labor Day daily 10am to 4pm; March through June and September to November Thursday through Monday 10am to 4pm; winter Monday through Friday 10am to 4pm. The center is 5 miles west of Chincoteague.

On Maddox Boulevard, between the traffic circle and the bridge to Assateague, are two small marine-themed museums. The **Oyster and Maritime Museum** (© 757/336-6117) tells the area's history and the role played by the vital seafood industry from the 1600s to the present, with examples of marine life (some of them live). The highlight is the original lens from the Assateague Lighthouse, which mariners could see 23 miles offshore from 1865 to 1961. The museum is open Memorial Day to Labor Day Monday through Saturday 10am to 5pm, Sunday noon to 5pm. Admission is free; donations are accepted.

Nearby, the **Refuge Waterfowl Museum** (© 757/336-5800) has a variety of antique decoys, boats, traps, art, and carvings by outstanding craftspeople, some of whom do their carving here. There's very good shopping at this museum; in fact, you should come here before buying decoys elsewhere. It's open Memorial Day through Labor Day daily 10am to 5pm. Call for off-season hours. Admission is $3 for adults, $1.50 for children younger than 12.

> ## ⎛Tips Mosquitoes, Mosquitoes & More Mosquitoes
>
> I grew up in coastal North Carolina and thus am accustomed to fighting off my share of mosquitoes, but Chincoteague, Assateague, and Tangier islands set a new standard for slapping, itching, and scratching. The Chincoteague mosquitoes seem more prone to make meals of my blood at dawn and dusk, but the Assateague variety is not nearly so finicky. Consequently, I seldom go outside here before applying insect repellent.

WHERE TO STAY

My friends and I used to rent a cottage when we came to Chincoteague, since it was more economical than a hotel for four or more of us, and we liked having our own kitchen and room to roam around. Among several companies handling cottage rentals are **Chincoteague Resort Realty,** 6378A Church St., Chincoteague Island, VA 23336 (© 800/668-7836 or 757/336-3100; www.chincoteagueresort.com), and **Chincoteague Vacation Rentals,** 7038 Maddox Blvd., Chincoteague, Virginia 23336 (© 757/336-1236; www.igetaway.net).

You will pay much less for all properties here during the off season, and especially during the slow winter months of December through February. Highest rates occur from mid-June through Labor Day weekend.

MOTELS

Most of Chincoteague's accommodations are small, family-run motels and bed-and-breakfasts. Even the Best Western Chincoteague Island falls into this category (see below). The island's other chain motels are the **Comfort Suites,** 4195 Main St. (© 800/228-5150 or 757/336-3700; fax 757/336-5452; www.chincoteaguechamber.com/comfortsuites), and the **Hampton Inn & Suites,** 4179 Main St. (© 800/426-7866 or 757/336-1616; www.hamptoninnsuiteschincoteague.com). They stand next to each other beside Chincoteague Channel in town. Both have heated indoor pools but neither has a restaurant.

Best Western Chincoteague Island   Between the traffic circle and the bridge to Assateague Island, this motel—formerly known as the Driftwood Lodge—and the Refuge Inn (see below) are Chincoteague's closest accommodations to the wildlife refuge and national seashore. Entered from the rear, the guest rooms in the gray, three-story shiplap building all have balconies facing the road (those on the third floor overlook the marshes). Most contain two double beds, tables and chairs, and full tiled bathrooms. The one suite has two bedrooms, one bathroom, whirlpool tub, and a kitchenette. Owners Scot and Lisa Chesson renovated the entire motel as part of their switch to Best Western. Breakfast is included in their rates, and the island's McDonald's is across Maddox Boulevard.

7105 Maddox Blvd. (P.O. Box 575), Chincoteague Island, VA 23336. © 800/553-6117 or 757/336-6557. Fax 757/336-6558. www.bestwestern.com/chincoteagueisland. 52 units. $69–$209 double; $139–$229 suite. Rates include continental breakfast. AE, DC, DISC, MC, V. From the bridge, turn left on Main St., right on Maddox Blvd. **Amenities:** Outdoor pool; coin-op washers and dryers. *In room:* A/C, TV, Wi-Fi, fridge, coffeemaker, iron.

Island Motor Inn Resort 🐠🐠   The best-equipped motel here, the inn sits on Chincoteague Channel just north of the business district, giving its spacious rooms great views across the bay to the mainland. Reception is in a three-story building whose rooms are better appointed than the standard units in the older, two- and three-story motel blocks adjoining. Rooms on the ends of this new building have bay windows on their sides, giving them two-way views. All rooms have private balconies. On the water side of the property, you'll find a 600-foot-long boardwalk and boat dock, a covered barbecue area with hammock for lounging, an outdoor pool, and glass-enclosed indoor pool and fitness center (with a trainer on duty year-round). On the road side, owners Reggie and Anna Stubbs have built a landscaped garden with lily ponds and benches for relaxing. The **Island Cafe** only serves breakfast, but it's exceptionally good (see box below). Also note that the minisuites are reserved for adults only.

4391 N. Main St., Chincoteague Island, VA 23336. © **757/336-3141.** Fax 757/336-1483. www.islandmotorinn.com. 60 units. $68–$195 double; $88–$195 suite. AE, DC, DISC, MC, V. From the bridge, turn left on Main St. to motel on left. **Amenities:** Restaurant; indoor/outdoor pool; 2 exercise rooms; Jacuzzi; room service (6:30am–noon); free washers and dryers; concierge-level rooms. *In room:* A/C, TV, Wi-Fi, fridge.

Refuge Inn 🏠🏠 *Kids* This charming motel with weathered gray siding nestled on beautifully landscaped grounds shaded by tall pines is, like the Best Western Chincoteague Island across the street (see above), as close to Assateague Island as you can stay. You won't have to go across the bridge to see the ponies, however, for several live in a small corral on the grounds. The care and attention that Arthur Leonard and sisters Donna Leonard and Jane Wolffe lavish on the decor are evident everywhere. Furnishings are charming: Some rooms have country inn–style Colonial pieces, bleached-pine headboards, decoys, handmade wall hangings, and all the elements of country style. First-floor rooms facing the back have sliding doors to private patios where guests can use outdoor grills. One of the two suites is a one-bedroom apartment with a fully equipped kitchen, a screened porch across the front, a bathroom with whirlpool tub, and a spiral staircase leading to a loft with a double bed–size convertible futon (the unit can sleep up to six people). Other facilities include an observation sun deck on the roof, an enclosed pool and whirlpool, a children's playground, and an excellent gift/crafts shop. Note that suites are rented on a weekly basis in summer. The Bike Depot is here, so you can rent a cycle virtually at your front door.

7058 Maddox Blvd., Chincoteague Island, VA 23336. © **888/868-6400** or 757/336-5511. Fax 757/336-6134. www.refugeinn.com. 72 units. $80–$170 double; $160–$285 suite. AE, DC, DISC, MC, V. **Amenities:** Heated indoor/outdoor pool; health club; Jacuzzi; sauna; watersports equipment/rentals; bike rentals; coin-op washers and dryers. *In room:* A/C, TV, Wi-Fi, fridge, coffeemaker.

Waterside Motor Inn 🏠 All the accommodations at Tommy and Donna Mason's three-story motel feature private wooden balconies overlooking Chincoteague Channel, guaranteeing some breathtaking sunset views, especially on the end units directly facing the water (they're worth requesting). Shingle-look siding gives the property a Victorian appearance. The spacious units are decorated in comfortable contemporary style, and some have a king- or queen-size bed and a pullout sofa bed. Four suites in a nearby Victorian house have two bedrooms and kitchens. The Waterside has an outdoor pool with deck and its own fishing and crabbing pier. The complimentary continental breakfast includes made-to-order waffles, or you can opt for coffee and muffins in your room.

3761 Main St. (P.O. Box 347), Chincoteague Island, VA 23336. © **877/870-3434** or 757/336-3434. Fax 757/336-1878. www.watersidemotorinn.com. 49 units. $80–$200 double; $150–$225 suite. Rates include breakfast and morning coffee and muffins in room. AE, DC, DISC, MC, V. At the bridge entering Chincoteague, turn right; the motel is on the right, about ½ mile from the bridge. **Amenities:** Heated outdoor pool; tennis court; health club; Jacuzzi; business center; coin-op washers and dryers. *In room:* A/C, TV, Wi-Fi, fridge, coffeemaker.

Virginia's Barrier Islands Center & Museum

Chincoteague and Assateague are but two of Virginia's 23 barrier islands, those long slivers of sand separating the Atlantic Ocean from the bays and backwaters along the eastern seaboard. They are now owned by governments or by organizations such as the Nature Conservancy, which are protecting them in their natural state. People once lived on the islands, and rich and famous folk like President Grover Cleveland came out to hunt and fish. But no more.

The former residents and their water-oriented life-style are fondly remembered at the **Barrier Islands Center & Museum** ◉◉, on U.S. 13 just north of Machipongo (© **888/678-5572** or 757/678-5550; www.barrierislands center.com). That's 20 miles north of the Chesapeake Bay Bridge-Tunnel, about 55 miles south of Chincoteague. The white-clapboard building looks like a farmhouse standing in the fields beside the highway, but in fact it was built by Northampton County as the Almshouse Farm at Machipongo—a place for poor people to live, in other words. The barrier island residents and their descendants donated the many artifacts on display, and they lead 30-minute museum tours twice daily. Admission is $4 adults, $3 seniors, $2 children 6 to 18, free for kids under 6. Open Tuesday through Saturday 10am to 4pm, it's well worth a brief stop.

You can cruise through the narrow channels and take a walk on a deserted beach with Capt. Buddy Vaughn of **Eastern Shore Adventures** (© **757/615-2598;** www.easternshoreadventures.com), whose wife, Laura Vaughn, is director of the Barrier Islands Center & Museum. Call Buddy well in advance to make arrangements.

BED & BREAKFASTS

In addition to the 1848 Island Manor House listed below, Chincoteague has several bed-and-breakfasts, including **Cedar Gables Seaside Inn,** 6905 Hopkins Lane (© **888/491-2944** or 757/336-1096; www.cedargable.com), with a screened outdoor swimming pool and a master suite with climb-up cupola rendering a 360-degree view of the marshes. In the village are **Inn at Poplar Corner,** 4248 Main St. (© **877/336-6111** or 757/336-6115; www.innatpoplarcorner.com); **The Watson House,** 4240 Main St. (© **800/336-6787** or 757/336-1564; www.watsonhouse.com); **The Channel Bass Inn,** 6228 Church St. (© **800/249-0818** or 757/336-6148; www.channel bassinn.com); and **Miss Molly's Inn,** 4141 Main St. (© **800/221-5620** or 757/336-6686; www.missmollys-inn.com).

1848 Island Manor House   This B&B consists of two gray-clapboard houses joined by a magnificent one-story, light-filled garden room with fireplace. It opens to a brick patio and fountain, where guests enjoy breakfast in good weather and watch the resident ducks waddling across the lawn. Originally, there was only one house, built before the Civil War by two young men. They eventually married sisters, who did not enjoy living under the same roof, so they split the structure and moved one half next door. Today, both have been handsomely restored and are furnished in Federal style, along with 17th-, 18th-, and 19th-century pieces. In the three first-floor sitting rooms are fireplaces and telephones for guest use. Hosts Jerry Pruitt and Andrew "A. D." Dawson serve full Southern-style breakfasts each morning.

4160 Main St., Chincoteague Island, VA 23336. (℃ **800/852-1505** or 757/336-5436. Fax 757/336-1333. www.island manor.com. 8 units (6 with private bathroom). $95–$225 double. Rates include full breakfast. AE, DISC, MC, V. From the bridge into Chincoteague, turn left onto Main St. and continue about 1½ blocks; the inn is on the right. *In room:* A/C, TV (1 unit), Wi-Fi, no phone.

WHERE TO DINE

You won't find fine dining here (locals will drive to Onancock for that; see the "A Cruise to Tangier Island" box, above), but you will be served seafood fresh from the boat. The famous Chincoteague oysters are harvested September to March. The area is also known for flounder, caught year-round. Most Chincoteague restaurants, however, are seasonal operations and close October until Easter weekend the following spring.

In addition to those below, also open year-round are the venerable **Bill's Seafood Restaurant,** 4040 Main St. (℃ 757/336-5831), which opens daily at 5am to feed breakfast to the watermen headed to work, and **Don's Seafood Restaurant and Chattie's Lounge,** 4113 Main St. (℃ 747/336-5715), which opens daily at 7am. Don's upstairs Chattie's Lounge has live or DJ music on weekend nights.

AJ's on the Creek ⨂ SEAFOOD/STEAKS   The island's most romantic restaurant, AJ's offers dining either on a screened-in patio beside a narrow creek or inside, where candles and dried-flower arrangements adorn a mix of tables and booths. Most romantic of all is table no. 20 in a private corner; it's worth a wait. The menu offers a mix of Italian-style pastas—Chincoteague oysters in a champagne cream sauce is a house specialty—and traditional dishes such as fried or steamed shrimp and oysters, plus chargrilled steaks. A popular local hangout, the friendly (and sometimes smoky) bar offers sports TVs and its own snack menu (with money-saving half-sizes of regular menu main courses). It has live music on weekends.

6585 Maddox Blvd. (℃ **757/336-5888.** Reservations not accepted. Lunch $5–$10; main courses $14–$26. AE, DC, DISC, MC, V. Summer Mon–Sat 11:30am–9pm (lounge until 1am); winter Mon–Sat 11:30am–2pm and 5–9pm.

Mr. Baldy's Family Restaurant *Finds* SEAFOOD   Opened in 2007 by the very bald Robert Zoller, who relocated his family here from Hoboken, New Jersey, this lively family-style restaurant serves a variety of fare, most of it made from fresh ingredients. The day begins with traditional breakfasts and moves on to a variety of salads and sandwiches, including soft-shell crabs and very good crab cakes made the traditional Chesapeake way with back fin meat and a touch of Old Bay seasoning. Main courses also include soft shells and crab cakes plus oysters, shrimp, flounder, steaks, and a few pastas. All in all, it's very good value.

Tips **Best Breakfast in Chincoteague**

The best breakfast place in town is the **Island Cafe,** a cottage in front of the Island Motor Inn, 4391 Main St. (℃ **757/336-3141**). The front porch is ideal for enjoying the chef's specialty, French toast laced with Grand Marnier, Amaretto, and Bailey's Irish Cream. Prices range from $4 to $14. Open daily 6:30 to 11:30am.

3447 Ridge Rd. (in middle of the island). © 757/336-1198. Reservations not accepted. Breakfast $2–$5.50; sandwiches and salads $2.50–$8; main courses $8–$19. MC, V. Daily 6:30am–9:30pm.

Village Restaurant SEAFOOD   Across Maddox Boulevard from AJ's on the Creek, the gardenlike Village Restaurant enjoys a fine view over a creek and a marsh. The specialties are traditionally prepared seafood such as fried or broiled oysters, flounder, and shrimp. The house seafood platter is piled with fish filet, shrimp, scallops, oysters, clams, and lobster tail. Nonseafood main dishes include veal or chicken Parmesan, fried chicken, and filet mignon.

6576 Maddox Blvd. © 757/336-5120. Reservations recommended. Main courses $11–$26. AE, DISC, MC, V. Daily 5–9pm. Closed 1 weekday in the off season and most of Jan–Feb.

Appendix:
Virginia in Depth

Below, we take a look at modern Virginia and examine the state's illustrious past. The history of English-speaking America began here 400 years ago, the fires of independence were flamed here, the American Revolution was won here, and much of the Civil War was fought here. Virginia's history will play a very important role in your visit, for many of the state's major attractions are houses, buildings, monuments, sites, and battlefields marking 4 centuries of America's past.

1 Virginia Today

The memory of the state's past still exerts its influence, as it surely must in towns where descendants of America's first patriots still live and where the homes, monuments, and battlefields that shaped the country's history comprise their daily landscape. So revered is history here that sometimes you would think George Washington still stands siege outside Yorktown, Thomas Jefferson still writes great political prose up at Monticello, and Robert E. Lee and Stonewall Jackson still ride at Fredericksburg and Chancellorsville.

Prominent in Virginia Tidewater plantation society since the 1600s, the Byrd family dominated the state's politics from World War I until the 1980s. Under their conservative control, the "Mother of Presidents" virtually withdrew from national leadership. The state government fought federally mandated public school integration in the 1950s, with one county actually closing its schoolhouse doors rather than admit African Americans to previously all-white institutions. Although racial relations have improved greatly since then, the old animosities still raise their ugly heads from time to time.

Back in 1989, however, Virginians chose Democrat L. Douglas Wilder as the nation's first elected African-American governor (he is now serving as mayor of Richmond). We Virginians have been narrowly splitting our votes between Republicans and Democrats. Conservative Republicans control the state legislature, but Gov. Tim Kaine is the second moderate Democrat in a row in the Governor's Mansion. In 2006, novelist and former Secretary of the Navy James Webb narrowly defeated Republican U.S. Senator George Allen, thus giving the Democrats control of the Senate.

Economically, the state has done reasonably well since the 1990s, thanks in large part to the growth of northern Virginia's high-tech corridor, where considerable business is done with the federal government.

Although colonist John Rolfe is best remembered for marrying Indian princess Pocahontas, he essentially founded the tobacco industry, which is still important to Virginia's economy despite the anti-smoking movement. As tobacco wanes, the state is encouraging the planting of grapes and the building of wineries (it strikes me as ironic that the home state of teetotaling preachers Pat Robertson and the late Jerry Falwell is switching from tobacco to alcohol!). Farm income also sprouts from apple orchards in the Shenandoah Valley; livestock, dairies, and poultry in the Piedmont; the state's famous Smithfield hams and peanuts from the Tidewater country; and seafood from the Chesapeake Bay. Industry includes the manufacturing of clothes, chemicals, furniture, and transportation equipment, plus shipbuilding at Newport News.

2 History 101

Virginia's recorded history began on April 26, 1607, when 104 English men and boys arrived at Cape Henry on the Virginia coast aboard the *Susan Constant,* the *Godspeed,* and the *Discovery.* The expedition—an attempt to compete with profitable Spanish encroachments in the New World—was sponsored by the Virginia Company of London and supported by King James I.

A MODEST BEGINNING

Although the colonists were heartened to find abundant fish and game, if not streets paved with gold, their optimism was short-lived, for American Indians attacked them on their first day in the New World. Fleeing Cape Henry, they settled on Jamestown Island, which offered greater protection from the Spanish and the Indians but was a lousy, mosquito-infested place to live. They also had arrived in the midst of an extended drought. As one on-the-scene chronicler described it, "a world of miseries ensued." Only 50 settlers were alive by autumn.

When Capt. John Smith tried to barter for corn and grain, the Indians took him prisoner and carried him to Chief Powhatan. According to legend, they would have killed him, but Powhatan's teenage daughter, the beautiful princess Pocahontas, interceded and saved his life.

But the colony survived that first year, and soon more men and women, among them some of my ancestors. ("It's true we arrived at Jamestown in 1613," my late Aunt Ola Williford wisecracked, "and we have never amounted to anything since!")

Also in 1613, John Rolfe (who later married Pocahontas) brought from the New World a new aromatic tobacco that proved popular in England. The settlers had discovered not the glittery gold they expected, but the "golden weed" that would be the foundation of Virginia's fortunes and its "First Families," including the Carters, the Hills, the Randolphs, and the Lees.

In 1619, the Virginia Company sent a shipload of 90 women to suitors who had paid their transportation costs, and 22 burgesses were elected to set up the first legislative body in the New World. That same year, 20 Africans arrived in a Dutch ship to work as indentured servants, a precursor of slavery.

In 1699, the capital of the colony was moved from Jamestown, which had suffered a disastrous fire, to the planned town of Williamsburg. It was from Williamsburg that Colonial patriots launched some of the first strong protests against Parliament.

UNREST GROWS   The French and Indian War in the 1750s proved to be a training ground for America's Revolutionary forces, including George Washington. In the field Washington acquitted himself with honor, and after General Braddock's defeat, he was appointed commander in chief of Virginia's army on the frontier.

Expenses from the war and economic hardships led the British to increase taxes in the colonies, and protests in Virginia and Massachusetts escalated. The 1765 Stamp Act met with general resistance. Patrick Henry inspired the Virginia General Assembly to pass the Virginia Resolves, setting forth Colonial rights according to constitutional principles. The young orator exclaimed, "If this be treason, make the most of it." The Stamp Act was repealed in 1766, but the Revenue Acts of 1767, which included the hated tax on tea, exacerbated tensions.

Ties among the colonies were strengthened when Virginia's burgesses, led by Richard Henry Lee, created a committee to communicate their problems in dealing with England to similar committees in the other colonies. When the Boston Post Bill closed that harbor in punishment for the Boston Tea Party, the Virginia Assembly moved swiftly. Although Governor Dunmore had dissolved the legislature, they met at Raleigh Tavern and recommended that a general congress be held annually. Virginia sent seven representatives to the First Continental Congress in 1774, among them Lee, Patrick Henry, and George Washington.

The following year, Patrick Henry made a plea for arming Virginia's militia. He concluded his argument with these immortal words, "Is life so dear or peace so sweet as to be purchased at the price of chains and slavery? Forbid it, Almighty God! I know not what course others may take, but, as for me, give me liberty, or give me death!"

Later in 1775, upon hearing news of the battles of Lexington and Concord, the Second Continental Congress in Philadelphia voted to make the conflict near Boston a colonywide confrontation and chose Washington as commander of the Continental Army. War had begun.

BIRTH OF THE NATION

Meeting in Williamsburg on June 12, 1776, the Virginia Convention adopted George Mason's Bill of Rights and instructed Virginia's delegates to the Continental Congress to propose independence for the colonies. Mason's document stated that "all power is vested in, and consequently derived from, the people," and that "all men are created free and independent, and have certain inherent rights . . . among which are the enjoyment of life and liberty, with the means of acquiring and possessing property . . ." He also firmly upheld the right of trial by jury, freedom of the press, and freedom of religion. The Congress meeting in Philadelphia adopted Thomas Jefferson's Declaration of Independence, based on Mason's bill, on July 4, 1776. The United States of America was born.

The Revolution was a bloody 7-year conflict marked by many staggering defeats for the patriots. Historians believe it was only the superb leadership and pertinacity of Gen. George Washington that inspired the Continental Army to continue so long in the face of overwhelming odds.

VICTORY AT YORKTOWN The turning point came in March 1781, when British Gen. Lord Cornwallis arrived with his army at Yorktown. At the end of a long and rather fruitless march through the Carolinas, Cornwallis waited for the British navy to evacuate him and his men to New York.

While Cornwallis waited, Washington received word that a French admiral, the Comte de Grasse, was taking his squadron to the Chesapeake and would be at Washington's disposal through October 15. After conferring with the Comte de Rochambeau, commander of the French troops in America, Washington marched his 17,000-man allied army 450 miles to Virginia in hopes of trapping Cornwallis.

On September 5, 1781, a fleet of 19 British ships under Adm. Thomas Graves appeared at the entrance to Chesapeake Bay to evacuate Cornwallis. By coincidence, De Grasse's 24 French ships arrived at the same time. The naval battle ended in a stalemate, but Graves was forced to return to New York without Cornwallis. The French remained to block further British reinforcements or their escape by water, while Washington arrived at Yorktown. The trap had worked.

After 2 weeks of bombardment, Cornwallis waved the white flag. Although the war didn't officially end until the Treaty of Paris 2 years later, the colonists had won.

FRAMING THE CONSTITUTION

At first the new country adopted the Articles of Confederation, which created a weak and ineffectual national government. To remedy the situation, a Constitutional Convention met in Philadelphia in 1781. Washington was elected the convention's president. He and fellow Virginian James Madison fought to have the new Constitution include a Bill of Rights and gradual abolition of the slave trade. Although both measures were defeated, the two Virginians voted to adopt the Constitution.

In 1788, Virginia became the 10th state to ratify the Constitution, and by 1791 the first 10 amendments—the Bill of Rights—had been added. Madison was author of the first nine amendments, Richard Henry Lee the tenth.

THE COUNTRY'S EARLY VIRGINIAN PRESIDENTS

Washington was elected president under the new Constitution and took office on April 30, 1789. Although he could have stayed in office, he stepped down after two terms, thus setting a precedent that ruled until Franklin D. Roosevelt was elected to a third term in 1940.

As third president of the United States, Jefferson nearly doubled the size of the country by purchasing the Louisiana Territory from Napoleon.

James Madison took office as president in 1809. Unable to maintain Jefferson's peacekeeping efforts in the face of continued provocations by England, Madison was swayed by popular demand for armed response, and in 1812, Congress declared war. Although British warships

attacked some coastal plantations, the only suffering Virginia witnessed was the burning of nearby Washington, D.C.

James Monroe followed, and during his two terms, the nation pushed westward, and he faced the first struggle over slavery (which resulted in the Missouri Compromise), established the Monroe Doctrine, and settled the nation's boundary with Canada.

THE CIVIL WAR

It was not long before the United States became a nation divided. The issues were states' rights and the conflicting economic goals between an industrial North and an agricultural South that relied on slavery. In the election of 1860, the Republicans nominated Abraham Lincoln, whom the South vowed it would not accept; but the Democrats split and Lincoln was elected. On April 12, 1861, guns sounded at Fort Sumter in Charleston harbor. Secession had become war.

FIRST MANASSAS In May 1861, the Confederate capital was transferred to Richmond, only 100 miles from Washington, dooming Virginia to be the major battleground of the Civil War. The Union strategy was to advance south and capture Richmond while at the same time taking the Shenandoah Valley to cut off the "breadbasket" of the Confederate Army of Northern Virginia. The first of six attempts was decisively repulsed on July 21, 1861, at the battle of First Manassas (Bull Run), where a stonewall-like stand by the Virginia Brigade of Gen. Thomas J. Jackson swept Union forces back to Washington. In addition to the victory, the South had found a new hero: "Stonewall" Jackson. Total casualties in this first major engagement of the war— 4,828 men—made it apparent that this would be a long and bloody conflict.

THE PENINSULA CAMPAIGN The second major offensive against Richmond, the Peninsula Campaign, devised by Union Gen. George B. McClellan, was the setting for a famous naval engagement. On March 9, 1862, two ironclad vessels, the USS *Monitor* and the CSS *Virginia* (formerly the *Merrimac*) pounded each other with cannon. Although the battle was a draw, the advent of ironclad warships heralded a new era in naval history.

Yorktown was reduced to rubble 2 months later, and the Union army advanced up the Peninsula. The Confederates retreated until taking a stand only 9 miles from Richmond. The Confederate leader, Gen. Joseph Johnson, was badly wounded during the battle. Robert E. Lee, son of Revolutionary War hero Henry "Light Horse Harry" Lee, was appointed head of the Army of Northern Virginia. Personally opposed to secession, Lee had sadly resigned his commission in the U.S. Army when Virginia joined the Confederacy, saying, "My heart is broken, but I cannot raise my sword against Virginia." In a series of victories beginning on June 26, 1862, Lee defeated McClellan and Richmond was saved.

SECOND MANASSAS, FREDERICKSBURG & CHANCELLORSVILLE
The third Union drive against Richmond was repulsed at the Second Battle of Manassas, where Lee's 55,000 men soundly defeated 70,000 Union troops under Gen. John Pope. On December 13, 1862, Gen. Ambrose Burnside, newly chosen head of the Army of the Potomac, crossed the Rappahannock and struck Fredericksburg while Lee's army was in northern Virginia. The Federal advance was so slow that by the time the Union armies moved, Lee's forces were entrenched on a hill. The result was a Union massacre, and the fourth Union drive against Richmond was turned back.

Gen. Joseph Hooker took command of the Union army early in 1863, and, once again, Federal forces crossed the Rappahannock. Fighting raged for 4 days at Chancellorsville. The Union army retreated, and the fifth drive on Richmond failed. Among the heavy casualties, Stonewall Jackson was wounded by his own troops and died of complications resulting from the amputation of his arm. Jackson's loss was costly, as Lee learned in July 1863 at the small Pennsylvania town of Gettysburg.

A WAR OF ATTRITION
In March 1864, Gen. Ulysses S. Grant was put in command of all Federal armies. His plan for victory called for total unrelenting warfare that would put constant pressure on all points of the Confederacy. The first great confrontation between Lee and Grant, the Battle of the Wilderness, resulted in a Confederate victory, but instead of retreating back to Maryland, Grant pushed on toward Richmond. The campaign was the heaviest fighting of the Civil War. Three times Grant tried and failed to interpose his forces between Lee and Richmond. More than 80,000 men were killed and wounded.

LAYING SIEGE TO PETERSBURG
Lee's resistance strengthened at Richmond, and unable to capture the capital, Grant secretly moved his army across the James River toward Petersburg, an important rail junction south of Richmond and the city's main supply line. Improvised Southern forces managed to hold Petersburg until Lee arrived. Grant then resorted to ever-tightening siege operations. If he left his trenches, Lee would be abandoning Petersburg and Richmond. Subjected to hunger and exposure, the Confederate will began to wane and periodic skirmishes weakened Confederate morale.

Lee, hoping to divert Grant, dispatched a small army under Jubal Early to the menaced Shenandoah Valley. Grant instructed Union Gen. Philip Sheridan: "The Shenandoah is to be so devastated that crows flying across it for the balance of the season will have to bring their own provender." This second major valley campaign resulted in the destruction of Early's army and Lee's main source of food.

LEE'S RETREAT   Back in Petersburg, Grant launched his inevitable onslaught on April 1, 1865, when Federal forces smashed through Confederate lines at Five Forks. Petersburg fell, and Richmond was soon occupied by Federal forces and visited by Lincoln and his young son, Todd. Lee's last hope was to rendezvous with Joe Johnson's army, which was retreating northward through North Carolina before Sherman's advance. However, on April 8, the vanguard of Grant's army succeeded in reaching Appomattox Court House ahead of Lee, thus blocking the Confederates' last escape route.

On April 9, 1865, the Civil War ended in Virginia at Appomattox in Wilbur McLean's farmhouse. Grant, uncompromising in war, proved compassionate in peace. Confederate soldiers were permitted to return home on parole, cavalrymen could keep their horses, and officers could retain their side arms. Rations were provided for the destitute Southerners. Speaking to his 28,000 soldiers, the remnants of the once-mighty Army of Northern Virginia, Lee said, "I earnestly pray that a merciful God will extend to you his blessing and protection. With an unceasing admiration of your constancy and devotion to your country, and a grateful remembrance of your kind and generous consideration for myself, I bid you all an affectionate farewell."

RECOVERY & RENEWAL & THE 20TH CENTURY

To a state devastated by a conflict that pitted brother against brother, recovery was slow. Besides the physical and psychological damages of the conflict, the Reconstruction era brought Virginia under federal military control until 1870.

However, by the turn of the 20th century, new railroad lines connecting remote country areas in the west with urban centers characterized Virginia's economic growth. Factories were bringing more people to the cities, and the economy, once based entirely on agriculture, now had a growing industrial base. The Hampton Roads ports enjoyed growing importance as steamship traffic carried an increasing volume of commercial freight (today, it's the world's largest coal port). During this period, the great scholar, author, and educator Booker T. Washington, who had been born in slavery, studied at Virginia's Hampton Institute and achieved fame as an advisor to presidents.

Although he was serving as governor of New Jersey at the time, Virginia-born Woodrow Wilson was elected president in 1912. Noted for his peace-loving ideals, Wilson nevertheless led the United States into World War I in 1917. War brought prosperity to Virginia with new factories and munitions plants and the expansion of military-training camps throughout the state.

World War II brought a population explosion, with men and women of the armed forces flocking to northern Virginia suburbs near Washington, D.C., and the port area of Hampton Roads. Many of these people stayed after the war, and by 1955, the majority of Virginians were urban-dwelling. Today, the state's population is about seven million.

Index